terra australis 56

terra australis 56

Quaternary Palaeontology and Archaeology of Sumatra

Edited by Julien Louys, Paul C.H. Albers
and Alexandra A.E. van der Geer

Australian
National
University

ANU PRESS

Australian National University

ANU PRESS

Published by ANU Press
The Australian National University
Canberra ACT 2600, Australia
Email: anupress@anu.edu.au

Available to download for free at press.anu.edu.au

ISBN (print): 9781760466312
ISBN (online): 9781760466329

WorldCat (print): 1424840797
WorldCat (online): 1424841120

DOI: 10.22459/TA56.2024

Terra Australis Editorial Board: Sue O'Connor, Sally Brockwell, Ursula Frederick, Tristen Jones, Ceri Shipton and Mathieu Leclerc
Series Editor: Sue O'Connor

Cover design and layout by ANU Press. Cover photograph by Julien Louys

This book is published under the aegis of the Terra Australis editorial committee of ANU Press.

Contents

List of figures

List of tables

Acknowledgements

The editors would like to thank their respective institutions for the support provided during the compilation of this volume: the Australian Research Centre for Human Evolution, Griffith University, Brisbane, Australia; the College of Asia and the Pacific at The Australian National University, Canberra, Australia; and the Naturalis Biodiversity Center, Leiden, the Netherlands. Julien Louys would also like to acknowledge the generous funding provided by the Australian Research Council for the project 'Assessing Sumatra's role in ancient human movements and evolution' (FT160100450), as well as past and current funding for Sumatran research provided by the Leakey Foundation grant 'Palaeontological and archaeological investigations of Pleistocene cave deposits from Sumatra', an Australian National University Research School of Asia and the Pacific Grant Development Support grant ('The Toba Eruption and Human Evolution – Evidence from Sumatra') and the National Geographic Society grant 'Remote sensing human evolution in ancient Sumatra' (NGS-59859R-19).

Work in the field would not have been possible without the support and cooperation of staff and students from Institut Teknologi Bandung, Indonesia, who have been instrumental in these projects' palaeontology field programs, which were initiated in 2015 and have continued ever since. In particular, deep gratitude is expressed to Drs Jahdi Zaim, Yan Rizal, Aswan, Mika Rizki Puspaningrum and Agus Tri Hascaryo for their assistance in the laboratory and the field. We also thank them for their valuable assistance in translating the chapter abstracts for this volume.

Finally, we thank the following for their assistance in publishing this volume: the two anonymous reviewers, who provided detailed and constructive comments that helped improve all the chapters in this volume; Sue O'Connor, the editor of the Terra Australis series; the College of Asia and the Pacific; and ANU Press.

1

Quaternary palaeontological and archaeological research in Sumatra

Julien Louys

Abstract

The late Quaternary history of Sumatra has experienced relatively little attention compared to that of the other large islands in the Indonesian archipelago. The first reports of fossils from the island date to the 1880s; they were discovered largely through the efforts of Dubois in the caves of the Padang Highlands. Following these efforts, focus shifted in the 1920s and 1930s to the archaeological records of the midden deposits of northern Sumatra and the Hoabinhian cultures preserved therein. There was little new fieldwork between 1940 and 1970, but by the mid-1970s several new campaigns seemed to herald a renewed interest in the history and prehistory of the island. This enthusiasm does not appear to have been sustained, however, and work was intermittent again in the 1980s and 1990s. Beginning in the mid-1990s and extending into the first two decades of the twenty-first century, more work at existing sites and new investigations have both taken place, extending our knowledge of both the deep-time and more recent history of the island. The application of new techniques on existing sites and the exploration and excavation of new sites are making an increasingly significant contribution to understanding the role of Sumatra in human biological and cultural evolution.

Keywords: Hoabinhian, Dubois, van Stein Callenfels, caves, fossils, history of archaeology, sumatralith

Abstrak

Perkembangan sejarah Kuarter Akhir di Sumatra sangat sedikit diketahui dan kurang mendapat perhatian dibandingkan dengan pulau-pulau besar lainnya di Indonesia. Rekaman penemuan adanya fosil di Sumatra pertama kali telah dilaporkan secara luas oleh Dubois pada tahun 1880-an melalui berbagai upaya kerja yang dilakukan di beberapa gua di Dataran Tinggi Padang. Menindaklanjuti berbagai upaya tersebut, pada tahun 1920-an dan 1930-an fokus penelitian kemudian diarahkan pada pekerjaan untuk mendapatkan data arkeologi dalam endapan/tumpukan sisa makanan yang terdapat di Sumatra bagian utara dan budaya Hoabinhian yang terawetkan di dalamnya. Setelahnya, diikuti oleh periode lapangan lanjutan antara tahun 1940 dan 1970, namun baru pada pertengahan 1970-an diperoleh berbagai keterangan baru yang menunjukkan adanya perhatian baru pada sejarah dan prasejarah Pulau Sumatra. Gairah melakukan penelitian ternyata tidak berlangsung secara menerus, meskipun demikian masih terdapat pekerjaan lapangan secara berselang yang tidak menerus selama beberapa decade berikutnya. Berawal pada pertengahan tahun 1990-an, dan menerus sampai pada awal dua dekade abad 21, lebih banyak pekerjaan dan penyelidikan lapangan baru telah dilakukan, yang hasilnya menambah pengetahuan tentang waktu yang makin mendalam dan sejarah tentang Pulau Sumatra yang lebih baru. Penerapan teknologi terbaru di situs-situs lama, begitupula eksplorasi dan ekskavasi yang dilakukan di situs-situs baru telah memberikan kontribusi yang lebih sigifikan untuk memahami peranan evolusi budaya dan manusia di Sumatra.

Kata kunci: Hoabinhian, Dubois, van Stein Callenfels, gua-gua, fosil, sejarah arkeologi, sumatralith

Introduction

Among the late Quaternary histories of the major Indonesian islands, that of Sumatra is one of the most poorly known. In 1973, Bronson and Wisseman noted:

> Despite its prominence in South-East Asian history books, Sumatra remains terra incognita to archaeology. A limited amount of archaeological fieldwork was done there in the early decades of this century, mostly by amateurs or self-trained professionals. Some of these succeeded in producing a respectable body of work; most were doubtfully competent even by the then-prevailing standards of archaeology in South-East Asia. The interpreters and synthesizers of field data tended to be better qualified than the fieldworkers but, unfortunately, few of these found it necessary to see Sumatra for themselves.

> Perhaps because of this lack of field orientation, the work of interpreters was not seriously interrupted by World War II and Indonesia's subsequent independence. Interpretive syntheses of Sumatran history have continued to be produced down to the present day. Field research, on the other hand, went into a decline from which it has still not recovered. (Bronson and Wisseman 1974:87)

Almost half a century later, the situation has not improved substantially, at least at the global level and regarding late Quaternary archaeology (and palaeontology). There are still only a handful of Pleistocene sites known on Sumatra, and most of these are poorly known or under-studied. The Holocene record is not much better, particularly outside the 130 km stretch on the northeast coast of Sumatra where numerous shell midden deposits, preserving a Hoabinhian cultural complex, have been reported.

In this chapter, I provide a brief and necessarily incomplete timeline of the archaeological and palaeontological field research that has been undertaken on the island, focusing on sites and finds dating from the Middle Pleistocene to the Hoabinhian. (For a history of archaeological research after the Hoabinhian, see Bonatz et al. 2009.) This list is incomplete because it includes very few references to unpublished primary Indonesian sources (and cites only a small proportion of the published ones), due to the difficulty in identifying and locating such reports. No doubt a full review of the Indonesian grey literature would identify many more recent local, regional and national field expeditions in Sumatra. However, such sources have not been reported beyond Indonesia, suggesting that any data collected have not significantly altered our understanding of Sumatra's late Quaternary history.

Preliminary timeline of archaeological and palaeontological field research in Sumatra up to the Hoabinhian

While European interest in the prehistoric record of the 'Netherlands Indies' dates to the beginning of the eighteenth century, through the work of G.E. Rumphius in his *D'Amboinsche Rariteitkamer*, it was not until the end of the nineteenth century that systematic research took place (von Heine-Geldern 1945). In the first such report, Martin (1884) described the fossil molar fragments of the Asian elephant recovered from the 'Ore Bed of Banhin N°. 8 Mine, Sungei Liat', on Bangka Island, southeastern Sumatra (Figure 1.1). This was probably an incidental find by tin miners, and the Naturalis Biodiversity Center, Leiden, where the fossils are lodged, records that they were found by 'van Dijk', no doubt in reference to the 'van Dijk' referred to by Martin (1884:3). More recent efforts to locate the source of these fossils encountered mixed success (Louys et al. 2021).

Four years after Martin's publication, Dubois was posted to Sumatra and began his exploration and excavations of the caves in the Padang Highlands, West Sumatra (Chapter 2, this volume). These continued from 1888 until 1890, when Dubois relocated to Java.

Figure 1.1: Tin mine dredging operations on Bangka Island near the probable source of the first fossils recovered from Sumatra.

Note: The fossils were found by van Dijk and described by Martin (1884).

Source: Photograph by author.

Figure 1.2: Eugène Dubois (left) and Pieter van Stein Callenfels (right). Dubois undertook the first systematic exploration of caves for fossils in Sumatra during the 1880s. Van Stein Callenfels explored and excavated midden sites in northern Sumatra during the 1920s.

Source: Images in public domain.

Following Dubois' efforts, there appears to have been a hiatus in archaeological field research on Sumatra until 1908, when the geologist Tobler, while working for the Dienst van het Mijnwezen in southern Sumatra, identified and excavated Ulu Tjangko Cave in Jambi. He collected material including 'obsidian shards, bone fragments of vertebrates and human skeletal parts, including upper arm bone, femur, skull fragments, lower jaw with chin and a few loose molars' (Zwierzycki 1926:63). Tobler also collected surface finds from Kikim River in Palembang Province. All Tobler's material was subsequently described by Sarasin (1914).

Beginning in the early twentieth century, attention was increasingly paid to the large shell mounds of northern Sumatra. Van Heekeren (1957) cited the *Yearbook 1917* of the mining department at Bandung as containing the first reports of large shell mounds on the lower course of the Tamiang River near Seruwai in eastern Sumatra. In 1920, van Stein Callenfels (Figure 1.2) reported shell middens near Deli in eastern Sumatra, commenting on their size and thus probable antiquity (van Stein Callenfels 1920). He described collecting several bones from the middens, including tiger, rhinoceros, monkey and dolphin, noting that some of the bones had been slit for marrow extraction. In the same year, the first Hoabinhian biface was found by Neumann at Batu Kenong near Deli. It was described by van Stein Callenfels (1924) as a surface find, not in situ, but thought to be identical to tools found near Medan in the same year. Also in 1920, Huesser and Mjöberg reported on shell mounds located near Medan, in 'Boeloe Tjina and Tandem Hilir' (Huesser and Mjöberg 1920:443). They reported the collection of bones (monkey), shells and stone tools from the mounds. Lastly, at the beginning of this busy year, Witkamp visited and described several midden sites in the same vicinity (Witkamp 1920).

By 1925–26, van Stein Callenfels had organised excavations at Saentis near Medan. These excavations were never published by van Stein Callenfels, but his field notebooks were briefly summarised by van Heekeren (1957). His excavation produced in situ worked stone tools, including 'unifacial Hoabinhian tools of the common Sumatran type', a bifacial tool, a mortar and pestle, and haematite (van Heekeren 1957:71), as well as abundant faunal remains (Forestier 2007). The finds and excavations undertaken in the Sumatran shell mounds in the 1920s had a long-lasting (nomenclatural) legacy for Southeast Asian archaeology, as the unifacial tool description by van Stein Callenfels and Evans (1926:184) as a 'Sumatra-type' tool led to the term sumatralith (Brandt 1976). This term describes cobbles of an oblong shape with one side chipped and the other in original waterworn condition (Brandt 1976).

In 1926, Zwierzycki returned to Tobler's Ulu Tjangko Cave in Jambi, but finding it depleted, he moved on to excavate another nearby cave—the unnamed cave eventually called Tianko Panjang Cave by Bronson and Asmar (1975). His excavations uncovered pots and iron tools in the top layers and, at a depth of about 45–60 cm, obsidian flakes he likened to those from Ulu Tjangko described by Sarasin (1914) as well as fragments made from quartz, limestone and cobbles. A rich fauna was also described, partially burnt and including deer, rodents, insectivores, pigs, fish and/or snakes, frogs, turtles and crustaceans (Zwierzycki 1926). Van der Hoop and Dinas Purbakala may also have worked on Tianko Panjang or its material (cited in Bronson and Asmar 1975).

In 1927, Heyting recovered sumatralith-type unifacial tools from the Upper Serdang region (L.C. Heyting, *Memorie van Overgave van der Controleur te Pangkalan Brandan 21 April 1927–1 Juni 1928*, cited in Edwards McKinnon and Sinar 1981; see also van Heekeren 1957:73). Around 1928, excavations in Aceh took place: Schürmann excavated the shell midden Binjai Tamieng, situated on the Tamieng River in Aceh (Schürmann 1928). The site included stone tools and faunal and human remains, which were described by Schürmann (1928, 1931) and Gruwier (2017) and thought to represent typical Hoabinhian characteristics (Gruwier 2017). Finally, Küpper, in or just before 1930, collected stone tools from the surface, or very near the surface, from near Aceh, as well as archaeological material from the middens nearby (Küpper 1930); these tools and materials were subsequently described in more detail by Lebzelter (1935).

There followed a gap of about 10 years, after which Schnitger (1940) reported the recovery of human bones from the Kampar Kanan River in central Sumatra in 1938. Although they were described as Palaeolithic and even named *Homo 'kamparensis'*, the antiquity and indeed nature of these remains has yet to be convincingly established (see also Movius 1955). In 1938, van der Hoop recovered obsidian artefacts from 'Danau Gadang Estate'; however, as bronze and Neolithic artefacts have also been recovered from this site, the obsidian is probably not of great antiquity. Finally, in 1939, Houbolt (1940) recovered a surface Palaeolithic artefact from Benkulen Residence, north of Tambangsawah.

Bronson and Wisseman (1974) indicated that from 1940 to 1970, only three archaeological projects took place in Sumatra, only two of which investigated the period considered here. The first of these was a survey of the southern part of the island by Dinas Purkala in 1954. Soejono (1961) described this as a field program arranged by the Ministry of Education, with finds from the Saling River and the Kikim River. Forestier (2007) also mentioned surveys undertaken by Soejono in South Sumatra

(Bungamas and Lahat), Lampung (Kalianda and Kedaton) and Bengkulu, but did not clarify when these were conducted. Also in 1954, Verstappen reported an incidental artefact find at Kalianda (Soejono 1961). The second project mentioned by Bronson and Wisseman was an examination of shell middens in Aceh by Jacob in the 1960s, although no further details were provided. Adding to Bronson and Wisseman's reports, suggestions of further chance finds during 1940–1970 came from Movius (1955:526), who referred to discoveries of Palaeolithic tools, made from fossil wood, by Erbrink on 'the Kedaton rubber estate, near Tanjong Karang, Lampong District (near Telukbetung)', citing a letter dated 1951.

In the 1970s, two major field surveys were conducted. The first of these (Bronson and Wisseman 1974), a joint venture by the University Museum of the University of Pennsylvania and the Archaeological Institute of Indonesia, involved a two-month, north–south survey of all Sumatran colonial-period sites then known. The team located 20 possible prehistory sites during a survey that was broad and included visits to inscriptions sites, earthworks sites and more. This survey was followed up in 1974 with excavations of Zwierzycki's cave (by this point named Tianko Panjang), with an interim report published in 1975 (Bronson and Asmar 1975). The second project, a 1974 survey and fieldwork investigation conducted by Edwards McKinnon (1975), re-evaluated the Hinai Midden Complex of northern Sumatra, both finding new sites and examining some of the mounds identified in the 1920s, where these remained (see also Edwards McKinnon 1991).

Sadly, this 1970s enthusiasm for field research was short-lived, and few records of 1980s fieldwork exist. The most significant were presented in *Pertemuan Ilmiah Arkeologi III*, wherein Djubiantono (1985) described a survey of the island of Nias undertaken in 1982 with a focus on the Muzoi River, where several Palaeolithic artefacts were recovered.

In 1995, researchers from Pusbang Arkeologi Jakarta began a campaign of fieldwork in southern Sumatra, focusing particularly on the Ogan River watershed (Simanjuntak 2015; see also Jatmiko [1995, 2001] cited in Forestier 2007). In 1999–2000, researchers from Balai Arkeologi Medan and the Prehistory-Archeometry Division, Archaeological Center returned to the Muzoi River to examine the Palaeolithic tools reported by Djubiantono (1985) (cited in Forestier et al. 2005 and Intan 2001). Also, starting in 1995 and continuing for over a decade, Drawhorn conducted a systematic survey of the caves in Padang Highlands; this was partly an attempt to locate the caves visited by Dubois in the late 1880s (Chapter 4, this volume). De Vos, alongside Aziz and Gjohan, also travelled to Padang in 1995 to investigate Dubois' old sites (John de Vos pers. comm. 2022).

The early 2000s brought new fieldwork efforts in the form of a collaboration between Pusbang Arkeologi Jakarta and France's Institut de Recherches pour la Dévelopment (IRD). Their teams undertook archaeological fieldwork in Nias in association with Balai Arkeologi Medan, focusing on the excavation of Tögi Ndrawa. This cave site yielded classic Hoabinhian tools, forest and coastal fauna, and human remains dated to the Terminal Pleistocene (Driwantoro et al. 2004; Forestier et al. 2005). From 2000 to 2004, Pusbang Arkeologi Jakarta and IRD expanded their focus to the area around Padang Bindu in South Sumatra (Chapter 10, this volume; Simanjuntak 2015), recovering what they describe as Acheulean tools from the beds of the two small rivers Air Tawar and Air Semuhun, as well as an early Holocene assemblage from Gua Pandan (Forestier et al. 2006).

Pusbang Arkeologi Jakarta continued working in South Sumatra, and in 2008, they identified a cave in Padang Bindu that would prove extremely fruitful. This cave, Gua Harimau, was excavated between 2009 and 2014 and has produced a wealth of data on periods from the Late Pleistocene to the Neolithic, including extensive burials (Simanjuntak 2015). It is a site currently unmatched in Sumatra and is likely to prove as significant for understanding the early human history of Sumatra as Niah Cave is for understanding that of Borneo. Also in 2008, an Australian–Indonesian team revisited Dubois' Lida Ajer site; the results of this expedition, including direct dates for the deposit, were published in Westaway et al. (2017).

In the early to middle 2010s, additional work was conducted at Hoabinhian sites in the highlands of northern Sumatra (as opposed to the coastal sites investigated in the 1920s), with Late Pleistocene to Early Holocene dates reported for Bukit Kerang Pang, Gua Kampet and Loyang Mendale (Wiradnyana 2016).

After a hiatus of over 100 years, Pleistocene palaeontological fieldwork restarted in 2015 through a collaboration between the Institut Teknologi Bandung (ITB) and The Australian National University. It involved the exploration of the caves in Padang Highlands, focusing partly on Dubois' old cave sites but having the primary objective of finding new palaeontological deposits. The results of this survey were published by Louys et al. (2017). The collaboration moved to ITB and Griffith University in 2017, and further fieldwork was conducted in 2018 and 2019 (Louys et al. 2021). As a result of these expeditions, new fossil sites have been discovered, including the first extinct mammal taxon recorded for the island, namely *Hexaprotodon* (Smith et al. 2021).

Influence of Sumatran palaeontology and archaeology

The Sumatran contribution to our understanding of the Quaternary history of Southeast Asia has been muted compared to those of other regions. From a natural history perspective, this stems from interpretations dating back to Dubois—namely the idea that the fossil faunas from the island were composed of essentially modern rainforest animals, and the long-lasting idea that these were at best only a few thousand years old. The lack of any notable differences between fossil and modern faunas of Sumatra meant there were no markers, events or index fossils to tie in with any regional biochronological or palaeogeographical schemes. While work by de Vos in the 1980s helped increase the time depth of fossil deposits from Sumatra (de Vos 1983), it was not until the advent of geochemical techniques that both the ages and environmental contexts of some of these deposits were more fully realised (e.g. Chapter 2, this volume; Duval et al. 2021; Janssen et al. 2016; Louys et al. 2022; Westaway et al. 2017). This was facilitated by the physical re-examination of the mode of fossil preservation in the caves, Lida Ajer in particular (Louys et al. 2017; Westaway et al. 2017). New finds from fossil sites in Sumatra have extended both the time depth and taxonomic breadth of the cave deposits (Smith et al. 2021).

Archaeologically, the island of Sumatra is still very poorly known. The discovery and excavation of Hoabinhian sites in northern Sumatra in the 1920s no doubt made important contributions to our understanding of the Hoabinhian period and its peoples across that region. The location of Hoabinhian sites other than the middens—in the highlands of Aceh and the island of Nias, for example—demonstrates that this was a widespread and versatile culture (Brandt 1976). Despite these early records, however, the archaeological record of Sumatra had little influence on the development of the Hoabinhian concept (Brandt 1976). Earlier habitation of the island, as evidenced by chance and surface finds of stone tools in southern Sumatra, hint that perhaps earlier hominins were present on the island. Probably, this would have taken place under environmental conditions very different from those currently known from the Late Pleistocene fossil record; however, Middle Pleistocene deposits potentially recording these remain elusive (Chapter 2, this volume).

While this volume largely deals with the earliest history of Sumatra, historical archaeological research has been fundamental in establishing the diversity of Sumatran interactions beyond the famous coastal entrepôts of the island (e.g. Bonatz 2012; Bonatz et al. 2009; Tjoa-Bonatz 2019).

Archaeological finds and antiquities from the island were first recorded in the reports and minutes of the meetings of the Batavian Society in the 1860s (Bonatz et al. 2009). Europeans became attracted to highland megaliths early in the twentieth century (Bonatz 2012), initially in the areas of Kerinci and Sungai Tenang (Adam 1922; de Bont 1922; Witkamp 1922), but most famously on the Pasemah Plateau in southern Sumatra through the work of van der Hoop (1940). Other significant early work included the systematic survey of western Sumatran archaeology by Krom (1912), who listed 24 inscriptions and 31 other types of sites from an area covering Muara Takus in the northeast to Padang Roco in the south (Bonatz et al. 2009). Despite initial interest in the highlands, archaeological interest shifted to the lowlands, and the identification of Srivijaya as a kingdom rather than a king in 1918 (Coedès 1918) spurred much research on this realm, which was famous for its wealth and learning. Archaeological efforts to find the location of Srivijaya, complicated by a dearth of physical finds, engendered important debate (e.g. Bronson 1975; Bronson and Wisseman 1976; Edwards McKinnon and Milner 1979). Most scholars now accept Palembang as the modern location of the city (Miksic 1980), and archaeological research in the early 1990s yielded the first systematically recovered evidence that Srivijaya was in the Palembang area (Manguin 1992, 1993). Another interesting and important historical archaeological port complex in Sumatra is Lobu Tua in Barus (Guillot 1998). However, the first early emporium and site in Sumatra to be excavated was Kota Cina, located in the northeast of the island near Medan. This was excavated thanks to the efforts of E. Edwards McKinnon, who followed up on the presence of numerous fragments of Chinese pottery in the area with systematic study that revealed Kota Cina's short but intense importance for trade in the region during the twelfth to fourteenth centuries (Edwards McKinnon 1977). Further excavations in Palembang were conducted by a joint Indonesian–French team (Guillaud 2006). This team also reported research into earlier sites such as Gua Pondok Selabe 1, Gua Pandan and Benua Keling Lama, which is very important as a rare example of a dated open Neolithic site in Indonesia. Other important pre-Neolithic and Neolithic sites include Loyang Mendali (Setiawan 2018), Lake Kerinci (van der Hoop 1940, Watson 1979), the Pasemah Plateau (Guillaud et al. 2009) and Pondok Silabe I (Forestier et al. 2006; Simanjuntak et al. 2005; Simanjuntak and Forestier 2004). Finally, the remarkable deposits of Gua Harimau are only just beginning to reveal their secrets (Simanjuntak 2015). It is likely that once fully analysed, the data from this cave will dramatically improve our knowledge of the nature of human habitation of the island and how it has changed.

Introduction to the volume

The chapters in this volume can be grouped under three broad themes. The first concerns the historical perspective on palaeontological and archaeological research in Sumatra. This theme is introduced by the current chapter, which has sought to lay out in chronological order some of the major field campaigns in Sumatra. In subsequent chapters addressing this theme, Albers et al. provide translations of Dubois' Sumatran fieldwork and a modern perspective on the science undertaken by Dubois in the Padang caves. Albers, in the following chapter, expands on this to explore Dubois' efforts in Sumatra against the backdrop of Dutch colonial rule. Finally, Drawhorn gives a detailed historical perspective on cave exploration in Sumatra, particularly discussing work done by scholars other than Dubois and its ramifications for our understanding of Sumatran prehistory.

Here, it is important to make a note regarding the spelling of site names. The Indonesian language has undergone several changes of spelling system. Prior to 1901, no standardised spelling for Indonesian words existed. From 1901 to 1947, the Van Ophuijsen Spelling System was in use; it was replaced by the Republican Spelling System used from 1947 to 1972. Finally, since 1972 the Indonesian Spelling System has been in place. Thus, commonly used site names described in the nineteenth century, such as Lida Ajer and Djamboe, should, under the current Indonesian Spelling System, be transcribed—to Lidah Air and Jambu in these two cases. Because name use can be context-dependent, no efforts to standardise the spelling of the sites have been made in this volume; instead, use and nomenclature has been dictated by individual authors.

The second theme of the volume involves new data and interpretations derived from the extensive palaeontological collections from Sumatra, primarily those collected by Dubois. Louys et al. report new direct dates on two critical Dubois sites, Sibrambang and Djamboe, as well as a reconstruction of their palaeoenvironments based on stable isotopes of carbon and oxygen. Gruwier et al. examine in detail the deer fossils from the Padang Highlands and explore their taxonomic and palaeobiological implications. Bacon et al. take a broader approach, examining the Dubois sites, particularly Lida Ajer and Sibrambang, in the context of palaeoecological reconstructions of Southeast Asia during the Late Pleistocene. Finally under this second theme is a chapter by Basilia et al. describing unique histological aspects of fossil elephants from the island of Bangka, which, although not administratively part of Sumatra, was connected to it for most of the Pleistocene.

The third theme is key archaeological sites and new interpretations of new and previously recovered materials and data. Louys and Kealy model the possible routes that *Homo erectus* took between mainland Southeast Asia and Java, with special attention to the pathways through emergent parts of Sumatra. Forestier provides an overview of the lithic technologies recorded from Sumatra. Sofian and Simanjuntak describe the remarkable Metal Age artefacts recovered from Gua Harimau and their context within the Southeast Asian Metal Age diaspora. Bonatz details the megaliths from several key locales in Sumatra and moves the discussion from the prehistoric to the historical period, which, in a way, brings the reader back to the period in which the volume started. Finally, Price et al. use the past to look towards the future, emphasising the heritage value of, and the protection needed by, one particular site among the many in Sumatra.

It is hoped that this volume will not only provide a ready resource for anyone wishing to understand the past of this fascinating island, but also spur additional attention and new research avenues going forward.

Acknowledgements

Funding for this research was generously provided by the Australian Research Council (FT160100450). I thank two anonymous reviewers and Peter Bellwood for their constructive comments on this chapter.

References

Adam, T. 1922. Oudheden te Djambi II. *Oudheidkundig Verslag* 1:38–41.

Bonatz, D. 2012. A highland perspective on the archaeology and settlement history of Sumatra. *Archipel* 84(1):35–81. doi.org/10.3406/arch.2012.4361

Bonatz, D., J.N. Miksic, J.D. Neidel and M. Tjoa-Bonatz (eds) 2009. *From Distant Tales: Archaeology and Ethnohistory in the Highlands of Sumatra*. Cambridge Scholars Publishing, Newcastle upon Tyne.

Brandt, R.W. 1976. The Hoabinhian of Sumatra: Some remarks. *Modern Quaternary Research in Southeast Asia* 2:49–52.

Bronson, B. 1975. A lost kingdom mislaid: A short report on the search for Srivijaya. *Bulletin, Field Museum of Natural History* 46:416–420.

Bronson, B. and T. Asmar 1975. Prehistoric investigations at Tianko Panjang Cave, Sumatra: An interim report. *Asian Perspectives* 18(2):128–145.

Bronson, B. and J. Wisseman 1974. An archeological survey in Sumatra, 1973. *Sumatra Research Bulletin* 4(1):87–94.

Bronson, B. and J. Wisseman 1976. Palembang as Sriwijaya: The lateness of early cities in southern Southeast Asia. *Asian Perspectives* 19:220–239.

Coedès, G. 1918. Le royaume de Çrivijaya. *Bulletin de l'Ecole française d'Extrême-Orient* 18:1–36. doi.org/10.3406/befeo.1918.5894

de Bont, G.K.H. 1922. De batoe's larong (kist-steenen) in Boven Djambi, Onderafdeeling Bangko. *Nederlandsch-Indië Oud en Niew* 7:31–32.

de Vos, J. 1983. The *Pongo* faunas from Java and Sumatra and their significance for biostratigraphical and paleo-ecological interpretations. *Proceedings of the Koninklijke Nederlandse Akademie van Wetenschappen, Series B* 86:417–425.

Djubiantono, T. 1985. Posisi stratigrafi artefak di Lembah Muzoi, Nias. In R.P. Soejono (ed), *Pertemuan Ilmiah Arkeologi III*, pp. 1026–1033. Pusat Penelitian Arkeologi Nasional, Jakarta.

Driwantoro, D., H. Forestier, T. Simanjuntak, K. Wiradnyana and D. Siregar 2004. Tögi Ndrawa cave site at Nias Island, New datas on life during the Holocene Period based on dating. *Berkala Arkeologi Sangkhakala* 13:10–15.

Duval, M., K. Westaway, Y. Zaim, Y. Rizal, Aswan, M.R. Puspaningrum, A. Trihascaryo, P.C.H. Albers, H.E. Smith, G.M. Drawhorn, G.J. Price and J. Louys 2021. New chronological constraints for the Late Pleistocene fossil assemblage and associated breccia from Ngalau Sampit, Sumatra. *Open Quaternary* 7:1–24. doi.org/10.5334/oq.96

Edwards McKinnon, E. 1975. A brief note on the current state of certain of the kitchen middens of East Sumatra. *Sumatra Research Bulletin* 4(2):45–50.

Edwards McKinnon, E. 1977. Research at Kota Cina, a Sung-Yüan period trading site in East Sumatra. *Archipel* 14(1):19–32. doi.org/10.3406/arch.1977.1355

Edwards McKinnon, E. 1991. The Hoabinhian in the Wampu/Lau Biang Valley of northeastern Sumatra: An update. *Bulletin of the Indo-Pacific Prehistory Association* 10:132–142. doi.org/10.7152/bippa.v10i0.11302

Edwards McKinnon, E. and A.C. Milner 1979. A letter from Sumatra: A visit to some early Sumatran historical sites. *Indonesia Circle* 7:3–21. doi.org/10.1080/03062847908723730

Edwards McKinnon, E. and T.L. Sinar 1981. A note on Pulau Kompei in Aru Bay, northeastern Sumatra. *Indonesia* 32:49–73. doi.org/10.2307/3350855

Forestier, H. 2007. Les éclats du passé préhistorique de Sumatra: Une très longue histoire des techniques. *Archipel* 74(1):15–44. doi.org/10.3406/arch.2007.3914

Forestier, H., D. Driwantoro, D. Guillaud and Budiman 2006. New data about prehistoric chronology of South Sumatra. In H.T. Simanjuntak, M. Hisyam, B. Prasetyo and T.S. Nastiti (eds), *Archaeology, Indonesian perspective: R.P. Soejono's Festschrift*, pp. 177–192. Lipi, Jakarta.

Forestier, H., T. Simanjuntak, D. Guillaud, D. Driwantoro, K. Wiradnyana, D. Siregar, R.D. Awe and Budiman 2005. Le site de Tögi Ndrawa, île de Nias, Sumatra nord: Les premières traces d'une occupation hoabinhienne en grotte en Indonésie. *Comptes Rendus Palevol* 4(8):727–733.

Gruwier, B.J. 2017. The large vertebrate remains from Binjai Tamieng (Sumatra, Indonesia). *Journal of Indo-Pacific Archaeology* 41:22–29. doi.org/10.7152/jipa.v41i0.15027

Guillaud, D. 2006. *Menyelusuri Sungai, Merunut Waktu: Penelitian Arkeologi di Sumatera Selatan*. Puslitbang Arkeologi Nasional/IRD/EFEO, Jakarta.

Guillaud, D., H. Forestier and T. Simanjuntak 2009. Mounds, tombs, and tales: Archaeology and oral tradition in the South Sumatra Highlands. In D. Bonatz, J.N. Miksic, J.D. Neidel and M.L. Tjoa-Bonatz (eds), *From Distant Tales: Archaeology and Ethnohistory in the Highlands of Sumatra*, pp. 416–433. Cambridge Scholars Publishing, Newcastle upon Tyne.

Guillot, C. 1998. *Histoire de Barus, Le Site de Lobu Tua: 1: Études et Documents*. Cahier d'Archipel, Paris.

Heusser, C. and E.M. Mjöberg 1920. De schelpheuvel van Boloe Tjina. *Teysmannia* 31:443–446.

Houbolt, J.H. 1940. Bijdrage tot de kennis van der verspreiding van Palaeolithische artefacten in Nederlandsch-Indië. *Tijdschrift voor Indische Taal-, Land-, en Volkenkunde* 80:614–617.

Intan, M.F.S. 2001. Geologi situs Muzoi-Sinoto, kabupaten Nias, provinsi Sumatera Utara. *Berkala Arkeologi Sangkhakala* 9:59–66.

Janssen, R., J.C. Joordens, D.S. Koutamanis, M.R. Puspaningrum, J. de Vos, J.H. van der Lubbe, J.J. Reijmer, O. Hampe and H.B. Vonhof 2016. Tooth enamel stable isotopes of Holocene and Pleistocene fossil fauna reveal glacial and interglacial paleoenvironments of hominins in Indonesia. *Quaternary Science Reviews* 144:145–154. doi.org/10.1016/j.quascirev.2016.02.028

Krom, N.J. 1912. Inventaris der oudheden in de Padangsche Bovenland. *Oudheidkundig Verslag* Bijlage G:33–50.

Küpper, H. 1930. Palaeolitische werktuigen uit Atjeh, Nord Sumatra. *Tijdschrift van het Koninklijk Nederlands Aardrijkskundig Genootschap* 47:985–989.

Lebzelter, V. 1935. Paläolithische Funde aus Atjeh (Nord-Sumatra). *Archiv für Anthropologie* 23:318–325.

Louys, J., M. Duval, G.J. Price, K. Westaway, Y. Zaim, Y, Rizal, Aswan, M. Puspaningrum, A. Trihascaryo, S. Breitenbach, O. Kwiecien, Y. Cai, P. Higgins, P.C.H. Albers, J. de Vos and P. Roberts 2022. Speleological and environmental history of Lida Ajer cave, western Sumatra. *Philosophical Transactions of the Royal Society B* 377:20200494. doi.org/10.1098/rstb.2020.0494

Louys, J., S. Kealy, S. O'Connor, G.J. Price, S. Hawkins, K. Aplin, Y. Rizal, Y. Zaim, Mahirta, D.A. Tanudirjo, W.D. Santoso, A.R. Hidayah, A. Trihascaryo, R. Wood, J. Bevitt and T. Clark 2017. Differential preservation of vertebrates in Southeast Asian caves. *International Journal of Speleology* 46:379–408. doi.org/10.5038/1827-806X.46.3.2131

Louys, J., Y. Zaim, Y. Rizal, G.J. Price, Aswan, M.R. Puspanigrum, H. Smith and A. Trihascaryo 2021. Palaeontological surveys in Central Sumatra and Bangka. *Berita Sedimentologi* 47:50–56. doi.org/10.51835/bsed.2021.47.3.358

Manguin, P.Y. 1992. Excavations in South Sumatra, 1988–1990: New evidence for Sriwijayan sites. In I. Glover (ed.), *Southeast Asian Archaeology 1990: Proceedings of the Third Conference of the European Association of Southeast Asian Archaeologists*, pp. 63–73. Centre for Southeast Asian Studies, Hull.

Manguin, P.Y. 1993. Palembang and Sriwijaya: An early Malay harbour-city rediscovered. *Journal of the Malaysian Branch of the Royal Asiatic Society* 66:23–46.

Martin, K. 1884. Ueberreste vorweltlicher Proboscidier von Java und Banka. *Sammlungen des Geologischen Reichs-Museums in Leiden, Serie 1, Beiträge zur Geologie Ost-Asiens und Australiens* 4:1–24.

Miksic, J. 1980. Classical archaeology in Sumatra. *Indonesia* 30:43–66. doi.org/10.2307/3350825

Movius, H.L. Jr 1955. Palaeolithic archaeology in southern and eastern Asia, exclusive of India. *Journal of World History* 2(3):520–553.

Sarasin, P. 1914. Neue lithochrone Funds im Innern von Sumatra. *Verhandlungen der Naturforschenden Gesellschaft in Basel* 25:97–111.

Schnitger, F.M. 1940. Der Paläolithische Mensch von Sumatra. *Zeitschrift für Ethnologie* 72:372–373. doi.org/10.1007/978-3-662-41260-2_7

Schürmann, H.M.E. 1928. Kjökkenmöddinger en Paleolithicum in Noord Sumatra. *De Mijningenieur* 12:235–243.

Schürmann, H.M.E. 1931. Kjökkenmöddinger und Paläolithicum in Nord-Sumatra. *Tijdschrift van het Koninklijk Aardrijkskundig Genootschap* 48:905–923.

Setiawan, T. 2018. Loyang Mendale situs hunian prasejarah di pedalaman Aceh: Asumsi awal terhadap hasil penilitian gua-gua di Kabupaten Aceh Tengah, Provinsi Naggore Aceh Darrussalam. *Berkala Arkeologi Sangkhakala* 12:229–239.

Simanjuntak, T. 2015. *Harimau Cave and the Long Journey of OKU Civilization*. UGM Press, Jogjakarta.

Simanjuntak, H.T. and H. Forestier 2004. Research progress on the Neolithic in Indonesia, with special reference to the Pondok Silabe Cave, South Sumatra. In V. Paz (ed.), *Southeast Asian Archaeology: Wilhelm G. Solheim II Festschrift*, pp. 104–118. University of Philippines Press, Manila.

Simanjuntak, H.T., H. Forestier and B. Prasetyo 2005. Gens des karsts au Néolithique à Sumatra. *Dossiers d'Archéologie* 302:46–49.

Smith, H.E., G.J. Price, M. Duval, K. Westaway, J. Zaim, Y. Rizal, Aswan, M.R. Puspaningrum, A. Trihascaryo, M. Stewart and J. Louys 2021. Taxonomy, taphonomy and chronology of the Pleistocene faunal assemblage at Ngalau Gupin cave, Sumatra. *Quaternary International* 603:40–63. doi.org/10.1016/j.quaint.2021.05.005

Soejono, R.P. 1961. Preliminary notes of new finds of Lower Palaeolithic implements from Indonesia. *Asian Perspectives* 5:217–232.

Swanenburg, B.D. 1951. *Iwan de Verschrikkelijke: Leven en werken van Dr. P.V. van Stein Callenfels*. Leiter Nypels, Maastricht.

Tjoa-Bonatz, M.L. 2019. *A View from the Highlands: Archaeology and Settlement History of West Sumatra, Indonesia*. ISEAS Publishing, Singapore. doi.org/10.1355/9789814843027

van der Hoop, A.N.J. Th. à Th. 1940. A prehistoric site near the lake of Kerinchi, Sumatra. In F.N. Chasen and M.W.F. Tweedie (eds), *Proceedings of the Third Congress of Prehistorians of the Far East, Singapore, 24th January–30th January 1938*, pp. 200–204. U.S. Government Printing Office, Singapore.

van Heekeren, H.R. 1957. *The Stone Age of Indonesia*. Verhandelingen van het Koninklijk Instituut voor Taal-, Land-, en Volkenkunde 21. Martinus Nijhoff, The Hague.

van Stein Callenfels, P.V. 1920. Rapport over een dienstreis door een deel van Sumatra. *Oudheidkundige Verslag* 1920:62–75.

van Stein Callenfels, P.V. 1924. Het eerste palaeolithische werktuig in den Archipel. *Oudheidkundige Verslag* 1924:127–133.

van Stein Callenfels, P.V. and I.H.N. Evans 1926. Report on the cave excavations in Perak. *Oudheidkundige Verslag* 1926:181–193.

von Heine-Geldern, R. 1945. Prehistoric research in the Netherlands Indies. In P. Honig and F. Verdoorn (eds), *Science and Scientists in the Netherlands Indies*, pp. 129–167. Natuurwetenschappelijk Tijdschrift voor Nederlandsch Indië, 102 (Special Supplement). Board for the Netherlands Indies, Surinam, and Curaçao, New York.

Watson, C.W. 1979. Some comments on finds of archaeological interest in Kerinci. *Majalah Arkeologi* 2(4):37–59.

Westaway, K.E., J. Louys, R. Due Awe, M.J. Morwood, G.J. Price, J.X. Zhao, M. Aubert, R. Joannes-Boyau, T. Smith, M.M. Skinner, T. Compton, R.M. Bailey, G.D. van den Bergh, J. de Vos, A.W.G. Pike, C. Stringer, E.W. Saptomo, Y. Rizal, J. Zaim, W.D. Santoso, A. Trihascaryo, L. Kinsley and B. Sulistyanto 2017. An early modern human presence in Sumatra 73,000–63,000 years ago. *Nature* 548:322–325. doi.org/10.1038/nature23452

Wiradnyana, K. 2016. Hoabinhian and Austronesia: The root of diversity in the western part of Indonesia. *European Scientific Journal* 12(32):131–145. doi.org/10.19044/esj.2016.v12n32p131

Witkamp, H. 1920. 'Kjokkenmoddinger' ter Oostkust van Sumatra. *Tijdschrift van het Koninklijk Nederlandsch Aardrijkskundig Genootschap* 37:572–574.

Witkamp, H. 1922. Drie 'steenen kanonnen', Zuid-Kerintji. *Tijdschrift van het Koninklijk Nederlandsch Aardrijkskundig Genootschap* 29:345–50.

Zwierzycki, J. 1926. Een vondst uit de Palaeolithische cultuurperiode in een grot in Boven Jambi. *De Mijningenieur in Nederlandsch-Indië* 4:63–67.

2

Eugène Dubois' work in Sumatra

Paul C.H. Albers, Julien Louys and Alexandra A.E. van der Geer

Abstract

This chapter presents the historical story of Dubois' cave research on Sumatra. Over two years in the Padang Highlands, Dubois explored a number of cave sites in his search for the 'missing link'. These include not only caves such as Lida Ajer, Jambu and Sibrambang that yielded large amounts of fossils, but also many other caves, often much smaller or with fewer or no fossils in them. As a supplement to the story, Dubois' field notes and official reports are disclosed and translated into English. Dubois' observations in the field indicate that he had a strong grasp of geological and palaeontological principles, given the knowledge current at the time. Dubois' later success in Java greatly overshadowed his accomplishments in Sumatra, which, although not as well known, have been significant for understanding its biological history.

Keywords: Lida Ajer, Jambu, Sibrambang, Padang Highlands, palaeontology, cave exploration

Abstrak

Bab ini menyajikan alur sejarah penelitian gua yang diakukan Dubois di Sumatra. Selama lebih dari dua tahun di Dataran Tinggi Padang, Dubois menjelajahi sejumlah situs gua untuk meneliti tentang 'mata rantai yang hilang'. Penelitiannya meliputi gua-gua, seperti Lida Ajer, Jambu dan Sibrambang, yang menghasilkan fosil dalam jumlah besar, juga telah ditemukan beberapa gua lainnya yang sering berukuran lebih kecil yang hanya mengandung sedikit fosil atau bahkan tidak ada fosilnya. Sebagai tambahan, ada catatan lapangan dan laporan resmi yang diterjemahkan dalam bahasa Inggris. Pengamatan Dubois di lapangan menunjukkan bahwa ia memiliki pemahaman yang sangat kuat tentang dasar-dasar geologi dan paleontologi yang telah memberikan pengetahuannya tentang aspek waktu. Keberhasilan Dubois di Jawa di kemudian hari sangat dipengaruhi oleh keberhasilan dan prestasinya ketika di Sumatra, yang meski tidak banyak diketahui dengan baik, namun hal tersebut sangat penting untuk memahami sejarah biologis pulau tersebut.

Kata kunci: Lida Ajer, Jambu, Sibrambang, Dataran Tinggi Padang, paleontologi, penjelajahan gua

Very brief introduction to Eugène Dubois

Dubois' life and contemplations are well described in the dissertation of Bert Theunissen (1985). They are also the subject of the more imaginative life description that Pat Shipman wrote based on research into parts of the Dubois Archive that had been disclosed by Theunissen and Paul Storm (Shipman 2001). All this was made possible by John de Vos, curator of the Dubois collection and archive at Naturalis, the natural history museum in Leiden. De Vos then assisted with further disclosure of these archives, resulting in a book by Albers and de Vos (2010) and the accounts of Sumatran research in this special issue.

The following brief biography of Dubois is drawn from both aforementioned sources, while the bulk of the section after that references Dubois' notes, employing the coding system used at Naturalis for individual scans of Dubois Archive pages or groups of pages. For each reference, a translation (by PCHA, of either the entire page or the appropriate paragraph) is provided in the appendix. For example, '50-040' refers to [MM774C-000050-040].

Eugène Dubois was born in 1859 in Eijsden in the deep south of the Netherlands, as the son of a well-to-do family. His father was the local apothecary, and was the mayor for some time. Eugène received a good education at school, then took up the study of medicine in Amsterdam. He was soon recognised as a brilliant scientist and accomplished anatomist. He was intended to succeed anatomist Max Fürbringer, his promoter, but Dubois was disillusioned with the university system and became convinced that Fürbringer was stealing his ideas to present them as if they were his. Whether or not Fürbringer indeed did so is not at all certain, but once this idea became fixed in Dubois' mind, he saw no other way out than to leave Amsterdam and pursue a dream he had: to find the 'missing link' between ape and humans. Dubois mentioned Lyell, Wallace and Virchow as the people who influenced him to look for it in Indonesia (50-040).

Aware of their favourable conditions for the preservation of fossils, Dubois chose to focus on examining caves, and the Padang Highlands in Sumatra seemed a good place to start. In one of the first caves he examined, Ngalau Lida Ajer, which he explored in 1888, he immediately met with success. He even found a hominin fossil tooth, but he was sure it belonged to *Homo sapiens* and that the faunal assemblage was young; thus, he concluded that these caves did not contain material old enough to deliver the 'missing link' he was looking for. Meanwhile, fossils had been found at Wajak on Java, and in 1890, he shifted his attention to that island, where he was again successful almost immediately. Within months, he found a *Homo erectus* jaw fragment in Kedung Brubus. He did recognise this fragment as fossil hominin, but he put it aside as it was too incomplete to persuade anybody that it represented the missing link. In 1891, he found a tooth and skullcap in Trinil, and initially assumed it to be that of a fossil chimpanzee. A year later, however, he found the famous hominin Femur 1, and with the arrival of a recent chimpanzee skull for comparison, it all fell into place and Dubois no longer considered the previous 'chimpanzee' finds to be of an anthropoid. He then named them and Femur 1 *Pithecanthropus erectus*, making Femur 1 the pivotal fossil of the species we now know as *Homo erectus*. Although Dubois found more *H. erectus* fossils in Java, with the exception of one tooth these did not play any role in the initial conception and description of *H. erectus* because they were not recognised in the Dubois collection until 40 years later when the first Ngandong skulls were also unearthed. Until his death in 1940, Dubois never acknowledged any finds other than his own as being *H. erectus*, leaving Ralph von Koenigswald in particular (but also many others) with a grudge that resulted in Dubois not being very warmly remembered. However, his contribution to science is unquestionable, as we will see in the following account of Dubois' life.

Arrival in Sumatra and discovery of Ngalau Lida Ajer

Dubois arrived as an army doctor in Padang, Sumatra, on 16 December 1887 with his pregnant wife Anna and their infant daughter Eugènie. Within three months, while still in Padang, he had already started exploring in his spare time (7-501, 7-502). He applied to be transferred, probably to be closer to the limestone caves as well as to be in a better climate, higher up in the mountains. In the second half of April, he finally moved from Padang to Payakumbuh. He performed his service as an army doctor in the local hospital but made no secret of his intentions for exploring science rather than a medical career. That this was a premeditated plan is abundantly clear from his correspondence. Jentink, the director of the natural history museum in Leiden, who was aware of Dubois' intentions, wrote to him to keep his head down and quietly be an army doctor for a year or two before making his intentions known, to avoid the risk of being sacked (e.g. 6-310, 6-313). Jentink wrote these words in vain: by the time they arrived in Indonesia, Dubois had already submitted a paper stating the desirability of palaeontological research in the Dutch Indies (Dubois 1888), contacted a high government official for support (Kroesen; 7-467) and further explored in his spare time (40-447).

On 1 June 1888, he noted his first visit to a cave near Payakumbuh (40-447). According to his route description, this was most probably Ngalau Sampit (see Figure 2.1; see also Duval et al. 2021 for current location details). These route descriptions mention names of places nearby, distances and directions. Maps copied into his notebook make it clear that Dubois had at his disposal the book *Topographische en geologische beschrijving van een gedeelte van Sumatra's westkust* (*Topographical and Geological Description of a Part of Sumatra's West Coast*) by geologist R.D.M. Verbeek (1883), chief engineer of the Dutch government mining department and famous for his work on the Krakatau volcano (Verbeek 1888). This book contains an extensive atlas, scaled 1:100.000, of this region, with geological descriptions of the soil; most of the names of locations that Dubois mentioned in his writings can be found on these maps in the old spelling. This book has proven to be an important key to unravelling Dubois' notes.

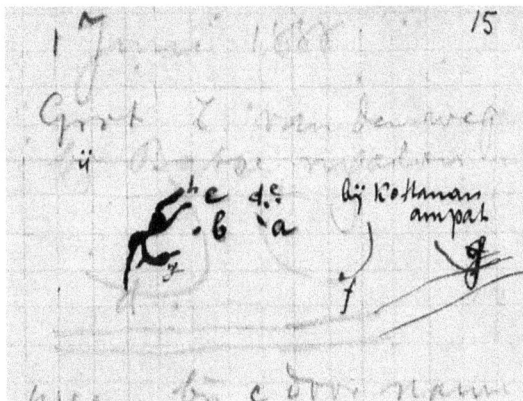

Figure 2.1: Dubois' first sketch of the cave entries and layout of a site most likely to be Ngalau Sampit.

Source: Field notes of Dubois, page 40-447. Dubois Archive, Naturalis Biodiversity Center, Leiden.

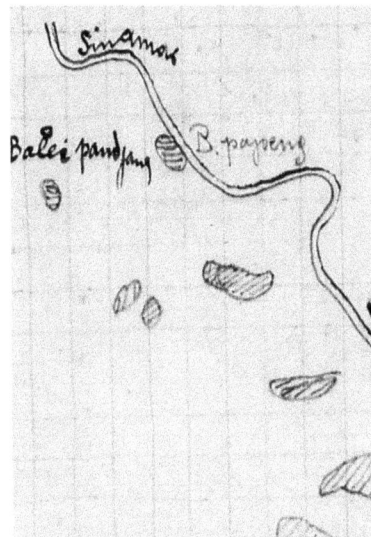

Figure 2.2: Drawing from Dubois' notebook showing the position of the Balei Pandjang cave in relation to the Sinamar River, which situates this cave near the location now called Nagari Bukik Sikumpa.

Source: Field notes of Dubois, page 40-446. Dubois Archive, Naturalis Biodiversity Center, Leiden.

Shortly afterwards, on 3 June 1888, he seems to have visited another cave close by—possibly Ngalau Indah—of which his description is merely 'being South of Balei Pandjang', which is ambiguous because Balei Pandjang is a name that occurs both southwest and southeast of Payakumbuh, giving us reason for uncertainty. However, given the small map in the notebook indicating the course of the Sinamar River in relation to this cave, its position can be established as the southeast alternative (see Figure 2.2).

In the Balei Pandjang cave he had a hole dug of 2 m depth. Dubois described it as containing a yellowish loam at the top; further down, this gradually became darker, as if bat excrements had been mixed in, until at 2 m depth, it overlaid a reddish-brown soil, which he described as 'baked' into a solid mass (40-448).

On 10 June 1888, his next free weekend, he apparently started again in the vicinity of Ngalau Sampit, further exploring the layout of the caves, but did not report any digging. On 15 June, his son Jean was born, and Dubois did not report any further explorations that month.

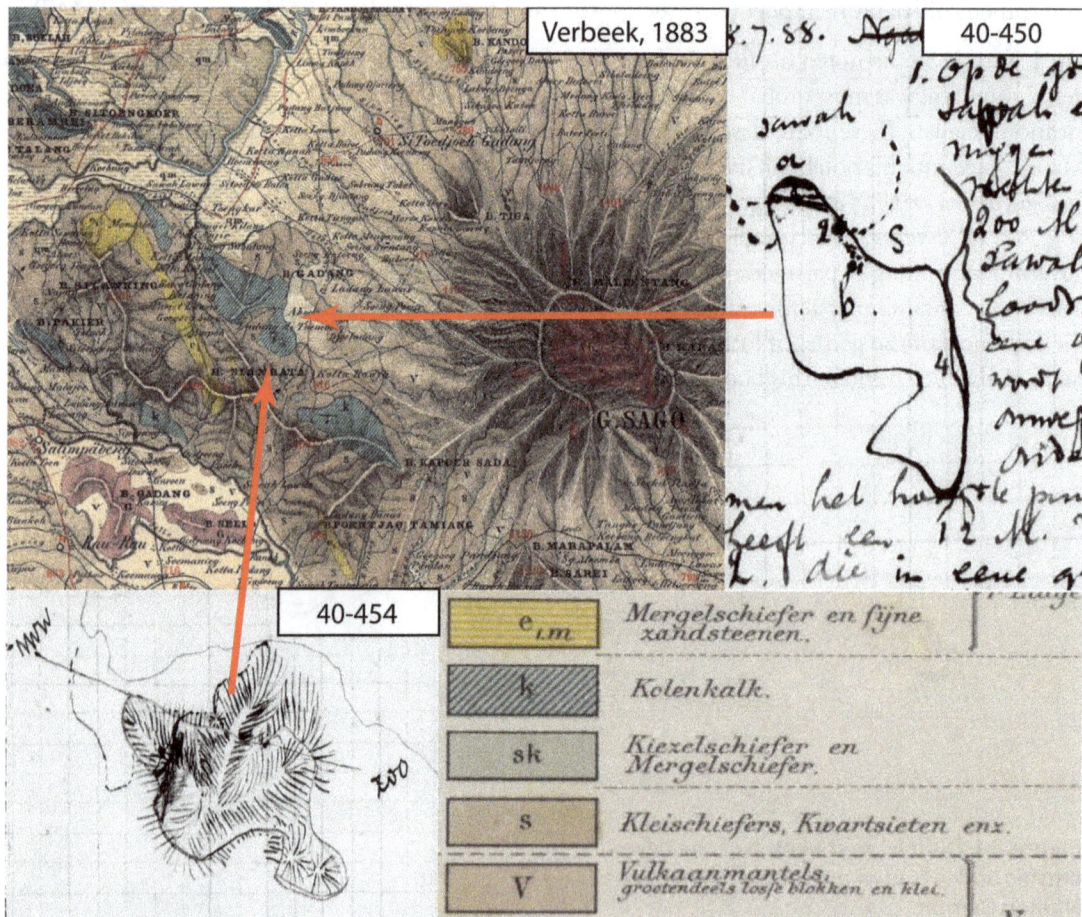

Figure 2.3: Part of a map from the Verbeek atlas and two excerpts from the Dubois notebooks concerning the surroundings of Ngalau Lida Ajer.

Note: To the right on the map is the old volcano Gunung Sago. The green-blue areas are indicated in the Dutch legend as 'Kolenkalk', coal limestone, which is the terrain where caves are most likely to be found. At that time, this terminology was mostly used to describe dark-coloured Carboniferous limestones.

Sources: Verbeek (1883); Dubois Archive and Library, Naturalis Biodiversity Center, Leiden.

On 1 July 1888, Dubois continued exploring for caves near Situdjuh Batu. He started at the north of a 'coal' (Dubois' description in translation) limestone ridge west of Mount Sago, where he located three caves (see Figure 2.3). From the descriptions he made in the following week (on 8 July) it is apparent that the third of these caves must have been Ngalau Lida Ajer (even though the notebook is not conclusive on this point), as later he clearly stated that in 'Ngalau Lida-ajer, cave 3 excavations have started 15.7.88' (40-452). In the official report, this date is stated to be 18 July 1888, but this could have been for political reasons, as some support and manpower for the excavations were supplied by the Assistant-Resident, and this date might reflect that transaction (50-035). Strictly speaking, that is also the date they actually began to dig a hole inside the cave (40-452). The cave opens in the mountain wall at about 150 m above the current level of the *sawahs* (rice fields). Dubois noted that the small brook, Betang Babuwe, that dug a course alongside this wall must have been much larger at some point, given the thick layers of large pebbles that could be observed in several places, and that it was also likely that a small waterway had once run through this cave (50-035). Dubois used the atlas of Verbeek (1883) to situate this cave within its geological context (see Figure 2.3). Also, sandy layers were present inside the cave but absent in the immediate vicinity outside, and Dubois considered this further evidence that the cave had previously channelled water (50-035). This demonstrates that Dubois was a keen observer of geological clues and well prepared for the task he had set himself.

Excavation of Ngalau Lida Ajer

Our written sources for the excavation of Ngalau Lida Ajer are his notebooks and reports and several letters he wrote. He kept copies or drafts of these letters with his received correspondence. Whereas the notebooks are just that—lists of short notes or reminders made in the field in pencil, sometimes later overwritten with ink—the reports and correspondence give a clear chronological account of the work that was done.

After Dubois had gained access to the cave and visually inspected it, men were put to work, but he did not have the manpower to systematically clear it out as he would have liked (50-036). From the start, soil samples were taken (40-451), but, alas, many of these samples were lost during World War II when a bomb hit the part of the museum in Leiden where all Dubois' soil samples were kept. Those irretrievably lost, were, together with the damaged part of the building, used to fill an adjacent canal (Natasja den Ouden, pers. comm. 2021).

Once Dubois had inspected the cave and taken soil samples, irregular pieces of stalagmite and fallen parts of stalactites were removed. On 18 July 1888, they started to dig a hole in the second chamber. This is shown at x in the top right part of Figure 2.4.

Whereas in the first chamber, the top layer was a continuation of the topsoil outside the cave, a 20–30 cm–thick black soil, in the second chamber, the top layer was described by Dubois as a loose loam or a brownish-yellowish claylike soil. In this, a piece of turned pottery was found. Underneath, there was an irregular stalagmite floor, very hard and crystalline, with a very broad foot expanding to most of the surface of the chamber, and with its top 45 cm underneath the ground level in the middle of the room. A large piece of petrified charcoal was found at its base, at a depth of 1 m, on its right side when coming from outside (40-453, 50-036). Dubois claimed that it was possible that this piece of charcoal pointed to human occupation of the cave long ago (50-036).

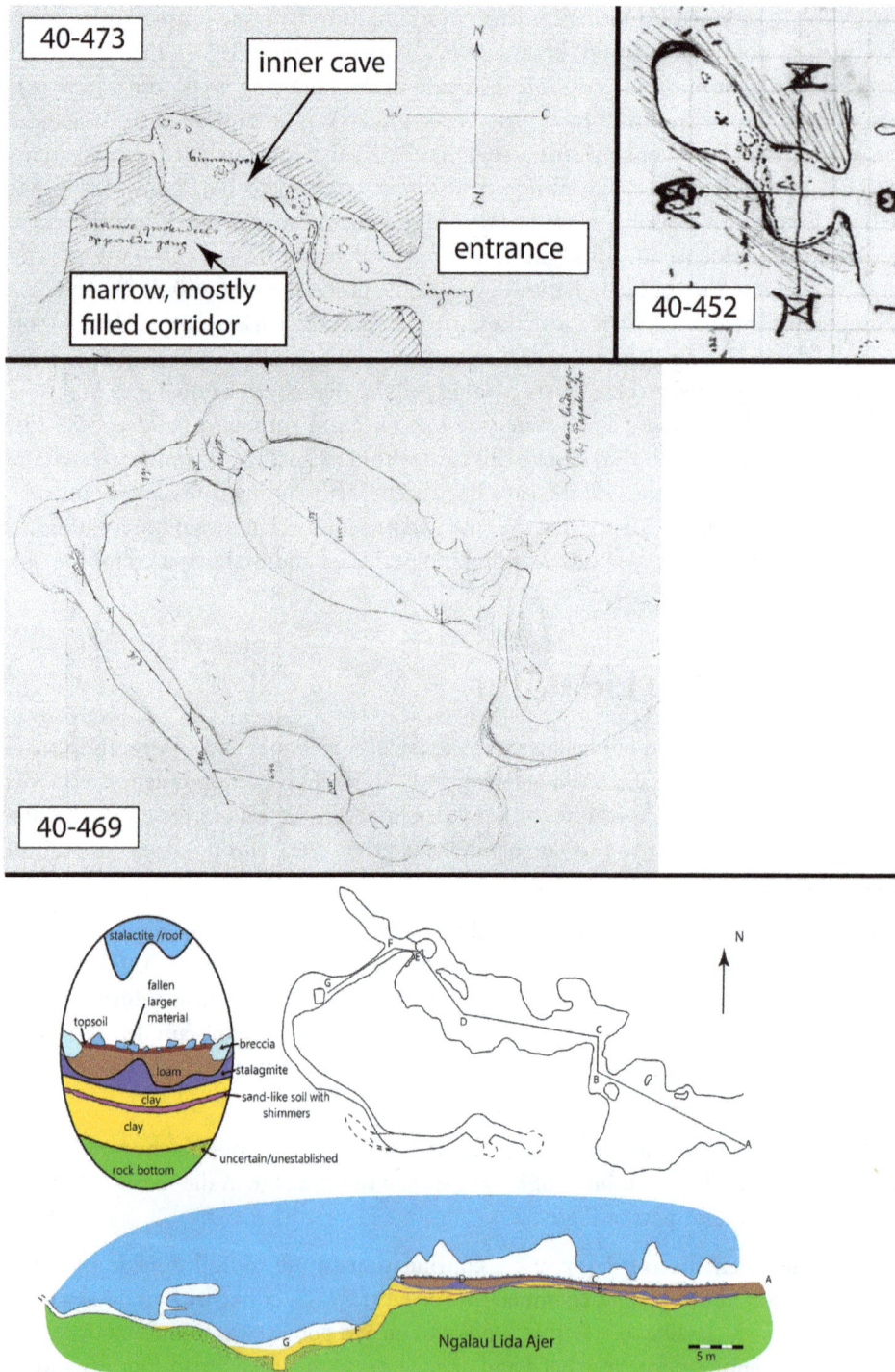

Figure 2.4: Sketches and drawings from Dubois' notebook and letter and their interpretation.

Top left (40-473): drawing in draft letter dated 17 September 1888.

Top right (40-452): sketch in notebook, dated 15 July 1888.

Middle (40-469): sketch in notebook, probably drawn towards the end of the excavation around the middle of October 1888.

Bottom: PCHA's interpretation of Dubois' layering superimposed on recent drawing of Ngalau Lida Ajer; the oval shape is the legend, top view and lateral view.

Sources: Dubois Archive, Naturalis Biodiversity Center, Leiden; Louys et al. (2022).

The stalagmite cone was removed using dynamite on 23 July 1888 (40-453). Underneath, they encountered a fine, yellowish, plastic clay. The excavation was expanded towards the rear of the cave, but to do that, the breccia, which extended about 1 m inwards from the walls and which so far had been neglected, had to be removed. This breccia was present over the whole width of the chamber and was about 70 cm thick. Besides both sharp and rounded pieces of limestone, it contained andesite pebbles, terrestrial gastropods next to a large number of teeth, and some bone fragments of several mammals (50-036). Thus, on 17 August 1888, the first fossils were found and brought to Dubois, who was not present at that time due to his medical duties (40-471). On 31 August, he inspected the location again and reported that he himself had dug up teeth (40-455), which were abundant in the calcified breccias and at the feet of the dripstones in the back of the cave, and even more abundant in the silt layer underneath (50-036).

He reported his finds to Kroesen, the governor of Sumatra, on 17 September 1888 (40-471), and after that, Dubois' position quickly improved. His paper arguing for palaeontological research (Dubois 1888), which had now been published, and his immediate success in finding a cave littered with fossils, did the trick. One thing that substantially boosted Dubois' efforts would have been that his work had immediately attracted the attention of Verbeek, who had been among the first to congratulate Dubois on his results and praise him for finding just what he had been looking for (12-400). In his reply on 1 October 1888, Dubois told Verbeek that after a month's work he had already recovered thousands of fossils from Ngalau Lida Ajer. He also stated that he had no doubt about them being fossil but did not dare to say anything about their true age yet (33-506). Verbeek would have recognised the scientific value of these finds, and, because of his high position at the mining department, would have been asked for his expert opinion by any office deciding on Dubois' future.

The other very influential person with whom Dubois was in correspondence was Melchior Treub, the effective head of all scientific research in the Dutch Indies (the actual head being the Minister). He, too, applauded Dubois' success and offered support as well as advice on how to deal with the politics (12-265). As a result of all this, Dubois was granted leave from his medical duties (as soon as a replacement for him had arrived) and could from then on spend all his time on palaeontological research. As early as his first official report, dated 15 October 1888, he had already presented a faunal list (50-037; shown in Table 2.1) that later changed only a little.

The whole report (50-032–50-039) has a long introduction, as if it is a scientific article, in an effort to convince any readers of the importance of the work. The subsequent chronological account of the work has all kinds of details that anyone working in the field today recognises, but which, at that time, were not common knowledge: for example, that fossils from cave deposits can be recognised because they 'stick to the tongue' (50-036).

Dubois also recognised that almost all the fossils had been gnawed by porcupines, a feature he knew from the literature (Lydekker 1886). In a cave nearby, Ngalau Gudja (Porcupine Cave), he also saw 'innumerable traces of these animals [that] are proof of their quite recent stay' (50-037). To further test his hypothesis that porcupines had indeed gnawed the fossil bones, he offered fresh bones to a living porcupine in captivity, in order to compare the gnawing patterns of modern porcupines with what he saw on his fossils and to deliver 'the final convincing proof that porcupines had been the destructors of the bones here' (50-037). Dubois was quite possibly the first to conduct such neotaphonomic experiments (see Figure 2.5).

Table 2.1: Species reported by Dubois for Ngalau Lida Ajer.

Species as reported by Dubois	Dubois' remarks (translated by PCHA)	Current identification in the Dubois collection catalogue
Simia satyrus	large differences in size	*Pongo pygmaeus palaeosumatrensis*
Hylobates	probably more than one species	*Symphalangus syndactylus* subfossilis, *Hylobates* sp. indet.
Semnopithecus		currently not identified in the collection
Macacus		*Macaca* sp. indet.
Cercocebus		currently not identified in the collection
Felis	of the tiger	currently not identified in the collection
Smaller *Felis species*	maybe	*Profelis temmincki temmincki, Paguma* sp. indet.
Elephas	probably two species	*Elephas maximus*
Rhinoceros		*Dicerorhinus sumatrensis,*
Tapirus		*Tapirus indicus intermedius*
Sus	probably more than one species[3]	*Sus* sp. indet.
Bos	or *Bubalus*	*Bibos javanicus*
Cervus	probably distinguishable species	*Muntiacus muntjak, Rusa* sp. indet.
Other ruminants		*Capricornis sumatraensis*
Hystrix		*Hystrix* sp. indet.
Other rodents		*Leopoldamys sabanus*
Homo sapiens[1]	molar superior III	*Homo sapiens*
Gastropods[2]		currently not identified in the collection

Note: All these fauna were present in the report of 15 October 1888 (50-037), except the last two entries which are in the following two notebooks:

[1] 31 October 1888 (40-459).

[2] Already mentioned on 15 July 1888 (40-452).

[3] There might have been more species indeed, but he also might have mistaken some of the more than 10 *Ursus malayanus* dental elements as being *Sus*.

Source: Dubois Archive, Naturalis Biodiversity Center, Leiden.

Figure 2.5: Recent *Sus barbatus* jawbone (RGM.1333508) at Naturalis Biodiversity Centre, Leiden, originally collected in Borneo by Büttikofer in 1894 but later added to the Dubois collection as a clear example of porcupine gnawing marks.

Source: Photograph by Natasja den Ouden.

The drawing included with Dubois' letter to Kroesen of 17 September 1888 (Figure 2.4; 40-473) shows that by this date they had already reached the corridor at the end of the first large inner chamber, going down between F and G in the modern drawing in Figure 2.4 (this is the 'sinkhole' mentioned by Louys et al. [2022:2]). This corridor was largely filled in; in fact, its entrance was found at a depth of about 3–4 m when most of the inner chamber had been emptied.

Dubois reported that while excavating this chamber, at some 2 m below the original surface, they came across a sandy layer containing numerous 'shimmers'. He had no time to examine these but suspected a pumice tuff origin. Samples were no doubt collected for later examination. Below the sand, a brownish clay layer like the one above the sandy layer was encountered, and this again contained teeth and bone fragments despite its depth.

The corridor yielded many teeth, among which were two intact molars of *Elephas* lying on top of the soil, and, according to Hooijer (1955), so alike they were probably from the same individual. The passage was followed for some 10 m more, but lack of fresh air (the candles would not burn any longer) prevented further examination (50-037). Along the way, Dubois noticed that two small stalactite pillars had been polished on the sides facing each other, and he assumed this to have been caused by larger animals living in the cave, passing between them, in times before the cave was filled with a 4 m–thick layer of soil. He argued that the large number of remnants, mainly teeth, sometimes of very large species, could only have been dragged in, meaning the cave had been the den of large predators. Dubois did not conclude which predator was responsible, but he did mention that some tiger and small-bear teeth had been found. He further remarked that although the work progressed slowly, and under insufficient supervision, thousands of teeth and many bone fragments were found, resulting in a preliminary faunal list (see Table 2.1). Given the contents of the list, and particularly the presence of about 600 orangutan teeth, Dubois concluded that the whole flats around Payakumbuh must have been a continuous, single forest in the past.

Dubois started a new notebook titled 'Ngalau Lida Ajer and Gua Balei-Pandjang 1888'(40-458), in which the first dated entry reads: '31 October 1888 at 4 to 4½ m. depth below the original level in the narrow corridor, 1½ m from the entrance a human molar was found (mol. sup. III)' (40-459).

He further described the corridor as having had a yellow loam layer with a sandier top layer 4–5 cm deep. The yellow loam, which he described as plastic, was:

> [...] present in the whole corridor at ± the same level slightly descending towards the deeper chamber and 40–70 cm below the surface of the less humic, slightly darker than ordinary clay, which is present everywhere in the cave and in which the fossils can be found. In the sandy layer et cetera in the first inner chamber they do also appear, but very scarcely and likely only ending up there because of them being dug or tossed up. (40-459)

He continued on the next page, stating:

> At the entrance of the second inner chamber the deeper layer of the plastic loam has, because of infiltration by chalk, been baked together to a hard mass.

> Everywhere this hard plastic loam is sharply separated from the above more porous loose and less homogeneous dark clay.

> It is apparent and without doubt that this loam and the accompanying layer of sand have been the result of deposition by a very slow-moving stream of water.

From the second inner chamber we had access to a 10-m long corridor on 8 November 1888, which after using dynamite gave access to a third small chamber with a second floor higher up. This corridor, which on one side has not been completely filled, is widening strongly and actually (40-460)

forms one room with the so-called second inner chamber.

First from there the subsidence became apparent. (40-461)

The same page contains another small map of the cave and the remark that the excavation ended on 12 December 1888. (For the complete notebooks, with transcriptions and translations, please see the appendix).

Other caves in the area of Payakumbuh

Dubois had his workforce divided over several locations at the same time, so the reader should keep in mind that we here present a list of descriptions of the work done in the caves that necessarily can only loosely follow the timeline as the work in different caves overlapped and in some caves their work was long and in others it was short.

Ngalau Gundja (Porcupine Cave)

About 200 m from Ngalau Lida Ajer, Dubois started a preliminary examination of Ngalau Gundja: Porcupine Cave. At a depth of 0.75 m, he recorded that a 'horizontal layer of pumice tuff of 80–90 cm thickness was found, under which a similar reddish-brown clay was present [to that which] currently forms the surface' (May 1889 report; 50-039). Another notebook states about this cave:

> […] opening clearly shaped later.
>
> Descending strongly into a deep crevasse which is also shaped later. Above these, one can however along the wall reach into the farthest point of the cave, entering a spacious round chamber which is communicating with a small one to the left. Both bear the traces of numerous porcupines. In the large chamber I had a transverse section made more than 2 m wide.
>
> At a depth of 75 cm the dry red clay changed into a dry white sandy mass. (pumice tuff, marl or sand) probably sand. (40-456)

Further documenting this cave, there are field notes (Figure 2.6), which state:

> In the deepest (farthest from the entrance) part, in a spacious room (of 8 by 10 m) I had an incision made over the length, which was 2½ metres wide, into the soil which was brown-yellow at the top, and red further on. Getting grainier further down (75–130 cm), whitish with lots of shimmers. Followed up to a max depth of 2.70 m. To the back part there are layers of gravel (not horizontally but irregularly crossing each other) which have largely baked together to a conglomerate. In the deeper layers sandy. Also irregularly a layer of speleothem is interspersed with the gravel mass. It was followed up to a max depth of 2.60 m below the surface where there was sandstone and it was 20 cm thick. It starts completely at the back 60 cm below the surface. The speleothem is not fully covering the gravel. The gravel is only present to about 2.25 m from the rear wall. Largest depth of the whitish soil 2.70 m. (49-264)

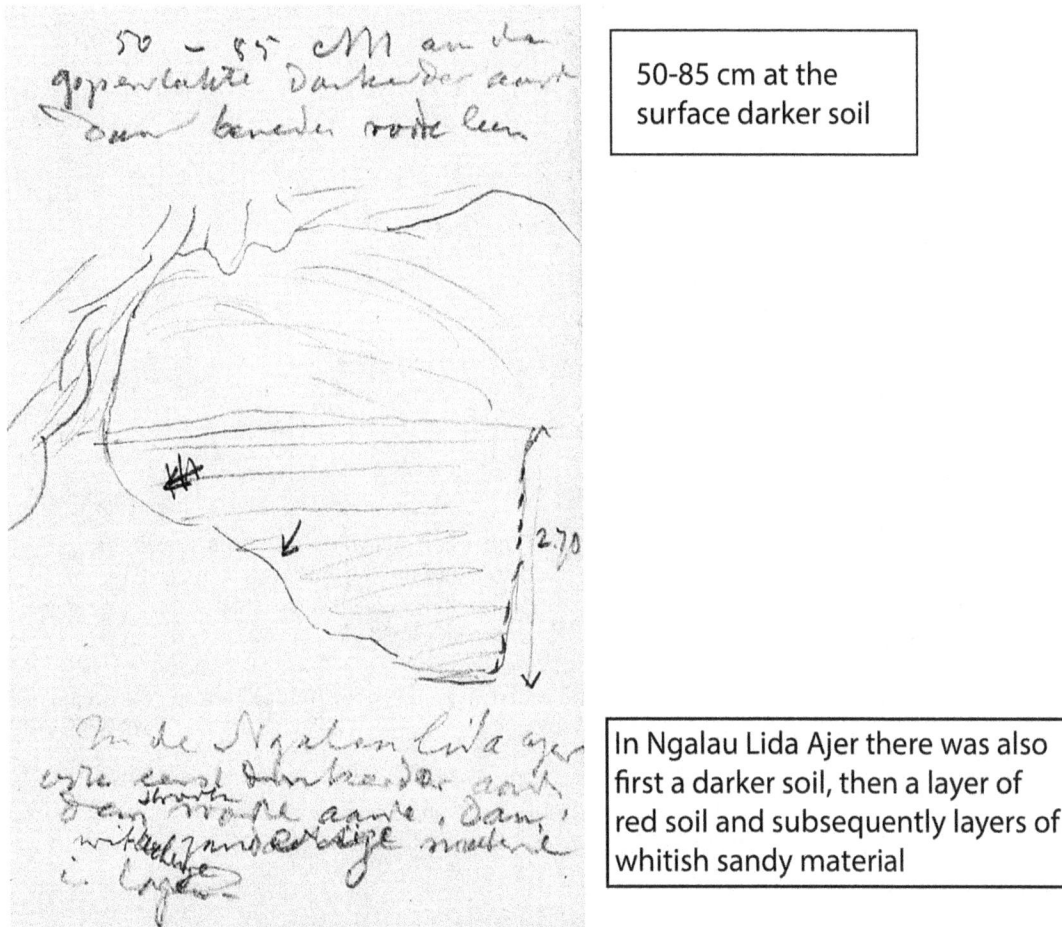

50-85 cm at the surface darker soil

In Ngalau Lida Ajer there was also first a darker soil, then a layer of red soil and subsequently layers of whitish sandy material

Figure 2.6: Dubois' sketch of Ngalau Gundja.

Note: The arrow in the centre seems to indicate where the gravel reached.

Source: Field notes of Dubois (49-265). Dubois Archive, Naturalis Biodiversity Center, Leiden.

Balei Pandjang Cave

In Dubois' notes, the descriptions of this so-called 'cave' suggest a complex of caves within one mountain. His notes say:

> Gua Balei-Pandjang
>
> Started 13 December 1888
>
> At the first point (deepest) at 90–100 cm underneath the yellow clay which was deposited in horizontal layers, a dark brownish clay with small calcium-concretions was found.
>
> At point 2, to the right of the first corridor 1½ m yellow clay in layers, then 30 cm bat guano (on top of which a piece of charcoal) sharply separated from it and basically removable by peeling it off.
>
> a. Cave with a 12 m deep pit at ± 300 m above the sawah.
>
> b. Cave at ± 250 m height above the sawah
>
> 35 m. deep vault at the bottom of which there is a second entrance in the perpendicular wall
>
> 1 [? hard] upper vault of cave b

3 hard stalagmite mass to the right

2— ditto

4? Soft " " [stalagmite mass] left

6 out of (crater pit) (40-462, 40-463)

The text and the numbering of the drawing on the next page of the notebook (Figure 2.7) suggest that a much more detailed drawing probably existed, but we have not been able to identify it.

The other notebook states:

> 13 October, 1888 started with the Ngalau (gua) Balei pandjang, which we had to abandon again on 24 February 1889 without any result because of lack of decent surveillance and difficulties because of the water dripping down. (40-457)

Figure 2.7: Drawing in Dubois' notebook related to Balei Pandjang.
Source: Dubois Archive, Naturalis Biodiversity Center, Leiden (40-464).

In his report, Dubois also mentioned the cave he called 'a' in the notes quoted above (we cannot be certain as the report did not identify the cave clearly, but the timing makes any other option unlikely):

> In the same mountain slightly below the top at about 300 m. height above the valley lies a natural pit of ±15 m. depth. This pit widens below to a beautiful cave and in the corner of this cave, almost directly below the surface of a very thin layer of clay, a layer of pumice tuff of about ½ m. thick was found. (50-039)

He further stated that this pumice tuff must have been deposited at the same time as the pumice tuff layers present 'outside' in the Payakumbuh valley (50-039).

Ngalau Sampit

In early 1889, Dubois also started working in Ngalau Sampit, which was probably the very first cave he had visited in June 1888, but which he excavated only after he finished with Lida Ajer. In a popular-science account of the time (Pijnappel 1897), an anecdote is told about Dubois entering a cave with a fellow countryman. After crawling for some time through a narrow entrance, they reach a larger chamber, from which many corridors continue. The description and timing make it likely that this refers to Ngalau Sampit. After some time, they cannot remember which entrance they came in through, which causes some panic in Dubois' companion. Dubois calms him down, then examines the corridors one by one to find the one through which they came; when he sees light at the end of the tunnel he is examining, he goes back to fetch his companion, and they both crawl out—only to find themselves on the other side of the mountain.

The report Dubois wrote about Ngalau Sampit (April 1889 report; 50-011) has already been published in full (translated into English by PCHA) in Duval et al. (2021), to which we refer readers for more details, except to mention that the fossil species encountered in Ngalau Sampit resembled those recovered from Lida Ajer, with remains of *Elephas*, *Rhinoceros*, *Sus*, *Bos* or *Bubalus*, *Cervus* and *Simia satyrus* (= *Pongo*), but in much lower frequencies. Dubois also described a more recent 'cave-in' in which remains of *Sus vittatus*, *Cervus muntjac*, *Antilope* (= *Capricornus*) *sumatraensis* and some *Canis* were found (50-011).

Meanwhile, his work and his success were being picked up by newspapers (e.g. *de Locomotief* of 11 and 29 November 1888; these clippings are in the Dubois Archive; 42-211; 42-212). He had really only barely started, but he now had formal support, and as soon as his replacement arrived, he would be able to dedicate his full attention to excavating. He asked to be transferred to Bua, where he started his explorations of the Ngalau Saribu mountain range, for which the Assistant-Resident of Tanah Datar had provided him with an extensive list of caves (50-006). He was also granted the use of convicts for labour (e.g. 50-005) and supplied with tools (50-007), and by 22 April 1889, two workmen from the engineer corps had been assigned to him, namely Franke and van de Nesse (50-009). His replacement, Vollema, arrived on 2 May, and Dubois was finally free to spend all his time on excavating (50-010).

Two caves are mentioned in his report for May 1889—'Ngalau kapala sawah liat' and 'Ngalau bateng pangean'—but excavations did not start until 1 June (50-039). The monthly report for June was not submitted until the end of July because Dubois had suffered a severe attack of malaria (50-013).

Caves approached from Bua

Ngalau Kapala Sawah Liat, or Ngalau Pandjang

The cave Ngalau Kapala Sawah Liat, which Dubois also referred to as 'Ngalau Pandjang', near Sibalen was described in the June 1889 report (50-040) as being a 45 m long corridor with an average width of 5 m, which widened to form some kind of chamber only for the first 8.5 m from the entrance and again at a depth of 30 m, where there was a width of 10 m. The cave did not actually end at 45 m and was thought to continue to the other side of the mountain, but further access was impossible because of narrowness and a collapsed roof. Dubois thought it had originally been a waterway through the mountain. He started digging at three points 10 m apart and found the stratigraphy to be similar at all three. The work was so hard, however, that he soon decided to concentrate all his workforce on one point. The topsoil was a yellow clay 0.30 m deep, which in the more inward parts of the cave was covered with 0.25 m of speleothem. The report states:

> Next was a very hard mass, a conglomerate of pebbles of different sizes, gravel and pieces of limestone, with here and there thin layers of sand interspersed with very hard clay, and locally sometimes thin layers of dripstone [speleothem]. This reached a thickness of 2–3 m. Next to that on some parts we already hit the bedrock, otherwise yellow clay which mainly expanded far into a small hollow left of the entrance. This 'corridor-shaped' small hollow started at 4.75 m depth and continued in a diagonal southeast direction into the mountain. Whilst in the clay at the surface only a few incisors of the common porcupine were found, apparently of rather recent date, more bones were found in this deep clay, of which a greater age cannot be doubted. In the mentioned small hollow a number of bones, predominantly of rodents and bats were found. An important find however was done on 30 June at a depth of 3.75 m in the middle of the chamber at the entrance, being the humerus of a species of Rhinoceros, which judging from the size of the bone was significantly larger than the current Sumatran species. (50-040)

Figure 2.8 shows this bone.

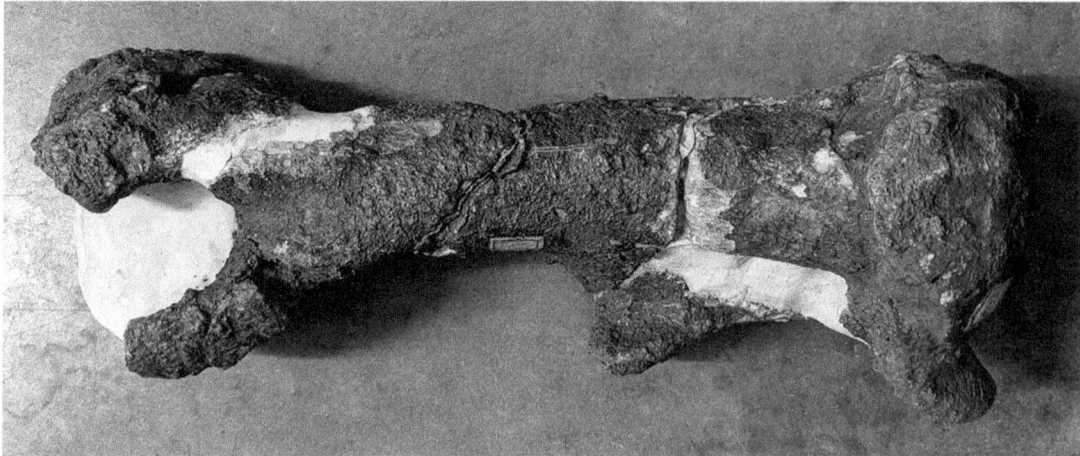

Figure 2.8: Humerus of *Dicerorhinus sumatrensis* (DUB9276) from Ngalau Pandjang near Sibalen.
Note: Length: 421 mm, according to Hooijer (1946).
Source: Photograph by Natasja den Ouden.

By July 1889, Dubois stated in his report on June:

> [The] work was continued up to a maximum depth of 8 m. where the bedrock of the cave was reached. Underneath the yellow clay that was reached last month, locally a layer of gravel impregnated with chalk was found, which was resting at the bottom of the cave. Fossils of any importance were not found, with the exception of a plastron of tortoise, which however upon removing the hardened clay mass by carelessness of the workmen was broken into many pieces. (50-048)

On 20 July 1889, Ngalau Pandjang was exhausted after they had reached the bottom.

In the September 1889 report, Dubois briefly mentioned a cave—close to a *dusun* [village] named Sibalin—whose:

> […] local name is not known to me, is located in the same valley at the right bank of the Sumpur as the other caves examined here so far, ± 40 m above the floor of it and consists of a 150-m long corridor with an average width of 7 m whilst its yellowish clay floor is rather even and almost horizontal. (50-050)

The October 1889 report speaks of a large cave at Sisawah that:

> […] turned out to be the earlier southern extension of the Ngalau pandjang (Ng kapala sawah luat), with which it was connected by a narrow passage, which now could be slightly widened. (50-050)

> The entrance of [that part of] the cave is located 20 m. above the valley floor (erroneously in the previous report it was stated to be 40 m) and it is facing Southward; it consists of a 150-m long corridor in north-northwest direction, which is on average 6–8 m wide, but at the end widens to a wide chamber 40 m long and in the middle 20 m wide.

> Its smooth and almost horizontal floor consists of a thick layer of chalk tuff, which in some spots is absent. Only near the entrance (up to 15–20 m), this chalk mass is missing and the floor, which is 2 metres lower, consists of yellow clay.

> Excavations were started at two points; one near the entrance, whereby the end of October they had reached a depth of 3.50 m, while the soil continued to consist of the same clay. A further excavation was started at 30 m distance from the entrance where they encountered:

1.35 m chalk tuff, a 0.30 m. thick breccia of small limestone parts and fine quartz gravel, baked together by the hard chalk tuff, 20 cm fine gravel mixed with clay and finally (at 1.85 m.) yellow clay. Fossils had not been found by the end of October. (50-051)

In November 1889, the southern extension yielded teeth and bones from:

> […] the yellow clay next to the entrance at a depth between 4.20 m. and 5.50 m. The latter however were in such a bad state of conservation that the majority were mere fragments which for the time being cannot be identified. They chiefly originate from elephant, rhinoceros, tapir, pig, porcupine (*Hystrix*) and the orangutan (*S. satyrus*), so represent the same species, of which the existence also became apparent in other caves that have been examined.

> The geological age of these fossils cannot rightly be ascertained and can only somewhat be established by comparison with others. The greatest depth by the end of November was 5.75 m. From 4.50 m down, the yellow clay from before was found to be strongly mixed with a moderately fine gravel delivered by weathering of tertiary conglomerate.

> The hole we dug at 30 m distance from the entrance of the cave with the size of 6.50 m by 5.50 m delivered the following profile starting from the top: 1.35 chalk tuff, 0.30 breccia of limestone pieces [50-051 up to here] and fine quartz gravel baked together by chalk tuff, 0.20 m fine gravel mixed with clay; underneath this, in total 1.85 m thick top layer the same yellow clay was found as near the entrance, at 2.75 m the bottom of the cave was found, which only along its east wall was covered with a maximally 0.75 m thick layer of clay stones.

> It was regrettable that the mentioned clay did not contain any fossils, as especially here one could have expected, underneath the strong limestone coverage that they would have [been] conserved well by calcification. (50-044)

By early December 1889, fossils were becoming scarce, and the site was abandoned (50-051).

Unnamed cavity near the southern entrance of Ngalau Pandjang

In his annual report for 1889, Dubois mentions a small cavity in the same valley as the one into which the entrance to the southern extension of Ngalau Pandjang opened; finding this led him to an elaborate insight on the local geology, which is presented here in full:

> At a short distance of the southern Ng. pandjang and completely at the same height a small hole found in the rocks at the east side of the valley was further examined. Although it was only 0.80 m long and 0.60 m high, it seems to be the remains of an earlier cave which had become filled up in later times with boulders and pointy limestone pieces connected to a conglomerate by the chalk. After this conglomerate breccia was broken away to the west the entrance of a small cave opened up, however only 3 m wide and 1.80 m high. Against the ceiling a 25 cm thick layer of hardened clay had remained which contained a number of teeth and some bones, most of which had completely calcified. By further breaking away the mentioned stone mass we could finally enter up to 20 m deep, where the cave seemed to end after it had widened, but it [the ceiling] remained as low as it was near the entrance.

> The teeth and bones originated from a Rhinoceros, a Tapir, a kind of buffalo (*Bos*), a deer (*Cervus*), one or more species of pig (*Sus*), the orangutan (*Simia*) and a common Karo-monkey (*Cercopithecus*) or some species closely related to that; so here yet again the same company we found everywhere. This is now however of great significance and confirms again the great age of this fauna. It is namely a peculiar phenomenon that here at a height of about 20 m above the floor, where both these caves are located and at many places apparently in the same horizon crevices in the rock can be observed which are of the same nature like for instance those along the Kuantan near Muka-Muka at the height of the water level. Surely the water must have

gnawed out these crevices and is now depositing pebbles and gravel and clay in them. This must also have been the case for the caves we have examined. The small cave is but an extension of such a crevice and also the southern Ngalau pandjang shows this at the entrance. (50-044)

In this valley, which now doesn't even have a brook anymore, the water level must have been 20 m above the current valley floor, and this will certainly not have been a small brook, for the crevices can be found along the whole length of the valley and quite strongly so. The water must also have deposited the boulders, the gravel and the fossil-bearing clay and such large changes demand a very long time which contributes to the decision of a substantial age of the fossils.

It is furthermore noteworthy, that higher up in the valley there is a rock wall in which there are three such crevices with a distance between them of 8–10 m and at which the same phenomenon can be seen where the valley of the Sisawah leads in southeastern direction towards the *tarata* Kabun.

Traces of such higher water levels and the rerouting of rivers are a well-known phenomenon and a consequence of the erosion doing its work over the whole globe, but what is noteworthy here is that these phenomena seem to have some periodicity.

Up to three or four times at least the water level was able to do its erosive action for a longer time (because the formation of these crevices must have taken quite some time), after which every time an abrupt decrease of the water level took place. Note it is not completely sure whether this water, which was a river, was as far from the shore as it is now. If it turns out, that during the diluvial times, as assumed by Verbeek, at the west coast of Sumatra the sea was yet covering part of the current land (up to a height of 180 m) then the phenomenon observed here might be related to these changes of sea-level and the here observed repeated rather local changes might have bearing on the work that by Inesz has been turned into a *question coulante* on the changes of the beach lines and the borders between sea and land and may be of no little significance. But this is only a suspicion, which I however not thought I should keep quiet, because the observed phenomena might deserve further investigation at other locations. (50-045)

The ideas highlighted in these reports and field notes again show Dubois to have been a keen observer of geology and thoroughly conversant with the geological knowledge of that time; he was able to combine information from the geological and palaeontological or physical anthropological disciplines to create logical and defendable hypotheses. Dubois finds reasonable geological explanations for his observations, even if the knowledge existing at the time meant that he was wrong in some details. Dubois considers observations of boulders, gravels and fossil-bearing clays in high crevices evidence that the fossils must be of significant antiquity, accurately using his geomorphological observations to deduce relative chronological information. More significantly, his observation that crevices are found together at different heights, and that these patterns are repeated across valleys and outcrops with an indication of periodicity, anticipates much later cave terrace development concepts (e.g. Duringer et al. 2012; Palmer 1991). His explanation for such phenomena relied on Verbeek's diluvial interpretation (i.e. eustatic variations due to glacial–interglacial cycles), which, although incorrect, was the best available knowledge at the time (it predated the concept of plate tectonics, from which we now understand that the Barisan Mountains are the result of a series of orogenies beginning in the Miocene). Nevertheless, the idea that sea-level changes can control the formation of limestone caves is not without merit and has been used to explain cave formation in limestone islands (e.g. Mylroie and Carew 1990).

Ngalau Bulan, or Ngalau Pandjang II

Work in this cave started at 20 July 1889 (50-048), but in the subsequent monthly report Dubois wrote:

> Ngalau bulan (Ngalau pandjang II) near Sibalin did not bring anything peculiar. Although rather many bones were found in the top, 0.60 m thick layer of loose black earth, these were also almost all broken into such tiny parts, that for most of them (at least for the time being) there can be no thought of having them identified. Most seem to be originating from small animals and must, after predators brought them in, have been shattered by porcupines whilst digging through the earth. They are however no big loss, as they are without doubt bones of a recent date.
>
> Upon further digging we came into 1.15 m of yellow clay, which at greater depth turns into a fine gravel. This yellow clay did contain some teeth of the ordinary wild pig (*Sus vittatus*), of the tapir (*Tapirus indicus*) and of the ordinary Karo (*Cercopithecus cynomolgus*), and a few bones of the Kidjang (*Cervulus muntjac*), all species still living today. (50-049)

In September 1889, no more fossils were found. Dubois reported that:

> Underneath the deepest layer of fine gravel we found in the previous month, which had a thickness of 30 to 40 cm, we found again a darkish yellow clay earth which we followed up to a depth of more than 5 m without finding anything important. This result and even more so the strong increase of fever amongst the workmen in this moist cave (up to 50% of the number of forced labourers were suffering from fevers) make me decide to quit the work here. (50-050)

Ngalau Batang Pangian and Ngalau Monsiu

The cave of Bua, Ngalau Batang Pangian, was abandoned after 12 days as too many workers were suffering from fever there. Instead, on 15 June 1889, they started excavating in Ngalau Monsiu (Gunpowder Cave, named for its saltpetre from bat guano):

> [...] at 4 paal [about 4 miles] from Bua on the opposite side of the Sinamar-river in the Gugug andjieng. It is a very deep cave; its main corridor is estimated to be 150–200 m long. It is connected to a cave at a lower level, through which the Batang Janki flows and it surely at one point was itself the conduit for this or some other river.
>
> We started excavating here close to the entrance on 15 June and we found a layer of sand lithified through impregnation of chalk 0.50 m., 1.60 m yellow loam, 0.20 conglomerate of silicates and pieces of limestone; all deposited in horizontal layers, apparently aquatic deposits. In the loam a few molars of a species of pig, a few incisors of the common porcupine and two molars of a deer were found. (50-047)

A few weeks later, however, the work was abandoned after no more fossils had surfaced (50-048). Dubois kept trying to track down suitable caves, and although a few were found, no further caves were opened in June (50-048).

Ngalau Bandar, or Ngalau Batang Chiparok

On 15 July 1889, excavations started in a small, shallow 8 m deep cave named after a *bandar* (water conduit) that transported water from the Sangtei brook to the *sawahs* (rice fields). It was excavated down to 2 m. Dubois stated that it:

> [...] almost completely consisted of limestone blocks that had fallen out of the ceiling and which, only with very little soil, had connected to a moderately vast and hard breccia. Completely at the surface, underneath only a few centimetres of loose clay, there was a 15 cm thick layer of

wood ashes, in which shards of pottery of more recent shapes appeared as well as some bones of the common goat and larger birds, of which some were clearly carrying the marks of having been cut with a knife, proving the cave has been in use by people. Any significant thickness of the ash layer makes us assume that throughout a number of years this cave has been inhabited and used up to recently as a temporary or permanent stay, probably for Malay people.

Up to the end of this month the limestone breccia did not deliver many bones. Just a few teeth of pigs, deer, porcupines and a tiger, were found, apart from the remains of bats. (50-048)

The August 1889 report shows that continuation was bothersome:

The sediment found, a breccia of limestone mixed with only very little soil, not hard enough to be successfully removed with dynamite, but then again so hard that removing it with ordinary tools results in very slow progress, which was partly the cause that this month we only reached a maximal depth of 2.75 m. The bones found were few in number and mostly small and broken into unidentifiable fragments, by the way apparently from the same animal species as we used to find before. (50-049)

In the September 1889 report, Dubois added that they found in the breccia:

[…] teeth of the ordinary wild hog (*Sus vittatus*), of the tapir (*Tapirus indicus*), the deer (*Cervus equinus*), the forest goat (*Antilope sumatrensis*) and the porcupine (*Hystrix mülleri*), all animals still present here today. Underneath the breccia we finally at 3.50 m found a brownish-red clay, of which we by the end of September had only removed a few centimetres. (50-050)

In the October 1889 report, Dubois stated that this brownish-red clay:

[…] turned out to be mixed with small pieces of limestone for 0.60 m until we encountered for 0.50 m pure clay and finally 1 m clayish quartz sand (originating from weathered Tertiary conglomerates); so now we have reached at a total depth of 5.60 m below the original surface floor the bottom of the cave. No more bones had been found and looking for them came to an unexpected end. It had already been noted lately that small cracks had appeared in the ceiling and when these started to increase, I had the work stopped. Luckily in time, for soon after a large part of the ceiling collapsed (some hundreds of cubic metres). Thus work that had been taken a long time remained fruitless. (50-050)

Ngalau Jambu

From Ngalau Jambu, Dubois brought back some 1,000 fossils. It is first mentioned in the July 1889 monthly report, in which Dubois stated:

Because of being indisposed I was not able to continue tracking down new caves during the larger part of this month. A Kampong chief however informed me about the existence of some thus far unknown caves near Tapi-Sello and in one of these, the Ngalau Jambu, on 31 July the Kampong chief together with one of the forced labourers, who was already more able in finding fossils, brought from there a great many teeth. They are of the same species, and in the same relative numbers towards each other and in the same state of conservation as those I found earlier in Ngalau Lida Ajer, near Payakumbuh; many teeth of pigs and of orangutan, further tapirs, rhinoceroses, elephants, deer, buffaloes, monkeys and porcupines are also here in abundance. (50-048)

In the following month's report, the description continued:

This cave is located at a short distance [of Tapi-Sello], north of the old little volcano Kuliet-monies, West of the brook Muara-panas, closer [than the previously described cave] to the top of the limestone mountain. It consists of two rather spacious chambers, which are in connection to each other by a high narrow opening. The front chamber opens to the outside and receives full daylight. Its floor consists entirely of heavy limestone blocks that have fallen from the ceiling. The inner chamber is completely devoid of daylight, it contains a few similar rocks like in the front chamber but in between the floor is flat and covered with an up to 0.50 M thick layer of earth.

Already in this dark red soil, which is of the same kind as is covering the old slate layers everywhere in this area, a great many teeth were found […] Underneath this layer we had a very irregular stalagmite mass which partly enveloped limestone blocks and which was followed to a maximum depth of 1.80 m. In its upper part there were still similar fossils present as in the red earth; further down these were completely lacking. We yet continued removing this mass, as there was the possibility that it was covering a deeper fossil-bearing layer or other soil. (50-049)

Excavations were stopped by the end of September 1889 after, at a depth of almost 3 m, the bedrock had been reached, and no more fossils had been found (50-050).

Ngalau Lebawah near Sisawah

In his September 1889 report, Dubois wrote of this cave:

On the right side of the road to the *dusun* Kabun, a few hours away from d.s. [*dusun*?] on top of a mountain ridge, this cave, which is a natural pit into which I climbed down along a rattan ladder for 28 m until I had reached its apparent floor; along a sideways crevice I could, from resting place to resting place, on rocks pointing out, climb down a further 25–30 m until I had reached its true floor. In there was like a very small bowl, in which there was hardly room for two people, but on the floor ± ½ m. of fine gravel mixed with earth, which looked very much tossed over and on top of it was a truly large bone, a thighbone, of which both the distal ends were missing and that turned out to be of an elephant. It had completely calcified, was very heavy and partly covered with a drip stone layer; there can be no doubt about its great age and fossil state, but lacking material for comparison it can for the time being not be ascertained as to which species of elephant it belongs; it is surely not of any other family than *Elephas*. Other remains were not found here although they might yet have been present in higher layers of earth (the top floor) of this pit; it is probably yet likely that this animal has fallen down this pit alive (like the complete Rhinoceros skeleton found in the Dream-cave near Wirksworth in England, which had fallen in the cave similarly [found by lead miners in 1822; see Mello 1880]). Quick attempts to find these gave no results and for a systematic exploration this cave, given its location on a mountain ridge hours away from any Kampong and drinking water, is unsuitable. So here we experienced again to what extent the terrain limits the number of caves suitable to be opened in these areas. (50-050)

Caves approached from Singkarah

In December 1889, Dubois left the Bua area and started exploring close to Singkarah in the vicinity of Paningahan. The 'famous' cave of Paningahan, located under the *nagari* Tandjung Bonei through which the Batang Pigago flows (50-042), was considered unsuitable as it was located only 20 m above the current water level of Lake Singkarah, whereas 'there are clear signs everywhere on several spots, that the level in recent times must have been at least 70 m higher than it currently is'.

Ngalau Si Babantu

One of the two teams was set to work at Ngalau Si Babantu, a cave located about 120 m above the lake on the bank of the Paningahan brook. To gain entrance, they first had to remove a heavy rock, which was partly blocking the entrance, using dynamite, but they did not manage to do so until the end of December (50-051).

In January 1890:

> After removing limestone blocks the black earth was dug through to a depth of 0.50 m to 1.25 m and subsequently yellow earth, mixed with small pieces of limestone up to a depth of about 1 m. The latter contains numerous teeth, again richly representing the Lida-ajer fauna. (50-045)

By the end of the month, however, the cave was exhausted, so they abandoned it (50-046).

Ngalau Pala Pisang and another unnamed hole nearby

After leaving Bua the second team started work in Ngalau Pala Pisang, a cave about 250 m above the lake on the left bank of the Paningahan brook. They encountered:

> [...] near the entrance a yellow clay mixed with pieces of limestone of which up to 1.50 m was removed; further down at about 15 m from the entrance inward in a spacious room bat guano was removed up to a depth of 2 m.

On 20 January 1890, however, the cave:

> [...] was already abandoned, after the solid rock floor of the cave had been reached near the entrance without finding any fossils, whilst in the deeper 'hall' because of the meanwhile started heavy rains so much water had entered that working there became completely impossible. Not that there was much to look forward to for reward. The bat guano was reaching at least to a depth of 4 m and the rock walls were converging thus, that the floor would soon have been reached.

> This Ngalau pala pisang is therefore one of the few caves that did not contain any mammal remains at all.

> Near to this cave in the ravine of the Batang Paningahan we found a hole in the rocks, too narrow to crawl in, which however after being widened, turned out to be the remainder of an old cave. In the yellow earth, which was completely filling the space underneath a hanging drip stone, a number of teeth were found of the already so often encountered Lida-ajer fauna. The yellow earth was covering river sand that had been hardened by impregnation of limestone, which therefore must be younger than the deposits of this sand by the Paningahan that is currently incised 25 m lower. (50-045)

This second excavation was finished by the beginning of February 1890 (50-046).

Ngalau Agung Agung or Sibrambang

On 9 February 1890, digging started in Ngalau Agung Agung (50-046). This was the cave from which Dubois brought home the largest number of fossils, over 3,400. (A cave of this name has recently been located in the area indicated by Dubois and will be the subject of future research. This site is now known as Sibrambang due to the village nearby.) In his February report, Dubois wrote:

> [...] our efforts were soon rewarded. After from the floor of this 11 m wide and 8 m deep cave some large dripstones which had fallen off or were growing to the floor, had been removed one could start taking out a thin layer of yellow clay (± ½ m), which was covering a black soil. This black earth, of which by the end of February 2½ m had been dug up, was mixed with pieces of limestone and contained an immense amount of teeth and molars from the animals of the aforementioned fauna, in which now elephants and buffaloes were now more strongly represented than before. The remains of thousands of large animals must have been dragged in here and one cannot without amazement and wonder think about the rich animal life which must once have existed in an area where currently even the common Indian hog is rare. (50-046)

The cave kept yielding fossils until:

> [...] on 25 March at a depth of 3.50 m below the original surface the rocky bottom was reached and as at another location within the cave up to 2.50 m no results of a different kind were encountered than had already been obtained, on 26 March this cave was also abandoned. (50-046)

Ngalau Sibatie (Bukit Mengkapok)

On 13 February 1890, work started in Ngalau Sibatie, which was 'actually 2 caves with the same name', but no results were reported that month (50-046). By halfway through March, this cave was completely emptied. Dubois stated:

> This little cave with a depth of only 5 m and a width of 8 m contains, underneath a 0.50 m thick layer of black earth, about 2.50 m hard yellow clay mixed with smaller and larger pieces of limestone. In this breccia-like mass a few completely calcified but yet very much broken bones were found, presumably of a kind of deer. (50-046)

Leaving Sumatra

For Dubois, his time in Sumatra ended in disappointment. He had hoped to find a human forerunner, but the contents of the caves were not old enough—in his view—to produce what he was looking for. Furthermore, conditions had been harsher than he had anticipated. He had barely survived several malaria attacks, and one of the sergeants initially assigned to him, Franke, had died, probably of malaria, three and a half months after he started. The other sergeant, van de Nesse, had not been capable of handling the convicts, so it had been necessary to replace him.

The convicts were also often ill and unable to work. *Plasmodium* being the cause of malaria was at that time known, but mosquitoes as the intermediate hosts were not, and malaria was still thought to be caused by so-called 'bad air'. Because of this, work in some caves ceased if too many people got ill within a short time; this happened, for example, in Muka-Muka Cave near Muara (50-047) and in Ngalau Bulan (50-048).

Moreover, war had been ongoing in Aceh, Sumatra, since 1873; consequently, throughout Sumatra the local people were less inclined towards the Dutch than they were on other islands. Although Dubois' intentions were benign, he did not meet with the support of the local people. They were worried that Dubois was surveying the caves for gold and saltpetre, commodities they were mining themselves and that they did not want to lose to the Dutch. Someone just looking for ancient bones was beyond their experience. As a result, Dubois was led astray more than once, and his complaints about that to, for instance, Jentink (6-373), are well described in Theunissen (1989). However, further similar letters exist, to Martin (33-512), Treub (12-271) and Verbeek (33-551), for example. (A book containing the correspondence of Dubois during his Indonesian period is in preparation).

After the Wajak skull had been found in Java in October 1888, Verbeek in particular had been pushing Dubois to go there (12-405, 12-408). The success of Lida Ajer, however, made Dubois decide at first to keep trying in Sumatra. In the end, however, the jungle defeated him, and he chose to go to Java where circumstances were much better (e.g. there was more deforestation). His final trip in Sumatra, moving with his family to the harbour at Padang, is telling: he fell ill, had to rent a house far from major towns as he was not able to continue travelling, and when he finally did arrive in Padang a month later, people did not recognise him because of his emaciated state (33-665). He arrived in Java in May 1890.

Concluding remarks

Eugène Dubois' work on Sumatra never got much attention, being completely overshadowed by his *Homo erectus* discoveries on Java. His work on Sumatra, however, was clearly conducted at the highest standards of his time. He worked from the sound hypothesis that caves would be likely places to find fossil faunas. He used all geological knowledge available to him to locate the areas where these caves were most likely to be found, and subsequently found both caves and fossils. He did not just pick up the bones in these caves, but also collected sediment samples of the different layers he encountered and described them. He made astute observations on the geology of the caves and the relationship between geomorphology and the chronology of his finds. He even conducted a neotaphonomic experiment with a live porcupine, something never done before as far as we know.

Today, the Dubois collection at Naturalis Biodiversity Center in Leiden has over 10,000 collection numbers for finds from Sumatran caves. Had a World War II bomb not destroyed part of the museum where the sediment samples were stored, we would have had many hundreds more of those too. Dubois may have been disappointed by the results of his endeavours on Sumatra, but what he did achieve there was extraordinary.

Although the original locations of all the fossils Dubois found are not currently known, sampling the bones for chemical clues of those locations with, for instance, X-ray Fluorescence Spectrometry, if necessary in combination with revisiting the sites, might well resolve this question in the future. This possibility, in combination with the archival information, makes the Dubois collection extremely valuable to this day.

Acknowledgements

We thank the anonymous reviewers for their constructive comments. Naturalis Biodiversity Center is gratefully acknowledged for allowing access to the Dubois Archive, and we are grateful in particular to Karien Lahaise of Naturalis, for supporting our access to the Dubois Archive, and Antje Weeda, who was a Naturalis volunteer from 2010 to 2014, for valuable biographical information about the authors of the letters in the Dubois Archive. JL's funding for this research was generously provided by the Australian Research Council (FT160100450).

References

Albers, P.C.H. and J. de Vos 2010. *Through Eugène Dubois' Eyes: Stills of a Turbulent Life*. Brill, Leiden. doi.org/10.1163/ej.9789004183001.i-186

Dubois, M.E.F.T. 1888. Over de wenschelijkheid van een onderzoek naar de diluviale fauna van Ned. Indië, in het bijzonder van Sumatra. *Natuurkundig Tijdschrift voor Nederlandsch-Indië* 48:148–165.

Duringer, P., A.M. Bacon, T. Sayavongkhamdy and T.K.T. Nguyen 2012. Karst development, breccias history, and mammalian assemblages in Southeast Asia: A brief review. *Comptes Rendus Palevol* 11(2–3):133–157. doi.org/10.1016/j.crpv.2011.07.003

Duval, M., K. Westaway, Y. Zaim, Y. Rizal, Aswan, M.R. Puspaningrum, A. Trihascaryo, P.C.H. Albers, H.E. Smith, G.M. Drawhorn, G.J. Price and J. Louys 2021. New chronological constraints for the Late Pleistocene fossil assemblage and associated breccia from Ngalau Sampit, Sumatra. *Open Quaternary* 7:1–24. doi.org/10.5334/oq.96

Hooijer, D.A. 1946. Prehistoric and fossil rhinoceroses from the Malay Archipelago and India. *Zoologische Mededelingen* 26:1–138.

Hooijer, D.A. 1955. Fossil Proboscidae from the Malay Archipelago and the Punjab. *Zoologische Verhandelingen* 28:1–146.

Louys, J., M. Duval, G. Price, K. Westaway, Y. Zaim, Y. Rizal, Aswan, M. Puspaningrum, A. Trihascaryo, S. Breitenbach, O. Kwiecien, Y. Cai, P. Higgins, P.C.H. Albers, J. de Vos and P. Roberts 2022. Speleological and environmental history of Lida Ajer cave, western Sumatra. *Philosophical Transactions of the Royal Society B* 377:20200494. doi.org/10.1098/rstb.2020.0494

Lydekker, R. 1886. The fauna of the Karnul caves. *Palaeontologia Indica Series 10* 4:23–58.

Mello, J.M. 1880. On a short history of the Creswell caves. *Proceedings of the Yorkshire Geological and Polytechnic Society* 7:252–265. doi.org/10.1144/pygs.7.3.252a

Mylroie, J.E. and J.L. Carew 1990. The flank margin model for dissolution cave development in carbonate platforms. *Earth Surface Processes and Landforms* 15(5):413–424. doi.org/10.1002/esp.3290150505

Palmer, A.N. 1991. Origin and morphology of limestone caves. *Geological Society of America Bulletin* 103:1–21. doi.org/10.1130/0016-7606(1991)103<0001:OAMOLC>2.3.CO;2

Pijnappel, M.W. 1897. Fossiele overblijfselen op Java (de *Pithecanthropus erectus* Dubois). *Huis en haard* 1897:29–31, 43–45, 58–62 and 72–79.

Shipman, P. 2001. *The Man Who Found the Missing Link. The Extraordinary Life of Eugène Dubois*. Weidenfeld & Nicholson, London.

Theunissen, L.T.G. 1985. *Eugène Dubois en de Aapmens van Java*. Rodopi, Amsterdam.

Theunissen, L.T.G. 1989. *Eugène Dubois and the Ape-Man from Java* (E. Perlin-West, trans.). Kluwer, Dordrecht. doi.org/10.1007/978-94-009-2209-9

Verbeek, R.D.M. 1883. *Topografische en Geologische Beschrijving van een Gedeelte van Sumatra's Westkust*. Landsdrukkerij, Batavia.

Verbeek, R.D.M. 1888. *Krakatau. Eerste gedeelte*. (Tweede verbeterde druk.) Landsdrukkerij, Batavia.

Appendix: Extracts from Eugène Dubois' notes and letters

Code	Date	Description
6-310 6-311 6-312 6-313	7 June 1888	[Letter from Jentink (director of the natural history museum in Leiden) to Dubois] STATE MUSEUM OF NATURAL HISTORY. Leiden, the 7th of June 1888 *Amice* Dubois, you surely must have been wondering often, why still no messages from Leiden had arrived, but all kinds of obstructions, not mine, but from professor Fürbringer, prevented me from writing to you earlier about the important matter. Many times we had set a date and time to come together and then suddenly he cancelled. Careful reading of your letters to professor Fürbringer and to me has convinced us, that you yourself will be the cause if your plans don't succeed, for repeatedly we pressed you not to speak to anyone about your [6-311] future plans: I've clearly pointed out what the questionable results would be if people were to find out that you have put on the soldier's uniform with ulterior motives. And now you have not only spoken to many in Amsterdam about your plans, but also to your superiors in the Dutch Indies, yes and even held conferences, whilst it is also highly reprehensible that your wife has meddled in your affairs in writing! Friend, you know I am <u>very</u> dedicated towards you and you will forgive me for speaking out plainly, it is in your own interest. In my profession I have to deal with many people, whom, if I am to have my way, I need to approach very diplomatically and I could have told you up front (as I did) that laying your cards on the table in this stage could spoil everything. But enough of this. What's done is done. Take my advice for the time to come and you will with more certainty achieve the goal, if it is at all achievable, than going further down the road you have taken so far. Speak with nobody whatsoever about your plans, tell them, you have put them aside, be for the eyes of your colleagues and superiors a fully committed and diligent officer of health:, who has therein found his ideal for life and has great desire to climb in rank. This way people will (what would happen easily in the lethargic Insulinde) be put to sleep and within a few months everybody will have forgotten all about it and you will be known for your diligence and knowledge as an excellent army man, who is due for promotion. Don't just hide your reluctance towards the service and the medical practice, but speak about it like your respect for it is ever-growing. So if you keep completely silent about the main matter, you will make your way in the Indies and be well established. Meanwhile we will try to sort the matter out here and will one day or another [6-312] submit a proposal to the Governor-General and you will get an assignment for scientific research. What can be done about that, believe me, can only be done out of Holland. And even here, Fürbringer, Martin and I can only fight your corner, if we strictly exclude other committees and societies. The less people know about it, the less they can do to oppose this. The Royal Academy of Sciences, the Geographical Society, the Natural History Committee, nothing can be expected from them other than opposition, as they eventually would all propose to get their own candidate for that research. The 10,000 guilders mentioned will for at least two years be allocated to the Key-expedition: even if we could get this for you, it would take too much time to get it for you. You speak of an advantage to be given by the government! Dear friend, something like that has never been seen and will never happen in a well-administrated country, it not only needs to be put to the Budget every year, but also has to be approved by the Chamber of Commons. What should happen to an advantage already given, if the chamber of Commons subsequently voted against it or when the Minister decided to not put it in the Budget?

Code	Date	Description
		If you think the tone of this letter is too patronising, please excuse me, consider it is not written and tear it apart immediately. But I do think I have the right to speak, as I've had more experience in these matters and if you had followed my advice from the start, things would look better for you now. Mind that in the first year doing or speaking about research in the Indies is out of the question. Never forget that in the Indies 'making money' is the main reason for being there and they look at energetic people as strange beings, a mythical beast, and they cannot imagine what goes on in the mind of such a man. And now *basta*, I hope to receive letters from you from time to time; from my side I promise to keep you apprised and take all necessary steps to support your cause from here. But everything 'sub rosa'! Fürbringer's health is not as it should be: he overworked himself now with that giants task, that has now
		[6-313]
		been printed, the 'Morphology etc. of the Birds', two giant volumes. He needs '*Erholung*' [German: recreation]!
		I regret to hear that your wife is not doing very well: it has been a dreadful start for her, hardly arrived in the Indies and mother and sister die! I heartily hope that she will find courage for the future and will be able to forcefully support you in doing your duty.
		I wonder what the consequences for us all will be of this new ministry? And who will become the next Governor-General? Who knows whether under the given circumstances your Catholic background might give you unexpected support from this clerical ministry, maybe Schaepman can help you: I could go and visit him on your behalf. Do you know him? <u>Do write this to me!</u> Here all is well: we all fondly remember the time you have allowed us, and my relatives all send heartily greetings to their cheerful nephew. And now '*praesta te vivum*', receive with your wife the friendly hand pressed by your dedicated and interested F.A. Jentink.
7-467	8 September 1888	I was very pleasantly surprised by your message of the second of this month, which was just followed by your message of the 5<u>th</u> and I cordially congratulate you on your initial and so rapidly acquired success.
7-501 7-502	February 1888	[Letter from Dubois to Kroeze (possibly a government official) and Kroeze's answer to it]
		Noble and Severe Sir.
		By the kindness of Mr de Freytag I am pleased to be able to tell you that I have also been acquitted of my afternoon duty. I'm therefore pleased to be able to be at your disposal at a much earlier time which will allow us to be able to make the trip by daylight. If it suits you I could be at 4 o'clock on the back of my horse and wherever is convenient to you, such as at the hospital or at your office.
		Could you give a message to the bearer of this, where and when you want to meet me?
		After polite greetings, with the highest esteem
		towards your noble and severe Sir
		your willing servant
		Eug. Dubois
		[7-502]
		Dear Doctor
		In answer to the attached note I take the liberty to give you into consideration that we meet each other on horseback at about 16:30 near the house of the provost.
		Do you think about bringing pajamas, kabaja and a warm jacket? Nights can be very cold at Lubu kelangan. If you prefer taking a thin blanket, that is also good. — I will bring food and drink. Do also take a towel and a few stockings and shoes. We need to wade through a river and it is always preferable to take along dry stockings. My boys will start marching at about 3 o'clock. Please have your servant be at my house at that time to carry your clothes and such and then they can point him in the right direction. Until later, please accept my polite and respectful greetings, your willing servant Kroeze

Code	Date	Description
12-400	28 September 1888	[Letter from Verbeek (Head engineer of the Governmental Mining Department and head scientist of the Geological Survey of the West Coast, Sumatra) to Dubois]
		Yesterday I heard from Doctor Schmeling Kool, whom you seem to know, that you have already found fossilised bones, molars and human remains et cetera. You seem to have been more lucky than us—for we always looked for them in vain. Please write to me in which caves you have found these fossil remains.
12-405	1 October 1888	[Letter from Verbeek to Dubois]
		I [...] advised that you would be given immediately two years of leave, and that you would be summoned to not just examine the caves of Sumatra, but also, subsequently, those of Java, and pointed out that only regular systematic research will do for fruitful science; and further that such research cannot be done by the mining department as that would mean they would have to
		[12-406]
		do without a mining engineer for years and their number is too few as it is already. I hope this will be helpful.
12-408	8 December 1888	[Letter from Verbeek to Dubois]
		I have seen the skull from Wadjak at Sluiters' [office],
		[12-409]
		it is truly a human skull with nice molars in it, but alas broken; and completely covered with limestone. Sluiter will send it to you. You can preparate it by dissolving the limestone with diluted hydrochloric acid; we tried it on a small shard, it works excellently, the bone remains and the chalk within the limestone is naturally dissolved. The skull is not broken from back to front but crosswise and Sluiter did not succeed in fitting the chunks together. As soon as you have dissolved the matrix, you will probably be able to piece the largest part together; but some parts appear to have been lost in excavation. Whether we are truly dealing with a diluvial remains is somewhat unsure.
12-265 12-266	10 October 1888	[Letter from Treub (Director of the Botanical gardens in Bogor and the most senior scientist in the Dutch Indies) to Dubois]
		I had just also wanted to advise you to not ask for leave as yet; it's prudent to be careful. If you again have
		[12-266]
		obtained important results, there will be opportunity and cause to see what can be done.
		That these important results will not fail to come up, I doubt as little as you do. A few months ago I already, as president of the Committee for nature research in our colonies, brought up your research in our meeting and subsequently contacted the Chief of the Medical Service. I have had a long and extensive talk with Colonel Lokhorst about the scientific importance of the success of your plan. I am very pleased to learn from your writing that this meeting has not been without result. You can always fully count on my warm interest both as a person and as the president of the Committee.
		Allow me to yet again advise you to be careful with your contact with the official world; nice and easy does it! The matter is so important that it would be a shame if it were to falter through some rash steps, that would diminish the sympathies that have been raised for your research.
		Please do excuse these remarks. They spring up out of true interest.

Code	Date	Description
12-271	end of September 1889	[Letter from Dubois to Treub] This is also my first letter after starting the cave research. If I had not met with so much misfortune and had so little success I would surely have notified you sooner, as you have shown such a great interest in the work. In comparison however to the enormous amount of work we have put in, the results are so little, that I did not want to bother you with my whining. The local people, who are very distrustful towards the 'Company' and not very forthcoming, along with the immensely rugged terrain and the high incidence of fever among the workmen, were insurmountable adversities. And that is the reason, and even with all the support from the government, very little research could be done. How discouraging this is for me your noble Sir will certainly understand knowing what it is to be committed to research with heart and soul.
33-506	1 October 1888	[Letter from Dubois to Verbeek] The respective remains, thousands by now, I have found after a month of work in the [illegible word: cave?] Ngalau lida ajer in the coal limestone located south of Situdju batu, (south-southwest of Fort de Kock in your Atlas) and it is [33-507] certainly a happy coincidence that I made an important find so soon where better men than me have been looking in vain. There can be no doubt that the objects found are truly fossil, as is apparent from the high level of calcification that the bones have undergone as well as from their position. However I will not yet hazard an opinion about their true age and consider it more careful to await further research before I do so.
33-512 33-513	October 1889	[Draft or copy of letter from Dubois to Martin (director of the geological museum in Leiden)] Although it has been long since the arrival of your kind letter of 8 May last I do not want to fail to politely thank your highly learned Sir for it. I had hoped so much to be able to send you word about results that were such that they would be a worthy reciprocation to the interest that you have shown me. So far this was not to be. I have only been able to collect about as much as I had before and the reason for this relatively unsuccessful result is not, because there's nothing to find here, because in two out of three reasonably completely excavated caves fossils were found. The causes however are 1) the thickly grown jungle that is largely even without any path, which makes the caves difficult to find and a lot of them therefore not viable for research; further 2) the distrustful nature of the population, that fear that the Government is trying to get their hands on the gold and saltpetre, that they are mining in many caves, which they therefore carefully keep secret and they continuously keep deceiving me about where they are, and 3) the poor work, that the convicts are delivering because many are ill (currently some 50%) and there wasn't always good supervision (by the engineer workmen, that each had to supervise one of the groups in my absence; one died and the other had to be sent away for being inadequate, whilst they could not be immediately replaced) and as these convicts are poorer workers from their nature. It must however be said that the lonely and unhealthy life in the jungle is not encouraging for these people. Earlier, when we were near Payakumbuh, an area more inhabited and more civilised, their work was much better. This has all been very disappointing and my expectations have not been met at all and as I have little hope that things will improve here and currently—in the rainy season—it is not the time to work on Java, I do regret now not to have

Code	Date	Description
		[33-513]
		asked to first start opening caves on Java, where the conditions are so much better and such wonderful finds like the fossil (Papuan-like) human skull have been found and from many locations finds of bones in caves have become known.
		Whether the Government, if I do not get more luck than I had so far, will yet allow me to continue my excavations on Java, is something that I seriously doubt, which would destroy every further prospect. That would certainly be a shame, now that on several locations on Java find sites have been encountered and it would dissipate the other wish I had and that I hoped might come true on Java. What I mean is, should I be allowed to continue excavating on Java I would suddenly also be getting the opportunity to dig up more of the Javan Siwalik fauna that you have discovered. When you asked me, before I left to the Indies, after I told you about my plans, whether I not rather want to go and look for these fossils I rejected the idea because I was of the opinion that trying so would be more difficult for technical reasons as there were no find sites near any garrisons and thus as an officer of health I would not have the means to get there. Your research about the Siwalik fauna together with the description of mammals from the Karnool caves in Madras have actually brought me to my current cave plans and I realised then as I do now, that Miocene fauna might even be more important than anything that the caves could deliver. It now seems that finding these tertiary fossils is not as problematic as I originally thought and should I be given another year of leave, you certainly would not have any difficulty convincing the Government to also
		[transposed in left margin] entrust me with the task of finding these tertiary mammal remains. Obviously all the material would be for you, unless you would and could leave me some for later for me to get my teeth in.
		[33-512 transposed in left margin]
		Forgive me for pre-empting the situation so far, even though it's very doubtful whether I will be given a year's extension. But exactly because of that I take the liberty to bring the so important palaeontological preliminary research that I would do on Java to your Noble Sir's attention for a moment, and it would have a much larger chance of success than on Sumatra, where no find sites were known upfront and many more difficulties have been encountered. Thank you for eventually safeguarding the diluvialia.
33-551 33-552 33-550	November(?) 1889	[Draft letter from Dubois to Verbeek]
		Whilst I have already been doing cave research at Bua for four months I have not sent Your Honour any report, although you not only have continuously shown interest in my work but also supported it with more strength than anybody else. But after I have told you the cause for the long delay of this report I am certain you will understand and forgive my silence. Up to now I have not found what I wished for so furiously, not because the terrain here seems barren but because maybe expectations have been very high and the difficulties have been unexpectedly large. Having come to the Dutch Indies full of hope of achievement, the initial success and even more the large appreciation for my efforts, in particular by knowledgeable people like you, and being now well supported and equipped by the government I was filled with the best of hopes and more than ever enthused and fully intending to use all my powers to make this research succeed. And you yourself, knowing how much one can get attached to one's scientific research, will not be amazed that when these great expectations did not come to be—not because of the research itself—this experience made me very sad, in particular, because I felt obliged towards the Government and people like you, that have put their trust in me largely because of the expectations I raised, to repay them with a proportional result.
		The difficulties I faced were much larger than I could have suspected and on top of that it turned out that I largely overestimated the working ability of the forced labourers.

Code	Date	Description
		At first the preliminary examination of the terrain that the controller had recommended to me, and which took a month to do, hardly led to anything. The Malaysians, who look in the caves for gold and potassium nitrate feared that the 'Company' was going to compete with them or had other reasons for distrust with the consequence that without guides I could hardly find any suitable cave, although the area is much richer in caves than many an area in Europe. Later I did track some down and heard afterwards from more than one chief that they had known their existence but kept silent out of fear for the above-mentioned reasons.
		I tried now to find as many of them as I could myself and did succeed to some extent and did get some help later from some chiefs after they had renewed encouragement from the controller. But the
		[33-552]
		finds remained sporadic and I did not succeed in getting a good overview of the existing caves to choose the ones most appropriate. I had to make do with what was there. Beside this the terrain itself also caused great difficulties, not just in finding the caves, but also in getting enough supplies to support the forced labourers which again excluded a number of caves that would have been worthwhile for research but were too far into the jungle.
		But the largest adversity was caused by my means of research. I had largely overestimated the real working ability of the forced labourers. Without proper overseeing the largest amount of their working capacity remains latent and as I could only be present at one of the three places where we were working at one time, supervision was permanently insufficient and as a result on average half of the forced labourers were doing almost nothing, meaning that after subtracting overseers, cooks, those ill, and the ones that had run off, only a tiny number of the fifty forced labourers appointed to me were effectively working.
		I did not have much luck with the workers from the Engineer Corps either, one of the two was doing excellently but died within a couple of months and the other turned out to be completely useless and was subsequently replaced upon my request by the first engineer officer t.K. For more than one half month now I still have to cope with only one engineer worker. I do feel obliged to say however, that both with the replacement as well as before, when my tools had not arrived yet from the Department of Education, Religion and Trade, the engineer Corps were the ones who supported me most and offered me tools willingly. When the inadequate engineer was just replaced and the other one had just died I myself became gravely ill so that
		[33-550]
		other than the recently arrived engineer for some time there was no European overseeing the work.
		I will not bother you any longer with complaints, but it saddens me to see how little has yet been done and I am convinced that because of that, so little has been found. More than once I have felt remorse that I did not follow your advice to come to Java straightaway although there were a number of counterarguments. All the difficulties that I have faced here would certainly not have arisen there and what is leaning on me most is that because of the humble results here the Government might hold back on continuing the research on Java, so the treasures you already know to be there are not to be lifted by me.
33-665	5 June 1890	[Letter from Dubois to Jentink]
		The last while on Sumatra was the end of a period and the first time on Java was the beginning of a new period for me and the transition seems to equal that between geological periods for having huge changes taking place; I went from being unwell to mortally ill to healthy.
		Whilst travelling to Padang in order to ship to Java I fell ill and have for about a month with my wife and children and without goods (for all had been sent ahead already) been compelled to remain in a ruinous [illegible: merchant?] house, where I eventually lost the fever, but not the cachexia, so that when I arrived in Padang (after a difficult [illegible: cart?]-travel of 8.30 AM to midnight because of accidents to the vehicles and poor horses) was taken for a stranger by old acquaintances.

Code	Date	Description
40-446 40-473		See file Sumatra notebooks doi.org/10.6084/m9.figshare.22154882
43-073 43-074		See file Sumatra notebooks doi.org/10.6084/m9.figshare.22154882
46-003 46-006		See file Sumatra notebooks doi.org/10.6084/m9.figshare.22154882
46-117 46-118		See file Sumatra notebooks doi.org/10.6084/m9.figshare.22154882
49-264 49-265		See file Sumatra notebooks doi.org/10.6084/m9.figshare.22154882
50-005	25 March 1889	[Letter from Dubois to the governor of Sumatra's West Coast] I therefore have taken the liberty to address your Noble severe Sir politely with the request to already have the 50 forced labourers, that have been put at my disposal earlier, be sent here.
50-006	28 March 2889	[Letter from Dubois to the Director of Education, Religion and Trade] The Assistant-Resident of Tanah-Datar had the benevolence of sending me an extensive list of the most well-known caves, in his department from which it became apparent that in this government the Department Tanah-Datar—as I had also learned from other sources, has by far the largest number of caves, so that will give much possibility for research. Within Tanah-Datar the sub-departments Bua and Lintan, covering a large part of the Ngalau-Saribu-mountain range, looked the most promising in this respect. These subdepartments alone list 120 caves and by analogy to what I have found in Payakumbuh, the true number of existing caves can easily be estimated to be double that number.
50-007	28 March 1889	[Attachment to letter from Dubois to the Director of Education, Religion and Trade] Tools needed for the palaeontological research at Sumatra's west coast

kind of tools	number
Hand and axes of several sizes	12
Goloks	24
Sledgehammers	10
Crowbars	12
Patjols	24
Rock drills	12
Clearance spoons[1]	6
Hammers	6
Pliers for percussions	3
Pickaxes (double)	24
Shovels	18
Spades	24
Whetstones (round)	2
Files (large)	6
Hand saws	4
Chisels	12
Small hammers	4
Blocks (a few) and rigging	4
Sink buckets	12
Lamps with equipment	12

---

1   To clear the drill holes before dynamite can be put in.

Code	Date	Description
		Consumables that possibly could be provided
		Petrol for ½ a year 24 chests
		Dynamite for ½ year 4 chests
		Candles for ½ year 250 items
		White glue 3 kilos
50-009	18 April 1889	[Letter from Dubois to the Director of Education, Religion and Trade]
		[The engineer workmen] Franke and van de Nesse that have been put at my disposal have arrived here on the 1st and 10th of April respectively.
50-010	2 May 1889	[Letter from Dubois to the Director of Education, Religion and Trade]
		I have the honour to inform your very Noble severe Sir that as of today I have passed on my medical duties and from this moment on will be able to fully dedicate myself to the assignment you have given me.
50-011	5 May 1889	[Monthly report for April; see Duval et al. (2021: figure 3), www.openquaternary.com/articles/10.5334/oq.96/]
50-013	30 July 1889	[Letter from Dubois to the Director of Education, Religion and Trade]
		Serious indisposition (heavy fevers and the consequences thereof) did not allow me to present this any earlier than I do now. I therefore politely request your noble severe Sir to please forgive this late presentation.
50-032 50-033 50-034 50-035 50-036 50-037 50-039	15 October 1888 [monthly report September]	Preliminary report about the palaeontological explorations in caves near Payakumbuh (Padang Highlands).
		Whilst already for a long time great importance has been assigned to prehistoric and palaeontological research, for which limestone caves of Europe and other parts of the world have proven to be very fruitful, up to now in the Dutch Indies this area of research has only seen a few futile attempts.
		Such explorations demand too much time and undivided dedication to be also taken on as a responsibility for the mining department, to which science already has so much to be grateful for, or to be taken on by zoologists and other nature researchers travelling through the archipelago, who already have enough to do in the areas they are specialised in.
		It is obvious that in a land such as the Indies, where nature is so infinitely rich, that, which is most at hand and most easily accessible, will also be the first subject of study. And this is a likely explanation, that in spite of the highly important results, that just here could be expected of such research, our, on related areas already so fruitfully examined colonies are in this respect still a terra incognita.
		From the, by the way much less richly endowed my nature, Indian mainland however, more is already known and the only recently published description of a Pliocene fauna from Java, which is completely analogous with the northwest Siwalik fauna, has now importantly strengthened the opinion, that the union of the mainland of India with the archipelago in that sense must also have existed in earlier geological times.
		[50-033]
		It furthermore gives a base to the opinion that also the diluvial animal world of the archipelago, which is currently known from the caves of northwest India will be compatible and as well as the famous Siwalik fauna form a connection to animals currently alive.
		That further substantially increases the importance for cave research in our colonies, especially also, there is justified reason to expect that here—even more so than in North West India—during diluvial times, there was richly developed animal life.
		After by accident in the caves of the Kamul district in North West India bones had been found, Professor Huxley considered the matter important enough to urge that the British Government would pursue further exploration of these caves, with the result, that since 1883 regular excavations have taken place, which already brought forth important results, both to anthropology and to palaeontology and which are still being continued.

Code	Date	Description
		These and the discoveries which Lund did in caves in Brazil already more than half a century ago, where giant diluvial Edentata and other peculiar shapes (e.g., of the horse that was indigenous there at the time) and whereby also humans have been found, deliver direct proof, that diluvial animals and diluvial men too don't fail to be present in the grottoes of the tropics, where the ice age did not have a direct impact. These are facts, which are even more pleasing, as they leave all the more reason to assume, that in particular the tropics might deliver important results and be key to the solution of more than one important palaeontological and anthropological question.
		These considerations, put forward in an essay, which was published in the second issue of the current year
		[50-034]
		of the Natural History Journal of the Dutch Indies, partly treated more extensively, made me decide to try to start examinations myself hoping that by doing so, to deliver the practical proof for the existence of such remains and therewith create more special interest in this branch of nature research.
		As far as my duties allowed me I visited all the caves and crevices in the vicinity of Payakumbuh, that I could find. By acquiring knowledge about their location in relation to the surrounding terrain, their internal structure and their formation I just tried to decide, whether analogous with those of other countries, truly fossils could be expected in them and whether they could be retrieved without too much difficulty.
		These case studies turned out to be very instructive in this tropical country. Here the process of formation is fully active and one can see caves in all stages of emergence.
		[You can see] Small crevices in the rock which, by the dissolving properties of the water, are widening into spacious canals in which a stream is taking its course, and next to that smaller and larger caves, which are now out of reach of the current water level, completely drained dry, but yet showing the clear markings of their formation by the eroding work of the water, and sometimes still consisting of clear canals. Here [you can see] the formation of stalactites or of a stalagmite floor, certainly by a third dissolvement of the walls of an originally dry cave, because rainwater has found its way in through a more recent point of access, then again apparent complete rest, [and] like after the flash of these enormous masses of earth, the shape of these giant drip stones are the products of earlier, lively productivity, now have gone into an eternal, sleep, mute witnesses of days long gone.
		[50-035]
		These preliminary studies were also very instructive for the way these holes in the earth get filled up, and how animal remains can get in there and be conserved.
		It became apparent to me, that they were in no way different from the caves in Belgium, Germany, England and France, which have become famous for the fossils which were found in them and that, yes even although for a number the influence of the tropics with its extreme weathering had taken its effect, there were still those, which upon closer inspection would not pose any larger practical concerns then there would be for any European cave.
		These encouraging results urged me to request further support from his Excellency the Governor of Sumatra's West Coast, with whose prior knowledge and approval I had started these explorations, and which were also most benevolently supplied to me. With some workers put at my disposal by his Excellency and the Assistant-Resident of L. Kota and providing other necessities out of my own means, on the 18th of July 1888 the actual research started with an excavation in the so-called Ngalau lida ajer. A priori this cave met all the demands to be a bone cave, it had all the hallmarks of great age, and after exploratory drilling, seemed the best place to start given the modest means I had available.

Code	Date	Description
		The Ngalau lida ajer ('water-tongue-cave', named after the tongue-shaped stalactites which are still dripping), is located in the lime mass, which in the geological atlas of Verbeek is drawn south of the *kampong* [village] Situdju betul. The entrances are about ±150 M height above the valley floor. A small brook, the Batang Babuwe, coming from the G. Sago, rushing to the Batang Agam, has dug itself a bed in this valley. There must have been, according to the thick layers of gravel, that can be seen at some places, a much more considerable flow of water. The whole terrain bears the marks of being much changed by erosion. Even though the entrance of the cave is at the middle of a slope of a mountain, estimated at about 150 m above the nearest level of water, it is still very possible that once, when the landscape had quite different proportions, a small stream took its course through the cave. The state of its walls, as far as they have not yet been covered with dripstones, and more so the sandy layers which are at hand, but which are lacking in the immediate vicinity of the cave, are more direct proof for this hypothesis. The entrance is porch shaped and rather large. It leads to a spacious, round high chamber (of about 8 M width) in which heavy stalactites of all kinds of shapes beautifully cover the walls and the ceiling, whilst also a few stalagmite cones stick up out of the rather even earthy surface of the floor. This chamber seems to be the end of the cave, because a colossal, largely double, dripstone wall has formed, which prevents the eye from examining it further. One can however pierce through this double wall and get into the actual inner cave. This is more longitudinal shaped (15 M long and 6-8 M wide) rather high and only has a few dripstone columns along the sides and near the wall, parting it from the front chamber. The floor was flat, but had a shallow dip towards the back and consisted at the surface of a loose brownish-yellow clay-like soil, on which along the wall locally present dripstone columns rested their wide stalagmite feet and over which at the front and back along the wall there was also an amount of stalagmite breccia. It is of importance, that these mentioned stalagmite masses were all located at about the same level and that many pieces of that mass

[50-036]

were found just below the surface, when we started to dig a hole in the middle of the cave.

The suspicion is therefore obvious, that they used to be a more fully covering stalagmite cover, which has later dissolved again; in later times in visible cracks must have formed in the ceiling, through which now at several points water is dripping down to the floor, such that there is even a pool present. The speed with which this water is coming through the ceiling, not yet saturated with chalk, will have had its dissolving effect on the mentioned stalactite cover on the floor.

The whole cave bears signs of great age. Not just by its location out of reach of every water stream, but also by its gigantic dripstone shapes and the immense amount of soil, which is present inside and which must have been deposited there under completely different circumstances as are present now, thereby proving its age.

As, given the limited means available but mostly also because of the limited time given the nature of my job, a systematic research, like removing all the earth out of the cave layer by layer, was out of the question, so I started with having a hole dug in the middle of the inner cave.

Apart from the above mentioned, almost immediately at the surface located plate-shaped pieces of stalagmite and locally present layers of soil glued with chalk were found in the middle of the cave with at its top about 45 cm underneath the original surface, a gigantic crudely crystalline very hard stalagmite cone, of which the foot turned into a stalagmite mass which seemed to expand over the whole cave.

At 1 M. depth near this foot we found a large piece of charcoal covered with limestone, of which I do not think it is daring to assume, that this points to the presence of humans in days long gone by. This and a shard of turned pottery, of the same shape as is still in use nowadays, which was found at the topmost layer of the soil, are so far the only objects found, that point to an earlier presence of men. |

Code	Date	Description
		As now the stalagmite mass had to be cleared with gunpowder and dynamite, but as it – as far as I could see –spread as a thick layer over the whole cave and the space available and, as the work continued deeper, was automatically getting narrower, we soon faced the necessity to enlarge the hole up to the back end of the cave. To this purpose we had to break out the stalagmite breccia, which spanned almost over the complete width of the cave and was lying as a mass extending up to 1 m inward with a thickness of 70 cm on top of the earth and it now turned out too that this so far neglected breccia, except for both sharp and rounded pieces of limestone also contained andesite pebbles and terrestrial snails, and also a large number of teeth and some fragments of bones of several mammals. Also within the platelike pedestals of the dripstone columns in the back part of the cave these were numerous and in particular the soil underneath was extremely rich of these remains.
		So on the 17th of August 1888 for the first time remains of a fossil cave fauna had been found, as far as I know, for the first time in the Dutch Indies. That the objects found were truly fossil was apparent from the state in which they were found: a stone-like hardness, a partial translucency sometimes, and that they stick to the tongue are characteristics,
		[50-037]
		which are valued much [as evidence of fossil status], and their orientation is consistent with it.
		The work here was now continued and the earth was removed up to a maximum depth of 4 M. The wealth of fossils—predominantly molars—did not diminish. Bones cropped up only rarely, but it also became clearer and clearer what the cause of that was. Almost all bones and many roots of teeth had been gnawed on, even to such extent, that of many teeth only the crowns had remained whilst of some pipe bones only a very small piece like a bead had remained. One could clearly recognise on the roots of the teeth as well as on the bones parallel traces of the incisors of a large rodent. The suspicion was obvious, that, as in British India, also here porcupines were the culprits of this vandal's work. Their incisors and molars—the first largely still having their peculiar orange colour—were found in great amounts, from which it is apparent that these animals in earlier days, probably earlier than those from which the other remains originate, have lived in the cave in great numbers and have dug through the soil. Experiments whereby a living porcupine was offered bones resulted in completely analogous results, thereby delivering the final convincing proof that porcupines had been the destructors of the bones here. A short distance of Ngalau lida ajer is the Ngalau gundja (porcupine cave), in which even now innumerable traces of these animals are proof of their quite recent stay.
		At about 2 M. depth below the original surface there were layers of a sand-like soil (with numerous shimmers). To what extent this consists of pumice tuff I did not yet have time to examine. Below this sand-like layer of ±60 cm thickness, which in any case points to flowing water, there is another brownish clay similar to the one above that. Teeth and bones are also present in these deeper layers.
		At 3 M depth we found in the back wall of the cave a ±80 cm wide opening which, as well as the hallway of which this was the start, was completely filled with earth. After this had been removed, up to a depth of 4 M. below the original level, one got into the mentioned small hallway, which after it extended 2 M further in the direction of the inner cave turned into a similar but only partly filled up hallway more to the left and upwards.

Code	Date	Description
		In the latter we found many teeth, amongst which two beautiful, completely intact elephant molars, lying on top of the soil; others were excavated. With some difficulty now, this long hallway which is going down strongly, was followed for some 10 m, until it widened into a room, which though spacious, was almost filled up to the ceiling. The air supply here was so insufficient that our candles did not want to burn any more, so for the time being further research had to be ceased. Before reaching this room another interesting fact could be observed. Of two little stalactite columns the surfaces turned to each other had been like buffed and polished, as like in the English hyena caves must have happened by numerous passing by and grinding of large animals, which in earlier times, when the 4 M. thick layer of soil had not yet been deposited, therewith closing the entrance, must have lived in the cave.
		The large gathering of bones, predominantly teeth, pointing to thousands of animals, most of which large or even very large species, cannot be otherwise explained than that they are the remains of quarry which has been dragged in for many, long years by large predators, which have lived in this cave. Finding polished dripstone shapes is a surprising confirmation of that. What predators these must have been, I do not yet dare to decide. Some teeth of tigers have been found as well as of a small type of bear but I do not think to it is yet justifiable to decide that these have been the former inhabitants who brought in their quarry.
		Although the work, on which there has been insufficient supervision, has only progressed depressingly slowly, already thousands of teeth and very many fragments of bone have been found. An accurate list of species I will have to postpone until later, but I can already establish the presence of a number of species:
		Simia, probably Simia satyrus, the orangutan. There are however large differences amongst the remains found. Some teeth are gigantic, larger than ever known of the largest orangutans, others, although originating from an old animal, are only mediocre in size. Also the shape varies much,
		Hylobates, likely of more than one species,
		Semnopithecus,
		Macacus,
		Cercocebus,
		Felis, of a tiger and maybe also of a smaller species,
		Elephas, probably two species,
		Rhinoceros,
		Tapirus,
		Sus, probably more than one species,
		Bos or *Bubalus*,
		Cervus, probably distinguishable species,
		other ruminants,
		Hystrix,
		other rodents.
		Although before establishing well-founded conclusions with regard to the right time and the condition of the land, when all these animals were living here, it would be good to await further results, one can however already assume that their presence implies the existence of enormous forests, which are currently completely absent.
		In particular the numerous presence of orangutan, of which we now have already dug up about 600 teeth, point to completely different circumstances than are currently here. As this animal exclusively seems to live in swampy jungles one has to assume that these were formerly here in the vicinity of the cave and it cannot but be that the whole flat of Payakumbuh, which is now built-up and densely populated must have been covered with one forest.

Code	Date	Description
		The orangutan is currently on Sumatra only known from the swampy forests of Tapanulie and Aceh, but its large distribution on Borneo and its presence in northwest India during the Pliocene, already raised the suspicion, that the distribution of this species in earlier times must have been much wider. These finds are now a pleasing confirmation of that. Should it moreover turn out, that truly amongst the species found, next to the common orangutan, there are also remains of related species, this would herewith become a fact of higher significance. I allow myself to also in this respect refer to my earlier mentioned essay. Although about these and other fossils still little can be said with certainty, the suspicion will yet not be unfounded, that amongst the species that are still living today, also some extinct or new species will be found. [50-039] In any case it has now been proven that there are truly fossils to be found in the caves of the Dutch Indies. With limited means, one [of them] has now been examined, albeit only partially, and was shown to be relatively richer than most of the known bone caves. A preliminary research of other caves learned that its content originates from a very old time. At 200 M. distance of the *Ngalau lida ajer* and at the same height in the same mountain lies the earlier already mentioned *Ngalau gundja*. In a beautiful chamber of this cave I had an incision made in the soil that forms the floor of it. In it at a depth of 75 cM a rather horizontal layer of pumice tuff of 80–90 cM thickness was found, under which there was a reddish-brown clay similar to that which currently forms the surface. In the same mountain slightly below the top at about 300 M. height above the valley lies a natural pit of ±15 M. depth. This pit widens below to a beautiful cave and in the corner of this cave, almost directly below the surface of a very thin layer of clay, a layer of pumice tuff of about ½ M. thickness was found. This pumice tuff, which must have been deposited here in a time when the terrain was completely different with regard to heights and, one can assume, as Dupont did for the Belgian caves, that these layers have been deposited here at the same time as those outside, and therefore these pumice tuff layers must be as old as for instance those present in the Payakumbuh-valley, which Verbeek presumes to have a diluvial character. From these facts one can, not without reason, hope that a research on a larger scale of the caves that are so immensely abundant in the Padang Highlands of which I was only granted to visit a few, may bring forth more shining results than cave research has delivered anywhere else in the world. Payakumbuh, 15 October 1888 Eug Dubois.
50-039 50-040	6 June 1889 [monthly report May]	Short overview of the work done for the palaeontological research on Sumatra's West Coast during the month of May 1889 Arriving in Bua on 3 May, the first thing to do was to arrange quarters for the forced labourers, so we could not leave before the 7th on our journey to the *Ngalau saribu mountains* to visit a number of the caves known to the natives as well as possibly find others. With the help of guides, who constantly had to be changed by others, acquainted with other parts of the jungle, we got an overview of the aforementioned mountains between Bua and Sidjunjung and I could form an opinion about the nature of the terrain and the location of the caves.

Code	Date	Description
		This terrain turned out to pose many difficulties for eventual working in caves, both by its remoteness and the extremely difficult traffic with inhabited areas as well as because of the colossal *rimbu* [dense forest], with which it is covered everywhere. Some points closer to the roads or the larger rivers were found more suitable in this respect. In general the number of visited and useful caves was much less than the name of the mountains would suggest. Some natives assured that the name in fact was *Gunung saribu*, after the great abundance of tops, out of which this range is composed. Furthermore it is custom in this area to call every overhanging rock, without any trace of a true cave, *ngalau* and finally in the thick *rimbu* it is difficult to find caves, even for the natives, who within the forest always follow the same paths. The time of *puasa* [lent], in which this journey took place, was also not favourably timed; the indolence of the natives is then particularly large.
		After returning on 18 May, I soon made another trip to the northern part of the Ngalau saribu mountains and to the limestone mountains west of Bua. Over there were also a relatively few number of caves suitable to be opened up and as there was nothing else to expect, than that in such an expansive terrain of limestone mountains, caves—as everywhere else—should be abundant and they were here only more difficult to find and less well known, I now decided to have the work started at two points and from these two points slowly track down new caves myself.
		[50-040]
		On the 23rd, 21 forced labourers under the supervision of the engineer workman Franke were directed to Sibalen where the *Ngalau kapala sawah liat* because of its location in the vicinity of a navigable river and because of its nature could without great difficulty with a chance of success be opened, whilst the remaining forced labourers with the engineer workman van de Nesse were put to work in the well-known cave of Bua—*Ngalau bateng pangean*. The first-mentioned cave is an about 30 M. deep wide corridor with a largely flat earthen floor, at ± 1 KM of the right bank of the Bateng sumpur; it is completely dry.
		The cave of Bua, through which the Bateng pangean flows, only has a relatively small dry spot, which however is a higher positioned corridor to the side, which makes it not improbable, that it is an older part, from the time when the Bateng Pangean did not have its current route through the cave.
		After at both locations barracks for the forced labourers and the engineer workmen had been erected, at 1 June excavations could make a start.
50-040 50-047 50-048	30 July 1889 [monthly report June]	Short overview of the work done for the palaeontological research at Sumatra's West Coast during the month of June 1889.
		The *Ngalau kapala sawah liat* or *Ng pandjang* near Sibalin turned out upon accurate inspection to have a length of 45 M and a corridor going from north to south with an average width of 5 M; only at the entrance and at about a depth of 30 M is it somewhat widened to form a chamber (respectively 8.50 and 10 M). One cannot actually say the cave ends but rather that it is not further accessible; in truth it continues with small openings further into the mountain and old Malay people are sure that the mountain is completely pierced through and that the connection to the other side is only broken by a cave-in. Going through it and the gentle rise of the floor inwards confirms what the examination of the floor suggested: that this once was the route along which water flowed from the other side of the mountain to this side.
		We now started excavating at three different points, 10 M apart from each other and we found thereby almost completely similar layers of soil. As we went deeper these soon turned out to be of such nature, that all workforce had to be brought together to one point and therefore after 10 days all the available forced labourers were put to work in the widened part.

Code	Date	Description
		[50-047]
		The layers we encountered were here: 0.30 M yellow clay. Further down the cave this was covered with a 0.25 M thick widely extended dripstone plate [speleothem]. Next was a very hard mass, a conglomerate of pebbles of different sizes, gravel and pieces of limestone, with here and there thin layers of sand interspersed with very hard clay, and locally sometimes thin layers of dripstone. This reached a thickness of 2–3 M. Next to that on some parts we already hit rock bottom, otherwise yellow clay which mainly expanded far into a small hollow left of the entrance. This corridor is shaped like a small hollow starting at a depth of 4.75 M and continuing in a diagonal southeast direction into the mountain. Whilst in the clay at the surface only a few incisors of the common porcupine were found, apparently of rather recent date, more bones were found in this deep clay, of which a greater age cannot be doubted. In the mentioned small hollow a number of bones, predominantly of rodents and bats were found. An important find however was done on 30 June at a depth of 3.75 M in the middle of the chamber at the entrance, being the humerus of a species of Rhinoceros, which judging from the size of the bone was significantly larger than the current Sumatran species. Further identification of the species, as well as of the animals, to which the smaller bones belong, will have to be postponed for the moment because of the lack of material for comparison; it is however not unlikely that this rhinoceros is closely related or identical to the species which is currently living in the mainland of India.
		The cave of Bua, *Ngalau batang pangian* already had to be abandoned after 12 days, because on average 30–40% of the workmen were suffering there from fevers. They were therefore put to work in the cave that I had meanwhile visited *Ngalau monsiu* (= gunpowder cave, named for the saltpetre, which the Malay people used to prepare out of the excrements of the bats that were found in there). It is located at 4 paal [± 5 km] distance of Bua on the opposite side of the Sinamar-river in the Gugung andjieng. It is a very deep cave; its main corridor is estimated to be 150–200 m long. It is connected to a cave at a lower level, through which the Batang Janki flows and it surely at one point was itself the conduct for this or some other river.
		We started excavating here close to the entrance on 15 June and we found a 0.50 M layer of sand lithified by impregnation with chalk, 1.60 M yellow loam, 0.20 [M] conglomerate of silicates and pieces of limestone; all deposited in horizontal layers, apparent water deposits. In the loam a few molars of a species of pig, a few incisors of the common porcupine and two molars of a deer were found.
		We excavated yet at another point in the cave and there we met with
		[50-048]
		about the same layers, it is just that here on the surface there were still blocks of a similar conglomerate to that further up the cave. Animal remains were not found.
		I continued tracking down other caves, without however finding many like *Ngalau bulan* near Sibalen and the *Ngalau bandar* near Bua, that were suitable to be opened.
		Having received information, that near Muara (subdepartment Sidungjung) years ago, whilst looking for gold, many bones had been found in the *Ngalau tambang sa puluk*, I started out on the 26ᵗʰ to travel there in the company of an old Malay, who used to wash gold there and claimed to know the way there very well. Three days long we have been looking with full effort for this palaeontological goldmine, without having any success in the thick *rimbu*, where every trace of a previous road had been eradicated. A test to examine the cave of *Muka-muka* near Muara was unsuccessful, because the workmen were suffering too much from fevers.

Code	Date	Description
50-048	23 August 1889 [monthly report July]	Short overview of the work done for the palaeontological research at Sumatra's West Coast during the month of July 1889.
		After it had become apparent that the *Ngalau mansiu* on the opposite side of the Sinamar River was not yielding any fossils the work there was abandoned and excavations were started in the [in pencil: 15 July] *Ngalau bandar* (also known as *Ngalau batang chiparok*). This cave thanks its name to a *bandar* = water conduit which transports water from the Bateng Sangtei to the sawahs. It is a small and shallow only about 8 m deep cave, which just like the *Ngalau mansiu* is located in the Gunung andjeng, at the right bank of the Bateng Sangtei, about 12 M. above the river bed of this mountain stream. Particularly at the back, at its deepest half, it is very low, because a strong erosion mainly affected the ceiling, with the result that the more spacious hollow of the cave has in earlier days become largely filled up with large and small rocks and gravel. The floor therefore also—apart from a very shallow surface layer—up to the largest excavated depth (of 2 M) almost completely consisted of limestone blocks that had fallen out of the ceiling and which, only with very little soil, had connected to a moderately vast and hard breccia. Completely at the surface underneath only a few centimetres of loose clay there was a 15 cm thick layer of wood ashes, in which shards of pottery of more recent shapes appeared as well as some bones of the common goat and larger birds, of which some were clearly carrying the marks of being cut with a knife, proving the cave has been in use by men and the important thickness of the ash layer makes us assume that for a number of years this cave has been inhabited and used up to recently as a temporary or permanent stay, probably for Malay people.
		Up to the end of this month the limestone breccia did not deliver many bones. Just a few teeth of pigs, deer and porcupines and of a tiger, were found, next to the remains of bats.
		In the *Ngalau pandjang* near Sibalin work was continued up to a maximum depth of 8 M. where rock bottom of the cave was reached. Underneath the yellow clay that was reached last month, locally a layer of gravel impregnated with chalk was found, which was resting at the bottom of the cave. Fossils of any importance were not found, with the exception of a plastron of tortoise, which however upon removing the hardened clay mass by carelessness of the workmen was broken in many pieces.
		The relatively low amount of fossils in this cave, as in that of *Ngalau mansiu* and in the caves I examined earlier near Balei-pandjang (L Kota), which at best only delivered a few scattered bones or fragments, seems with certainty to be explained by the fact that these caves, only have been dry for short intermittent periods, and during their existence up to recent times have had a brook running its course through them (as is still the case in many caves).
		In general it seems that the presence of animal remains in caves of Sumatra, as far as the origin is concerned, leads to another conclusion than is the case in Europe. Equally to what research in the Karnul caves in tropical British India seems to have taught us, here, much less than in Europe, where the ice age has had its direct influence, water seems not to have played such an important role in transporting bones into the caves, but a rather more important role, however, was played by large predators. Important stashes of diluvial fossils here will likely only have been brought about that way.
		What role men might have played in that respect is still unclear as, with the exception of the peculiar human skull found in Kediri and the manmade stone object I found in *Ngalau lida ajer* near Payakumbuh, as far as is known to me, in no cave of the archipelago have traces of prehistoric man ever been discovered. –
		Since 20 July *Ngalau pandjang*, where we have now reached the bottom, was abandoned and the men were put at work at close distance in the *Ngalau bulan* (also called *Ngalau pandjang* too) which apart from some molars of pigs close to the surface in the loose black earth and some bones of little bats did not bring anything of importance.

Code	Date	Description
		Because of being indisposed I was not able to continue tracking down new caves during the larger part of this month. A Kampong chief however informed me about the existence of some so far unknown caves near Tapi-Sello and in one of these, the *Ngalau Jambu*, on 31 July the Kampong chief together with one of the forced labourers, who was already more able in finding fossils, brought from there a great many teeth. They are of the same species, and in the same relative numbers towards each other and in the same state of conservation as those I found earlier in *Ngalau Lida ajer*, near Payakumbuh; many teeth of pigs and of orangutan, further tapirs, rhinoceroses, elephants, deer, buffaloes, lower monkeys and porcupines are also here in abundance.
50-049	8 September 1889 [monthly report August]	Short overview of the work done for the palaeontological research at Sumatra's West Coast during the month of August 1889.

In the *Ngalau bandar* (*Ngalau batang chiparok*) near Bua work was continued. The sediment found, a breccia of limestone mixed with only very little soil, not hard enough to be fruitfully removed with dynamite, but then again so hard that removing it with ordinary tools results in very slow progress, which was partly the cause that this month we only reached a maximal depth of 2.75 M. The bones found were few in number and mostly small and broken into unidentifiable fragments, by the way apparently from the same animal species as we used to find before.

Also the *Ngalau bulan* (*Ngalau pandjang II*) near Sibalin did not bring anything peculiar. Although rather many bones were found in the top, 0.60 M thick layer of loose black earth, these were also almost all broken into such tiny parts, that for most of them (at least for the time being) there can be no thought of having them identified. Most seem to be originating from small animals and must, after predators brought them in, have been shattered by porcupines whilst digging through the earth. They are however no big loss, as they are without doubt bones of a recent date.

Upon further digging we came into 1.15 M of yellow clay, which at greater depth turns into a fine gravel. This yellow clay did contain some teeth of the ordinary wild pig (*Sus vittatus*), of the tapir (*Tapirus indicus*) and of the ordinary Karo (*Cercopithecus cynomolgus*), and a few bones of the Kidjang (*Cervulus muntjac*), all species still living today.

More important results were almost immediately obtained in the *Ngalau Jambu* near Tapi-Sello. This cave is located at a short distance [thereof], north of the old little volcano Kuliet-monies, West of the brook Muara-panas, close to the top of the limestone mountain. It comprises two rather spacious chambers, which are in connection to each other by a high narrow opening. The front chamber is open to the outside and receives full daylight. Its floor entirely consists of heavy limestone blocks that have fallen from the ceiling. The inner chamber is completely devoid of daylight, it contains a few similar rocks like in the front chamber but in between the floor is flat and covered with an up to 0.50 cM. thick layer of earth.

Already in this dark red soil, which is of the same kind as is covering the old slate layers everywhere in this area, a great many teeth were found, which, as I already had the opportunity to note in my previous report, originated from the same species, and at about in the same ratio and the same state of conservation as those which were collected earlier in *Ngalau lida ajer* near Payakumbuh. Underneath this layer we had a very irregular stalagmite mass which partly enveloped limestone blocks and which was followed to a maximum depth of 1.80 M. In its upper part there were still similar fossils present as in the red earth; further down these were completely lacking. We yet continued removing this mass, as there was the possibility that it was covering a deeper fossil-bearing layer or other soil. |

Code	Date	Description
50-049 50-050	17 October 1889 [monthly report September]	Brief overview of the palaeontological research on Sumatra's West Coast during the month September 1889.
		Also in this month the excavation of the *Ngalau bandar* (*batang chiparok*) was continued; the work however was progressing slowly both because of the nature of the stony mass that had to be removed as well as the large number of forced labourers suffering from fever. In the earlier described breccia we found yet a very few more
		[50-050]
		teeth of the ordinary wild hog (*Sus vittatus*) of the tapir (*Tapirus indicus*), the deer (*Cervus equinus*), the forest goat (*Antilope sumatrensis*) and the porcupine (*Hystrix mülleri*) all animals still present here today. Underneath the breccia we finally at 3.50 M found a brownish-red clay, of which we by the end of September had only removed a few centimetres.
		In the Ngalau Bulan near Sibalin no fossils were found this month. Underneath the deepest layer of fine gravel we found in the previous month, which had a thickness of 30 to 40 cm, we found again a darkish yellow clay earth which we followed up to a depth of more than 5 m without finding anything important. This result and even more so the strong increase of fever amongst the workmen in this moist cave (up to 50% of the number of forced labourers was suffering from fevers) make me decide to quit the work here and start on 1 October in a meanwhile discovered cave at a short distance from the *dusun* Sibalin. This cave, of which the local name is not known to me, is located in the same valley at the right bank of the Sumpur as the other caves examined here so far, ±40 m above the floor of it and consists of a 150-m long corridor with an average width of 7 m whilst its yellowish clay floor is rather even and almost horizontal.
		Also in the *Ngalau Jambu* near the Tapi Sello excavations were ceased by the end of the month, after a depth of almost 3 m a solid rock mass was encountered and therefore the bottom of the cave had been reached. No more fossils had been found. The forced labourers who became available were added to the ones working in the *Ngalau bandar*.
		Some Malay, who claimed that whilst searching for gold they had found huge bones some years ago in a deep pit, the *Ngalau lebawah* near Sisawah accompanied me there at the start of the month. On the right side of the road to the *dusun* Kabun, a few hours away from d.s. on top of a mountain ridge, this cave, which is a natural pit in which I climbed down along a rattan ladder for 28 M. until I had reached its apparent floor; along a sideways crevice I could, from resting place to resting place, on rocks pointing out, climb down a further 25–30 M. until I had reached its true floor. In there was like a very small bowl, in which there was hardly room for two people, but on the floor ±½ M. of fine gravel mixed with earth, which looked very much tossed over and on top of it was a truly large bone, a thighbone, of which both the distal ends were missing and that turned out to be of an elephant. It had completely calcified, was very heavy and partly covered with a dripstone layer; there can be no doubt about its great age and fossil state, but lacking material for comparison it can for the time being not be ascertained as to which species of elephant it belongs; it is surely not of any other family than *Elephas*. Other remains were not found here although they might yet have been present in higher layers of earth (the top floor) of this pit; it is probably yet likely that this animal has fallen down this pit alive (like the complete Rhinoceros skeleton found in the Dream-cave near Wirksworth in England, who had fallen in the cave similarly). Quick attempts to find these gave no results and for a systematic exploration this cave is unsuitable given its location on a mountain ridge hours away from any *kampong* and drinking water. So here we experienced again to what extent the terrain is limiting the number of caves suitable to be opened in these areas.

Code	Date	Description
50-050 50-051	8 November 1889 [monthly report October]	Short overview of the palaeontological research at Sumatra's West Coast, during the month October 1889.
		The brownish-red clay which we encountered by the end of the previous month in the Ng. bandar at a depth of 3.50 M turned out to be mixed with small pieces of limestone for 0.60 M until we encountered for 0.50 M. Pure clay and finally 1 M. clayish quartz sand (originating from weathered Tertiary conglomerates); so now we have reached at a total depth of 5.60 M. below the original surface floor the bottom of the cave. No more bones had been found and looking for them came to an unexpected end. It had already been noted lately that small cracks had appeared in the ceiling and when these started to increase I had the work stopped. Happily in time, for soon after a large part of the ceiling collapsed (some hundreds of cubic metres). Thus work that had taken a long time remained fruitless.
		As meanwhile the attempts to find suitable caves in the mountain range near Tandjung Banei had failed and no others were known to me, the forced labourers that had become available here were also put to work in the large cave at Sisawah.
		This cave turned out to be the earlier southern extension of the *Ngalau pandjang* (*Ngalau kapala sawah luat*), with which it was connected by a narrow passage, which now could be slightly widened.
		[50-051]
		The entrance of the cave is located 20 M. above the valley floor (erroneously in the previous report it was stated to be 40 m) and it is facing Southward; it consists of 150-m long corridor in north-northwest direction, which is on average 6–8 m wide, but at the end widens to a 40-m long and in the middle 20-m wide chamber.
		It's smooth and almost horizontal floor consists of a thick layer of chalk tuff, which at some spots is absent. Only near the entrance (up to 15–20 M), this column mass is missing and the floor consists of a surface 2 m further down of yellow clay.
		Excavations were started at two points; [first] near the entrance, and here by the end of October they had reached a depth of 3.50 M, while the soil remained to be the same clay. An excavation was further started at 30 m distance from the entrance where they encountered: 1.35 m chalktuff, a 0.30 M. Breccia of small limestone parts and fine quartz gravel, baked together by the hard chalk tuff, 20 cM fine gravel mixed with clay and finally (at 1.85 M.) yellow clay. Fossils had not been found by the end of October.
50-051 50-044 50-045	2 December 1889 [monthly report November]	Brief overview of the palaeontological research on Sumatra's West Coast during the month November 1889.
		In the south extension of the *Ngalau pandjang* near Sisawah teeth and bones were found in the yellow clay next to the entrance at a depth between 4.20 M. and 5.50 M. The latter however were in such bad state of conservation that the main part of them consisted of mere fragments which for the time being cannot be identified. They chiefly originate from elephant, rhinoceros, tapir, pig, porcupine (*Hystrix*) and the orangutan (*S. satyrus*), so represent the same species, of which the existence also became apparent in other caves that have been examined.
		The geological age of these fossils cannot rightly be ascertained and can only somewhat be established by comparison with others. The greatest depth by the end of November was 5.75 m. From 4.50 m down the yellow clay of earlier was found to be strongly mixed with a moderately fine gravel delivered by weathering of tertiary conglomerate.
		The hole we dug at 30 M. distance of the entrance of the cave with the size of 6.50 m by 5.50 m delivered the following profile starting from the top: 1.35 chalktuff, 0.30 breccia of limestone pieces
		[50-044]
		and fine quartz gravel baked together by chalk tuff, 0.20 M. fine gravel mixed with clay; underneath this—in total 1.85 M. thick—top layer, the same yellow clay was found as near the entrance, at 2.75 the bottom of the cave was found, which only along its east wall was covered with a maximally 0.75 M. thick layer of stones.
		It was regrettable that the mentioned clay did not contain any fossils, as especially here one could have expected, underneath the strong limestone coverage that they would have conserved well by calcification.

Code	Date	Description
		At a short distance from the southern *Ngalau pandjang* and completely at the same height a small hole found in the rocks at the east side of the valley was further examined. Although it was only 0.80 M long and 0.60 M. high, it seems to be the remains of an earlier cave which had become filled up in later times with pointy limestone pieces and boulders glued together to a conglomerate by the chalk. After this conglomerate breccia was broken away to the west the entrance of a small cave opened up, however only 3 m wide and 1.80 m high. Against the ceiling a 25 cm thick layer of hardened clay had remained which contained a number of teeth and some bones, most of which had completely calcified. By further breaking away of the mentioned stone mass we could finally enter up to 20 m deep, where the cave seems to end, after it had widened but it remained as low as near the entrance.
		The teeth and bones originated from a Rhinoceros, a Tapir, a kind of buffalo (*Bos*), a deer (*Cervus*), one or more species of pig (*Sus*), the orangutan (*Simia*) and a common Karo-monkey (*Cercopithecus*) or some species closely related to that; so here yet again the same company we found everywhere. This is now however of great significance and confirms again the great age of this fauna. It is namely a peculiar phenomenon that here at a height of about 20 M. above the floor, where both these caves are located and at many places apparently in the same horizon crevices in the rock can be observed which are of the same nature like for instance those along the Kuantan near Muka-Muka at the height of the water level. Surely the water must have gnawed out these crevices and is now busy depositing pebbles and gravel and clay in them. This must also have been the case for the caves we have examined. The small cave is but an extension of such a crevice and also the southern *Ngalau pandjang* shows this at the entrance.
		[50-045]
		In this valley, which now does not even have a brook any more, the water level must have been 20 m above the current valley floor, and this will certainly not have been a small brook, for the crevices can be found along the whole length of the valley and quite strongly so. The water must also have deposited the boulders, the gravel and the fossil-bearing clay and such large changes demand a very long time which contributes to the determination of a substantial age of the fossils.
		It is furthermore noteworthy, that higher up in the valley there is a rock wall in which there are three such crevices with a distance between them of 8-10 m and that the same phenomenon can be seen where the valley of the Sisawah leads in southeastern direction towards the tarata Kabun.
		Traces of such higher water levels and the rerouting of rivers are well-known phenomena and a consequence of the erosion doing its work over the whole globe, but what is noteworthy here is that these phenomena seem to have some periodicity.
		Up to 3 or four times at least the water level was able to do its erosive action for a longer time (because the formation of these crevices must have taken quite some time), after which every time an abrupt decrease of the water level took place. Note it is not completely sure whether this water, which was a river, was as far from the shore as it is now. If it turns out, that during the diluvial times as assumed by Verbeek on the west coast of Sumatra the sea was yet covering part of the current land (up to a height of 180 m) then the phenomenon observed here might be related to these changes of the sea-level and the here observed repeated rather local changes might have bearing on the work that by Inesz has been turned into a *question coulante* on the changes of the beach lines and the borders between sea and land and may be of no little significance. But this is only a suspicion, which I however not thought I should keep quiet, because the observed phenomena might deserve further investigation at other locations.
		[In left margin rewrite:]
		Should it turn out, that the drop, which Verbeek assumes for the west coast of Sumatra during diluvial times also expands towards the eastern shores, then the phenomenon observed here might be related to the changes in the level of the sea,—

Code	Date	Description
50-051	23 January 1890 [monthly report December]	Short overview of the palaeontological research at Sumatra's West Coast during the month December 1889.
		Already at the start of the month the fossils in the southern extension of the *Ngalau pandjang* near Sisawah were getting scarce, such that it was soon to be expected that further work would be fruitless. The little cave close by was already abandoned for the same reasons.
		As there soon would be no more caves within the vicinity of Bua suitable for the purpose and as currently the terrains of the lake of Singkarah seem to be the most rewarding, a proposition was made to your Noble severe Sir to have the work transferred to that area. Meanwhile the work had to cease earlier than expected because already on the 5th we hit in the *Ngalau pandjang* on large boulders and subsequently on the bottom of the cave and I thought it wise not to lose any time even though your Noble severe Sir had not yet officially transferred me to Singkarah I transferred the whole operation there to be able to continue the work as soon as possible.
		On the 11th we started with exploring for caves starting firstly in the vicinity of Paningahan, where the most appeared to be, whilst the distance to Singkarah is relatively small. Only a few of the caves we visited with the help of guides turned out to be suitable; the famous cave of Paningahan (along the road from the pasar to the coffee storage) the least of all, as this cave is only 20 M. above the current water level of the lake and there are clear signs everywhere on several spots, that the level in recent times must have been at least 70 M. higher than it currently is.
		On the 20th the workmen were divided over two caves higher up; half of them were put at work at the Ngalau siba bantu ±120 M. above the lake on the bank of the Paningahan-brook, the other half in the *Ngalau pala pisang* ±250 M. above the lake on the left bank of the Bateng Paningahan. In the first cave we first had to remove a heavy rock, which was partly blocking the entrance, with dynamite, with which [task] they had not yet finished by the end of December. In the *Ngalau pala pisang* we encountered near the entrance a yellow clay mixed with pieces of limestone of which up to 1.50 M. was removed; further down at about 15 M. from the entrance inward in a spacious room bat guano was removed up to a depth of 2 M.
50-045	8 February 1890 [monthly report January]	Short overview of the palaeontological research at Sumatra's West Coast during the month of January 1890.
		On 20 January the *Ngalau pala pisang* near Paningahan was already abandoned, after the solid rock floor of the cave had been reached near the entrance without finding any fossils, whilst in the deeper 'hall' because of the meanwhile started heavy rains so much water had entered that working there became completely impossible. Not that there was much to look forward to for reward. The bat guano was reaching at least to a depth of 4 M. and the rock walls were converging in such a way, that the floor would soon have been reached.
		This *Ngalau pala pisang* is therefore one of the few caves that did not contain any mammal remains at all.
		Near to this cave in the ravine of the Batang Paningahan we found a hole in the rocks, too narrow to crawl in, which however after being widened, turned out to be the remainder of an old cave. In the yellow earth which was completely filling the space underneath a hanging dripstone a number of teeth were found of the already so often encountered Lida-ajer fauna. The yellow earth was covering river sand that had been hardened by impregnation of limestone, which therefore must be younger than the deposits of this sand by the Paningahan that is currently incised 25 m lower.
		The *Ngalau si babantu*, a beautiful small cave delivered a considerable amount of such remains like this hole in the rocks. After removing limestone blocks the black earth was dug through to a depth of 0.50 M to 1.25 M. and subsequently yellow earth, mixed with small pieces of limestone up to a depth of about 1 M. The latter contains numerous teeth, again richly representing the Lida-ajer fauna.

Code	Date	Description
50-046	8 March 1890 [monthly report February]	Short overview of the palaeontological research at Sumatra's West Coast during the month of February 1890.
		The small hole in the rocks in the ravine of the Batang Paningahan, which had been opened by the end of January, was already emptied at the start of this month, without the finds showing any important changes.
		The excavations in the *Ngalau Sibantu* were abandoned for the same reason. The cave did, however, still yield a rather large amount of teeth from animals which belong to the oft-mentioned Lida-ajer fauna.
		As the state of health of the personnel on this moist West side of the lake was again deteriorating and as there were no further caves at hand, the work was moved to the east side, which has a drier and more healthy climate. As usual we also had to find the caves here ourselves, but yet already on the 9th the digging could start in the *Ngalau agung agung*, about 2 paal east of the Kampong Sibrambang and on the 13th in the *Ngalau Sibatie* (Bukit Mengkapok).
		In the first our efforts were soon rewarded. After from the floor of this 11 m wide and 8 m deep cave some large dripstones which had fallen off or were growing to the floor, had been removed one could start taking out a thin layer of yellow clay (±½ M), which was covering a black soil. This black earth, of which by the end of February 2½ M. has been dug up, was mixed with pieces of limestone and contained an immense amount of teeth and molars from the animals of the aforementioned fauna, in which now elephants and buffaloes were now more strongly represented than before. The remains of thousands of large animals must have been dragged in here and one cannot without amazement and wonder think about the rich animal life which must have once existed in an area where currently even the common Indian hog is rare.
		Contrary to that the work in the *Ngalau Sibatie* — actually 2 caves with the same name — remained without result up to the end of this month.
50-046	26 March 1890 [monthly report March]	March 1890.
		Halfway through this month the *Ngalau Sibatie* in the Bukit mentapok (Nagarie Sullied ajer) was completely emptied. This little cave with a depth of only 5 M and a width of 8 M contains underneath a 0.50 M. thick layer of black earth about 2.50 M. hard yellow clay mixed with smaller and larger pieces of limestone. In this breccia-like mass a few completely calcified but yet very much broken bones were found, presumably of a kind of deer.
		The *Ngalau agung-agung* near Sibrambang kept yielding a numerous amount of teeth and molars of the fauna mentioned in the previous report. However on the 25th of March at a depth of 3.50 M. below the original surface the rocky bottom was reached and as at another location within the cave up to [a depth of] 2.50 M no results of a different kind were encountered than had already been obtained, at the 26th of March this cave was also abandoned.
56-142 56-144		See file Sumatra notebooks doi.org/10.6084/m9.figshare.22154882

Note: Dutch formulaic greetings, that may seem odd in English, have been translated literally, as they convey the status of the addressee; for instance, someone addressed as 'severe' has either studied law or holds a civil or military position of power.

Source: Dubois Archive, Naturalis Biodiversity Center, Leiden. The code numbers refer to those in the archive. For example, 6-310 refers to [MM774C-000006-310].

3

An expedition in colonial times: Some notes regarding Dubois' fieldwork in Sumatra

Paul C.H. Albers

Abstract

When Dubois travelled to Sumatra, Indonesia had already been under Dutch colonial rule for almost 300 years. This obviously had implications and benefits for Dubois and his expedition. By enlisting in the army—following the example of Junghuhn—he was able to obtain government support for his plans. Without such support, he could never have financed the expedition. His army status gave him the advantage of being on speaking terms with high government officials, and being assigned convicts enabled him to get the laborious work done cheaply. (Of course, the use of convict labour was not limited to the colonies.) Dubois was appreciative of the support he received from local people. His trust was not always reciprocated, however—but the biggest difficulty was health. In particular, Dubois and the soldiers and local people who worked for him suffered from malaria. As a physician, Dubois endeavoured to take care of his employees' health, but he could not prevent one of his sergeants from dying. Despite the adversities—and contrary to Dubois' own perception— his Sumatra expedition was hugely successful.

Keywords: Padang Highlands, palaeontology, cave exploration, Dutch, fieldwork history

Abstrak

Pada saat Dubois melakukan perjalanan ke Sumatra, Indonesia telah berada di bawah kekuasaan kolonial Belanda selama hampir 300 tahun. Ini jelas berimplikasi dan menguntungkan bagi Dubois dan ekspedisinya. Dengan mendaftar sebagai tentara, mengikuti contoh Junghuhn, ia mampu menggalang dukungan pemerintah untuk rencananya. Tanpa dukungan seperti itu, dia tidak akan pernah bisa membiayai ekspedisinya. Statusnya sebagai tentara memberikan keuntungan sehingga dia bisa berbicara dengan pejabat tinggi pemerintah. Ditugaskan sebagai pengawas narapidana, memungkinkannya untuk menyelesaikan pekerjaan yang melelahkan dengan biaya murah, meskipun ini, bagi dia sendiri merupakan praktik universal, tidak terbatas pada koloni. Dubois menghargai dukungan lokal, meskipun kepercayaan tidak selalu saling menguntungkan. Namun persoalan yang terbesar adalah masalah kesehatan. Dubois serta penduduk setempat dan tentara yang bekerja untuknya khususnya menderita penyakit malaria. Sebagai tenaga medis sendiri, Dubois menjaga kesehatan orang-orang bekerja dengannya sebaik mungkin, tetapi hal ini tidak dapat mencegah, salah satu sersannya meninggal. Terlepas dari kesulitan, dan bertentangan dengan persepsi Dubois sendiri, ekspedisi Sumatra-nya sangat sukses.

Kata kunci: Dataran Tinggi Padang, paleontologi, penjelajahan gua, Belanda, sejarah kerja lapangan

Introduction

This chapter aims to address some of the speculations and ideas people might have about the colonial circumstances under which the Sumatran (and other Dutch Indies) expeditions of Dubois took place and from which Dubois undoubtedly benefited. By explaining some of the circumstances that existed during Dubois' time in Sumatra, I hope to show some of the colonial aspects of his expeditions that sometimes did (and sometimes did not) have an influence on Dubois' contributions to science.

References to Dubois' notes and correspondence are provided using the coding system used at Naturalis Biodiversity Center for scans of Dubois Archive pages or groups of pages. For example, '50-040' refers to [MM774C-000050-040]. Translations of these scans (by PCHA, of either the entire page or the appropriate paragraph) are provided in the appendix.

Figure 3.1: Dubois and his wife Anna Lojenga on the SS *Amalia* bound for Sumatra.
Source: Dubois Archive, Naturalis Biodiversity Center, Leiden.

Why did Dubois go to the Dutch Indies and to Sumatra in particular? The first part of this question—why did he go to the Dutch Indies?— has been posed and answered before, and his scientific reasons are clear: he was convinced that human forerunners were to be expected in historically tropical environments (e.g. Albers and de Vos 2010; Chapter 2, this volume; Theunissen 1989), and Lydekker's (1886) publication of a fossil primate jaw fragment from the Siwalik hills in British India (now Pakistan) gave Dubois sufficient reason to target Sumatra, where geological conditions were also favourable. However, his decision to go to the Dutch Indies to find these forerunners was not only scientific: it also had a strong colonial aspect. The Dutch Indies were available to Dubois in ways that other suitable places, such as Africa, were not. By the time Dubois arrived in Indonesia, it had already seen Dutch colonial presence for almost 300 years, and large parts were relatively safe for a Dutch family to visit. Figure 3.1 shows Dubois and his wife Anna Lojenga on their way to the Dutch Indies.

Because of the colonial connection between the Netherlands and Indonesia, Dubois also had easier access to the scientific literature about Indonesia than he would have had to the scientific literature about other parts of the world. Dubois lived during a time when books were sent from scientist to scientist and required passages were copied by hand (this is one of the reasons why the Dubois Archive consists of over 30,000 scanned pages). Dubois pieced together all the clues he needed. The geological maps of Verbeek (1883) and Junghuhn (1855) were known to him, as were the fossils found in Java by Junghuhn (1857) and Radèn Saléh (1867) and the publications of Martin on these fossils (Martin 1879–1880, 1884–1889a, 1884–1889b). He also knew about the stories of mythological giants whose bones could be found scattered throughout Java. For instance, Cohen Stuart (1867:468) noted, in a response in the same journal to the finds of Radèn Saléh and his reference to a publication on the travels of Rhaden Mas Arja Purwa Lelana, that these stories had been well known for a long time.

From a practical viewpoint, too, the Dutch Indies had advantages. Dubois had the scientific and political connections needed for an enterprise there, partly through his marriage to Anna Lojenga, who had two brothers already stationed in the Dutch Indies and a sister married to the Assistant-Resident (government official) in Borneo. Moreover, his mother-in-law was a full cousin of Jentink, the director of the natural history museum in Leiden, who was a major contributor to his cause (6-319).

Choosing Sumatra instead of Java, from where fossils had already been reported (Junghuhn 1857; Radèn Saléh 1867), was done purely for geological reasons. Conditions favourable for fossilisation are rare—particularly rare in tropical environments—and caves are optimal for finding fossils (e.g. Louys et al. 2017; Morley and Goldberg 2017). This is not just because of the higher preservation potential, but also because fossils tend to accumulate in caves due to sinkholes, natural shelters, and rodents and predators that can den or bring their prey there. The geological circumstances for the right type of caves to occur are simply much better in Sumatra than in Java, where there are fewer limestone outcrops. To Dubois, the choice was a matter of calculation, and Sumatra presented the greatest chance of finding the right fossils of the right age.

Government support

Without government support, Dubois could never have financed his trip to the Indies and certainly could not have supported himself and his family for the seven years he was there. By enlisting in the army, he achieved the first step—actually getting there—as transport for army personnel to the Dutch Indies was paid for. The big gamble Dubois took was on whether he would gain financial support for the enterprise while he was there. Dubois followed the example set by Franz Wilhelm Junghuhn, who had also entered the Dutch Indies as an army doctor (Nieuwenhuys and Jaquet 1980 provide more extensive biographical information on Junghuhn), and it is evident that Junghuhn's career switch, from officer of health to government geological scientist, was exactly the precedent that Dubois sought and copied. This is mentioned in a letter dated 10 April 1889 to Dubois from Kroeze (possibly a government official):

> I have no doubt that, if you ask, your term of detachment to the Department of Education, Religion and Trade will be extended, to allow you, as they did Junghuhn in Sumatra and other islands, to extensively continue your research.' (7-505)

In many ways, Dubois played this out brilliantly, convincing and interesting the right people, promising a rich haul of fossils and delivering results quickly due to both skill and his luck in finding his first Sumatran caves full of fossils (Chapter 2, this volume).

The Dutch government and the government of the Dutch Indies essentially paid for almost everything (although at the start, Dubois did contribute personally; 10-361), but the costs were distributed over several departments so that all of them initially seemed to be getting a cheap deal. The Department of War paid the wages and sustenance of Dubois and his engineer workmen and also arranged and paid for a replacement doctor to release him from his hospital duties (9-286). The mining department supplied tools (42-274). A list of tools and Dubois' assessment of their costs (50-007) is presented in Tables 3.1 and 3.2. On Sumatra, the governor allowed Dubois to use the labour of 50 convicts, who also needed to be housed and fed and looked after (10-361, 42-349). The Department of Education, Religion and Trade paid many other costs, such as the printing costs of the 1894 publication on *Pithecanthropus* (42-284) and Dubois' trip to the Siwalik hills and the museum in Kolkata (then Calcutta) for comparative research. To what extent the Dutch Department of Colonies contributed—for instance, towards the cost of the sea transport of the over 400 crates of fossils and rock and soil samples—has not yet been a subject of any study, nor have all the bills available in the archive yet been transcribed and disclosed, so the above are merely examples.

Table 3.1: Dubois' assessment of the tools needed for his palaeontological research on Sumatra's west coast.

Kind of tools	Number	Kind of tools	Number
Hand and [other] axes of several sizes	12	Whetstones (round)	2
Goloks	24	Files (large)	6
Sledgehammers	10	Hand saws	4
Crowbars	12	Chisels	12
Patjols	24	Small hammers	4
Rock drills	12	Blocks (a few) and rigging	4
Clearance spoons[1]	6	Sink buckets	12
Hammers	6	Lamps with equipment	12
Pliers for percussions	3	**Consumables that possibly could be provided**	
Pickaxes (double)	24	Petrol for ½ a year	24 chests
Shovels	18	Dynamite for ½ year	4 chests
Spades	24	Candles for ½ year	250 items
		White glue	3 kilos

[1] To clear the drill holes before dynamite can be put in.

Source: Missive of Dubois to the Director of Education, Religion and Trade at Batavia, dated 29 March 1889 (50-007).

Table 3.2: Dubois' assessment of the finances needed for his palaeontological research on Sumatra's west coast.

Type of expenses	Money	Explanation
Obtaining tools and lamps	ƒ 400	this post is only needed for 1st month and can be completely omitted if the Department provides everything herself
Petrol candles et cetera for a year	ƒ 450	
Dynamite for a year	ƒ 500	
Maintenance of tools and lamps and possible replacement	ƒ 300	
Erecting temporary barracks for the forced labourers near the caves (material) – for one year	ƒ 180	
Transport costs for a year – including those of the officer Dubois	ƒ 300	These do not include transport cost in case of change of workplace, nor for transport of goods overseas.
Wages for two army engineers	ƒ 600	
Unforeseen	ƒ 100	
Total	**ƒ 2,830**	

Note: ƒ = Dutch guilders (*florijn*).

Source: Missive of Dubois to the Director of Education, Religion and Trade at Batavia, dated 29 March 1889 (50-007).

This whole investment of the government into Dubois' research was made with only two requirements. Firstly, all the fossils—this was very clearly stated before any fossils were collected (7-481, 8-339)—were to become government property and to go to the Leiden State Geology Museum; and secondly, scientific publications were to be written to radiate the prestige of this project onto all who contributed.

What should also be discussed is to what extent this support can be called colonial: that is, was it only because the Dutch Indies were a colony that such support was given or available? Universities in the Netherlands itself also got support for scientific enterprises that produced no gains other than knowledge and sometimes prestige. The use of convicts for work was also not limited to the Dutch colonies, and at around this time, large moors and wilderness areas in the Netherlands were cleared for agriculture using convicts and outcasts for labour (Canon van Nederland n.d.). Making convicts work is still practised today in the Netherlands (Dienst Justitiële Inrichtingen n.d.) and has been considered more humane and enlightened than corporal punishment for a very long time (Coornhert 1587). I am not claiming that *abuse* of forced labour did not happen in the colonies, just that the use of convicts for forced labour was not restricted to colonies and, therefore, the evaluation of forced labour as being a typical colonial practice seems unjustified. That abuse of forced labour took place, especially on plantations, is well documented and unquestionable (e.g. Minasny 2020). The question of how Dubois treated the people indentured to him is discussed below.

A widespread presence of the Dutch soldiers was, however, keeping the colonial system in place, and to Dubois, one of the advantages of that was that he could be stationed wherever he liked in the colonies; he was able to start at the army hospital in Payakumbuh, near to where he expected caves to be. Overall, wearing a uniform no doubt helped Dubois in some circumstances when he needed to get things done. This applies not just to his dealings with local people: his rank as an officer would also have helped him to deal with government officials, as the army and local politics were closely connected. This advantage alone justifies concluding that Dubois made use of the colonial system.

Local support and Dubois' attitude towards the local people

For any expedition anywhere, local support is invaluable and greatly contributes to its success. As soon as Dubois arrived in Sumatra, he started inquiring about locations of caves, asking local administrators as well as village heads and local regents (50-006). In Sumatra, however, the Aceh war had been ongoing since 1873. It was an armed military conflict between the so far independent Sultanate of Aceh and the Kingdom of the Netherlands; it lasted until 1904. While in Sumatra, Dubois had nothing to do with the Aceh war and never came close to it, nor was he ever in any danger because of it. However, distrust towards soldiers was present everywhere. The local people mined the caves for gold and guano—the latter to obtain saltpetre to make gunpowder. That Dubois was interested merely in prehistoric bones was beyond the comprehension of the local people. They assumed it to be a deception, too ludicrous to be true, and thought Dubois to be surveying for gold and guano. Dubois received large lists of caves that proved useless as most were little more than overhanging rocks or small wells. In the jungle, with no roads to speak of, he was continually misled, and true caves were concealed from him. All this was discussed by Theunissen (1989), who deduced it from a letter dated 17 October 1889 from Dubois to Jentink, the director of the natural history museum in Leiden. In the letter, Dubois stated that he finally went looking for caves by himself without relying on local guides, and only then did he find caves that were useful (6-373; see the appendix for a translation). There are several other letters with similar content (Albers in prep).

During Dubois' lifetime, attitudes towards racial differences were not the same as they are today, and among the correspondence of Dubois (and any of his contemporaries), expressions can be found that would not be acceptable now (Albers in prep). The letter to Jentink mentioned above, most probably written in a depressed state while recovering from a malaria attack, painted Sumatra as a hostile environment (6-373). Dubois referred to the Sumatran people as Malays—and thus clearly distinguished them from the Javanese—and was critical of their agricultural strategies. He was also unhappy with the amount of work done by the convicts assigned to him—however, he also noted as causes not only health issues, but also poor oversight: one of his sergeants, van der Nesse, was not sufficiently competent and had to be replaced (6-373).

Dubois' Sumatran notebooks contain one list of names, crimes, and sentences of convicts apparently working for Dubois (Table 3.3), but other than that, we know very little about their background. The list presents some surprisingly serious crimes such as murder and arson.

Table 3.3: Sentences of convicts working for Dubois in Sumatra.

Name	Crime	Number of years on the chain
1 Soeredjo alias Rebo	Theft of cashier's tickets with burglary	5
2 Mas joedjo admodjo	Fraud as storage master, embezzlement, forgery	5
3 Mas anggadjoedo	Killed the *wedono* of Sampang, whom he blamed for not being promoted to police overseer.	19
4 Soemo	Theft	[not mentioned]
5 Oesodikromo	Contract killing	20
6 Diporedjo (fusilier)	Killed his housekeeper	20
7 Setrawitana	Thefts with undermining	6
8 ~~Soerokarto Kartosrito~~	Thefts with undermining	5
9 Kamedjokel Towirio	Arson	10
10 Rasoet	Theft of [manufactured cloths?], et cetera	4

Name	Crime	Number of years on the chain
11 Troenokorio al. Troenoredjo Rasiman	Wounding	6
12 Soeroredjo	Cat-burglary	7
13 Tistowirono al. Kastodono (Foegiman)	Breaking and entering and theft	5
14 P Dallien	Theft of cattle by night	6
15 Asli	Theft with illegal entering	5
16 Pa Saetie	Theft of cattle	5
17 Arsidien al Pa Arsidja	Theft with illegal entering	5
18 Klimin	Murder	20
19 Mohamed al. Alie	Theft by night in gardens	5
20 Latoengangtoeng	Ditto	5
21 Pa Gloendoeng	Ditto	7
22 Ekoleksono	Arson	5
23 Gimin	2 thefts with undermining	4
24 Kromotanoeno	Theft with illegal entering and use of weapons with several persons	19
25 Kardi	Thefts—one with undermining	4 y 8 months
26 Kiting	Arson	5
27 Janoe Gapa Dalim (Ketjel)	Theft with undermining	5
28 Sangid	Theft of water buffaloes	6
29 Tarmo	Arson	6
30 Troenokarto al Simon	Theft with undermining	4
31 Gentaroedjin	Premeditated manslaughter	20
32 Pa Kadir	Killing his father with a spear	6
33 Pa Sarijo	Vengeance murder because of adultery	15
34 Pa Sijot	Theft with undermining	5
35 Pa Jalim	Theft by night from a house	4 y 4 months
36 Saiman al. Pa Sawie	Ditto	5
37 Sariman	Ditto	4
38 Najawitoma	Ditto	3
39 Najawi al. Ichodikromo	Arson	3
40 Rasjan Moentalip al. Sarimin	Theft and burglary	4
41 Karnin al Pa Karnina	Ditto (with undermining)	4
42 Pa Beng	Ditto	3
43 Rasim al. Oedin	Fraud, escaping	9
44 Jodjo al Wongsavinangoen	Theft by night	3
45 Pa Ramdjaeno	Wounding and stealing cattle	[?]
46 Kromodrono	Theft by night	4
47 Tanda al Pak Wadniak al. Soetawirija al. Wirjadirana	Theft by night	5
48 Doerahunoa	Ditto by day	3
49 Ripin	Ditto	4
50 Samir al. Karijawitana	Arson	4
Marijam	Theft	3

Source: Based on translation of pages (46-117, 46-118) from one of Dubois' Sumatran notebooks (doi.org/10.6084/m9.figshare.22154882).

It is not surprising that some of the convicts used working outside prison walls as an opportunity to escape (33-550). It is interesting to note that Dutch texts in the Dubois archives often speak of 'running off' or 'desertion' rather than using words equivalent to 'escaping'. This could suggest that although these men were forced labourers, this may, to some extent, have been their choice, as it earned them reduced sentences. They were certainly not heavily guarded, and escaping would not have been difficult—so we can, at least, conclude that most of them chose not to escape. However, slavery had only been abolished some 30 years before, and forced labourers were effectively temporarily enslaved, so these people would have considered themselves enslaved.

Undoubtedly, Dubois was unlikely to have been pleased with people 'running off', as he states this as one of the problems he faced in Sumatra in for instance the previously mentioned letter to Jentink (6-373), but there is no reason to assume that he actually blamed them for doing so. In fact, later, in Java, he asked to be assigned less severely sentenced men because they were less likely to abscond (50-020, 50-021), demonstrating that he understood very well why they ran away. It is, however, important to realise that we should not confuse Dubois' comments on the forced labourers with those expressing his attitude to the local people, as the former are a very specific subset of the latter.

In the Dubois Archive, examples of both positive and negative inclinations towards the local people can be found. While the modern trend of focusing on negative or racist attitudes is important to make certain such cases do not remain hidden from view and are not used to glorify an unrealistic colonial past (and some remarks in 6-373, for example, could be seen in such light), it is also worth noting that positive experiences did also occur, such as that local people, strange to Dubois, apparently regarded him sufficiently well to approach him on the street for medical advice, which he provided (33-513). Another clearly positive example concerned fellow scientist Hubrecht, who had visited Dubois in Java in 1891 and was about to continue to move on to Sumatra. Dubois then wrote to him:

> I am truly convinced, that you will have more success in Sumatra, I however do advise you again, not to take too much notice of the talk of 'rural Sirs' and the like, who haven't got the least notion of natural history. Native boys and men like resident van Hasselt or registrar Rost [both local Sumatran officials], who are used to observing the living nature, I believe to be the only reliable guides. (6-113)

It is clear from this quotation that Dubois preferred local guides over most European settlers and was very appreciative of local knowledge and people, even in Sumatra where his own experiences with local guides were not always positive, as discussed above.

When, in 1895, Dubois was finally about to leave Java and return to the Netherlands, there is some exchange of correspondence that suggests he had 'befriended' some local people (Albers in prep), but whether this was on an equal basis cannot be ascertained. His knowledge of the local languages is likely to have been very limited. Even his sergeants, who were in far closer contact with the local people than he was, were not proficient in the rural Javanese languages, and it is therefore safe to assume that Dubois was even less so. Moreover, although his interests were broad, there is little evidence of Dubois having had much interest in the local culture except where it related to his scientific interests.

Health

From the letters, we can conclude that sick workers were treated with medicines and not forced to work. This work could only be done by healthy people, and the work in some caves in Sumatra (such as Ngalau Bulan, and Muka-Muka Cave near Muara) was ceased altogether because the cave air was thought to cause malaria (50-048, 50-050). That malaria was actually transmitted by mosquitoes was only discovered in 1897 by Ronald Ross, two years after Dubois had returned to Europe (CDC 2015). We should also realise nowadays that the average life expectancy of people born in Indonesia in Dubois' day was only 30 years (O'Neill 2020), and, although much higher, still only about 45 in the Netherlands (O'Neill 2019). Dubois only barely survived several malaria attacks in Sumatra. One of his first sergeants (Franke) died in Sumatra within two months after he started working for Dubois. The report of Franke's death (42-369) clearly demonstrates that entering the Sumatran jungle in 1889 was not without risk. Suffering from malaria can change one's mental state, and in Dubois' case there are clear signs of that, which he himself recognised. In a letter to Jentink, he apologised for not writing earlier, saying that he waited because the letter would otherwise have been terribly gloomy (33-665). When assessing the content of letters from Dubois that seem overly negative or gloomy, possible coinciding malaria attacks ought to be considered.

We do not have as much factual evidence that Dubois provided medicine to his workers in Sumatra as we have from Java, but for the latter, it is quite clear from many letters (see Albers in prep) that he, as a trained medic, provided his workers (including the convicts) with medicine and treatment that they might otherwise not have received and thereby improved their general circumstances. (See 42-369 for one example of Dubois sending medicine in Sumatra.) So it is unlikely that he did not provide such support in Sumatra, even though this one incident occurred that resulted in the death of his sergeant Franke; Franke simply had the bad luck of deteriorating rapidly in the absence of Dubois, far away from any other medical support, while Dubois, seriously ill himself at the same time, could not go to him.

Concluding remarks

Dubois grossly underestimated the difficulties he would face in Sumatra. Tropical circumstances were hard, and the jungle was unforgiving, not only for the Dutch but also for the local people, who suffered equally from diseases such as malaria, although they were undoubtedly better accustomed to the slower pace of life required to survive. For his success, Dubois partly depended on people who were forced to work as part of their imprisonment. The need to treat these people well was in Dubois' own interest. Had they wished, they would have been able to sabotage his whole campaign, so the fact that it was so successful gives us a strong indication that he treated them well by the standards of the time. In slightly over a year, he collected over 10,000 fossils from Sumatra, whereas from Java he brought back only about 30,000 collected over five years. Although circumstances in Java were completely different (there was no cave work), it is still clear that compared to Java, Sumatra was at least as successful, and in some ways even more so.

Dubois' disappointment with his Sumatran results was caused more by his own expectations than by the actual results. He had not found a human forerunner of the 'ape-man' kind he had hoped to find, and the fossils and human teeth he had found in Lida Ajer were not sufficiently old to give him any hope of success in Sumatra with regard to that research priority. Moreover, the local people were not inclined to support his efforts, as they had their own interests to defend. Dubois must have realised that with their full support he would have achieved much more. However, the lack of support was not as dire as it sometimes seems from his letters. He could not have achieved what he did without local support, and his letter to fellow scientist Hubrecht in 1891 clearly indicates that he both received local support and appreciated it (6-113).

Acknowledgements

I thank the anonymous reviewers for their constructive comments. Naturalis Biodiversity Center is gratefully acknowledged for allowing access to the Dubois Archive, and I am grateful in particular to Karien Lahaise of Naturalis, for supporting my access to the Dubois Archive, and Antje Weeda, a Naturalis volunteer from 2010 to 2014, for valuable biographical information about the authors of the letters in the Dubois Archive. Bianca Janssen Groesbeek, Christine Hertler and my co-editors are thanked for discussion and comments on the earlier version.

References

Albers, P.C.H. in prep. *The Correspondence of Eugène Dubois (from 1881–1900)*. Noordboek, Gorredijk.

Albers, P.C.H. and J. de Vos 2010. *Through Eugène Dubois' Eyes: Stills of a Turbulent Life*. Brill, Leiden. doi.org/10.1163/ej.9789004183001.i-186

Canon van Nederland n.d. *Dwangkolonie Veenhuizen*. canonvannederland.nl/nl/drenthe/drenthe-po/dwang kolonie-veenhuizen (accessed 21 January 2022).

CDC (Centers for Disease Control and Prevention) 16 September 2015. *Ross and the discovery that mosquitoes transmit malaria parasites*. cdc.gov/malaria/about/history/ross.html (accessed 21 January 2022).

Cohen Stuart, A.B. 1867. Missive dd. 8 Mei etc. *Natuurkundig Tijdschrift voor Nederlandsch-Indië* 29:468.

Coornhert, D.V. 1587. *Boeventucht ofte Middelen tot Mindering der Schadelyke Ledighghanghers*. Harmen Muller, Amsterdam.

Dienst Justitiële Inrichtingen n.d. *Arbeid*. Dienst Justitiële Inrichtingen, Nederland.

Junghuhn, F.W. 1855. *Kaart van het Eiland Java*. A.J. Bogaerts, Breda.

Junghuhn, F.W. 1857. Over fossiele zoogdierbeenderen te Patihajam, in de residentie Djapara, eiland Java. *Natuurkundig Tijdschrift voor Nederlandsch-Indië* 14:215–219.

Louys, J., S. Kealy, S. O'Connor, G.J. Price, S. Hawkins, K. Aplin, Y. Rizal, J. Zaim, Mahirta, D.A. Tanudirjo, W.D. Santoso, A.R. Hidayah, A. Trihascaryo, R. Wood, J. Bevitt and T. Clark 2017. Differential preservation of vertebrates in Southeast Asian caves. *International Journal of Speleology* 46:379–408. doi.org/10.5038/1827-806X.46.3.2131

Lydekker, R. 1886. The fauna of the Karnul caves. *Palaeontologia Indica Series 10* 4:23–58.

Martin, K. 1879–1880. *Die Tertiärschichten auf Java nach den Entdeckungen von Fr. Junghuhn*. Brill, Leiden.

Martin, K. 1884–1889a. Überreste vorweltlicher Proboscidier auf Java und Banka. *Sammlungen des Geologischen Reichs-Museums in Leiden* 4:1–24.

Martin, K. 1884–1889b. Fossile Säugethierreste von Java und Japan. *Sammlungen des Geologischen Reichs-Museums in Leiden* 4:25–69.

Minasny, B. 2 July 2020. The dark history of slavery and racism in Indonesia during the Dutch colonial period. *The Conversation*. theconversation.com/the-dark-history-of-slavery-and-racism-in-indonesia-during-the-dutch-colonial-period-141457 (accessed 21 January 2022).

Morley, M.W. and P. Goldberg 2017. Geoarchaeological research in the humid tropics: A global perspective. *Journal of Archaeological Science* 77:1–9. doi.org/10.1016/j.jas.2016.11.002

Nieuwenhuys, R. and F. Jaquet 1980. *Java's Onuitputtelijke Natuur, Reisverhalen, Tekeningen en Fotografiën van Franz Wilhelm Junghuhn.* A.W. Sijthof, Alphen aan den Rijn.

O'Neill, A. 2019. *Life expectancy (from birth) in the Netherlands, from 1800 to 2020.* Statista. statista.com/statistics/1041455/life-expectancy-netherlands-all-time (accessed 16 January 2022).

O'Neill, A. 2020. *Life expectancy (from birth) in Indonesia from 1875 to 2020.* Statista. statista.com/statistics/1072197/life-expectancy-indonesia-historical (accessed 28 December 2021).

Radèn Saléh 1867. Over fossiele beenderen van den Pandan. *Natuurkundig Tijdschrift voor Nederlandsch-Indië* 29:423, 426–429, 433–437, 448–451 and 455–459.

Theunissen, L.T.G. 1989. *Eugène Dubois and the Ape-Man from Java* (E. Perlin-West, trans.). Kluwer, Dordrecht. doi.org/10.1007/978-94-009-2209-9

Verbeek, R.D.M. 1883. *Topographische en Geologische Beschrijving van een Gedeelte van Sumatra's Westkust.* Landsdrukkerij, Batavia.

Appendix: Unpublished references from the Dubois Archive

Code	Date	Description
6-113	? January 1891	[Letter from Dubois to Hubrecht (a fellow scientist)] Quotation in main text
6-319	30 July 1890	[Letter from Jentink (director of the Leiden natural history museum) to Dubois] *Amice,* I was tempted to also start this letter with 'your noble and very learned Sir', like you do so faithfully. It seems to me, you are to follow my example and start on a more familiar tone. And there is every reason to do so—unless you have reasons that carry more weight to put against this—as we are as good as 'amongst family'; for your mother-in-law and my father were full siblings. What more do you want!
6-373	17 October 1889	[Letter from Dubois to Jentink (director of the Leiden natural history museum)] All your kind writing in which you wish me so much prosperity is now already in my possession, and only very important causes could have motivated me not to reply sooner. And alas they have. Now, upon rereading your letter, I am more than ever touched by its friendly tone, but it also makes me sad that I have not yet been able to do enough to be worthy of the interest you have shown in me. And may I therefore please be excused, that this letter is not written in a joyful tone and that it arrives so late. I kept hoping to be able to finally send you completely different messages than I have to do now. Everything here has been disappointing and with the utmost efforts from my side I have not been able to do even 1% of what I had imagined.

Code	Date	Description
		My first misfortune for the cave research was that I arrived here early May, at the *puaza* [lent], when the Malays are as indolent as frogs in winter.
		A trip that I had undertaken at the advice of the Controller to get to know the cave area brought, because of that, but even more because of the distrust of the locals against anything to do with the 'Company' no result whatsoever; only by accident I did find a suitable cave, which was far off the road which had not been pointed out to me for reasons I'll state later. A list of caves given to me by the Assistant-Resident of Tanah-Datar, head of this Department, turned out to be only useful to put me off track. Keeping to that I had to find out after a month of difficult travels and hardship, that the list only contained leaning rocks and natural wells (which the locals also call ngalau) but that there were very few true caves amongst them. Yet they did exist as I found out later and they had simply concealed them from me—despite encouragement to the local chiefs—because they were afraid that the 'Company' was going to usurp the gold and saltpetre that the locals harvest from these caves. Later on many local chiefs told me that was the reason for being so secretive, but—as is characteristically Malay—despite being open about it in words, they did not change their ways.
		The *pengkulu kapala* of Sisawah, where I have now been digging for five months, whose trust I thought I to have completely gained, but what do you think? Whilst the man has brought me to all kinds of impossible caves, up to three or four hours away from Sisawah, there turns out to be a wonderful cave no more than 150 steps, from where we have been working for so long and which turned out to be fully known, but was used as a source for saltpetre.
		After these experiences I've started looking for caves myself and found a few very useful ones, but still never the best that one would wish for. Therefore it was necessary to remain in the jungle four weeks, with little more cover than a leaning rock or an improvised hut and in the long run I could not withstand that, however well I can take hardship. After being brought home having had severe fevers for the third time, that almost ended all searching for Diluvialia,—I must cease doing so for good. The expats are right, you just can't do here what you can do in Europe. But even worse than this adversity was what I experienced with the workforce. Firstly one of the two army engineers that had been put at my disposal as overseers for the forced labourers was completely inadequate for his job and after repeated injunctions and encouragement to do his duty he has been transferred at my request, but only after a few months, and because I could not be present all the time, the work done was virtually zero. Meanwhile the other army engineer died of fevers, but I myself was ill with fever and confined to the Gunung Sago for three weeks. So for a long time the forced labourers were completely left to their own devices. Happily they soon sent a new army engineer, and after a few months a second arrived, and these seem to be capable men. But now considering the forced labourers. The number put at my disposal is 50. Thereof some (7) ran off or were sent off for misconduct; currently (in the rainy season) the number who are ill is 50%. And then some of them are overseers and cooks so currently—it is sad but true—only 12–15 forced labourers are actually working. What to do about it?
		The third adversity is the terrain itself. That the whole area is heavily vegetated would not have been so bad, had there been roads or paths and had not those steep chalk mountains made communication with most points virtually impossible, and had not drinking water at many places in the mountains been completely lacking. For that reason only a small amount of the caves could be considered for excavation. Whilst I was scurrying around in the jungle for a month the Controller had to go away for a few weeks on a mission without appointing a replacement, which not only broke the connection to the local population, but also caused large problems having rations delivered for the forced labourers et cetera—but I will now end my enumerations.
		All the time I have been here, with all the resources put at my disposal I have so far only examined 3 caves (and only examined partly). In two of them I found fossils, very few in the one, but the other one turned out to be as rich as the one in Payakumbuh.

Code	Date	Description
		The help that I have received so generously to which the results up to now (almost half of the time appointed to me) don't match up, obviously cannot evoke a cheerful mood in me and now the fever has slowly diminished my old strength, things are not getting any better. I worry most about having not been able to meet expectations and losing the trust that has been put in me, although it's all truly not my fault, but due to the circumstances, which I haven't been able to change despite all my efforts.
		Verbeek proposed to me at the time, after being appointed, to first come to Java and in particular pointed out that the terrain would cause much less troubles. I thought at the time that I should not accept, having already been successful in Sumatra and feeling so healthy and strong and full of courage, that I considered the adversities of the jungle to be small. Now I often contemplate, how different the present and most certainly also the future would have looked had I followed his advice.
		What I had assumed to be able to do for your museum has even less come true. *Lepus netscheri* does not seem to be living here. A certain registrar Scholten from Dolog—a famous hunter—does however claim to have seen the animal in the lowlands of Padang. I will write to that gentleman—now I have been free from fever for some time—about it and hope to meet him later on. For mouselike animals I've even put out an award of ƒ 2,50 each, but even after a month of waiting not a single one has been brought to me. As often as I am in the jungle traps and slings have been put up. But only once I've got a rat, that I keep in methylated spirit. For all the other animals that you listed to me as desired I've put in efforts or offered money. The local population here however is so lazy and careless, that they can't be bothered to put in the effort. For an antelope I've offered twice the usual price and also promised them the meat—yet I can't get hold of one. But that's how everything is here. And how could it be different with a population that leaves its sawahs [rice fields] unused and is not growing any more rice than is just sufficient not to starve. Even the chiefs rarely eat anything different than rice with salt and Spanish peppers.
		I've also—in particular by being incapacitated again and again with fever—not had a lot of opportunity to go out myself. I have been out with a few hunters in the forest, but I did not bring anything home but fever. Never let a zoologist expect from Bua the same as he has met in Pajakumbuh.
7-481	18 January 1891	[From Letter from Dubois to R.C. Kroesen (the governor of Sumatra's West Coast)] The collection is obviously the property of the government [...]
7-505	10 April 1889	[From Letter from F.J. Kroeze (possibly a government official) to Dubois] Quotation in main text
8-339	11 February 1891	[From Letter from Dubois to Martin (the director of the Leiden Geology Museum)] With regard to my collection, allow me to speak my opinion frankly. Not me, but the government is the owner.
9-286	5 April 1889	[From Letter from Oosterhoff (head of the army medical troops in Sumatra) to Dubois] I have the honour to notify your noble severe Sir that by disposition of the Commander of the Army IInd Department 1st Bureau dd. 22 March last N° 25, to replace the officer of Health 2nd Class M.E.F.T.Dubois, who by Governmental Decision of 6 March 1889 N° 6, was put at the disposal of the Director of Education, Religion and Trade, the officer of Health 2nd Class J. Vollema has been transferred to the garrison of Pajakombo.
10-361	15 March 1891	[From letter from Dubois to Renaud (the chief of the mining department)] Of all the fossils collected on Sumatra about half were collected in the 10 months of Governmental appointment, be it with the forced labourers that had benevolently been put at my disposal by the Governor at that time (Mr Kroesen), however with overseers, tools and lighting that I paid for myself.

Code	Date	Description
33-513	August 1889	[From draft letter from Dubois to an unknown recipient] One afternoon August 1889 I left from Socka Radja to catch water beetles with a net I had attached to my cane, when I met, when I had come on the road to Tandjung Bonei at about the first little house to the right, three women who stopped when I passed them which made me suspect they needed medical care and *obat*. This turned out to be the case and the woman told me they were sent by the village chief to come and ask for help. One of the 3, a girl of about 16 years old, asked me through one of the women whether I could cure her goitre. I have examined this cancer.
33-550	17 September 1889	[From draft letter from Dubois to Kroesen (the governor of Sumatra's West Coast)] [...] the prisoners, of which on average about half is not working because they are *mandor* [foremen], cook, ill or had escaped, even if I was myself present as overseer [...]
33-665	5 June 1890	[From draft letter from Dubois to Jentink. 'Hartmann' means Eduard von Hartmann (1842–1906), a German philosopher who had a very pessimistic view on the usefulness of being alive.] Forgive me for speaking so much about my personal wellbeing; it was necessary to explain why you have not heard of me for such a long time. You must surely be familiar with the 'Hartmann'-like moods of one suffering from malaria and therefore I did not want to write any letter.
42-349 42-350	6 March 1889	Extract from the Register of Decisions of the Governor-General of the Dutch Indies. Copy N$^{\circ}$6. Buitenzorg 6 March 1889 Taking into account the missive of the 1st Government Secretary of 6 November 1888, N$^{\circ}$2103 and 2104; Having read the missives: a. of the Commander of the Army and Chief of the Department of War in the Dutch Indies of 1 Nov. 1888, VIth department, N$^{\circ}$2853/7; b. of the Director of Education, Religion and Trade of 7 February 1889, N$^{\circ}$1387 and attachments; and also having read the missive of the Minister of colonies of 11 January 1889, letter A$^{\downarrow}$, N$^{\circ}$35/5;— It has been accorded and understood: First. The officer of health 2nd class *à la suite* <u>M.E.F.T. Dubois</u>, while being awarded an allowance of *f* 250 (two hundred and fifty guilders) per month on top of his usual income, and is to be put at the disposal of the Director of Education, Religion and Trade, for the purpose of doing palaeontological research in caves in the governmental West Coast of Sumatra and possibly on Java; with an assignment to, at the due time report, the results of his research to the Director mentioned and put the obtained fossils at the disposal of the Government; with the condition that a, he will have free use of transport or his expenses paid according to regulations for any travelling in the interests of his research. b, that, as long as he remains at the disposal of the Director of Education, Religion and Trade he will perform his service *à la suite.—* Secondly. To mandate the Commander of the Army and Chief of the Department of War in the Dutch Indies to make two engineer workmen available for the aforementioned research; with stipulation, that these beside their income will receive an allowance of *f* 25 (twenty-five guilders) per month each.

Code	Date	Description
		[42-350]
		Thirdly. To invite the Governor of Sumatra's West Coast, to make available for the research mentioned under paragraph 1 of this decision, as far as this is going to take place under his rule, to make as many convicts available as Mr M.E.F.T. Dubois will desire, up to a maximum of no more than fifty at the same time; with stipulation that the care and supervision over these convicts will be as much as possible, according to the demands of the Rulebook for order and discipline for convicts in the Dutch Indies which are to be practised by the heads of the local government of the locations where they are being put to work.
		Fourth. To make note, that the expenses arising from this decision—and other expenses for this research, with the exception of already-established wages and indemnities, as well as the usual care and food costs for the convicts, as far as they concern the year 1889, are to be charged to the budget of paragraph 305, of the account of this year.
		A copy of this will be sent to the Council of the Dutch Indies for information, and an extract will be sent to the commander of the army, the Directors of Education, Religion and Trade and of Justice, the Court of Audit, the Governor of Sumatra's West Coast, the military widows and orphans fund and the officer of health Dubois for information and checking afterwards.
		In accord with the Register of provisions; the Government-Secretary (signed) O vd Wijck
42-369 42-370	18 July 1889	Report written by Soeromedjo alias Robo, age ±42 years, working as *mandor* [foreman] of the convicts in the place of Tuban of the residency Rembang.
		Report about a certain [Sopir], about how this man died, has been described below.
		On Tuesday Mr the doctor came from ngalau Muka, bringing with him nine men in chains and one Mandur, at about 4 o'clock in the afternoon. They remained near cave Sabalin for one night. Wednesday morning the doctor went to cave Munte, next to cave Sabalin, together with Sopir and two other convicts, Satro and Sariman. They returned to Sabalin shortly before 4 o'clock in the afternoon. He [Sopir] was then ill and remained so into the night. Thursday morning the doctor returned to Bua, Sopir accompanied the doctor along the banks of the Kali Sabalin with another seven chained convicts; about 12:30 Sopir returned to Sabalin, saying that he was feverish and feeling cold. Upon my question where the convicts were he answered that they had gone to the back to bathe.
		He then immediately went to his bunk, but returned to the cave at 1 o'clock, and told me as Mandor, that I should look after the workmen, because he wanted to return because his body was ill. After that he went to the place he stayed. Saturday afternoon he called on me again and commanded me to send a letter to Mr, to let him know that he was ill. I sent this letter to Mr on Sunday. I gave it to the Penkulu chief of the kampong Sisawah, early in the morning.
		[42-370]
		After the letter left I waited; by Tuesday I did not yet receive any reply. I then sent another letter, Tuesday morning, with a coolie from Sabalin, and with a sum of ƒ 1,50, to bring back medicine. By 8 o'clock Wednesday evening there came a letter from Mr, with a medicine, a white powder wrapped in paper; and the command to give it to him at 7 o'clock in the morning to eat. After reading the letter to him Sopir asked permission to go to Bua, because, as he said, the illness of his body had become worse.
		At 7 o'clock in the morning Sopir took the medicine and subsequently asked to be allowed to go to Bua and I then carried him on a stretcher with 13 convicts, 14 counting me [illegible word] and also his luggage by two rowers, who were steering the *proa*. Close to the hill Padang lawas about 2:00 o'clock in the afternoon Sopir died in the proa. Near Tapian Kumanis I had him brought up on a stretcher to Bua.
		I have no other things worth knowing to convey.
		I, (yours truly) am telling the truth in this message. [Signature]

Code	Date	Description
42-274	29 January 1892	[From letter from Dubois to Renaud (the chief of the mining department)] As there is a need for new pickaxes for the fieldwork, I politely take the liberty to call upon your noble severe Sir to have the intended tools needed for the research bought and sent to Tulung Agung. The ones most suitable are the small double pickaxes with matching handles, which I also received from you in 1889 and that had been bought from the firm Schlieper in Batavia. With regard to the number 30 are needed and will suffice.
42-284	31 October 1894	[From letter from Dubois to the Director of Education, Religion and Trade] I respectfully thank your Noble severe Sir and the government of the Dutch Indies for the gift of forty copies of the book published by the State publishers titled: 'Pithecanthropus erectus [...]
50-006	28 March 1889	[From letter from Dubois to the Director of Education, Religion and Trade] The Assistant-Resident of Tanah-Datar had the benevolence of sending me an extensive list of the most well known caves, in his department from which it became apparent that in this government the Department Tanah-Datar—as I had also learned from other sources, has by far the largest number of caves, so that will give much possibility for research. Within Tanah-Datar the sub departments Bua and Lintan, covering a large part of the Ngalau-Saribu-mountain range, looked the most promising in this respect. These subdepartments alone list 120 caves and by analogy to what I have found in Pajakombo, the true number of existing caves can easily be estimated to be double that number.
50-020 50-021	28 July 1890	[From letter from Dubois to the Director of Education, Religion and Trade] Referring to your Missive dated 10 July last, N°6549, I take the liberty to politely give into the benevolent consideration of your very Noble Sir the possibility to have these convicts from Surabaya replaced by men who are convicted to forced labour for less than a year from the Department Madiun, or of those departments, where [50-021] they are being put to work. In the Department Ngrowo (Kediri), where the work is being done by 25 belonging to the just named category, none of the convicts so far has escaped nor is there any other reason for dissatisfaction.
50-048	30 July 1889	[From Dubois' monthly report for June 1889] A test to examine the cave of Muka-muka near Muara was unsuccessful, because the workmen were suffering too much from fevers
50-050	17 October 1889	[From Dubois' monthly report for September 1890] In the Ng. Bulan near Sibalin no fossils were found this month. [...] This result and even more so the strong increase of fever amongst the workmen in this moist cave (up to 50% of the number of forced labourers was suffering from fevers) make me decide to quit the work here.

Source: Dubois Archive, Naturalis Biodiversity Center, Leiden. Entries are ordered according to the code numbers that refer to those in the archive. For example, 6-313 refers to [MM774C-000006-313]. (The complete correspondence of Dubois for this period can be found in Albers [in prep].)

4

Dubois and beyond: The historical background of cave exploration in Sumatra

Gerrell M. Drawhorn

Abstract

Although references to cave discovery and exploration on the island of Sumatra are sparse and intermittent, they are not entirely absent. The human use of caves in Sumatra can be divided into five phases: 1) an initial period of use of caves as shelters or burial sites; 2) exploitation by indigenous populations for birds' nests, guano and saltpetre; 3) the Dutch colonial period, in which caves were identified and explored, culminating in the excavations of Eugène Dubois from 1888–90; 4) followed by a decline of interest in the exploration of caves except as objects of curiosity and tourism; and 5) in the 1970s, sporadic scientific research in Sumatra's caves resumed, with a pronounced upsurge of interest during the new millennium. A historical review of these phases of exploration provides not only important context and insights for understanding the rationale behind Dubois' expeditions but also important clues about why there was a decline in archaeological and palaeontological research until the recent renaissance.

Keywords: speleology, Verbeek, palaeontology, karst

Abstrak

Meskipun referensi penemuan dan eksplorasi gua di Pulau Sumatra jarang dan terputus-putus, bukan berarti sepenuhnya tidak ada. Penggunaan gua oleh manusia di Sumatra dapat dibagi menjadi lima fase: 1) periode awal penggunaan gua sebagai tempat berteduh atau tempat pemakaman, 2) eksploitasi oleh penduduk asli untuk sarang burung, guano dan niter (kalium nitrat), 3) pada masa kolonial Belanda di mana gua-gua diidentifikasi dan dieksplorasi, yang puncaknya terjadi pada penggalian Eugène Dubois dari tahun 1888–90, 4) diikuti oleh penurunan minat eksplorasi gua kecuali sebagai objek keingintahuan dan pariwisata, 5) pada tahun 1970-an, penelitian ilmiah secara sporadis dimulai kembali di gua-gua Sumatra, dengan minat yang meningkat tajam pada milenium baru. Tinjauan sejarah dari fase eksplorasi ini tak hanya memberikan konteks dan wawasan penting untuk memahami alasan di balik ekspedisi Dubois, tetapi juga memberikan petunjuk penting mengapa terjadi penurunan penelitian arkeologi dan paleontologi hingga kebangkitannya baru-baru ini.

Kata kunci: speleologi, Verbeek, paleontologi, karst

Introduction

The island of Sumatra is the fifth largest island in the world (473,606 km^2) and extends for 1,760 km from the northwest to the southeast. At its widest point, it is approximately 400 km across. Sumatra and the Indian Ocean islands off its west coast were the product of tectonic uplift of the northwest-moving Sunda Plate encountering the Sunda subduction zone. To the west of the subduction zone, a chain of forearc islands (Nias, Simeulue, Mentawai, Pagai and Enggano) were formed, while to the immediate east, the crust of the Sunda Plate uplifted to form the Bukit Barisan range, which extends along the entire length of Sumatra. Separated from the Indian Ocean by only a narrow coastal plain, the volcanic peaks of the Bukit Barisan are typically over 2,000 m in altitude, while the highest, Gunung Kerenci, is 3,805 m high and is the second highest summit in Southeast Asia. Many of these peaks were formed during the Pleistocene, and many are still active (Hutchison 2005; van Gorsel 2018).

Fault-produced lakes and calderas serve as repositories for eroded sediments. Because of the rapid change in altitude, steep, attenuated river courses drain the Bukit Barisan range towards the west, producing deep gorges. To the east of the Bukit Barisan is a wide coastal plain interrupted by sinuous river systems that emerge from the Bukit Barisan and terminate in extensive deltas and swamps before disgorging into the South China Sea. During the glacial maxima of the Plio-Pleistocene, the area between Sumatra, Peninsular Malaysia and Borneo was periodically exposed to form the Sunda Shelf, which served as a zoogeographic dispersal route for terrestrial fauna (Voris 2000). The tin-producing islands of Bangka and Billiton and the Riau islands to the east are vestiges of the higher summits of this large Sundaland plain (Sathiamurthy and Rahman 2017).

Also tending to follow the same northwest–southeast plane as the volcanic mountains are numerous faults and rift systems that have exposed not only the basal granites of the Sunda Shelf but also the Late Carboniferous, Permian, Jurassic, Cretaceous and Tertiary folded seabeds and reefs, which developed prior to uplift (Barber et al. 2005; Zahirovic et al. 2014). When exposed, these sediments often produce extensive limestone outcrops that, under tropical weathering, develop into karst landscapes and which, of course, contain caves. Some of these limestone karst systems extend for hundreds of kilometres (e.g. the Gunung Ngalau Seribu—the 'Mountains of a Thousand Caves'—in western Sumatra) and are broken up by localised faulting, erosion, volcanic activity, and the passage of large rivers through them. The origin of the various karst systems of Sumatra and the relationships between them are still poorly understood, although these systems extend along the entire length of the island, from the islands north of Aceh to the Sunda Straits. For general reviews of the tectonics and economics and the geological and mineralogical exploration of Sumatra, see the extensive bibliographies of Barber et al. (2005) and van Gorsel (2018).

In Bahasa Indonesia, caves are called *gua*, which is derived from the Sanskrit *guha* (Kastawan et al. 2009). They are called *ngalau* in Minangkabau and *leang* in Acehnese; the latter probably has Austronesian origins based upon the Proto-Austronesian root **be-luŋ* (Sagart 2005). Caves have attracted the interest of both the Indigenous peoples and more recently the colonial and Indonesian national authorities.

The prehistoric period: Caves as shelters and mortuaries

Although there is, as yet, no evidence of early hominins having made use of caves in Sumatra, it seems reasonable that they were near locales that had karstic formations. For example, Acheulean tools and bifaces have been found along the Ogan River in South Sumatra (Forestier 2007; Forestier et al. 2005a, 2006).

Homo erectus and other archaic forms of the genus *Homo* are well recognised to have occupied caves in Africa, Europe, the Near East, and elsewhere in Southeast Asia (e.g. *H. floresiensis* at Liang Bua, Flores; Morwood et al. 2004), so it would be remarkable if they never used caves for shelter or mortuary purposes in Sumatra. However, the record of the human occupation of Sumatra in the Early to Middle Pleistocene remains scanty, and the first substantial record only emerges later (Forestier et al. 2010).

Two teeth of *Homo sapiens* were found at Ngalau Lida Ajer, dated to about 73 ka (Westaway et al. 2017). However, most of the faunal remains from this cave appear to consist of material that was transferred into the cave by the collecting activity of porcupines. The larger specimens are almost exclusively dental crowns, and where there are roots, there is the characteristic bevelling of rodent gnawing. There is also an absence of identifiable bones or artefacts. It thus seems unlikely that the human specimens are evidence of an occupation of the cave. Nevertheless, the existence of even a single human tooth here in the heart of the Gunung Seribu karst indicates that the area was occupied by Late Pleistocene *Homo sapiens*, who were thus not restricted to the proposed savanna grassland zone in the lower reaches of eastern Sundaland (Roberts 2019; Roberts and Amano 2019; contra Bird et al. 2005).

Evidence of Sumatran caves being used as occupation sites was first suggested by the Late Palaeolithic site of Tiangko Pandjang in central Sumatra (Asmar 1989; Bronson and Asmar 1975; Fauzi et al. 2020; Sarasin 1914; Tobler 1917; Zwierzycki 1926; Zwierzycki and Posthumus 1926), the Late Pleistocene and early Holocene Hoabinhian locality of Tögi Ndrawa, Nias Island, North Sumatra (Forestier et al. 2005b), and Loyang Mendali in Aceh (Setiawan 2009). Slightly younger cave occupations and mortuary activities occur at Gua Harimau in the Pasemah Highlands of South Sumatra (Simanjuntak et al. 2006; Simanjuntak 2021). The latter shows the important potential of intensive archaeological excavations and indicates that mortuary collections in the relatively stable conditions of caves, even in a subtropical environment, can generate sufficient DNA to be analysed for assessable relationships with modern and prehistoric populations (Matsumura et al. 2018). This includes some mortuary crypts in the Karo region of North Sumatra that may have been modified from natural caves (Edwards McKinnon 2011).

Caves are all the more important because, with a few potential exceptions (Gruwier 2017; Hooijer 1948a, 1948b; Schürmann 1928), there are no known open-country Upper Palaeolithic occupation sites in Sumatra. Many of the littoral Hoabinhian shell mound sites, which are principally found in North Sumatra and Aceh, have unfortunately been destroyed or greatly disturbed by the extraction of lime during the historic period (Edwards McKinnon 1991; Tieng 2016; van Stein Callenfels 1921).

The classical period: Chinese traders and edible swiftlet nests

The name Sumatra probably derives from the Sanskrit term *suvarnadvipa*, 'Gold Island' (Kulke et al. 2009), and appears to relate to the opening of maritime trade routes with India. Forest products from Southeast Asia, including Sumatra, played an important part in this commercial opening. Later, in the middle of the first century AD, there was mercantile contact with China for trade in spices, aromatic resins, diamonds and gold (Kulke et al. 2009). References to the Srivijayan capital at Palembang in Sumatra in Chinese records date to the time of the Buddhist monk Yijing's visits in AD 687 and 695 (Takakusu 1896; Manguin 2022). A major Chinese entrepôt existed at Kota Cina, near Medan in North Sumatra, from the twelfth to the fourteenth centuries (Edwards McKinnon 1977, 1984).

One unusual item exported to China was, until recently, exclusively found in caves. Although the Indigenous peoples of Southeast Asia appeared to have little interest in the dietary or medicinal consumption of the gelatinous nests of swiftlets (*Aerodramus fuciphagus; walet* in Bahasa Indonesia), the export of these nests to China became a highly lucrative industry. Hooyman found that in 1824, the swiftlet nest, which is called the *layang-layang, burung daija* in Sumatra and *lawit* in Java, was being sold to the Chinese market for nearly its weight in silver (Hooyman 1824; Erpp 1847).

For the Chinese, the consumption of bird's nest soup has historically been a symbol of wealth, prestige and power. Swiftlet nests also have value in traditional Chinese medicine. There are two traditions that relate to the exploitation of Sumatran caves. One legend holds that the culturally innovative and influential Tang Dynasty (AD 618–907) empress Wu Zhe Tian (AD 624–705) was served swiftlet nests by her royal chef (Suntory Beverage & Food Asia Pte Ltd 2019). Therefore, consumption of birds' nests as a quintessential delicacy in ancient China can be traced back to her influence. It was during her reign that Yijing returned to China from Srivijaya (Manguin 2022). Another tradition indicates that Admiral Zheng He brought back edible swiftlet nests to the imperial court of the Ming Dynasty (AD 1368–1644) as tribute from his voyage to various kingdoms in the South China Sea. The existence of this trade in swiftlet nests has been more firmly reported in Chinese pharmacopoeiae from both the Ming and the Qing (AD 1636–1912) Dynasties (Salmon 2008). What this might suggest is that, as local Chinese swiftlet nesting colonies became depleted, the value of finding alternative sources outside China became apparent.

The fact that China and India had already opened trade routes to Sumatra, Borneo and Java prior to the voyages of Admiral Zheng He might explain the various Hindu and Buddhist mythological references associated with Indonesian caves. References to protective giant serpents, or *nagas*, are common in the mythologies of areas with edible swiftlet nest caves. For example, nest collecting at Goa Nangosari in southern Java involved a complex sequence of ceremonies, *wayang* [puppet] plays and sacrifices to the goddess Nyai Rata Laut Kidul (Erpp 1847).

Initially, European colonialists showed little interest in the economic exploitation of the trade in swiftlet nests, only realising later that regulating the pre-existing Indigenous system of trade could be quite lucrative. In 1778, they imposed a system of licences sold at public auction as a means of settling disputes over ownership and over-exploitation (Hooyman 1824). Licences for two caves, Kalapa Nongal and Sampia, fetched over R.100,000—the equivalent of US$1.6–2.24 million in 2015 dollars (Edvinsson 2016; Hooyman 1824). To the government, this was a shockingly high price that suggested to them that they had been given poor intelligence regarding the caves' actual value (Hooyman 1824). The south-coast caves of Nangosarie and Goa Dahar, as well as Goa Gede near Samarang were under the control of various Javanese rajas. Hooyman noted that other islands, such as Ternate and Borneo, also supplied nests, but he did not indicate sources in Sumatra, perhaps because Dutch control over these source areas was incomplete. De Bruyn Kops (1854) noted swiftlet caves on Lingga and Tarong in the Riau Islands. Aceh, also outside Dutch control, had a well-developed swiftlet nest harvesting operation on the west-coast island of Kluang (de St. Pol Lias 1879, 1891; Wallon and Hervey 1881). Nests from Aceh were exported through the ports of Junk Ceylon (now Phuket), Penang and Singapore (Salmon 2008).

Marsden (1811), in his *History of Sumatra*, noted that there was an important trade in *layang-layang* nests on the river Krui, extending about four miles inland from the southwest coast of Sumatra. Palembang also became an entrepôt for edible birds' nests, and Marsden mentions the village of Ampat Sawah on the Kawes River and several caves on the Sungai Ogan River as the source of these. The caves on the Sungai Ogan River may be the caves later explored by Musper (1934).

As well as caves producing edible swiftlet nests, Marsden (1811) found in 1783 that the saltpetre (*mesiyu mantah*) derived from the bird and bat guano inside the caves of Kattuan near the headwaters of the Urai River near Bencoolen (Bengkulu) was being exploited for producing gunpowder. Marsden noted that the surveyor at the English Fort Marlboro at Bencoolen, Mr Whalfeldt, had penetrated two caves 743 and 600 feet, and that one of these had an interior chamber about 40 feet high. Marsden also reported the same caves had been explored by Christopher Terry and Charles Miller. During the unrest of the Padri Wars (1803–37), saltpetre became even more sought after.

During this period, caves also served other functions. Ngalau Pinto Air near Ladang Lawas on the northwestern flank of the mountain Gunung Sago was used as a refuge to conceal members of the Minangkabau royal family during the Padri Wars, while caves in the Kamang area north of Fort de Kock (Bukittinggi) were reportedly used in the mid-1800s as staging areas and redoubts by anti-Dutch revolutionaries such as Tuanku Nan Renceh (Zakariya and Salleh 2011).

Eugène Dubois and his precursors

Interest in the palaeontological and archaeological value of Southeast Asian caves even precedes the publication of Darwin's *On the Origin of the Species*. In 1839, Captain Thomas Newbold suggested 'the careful examination of the caves with a view to the discovery of fossiliferous remains. But situated as it is in a very modern alluvial plain and surrounded by a swamp it is not probable that any of the caves are ossiferous' (Newbold 1839:119; Logan 1848).

The Bukit Barisan region near Danau Toba and Pasaman was explored and mapped for the first time by the geologist Franz Junghuhn and the botanist C.B.H. Rosenberg in 1844. Junghuhn is best known for his work for the Natuurwetenschappelijke Commissie from 1842–49, which resulted in a famous monograph and maps detailing the natural history of Java, but he was also critical to the successful introduction of cinchona in Java (Wichmann 1909; Wormser 1941). It was also Junghuhn (1857) who first noted the Pleistocene fossil proboscidean bones in central Java. His work was later followed up by the acclaimed Javanese artist and naturalist Radèn Saléh (1867a, 1867b). Both Junghuhn's and Radèn Saléh's collections of fossil mammals from the Pati Ayam and Pandan regions in central Java were later described by Karl Martin (1884). Martin (1884) also noted additional discoveries of fossil proboscideans in Bangka.

All these researchers were cited by Eugène Dubois in his prospectus for undertaking palaeontological research in the Netherlands Indies (Dubois 1888). Indeed, Junghuhn moved to the Netherlands Indies in 1836, enlisting as a military doctor upon the recommendation of Dutch mycologist Christiaan Hendrik Persoon (Schmidt 1909). Once there, Junghuhn was able to get relief from his medical duties to undertake mapping and natural science. This was probably the major rationale for Dubois' research strategy (Chapter 3 discusses this further). Dubois' scheme of quitting his university post and joining the military as a medical officer had a precedent.

In 1863, Alfred Russel Wallace visited Sumatra and made natural history collections near Palembang in central Sumatra. In 1878–89, the botanist Odoardo Beccari visited western Sumatra. Unfortunately, neither of these well-known naturalists explored the nearby karst regions. However, the Scandinavian-born English collector Carl Bock (1881) arrived the same year as Beccari (1878) and hired some of the local people who had been trained by Beccari. Bock proceeded deeper into the interior of the Padang region and explored the interior of Ngalau Pangian near Boea (Bua?), where he collected cave arthropods. He also collected a snake, the Asian cave racer, sometimes called the beauty rat snake (*Orthriophis taeniura*).

Another researcher who mapped the geology, natural history and resources of western and central Sumatra was Pieter Johannes Veth, who directed the massive First Midden [Central]-Sumatra Expedition of 1877–79 (Veth and van Hasselt 1881). Veth's expedition explored and investigated the economics of the collection of edible birds' nests from caves at Maura Bliti in Musi Rawas, southern Sumatra. Veth also explored an extensive swiftlet nest cave above Padang (perhaps at Indaorung) and visited caves at (perhaps) Muka-Muka on the Kuantan River, Pangian (at Bua), Laras Magek (at Biaro near the Agam River) and at Gasing (at Solok). Some cavernicolous fauna was collected, including a water-beetle taken at Ngalau Pangian, *Orectochilus subsulcatus*, which was described as an endemic species by Régimbart (1880).

However, it was Rogier Diederik Marius Verbeek (1845–1926) who appears to have provided Dubois with the essential techniques to make the latter's palaeontological explorations successful. Verbeek is best known for his extensive studies of the 1883 Krakatoa eruption, but prior to this he had already spearheaded the geological mapping and survey teams of central and western Sumatra. Intent on finding the extent of the newly discovered Ombilin coalfields, Verbeek's team consisted of more than a dozen geologists, mining engineers and topographers, who were helped by a small army of porters, local assistants, troops and camp assistants. Verbeek's team mapped cave entrances as well as dolines and resurgences ('onderaardsche loop', underground river), but with a few limited exceptions, the interiors of caves were rarely scrutinised. Verbeek's team also noted the local toponym for indicating caves, *ngalau*, which was used for many of the cavern-rich karst hills (Verbeek 1883).

Eugène Dubois not only used Verbeek's (1883) *Geologische Kaart van Sumatra's Westkust*, an atlas produced during 1875–80, to identify probable limestone (*kolenkalk*) karst exposures, but also inspected its maps in great detail to identify caves, dolines and resurgences. In fact, almost all of the caves explored by Dubois can be identified on Verbeek's maps as a small emerald-coloured dot (which may even be labelled *grot*, Dutch for cave). Dubois copied Verbeek's maps to make a field map, and sections of them are copied in his notebooks, right down to the roads and footpaths. Figure 4.1 compares Verbeek's map (a) of the region of Lintau-Bua with Dubois' linen field map (b). Dubois also copied the geological exposure profiles made by Verbeek's team.

One of the most significant of the groups involved in exploring Sumatra was the Topographische Dienst Batavia (Topographic Service of Batavia) in Weltevreden (now part of Jakarta), which began to make detailed (1:40,000) survey maps in the mid-nineteenth century and continued to do so until the advent of the Second World War in 1940. Most of their maps were not published until after Dubois' departure from the region, but many of their mapping teams were active at the same time as Dubois and in precisely the same areas as his palaeontological expeditions.

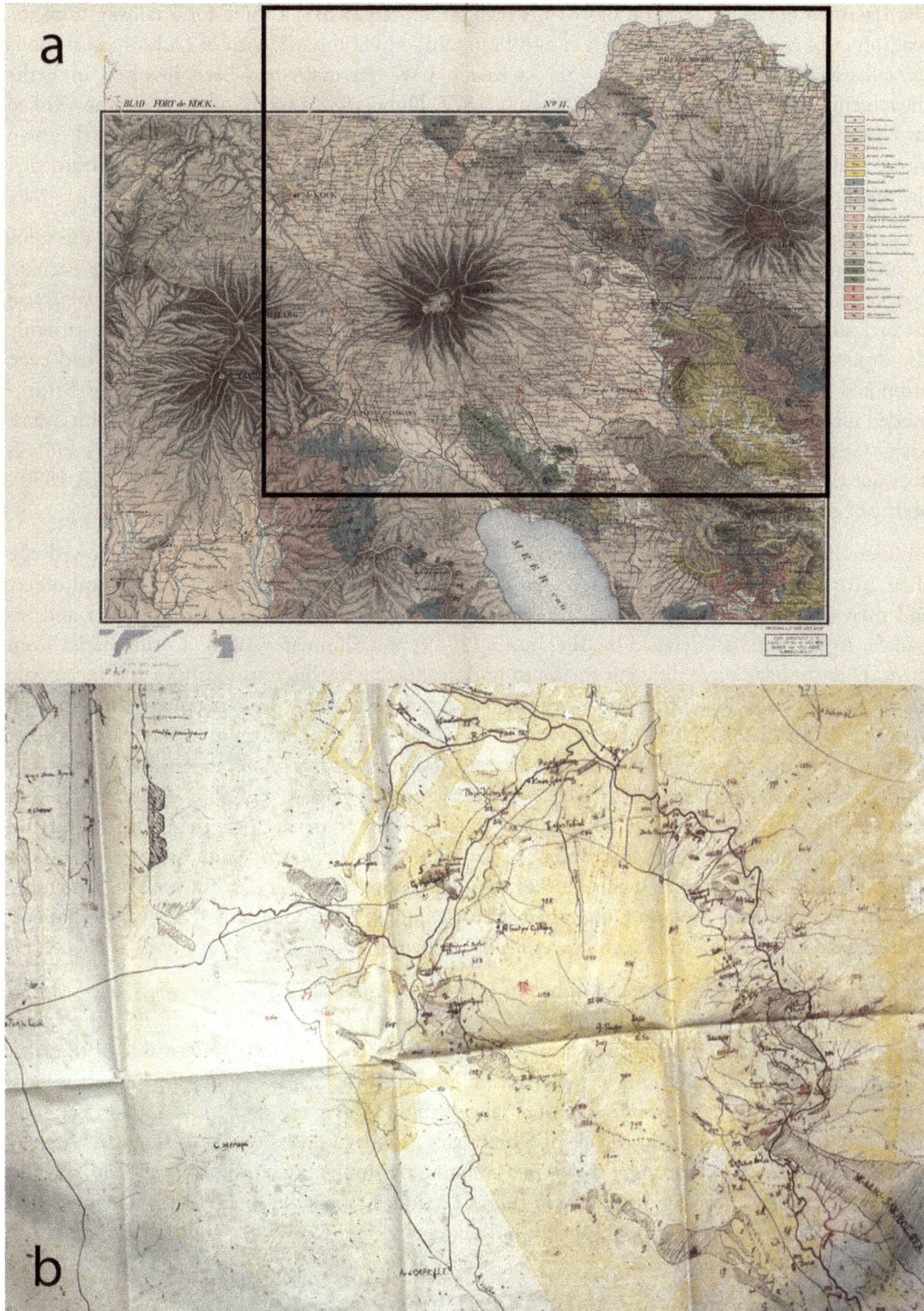

Figure 4.1: Verbeek's and Dubois' maps of the same area of the Padang Highlands.

(a) Blad Fort de Kock, Verbeek Geological Map D D 6,3, sheet 2.

(b) Dubois' hand-drawn copy of the rectangular area inset in (a).

Sources: (a) Universitaire Bibliotheek Leiden, reproduced under CC-BY 3.0 (creativecommons.org/licenses/by/3.0); (b) unpublished Dubois notes, 1888–1890, Dubois Archive, Naturalis Biodiversity Center, Leiden, photograph by author.

The IJzerman Survey Expedition of 1895, which attempted to find a route for a railway from the coal mines of Sawahlunto to the east coast of Sumatra, noted the evidence of Dubois' excavations at Muka-Muka Cave (IJzerman 1895). Its leader, J.W. IJzerman, had been involved in Veth's abovementioned exploration of the Kuantan in 1877. Dubois was a friend of Delprat, who worked for IJzerman, and was in contact with IJzerman himself, as indicated by several letters by IJzerman in the Dubois collection, such as one from Padang dated 26 July 1888 from which we learn that IJzerman provided dynamite to Dubois for his cave explorations.

To strongly encourage support for his mission to find the 'missing link' and suggest that the value of such an expedition was at an inflection point, Dubois mentioned in his prospectus Richard Lydekker's discovery at Siwalik (in what is now Pakistan) of the extinct Asian ape *Palaeopithecus* and his excavations in the Karnul caves in India (Lydekker 1879, 1886). Dubois was almost certainly also aware of British efforts in the 1860s and 1870s to explore caves in Borneo, which had been promoted by Wallace (1864, 1873), and Thomas Huxley (1864). Subscriptions for this British-funded project were made by Darwin, John Lubbock, Charles Lyell, Royal Society chair John Evans, Major General Lane Fox (Pitt-Rivers), Henry Willett, and other luminaries (Sherratt 2002). Dubois does not cite the Royal Society–funded excavations in Sarawak of A.H. Everett (1873, 1877, 1880), perhaps because they were unsuccessful (Drawhorn 2005).

Ultimately, Dubois went forward without direct funding. As already noted, he followed the alternative course already undertaken by Junghuhn, joining the Dutch military as a medical officer and then obtaining leave to explore the region scientifically. Dubois' travels in Sumatra and his transfer to Java are well detailed by Theunissen (1989) and Shipman (2001). To summarise from them, Dubois made three different sorties to find productive fossiliferous localities and investigate them. His efforts were interrupted by the rainy seasons. His first two exploratory trips are well discussed in his field reports (Anonymous 1889, 1890; Dubois 1889) and notebooks. The first journey, from June to August 1888, involved excavations and surveys first in the region southwest of Dubois' hospital in Payakumbuh. These included the caves Ngalau Lida Ajer, Ngalau Sampit, and caves along the Sinamar River in the Gunung Ngalau Seribu mountains (Mountains of a Thousand Caves) from Lintau-Boea (Ngalau Djamboe or Siambok), Ngalau Pangian, and caves in the 'Andjing Hills' (Ngalau Sangki) and near Sibalin/Sisawah. The second expedition, from June to September 1889, covered the southern area Dubois had already explored and also extended down the Kuantan/ Indragiri River to Moeka-Moeka and caves nearby (Chapter 2, this volume).

Dubois' third expedition, from December to February 1890, just prior to his transfer to Java, is not as well detailed. He reported some work on the west side of Lake Singkarah near the village of Paningahan, as well as some caves near Soliet Air, which overlooks the eastern side of the lake. He even mapped the excavations of these sites. However, these caves were depauperate. It is clear that he, or his assistants, did make a substantial collection in one additional cave (almost certainly Ngalau Agung Agung) near the village of Sibrambang, south of Soliet Air. Subsequent researchers have called this cave Sibrambang. Perhaps in a rush to move to the more promising sites in Java, and finding, in his view, nothing distinctive in this collection, Dubois did not publish it in any detail (Anonymous 1891), but his unpublished monthly reports do give us some additional information about it (Chapter 2, this volume).

Studies and tourism after Dubois

Dubois' (1890, 1891) assessment that the materials he collected from the sites in the Padang Highlands were relatively recent and largely undifferentiated from modern faunas had a notable negative effect on continuing research at these sites. Dubois also did not report any of the archaeological materials from these sites. Moreover, his success in Java was extremely detrimental to the study of the caves of Sumatra. With a few exceptions, the centre of attention shifted to the Pleistocene deposits in Java and to other locations in Indonesia. For almost five decades, even the materials in Leiden that had already been collected by Dubois from the caves of the Padang Highlands remained unstudied.

On the eve of the Second World War, Leo Daniel Brongersma (1936, 1941) initiated some comparative studies of the fossil carnivores in Dubois' collections from the Padang Highlands caves and Java. Brongersma was a herpetologist, however, and these are the only mammalian fossil collections he ever published on.

Immediately after the war, Dirk Hooijer conducted extensive studies of Dubois' Sumatran collections of the remains of rhinoceroses (Hooijer 1946a, 1946b, 1948a) porcupines (Hooijer 1946c), tapirs (Hooijer 1947), orangutans (Hooijer 1948b; see also Drawhorn 1995), proboscideans (Hooijer 1955), bovids (Hooijer 1958) and primates (Hooijer 1960, 1962). However, because Dubois had described the materials as recent or subfossil (Dubois 1891; see also Hooijer 1946a) and the locations of the caves were considered lost (although Hooijer [1946:16–17] did provide a roster of the caves visited by Dubois with associated larger towns), there were few efforts to relocate Dubois' western Sumatran caves. Because the chronology remained uncertain (see de Vos 1983), renewed surveys were initiated to relocate Dubois' caves in the 1990s (see below).

From 1890 to 1940, many of the caves became tourist attractions because of their ease of access. This period could be called the 'Tourism Phase' because Dutch administrators and foreign and local visitors visited the caves recreationally, often leaving graffiti and taking photographs (Figure 4.2). The noted photographer C.W. Nieuwenhuys took many of these, sometimes in artistically posed high-contrast albumin prints or for postcards. The firm of Woodbury & Page in Batavia also had a set of Sumatran postcards whose images included photographs of Kamang Cave north of Fort de Kock (Bukittinggi). Celebrities such as the grand duke of Mecklenburg-Schwerin, Germany, visited the Samang Caves with large delegations of over 100 participants (Figure 4.3 shows the Mecklenburg-Schwerin delegation in front of Kamang Cave). Traditional dances and pig hunts were hosted for visitors. Popular articles were written by many visitors about their experiences exploring the caves (van Boekhoven 1928). See the appendix for a list of Dutch colonial photographs of Sumatra.

Some geological, and even archaeological, efforts in caves continued during the Dutch colonial period after Dubois' time, but outside western Sumatra. The German geologist Hugo Bucking (1904) explored the sedimentology of northern and eastern Sumatra and visited several caves and limestone exposures (e.g. Liang Nampiring and Liang Mergandjang along the Wampu River), north of the volcanic cones of Gunung Sibayak and Gunung Simabur. G.E. Bekkering explored Gua Marike, Lobang Angin and karst outcrops on the Sei Bohorok River near Binjai (Tichelman 1939). Batak crypts, some using natural caves, were explored by Pieter van Stein Callenfels (1921, 1924) and G.L. Tichelman (Tichelman 1939; see also Edwards McKinnon 2011).

Figure 4.2: Tourist Cave in the Padang Highlands, western Sumatra, in 1939, showing evidence of graffiti.

Source: Leiden University Libraries Digital Collections (KITLV 69930), reproduced under CC-BY 3.0 (creativecommons.org/licenses/by/3.0).

Grot van Kamang (Fort de Kock)
opname tijdens het bezoek van Z. K. H. Groothertog van Mecklenburg-Schwerin

Figure 4.3: The Mecklenburg-Schwerin tourist group in front of Kamang Cave, western Sumatra, 1910.

Source: Courtesy of J. Louys.

In southern Sumatra, Paul Sarasin (1914), Józef Zwierzycki (1926) and August Tobler (1917) reported on the archaeology of the Tiangko caves in the headwaters of the Jambi River. Karl A.F.R. Musper (1934) explored the palaeobotany of the region and found several extensive caves within Cretaceous limestone formations in the Gunung Gumai mountains near Palembang. One, Soeroeman Besar, was explored for 425 m, and others appeared to be more than 1 km long.

Revolution and independence period: West Sumatra

According to local people, Ngalau Lida Ajer served as a refuge for Indonesian fighters during the 1945–47 Indonesian Revolution (Chapter 13, this volume; Damhoeri 1949). Fragments of hand grenades were found there by the present author in 1998 and later by a joint Australian–Indonesian team in 2018 (Chapter 13, this volume). After the Indonesian Revolution, there was a focus on palaeontological and archaeological resources in Java, to the detriment of research in other provinces. Major academic and research institutions were located in Java, so provincial exploration was relatively costly and inconvenient. Beginning in the 1970s, a few archaeological surveys of Hoabinhian and classical-period archaeological sites were conducted in North Sumatra and Aceh (Edwards McKinnon 1977, 1984), South Sumatra (Bronson and Asmar 1975) and West Sumatra (Asmar 1989; Bronson and Wisseman 1974; Bronson et al. 1973). Tangentially, Morley et al. (1973), Maloney (1980), Maloney and McCormac (1995) and Newsome and Flenley (1988) undertook palaeoclimatological studies on Holocene peat deposits in several volcanic lakes near the Padang Highlands cave sites. Brief visits to Ngalau Pangian were made by Nicolas Tofts around 1977 (pers. comm.) and by Peter Bellwood around 1985 (pers. comm.). These two individuals, both experienced archaeologists, surveyed for archaeological sites and visited one of the Dubois localities:

the well-known tourist cave of Ngalau Pangian near Buo. This site was, however, not fruitful for Dubois' collectors. More extensive surveys by the present author from 1996 to 2008 (Drawhorn 2003, 2005; Drawhorn and Makmur 2008) and intermittently thereafter allowed the identification of several of Dubois' localities. Zoological and hydrological mapping work in caves in both West Sumatra and Aceh was conducted between 1990 and 2004 by a team led by Louis Deharveng and Anne Bedos (Deharveng and Bedos 2003).

Conclusion

It is regrettable that research on the Sumatran caves lapsed after Dubois' ambitious expedition in the late 1880s came to an end. His lukewarm descriptions of the Sumatran palaeofaunas and his impressive success in Java created a momentum that was difficult to stem. In addition, Jakarta has been the political and commercial centre of the Archipelago since the Dutch colonial period, and this continued after independence. Higher educational and research institutions were also mainly based in Java. However, research questions, and the resolutions to those questions, are largely based upon collection locations, which can bias our understanding of the broader context of events if important areas are undersampled (see also Raja et al. 2022).

Dubois and his successors' unfortunate abandonment of Sumatra as a worthwhile location for palaeontological and archaeological research appears to be coming to an end. Since 2000, there has been something of a renaissance in the re-examination of cave and open sites in Sumatra (Bonatz et al. 2009; Chapter 10, this volume; Forestier et al. 2005a, 2005b, 2006, 2010; Louys et al. 2017, 2021; Prasetyo et al. 2017; Setiawan 2009, 2020; Simanjuntak 2021; Westaway et al. 2017). Research on the island is no longer considered as merely providing confirmation of findings from elsewhere; rather, it is considered integral to understanding the movement and subsequent isolation of faunas and human populations throughout the Pleistocene and Holocene (Matsumura et al. 2018). Revived interest in the palaeontological and archaeological value of the caves has spurred Indonesian–international collaborations, in both the field and the laboratory, to assist in resolving many biogeographic and archaeological issues.

References

Anonymous 1889–1890 (E. Dubois). Palaeontologische Onderzoekingen ter Westkust van Sumatra. *Verslag Mijnwezen,* 2e kwartaal 1889:8–9, 3e kwartaal 1889:10, 4e kwartaal 1889 (1890):10–11.

Anonymous 1891 (E. Dubois). Palaeontologische Onderzoekingen op Java. *Verslag Mijnwezen*, 4e kwartaal 1890:14–18.

Asmar, T. 1989. Catatan atas alat serpih obsidian Gua Ulu Tiangko. In N. Magetsari, B. Sumadio, Nurhadi, H. Santiko and R.P. Soejono (eds), *Dalam Pertemuan Ilmiah Arkeologi V*, II B, pp. 343–336. Kajan Arkeologi Indonesia, Yogyakarta; Skatan Ahli Arkeologi Indonesia, Yogyakarta.

Barber, A.J, M.J. Crow and J.S. Milsom (eds) 2005. *Sumatra: Geology, Resources and Tectonic Evolution*. Geological Society Memoir No. 31. Geological Society, London. doi.org/10.1144/GSL.MEM.2005.031

Bird, M.I., D. Taylor and C. Hunt 2005. Palaeoenvironments of insular Southeast Asia during the Last Glacial Period: A savanna corridor in Sundaland? *Quaternary Science Reviews* 24(20–21):2228–2242. doi.org/10.1016/j.quascirev.2005.04.004

Bock, C. 1881. *The Head-Hunters of Borneo: A Narrative of Travel Up the Mahakkam and Down the Mario. Also, Journeyings in Sumatra.* Sampson Low, Marston, Searle and Rivington, London.

Bonatz, D., J.N. Miksic, J. Neidel and M.L. Tjoa-Bonatz (eds) 2009. *From Distant Tales: Archaeology and Ethnohistory in the Highlands of Sumatra.* Cambridge Scholars Publishing, Newcastle upon Tyne.

Brongersma, L.D. 1936. Notes on some recent and fossil cats chiefly from the Malay Archipelago. *Zoologische Mededelingen* 18:1–89.

Brongersma, L.D. 1941. On the remains of carnivora from cave deposits in Java and Sumatra, with notes on recent specimens, I. *Zoologische Mededelingen* 23:114–148.

Bronson, B. and T. Asmar 1975. Prehistoric investigations at Tianko Panjang Cave, Sumatra. *Asian Perspectives* 28(2):128–145.

Bronson, B., M. Suhrdi Basoeki and J. Wisseman 1973. *Laporan Penelitian Arkeologi di Sumatera.* Lembaga Purbakala, Jakarta.

Bronson, B. and J. Wisseman 1974. An archeological survey in Sumatra in 1973. *Sumatra Research Bulletin* 4(1):84–94.

Bücking, D.H. 1904. *Zur Geologie von Nord- und Ost-Sumatra.* Sammlungen des Geologischen Reichs-Museums in Leiden 8. Brill, Leiden.

Damhoeri, A. 1949. *Perestiwa Sitadjuh Batur 15-1-1949: Pewarta Hayat Syamsul Bahar.* commons.wikimedia. org/wiki/File:ADH_0009_A._Damhoeri_-_Peristiwa_Situjuh_Batur_15-1-1949.pdf (accessed 20 February 2023).

de Bruyn Kops, G.F. 1854. Sketch of the Rhio-Lingga Archipelago with a Map. *Natuurkundig Tijdschrift voor Nederlandsch Indië* 1854:386–402.

de St. Pol Lias, X.B. 1879–1880. Klouwang et ses grottoes sur la Côte Ouest d'Achin. *Annales d'Extrême-Orient* 2:37–41.

de St. Pol Lias, X.B. 1891. *La Côte du Poiré, Voyage à Sumatra.* Lecéne Oudin, Paris.

de Vos, J. 1983. The *Pongo* faunas from Java and Sumatra and their significance for biostratigraphical and paleo-ecological interpretations. *Proceedings of the Koninklijke Nederlandse Akademie van Wetenschappen Serie B* 86:417–425.

Deharveng, L. and A. Bedos 2003. *Expédition Sumatra 2000: Rapport Spéléologique et Scientifique.* Association Pyrénéenne de Spéléologie, Toulouse.

Drawhorn, G.M. 1995. Paleodemography and Systematics of the Orangutan (*Pongo pygmaeus*). Unpublished doctoral dissertation. Department of Anthropology, University of California, Davis.

Drawhorn, G.M. 2003. The prospect of archeological and vertebrate paleontological investigation in the karst regions of West Sumatra. In L. Deharving and A. Bedos (eds), *Expédition Sumatra 2000: Rapport Spéléologique et Scientifique*, pp. 58–62 Association Pyrénéenne de Spéléologie, Toulouse.

Drawhorn, G.M. 2005. Seeking the 'missing link': A.R. Wallace's significance in fostering the science of palaeoanthropology. In A.A. Tuen and I. Das (eds), *Wallace in Sarawak: 100 Years Later, an International Conference on Biogeography and Biodiversity*, pp. 45–56. IBEC, UNIMAS, Kota Samarahan.

Drawhorn, G.M. and D. Makmur 1 April 2008. Sumatra caves. *Wisata Ranah Minangkabau.* thewestcoast. wordpress.com/2008/04/08/sumatra-caves/ (accessed 2 August 2022).

Dubois, M.E.F.T. 1888. Over de wenschelijkheid van een onderzoek naar de diluviale fauna van Nederlandsch-Indië, in het bijzonder van Sumatra. *Natuurkundig Tijdschrift voor Nederlandsch Indië* 48:158–165.

Dubois, M.E.F.T. 1889. Uittreksel van een schrijven van het Heer Dubois te Pajacombo naar aanleiding van den aan dien Heer toegezonden schedel, door den Heer van Rietschoten in zijn marmergroeven in het Kedirische opgegraven. *Natuurkundig Tijdschrift voor Nederlandsch Indië* 49:209–210.

Dubois, M.E.F.T. 1890. Beschrijving van een bloeienden *Amorphophallus titanium*, Beccari, aangetroffen te Boea bij de grot der Batang Pangian, den 24st November 1889. *Teysmannia* 1:89–91.

Dubois. M.E.F.T. 1891. Voorloopig bericht omtrent het onderzoek naar de Pleistocene en Tertiaire Vertebraten-fauna van Sumatra en Java, gedurende het Jaar 1890. *Natuurkundig Tijdschrift voor Nederlandsch Indië* 51:93–100.

Edvinsson, R. 10 January 2016. *Historical Currency Converter (test version 1.0)*. historicalstatistics.org/Currencyconverter.html (accessed 2 August 2022).

Edwards McKinnon, E. 1977. Research at Kota Cina, a Sung-Yuan period trading site in East Sumatra. *Archipel* 14:19–32. doi.org/10.3406/arch.1977.1355

Edwards McKinnon, E. 1984. Kota Cina: Its Context and Meaning in the Trade of Southeast Asia in the Twelfth to Fourteenth Centuries. Unpublished doctoral dissertation. Department of Art History, Cornell University, Ithaca, New York.

Edwards McKinnon, E. 1991. The Hoabinhian in the Wampu/Lau Biang Valley of northeast Sumatra: An update. *Bulletin of the Indo-Pacific Prehistory Association* 10:132–142.

Edwards McKinnon, E. August 2011. *Rock-cut Chambers on the East Coast of Sumatra: A Translation and Review of G.L. Tichelman's Felsengänge an Sumatras Ostküste, with Additions and Amendments (with Translation by Dieter Bartels)*. Nalanda-Sriwijaya Centre Working Paper 5. nsc.iseas.edu.sg/documents/working_papers/nscwps005.pdf (accessed 2 August 2022).

Erpp, F. 1847. Description of Karrang Bollong in Java and some birds nest rocks there. *Journal of the Indonesian Archipelago and East Asia* 1(11):101–108. Translated from 'Beschrijving van Karrang Bollong, en de vogelnest-klippen aldaar', *Tijdschrift voor Ned. Indië* 1846:313–327.

Everett, A.H. 1873. Cave deposits in Borneo. *Nature* 181:462.

Everett, A.H. 1877. Cave exploration in Borneo. *Athenaeum* 2594:53–54.

Everett, A.H. 1880. Report on the exploration of the caves of Borneo. *Proceedings of the Royal Society of London* 30(203):310–321. doi.org/10.1098/rspl.1879.0123

Fauzi, M.R. 2015. Karakterisasi tipe dan teknologi alat batu dari Gua Harimau. In T. Simanjuntak (ed.), *Gua Harimau dan Perjalanan Panjang Peradaban OKU* 1, pp. 105–119. UGM Press, Yogyakarta.

Fauzi, M.R., A.S. Wibowo and R.E. Wibawa 2020. Indentifikasi sumber-sumber Obsidian di Merangin dan Sarolangun (Jambi, Sumatra) berdasarkan analysis Portable X-Ray Fluorescence Spectrometry (PXRF). *AMERTA* 37(2):93–108. doi.org/10.24832/amt.v37i2.93-108

Forestier, H. 2007. Les éclats du passé préhistorique de Sumatra: Une très longue histoire des techniques. *Archipel* 74:15–44. doi.org/10.3406/arch.2007.3914

Forestier, H., D. Driwantoro, D. Guillaud, Budiman and D. Siregar 2006. New data for the prehistoric chronology of South Sumatra. In T. Simanjuntak, M. Hisyam, B. Prasetyo, T.S. Nastit and D. Bulbeck (eds), *Archaeology: Indonesian perspective, R.P. Soejono's Festschrift*, pp. 177–192. LIPI Press, Jakarta.

Forestier, H., T. Simanjuntak, F. Detroit and V. Zeitoun 2010. Unité et diversité préhistorique entre Java et Sumatra. *Archipel* 80:19–44. doi.org/10.3406/arch.2010.4175

Forestier, H., T. Simanjuntak and D. Driwantoro 2005a. Les premiers indices d'un faciès Acheuleen a Sumatra-Sud, Indonesia. Asie du Sud-Est: de l'*Homo erectus* a l'*Homo sapiens*. *Dossiers d'Archéologie* 302:16–17.

Forestier, H., T. Simanjuntak, D. Guillaud, D. Driwantoro, K. Wiradnyana, D. Siregar, R. Due Awe and Budiman 2005b. Le site de Tögi Ndrawa, île de Nias, Sumatra nord: Les premières traces d'une occupation hoabinhienne en grotte en Indonésie. *Comptes Rendus Paleoevol* 4:727–733. doi.org/10.1016/j.crpv.2005. 08.004

Gruwier, B.J. 2017. The large vertebrate remains from Bindjai Taming (Sumatra, Indonesia). *Journal of Indo-Pacific Archaeology* 41:22–29. doi.org/10.7152/jipa.v41i0.15027

Hooijer, D.A. 1946a. Prehistoric and fossil rhinoceroses from the Malay Archipelago and India. *Zoologische Mededelingen* 26:1–138.

Hooijer, D.A. 1946b. The evolution of the skeleton of *Rhinoceros sondaicus* Desmarest. *Proceedings of the Koninklijke Nederlandse Akademie van Wetenschappen* 49:671–676.

Hooijer, D.A. 1946c. Some remarks on recent, prehistoric and fossil porcupines from the Malay Archipelago. *Zoologische Mededelingen* 26(8):251–267.

Hooijer, D.A. 1947. On fossil and prehistoric remains of *Tapirus* from Java, Sumatra and China. *Zoologische Mededelingen* 27(3):253–299.

Hooijer, D.A. 1948a. *Rhinoceros sondaicus* Desmarest from kitchen-middens of Binjai Tamiang, north Sumatra. *Geologie en Mijnbouw* 10(5):115–116.

Hooijer, D.A. 1948b. Prehistoric teeth of man and of the orang-utan from central Sumatra, with notes on the fossil orang-utan from Java and southern China. *Zoologische Mededelingen* 29(2):175–301.

Hooijer, D.A. 1955. Fossil Proboscidea from the Malay Archipelago and the Punjab. *Zoologische Verhandelingen* 28(1):1–146.

Hooijer, D.A. 1958. Fossil Bovidae from the Malay Archipelago and the Punjab. *Zoologische Mededelingen* 38:1–112.

Hooijer, D.A. 1960. Quaternary gibbons from the Malay Archipelago. *Zoologische Verhandelingen* 46(1):1–42.

Hooijer, D.A. 1962. Quaternary langurs and macaques from the Malay Archipelago. *Zoologische Verhandelingen* 55(1):1–64.

Hooyman, J. 1824. Beschrijving der vogelnestjes. *Bataviaasch Genootschap van Kunsten en Wetenschappen* January 1824:91–103.

Hutchison, C.S. 2005. The geological framework. In A. Gupta (ed.), *The Physical Geography of Southeast Asia*, pp. 3–23. Oxford University Press, Oxford. doi.org/10.1093/oso/9780199248025.003.0011

Huxley, T.H. 1864. Cave explorations in Borneo. *Natural History Review* 15:472–473.

IJzerman, J.W., J.F. van Bemmelen, S.H. Koorders and L.A. Bakhuis 1895. *Dwars door Sumatra: Tocht van Padang naar Siak.* G Kolff, Haarlem.

Junghuhn, F. 1857. Over fossiele zoogdierbeenderen te Patihajam, in de residentie Djapara, eiland Java. *Natuurkundig Tijdschrift voor Nederlandsch Indië* 14:215–219.

Kastawan, I., Y. Nagafuchi and K. Fumoto 2009. Morphological typology and origins of the Hindu-Buddhist Candi architecture in Bali Island. *Journal of Architecture and Planning (Transactions of AIJ)* 74(6):1857–1866. doi.org/10.3130/aija.74.1857

Kulke, H., K. Kesavapany and V. Sakuja 2009. *Nagapattinam to Suvarnadwipa. Reflections on the Chola Naval Expeditions to Southeast Asia.* Institute of Southeast Asian Studies, Singapore.

Logan, J.R. 1848. Sketch of the physical geography and geology of the Malay Peninsula. *Journal of the Indian Archipelago and East Asia* 2(2):83–138.

Louys, J., S. Kealy, S. O'Connor, G.J. Price, S. Hawkins, K. Aplin, Y. Rizal, Y. Zaim, Mahirta, D.A. Tanudirjo, W.D. Santoso, A.R. Hidayah, A. Trihascaryo, R. Wood, J. Bevitt and T. Clark 2017. Differential preservation of vertebrates in Southeast Asian caves. *International Journal of Speleology* 46:379–408. doi.org/10.5038/1827-806X.46.3.2131

Louys, J., Y. Zaim, Y. Rizal, G.J. Price, Aswan, M.R. Puspanigrum, H. Smith and A. Trihascaryo 2021. Palaeontological surveys in Central Sumatra and Bangka. *Berita Sedimentologi* 47:50–56. doi.org/10.51835/bsed.2021.47.3.358

Lydekker, R. 1879. Notices of Siwalik mammals. *Records of the Geological Survey of India* 12:33–52.

Lydekker, R. 1886. The fauna of the Karnul caves. *Palaeontologia Indica Series 10* 4:23–58.

Maloney, B.K. 1980. Pollen analytical evidence for early forest clearance in North Sumatra. *Nature* 287:324–326. doi.org/10.1038/287324a0

Maloney, B.K. and F.G. McCormac 1996. A 30,000-Year Pollen and Radiocarbon Record from Highland Sumatra as Evidence for Climatic Change. *Radiocarbon* 37:181–190. doi.org/10.1017/S003382220003 0629

Manguin, P.-Y. 2022. Srivijaya. In C.F.W. Higham and N.C. Kim (eds), *The Oxford Handbook of Early Southeast Asia.* Oxford University Press, Oxford. doi.org/10.1093/oxfordhb/9780199355358.013.37

Marsden, W. 1811. *The History of Sumatra.* 3rd edition. M'Creery, London.

Martin, K. 1884. Ueberreste vorweltlicher Proboscidier von Java und Banka. *Sammlungen des geologischen Reichs-Museums in Leiden, Serie 1, Beiträge zur Geologie Ost-Asiens und Australiens* 4:1–24.

Matsumura, H., K.-I. Shinoda, T. Simanjuntak, A.A. Oktaviana, S. Noerwidi, H.O. Sofian, D. Prastiningtyas, N.L. Cuong, T. Kakuda, H.K. Kiriyama, N. Adachi, H.C. Hung, X. Fan, X. Wu, A. Willis and M. Oxenham 2018. Cranio-morphometric and aDNA corroboration of the Austronesian dispersal model in ancient island Southeast Asia: Support from Gua Harimau, Indonesia. *PLoS One* 13(6):e0198689. doi.org/10.1371/journal.pone.0198689

Morley, R.J., J.R. Flenley and M.K. Kardin 1973. Preliminary notes on the stratigraphy and vegetation of the swamps and small lakes of the Central Sumatran Highlands. *Sumatra Research Bulletin* 2(2):50–60.

Morwood, M.J., R.P. Soejono, R.G. Roberts, T. Sutikna, C.S.M. Turney, K.E. Westaway, W.J. Rink, J.-X. Zhao, G.D. van den Bergh, Rokus Awe Due, D.R. Hobbs, M.W. Moore, M.I. Bird and L.K. Fifield 2004. Archaeology and age of a new hominin from Flores in eastern Indonesia. *Nature* 431:1087–1091. doi.org/10.1038/nature02956

Musper, K.A.F.R. 1934. Een bezoek aan de grot Soeroeman Besar in het Goemaigebergte (Palembang, Zuid-Sumatra). *Tijdschrift van het Koninklijk Nederlandsch Aardrijkskundig Genootschap* 51(4):521–531.

Newbold, T.J. 1839. *Political and Statistical Account of the British Settlements in the Straits of Malacca, Volume 2.* John Murray, London.

Newsome, J. and J.R. Flenley 1988. Late Quaternary vegetational history of the Central Highlands of Sumatra. II. Palaeopalynology and vegetational history. *Journal of Biogeography* 15:555–578. doi.org/10.2307/2845436

Prasetyo, B., T.S. Nastiti and T. Simanjuntak (eds) 2017. *Austronesian Diaspora: A New Perspective.* Gajah Mada University Press, Yogyaarta.

Radèn Saléh 1867a. Letters by Radèn Saléh on Fossil sites near Banjoengantie, Kalisono, and Goenoeng Plawangan to the Directorate. *Notulen van de Algemeene en Directie-vergaderingen van het Bataviaasch Genootschap van Kunsten en Wetenschappen 4, 2*, pp. 41–42. Lange & Co, Batavia.

Radèn Saléh 1867b. Over fossiele beenderen van den Pandan. *Natuurkundig tijdschrift voor Nederlandsch-Indië* 29:422–423, 426–429, 433–437, 448–451, 455–459.

Raja, N.B., E.M. Dunne, A. Matiwane, T.M. Khan, P.S. Nätscher, A.M. Ghilardi and D. Chattopadhyay 2022. Colonial history and global economics distort our understanding of deep-time biodiversity. *Nature Ecology and Evolution* 6:145–154. doi.org/10.1038/s41559-021-01608-8

Régimbart, M. 1880. The new Dytiscidae and Gyrinidae collected during the recent scientific Sumatra Expedition. *Notes from the Leyden Museum* 4(2):209–216.

Roberts, P. 2019. *Introducing Tropical Forests in Prehistory, History, and Modernity.* Oxford University Press, Oxford. doi.org/10.1093/oso/9780198818496.003.0005

Roberts, P. and N. Amano. 2019. Plastic pioneers: Hominin biogeography east of the Movius Line during the Pleistocene. *Archaeological Research in Asia* 17:181–192. doi.org/10.1016/j.ara.2019.01.003

Sagart, L. 2005. Sino-Tibetan-Austronesian: An updated and improved argument. In R. Blench, L. Sagart and A. Sanchez-Mazas (eds), *The Peopling of East Asia: Putting Together Archaeology, Linguistics and Genetics,* pp. 161–176. Routledge Curzon, London. doi.org/10.4324/9780203343685

Salmon, C. 2008. Le goût Chinois pour les nids de salaganes et ses répercussions économiques en Indonésie (XVe/XVIe-XXIe s.). *Archipel* 76:251–290. doi.org/10.3406/arch.2008.4106

Sarasin, P. 1914. Neue lithochrone Funde im Innern von Sumatra. *Verhandlungen der Naturforschenden Gesellschaft in Basel* 25:97–111.

Sathiamurthy, E. and M.M. Rahman 2017. Late Quaternary paleo-fluvial system research of Sunda Shelf: A review. *Bulletin of the Geological Society of Malaysia* 64:81–92. doi.org/10.7186/bgsm64201708

Schmidt, M.C.P. 1909. *Franz Junghuhn. Biographische Beiträge zur 100. Wiederkehr seines Geburtstages-1909.* Verlag der Dürr'schen Buchhandlung, Leipzig.

Schürmann, H. 1928. Kjökkenmöddinger en Paleolithicum in Noord Sumatra. *De Mijningenieur* 12:1–19.

Setiawan, T. 2009. Loyang Mendale situs hunian prasejarah di pedalaman Aceh: Asumsi awal terhadap hasil penelitian gua-gua di Kabupaten Aceh Tengah, Provinsi Nanggroe Aceh Darrussalam. *Berkala Arkeologi Sangkhakala* 12(24):1–12.

Setiawan, T. 2020. Cave settlement potential of caves and rock shelters in Aceh Besar Regency. *Berkala Arkeologi* 40(1):23–44. doi.org/10.30883/jba.v40i1.506

Sherratt, A. 2002. Darwin among the archaeologists: The John Evans nexus and the Borneo Caves. *Antiquity* 76:151–157. doi.org/10.1017/S0003598X00089924

Shipman, P. 2001. *The Man Who Found the Missing Link: Eugene Dubois and His Lifelong Quest to Prove Darwin Right.* Simon and Schuster, New York.

Simanjuntak, T. (ed.) 2021. *Gua Harimau dan Perjalanan Panjang Peradaban OKU*. UGM Press, Yogyakarta.

Simanjuntak, T., H. Forestier, D. Dwiwantoro, Jatmiko and D. Siregar 2006. Berbagai Tahat Zaman Batu. In D. Guillaud (ed.), *Menyusuri Sungai, Menurut Waktu: Penelitian Arkeologi do Sumatran Seletan*, pp. 23–35. IRD-Enrique Indonesia, Jakarta.

Suntory Beverage & Food Asia Pte Ltd 21 January 2019. *Edible Bird's Nest – Top 7 Facts*. Avian Science Institute. avianscienceinstitute.com/edible-birds-nest-top-7-facts

Takakusu, J. (trans.) 1896. *A Record of the Buddhist Religion as practised in India and the Malay Archipelago (A.D. 671-695)* (Yi Jing [635–713], author). Clarendon Press, Oxford.

Theunissen, L.T.G. 1989. *Eugène Dubois and the Ape-Man from Java* (E. Perlin-West, trans.). Kluwer, Dordrecht. doi.org/10.1007/978-94-009-2209-9

Tichelman, G.L. 1939. Felsengänge an Sumatras Ostküste. *Paideuma* 1(4):179–191.

Tieng, F.S. 2016. The Guar Kepah shell middens: Evidence and questions. In N. Hidalgo Tan (ed.), *Advancing Southeast Asian Archaeology 2013: Selected Papers from the First SEAMEO SPAFA International Conference on Southeast Asian Archaeology, Chonburi, Thailand, 2013*, pp. 114–128, 139. SPAFA Publications, Bangkok.

Tobler, A. 1917. Über Deckenbau im Gebiet von Djambi (Sumatra). *Verhandlungen der Naturforschenden Gesellschaft in Basel* 28(2):123–147.

van Boekhoven, J. 1928. Vacantieschetsen der Fraters van Padang 1927. *Tropisch Nederland* 18:20, 22–25.

van Gorsel, J.T. 2018. *Bibliography of the Geology of Indonesia and Surrounding Areas, Edition 7.0, July 2018*. vangorselslist.com/pdf/BIG_2018_All_7.pdf

van Stein Callenfels, P.V. 1921. Rapport over een dienstreis door een deel van Sumatra. *Oudheidkundig Verslag* 1921:62–75.

van Stein Callenfels, P.V. 1924. De Batoe Kemang. *Oudheidkundig Verslag* 1924:134–136.

Verbeek, R.D.M. 1883. *Topographische en Geologische Beschrijving van een Gedeelte van Sumatra's Westkust*. Stemler, Batavia.

Veth, P.J. and A.L. van Hasselt 1881. *Midden-Sumatra Reizen en Onderzoekingen der Sumatra-Expeditie Uitgerust door het Aardrijkskundig genootschap 1877–79*. Brill, Leiden. doi.org/10.5962/bhl.title.119451

Voris, H.K. 2000. Maps of Pleistocene sea levels in Southeast Asia: Shorelines, river systems and time durations. *Journal of Biogeography* 27:1153–1167. doi.org/10.1046/j.1365-2699.2000.00489.x

Wallace, A.R. 1864. The bone caves of Borneo. *Natural History Review* 4:308–311.

Wallace, A.R. 1873. Cave-deposits of Borneo. *Nature* 181:461–462. doi.org/10.1038/007461c0

Wallon, M.L.H. and D.F.A. Hervey 1881. Klouwang and its caves, west Coast of Atchin. *Journal of the Straits Branch of the Royal Asiatic Society* 8:153–158.

Westaway, K.E., J. Louys, R. Due Awe, M.J. Morwood, G.J. Price, J.X. Zhao, M. Aubert, R. Joannes-Boyau, T. Smith, M.M. Skinner, T. Compton, R.M. Bailey, G.D. van den Bergh, J. de Vos, A.W.G. Pike, C. Stringer, E.W. Saptomo, Y. Rizal, J. Zaim, W.D. Santoso, A. Trihascaryo, L. Kinsley and B. Sulistyanto 2017. An early modern human presence in Sumatra 73,000–63,000 years ago. *Nature* 548:322–325. doi.org/10.1038/nature23452

Wichmann, A. 1909. Franz Wilhelm Junghuhn 26 Oktober 1809 bis 24 April 1864. *Petermanns Mittelungen* 55:297–300.

Wormser, C.W. 1941. *Franz Junghuhn Biografie.* Van Hoeve, Den Haag.

Zahirovic, S., M. Seton and R.D. Müller 2014. The Cretaceous and Cenozoic tectonic evolution of Southeast Asia. *Solid Earth* 5:227–273. doi.org/10.5194/se-5-227-2014

Zakariya, H. and M.A. Salleh 2011. From Makkah to Bukit Kamang?: The moderate versus radical reforms in West Sumatra (ca 1784-1819). *International Journal of Humanities and Social Science* 1(14):195–203.

Zwierzycki, J. 1926. Een vondst uit de Palaeolithische cultuurperiode in een Grot in Boven Jambi. *De Ingenieur in Nederlandsch-Indië* 4:63–67.

Zwierzycki, J. and O. Posthumus 1926. De Palaeo-Botanische Djambi-Expeditie. *Tijdschrift van het Aardrijkskundig Genootschap* 1926:202–216.

Appendix: List of Dutch colonial photographs of Sumatran caves

Location	Code	Date	Description	Notes
A. West Sumatra				
Kamang	KITLV A320 (37397)	1911	*"Jagers en drijvers van een jachtgezelschap verzameld in de grot van Kamang bij Tilatang"*	Series by de Tulp, Haarlem, number 68
Kamang	KITLV 69771	1939	Same as H1349 ~782 [Interior of cave facing outward]	
Kamang	H1349-783	1916–39	Exterior of cave, with fancy car demonstrating graffiti dating from 1916 through 1939	From the same album as above
Kamang	KITLV 26464	c. 1900	*"Grot van Kamang. Een geheel doorlopende grot bij Ft. De Kock"* [View from across sawah (rice field)]	Photograph by C.C. Jasper
Kamang	KITLV 151377	c. 1890	*"Man in de Grot Kamang bij Fort de Kock"* [Man with arms extended upward]	Same as A773 (KITLV 102843) and A26466
Kamang	KITLV 69930	1939	*"PRW van Gesselar Verschuir (rechtsachter) bezoekt een grot mogelijk op Sumatra 1939"* [Fancy car in front of Batoe Biaroe (Kamang)]	Graffiti indicates latest date is 1939 (some date back to 1916). Bags of guano fertiliser (or possibly cement) at the mouth of the cave
Simarasop	KITLV A416	c. 1910	*"Grot te Payakoemboh"*	Same as entry below
Simarasop	KITLV 85160		*"Grot te Payakoemboh"*	Same as entry above
Simarasop	KITLV 85161		*"Grot te Payakoemboh"*	
Simarasop	A1300-65167	1910–25	*"Rivier stroomt vanuit een grot in een kloof of ravijn vermoedelijk op West-Sumatra"*	Same photographer as the series KITLV 65183-89 (1910–25)
Ngalau Indah	KITLV A1119-75247	c. 1895	*"Grot nabij Payamkoeboh (@1895)"* in *"Reis door Padangsche Bovenlanden Sumatra's Westkust"* W.D, Harvant	Album print Photograph possibly by C. Nieuwenhuys

Location	Code	Date	Description	Notes
Batoe Biaro (Ng. Sangkar Poejoeh)	KITLV 26467		*"Grot te Payakoemboh, Lima Puloh Koto"*	Cement steps
Batoe Biaro (Ng. Sangkar Poejoeh)	A881-107367	c. 1915	*"3/265"*	Cement steps, same as above. Album print
Baso	KITLV 26463	c. 1905	*"Grot van Baso in het Padangsche Bovenland, Sumatra's Westkust"*	Man with arm raised, in front of cave mouth near fig tree with descending roots. Graffiti with Indonesian names. Photograph by Nieuwenhuys
Baso	1300-65166		*"Vermoedelijk een grot in West Sumatra"*	From the same album as 61583-65189
Katoembang	KITLV 32431			
Ng. Pangian (Boea)	KITLV 106052		*"Grot van Boea bij Fort Van der Capellen"*	
Paoeh	KITLV A320 (37398)	1911	*Ingang van de grot bij Paoeh*	Cave near Padang
B. North Sumatra				
	99415	1937–41	*"Grot en de Batakland"*	*"r. Neg. XVII,4 1937-41"*
Batoe Tulis	KITLV 79200-A179	1934	*"Batoe tulis leistenen grot aan de Koeala (Aek Linkoengang) tussen Pematang Siantar en Rantau Prapat"*	Europeans being shown the cave, with canoes beached on riverbank
Batoe Tulis	KITLV 79201-A179	1934	*"Rotstekengingen in een leisteen (Batoe Tulis) grot aan de Koeala (Aek Lingkoengan) in de Oostkust van Sumatra"*	Engravings on a crypt tomb
Batoe Tulis	KITLV 79202-A179		*"De tengoe-besen van Bilah en Koeala bij grenssteen tussen hun dorpen bij Rantau Prapat"*	Indonesian administrators at a boundary marker
Aek Simare, Toba	KITLV 34008-145	1938	*"Bataksche inscriptie op een rotsblok rechts van de ingang van de grot aan de westelijke oever van de bovenloop van de Aek Simare in de onder afdeling van Toba"*	Photograph by P. Voorhoeve
Aek Simare, Toba	KITLV 32316	c. 1920	*"Rotswoningen of toegangen tot dodenmis, Sumatra's Westkust"*	Hewn crypts in rock
Aek Simare, Toba	KITLV 32317		*"Europees meisje in een grotwoning, Sumatra's Westkust"*	*"H963"*
C. Aceh				
Takengon	KITLV A149 (KITLV 78149)	c. 1913	*Sajeuëng, Takengon, Aceh Tengah, Grot aan een rivier Sajeuëng bij Takingeun*	
Ng. Kloeang	KITLV 11768-A33	c. 1894	*"Grot op het voor de Westkust van Atjeh nabij Tjalang gelegen eiland Kloeang gezien vanuit zee"*	Nr. Tjalang = Calang, West Coast, Aceh. A well-known bird nest cave on a coastal island

Location	Code	Date	Description	Notes
Ng. Kloeang	KITLV 11769-A33	c. 1894	*"Grot op het voor de Westkust van Atjeh nabij Tjalang gelegen eiland Kloeang gezien vanuit zee"* *"Van Hr. Ms. Flottieljevaartuig Benkoelin zichtbaar in het midden van de grot"*	Men deep within cave with massive cursive graffiti
Ng. Kloeang	KITLV 11770-A33	c. 1894	*"Grot op het voor de Westkust van Atjeh nabij Tjalang gelegen eiland Kloeang gezien vanuit zee"*	
Ng. Kloeang	KITLV 11771-A33	c. 1894	*"Grot op het voor de Westkust van Atjeh nabij Tjalang gelegen eiland Kloeang gezien vanuit zee"*	Large waves breaking at entrance

Source: Leiden University Libraries Digital Collections (collection KITLV: Southeast Asian & Caribbean Images).

5

Geochronology and palaeoenvironments of Sibrambang and Djambu caves, western Sumatra

Julien Louys, Gilbert J. Price, Pennilyn Higgins, John de Vos, Jahdi Zaim, Yan Rizal, Aswan, Mika Rizki Puspaningrum, Agus Tri Hascaryo, Gerrell M. Drawhorn and Paul C.H. Albers

Abstract

Fossils from Sibrambang and Djambu, two sites in the Padang Highlands, were collected by Dubois in the late 1880s. These collections, alongside the deposits from Lida Ajer, have for over 100 years been our only insights into the Pleistocene mammalian history of Sumatra. Despite their importance, their chronological context has remained elusive. Here, we provide the first direct dates of fossils from Sibrambang and Djambu. Uranium–thorium series dating indicates that it is likely that the fossils from Djambu were derived from at least three periods: (1) >500 ka (beyond or close to the limit of the applied dating technique); (2) close to 85 ka (but not younger); and (3) close to 38 ka (but not younger). Sibrambang, too, has a mix of fossils with different ages, and it is hard to say how many distinct time intervals may be present. Conservatively, there are at least two: (1) >149 ka; and (2) >55 ka (but not younger than that). Stable carbon and oxygen isotope analyses of fossils from both sites indicate largely rainforest conditions during this period, except for one elephant specimen (>500 ka), which is reconstructed here as a mixed feeder. These data, combined with previous studies, hint at more open environments in Sumatra during (periods of) the Middle Pleistocene, although significantly more data will be required to confirm this. Our results have implications for previous palaeoecological analyses involving these sites, as well as for the taxonomy of fossil orangutan (*Pongo*).

Keywords: Pleistocene, rainforest, orangutan, carbon isotope, oxygen isotope

Abstrak

Banyak fosil hasil koleksi Dubois pada tahun 1880-an dari dua lokasi di Dataran Tinggi Padang, Sibrambang dan Djambu. Dari koleksi tersebut, selain yang dikoleksi dari endapan gua Lida Ajer, selama lebih dari 100 tahun telah menjadi satu-satunya sumber wawasan kita dalam memahami sejarah mamalia Pleistosen di pulau Sumatra. Terlepas dari pentingnya fosil tersebut, konteks kronologinya masih sulit untuk dipahami. Di sini, kami sampaikan hasil pertanggalan fosil-fosil dari Sibrambang dan Djambu menggunakan metode pertanggalan Uranium–Thorium. Pertanggalan deret U–Th menunjukkan bahwa setidaknya fosil-fosil dari Djambu setidaknya berasal dari tiga periode: (1) >500 ka (melampaui atau mendekati batas teknik pertanggalan yang diterapkan); (2) mendekati 85 ka (tetapi tidak lebih muda) dan (3) mendekati 38 ka (tetapi tidak lebih muda). Sibambrang juga memiliki campuran fosil dengan umur yang berbeda, sehingga menyulitkan untuk menyimpulkan berapa banyak interval umur yang berbeda yang mungkin ditemukan. Secara konservatif, setidaknya terdapat dua umur: (1) >149 ka; dan (2) yang lebih muda >55 ka (tetapi tidak lebih muda dari umur tersebut). Analisis isotope karbon dan oksigen stabil untuk fosil yang berasal dari kedua lokasi tersebut menunjukkan sebagian besar kondisi hutan hujan yang stabil selama periode ini, kecuali untuk satu spesimen gajah (>500 ka), yang di sini direkonstruksikan sebagai pemakan tumbuhan campuran. Data ini, dikombinasikan dengan data dari kajian-kajian sebelumnya mengisyaratkan lingkungan yang lebih terbuka di Sumatra selama periode Plestosen Tengah, meskipun masih diperlukan lebih banyak data yang signifikan untuk mengkonfirmasi hal ini. Hasil kami telah memberikan implikasi pada analisis paleoekologi yang telah dilakukan sebelumnya yang melibatkan situs-situs tersebut, begitu pula dengan taksonomi fosil orangutan (*Pongo*).

Kata kunci: Plestosen, hutan hujan, orangutan, isotop karbon, isotop oksigen

Introduction

In the late 1880s, Dubois began his search for the 'missing link' of human evolution in the Padang Highlands in western Sumatra. His exploration and excavation of several caves were initially met with a great deal of excitement, particularly for Lida Ajer (Dubois 1888). However, this excitement was eventually tempered and ultimately dampened when the only fossils recovered represented extant species from the region (Chapter 2, this volume). Dubois, and Hooijer after him, considered these to belong only to the Holocene (Dubois 1888; Hooijer 1947). Dubois moved his exploration to Java in 1890, leaving the bulk of the fossil materials from the Sumatran caves to be described by Hooijer in a series of papers (Hooijer 1946a, 1946b, 1947, 1948, 1955, 1960, 1962). Although Dubois collected from numerous caves in the Padang Highlands, the most substantial material he recovered was derived from only three caves: Lida Ajer, Sibrambang and Djambu.

The Sumatran cave deposits were attributed to the Holocene until the 1980s, when de Vos (1983) first pointed out the close faunal similarities between Punung in Java and Lida Ajer and Sibrambang in Sumatra and contrasted these with the sites of Wajak and Ngandong, also in Java. He observed that Punung I and II and the Sumatran caves sampled taxa reminiscent of interglacial humid forests and argued that they should be considered of similar antiquity and had been connected by a land bridge between Java and Sumatra. Ngandong and Wajak, on the other hand, represented drier habitats indicative of glacial periods. This, combined with biochronological data available at the time, suggested that Punung dated to sometime between Ngandong and Wajak. The contemporaneity of Punung, Lida Ajer and Sibrambang was subsequently accepted by some (e.g. Bacon et al. 2008; Janssen et al. 2016; Louys et al. 2007; Louys and Meijaard 2010).

The environmental context of the biocorrelations was an explicit and important aspect of the faunal turnover scheme proposed for determining the ages of Javanese Pleistocene sites (de Vos 1983, 1985, 1996; de Vos et al. 1994; Leinders et al. 1985; Sondaar 1984; van den Bergh et al. 2001). In this scheme, the more open woodlands represented by Middle Pleistocene sites such as

Trinil, Kedung Brubus and Ngandong gave way to interglacial rainforest conditions, as represented by the Late Pleistocene Punung I and II, only to be replaced by the more open Holocene sites of Sampung, Hoekgrot, Goa Jimbe and Wajak. Wajak is now understood to be Late Pleistocene (Storm et al. 2013).

Breccia from Punung III, a collapsed cave site found in the vicinity of Punung I and II and thought to be contemporaneous with them due to faunal similarities, was dated to between 128 ± 15 and 118 ± 3 ka using thermoluminescence (TL), optically stimulated luminescence, thermal ionisation mass spectrometry and uranium-series (U-series) dating (Westaway et al. 2007). This age range was subsequently applied to the Sumatran assemblages on biostratigraphic grounds (Janssen et al. 2016; Louys and Meijaard 2010; Louys et al. 2007), although some expressed caution regarding the implied relationship between Punung III and Punung I and II (Bacon et al. 2015; Kaifu et al. 2022).

The first attempt to directly date Sumatran material used amino-acid racemisation. Randy Skelton (pers. comm. cited in Drawhorn 1995) attempted to date a sample of bone from Lida Ajer and calibrated the racemisation using two dated samples collected from the deepest layers of the Niah Cave deposits in Borneo. Skelton observed that if racemisation rates between Niah and Lida Ajer were equivalent, then the Lida Ajer material would be older than 80,000 years. Skelton also dated two bone fragments from Djambu. These returned dates of 70–85 ka and 56 ka respectively, leading Drawhorn (1995) to suggest a minimum of 6,000–14,000 years of time averaging for the Djambu assemblage.

More recently, new exploration and sampling of caves in western Sumatra, specifically Lida Ajer, Ngalau Gupin and Ngalau Sampit, allowed for an evaluation of the age of fossil-bearing breccias in the Padang Highlands as well as several Dubois legacy fossils (Duval et al. 2021; Louys et al. 2022; Smith et al. 2021; Westaway et al. 2017). For Lida Ajer, red TL and post-infrared infrared-stimulated luminescence (pIR-IRSL) dating of the breccia sediments in the main fossil chamber provided burial ages of 85 ± 25 ka and 62 ± 5 ka respectively, with the latter probably closer to the true age of burial (Westaway et al. 2017). U-series dating of a basal flowstone to 203 ± 17 ka provided a maximum age, while a straw stalactite derived from the breccia, dated to 84 ± 1 ka, provided a probable true age of the deposit. Overlying flowstones, providing a minimum age, were dated to 71 ± 7 ka and 11 ± 2 ka.

Direct dating on a fossil orangutan tooth (*Pongo*) from the Dubois collection (Naturalis Biodiversity Centre, Leiden) using U-series dating produced a date of 70–60 ka. While this probably represents a minimum age for the fossil, this was not confirmed by Westaway et al. (2017). A similar age (>80–75 ka) was obtained by direct dating fossil teeth extracted directly from the breccia by Westaway et al. (2017), with the overall breccia deposit probably deposited between 63 and 73 ka (Westaway et al. 2017).

Louys et al. (2022) provided further details on the ages and stratigraphic relationship of the new recovered fossils from Lida Ajer, paying particular attention to the deposits from the passages at the rear of the cave. They combined electron spin resonance (ESR) dating of several teeth from unconsolidated muds, luminescence dating of non-fossiliferous sediments, and stratigraphic observations to construct a model of deposition history for the cave. Although the 'sinkhole' fossil deposits, topographically lower in the cave, are probably (but not conclusively) older than the material dated by Westaway et al. (2017), the most parsimonious interpretation of the history of the site suggests that all the fossils were deposited during Marine Isotope Stage (MIS) 4, corresponding to 76–59 ka, using the composite marine $\delta^{18}O$ record provided by Westerhold et al. (2020). Stable isotope analyses of the fossil teeth from Lida Ajer (both Dubois fossils and newly recovered fossils) indicated rainforest conditions similar to today, although potentially slightly wetter and with some small open patches (Louys et al. 2022).

Ngalau Sampit is one of the caves that also appear in Dubois' notes, although no specific fossils present in the Dubois collections have been associated with deposits from this cave (Duval et al. 2021). Exploration and initial U-series dating of flowstone and calcite by Louys et al. (2017), suggesting an age of approximately 90 ka for the deposit, were confirmed through a more comprehensive dating study by Duval et al. (2021). This latter study combined U-series/ESR ages of individual fossils (obtaining a mean age of 105 ± 9 ka, 1 SD), and conducted breccia dating yielding internally 1σ-consistent pIR-IRSL mean ages of 93 ± 6 ka, 1 SD; it indicated deposition during MIS 5 (130–71 ka; Lisiecki and Raymo 2005). Thus, Ngalau Sampit is roughly coeval with Punung in Java. Although these sites have preserved relatively few fossil specimens, these specimens indicate that rainforest conditions were present in the Padang Highlands at that time (Louys et al. 2021).

Ngalau Gupin was first discovered during fieldwork in Padang Highlands in 2015 reported by Louys et al. (2017), and a detailed analysis of its fauna and age was described by Smith et al. (2021). The fauna is largely typical of already-known Pleistocene Sumatra, with the addition of several taxa not previously recorded from the fossils of the island, including the Indian rhinoceros (*Rhinoceros unicornis*) and the extinct Asian hippopotamus (*Hexaprotodon*). The fossils were recovered from cemented breccia and eroded material, with reconstructed ages between 160 and 115 ka based on combined U-series/ESR dating of teeth from the deposit. As such, the Ngalau Gupin fossils probably represent MIS 6 faunas (160–115 ka) and are currently the oldest directly dated remains from the region (Smith et al. 2021).

Here, we present the results of direct dating of Dubois legacy fossil teeth from Sibrambang and Djambu, complementing the renewed dating efforts at other sites in the Padang Highlands. We discuss the dates in the context of the probable depositional and taphonomic environment operating in these caves. We also present stable isotope analyses of the teeth from the three main cave sites and discuss these in the context of previous palaeoenvironmental and palaeoecological studies of the assemblages.

Materials and methods

Geographical context

Sibrambang (alternative spelling Simbrambang) is one of the most productive of Dubois' Sumatran cave localities. Dubois' notes suggest that material from this site was excavated from a cave called Agung Agung (Chapter 2, this volume). A cave bearing this name has been identified (but not yet explored) in the general vicinity of the modern village of Sibarambang (Louys et al. 2017). Drawhorn (1995) suggested that, given the importance of the cave site now known as Sibrambang, Dubois identified it not by the cave name but rather by the name of a nearby village or geological feature, and we argue it is likely that this village or feature name probably had one or two letters different from the site name and has been altered in transliteration to become Sibrambang. Djambu (original spelling Djamboe, modern alternative spelling Jambu) has better locality information recorded, although, like that of Sibrambang, its exact location remains to be determined. Dubois' notes indicate that the cave was located near and north of the Kuliet-monies Volcano, west of the Muara-panas River, and at a relatively high altitude (Chapter 2, this volume, Appendix, 50-049) and north of the town of Tapisello.

Material

From the Dubois material available from Sibrambang, two *Pongo,* one *Tapirus indicus,* two *Elephas maximus*, two *Capricornis sumatraensis* and six Rhinocerotidae enamel fragments were used as samples for carbon and oxygen isotope analysis, and the following teeth were dated: two *Pongo* (4 and 5 drill samples), one *Panthera pardus* (4 drill samples), one *Tapirus indicus* (4 drill samples) and one *Elephas maximus* (7 drill samples). From Dubois' Djambu collection, one *Capricornis sumatraensis*, three *Elephas maximus* and four Rhinocerotidae enamel fragments were used as samples for carbon and oxygen isotope analysis, and one *Pongo* tooth (5 drill holes), one *Tapirus indicus* tooth (4 drill holes), one *Panthera pardus* dental fragment (3 drill holes) and one *Elephas maximus* dental fragment (3 drill holes) were dated.

Each tooth or tooth fragment came from the bulk Dubois fossils housed at Naturalis Biodiversity Center, Leiden, the Netherlands. Bulk registration numbers for the fragments are listed in Tables 5.1 and 5.2 in the Results section. As each individual fragment listed under a bulk number did not have an individual registration number, we assigned each sample an internal number corresponding to the site they came from; samples were bagged with this number and returned to the bulk collections.

Carbon and oxygen stable isotope analysis

Carbon and oxygen isotope analysis was undertaken on samples of powdered enamel obtained using a diamond burr drill bit applied to the exposed surface of the enamel. Enamel powder was treated chemically to remove organics using 30% H_2O_2 and 0.1 N acetic acid. Samples were subsequently measured using a ThermoFinnigan DeltaPlus XP mass spectrometer at the University of Rochester's Stable Isotope Ratios in the Environment Analytical Laboratory. Carbon and oxygen isotopes are reported in permil (‰) and standardised to Vienna Pee-Dee Belemnite. Where sample size permitted, we ran repeat analyses. For these, we discarded the results with the highest standard deviation across both oxygen and carbon isotopes; where these were identical, the lower carbon standard deviation was retained.

U-series dating

Other than biochronology, geochronological methods applicable to the Djambu and Sibrambang fossil assemblages are limited to direct dating approaches. Because the caves have not been re-explored and sampled, stratigraphy-based geochronological methods are not currently applicable. Moreover, because the fossils are mostly isolated teeth that are well preserved but were prepared in a way that meant formerly adhering matrix was removed at the time of curation, luminescence and electron-based methods (which rely on knowledge of burial dose rates) are not possible. Hence, we were restricted to direct approaches such as uranium–thorium (U–Th) and radiocarbon dating. We chose the former because it is less destructive (a curatorial concern for the historic Dubois collections) than radiocarbon dating and has a far greater temporal application range (up to c. 500 ka versus c. 50 ka for radiocarbon dating).

Direct U–Th dating is based on the premise that vertebrate tissues such as teeth take up uranium (U) from the burial environment during the fossilisation process. ^{238}U then undergoes alpha and beta decay to produce a series of short-lived nuclides including ^{234}U, ^{234}Th and ^{230}Th (and eventually stable lead (Pb) daughter isotopes). The U–Th age is then calculated by measuring the ratio of the parent isotope, ^{238}U, to the daughter ^{230}Th. Because living tissues contain little or no U, direct U-series dating in most cases produces only minimum ages for the specimens, but in some situations, it can return dates that may approximate the true age (e.g. Price et al. 2021). Although teeth are open systems for U uptake and migration, they may often act as closed systems after recrystallisation. In some cases, U may be lost from the system through leaching, leading to maximum ages (and age overestimates) for the fossils of concern (Sambridge et al. 2012). However, the reliability of the U-series age can be estimated by considering the geometry of ^{230}Th age and U-concentration in a section (Pike et al. 2002).

We followed the sampling approach described in Price et al. (2013), which basically involved hand-drilling multiple dentine powders in transects across each tooth, with each sample then dated separately (see Figure 5.1). This approach allowed us to produce age and U-concentration profiles through the teeth and hence allows us to determine their suitability for U–Th dating. Again, to reduce the need to destructively sample the teeth—for example, by cut and slabbing as would be required for U–Th laser ablation approaches (e.g. Grün et al. 2014)—our hand-drilling utilised drill bits of only 1 mm diameter (producing c. 1 mg of dentine powder per sample) and targeted already-broken and naturally exposed dentine surfaces. The sample powders were measured on a Nu Plasma HR multi-collector inductively coupled plasma mass spectrometer following techniques described in Zhou et al. (2011) using the infrastructure in the Radiogenic Isotope Facility at The University of Queensland, Brisbane, Australia.

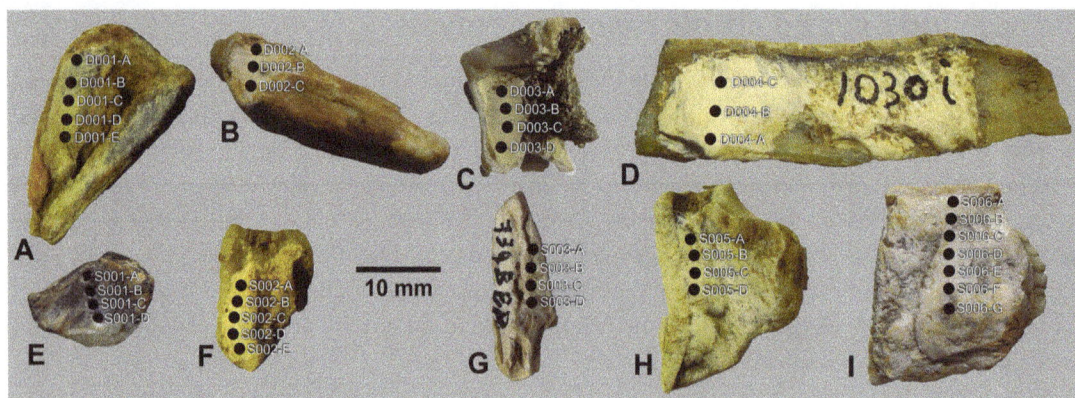

Figure 5.1: The nine dated teeth from the Dubois collections from Sibrambang and Djambu, showing sampling positions.

Note: See Table 5.2 for the results.

A. D001 (*Pongo* sp., Djambu).

B. D002 (*Panthera pardus*, Djambu).

C. D003 (*Tapirus indicus*, Djambu).

D. D004 (*Elephas maximus*, Djambu).

E. S001 (*Pongo* sp., Sibrambang).

F. S002 (*Pongo* sp., Sibrambang).

G. S003 (*Panthera pardus*, Sibrambang).

H. S005 (*Tapirus indicus*, Sibrambang).

I. S006 (*Elephas maximus*, Sibrambang).

Source: Image by G.J. Price.

Results

Stable isotopes

The carbon and oxygen isotope values are listed in Table 5.1. Elephants demonstrated the largest range of carbon isotope values, with a large C_4 contribution to diet in one individual from Djambu (Figure 5.2). However, all other elephant samples showed a carbon isotope either dominated by or having a large proportion of C_3. All the other taxa examined had carbon isotope values well towards or in the C_3 range, with rhinoceroses exhibiting the lowest $\delta^{13}C$ values of any of the sampled specimens.

Oxygen isotopes were all highly negative, as would be expected from a humid or rainforest environment. An elephant specimen from Sibrambang had the highest value, at –6‰ $\delta^{18}O$, while a rhinoceros specimen from this site had the lowest value, at –10.7‰ $\delta^{18}O$. The C_4-eating elephant had oxygen isotope ratios within the range of all the other elephants examined, and only one C_3 elephant had lower $\delta^{18}O$ values than modern elephants.

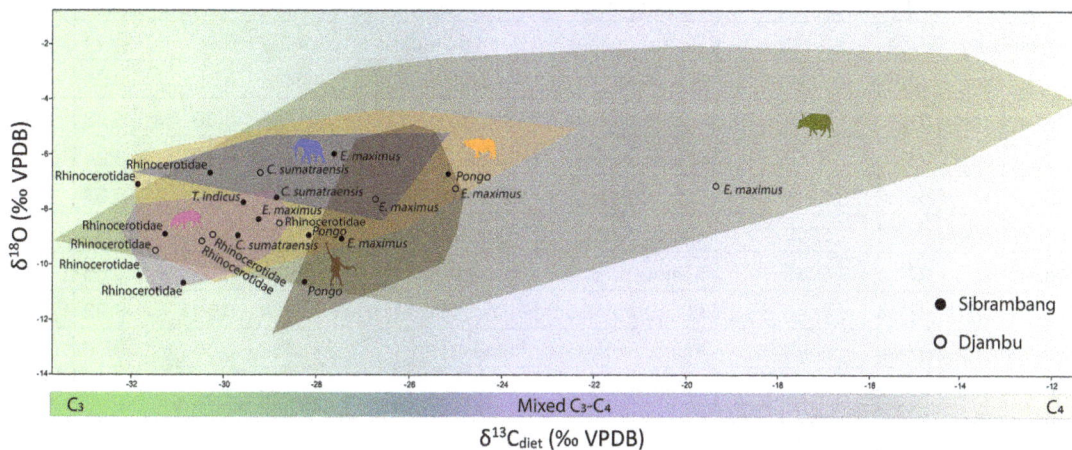

Figure 5.2: Stable isotope analysis of $\delta^{13}C_{diet}$ (‰ VPDB) and $\delta^{18}O$ (‰ VPDB) from faunal enamel of fossil mammals collected by Dubois from Sibrambang and Djambu compared with modern Southeast Asian representatives of their families.

Note: Modern representatives' data are shown as convex hulls; see Louys and Roberts (2020) for original data. Pink: Tapiridae; blue: Elephantidae; brown: Hominidae (*Pongo*); orange: Rhinocerotidae; green: Bovidae. *E. maximus* = *Elephas maximus*; *T. indicus* = *Tapirus indicus*; *C. sumatraensis* = *Capricornis sumatraensis*.

VPDB = Vienna Pee-Dee Belemnite.

Source: Image by J. Louys using animal silhouettes from phylopic.org (public domain) and CC-BY-SA 3.0. All animal silhouettes via phylopic.org: *Pongo abelii* by Gareth Monger (creativecommons.org/licenses/by/3.0/); *Mammuthus armeniacus* by Julián Bayona (creativecommons.org/licenses/by-nc/3.0/); *Tapirus pinchaque* by Steven Traver (creativecommons.org/publicdomain/zero/1.0/); *Bubalus arnee* by Cristopher Silva (creativecommons.org/public domain/zero/1.0/); *Rhinoceros unicornis* by H.F.O March (creativecommons.org/publicdomain/mark/1.0/). CC-BY-NC 3.0 Elephantini by Zimices.

Table 5.1: Carbon and oxygen isotope analysis values calculated for select taxa from Dubois' collections from Sibrambang and Djambu.

Site	Collec-tion no.	Internal sample ID	Taxon	Common name	Carbon, $\delta^{13}C_{diet}$ mean ‰ VPDB	SD	Oxygen, $\delta18O$ mean ‰ VPDB	SD
Djambu	1030i	D004	Elephas maximus	Asian elephant	−5.36	0.05	−7.14	0.10
Djambu	959aan	D005	Capricornis sumatraensis	Mainland serow	−15.21	0.05	−6.67	0.13
Djambu	1030i	D008	E. maximus	Asian elephant	−12.72	0.08	−7.62	0.10
Djambu	1030i	D009	E. maximus	Asian elephant	−10.99	0.05	−7.24	0.11
Djambu	1022a	D010	Rhinocerotidae	Rhinoceros	−17.46	0.05	−9.51	0.21
Djambu	1022a	D011	Rhinocerotidae	Rhinoceros	−16.48	0.07	−9.14	0.14
Djambu	1022a	D012	Rhinocerotidae	Rhinoceros	−16.23	0.05	−8.93	0.11
Djambu	1022a	D013	Rhinocerotidae	Rhinoceros	−14.8	0.1	−8.50	0.13
Sibrambang	739au	S001	Pongo sp.	Orangutan	−17.16	0.09	−8.95	0.16
Sibrambang	810q	S002	P. pygmaeus	Orangutan	−14.15	0.05	−6.70	0.20
Sibrambang	815g	S005	Tapirus indicus	Malayan tapir	−15.57	0.05	−7.74	0.10
Sibrambang	7989a	S006	E. maximus	Asian elephant	−13.44	0.06	−9.05	0.11
Sibrambang	810n	S007	E. maximus	Asian elephant	−13.6	0.06	−5.98	0.10
Sibrambang	961t	S008	C. sumatraensis	Mainland serow	−15.69	0.03	−8.94	0.09
Sibrambang	961s	S009	C. sumatraensis	Mainland serow	−14.87	0.08	−7.57	0.14
Sibrambang	809	S012	E. maximus	Asian elephant	−15.24	0.06	−8.35	0.14
Sibrambang	971aa	S013	Rhinocerotidae	Rhinoceros	−16.87	0.07	−10.65	0.11
Sibrambang	971aa	S014	Rhinocerotidae	Rhinoceros	−17.24	0.06	−8.93	0.21
Sibrambang	971aa	S015	Rhinocerotidae	Rhinoceros	−16.32	0.06	−6.66	0.09
Sibrambang	971aa	S016	Rhinocerotidae	Rhinoceros	−17.85	0.07	−7.11	0.13

Note: VPDB = Vienna Pee-Dee Belemnite.

Source: Data from the authors.

U–Th dating

We produced a total of 40 U–Th dates for nine fossil teeth (four from Djambu and five from Sibrambang) and included specimens referable to *Pongo* sp., *Tapirus indicus*, *Panthera pardus* and *Elephas maximus* (see Figure 5.3 and Table 5.2). Although the dating of each dentine sample was relatively straightforward, interpretation was more challenging due to the apparent variable nature of U uptake and loss in the teeth; this complicated the interpretation of the respective assemblages.

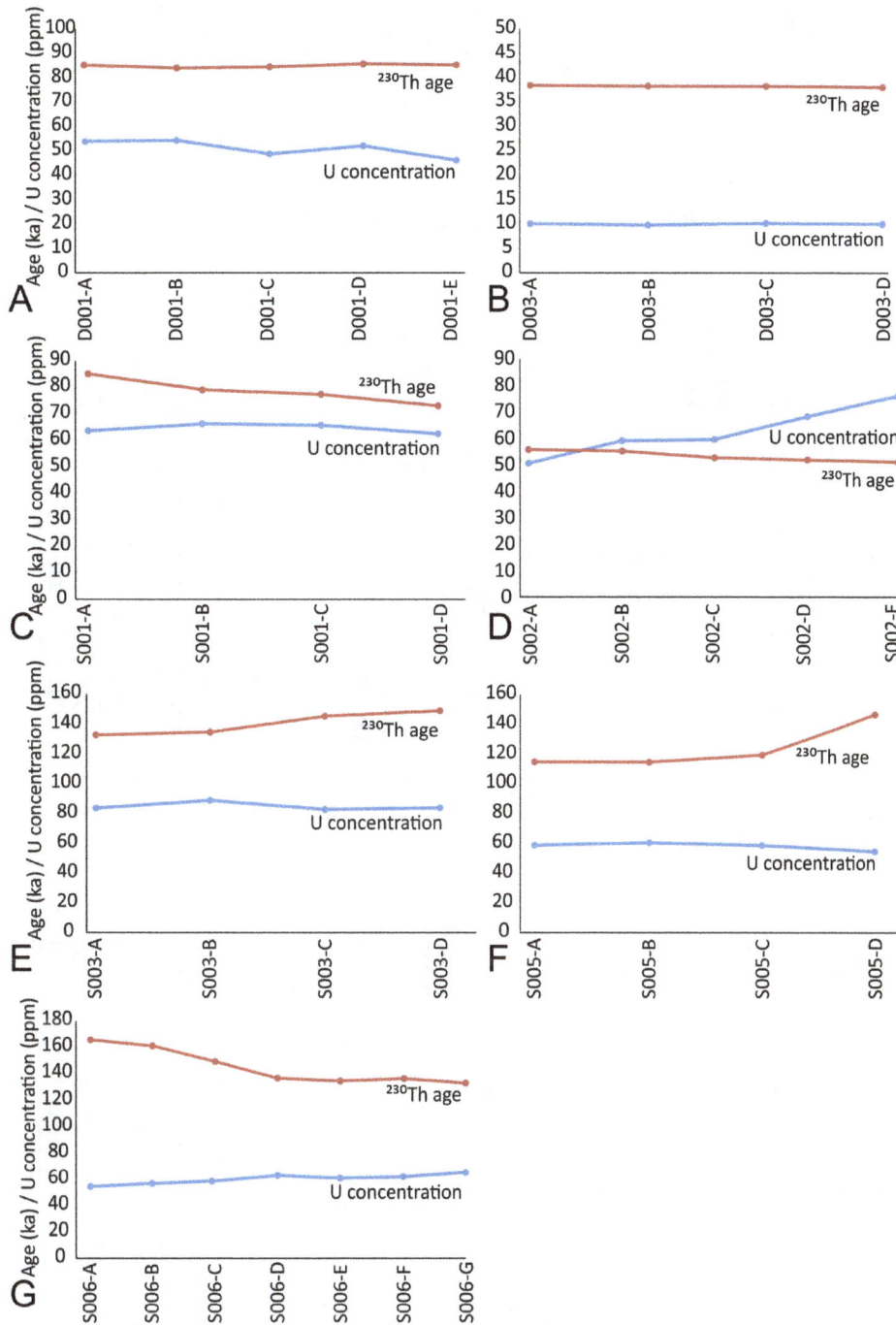

Figure 5.3: ^{230}Th age and U-concentration profiles in sections of dated fossil teeth from Dubois' collections from Sibrambang and Djambu.

Note: Specimens that exhibited clear U loss — D002 and D004 — are not plotted. See Table 5.2 for specific isotopic data for all teeth (including D002 and D004).

A. D001 (*Pongo* sp., Djambu).

B. D003 (*Tapirus indicus*, Djambu).

C. S001 (*Pongo* sp., Sibrambang).

D. S002 (*Pongo* sp., Sibrambang).

E. S003 (*Panthera pardus*, Sibrambang).

F. S005 (*Tapirus indicus*, Sibrambang).

G. S006 (*Elephas maximus*, Sibrambang).

Source: Image by G.J. Price.

Table 5.2: Uranium-series isotopic and concentration data for fossil teeth from Dubois' collections from Sibrambang and Djambu.

Sample name[1]	Collection no.	Taxon	U (ppm)	232Th (ppb)	230Th/232Th	230Th/238U	234U/238U	Uncorrected age (ka)	Corrected age (ka)	Corrected initial (234U/238U)
D001-A	937d	Pongo sp.	53.94 ± 0.03	7.48 ± 0.10	14383	0.657 ± 0.003	1.190 ± 0.001	85.3 ± 0.6	85.3 ± 0.6	1.2417 ± 0.0013
D001-B	937d	Pongo sp.	54.35 ± 0.03	4.85 ± 0.09	22197	0.653 ± 0.003	1.193 ± 0.001	84.1 ± 0.5	84.1 ± 0.5	1.2451 ± 0.0016
D001-C	937d	Pongo sp.	48.76 ± 0.02	1.18 ± 0.03	82095	0.654 ± 0.002	1.191 ± 0.002	84.5 ± 0.4	84.5 ± 0.4	1.2427 ± 0.0018
D001-D	937d	Pongo sp.	52.08 ± 0.03	2.34 ± 0.05	44394	0.658 ± 0.002	1.188 ± 0.001	85.8 ± 0.4	85.8 ± 0.4	1.2389 ± 0.0010
D001-E	937d	Pongo sp.	46.23 ± 0.02	1.80 ± 0.04	50750	0.652 ± 0.002	1.181 ± 0.001	85.3 ± 0.5	85.3 ± 0.5	1.2300 ± 0.0012
D002-A	937b	Panthera pardus	37.53 ± 0.03	1.80 ± 0.05	81298	1.286 ± 0.003	1.218 ± 0.001	473.6 ± 17.1	473.6 ± 17.1	1.8286 ± 0.0387
D002-B	937b	P. pardus	34.15 ± 0.02	503.78 ± 1.17	277	1.345 ± 0.004	1.217 ± 0.001	>500	>500	
D002-C	937b	P. pardus	37.79 ± 0.01	39.67 ± 0.11	3833	1.326 ± 0.004	1.228 ± 0.001	746.0 ± 137.7	746.0 ± 137.7	2.8761 ± 0.7253
D003-A	10061	Tapirus indicus	10.16 ± 0.01	65.16 ± 0.17	161	0.339 ± 0.003	1.129 ± 0.001	38.7 ± 0.5	38.5 ± 0.5	1.1441 ± 0.0014
D003-B	10061	T. indicus	9.87 ± 0.01	13.91 ± 0.03	727	0.338 ± 0.001	1.131 ± 0.001	38.4 ± 0.2	38.4 ± 0.2	1.1466 ± 0.0016
D003-C	10061	T. indicus	10.26 ± 0.01	4.32 ± 0.02	2430	0.337 ± 0.002	1.131 ± 0.001	38.3 ± 0.2	38.3 ± 0.2	1.1458 ± 0.0014
D003-D	10061	T. indicus	10.10 ± 0.01	8.46 ± 0.05	1214	0.335 ± 0.002	1.129 ± 0.002	38.1 ± 0.3	38.1 ± 0.3	1.1438 ± 0.0019
D004-A	1030i	Elephas maximus	7.594 ± 0.002	12.12 ± 0.03	2872	1.511 ± 0.005	1.361 ± 0.002	659.7 ± 73.1	659.7 ± 73.1	3.3232 ± 0.4748
D004-B	1030i	E. maximus	7.658 ± 0.004	25.64 ± 0.08	1464	1.615 ± 0.004	1.359 ± 0.001	>500	>500	
D004-C	1030i	E. maximus	7.846 ± 0.004	16.62 ± 0.04	2259	1.578 ± 0.006	1.349 ± 0.001	>500	>500	

Sample name[1]	Collection no.	Taxon	U (ppm)	232Th (ppb)	230Th/232Th	230Th/238U	234U/238U	Uncorrected age (ka)	Corrected age (ka)	Corrected initial (234U/238U)
D004-D	1030i	E. maximus	7.135 ± 0.002	111.94 ± 0.23	301	1.554 ± 0.004	1.350 ± 0.001	>500	>500	
S001-A	739au	Pongo sp.	63.52 ± 0.03	4.70 ± 0.10	26068	0.636 ± 0.002	1.157 ± 0.001	84.9 ± 0.5	84.9 ± 0.5	1.1993 ± 0.0011
S001-B	739au	Pongo sp.	66.24 ± 0.06	11.34 ± 0.07	10710	0.604 ± 0.002	1.156 ± 0.001	79.0 ± 0.5	79.0 ± 0.5	1.1946 ± 0.0010
S001-C	739au	Pongo sp.	65.69 ± 0.03	9.46 ± 0.09	12530	0.595 ± 0.002	1.156 ± 0.001	77.3 ± 0.4	77.3 ± 0.4	1.1937 ± 0.0012
S001-D	739au	Pongo sp.	62.43 ± 0.02	9.30 ± 0.06	11588	0.569 ± 0.002	1.151 ± 0.001	73.0 ± 0.3	73.0 ± 0.3	1.1856 ± 0.0015
S002-A	810q	Pongo sp.	51.26 ± 0.03	9.78 ± 0.07	7311	0.460 ± 0.002	1.129 ± 0.001	56.4 ± 0.3	56.4 ± 0.3	1.1514 ± 0.0010
S002-B	810q	Pongo sp.	59.75 ± 0.03	3.28 ± 0.06	25108	0.454 ± 0.002	1.122 ± 0.001	55.9 ± 0.3	55.9 ± 0.3	1.1429 ± 0.0010
S002-C	810q	Pongo sp.	60.24 ± 0.05	4.61 ± 0.10	17367	0.438 ± 0.002	1.122 ± 0.001	53.4 ± 0.3	53.4 ± 0.3	1.1419 ± 0.001
S002-D	810q	Pongo sp.	68.83 ± 0.04	3.08 ± 0.07	29333	0.433 ± 0.002	1.123 ± 0.001	52.6 ± 0.3	52.6 ± 0.3	1.1426 ± 0.0012
S002-E	810q	Pongo sp.	76.59 ± 0.04	10.18 ± 0.14	9750	0.427 ± 0.002	1.121 ± 0.001	51.8 ± 0.3	51.8 ± 0.3	1.1401 ± 0.0009
S003-A	739bbd	P. pardus	83.62 ± 0.06	3.11 ± 0.10	67568	0.828 ± 0.003	1.151 ± 0.001	132.7 ± 0.8	132.7 ± 0.8	1.2196 ± 0.0014
S003-B	739bbd	P. pardus	88.62 ± 0.10	6.43 ± 0.13	34803	0.832 ± 0.003	1.148 ± 0.001	134.7 ± 0.9	134.7 ± 0.9	1.2166 ± 0.0015
S003-C	739bbd	P. pardus	82.66 ± 0.09	21.36 ± 0.16	10120	0.862 ± 0.003	1.144 ± 0.001	145.4 ± 1.2	145.4 ± 1.2	1.2170 ± 0.0018
S003-D	739bbd	P. pardus	83.68 ± 0.06	5.24 ± 0.11	41770	0.862 ± 0.003	1.132 ± 0.001	149.0 ± 1.0	149.0 ± 1.0	1.2017 ± 0.0018
S005-A	815g	T. indicus	60.16 ± 0.04	15.05 ± 0.10	9701	0.800 ± 0.003	1.192 ± 0.001	116.1 ± 0.7	116.1 ± 0.7	1.2667 ± 0.0012
S005-B	815g	T. indicus	61.73 ± 0.06	7.27 ± 0.11	20522	0.797 ± 0.002	1.188 ± 0.001	116.0 ± 0.6	116.0 ± 0.6	1.2613 ± 0.0016

Sample name[1]	Collection no.	Taxon	U (ppm)	^{232}Th (ppb)	^{230}Th/^{232}Th	^{230}Th/^{238}U	^{234}U/^{238}U	Uncorrected age (ka)	Corrected age (ka)	Corrected initial (^{234}U/^{238}U)
S005-C	815g	T. indicus	59.87 ±0.03	4.87 ±0.08	30593	0.820 ±0.003	1.194 ±0.001	120.7 ±0.9	120.7 ±0.9	1.2730 ±0.0015
S005-D	815g	T. indicus	55.90 ±0.02	16.30 ±0.09	9529	0.916 ±0.003	1.197 ±0.001	147.8 ±0.9	147.8 ±0.9	1.2994 ±0.0018
S006-A	7989a	E. maximus	54.33 ±0.04	29.01 ±0.09	5345	0.941 ±0.003	1.170 ±0.001	165.6 ±1.1	165.6 ±1.1	1.2712 ±0.0015
S006-B	7989a	E. maximus	56.67 ±0.04	24.12 ±0.08	6616	0.928 ±0.004	1.170 ±0.002	161.0 ±1.5	161.0 ±1.5	1.2670 ±0.0023
S006-C	7989a	E. maximus	58.65 ±0.04	21.47 ±0.09	7401	0.893 ±0.003	1.167 ±0.0001	149.2 ±1.2	149.2 ±1.2	1.2541 ±0.0018
S006-D	7989a	E. maximus	62.68 ±0.03	12.20 ±0.09	13248	0.850 ±0.004	1.162 ±0.001	136.5 ±1.1	136.5 ±1.1	1.2382 ±0.0016
S006-E	7989a	E. maximus	60.61 ±0.04	2.08 ±0.07	74368	0.842 ±0.003	1.161 ±0.002	134.4 ±1.0	134.4 ±1.0	1.2351 ±0.0024
S006-F	7989a	E. maximus	61.74 ±0.04	2.77 ±0.11	57476	0.850 ±0.003	1.164 ±0.001	136.2 ±0.9	136.2 ±0.9	1.2409 ±0.0017
S006-G	7989a	E. maximus	64.99 ±0.04	30.98 ±0.12	5321	0.836 ±0.003	1.160 ±0.001	132.8 ±0.9	132.8 ±0.9	1.2327 ±0.0017

[1] D = Djambu; S = Sibrambang.

Note: There is evidence of U leaching in D002 and D004; thus, ^{230}Th ages could not be calculated for all subsamples.

Ratios in parentheses are activity ratios calculated from the atomic ratios but normalised to measured values of secular-equilibrium HU-1 (Ludwig et al. 1992). Errors are given at the 2σ level. ^{230}Th ages were calculated using Isoplot EX 3.0 (Ludwig 2003) with decay constants λ238 = 1.551x10^{-10} yr^{-1} for ^{238}U, λ234 = 2.826x10^{-6} yr^{-1} for ^{234}U and λ230 = 9.158x10^{-6} yr^{-1} for ^{230}Th (Cheng et al. 2000). 2σ errors in the uncorrected ages were propagated directly from the uncertainties in (^{230}Th/^{238}U) and (^{234}U/^{238}U). The corrected ^{230}Th age was calculated using an assumed bulk earth or upper crust value equivalent to a detrital ^{230}Th/^{232}Th activity ratio of 0.83.

Source: Data from the authors.

As shown in Figure 5.3, dating of the Djambu samples revealed two specimens with plateau-like ^{230}Th age and U-concentration profiles: D001 (*Pongo* sp.) and D003 (*T. indicus*). This suggests relatively rapid uranium uptake following burial, without subsequent leaching. Thus, these two teeth represent reliable minimum ages that may be close to the true age of these specimens. These are c. 85 ka and c. 38 ka respectively. Samples D002 (*P. pardus*) and D004 (*E. maximus*) are less ideal for constraining the age of Djambu. Both show some evidence of uranium loss and are probably older than 500 ka and therefore beyond the applicable temporal range of the U–Th method. Collectively, these results suggest that the curated Djambu fossil collection may be significantly time-averaged. Given the lack of stratigraphic context recorded by Dubois and his team, it is possible that the teeth were reworked into a single stratigraphic layer prior to excavation or were collected from three separate and variously aged strata (i.e. c. 38 ka, c. 85 ka, and >500 ka). We consider the latter to perhaps be a slightly more parsimonious interpretation, given the lack of evidence of abrasion (which would indicate transport or reworking) on the fossils, and the fact that it is not uncommon for other caves in the Padang Highlands to contain stratigraphically complex and temporally various deposits (e.g. Louys et al. 2022; Smith et al. 2021).

U-migration behaviour in dated specimens from the Sibrambang assemblage is slightly different from that of Djambu. While there is no strong evidence for U loss in any of the teeth, there are no plateau-like ^{230}Th age profiles either. The evidently youngest specimen, S002 (*Pongo* sp.), has a half-∩-shaped age profile where the ^{230}Th ages become progressively older from the outer margin of the tooth to the inner portion but with an inverse relationship with regard to U-concentration; that is, the highest U-concentration is closest to the outer margin (note that this tooth was only drilled for dateable samples from the outer margin to the middle rather than completely across the tooth, outer margin to outer margin). This profile resembles a tooth that has experienced more recent U uptake, without U loss (e.g. Pike et al. 2002). The tooth yields a reliable minimum age of >56 ka (i.e. from subsample S002-A, closest to the middle of the specimen), although we cannot be sure how close this may be to the true age of the fossil. Sample S001 (*Pongo* sp.) has a similar profile to S002 and is >85 ka; likewise, we also interpret that to be a reliable minimum age. Three specimens (S003, *P. pardus*; S005, *T. indicus*; S006, *E. maximus*) have half-∪-shaped ^{230}Th age profiles in which the oldest ages occur towards the outer margin of the tooth and are progressively younger interiorward. Due to the relatively plateau-like U-concentration profiles through the teeth, there is no evidence for U loss, and thus these three teeth yield reliable minimum ages. Perhaps noteworthily, these teeth all have late Middle Pleistocene minimal ages (S003 and S005 >148 ka; S006 >165 ka; see Table 5.2). Again, it is challenging to draw firm conclusions about the overall age of the complete Sibrambang assemblage, but it remains possible that multiple and/or temporally various strata were sampled during the Dubois excavations. The clustering of at least three Sibrambang teeth with evidently similar U-uptake histories and minimum ages may show that those particular specimens were excavated from a single stratum.

Discussion

The new dates produced here are useful in reconstructing, as a first approximation, both the time depth and likely time averaging present in the deposits of Sibrambang and Djambu. These new dates help place Dubois' sites in a regional geochronological framework and provide direct minimum ages for several taxa in the Padang Highlands. Both sites preserve orangutan fossils with minimum ages of around 85 ka, with the uptake interpretation suggesting this could be close to their true ages. Orangutan fossils are recorded from Ngalau Sampit (c. 100 ka; Duval et al. 2021), Ngalau Gupin (c. 160–115 ka; Smith et al. 2021) and the later Lida Ajer deposits (Westaway et al. 2017), so their presence elsewhere in the Padang Highlands at c. 85 ka is to be expected. The minimum age of c. 50 ka for *Pongo* from Sibrambang may indicate persistence of this taxon after the Lida Ajer deposits; however, such interpretations require further testing and analysis. A conservative interpretation would suggest an older age for this specimen.

The *P. pardus* dating records suggest that leopards lived in the Padang Highlands from at least 148 ka. Meijaard (2004) hypothesised that the leopard first migrated into Sundaland in the Middle Pleistocene. Our data would appear to support this hypothesis; moreover, given the presence of these fossils, it is evident that this taxon did not bypass Sumatra on its way to Java.

Of course, the leopard is no longer found on the island of Sumatra, and several hypotheses have been proposed regarding its absence. Meijaard (2004) suggested that the prey densities that could be supported by the evergreen rainforests of Borneo and Sumatra were too low to sustain leopards in competition with tigers. Wilting et al. (2012, 2016) strongly advocated that the Toba eruption (c. 74 ka) was the primary cause of the leopard's extinction. Wilkinson and O'Regan (2003) suggested that life history traits, specifically the leopard's smaller litter size and shorter reproductive life relative to the tiger, were key factors explaining the absence of leopards on Indonesian islands such as Sumatra. Volmer et al. (2017) used agent-based modelling to examine the extinction of the leopard on Sumatra, concluding that the leopard could have been driven to extinction by competition from other carnivores, specifically from two medium-sized cats and the Asiatic wild dog. Our data indicates that the leopard persisted on Sumatra from the Middle Pleistocene (>500 ka) until at least the MIS 4 (76–59 ka) deposits of Lida Ajer. Thus, while our data do not refute any of the abovementioned hypotheses, this long persistence through major climatic and geological events does suggest that other causes may need to be invoked to explain the extinction of the leopard on Sumatra.

Tapirus specimens from the two sites provided reliable minimum ages, meaning that the likely youngest specimen from Djambu is one of the youngest fossils reported from the Padang Highlands caves. *Tapirus* (the tapir) is a medium-sized ungulate that is recovered relatively commonly from the Padang Highlands, and these newly dated records of it, in conjunction with previously dated deposits in that region (Lida Ajer, Ngalau Gupin), indicate persistence of this taxon throughout at least the Late Pleistocene and very probably the Middle Pleistocene.

The *Elephas maximus* records indicate that the Asian elephant has been present in Sumatra since the Middle Pleistocene. Like the tapir, it is a relatively common large mammal recovered from the Padang Highlands caves and is still extant on Sumatra today.

At a site level, the dating resolution of all teeth examined herein is limited—by available techniques and destructive analytical ability; see Duval et al. (2021) for a detailed discussion of dating limitations in these cave environments—such that the geochronological picture that emerges for these sites can be interpreted in several ways. The Sibrambang material produced dates of approximately >52–56 ka, >85 ka, >148 ka, and >165 ka. The Djambu material produced dates of >38 ka, >85 ka, and >500 ka.

The dates obtained from both Sibrambang and Djambu demonstrate a potentially huge chronological range for each site, and it is possible that the teeth from the two sites were each derived from a single massively time-averaged original deposit in each cave (or a single deposit facilitating heterogeneous and complex uranium-uptake histories across incorporated teeth, with Sibrambang >165 ka and Djambu >500 ka). However, we consider it more likely that they came from different deposits in the respective cave systems. Older fossils may have become incorporated into younger assemblages through dissolution and re-formation of breccias in the system (see Louys et al. 2017 and O'Connor et al. 2017 for detailed discussions), such that what may have appeared to be a single deposit was the amalgamation of two or more palaeodeposits in a single setting. Unfortunately, without detailed field notes of the excavations or re-examination of the caves, determining which of these scenarios is most likely is currently impossible.

In a best-case scenario for the uranium-uptake histories of the teeth, it is most likely that the fossils from Djambu were derived from at least three periods: (1) >500 ka (beyond or close to the limit of the U–Th technique); (2) close to 85 ka (but not younger); and (3) close to 38 ka (but not younger). These could represent different collecting areas in the cave, or one or two massively time-averaged deposits. Sibrambang has a mix of fossils with different ages, and it is hard to determine how many distinct time intervals are present. Conservatively, there are at least two: one >149 ka and a younger one >55 ka (but no younger than that). Unlike the teeth from Djambu, the Sibrambang teeth included none that returned ages that appear potentially close to the true age of the individual.

Despite the huge age ranges demonstrated by the U-series dating, the carbon and oxygen isotope values showed remarkable consistency. Other than a single elephant, all taxa sampled from the sites are indicative of wet, tropical rainforests (as shown by Figure 5.2), quite unlike what would be expected from a Southeast Asian mixed to open woodland site—for example, Tham Wiman Nakin (Louys and Meijaard 2010; Louys and Roberts 2020; Pushkina et al. 2010). This suggests a high degree of stability in the Padang Highlands throughout glacial–interglacial cycles, or that the primary accumulating agent of fossils (likely to be porcupines in all the sites, based on the preservation of almost nothing but tooth crowns; Smith et al. 2020), operated only in rainforest conditions. Previous carbon and oxygen isotope analyses of suid remains from Sibrambang and bovid and cervid remains from unnamed Padang Highlands caves also demonstrated a C_3-dominated diet for these taxa, although the ingestion of some C_4 vegetation is indicated in at least some of the samples (Janssen et al. 2016). This accords with palaeocommunity analyses of Lida Ajer, Sibrambang, and Djambu that suggest the presence of more open areas in Sumatra during the Pleistocene (Spehar et al. 2018). Importantly, the one elephant sample from Djambu that plotted on the C_4 end of the spectrum (1030i, D004) is also one of two specimens dating to the Middle Pleistocene (i.e. >500 ka). This raises the intriguing possibility that the extensive savanna environments recorded for Southeast Asia during the Middle Pleistocene (Louys and Roberts 2020) may have extended into the Padang Highlands. More fossil deposits of this age will be required to confirm that; however, it hints that there may have been some faunal turnover events in Sumatra similar to those experienced in Java; the record of *Hexaprotodon* at Ngalau Gupin (Smith et al. 2021) supports this hypothesis. Relatively open savanna environments would have provided suitable habitats for several large mammals, including early hominins (Louys and Roberts 2020).

Our results have implications for previous palaeoecological arguments that have been based on these sites. Several researchers, including one present author, have treated each of the Sibrambang and Djambu assemblages as representing a single palaeocommunity for the purposes of palaeoecological analyses (e.g. Bacon et al. 2015; Louys 2012; Volmer et al. 2017). On one hand, the results presented here do not invalidate this treatment—at each site, there is an assemblage of fauna that were found together over a finite period, even if that period cannot yet be precisely bracketed. On the other hand, the large period represented by each site may necessitate critical re-examination of the ecological inferences derived from the deposits. At best, as a single palaeocommunity, Djambu represents a time-averaged assemblage dating from between 38 and >500 ka. At Simbrambang, the time averaging is somewhat better constrained, perhaps to between 55 and >149 ka, but this is probably still too broad to provide convincing evidence for ecological interactions between individuals.

The broad temporal span represented by the assemblages also has implications for the taxonomy of species erected based on fossil material from the caves. In Sumatra, two fossil orangutan species have been proposed from these sites: *Pongo palaeosumatrensis* and *P. duboisi*. The first of these was originally erected by Hooijer (1948) as a subspecies of *P. pygmaeus* (under which all extant orangutans were classified at the time). Hooijer erected this subspecies based on the larger-than-average teeth of the fossil taxon compared to the modern orangutan. In this subspecies, he grouped all the Sumatran samples together and selected as the holotype a left third upper molar (M_3) from Simbrambang. Badoux (1959) and Kahlke (1972) argued that the differences between *P. p. palaeosumatrensis* and modern orangutans were insufficient to merit taxonomic distinction. Drawhorn (1995), in his re-examination of fossil orangutans, also noted that the dimensions of orangutan teeth from this site were not significantly different from modern orangutan dental dimensions under a heteroscedastic *t*-test. However, Drawhorn (1995) was more circumspect than Badoux (1959) and Kahlke (1972) in rejecting this taxon, choosing to restrict the subspecies to specimens from Sibrambang while raising the possibility that the Sibrambang orangutans may be accommodated by the modern Sumatran orangutan species *P. abelii*. Conversely, Harrison et al. (2014) raised *P. p. palaeosumatrensis* to full species level, largely based on arguments by Harrison (2000), who, like Hooijer, grouped all Sumatran fossil orangutans together in his statistical analysis.

Pongo duboisi was proposed by Drawhorn (1995) to accommodate the orangutan fossils from Lida Ajer, which, unlike the Sibrambang sample, were statistically different from modern populations. To this hypodigm, Drawhorn (1995) added the material from Djambu under a subspecies, *P. duboisi djamboensis* (separate from the Lida Ajer subspecies *P. d. lidaajerensis*). Drawhorn also presciently suggested that the Djambu orangutans were derived from two separate assemblages; our results suggest that Djambu may in fact be derived from at least three different periods.

Our results also suggest that the fossil material derived from Sibrambang comes from at least two periods, one of which (at c. 55 ka) may have overlapped with both Lida Ajer and some Djambu fossils (the other, at >148 ka, may have overlapped with other Djambu fossils as well). Because it is not possible to determine which fossil orangutans from Sibrambang belong to which period without resorting to directly dating every specimen, any given orangutan sample from Sibrambang may represent one, two or even more biological populations. The relationship of these populations to orangutans preserved in Lida Ajer and Djambu is unclear, and while it is unlikely that several different species of sympatric ape coexisted in such a small region, we note that less than 100 km currently separates the two extant Sumatran orangutan species (Meijaard et al. 2021). *P. palaeosumatrensis* is only nominally distinguished from other orangutans based on average size (and only from *P. duboisi* if restricting the hypodigm to material from Sibrambang), necessitating a biological population to draw the average from; therefore, since no clear and single population is preserved, we suggest this taxon be considered a *nomen dubium*.

In contrast, *Pongo duboisi* is derived from a stratigraphically and chronologically well-constrained fossil deposit and is therefore statistically differentiable from other orangutans. However, there is an issue regarding the availability of the name *P. duboisi,* which has been described only in an unpublished PhD thesis (Drawhorn 1995). Under International Code of Zoological Nomenclature Article 8.1, for a work to be considered published, it must be issued for the purpose of providing a public and permanent scientific record (8.1.1) and it must have been produced in an edition providing simultaneously obtainable copies by a method that assures numerous identical, durable copies (8.1.3.1). As an unpublished PhD thesis does not fulfil these criteria, until the name is made available, we will refer to the Lida Ajer orangutans as *Pongo 'duboisi'*. Moreover, while *P. 'duboisi' lidaajerensis* derives from a temporally constrained deposit, *P. 'd.' djamboensis* almost certainly does not. Distinguishing which of the orangutans from Djambu belongs to the *P. 'duboisi'* hypodigm will require more-constrained deposits from Djambu. Thus, like *P. palaeosumatrensis*, this subspecies, even when available, should be considered a *nomen dubium*.

Conclusions

The Sumatran fossils recovered by Dubois have, until recently, provided the only insights into the island's palaeontological past. They have been interpreted as characteristically rainforest, closed-forest, or humid-forest faunas (de Vos 1983; Louys and Meijaard 2010), similar if not identical to those found today on the island. Despite a lack of detail about the age or geological context of the fossil assemblages from Sibrambang, Djambu and, until recently, Lida Ajer, these assemblages have continued to be used to infer environmental and ecological processes occurring in Pleistocene Southeast Asia. Our stable isotope results indicate that the Dubois fossil materials from Sibrambang and Djambu largely represent characteristically rainforest species and that such conditions have been present on the island since the Middle Pleistocene. The only exception is an elephant fossil hinting at more open conditions. Our dating results from these sites are less clear-cut. Nevertheless, they suggest that fossils were deposited during several periods in both caves, from at least the Middle Pleistocene until the Late Pleistocene. Moreover, they indicate that relatively open environments may have been present in the Padang Highlands during the Middle Pleistocene. These results are important for understanding the ecological and biological history of large mammals on this island and, by implication, of the hominins that would have been present in the broader region.

Acknowledgements

Naturalis Biodiversity Center is gratefully acknowledged for allowing access to the Dubois Archive, especially Reinier van Zelst for facilitating access. Funding for this research was generously provided by the Australian Research Council (FT160100450), the Leakey Foundation grant 'Palaeontological and archaeological investigations of Pleistocene cave deposits from Sumatra' and an Australian National University Research School of Asia and the Pacific Grant Development Support grant (to JL). Many thanks to two anonymous reviewers for their constructive comments on this chapter.

References

Bacon, A.M., F. Demeter, P. Duringer, C. Helm, M. Bano, V.T. Long, N.T.K. Thuy, P.O. Antoine, B.T. Mai, N.T.M. Huong and Y. Dodo 2008. The Late Pleistocene Duoi U'Oi cave in northern Vietnam: Palaeontology, sedimentology, taphonomy and palaeoenvironments. *Quaternary Science Reviews* 27:1627–1654. doi.org/10.1016/j.quascirev.2008.04.017

Bacon, A.M., K. Westaway, P.O. Antoine, P. Duringer, A. Blin, F. Demeter, J.L. Ponche, J.X. Zhao, L.M. Barnes, T. Sayavonkhamdy and N.T.K. Thuy 2015. Late Pleistocene mammalian assemblages of Southeast Asia: New dating, mortality profiles and evolution of the predator–prey relationships in an environmental context. *Palaeogeography, Palaeoclimatology, Palaeoecology* 422:101–127. doi.org/10.1016/j.palaeo.2015.01.011

Badoux, D.M. 1959. Fossil mammals from two fissure deposits at Punung (Java). Unpublished doctoral dissertation. University of Utrecht, Utrecht.

Cheng, H., R.L. Edwards, J. Hoff, C.D. Gallup, D.A. Richards and Y. Asmerom 2000. The half-lives of uranium-234 and thorium-230. *Chemical Geology* 169:17–33. doi.org/10.1016/s0009-2541(99)00157-6

de Vos, J. 1983. The *Pongo* faunas from Java and Sumatra and their significance for biostratigraphical and paleo-ecological interpretations. *Proceedings of the Koninklijke Nederlandse Akademie van Wetenschappen, Series B* 86:417–425.

de Vos, J. 1985. Faunal stratigraphy and correlation of the Indonesian Hominid sites. In E. Delson (ed.), *Ancestors: The Hard Evidence*, pp. 215–220. Liss, New York.

de Vos, J. 1996. Faunal turnovers in Java in relation to faunas from the continent. In Y. Kozawa (ed.), *Proceedings of the International Symposium on Biogeography of Vertebrates in Indonesian Islands and Adjacent areas, Kashiwa, Japan, June 1995*, pp. 32–36. Odontology 1. Association for Comparative Odontology, Terajima Cultural Hall Foundation, Japan.

de Vos, J., P.Y. Sondaar, G.D. van den Bergh and F. Aziz 1994. The *Homo* bearing deposits of Java and its ecological context. *Courier Forschungsinstitut Senckenberg* 171:129–140.

Drawhorn, G.M. 1995. Paleodemography and Systematics of the Orangutan (*Pongo pygmaeus*). Unpublished doctoral dissertation. Department of Anthropology, University of California, Davis.

Dubois, M.E.F.T. 1888. Preliminary Report about the Palaeontological Explorations in Caves near Payakombo (Padang Highlands). Unpublished report. The Dubois Archive, Naturalis Biodiversity Center, Leiden.

Duval, M., K. Westaway, Y. Zaim, Y. Rizal, Aswan, M.R. Puspaningrum, A. Trihascaryo, P.C.H. Albers, H.E. Smith, G.M. Drawhorn, G.J. Price and J. Louys 2021. New chronological constraints for the Late Pleistocene fossil assemblage and associated breccia from Ngalau Sampit, Sumatra. *Open Quaternary* 7:1–24. doi.org/10.5334/oq.96

Grün, R., S. Eggins, L. Kinsley, H. Moseley and M. Sambridge 2014. Laser ablation U-series analysis of fossil bones and teeth. *Palaeogeography, Palaeoclimatology, Palaeoecology* 416:150–167. doi.org/10.1016/j.palaeo.2014.07.023

Harrison, T. 2000. Archaeological and ecological implications of the primate fauna from prehistoric sites in Borneo. *Bulletin of the Indo-Pacific Prehistory Association* 20:133–146.

Harrison, T., C.Z. Jin, Y.Q. Zhang, Y. Wang and M. Zhu 2014. Fossil *Pongo* from the Early Pleistocene *Gigantopithecus* fauna of Chongzuo, Guangxi, southern China. *Quaternary International* 354:59–67. doi.org/10.1016/j.quaint.2014.01.013

Hooijer, D.A. 1946a. Prehistoric and fossil rhinoceroses from the Malay Archipelago and India. *Zoologische Mededelingen* 26(1):1–138.

Hooijer, D.A. 1946b. Some remarks on recent, prehistoric, and fossil porcupines from the Malay Archipelago. *Zoologische Mededelingen* 26(8):251–267.

Hooijer, D.A. 1947. On fossil and prehistoric remains of *Tapirus* from Java, Sumatra and China. *Zoologische Mededelingen* 27:253–299.

Hooijer, D.A. 1948. Prehistoric teeth of man and of the orang-utan from central Sumatra, with notes on the fossil orang-utan from Java and southern China. *Zoologische Mededelingen* 29:175–301.

Hooijer, D.A. 1955. Fossil Proboscidea from the Malay Archipelago and the Punjab. *Zoologische Verhandelingen* 28(1):1–146.

Hooijer, D.A. 1960. Quaternary gibbons from the Malay Archipelago. *Zoologische Verhandelingen* 46(1):1–42.

Hooijer, D.A. 1962. Quaternary langurs and macaques from the Malay Archipelago. *Zoologische Verhandelingen* 55(1):1–64.

Janssen, R., J.C. Joordens, D.S. Koutamanis, M.R. Puspaningrum, J. de Vos, J.H. van der Lubbe, J.J. Reijmer, O. Hampe and H.B. Vonhof 2016. Tooth enamel stable isotopes of Holocene and Pleistocene fossil fauna reveal glacial and interglacial paleoenvironments of hominins in Indonesia. *Quaternary Science Reviews* 144:145–154. doi.org/10.1016/j.quascirev.2016.02.028

Kahlke, H.D. 1972. A review of the Pleistocene history of the orang-utan (*Pongo* Lacépede 1799). *Asian Perspectives* 15(1):5–14.

Kaifu, Y., I. Kurniawan, D. Yurnaldi, R. Setiawan, E. Setiyabudi, H. Insani, M. Takai, Y. Nishioka, A. Takahashi, F. Aziz and M. Yoneda 2022. Modern human teeth unearthed from below the ~128,000-year-old level at Punung, Java: A case highlighting the problem of recent intrusion in cave sediments. *Journal of Human Evolution* 163:103122. doi.org/10.1016/j.jhevol.2021.103122

Leinders, J.J., M.F. Aziz, P.Y. Sondaar and J. de Vos 1985. The age of the hominid-bearing deposits of Java: State of the art. *Geologie en Mijnbouw* 64:167–173.

Lisiecki, L.E. and M.E. Raymo 2005. A Pliocene-Pleistocene stack of 57 globally distributed benthic $\delta^{18}O$ records. *Paleoceanography* 20:PA1003. doi.org/10.1029/2004PA001071

Louys, J. 2012. Mammal community structure of Sundanese fossil assemblages from the Late Pleistocene, and a discussion on the ecological effects of the Toba eruption. *Quaternary International* 258:80–87. doi.org/10.1016/j.quaint.2011.07.027

Louys, J., D. Curnoe and H. Tong 2007. Characteristics of Pleistocene megafauna extinctions in Southeast Asia. *Palaeogeography, Palaeoclimatology, Palaeoecology* 243(1–2):152–173.

Louys, J., M. Duval, G.J. Price, K. Westaway, Y. Zaim, Y, Rizal, Aswan, M. Puspaningrum, A. Trihascaryo, S. Breitenbach, O. Kwiecien, Y. Cai, P. Higgins, P.C.H. Albers, J. de Vos and P. Roberts 2022. Speleological and environmental history of Lida Ajer cave, western Sumatra. *Philosophical Transactions of the Royal Society B* 377:20200494. doi.org/10.1098/rstb.2020.0494

Louys, J., S. Kealy, S. O'Connor, G.J. Price, S. Hawkins, K. Aplin, Y. Rizal, Y. Zaim, Mahirta, D.A. Tanudirjo, W.D. Santoso, A.R. Hidayah, A. Trihascaryo, R. Wood, J. Bevitt and T. Clark 2017. Differential preservation of vertebrates in Southeast Asian caves. *International Journal of Speleology* 46:379–408. doi.org/10.5038/1827-806X.46.3.2131

Louys, J. and E. Meijaard 2010. Palaeoecology of Southeast Asian megafauna-bearing sites from the Pleistocene and a review of environmental changes in the region. *Journal of Biogeography* 37:1432–1449. doi.org/10.1111/j.1365-2699.2010.02297.x

Louys, J. and P. Roberts 2020. Environmental drivers of megafauna and hominin extinction in Southeast Asia. *Nature* 586:402–406. doi.org/10.1038/s41586-020-2810-y

Louys, J., Y. Zaim, Y. Rizal, M. Puspaningrum, A. Trihascaryo, G.J. Price, A. Petherick, E. Scholtz and L.R.G. DeSantis 2021. Sumatran orangutan diets in the Late Pleistocene as inferred from dental microwear texture analysis. *Quaternary International* 603:74–81. doi.org/10.1016/j.quaint.2020.08.040

Ludwig, K.R. 2003. *User's Manual for Isoplot/Ex Version 3.0: A Geochronological Toolkit for Microsoft Excel.* Berkeley Geochronology Centre, Berkeley.

Ludwig, K.R., K.R. Simmons, B.J. Szabo, I.J. Winograd, J.M. Landwehr, A.C. Riggs and R.J. Hoffman 1992. Mass-spectrometric ^{230}Th-^{234}U-^{238}U dating of the Devils Hole calcite vein. *Science* 258:284–287. doi.org/10.1126/science.258.5080.284

Meijaard, E. 2004. Biogeographic history of the Javan leopard *Panthera pardus* based on a craniometric analysis. *Journal of Mammalogy* 85(2):302–310. doi.org/10.1644/BER-010

Meijaard, E., S. Ni'matullah, R. Dennis, J. Sherman, Onrizal and S.A. Wich 2021. The historical range and drivers of decline of the Tapanuli orangutan. *PLoS ONE* 16(1):e0238087. doi.org/10.1371/journal.pone.0238087

O'Connor, S., A. Barham, K. Aplin and T. Maloney 2017. Cave stratigraphies and cave breccias: Implications for sediment accumulation and removal models and interpreting the record of human occupation. *Journal of Archaeological Science* 77:143–159.

Pike, A.W.G., R.E.M. Hedges and P. van Calsteren 2002. U-series dating of bone using the diffusion-adsorption model. *Geochimica et Cosmochimica Acta* 66(24):4273–4286. doi.org/10.1016/S0016-7037(02)00997-3

Price, G.J., Y.X. Feng, J.X. Zhao and G.E. Webb 2013. Direct U–Th dating of vertebrate fossils with minimum sampling destruction and application to museum specimens. *Quaternary Geochronology* 18:1–8. doi.org/10.1016/j.quageo.2013.07.003

Price, G.J., K.E. Fitzsimmons, A.D. Nguyen, J.X. Zhao, Y.X. Feng, I.H. Sobbe, H. Godthelp, M. Archer and S.J. Hand 2021. New ages of the world's largest-ever marsupial: *Diprotodon optatum* from Pleistocene Australia. *Quaternary International* 603:64–73. doi.org/10.1016/j.quaint.2021.06.013

Pushkina, D., H. Bocherens, Y. Chaimanee and J.J. Jaeger 2010. Stable carbon isotope reconstructions of diet and paleoenvironment from the late Middle Pleistocene Snake Cave in northeastern Thailand. *Naturwissenschaften* 97(3):299–309. doi.org/10.1007/s00114-009-0642-6

Sambridge, M., R. Grün and S. Eggins 2012. U-series dating of bone in an open system: The diffusion-adsorption-decay model. *Quaternary Geochronology* 9:42–53.

Smith, H.E., G.J. Price, M. Duval, K. Westaway, J. Zaim, Y. Rizal, Aswan, M.R. Puspaningrum, A. Trihascaryo, M. Stewart and J. Louys 2021. Taxonomy, taphonomy and chronology of the Pleistocene faunal assemblage at Ngalau Gupin cave, Sumatra. *Quaternary International* 603:40–63. doi.org/10.1016/j.quaint.2021.05.005

Smith, H.E., M.W. Morley and J. Louys 2020. Taphonomic analyses of cave breccia in southeast Asia: A review and future directions. *Open Quaternary* 6(1). openquaternary.com/articles/10.5334/oq.75

Sondaar, P.Y. 1984. Faunal evolution and the mammalian biostratigraphy of Java. In P. Andrews and J.L. Franzen (eds), *The Early Evolution of Man with Special Emphasis on Southeast Asia and Africa*, pp. 219–235. Senckenbergische Naturforschende Gesellschaft, Frankfurt.

Spehar, S.N., D. Sheil, T. Harrison, J. Louys, M. Ancrenaz, A.J. Marshall, S.A. Wich, M.W. Bruford and E. Meijaard 2018. Orangutans venture out of the rainforest and into the Anthropocene. *Science Advances* 4:e1701422. doi.org/10.1126/sciadv.1701422

Storm, P., R. Wood, C. Stringer, A. Bartsiokas, J. de Vos, M. Aubert, L. Kinsley and R. Grün 2013. U-series and radiocarbon analyses of human and faunal remains from Wajak, Indonesia. *Journal of Human Evolution* 64(5):356–365. doi.org/10.1016/j.jhevol.2012.11.002

van den Bergh, G.D., J. de Vos and P.Y. Sondaar 2001. The Late Quaternary palaeogeography of mammal evolution in the Indonesian Archipelago. *Palaeogeography, Palaeoclimatology, Palaeoecology* 171(3–4):385–408. doi.org/10.1016/S0031-0182(01)00255-3

Volmer, R., E. Hölzchen, A. Wurster, M.R. Ferreras and C. Hertler 2017. Did *Panthera pardus* (Linnaeus, 1758) become extinct in Sumatra because of competition for prey? Modeling interspecific competition within the Late Pleistocene carnivore guild of the Padang Highlands, Sumatra. *Palaeogeography, Palaeoclimatology, Palaeoecology* 487:175–186. doi.org/10.1016/j.palaeo.2017.08.032

Westaway, K.E., J. Louys, R. Due Awe, M.J. Morwood, G.J. Price, J.X. Zhao, M. Aubert, R. Joannes-Boyau, T. Smith, M.M. Skinner, T. Compton, R.M. Bailey, G.D. van den Bergh, J. de Vos, A.W.G. Pike, C. Stringer, E.W. Saptomo, Y. Rizal, J. Zaim, W.D. Santoso, A. Trihascaryo, L. Kinsley and B. Sulistyanto 2017. An early modern human presence in Sumatra 73,000–63,000 years ago. *Nature* 548:322–325. doi.org/10.1038/nature23452

Westaway, K.E., M.J. Morwood, R.G. Roberts, A.D. Rokus, J.X. Zhao, P. Storm, F. Aziz, G. van den Bergh, P. Hadi, Jatmiko and J. de Vos 2007. Age and biostratigraphic significance of the Punung Rainforest Fauna, East Java, Indonesia, and implications for *Pongo* and *Homo*. *Journal of Human Evolution* 53:709–717. doi.org/10.1016/j.jhevol.2007.06.002

Westerhold, T., N. Marwan, A.J. Drury, D. Liebrand, C. Agnini, E. Anagnostou, J.S. Barnet, S.M. Bohaty, D. De Vleeschouwer, F. Florindo, T. Frederichs, D.A. Hodell, A.E. Holbourn, D. Kroon, V. Lauretano, K. Littler, L.J. Lourens, M. Lyle, H. Pälike, U. Röhl, J. Tian, R.H. Wilkens, P.A. Wilson and J.C. Zachos 2020. An astronomically dated record of Earth's climate and its predictability over the last 66 million years. *Science* 369:1383–1387. doi.org/10.1126/science.aba6853

Wilkinson, D.M. and H.J. O'Regan 2003. Modelling differential extinctions to understand big cat distribution on Indonesian islands. *Global Ecology and Biogeography* 12(6):519–524. doi.org/10.1046/j.1466-822X.2003.00063.x

Wilting, A., R. Patel, H. Pfestorf, C. Kern, K. Sultan, A. Ario, F. Peñaloza, S. Kramer-Schadt, V. Radchuk, D.W. Foerster and J. Fickel 2016. Evolutionary history and conservation significance of the Javan leopard *Panthera pardus melas*. *Journal of Zoology* 299(4):239–250. doi.org/10.1111/jzo.12348

Wilting, A., R. Sollmann, E. Meijaard, K.M. Helgen and J. Fickel 2012. Mentawai's endemic, relictual fauna: Is it evidence for Pleistocene extinctions on Sumatra? *Journal of Biogeography* 39(9):1608–1620. doi.org/10.1111/j.1365-2699.2012.02717.x

Zhou, H., J. Zhao, W. Qing, Y. Feng and J. Tang 2011. Speleothem-derived Asian summer monsoon variations in central China, 54–46 ka. *Journal of Quaternary Science* 26(8):781–790. doi.org/10.1002/jqs.1506

6

Diversity, population structure and palaeoecology of the Pleistocene large cervids from the Padang Highlands, Sumatra

Ben Gruwier, John de Vos, Mathias Wirkner, Christine Hertler and Kris Kovarovic

Abstract

This chapter deals with the dentognathic remains of the Late Pleistocene large cervids from the Padang Highlands caves in Sumatra. We used linear and geometric morphometric techniques to investigate variation, taxonomic position and body size trends in a dataset of upper and lower molars. Dental mesowear was used to assess dietary preference in a subsample. The results suggest the Padang Highlands cervids belonged to multiple populations of an early stock of *Rusa* deer the size of sambar (*Rusa unicolor*), but morphologically reminiscent of Javan rusa (*Rusa timorensis*). The *Rusa* sp. of Sumatra was reconstructed as a mixed feeder with an increase in the grazing component with age.

Keywords: Cervidae, *Rusa*, taxonomy, Sundaland, morphometrics, mesowear

Abstrak

Bab ini membahas sisa-sisa dentognatik (rahang dan gigi) Cervidae berukuran besar yang berasal dari umur Pleistosen Akhir, yang ditemukan di gua-gua Dataran Tinggi Padang di Sumatra. Kami menggunakan teknik morfometrik linier dan geometris untuk menyelidiki variasi, posisi taksonomi, dan kecendrungan ukuran tubuh dalam kumpulan data geraham atas dan bawah. *Mesowear* gigi digunakan untuk menilai preferensi diet dalam sub-sampel. Hasil penelitian menunjukkan bahwa Cervidae Dataran Tinggi Padang termasuk dalam beberapa populasi dari stok awal jenis *Rusa* seukuran sambar (*Rusa unicolor*), tetapi secara morfologi menyerupai rusa Jawa (*Rusa timorensis*). *Rusa sp.* dari Sumatra direkonstruksi sebagai pemakan tumbuhan campuran, dengan peningkatan komponen merumput seiring bertambahnya usia.

Kata kunci: Cervidae, *Rusa*, taksonomi, Sundaland, morfometrik, *mesowear*

Introduction

Although Eugène Dubois has primarily been credited with the discovery of *Homo erectus* in Java (Dubois 1894; de Vos 2004), another, sometimes-neglected, accomplishment of his was the meticulous collection of large numbers of vertebrate fossils found in association with those hominin remains. These collections have allowed several generations of researchers to develop a more detailed understanding of the biostratigraphy of Java (de Vos 1985, 1996; van den Bergh et al. 2001; von Koenigswald 1933, 1934, 1935) and the palaeobiology of several mammalian groups (Badoux 1959; Hardjasasmita 1987; Hooijer 1958, 1960). However, a large part of Dubois' collection was discovered not on Java but during his preceding 1887–90 stay on Sumatra (de Vos 2004). The fossils he found there can mostly be traced to three karstic limestone caves in the Padang Highlands: the Jambu and Sibrambang caves, close to Tapisello, and the recently rediscovered Lida Ajer Cave near Pajakombo (de Vos 1983; Westaway et al. 2017). While the geological context of Lida Ajer is better understood, movements inside that cave may have redeposited the fossils (Louys et al. 2017), and it is not possible to reassign the finds from Lida Ajer to specific stratigraphic layers (Westaway et al. 2017). At present, very little is known about the geology and taphonomy of Jambu and Sibrambang (Wirkner and Hertler 2019). Therefore, temporal, spatial and altitudinal relationships within these three caves' individual fossil assemblages are unclear.

Although, due to porcupine gnawing (Bacon et al. 2015), the material from these sites consists almost exclusively of teeth, a wide range of mammals are represented (de Vos 1983). The faunal spectrum appears to be primarily composed of extant taxa and suggests the presence of closed forest (Bacon et al. 2015; de Vos 1983; Louys 2007). As a consequence, earlier researchers have generally considered the fossils to be of Holocene age (Dubois 1891; Hooijer 1960, 1962) and of limited relevance to questions of human evolution and palaeobiogeography. This assumption was later amended by de Vos (1983), who suggested that the Sumatran material is of early Late Pleistocene age and probably correlates with the Punung faunal stage of Java, a notion later confirmed by chronometric studies (Chapter 5, this volume; Skelton 1985; Westaway et al. 2007, 2017). Several absolute dates have been obtained for Lida Ajer (73–63 ka; Westaway et al. 2017), Sibrambang (80–60 ka; Bacon et al. 2015) and Jambu (>70 ka; Bacon et al. 2015; Skelton 1985), and today little doubt is left about their ages being Pleistocene. Nevertheless, a more recent study (Chapter 5, this volume) suggests that the individual cave assemblages may represent a mix of fossils with different ages, ranging widely between the Middle and Late Pleistocene. That being said, there is no doubt that our increased understanding of the chronology, in addition to the rediscovery of two Pleistocene *Homo sapiens* teeth in the Lida Ajer assemblage (Westaway et al. 2017) has reignited interest in Dubois' Sumatran collections.

Despite having attracted less attention than the Javan fossil record, the material from the Padang Highlands caves has been examined in several studies (Hooijer 1948, 1960, 1962). Although part of the ungulate fauna was described by Hooijer (1958), the Cervidae have only recently become the focus of more detailed study (Gruwier et al. 2015; Wirkner and Hertler 2019). In part, the omission of this family can be explained by the complexity of cervid evolution in the wider Indomalayan region (e.g. Heckeberg 2020). Most of the known Pleistocene taxa have been described from material found in Java, but the identification of individual fossils from that island remains problematic because the original descriptions have often been based on isolated teeth or antler fragments (Dubois 1891, 1908; Martin 1886; von Koenigswald 1933, 1934). In the absence of a comprehensive synthesis of the Javan cervids, it remains challenging to consider the position of the Sumatran fossils within a wider evolutionary framework for the region.

Regardless of these drawbacks, deer form a large and important component of the Lida Ajer, Jambu and Sibrambang assemblages. In the Dubois collection, of the approximately 10,000 remains from the three cave sites, about 24% are currently catalogued as cervid. More than half of these are of a small type identified as Indian muntjac (*Muntiacus* sp.) (de Vos 1983). Most of the other fossils belong to one or more larger forms, typically placed within the genus *Rusa* (de Vos 1983; Gruwier et al. 2015). The taxonomic status of these large deer, and whether one or multiple species are present, remains uncertain. Previous morphometric analyses have, nevertheless, suggested a close relationship between some of the large deer fossils and *Rusa unicolor*, *Rusa timorensis*, or *Cervus kendengensis*, a Javan species from the Pleistocene that is often considered a member of the genus *Rusa* (Gruwier et al. 2015).

In addition to contributing to our understanding of cervid evolution, the Sumatran fossils are also significant in that they represent a valuable resource that gives ecological context to the early presence of hominins in Southeast Asia. Irrespective of their taxonomic status, new methods—such as ecomorphological analysis, community structure analysis, dental wear studies and biomolecular analyses—make fossil deer remains useful for palaeoenvironmental reconstruction (Amano et al. 2016; Curran 2012; Li et al. 2017; Louys 2012). During the last few years, the Sumatran cervids have been included in broader palaeoecological studies of the region (Bacon et al. 2015; Louys 2007, 2012; Louys and Meijaard 2010), stable isotope analyses (Janssen 2017; Janssen et al. 2016) and mesowear studies (Wirkner and Hertler 2019). However, no study is currently available that deals specifically with the larger deer or that summarises the results of earlier work on them.

In this chapter, we examine the taxonomic status, population structure and ecology of the large cervids from the Padang Highlands using a multiproxy approach. To assess diversity and taxonomic status in the assemblage, we used a comparative morphometric approach on a number of extant and fossil deer molars. Dental measurements were also used to explore the sample for body size trends, sexual size dimorphism, and their potential ecological implications. Dental mesowear analysis on upper and lower molars was used to evaluate aspects of dietary ecology.

Materials

For our linear morphometric analyses, we used length and width measurements of 116 lower third molars of fossil *Rusa* sp. from Sumatra. The measurements were taken at Naturalis Biodiversity Center in Leiden. Five of the specimens could be specifically traced to Sibrambang cave, while the others came from Padang Highlands caves, most probably from either Jambu, Lida Ajer or Sibrambang. Our comparative sample consisted of 223 molars of extant species, primarily collected at the Natural History Museum, London; the Muséum National d'Histoire Naturelle, Paris; the National Museum of Scotland, Edinburgh; Naturalis Biodiversity Center, Leiden; the Royal Belgian Institute of Natural Sciences, Brussels; Natuurhistorisch Museum Rotterdam; Ghent University Museum; and the archaeozoology labs of the University of Lille and the Center for Artefact Research, Mechelen. (See Table 6.1; see doi.org/10.5281/zenodo.5876370 for the supplementary data.) A limited number of measurements were taken from the literature (Dong and Chen 2015; Sykes et al. 2011 and supplementary data therein).

Standardised photographs of a smaller number (*n* = 43) of upper third molars were taken at the same institutions for geometric morphometric (GMM) analysis (Table 6.1). This included eight fossil *Rusa* sp. specimens from the Padang Highlands collection at Naturalis Biodiversity Center and 35 specimens belonging to five extant species of the genus *Rusa*. Pathological teeth and specimens with a severe degree of attrition were excluded to avoid complicating the placement of the landmarks. When possible, right upper molars were selected, but in a few cases left ones were included by digitally mirroring them in tpsDig 2.16 (Rohlf 2004).

Table 6.1: Numbers of upper molars (m3 sup) and lower third molars (m3 inf) used in linear and geometric morphometric (GMM) analysis, calculation of body mass (see Figure 6.4) and sex determination.

Taxon	Number of specimens	
	Linear morphometric analysis (m3 inf)	GMM analysis (m3 sup)
Rusa sp. (Padang Highlands fossils)	116[a]	8
Rusa unicolor (sambar)	30	12
Rusa timorensis (Javan rusa)	20	10
Rusa alfredi (Prince Alfred's deer)	4	2
Rusa marianna (Philippine deer)	5	1
Cervus kendengensis (Javan fossils)	28	10
Cervus elaphus (red deer)	16	—
Rucervus eldii (Eld's deer)	12	—
Rucervus duvaucelii (swamp deer)	7	—
Axis axis (spotted deer)	71[b]	—
Axis porcinus (hog deer)	24	—
Axis kuhlii (Bawean deer)	2	—
Dama dama (fallow deer)	32	—
Total	367	43

[a] Includes five specimens specifically from Sibrambang.
[b] Includes 27 specimens of one population of *A. axis* from Kanha National Park, India.
Source: Authors' data.

After excluding a number of specimens that were insufficiently preserved, a sample of 27 upper and lower molars from the Padang Highlands was retained for mesowear analysis. Because both anterior and posterior cusps were assessed, this corresponded to 39 usable cusps (see Table 6.2). We included first, second and third molars, but in several instances the rank was unclear, and specimens were designated as upper molars (M1/2/3 sup) or lower first or second molars (m1/2 inf). As with the teeth used in our morphometric analyses, most of the material could be assigned only broadly to the Padang Highlands caves, not to a specific site. In only five cases could the provenance be traced to Sibrambang cave.

Table 6.2: Materials used for tooth age estimation, individual dental age stage, mesowear analysis, body mass estimation and sex determination.

Fossil site	Tooth position	Wear stage: number of teeth / usable cusps						
		Total	0	1	2	3	4	5
Padang Highlands	M1/2/3 sup	20/28	—	3/5	10/14	5/6	2/3	—
	m1/2 inf	1/1	—	—	—	—	1/1	—
	m3 inf	1/2	1/2	—	—	—	—	—
Sibrambang	m3 inf	5/8	—	—	2/4	2/3	1/1	—

Note: The numbers of teeth and cusps are sorted by fossil site, tooth position and wear stage.
Source: Authors' data.

Methods

Linear and GMM analyses were used to explore diversity and taxonomy in our dataset of fossil teeth. First, a linear morphometric analysis was conducted on a sample of lower third molars from the Padang Highlands caves, in comparison with a series of extant Southeast Asian species and a sample of *Cervus kendengensis* specimens from the Pleistocene of Java. Length (Dap) and width (Dt) measurements were taken following Heintz (1970) and plotted on an XY-graph using PAST 2.17b (Hammer et al. 2001). Statistical significance ($p < 0.05$) of between-group differences was tested using multivariate analysis of variance (MANOVA) followed by Mann-Whitney pairwise comparisons. Holm-Bonferroni corrected p-values were used to minimise the family-wise error rate (Holm 1979).

For the lower third molars used in our morphometric analyses (Table 6.1), and for the smaller, more diverse sample of upper and lower molars subsequently used for mesowear analysis (Table 6.2), body mass and sex were assessed. We reconstructed total body mass using regressions on linear dimensions, based on Janis (1990) (Table 6.3). Length (Dap), width (Dt) and surface area (Dap × Dt) were used as variables. To assess the precision of the estimate, we used the correlation coefficient for each of the regressions provided by Janis (1990), as well as the per cent standard error of the estimate (%*SEE* in Table 6.3) and the per cent prediction error (%*PE*). These values show that, despite the robust correlation coefficient, the standard error of the estimate and the prediction error are high in all of the equations. The regression gives values that indicate a range rather than an absolute value. The reason for this is that body mass is not a constant but varies with sex, age and other life history traits. In order to control for the effects of age, we used only permanent molars belonging to adult individuals. Furthermore, Janis's (1990) method accounts for the effects of sex by using a comparative dataset for body size based on males only. Although this leads to reconstructed values that overestimate body mass in female individuals, it is a useful approach in taxa with high sexual dimorphism such as cervids, because values based on an unsexed regression sample would result in averaged body masses, which do not represent either sex. Taking these potentially confounding factors into account, we used an average of the predicted body mass calculated for each of the three variables for further analysis.

Table 6.3: Regressions applied on upper and lower molars to calculate body mass and sex.

Regression used for body mass reconstruction per element	Slope	Intercept	R2	% SEE	% PE	Source
m3 inf length	3.143	0.799	0.957	27.4	19.1	Janis (1990)
m3 inf width	3.000	1.877	0.880	49.6	35.9	Janis (1990)
m3 inf area	1.561	1.346	0.953	28.8	19.9	Janis (1990)
M3 sup length	3.281	1.073	0.959	26.8	18.3	Janis (1990)
M3 sup width	3.286	1.375	0.921	38.7	23.8	Janis (1990)
M3 sup area	1.651	1.214	0.954	28.2	19.2	Janis (1990)
Female body mass inferred from male body mass in *Rusa* sp.	0.577	8.036	0.805	—	—	Data from Nowak (1999), A.T. Smith and Xie (2008), Francis (2008)

% *SEE*: per cent standard error of the estimate.

% *PE*: per cent prediction error.

Note: Where the rank of a molar (i.e. whether it was a first or second molar) was unclear, we considered the tooth a second molar for the purposes of the regressions.

Source: Authors' data based on regressions by Janis (1990), Francis (2008), Nowak (1999) and A.T. Smith and Xie (2008).

The calculated body masses were then used to predict sex for each specimen. This was done by considering the largest individual in the sample as male and inferring maximum body mass for the largest female by a regression based on published pairs of male and female body masses from recent representatives of the genus *Rusa* (Francis 2008; Nowak 1999; Smith A.T. and Xie 2008). Specimens with values below the maximum female body mass were considered female.

As it was unclear whether the Padang Highlands fossils represent one or multiple species, we conducted disparity analyses on the fossil molar dataset in comparison with a number of extant cervid species. To accomplish this, we took two approaches to test if the magnitude of variance was significantly larger in *Rusa* sp. than is normally expected in related species or populations. In our first approach, we calculated the standard deviation (SD) of the regressions of the linear data against body mass and expressed it as a percentage of body mass (% SD). As an additional coherence test, this value was then compared to the maximum prediction error of the regression. If % SD was lower than the maximum prediction error, this indicated that the value was coherent and not confounded by additional sources of variation.

Our second method to assess disparity in the samples consisted of conducting a series of pairwise Levene's tests (Cardini et al. 2007; Hallgrímsson et al. 2006) directly on tooth length (Dap) and on tooth surface area (Dap × Dt). Levene's F compares the within-group variance between different populations by calculating the deviation of each specimen from the group mean (Cardini et al. 2007). These deviations are then compared between different groups via MANOVA (Cardini et al. 2007). An F-statistic is used to test the null hypothesis that two compared groups are randomly drawn from the combined set of mean deviations (Hallgrímsson et al. 2006). If the (Holm-Bonferroni corrected) p-values are below the α-value ($p < 0.05$), the difference in variance between populations is not expected to be equal.

As a complementary technique to explore morphological variation, we conducted a GMM analysis on a small sample of upper third molars of fossil *Rusa* sp. from Sumatra, fossil *Cervus kendengensis* from Java and four extant *Rusa* species (Table 6.1). GMM not only allows for the exclusion of isometric size effects from the dataset (Zelditch et al. 2004) but also has the advantage of picking up subtle morphological differences and has already proven to be a powerful method for studying phenotypic diversity in artiodactyls (Brophy et al. 2014; Cucchi et al. 2009; Evin et al. 2013). The GMM model used here consisted of an improved version of an earlier model by Gruwier et al. (2015), where shape was defined by placing a number of homologous landmarks at discrete anatomical loci along the outline of the third molar (Gruwier et al. 2015; Zelditch et al. 2004). Standardised photographs were taken of the occlusal surface, using the protocol described in Gruwier et al. (2015). After placing eight type I and type II landmarks (Baab et al. 2012) on the outline of each tooth using tpsDig 2.16 (Rohlf 2004) (see Figure 6.1), the Cartesian coordinate data were extracted and further analysed in PAST 2.17b (Hammer et al. 2001). Here, we used a generalised Procrustes superimposition to scale, rotate and translate the objects, to exclude all information irrelevant to shape (Walker 2000). As this translation results in a projection of the data in a Euclidean space tangential to the Procrustes shape space (Viscosi and Cardini 2011), we tested the accuracy of this approximation with tpsSmall 1.20 (Rohlf 2003).

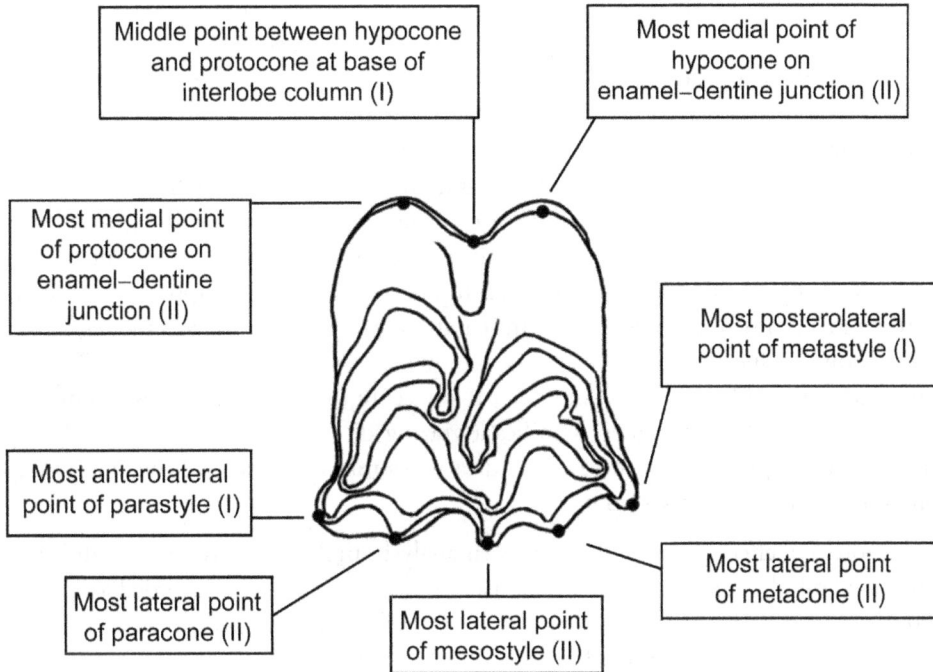

Figure 6.1: Landmarks recorded on the upper third molar, with illustration of the occlusal surface and description of landmark location and type.

(I) Type I landmark.

(II) Type II landmark.

Source: Image by the authors.

To explore morphological variation in the Procrustes-transformed coordinate data, we first conducted a between-groups principal component analysis (PCA). In this approach, eigenvectors are derived from the variance–covariance matrix of the group means instead of the individual specimens, which has the advantages that the original Procrustes distances in shape space are preserved and differences between populations are emphasised (Seetah et al. 2012). We used a non-parametric MANOVA, followed by Mann-Whitney pairwise comparisons, on the relevant principal component scores to assess the statistical significance ($p < 0.05$) of the cluster separations (Gruwier and Kovarovic 2021; Hou et al. 2021; Marramà and Kriwet 2017; Polly et al. 2013; Schutz et al. 2009). A permutational test was selected because the assumptions required for parametric testing are not necessarily met by data that results from GMM analysis (Cardini et al. 2015; Gruwier and Kovarovic 2021; Lopez-Lazaro et al. 2018). The number of relevant components retained for analysis was indicated by a scree plot of the eigenvalue distribution (Jackson 1993). Shape changes along the axes of variation were visualised with thin-plate spline deformation grids.

To further assess the relationship between different members of the genus *Rusa*, and to maximise between-group variation, a canonical variates analysis was run on a subsample including *R. unicolor*, *R. timorensis*, *C. kendengensis* and fossil *Rusa* sp. from Sumatra. As with the PCA, the significance ($p < 0.05$) of between-group differences was tested using a non-parametric MANOVA with associated pairwise comparisons. This was conducted on the first two axes, which together explained the majority of the variation. The Holm-Bonferroni procedure was used as a multiple correction technique (Holm 1979). Reclassification rates with jackknifed cross-validation were provided for the different assigned groups.

Finally, dental mesowear analysis was used to explore the dietary ecology of the cervids from the Padang Highlands. In this method, gross patterns of molar wear are categorised by assessing tooth cusp shape and relief, as these aspects are indicative of the abrasiveness of consumed dietary plant matter (Fortelius and Solounias 2000). Consequently, mesowear analysis can be used as a proxy for vegetation structure and to help infer palaeoenvironmental conditions. In this study, we recorded the mesowear signal on the buccal side of the upper molars and on the lingual side of the lower molars, from a series of digital photographs of the teeth. We used a ruler-based mesowear II approach that distinguishes seven mesowear stages (MWS) and combines cusp shape and relief into a single value (Ackermans 2020). This digital ruminant ruler is superimposed on the photographs of the molars and scored according to a protocol developed by Wirkner and Hertler (2019). In this model, MWS 0, 2, 4 and 6 correspond to specific combinations of mesowear variables, while MWS 1, 3 and 5 represent intermediate stages. On the ruminant ruler, a low score (MWS 0) indicates a browsing diet, while a high score (MWS 3 or higher) signifies a grazing diet with soft to increasingly dry grasses. The intermediate stages (MWS 1 and 2) are indicative of mixed diets with either a browsing or a grazing component (Wirkner and Hertler 2019).

To account for the potential effect of age in the mesowear analysis, molars were assigned to different tooth age classes. Based on photographs of the occlusal surface, wear stages were recorded according to Wirkner and Hertler's (2019) protocol. This tooth age reflects the degree of wear, but not necessarily the absolute age of an individual. In part this is because molars at different positions in the tooth row are subject to different rates of wear (Wirkner and Hertler 2019). To convert the wear stages of molar cusps of different rank to usable ontogenetic categories, we translated the wear stages into the individual dental age stages (IDAS) of Anders et al. (2011:547), adapted by Wirkner and Hertler (2019). Six age categories are identified in this scheme: 'prenatal' (0), 'infant' (1), 'juvenile' (2), 'adult' (3), 'late adult' (4) and 'senile' (5). Except for the lower third molars, we designated every tooth as a second molar, which is the standard tooth position in Fortelius and Solounias' (2000) mesowear method. Body masses were calculated using the regressions provided by Janis (1990), which are shown in Table 6.3, and the boundary value that was calculated for the whole *Rusa* dataset was used to delineate the presumably male portion of the sample from the potentially female specimens.

Results

When plotting the length and width measurements of the lower third molar of seven extant Southeast Asian species, Pleistocene *Cervus kendengensis*, and *Rusa* sp. from the Padang Highlands, there was visual separation between several groups (see Figure 6.2). A MANOVA confirmed that overall group differences were significant ($p < 0.01$). Associated pairwise comparisons indicated that most between-group differences were significant (Table 6.4). Members of the genus *Axis* gave lower scores than members of the genera *Rusa* and *Rucervus*. *Rusa unicolor* was the largest species and gave higher scores than the other extant species, except for *Rucervus duvaucelii*, whose score did not differ significantly from that of *Rusa unicolor* ($p = 1$). *Rusa timorensis* and *Cervus kendengensis* were significantly smaller than *Rusa unicolor* ($p < 0.01$) and *Rucervus duvaucelii* ($p < 0.01$). The fossil *Rusa* specimens from the Padang Highlands were visually of the same size as *Rusa unicolor*, but the MANOVA suggested that this group was significantly different from all the other groups ($p < 0.01$).

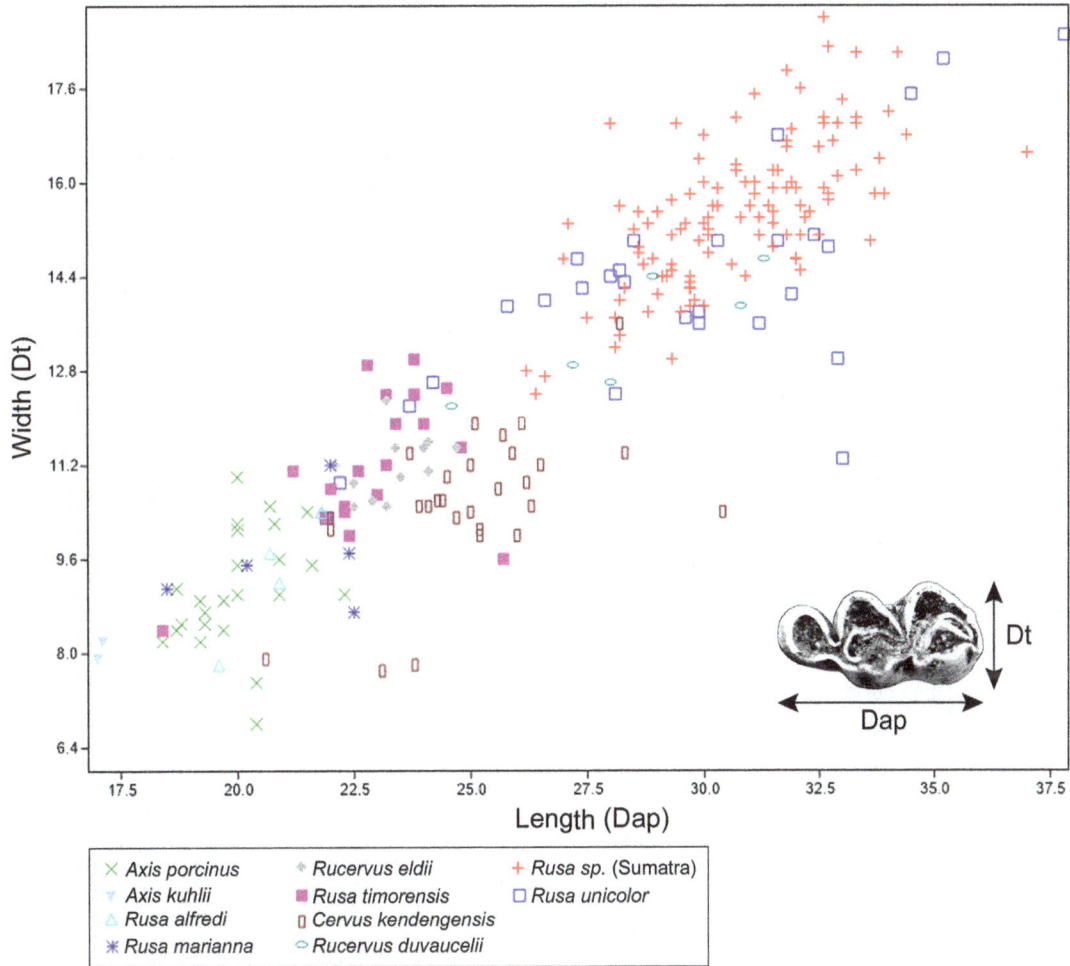

Figure 6.2: Length (Dap) and width (Dt) measurements of Padang Highlands *Rusa* sp., Pleistocene *Cervus kendengensis* and extant Southeast Asian Cervini.

Source: Image by the authors.

Table 6.4. Holm-Bonferroni corrected *p*-values of pairwise comparisons of a multivariate analysis of variance on length (Dap) and width (Dt) measurements of lower third molars.

Taxon	Rusa unicolor	Rusa timor-ensis	Axis porcinus	Rusa sp. (Padang)	Ruc-ervus alfredi	Rusa eldii	Axis kuhlii	Rucervus duvau-celii	Rusa marianna
R. timorensis	<0.01*	—	—	—	—	—	—	—	—
A. porcinus	<0.01*	<0.01*	—	—	—	—	—	—	—
R. sp. (Padang fossils)	<0.01*	<0.01*	<0.01*	—	—	—	—	—	—
R. alfredi	<0.01*	1	1	<0.01*	—	—	—	—	—
R. eldii	<0.01*	1	<0.01*	<0.01*	1	—	—	—	—
A. kuhlii	<0.01*	0.18	1	<0.01*	1	0.43	—	—	—
R. duvaucelii	1	<0.01*	<0.01*	<0.01*	<0.01*	0.05*	0.11	—	—
R. marianna	<0.01*	1	1	<0.01*	1	1	0.23	0.05*	—
C. kendengensis	<0.01*	<0.01*	<0.01*	<0.01*	0.12	0.02*	<0.01*	<0.01*	0.05*

* Significant values ($p \leq 0.05$).

Source: Authors' data.

Levene's test on lower third molar length and surface area gave insight into the intraspecific variation of seven different taxa (see Table 6.5 and Figure 6.3). In these results, F-values significantly deviating from 1 indicate a difference between the two groups' variances. This showed that, as far as molar length and surface area were concerned, intraspecific variability was unequal among the species. The species of the genera *Axis* and *Dama* demonstrated a relatively low variance, and the difference between these taxa was not significant (as shown in Table 6.5). However, when *C. elaphus*, and especially *R. unicolor*, were compared with the other species, Levene's F was in most cases significantly different from 1, suggesting that the variance of *C. elaphus* and *R. unicolor* was higher (Table 6.5). *R. timorensis* had a significantly lower variance in length than *R. unicolor*, but this was similar to that of the *Axis* species. In the *Rusa* fossils from the Padang Highlands, the variance was similar to that in *R. timorensis* and, especially, *C. elaphus*, lower than in *R. unicolor*, and higher than in the genera *Axis* and *Dama* (Table 6.5, Figure 6.3).

Table 6.5: Results of Levene's tests on tooth length (Dap) and surface area (Dap × Dt).

Taxa	Length (Dap)			Surface area (Dap × Dt)		
	Levene's F	*p*	*R2*	Levene's F	*p*	*R2*
A. axis × Rusa sp.[a]	13.44	<0.01*	0.06	12.97	<0.01*	0.06
A. axis × Axis porcinus	2.62	0.7	0.02	6.09	0.16	0.06
A. axis × Rusa unicolor	67.33	<0.01*	0.40	18.30	<0.01*	0.15
A. axis × Rusa timorensis	0.01	1	0.01	0.11	1	0.01
A. axis × Dama dama	0.10	1	0.01	11.37	0.01*	0.11
A. axis × Cervus elaphus	8.99	0.04*	0.09	5.39	0.18	0.05
A. porcinus × R. sp.[a]	12.77	<0.01*	0.09	13.31	<0.01*	0.08
A. porcinus × R. unicolor	29.60	<0.01*	0.37	11.27	<0.01*	0.18
A. porcinus × R. timorensis	1.33	1	0.03	3.17	0.49	0.07
A. porcinus × D. dama	1.33	1	0.02	1.73	0.77	0.03
A. porcinus × C. elaphus	6.59	0.14	0.14	9.64	0.03*	0.20
R. unicolor × R. sp.[a]	60.99	<0.01*	0.30	5.65	0.17	0.03
R. unicolor × R. timorensis	20.50	<0.01*	0.31	6.17	0.16	0.11
R. unicolor × D. dama	32.36	<0.01*	0.36	12.24	0.12	0.20
R. unicolor × C. elaphus	6.59	0.14	0.13	1.53	0.77	0.03
R. timorensis × R. sp.[a]	4.02	0.36	0.02	4.96	0.19	0.03
R. timorensis × C. elaphus	2.84	0.7	0.07	2.92	0.49	0.07
D. dama × R. sp.[a]	8.07	<0.01*	0.05	16.63	<0.01*	0.10
D. dama × C. elaphus	5.21	0.24	0.10	11.88	0.02*	0.24
C. elaphus × R. sp.[a]	1.75	0.93	0.01	0.01	1	0.01

* Significant values ($p < 0.05$).

[a] Padang Highlands fossils.

Source: Authors' data.

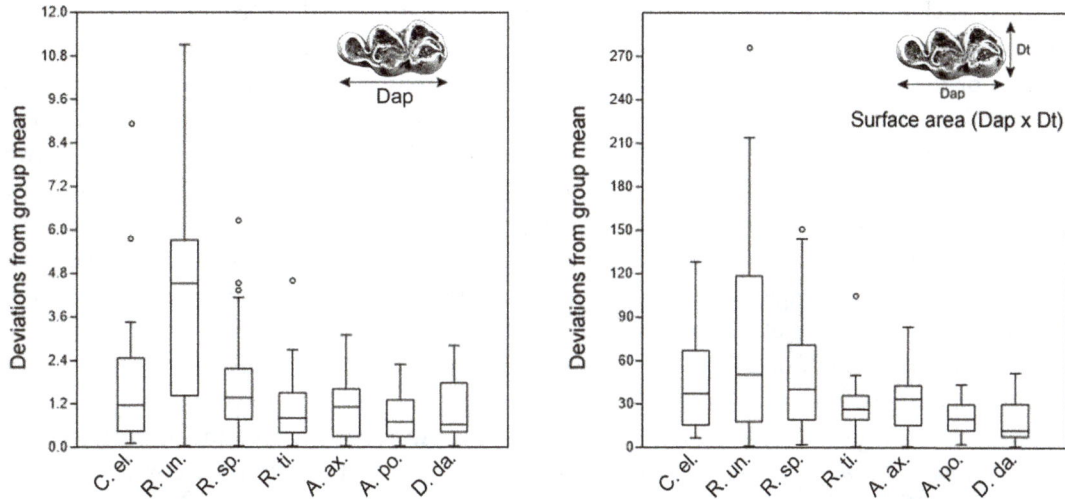

Figure 6.3: Box plots of deviations from group mean per species, for lower third molar length and surface area.

Note: C. el = *Cervus elaphus*, R. un = *Rusa unicolor*, R. sp. = *Rusa* sp. (Padang), R. ti = *Rusa timorensis*, A. ax = *Axis axis*, A. po = *Axis porcinus*, D. da = *Dama dama*.

Source: Authors' data.

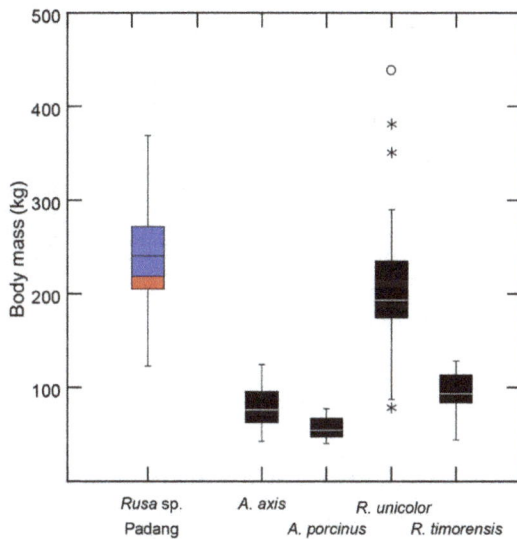

Figure 6.4: Reconstructed body masses of the *Rusa* species from the Padang Highlands compared to a sample of recent species, namely *Axis axis*, *Axis porcinus*, *Rusa unicolor* and *Rusa timorensis*.

Source: Authors' data.

We then calculated body masses for fossil *Rusa* sp. from the Padang Highlands based on teeth ($n = 134$), and for a subsample of four recent species ($n = 167$, Table 6.1) for comparative purposes (see Figure 6.4). The average body mass in the fossil *Rusa* sample was 241 ± 54 kg. Absolute values corresponded to recent representatives of *R. unicolor* rather than of the smaller *Axis* species or the endemic *R. timorensis* from Java. Individual body masses in the fossil *Rusa* sample ranged from 123 kg to 369 kg. The range covered by the values matched the corresponding range in the *R. unicolor* sample better than that in any other species included in our comparative sample. *R. timorensis* was substantially smaller.

Along with geographical range, another source of variability in a sample of body masses is sex, particularly in species with a high degree of sexual dimorphism. We assessed sex-specific body masses in our dataset by inferring a boundary value for female body masses from the largest individual body mass occurring in the sample (438 kg). This boundary value was 221 kg. Assuming all specimens displaying body masses with a higher value represent males, and all individuals with a lower body mass represent females, our dataset included 85 male and 52 female individuals.

For the GMM analysis, we first established that the projection of the shape coordinates in tangent shape space was adequate for further analysis (slope = 0.998, p = 1). A PCA on the Procrustes residuals of the Padang Highlands molars and of molars from five extant members of the genus *Rusa* revealed substantial shape variation (see Figure 6.5). As indicated by a plot of the eigenvalue distribution (see the supplementary data at doi.org/10.5281/zenodo.5876370), the first two components, which explained 90.4% of the variation, were retained as relevant. The thin-plate spline deformation grids revealed that the shape changes along the first axis were mainly expressed as a difference in relief between the parastyle, paracone, metastyle and metacone and a difference in medio-lateral depth (see Figures 6.1 and 6.5). The second axis showed that there was variation in the relief between the base of the interlobe column and the hypocone and protocone, a difference in antero-posterior length of the medial relative to the lateral side, and a variation in the more or less medial position of the parastyle and metastyle relative to the paracone, mesostyle and metacone. The scatter plot (Figure 6.5) revealed a substantial overlap in shape between the Sumatran fossils and *R. unicolor*, *R. timorensis* and *C. kendengensis*. *R. marianna* and *R. alfredi* were well separated, especially on PC1, and indicated the presence of a different morphology in each of these island forms. Pairwise comparisons following a MANOVA on the relevant components (PC1 and PC2, p < 0.01) confirmed that *Cervus kendengensis*, *R.timorensis*, *R. unicolor* and the Padang Highlands fossil *Rusa* sp. were not significantly different from each other (see Table 6.6). Despite their visual separation, *R. alfredi* and *R. marianna* did not significantly differ from the other species after multiple corrections (see Table 6.6).

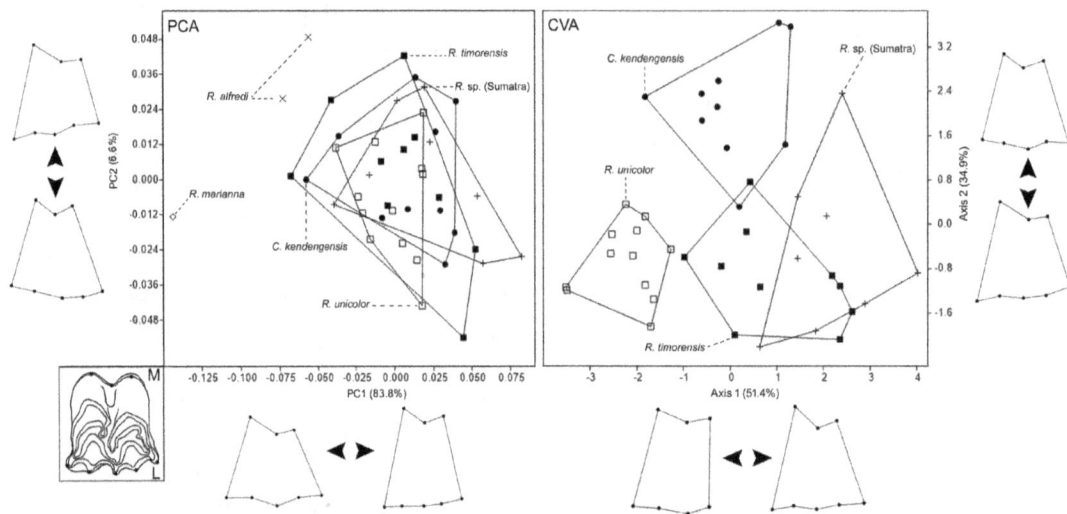

Figure 6.5: Principal component analysis and canonical variates analysis on *Rusa* sp. from the Padang Highlands and several species of the genus *Rusa* and the fossil *Cervus kendengensis* from Java.

Note: Shape changes along the axes are visualised with thin-plate spline deformation grids showing hypothetical extreme values at the end of each axis.

PC = principal component; CV = canonical variate.

L = lateral; M = medial.

R. = *Rusa*; C. = *Cervus*.

Source: Image by the authors.

Table 6.6: Pairwise comparisons of a multivariate analysis of variance (MANOVA) on the first two axes of the principal component analysis (PCA) and canonical variates analysis (CVA) on members of the genus *Rusa* and the closely related *Cervus kendengensis*, and reclassification rates with jackknifed cross-validation for the CVA.

MANOVA PCA					
Taxon	***R. timorensis***	***R. unicolor***	***R. sp. (Padang)***	***C. kendengensis***	***R. alfredi***
R. unicolor	0.150	—	—	—	—
R. sp. (Padang)	0.168	0.190	—	—	—
C. kendengensis	0.168	0.198	1	—	—
R. alfredi	0.168	0.248	1	1	—
R. marianna	0.176	0.742	1	1	1

MANOVA CVA			
Taxon	***R. timorensis***	***R. unicolor***	***R. sp. (Padang)***
R. unicolor	<0.01*	—	—
R. sp. (Padang)	0.13	<0.01*	—
C. kendengensis	<0.01*	<0.01*	<0.01*

Reclassification rates CVA					
Taxon	***R. timorensis***	***R. unicolor***	***R. sp. (Padang)***	***C. kendengensis***	**Correct %**
R. timorensis	3	3	4	0	30
R. unicolor	2	10	0	0	83
R. sp. (Padang)	3	1	2	2	25
C. kendengensis	1	2	1	6	60

Note: Numbers represent p-values. * Significant value ($p \leq 0.05$).

R. = *Rusa*; *C.* = *Cervus*. Padang = Padang Highlands fossils.

Source: Authors' data.

To obtain a better understanding of the relationship between the Padang Highlands fossils and *C. kendengensis*, *R. unicolor* and *R. timorensis*, a CVA was run on a subsample that included only these species. A scatter plot of the first two axes revealed a better visual separation for these groups than the PCA. (Both the CVA and the PCA scatter plots are shown in Figure 6.5). The Padang Highlands specimens overlapped mostly with *R. timorensis* and were well separated from *R. unicolor* on the first axis. The extinct *C. kendengensis* from Java gave similar scores on the first axis as *R. timorensis* and *Rusa* sp. (Padang) but gave higher scores on the second axis than the other three forms. A MANOVA on the first two axes (see Table 6.6) showed that these differences were significant ($p < 0.01$), with pairwise comparisons indicating that only the difference between *R. timorensis* and *Rusa* sp. (Padang) was not significant ($p = 0.13$). In general, this was confirmed by the reclassification rates for the CVA (also shown in Table 6.6). Of the *R. unicolor* specimens, 83.3% were correctly reclassified with jackknifed cross-validation, suggesting an idiosyncratic shape for this group. *R. timorensis* and *Rusa* sp. (Padang) showed lower reclassification rates (respectively 30% and 25%), but the majority (66%) of the specimens in either of those two groups were reclassified correctly or as part of the other group. Morphologically, these between-group differences were expressed as a less medially extended protocone and a more laterally placed metacone and metastyle, relative to the parastyle and paracone, in specimens with a low score on the first axis (*R. unicolor*). Specimens with a higher score on this axis (*R. timorensis*, *C. kendengensis* and *Rusa* sp. [Padang]) had a more medially extended protocone and a more medially placed metacone and metastyle. Variation along the second axis was mainly expressed as a less laterally extended parastyle in specimens with a high score (*C. kendengensis*).

For the mesowear analysis, we first assigned teeth to different age classes. The analysed teeth ranged from MWS 2 to MWS 4. In IDAS terms, the sample comprised juvenile (IDAS 2), adult (IDAS 3) and late adult (IDAS 4) individuals. IDAS 3 was represented by the most specimens (over 60%), while the number of IDAS 2 and IDAS 4 specimens was almost even (see Figure 6.6). Our initial sample of teeth included 54 cusps from 27 teeth that each had at least one intact cusp. Because they were damaged, 15 cusps were excluded. Hence, 39 cusps were usable for further analysis (see Table 6.2). Body masses in this sample varied between 123 kg and 292 kg. The range of variability was thus smaller than in the extended sample of *Rusa* sp. The average body mass was 210 ± 44 kg. According to the higher boundary value obtained from the lower-molar dataset, 8 of the specimens represented male individuals and 19 represented females.

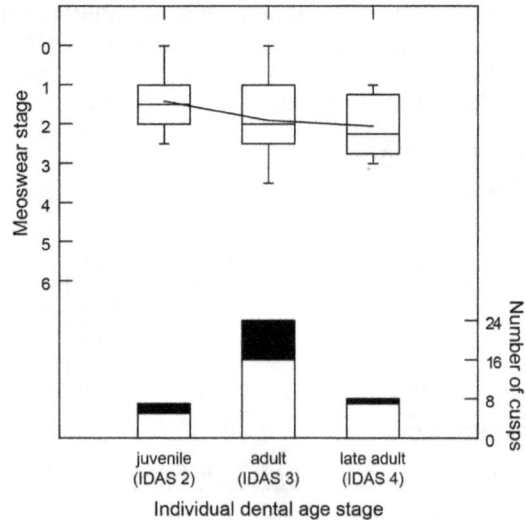

Figure 6.6: Mesowear signal of *Rusa* sp. (Padang Highlands fossils) at different individual dental age stages (IDAS).

Note: The line on the box plot shows the arithmetic mean. The bar chart shows the sample sizes; black = male; white = female. IDASs not represented in the sample are not shown.

Source: Image by the authors.

Our results illustrated an increase in the range of the mesowear score from juvenile to adult. As the box plots (see Figure 6.6) show, the greatest range occurred in IDAS 3 and the smallest range in IDAS 4. While IDAS 2 and IDAS 3 included cusps at MWS 0, the minimum MWS of IDAS 4 was 1. IDAS 3 had the highest maximum MWS (3.5), while IDAS 2 had the lowest maximum MWS (2.5). The interquartile ranges of the MWS of IDAS 3 and IDAS 4 were identical, while IDAS 2's was smaller. The median MWS of IDAS3 was higher than that of IDAS 2.

There was also a rise in the mean MWS as IDAS increased: from 1.4 ± 0.8 at IDAS 2 through 1.9 ± 0.9 at IDAS 3 to 2.1 ± 0.8 at IDAS 4 (see Figure 6.6). Therefore, the examined *Rusa* sp. from the Padang Highlands was classified as a mixed feeder at all three examined IDASs. However, there was an increase in the grazing component during ontogeny, resulting in a shift from the browsing side of the spectrum (at IDAS 2) to the grazing one (at IDAS 4).

Discussion

When considering the results of the dietary analysis (see Figure 6.6), we noted that our data showed a Gaussian age distribution. This was to be expected, as the adult stage covers the longest period of an individual's life history (Anders et al. 2011). Therefore, in a naturally accumulated population, most teeth are expected to be at this age stage. The mesowear analysis shows a mixed-feeder signal in all the represented age stages. Enamel stable isotope data published by Janssen et al. (2016), which was collected on a different series of Padang Highlands *Rusa*, showed a predominantly C$_3$ signal that frequently had δ^{13}C lower than −12 permil (Janssen et al. 2016 and supplementary data therein). Integrating these data with our mesowear results indicates that fossil *Rusa* sp. primarily fed on C_3 plants with mildly abrasive components. This is not surprising when we consider that during the Late Pleistocene, the Padang Highlands were probably covered by lowlands rainforest with patches of montane and limestone rainforest (Backer and Bakhuizen van den Brink 1980; Whitten et al. 2000); this environment would have contained plant materials matching the indicated characteristics, such as leaves from trees, shrubs and bushes, or along the rivers, ferns and bamboo leaves. The mesowear signals obtained in the present study did not indicate a diet consisting of dry grasses. However, two cervid teeth in the enamel isotope study displayed a clear C_4 signal (Janssen et al. 2016 and supplementary data therein). Possible candidates for herbaceous plants that follow a C_4 metabolism and that are available in higher densities but generate a mixed-feeder mesowear signal are *Amaranthus viridis* or *Portulaca* sp. (Maria Adelia Widijanto pers. comm. 2021). Unfortunately, none of the teeth examined in our sample were included in the study by Janssen et al. (2016), precluding direct comparison of data about individual molars.

The specimens in our sample evidenced an increasingly variable diet throughout the individual's lifespan (Figure 6.6). Our age-specific datasets indicated a mixed diet with a slight shift from a stronger browsing component to a stronger grazing component with increasing age. This mixed-feeder signal does not necessarily indicate an uninterrupted mixed diet, because a mixed diet may also result from seasonal shifts in vegetation (Rivals et al. 2011; Wirkner and Hertler 2019). However, in extant *Rusa* species (i.e. *R. timorensis* and *R. unicolor*), the juvenile stage persists for a maximum of only 1.2 years, whereas the adult stage has a duration of several years (Tacutu et al. 2018) and thus includes multiple seasons during which the mesowear signal can accumulate. Adults are therefore expected to exhibit a more varied diet than younger individuals. If animals consume a more resistive diet during the dry season, the mesowear signal from older individuals will reflect this seasonal shift. An increase in the grazing component of the signal may thus result from seasonally changing food resources. Yet the isotope data provided by Janssen et al. (2016) did not indicate seasonally varying diets. Moreover, present representatives of the genus *Rusa* are known to be extremely opportunistic feeders (Hedges et al. 2015; Timmins et al. 2015). Such an opportunistic diet will also lead to increasingly variable mesowear signals, obscuring any seasonal variations.

Extant *R. timorensis* and *R. unicolor* live in flexible, temporal groups (Hedges et al. 2015; Leslie 2011; Timmins et al. 2015) containing a higher number of individuals during peak mating season. The herds generally segregate by sexes and combine during the mating season only. This results in a strong numerical bias towards female individuals (Leslie 2011; Timmins et al. 2015). Although in the small subsample studied in our mesowear analysis, such a female-biased ratio is present (19 females to 8 males in our sample), this is unlikely to reflect an ecological pattern, as the precise geographic origin and geological context of our subsample are unknown and may cover a period of several thousand years or more. This is confirmed by our wider analysis of body mass dimorphism in a dataset of lower third molars. Here, the sex ratio reverses to 52 females and 85 males and does not contradict a scenario with several populations of *Rusa* in various seasons.

Besides providing indications regarding sexual dimorphism, the results of the body mass analyses were also informative about the taxonomic status and diversity of our sample of deer fossils. The body mass data indicate that the variability in the fossil dataset is relatively high compared with that of several medium-sized cervids (*Axis axis*, *A. porcinus* and *R. timorensis*), and is closer to that of *R. unicolor*. However, *R. unicolor* is a widely distributed species with a geographic range that extends across large parts of South and Southeast Asia (Timmins et al. 2015). Our sample of this species (*n* = 25) included specimens from across this range and from islands as well as continental ecosystems. The variability in this extant sample was relatively large for a single species: the sample included specimens of exceptionally heavy body mass (438, 381 and 351 kg) as well as individuals of lower than average body mass (78 kg).

Overall, the data indicated that the fossil *Rusa* sp. sample included specimens of a single species, but from various populations, corresponding to a dataset of mixed geological, chronological and/or spatial provenance. This is in line with our unbalanced male–female body mass ratio, which also may suggest the presence of more than one population.

Levene's test on tooth length and surface area further supports these interpretations, showing differences in the variance of several cervid species, but without indicating variance in the fossils beyond that expected at the species level (Figure 6.3, Table 6.4). In fact, the Sumatran fossil sample showed a relatively high degree of variation, somewhat lower than that of extant *R. unicolor*. With a variance similar to that of *Cervus elaphus*, also a wide-ranging species with several distinct subspecies and populations (Geist 1998), *Rusa* sp. fossils probably represented multiple populations of a single species.

If we assume that only one species is represented in the fossil dataset, that species' taxonomic status remains to be determined. The results shown in our plot of molar length and width (Figure 6.2) support the conclusion by earlier researchers that the large Padang Highlands cervids were similar to members of *Rusa*, especially *R. unicolor* (de Vos 1983; Gruwier et al. 2015). Their conclusion was, however, based on the assumption that tooth size can be used as a reliable indicator of taxonomic affinity. This assumption is only partially supported by our GMM analysis (see Figure 6.4 and Table 6.5). The PCA of the upper third molars supports the hypothesis that *Rusa* sp. was related to *Cervus kendengensis*, *R. unicolor* and *R. timorensis*, but the CVA provided deeper insight into the relationship between these four species. It showed that, after the removal of isometric size effects, the *Rusa* sp. molars had a greater morphological similarity to the *R. timorensis* and *C. kendengensis* molars than to those of *R. unicolor*. The *R. timorensis* molars were particularly similar to the Padang Highlands molars. If we accept that the observed phenotypic variation is phylogenetically driven, the possibility that the Sumatran fossils belonged to a large type of *Rusa timorensis*, or a related form, must be considered.

Although *R. unicolor* is currently the only large cervid species living on Sumatra (Francis 2008; Geist 1998), the notion that this may not necessarily have been the case during the Late Pleistocene is supported by palaeontological evidence from the region. Certain taxa, such as orangutans (*Pongo* spp.), tapirs (*Tapirus indicus*) and tigers (*Panthera tigris*), are known to have been more widely distributed across the Sundanese islands before the Holocene (Earl of Cranbrook and Piper 2009; Piper et al. 2007; van den Bergh et al. 2001). This is also seen in the Padang Highlands assemblages, in which the remains of leopard (*Panthera pardus*) (de Vos 1983), banteng (*Bos sondaicus*) (Hooijer 1958) and long-nosed monkey (*Nasalis* sp.) (Smith et al. 2021) represent taxa that are currently absent from Sumatra but are still found on either Java or Borneo. It is conceivable that *R. timorensis*, a species currently endemic to Java and Bali (Martins et al. 2017), previously had a wider distribution across Sundaland. The large size of the Padang Highlands teeth does not contradict such an interpretation. Several Sundanese taxa, such as *Pongo*, *Muntiacus* and *Bubalus bubalis*, are known to have been substantially larger than their extant conspecifics during the Late Pleistocene (Hooijer 1948, 1958; Medway 1964).

Perhaps the most tantalising evidence to support our hypothesis that *Rusa timorensis*, or a closely related form, may previously have been part of the Sumatran fauna comes from a recent genetic study of the genus *Rusa* by Martins et al. (2017). Although these authors confirmed the validity of the species *R. timorensis* and *R. unicolor*, they found clear evidence for introgression between Javan *R. timorensis* populations and Sumatran *R. unicolor* (Martins et al. 2017). This would suggest that during glacial stages, when the Sunda Shelf emerged, isolated *Rusa* populations on Java and Sumatra were connected and thus hybridised in a contact region (Martins et al. 2017). During the Late Pleistocene, this was by no means an exceptional condition, as for 60% of the last 150,000 years, sea-levels were at least 30 m below the current level, low enough for the narrow Sunda Strait to emerge between the two islands (Voris 2000). Although some palaeoenvironmental reconstructions suggest that the Padang Highlands assemblages accumulated during an interglacial stage (de Vos 1983, but see Chapter 5, this volume), it seems likely that the fossil *Rusa* deer were part of an early stock that was connected to Javan *Rusa* populations at intermittent intervals. Probably the *R. unicolor* populations currently present on Sumatra result mostly from a later dispersal event that brought their ancestors from the mainland (Martins et al. 2017). Whether the early stock consisted of a large *Rusa timorensis*, an extinct form or perhaps a *Rusa timorensis* x *Rusa unicolor* hybrid cannot be inferred from our data with any confidence. In this context, it is worth mentioning that when hybridisation does occur between the two species, individuals reach sizes more like that of *R. unicolor* (Forsyth et al. 2015; van Mourik and Schurig 1985). Whether this would result in large deer with *R. timorensis*-like dental traits in the palaeontological record is unclear. Nevertheless, our data suggest a complex evolutionary history of the genus *Rusa* in Southeast Asia.

Conclusion

Our study demonstrates the use of a multiproxy approach to reconstruct the characteristics of an extinct taxon. In summary, we conclude that the large cervid remains from the Padang Highlands belonged to a large *Rusa* deer, of a different type than extant *R. unicolor* from Sumatra, with morphological traits reminiscent of *R. timorensis*. *Rusa* sp. was reconstructed as a mixed feeder during all ontogenetic stages, and, based on comparison with published carbon isotope data, must have relied on a diet consisting mainly of trees, shrubs and bushes as well as ferns and bamboo leaves.

In the future, more extensive GMM and palaeogenomic analyses of Pleistocene deer could shed further light on the evolutionary history of the genus *Rusa*. Such studies would, ideally, be part of a wider revision of the cervid fossil record from the Sundaic region, including fossils of *R. timorensis* from Java. Additional palaeoecological analyses, such as dental microwear analysis or stable isotope analysis, would complement our mesowear analysis and provide further details about the dietary ecology of the Padang Highlands cervids.

Acknowledgements

We would like to thank Angela Bruch and Maria Adelia Widianto for their palaeobotanical insights and Andrea Cardini for his advice about the GMM analyses. We are also grateful to the collection managers and curators who made their collections available to us, and we wish to thank the Department of Anthropology (Durham University), the Heidelberg Academy of Sciences and Humanities and the ROCEEH Research Center in Frankfurt for contributing infrastructure and co-funding parts of the project.

References

Ackermans, N.L. 2020. The history of mesowear: A review. *PeerJ* 8:e8519. doi.org/10.7717/peerj.8519

Amano, N., F. Rivals, A.M. Moigne, T. Ingicco, F. Sémah and T. Simanjuntak 2016. Paleoenvironment in East Java during the last 25,000 years as inferred from bovid and cervid dental wear analyses. *Journal of Archaeological Science* 10:155–165. doi.org/10.1016/j.jasrep.2016.09.012

Anders, U., W. von Koenigswald, I. Ruf and B.H. Smith 2011. Generalized individual dental age stages for fossil and extant placental mammals. *Paläontologische Zeitschrift* 85(3):321–339. doi.org/10.1007/s12542-011-0098-9

Baab, K.L., K.P. McNulty and F.J. Rohlf 2012. The shape of human evolution: A geometric morphometrics perspective. *Evolutionary Anthropology* 21:151–165. doi.org/10.1002/evan.21320

Backer, C.A. and R.C. Bakhuizen van den Brink 1980. *Flora of Java*. Springer, New York.

Bacon, A.M., K. Westaway, P.O. Antoine, P. Duringer, A. Blin, F. Demeter, J.L. Ponche, J.-X. Zhao, L.M. Barnes, T. Sayavonkhamdy, N.T.K. Thuy, V.T. Long, E. Patole-Edoumba and L. Shackelford 2015. Late Pleistocene mammalian assemblages of Southeast Asia: New dating, mortality profiles and evolution of the predator–prey relationships in an environmental context. *Palaeogeography, Palaeoclimatology, Palaeoecology* 422:101–127. doi.org/10.1016/j.palaeo.2015.01.011

Badoux, D.M. 1959. Fossil Mammals from Two Fissure Deposits at Punung (Java). Unpublished doctoral thesis. University of Utrecht, Utrecht.

Brophy, J.K., D.J. de Ruiter, S. Athreya and T.J. DeWitt 2014. Quantitative morphological analysis of bovid teeth and implications for paleoenvironmental reconstruction of Plovers Lake, Gauteng Province, South Africa. *Journal of Archaeological Science* 41:376–388. doi.org/10.1016/j.jas.2013.08.005

Cardini, A., K. Seetah and G. Barker 2015. How many specimens do I need? Sampling error in geometric morphometrics: Testing the sensitivity of means and variances in simple randomized selection experiments. *Zoomorphology* 134(2):149–163. doi.org/10.1007/s00435-015-0253-z

Cardini, A., R.W. Thorington and P.D. Polly 2007. Evolutionary acceleration in the most endangered mammal of Canada: Speciation and divergence in the Vancouver Island marmot. *Journal of Evolutionary Biology* 20:1833–1846. doi.org/10.1111/j.1420-9101.2007.01398.x

Cucchi, T., M. Fujita and K. Dobney 2009. New insights into pig taxonomy, domestication and human dispersal in Island South East Asia: Molar shape analysis of *Sus* remains from Niah caves, Sarawak. *International Journal of Osteoarchaeology* 19:508–530. doi.org/10.1002/oa.974

Curran, S. 2012. Expanding ecomorphological methods: Geometric morphometric analysis of Cervidae post-crania. *Journal of Archaeological Science* 39:1172–1182. doi.org/10.1016/j.jas.2011.12.028

de Vos, J. 1983. The *Pongo* faunas from Java and Sumatra and their significance for bio-stratigraphical and paleo-ecological interpretations. *Proceedings of the Koninklijke Nederlandse Akademie van Wetenschappen, Series B* 86:417–425.

de Vos, J. 1985. Faunal stratigraphy and correlation of the Indonesian hominid sites. In Delson, E. (ed.), *Ancestors: The Hard Evidence*, pp. 215–220. Liss, New York.

de Vos, J. 1996. Faunal turnovers in Java in relation to faunas of the continent. *Odontology* 1:32–36.

de Vos, J. 2004. The Dubois collection: A new look at an old collection. In C. Winkler-Prins and S. Donovan (eds), *Cultural Heritage in Geosciences, Mining and Metallurgy: Libraries-Archives-Museums: Museums and Their Collections*, pp. 267–285. *Scripta Geologica* Special Issue 4. Naturalis Biodiversity Center, the Netherlands.

Dong, W. and S.K. Chen 2015. An extraordinary pattern of ruminant molars and associated cervids from the Pleistocene of Wushan, central China. *Vertebrata Palasiatica* 7:207–218.

Dubois, E. 1891. Voorloopig bericht omtrent het onderzoek naar de Pleistocene en Tertiaire vertebraten-fauna van Sumatra en Java, gedurende het jaar 1890. *Natuurkundig Tijdschrift voor Nederlandsch Indië* 51:93–100.

Dubois, E. 1894. *Pithecanthropus erectus, einen menschenaehnliche Uebergangsform aus Java.* Landesdruckerei, Batavia.

Dubois, E. 1908. Das geologische Alter der Kendeng oder Trinil Fauna. *Tijdschrift Koninklijk Nederlands Aardrijkskundig Genootschap* 25:1235–1270.

Earl of Cranbrook and P.J. Piper 2009. Borneo records of the Malay tapir, *Tapirus indicus* Desmarest: A zooarchaeological and historical review. *International Journal of Osteoarchaeology* 19(4):491–507. doi.org/10.1002/oa.1015

Evin, A., T. Cucchi, A. Cardini, U.S. Vidarsdottir, G. Larson and K. Dobney 2013. The long and winding road: Identifying pig domestication through molar size and shape. *Journal of Archaeological Science* 40:735–743. doi.org/10.1016/j.jas.2012.08.005

Forsyth, D.M., K. Stamation and L. Woodford 2015. Distributions of sambar deer, rusa deer and sika deer in Victoria. Arthur Rylah Institute for Environmental Research unpublished report for the Biosecurity Branch, Department of Economic Development, Jobs, Transport and Resources. Department of Environment, Land, Water and Planning, Heidelberg, Victoria, Australia. parliament.vic.gov.au/images/stories/committees/enrc/Invasive_Animals_on_Crown_land/210R._2016.09.13_Attachment_18_-_Sambar_Rusa_Sika_distributions_2015_FINAL.pdf

Fortelius, M. and N. Solounias 2000. Functional characterization of ungulate molars using the abrasion-attrition wear gradient: A new method for reconstructing paleodiets. *American Museum Novitates* 3301:1–36. doi.org/10.1206/0003-0082(2000)301<0001:FCOUMU>2.0.CO;2

Francis, C. 2008. *A Guide to the Mammals of South-East Asia.* Princeton University Press, Princeton NJ.

Geist, V. 1998. *Deer of the World: Their Evolution, Behaviour and Ecology.* Stackpole Books, Mechanicsburg, PA.

Gruwier, B., J. de Vos and K. Kovarovic 2015. Exploration of the taxonomy of some Pleistocene Cervini (Mammalia, Artiodactyla, Cervidae) from Java and Sumatra (Indonesia): A geometric and linear morphometric approach. *Quaternary Science Reviews* 119:35–53. doi.org/10.1016/j.quascirev.2015.04.012

Gruwier, B. and K. Kovarovic 2021. Ecomorphology of the cervid calcaneus as a proxy for paleoenvironmental reconstruction. *The Anatomical Record* 305(9):2207–2226. doi.org/10.1002/ar.24845

Hallgrímsson, B., J.J.Y. Brown, A.F. Ford-Hutchinson, H.D. Sheets, M.L. Zelditch and F.R. Jirik 2006. The brachymorph mouse and the developmental-genetic basis of canalization and morphological integration. *Evolution and Development* 8(1):61–73. doi.org/10.1111/j.1525-142X.2006.05075.x

Hammer, Ø., D.A.T. Harper and P.D. Ryan 2001. PAST: Paleontological statistics software package for education and data analysis. *Palaeontologia Electronica* 4(1):1–9.

Hardjasasmita, H.J. 1987. Taxonomy and phylogeny of the Suidae (Mammalia) in Indonesia. *Scripta Geologica* 85:1–68.

Heckeberg, N. 2020. The systematics of the Cervidae: A total evidence approach. *PeerJ* 8:1–76. doi.org/10.7717/peerj.8114

Hedges, S., J.W. Duckworth, R. Timmins, G. Semiadi and G. Dryden 2015. *Rusa timorensis* [article]. *The IUCN Red List of Threatened Species 2015*:e.T41789A22156866. doi.org/10.2305/IUCN.UK.2015-2.RLTS.T41789A22156866.en

Heintz, E. 1970. Les cervidés villafranchiens de France et d'Espagne. *Mémoires du Muséum National d'Histoire Naturelle Série C: Sciences de la Terre* 22(1–2):206–303.

Holm, S. 1979. A simple sequential rejective multiple test procedure. *Scandinavian Journal of Statistics* 6(2):65–70.

Hooijer, D.A. 1948. Prehistoric teeth of man and of the orang-utan from central Sumatra, with notes on the fossil orang-utan from Java and southern China. *Zoologische Verhandelingen* 29:175–293.

Hooijer, D.A. 1958. Fossil Bovidae from the Malay Archipelago and the Punjab. *Zoologische Verhandelingen* 38:1–112.

Hooijer, D.A. 1960. Quaternary gibbons from the Malay Archipelago. *Zoologische Verhandelingen* 46:1–112.

Hooijer, D.A. 1962. Quaternary langurs and macaques from the Malay Archipelago. *Zoologische Verhandelingen* 55:1–64.

Hou, S.Y., W. Zhou, D. Hongwei, M.W. Hai, Y.F. Wen and J. Zhou 2021. Soft tissue facial changes among adult females during alignment stage of orthodontic treatment: A 3D geometric morphometric study. *Oral Health* 21(57):1–9. doi.org/10.1186/s12903-021-01425-2

Jackson, D.A. 1993. Stopping rules in principal components analysis: A comparison of heuristical and statistical approaches. *Ecology* 74:2204–2214. doi.org/10.2307/1939574

Janis, C.M. 1990. Correlation of cranial and dental variables with body size in ungulates and macropodoids. In J. Damuth and B.J. MacFadden (eds), *Body Size in Mammalian Paleobiology*, pp. 255–299. Cambridge University Press, Cambridge.

Janssen, R. 2017. Isotope Records in Vertebrate Fossils: From Cretaceous Seas to Quaternary Sundaland. Unpublished doctoral thesis. Free University of Amsterdam, Amsterdam.

Janssen, R., J.C.A. Joordens, D.S. Koutamanis, M.R. Puspaningrum, J. de Vos, J.H.J.L. van der Lubbe, J.J.G. Reijmer, O. Hampe and H.B. Vonhof 2016. Tooth enamel stable isotopes of Holocene and Pleistocene fossil fauna reveal glacial and interglacial paleoenvironments of hominins in Indonesia. *Quaternary Science Reviews* 144:145–154. doi.org/10.1016/j.quascirev.2016.02.028

Leslie, D.M. 2011. *Rusa unicolor* (Artiodactyla: Cervidae). *Mammalian Species* 43(871):1–30. doi.org/10.1644/871.1

Li, D., C. Hu, W. Wang, W. Chen, F. Tian, S. Huang and C.J. Bae 2017. The stable isotope record in cervid tooth enamel from Tantang Cave, Guangxi: Implications for the Quaternary East Asian monsoon. *Quaternary International* 434:156–162. doi.org/10.1016/j.quaint.2015.11.049

Lopez-Lazaro, S., I. Aleman, J. Viciono, J. Irurita and M.C. Botella 2018. Sexual dimorphism of the first deciduous molar: A geometric morphometric approach. *Forensic Science International* 290:94–102. doi.org/10.1016/j.forsciint.2018.06.036

Louys, J. 2007. Ecology and extinction of Southeast Asia's megafauna. Unpublished doctoral thesis. University of New South Wales, Sydney.

Louys, J. 2012. Mammal community structure of Sundanese fossil assemblages from the Late Pleistocene, and a discussion on the ecological effects of the Toba eruption. *Quaternary International* 258:80–87. doi.org/10.1016/j.quaint.2011.07.027

Louys, J., S. Kealy, S. O'Connor, G.J. Price, S. Hawkins, K. Aplin, Y. Rizal, J. Zaim, Mahirta, D.A. Tanudirjo, W.D. Santoso, A.R. Hidayah, A. Trihascaryo, R. Wood, J. Bevitt and T. Clark 2017. Differential preservation of vertebrates in Southeast Asian caves. *International Journal of Speleology* 46(3):379–408. doi.org/10.5038/1827-806X.46.3.2131

Louys, J. and E. Meijaard 2010. Palaeoecology of Southeast Asian megafauna-bearing sites from the Pleistocene and a review of environmental changes in the region. *Journal of Biogeography* 37:1432–1449. doi.org/10.1111/j.1365-2699.2010.02297.x

Marramà, G. and J. Kriwet 2017. Principal component and discriminant analyses as powerful tools to support taxonomic identification and their use for functional and phylogenetic signal detection of isolated fossil shark teeth. *PLoS One* 12(11):1–22. doi.org/10.1371/journal.pone.0188806

Martin, K. 1886. Fossile Säugethierreste von Java und Japan. *Sammlungen des Geologischen Reichs-Museums in Leiden, Serie 1, Beiträge zur Geologie Ost-Asiens und Australiens* 4:25–69.

Martins, R.F., A. Schmidt, D. Lenz, A. Wilting and J. Fickel 2017. Human-mediated introduction of introgressed deer across Wallace's line: Historical biogeography of *Rusa unicolor* and *R. timorensis*. *Ecology and Evolution* 8:1465–1479. doi.org/10.1002/ece3.3754

Medway, L. 1964. Post-Pleistocene changes in the mammalian fauna of Borneo. *Studies in Speleology* 1:33–37.

Nowak, R.M. 1999. *Walker's Mammals of the World*, Volume 2. 6th edition. Johns Hopkins University Press, Baltimore.

Piper, P., Earl of Cranbrook and R. Rabett 2007. Confirmation of the presence of the tiger *Panthera tigris* (L.) in Late Pleistocene and Holocene Borneo. *Malayan Nature Journal* 59(3):259–267.

Polly, P.D., A.V. Polyakov, V.B. Ilyashenko, S.S. Onischenko, T.A. White, N.A. Shchipanov, N.S. Bulatova, S.V. Pavlova, P.M. Borodin and J.B. Searle 2013. Phenotypic variation across chromosomal hybrid zones of the common shrew (*Sorex araneus*) indicates reduced gene flow. *PLoS One* 8(7):1–12. doi.org/10.1371/journal.pone.0067455

Rivals, F., N. Solounias and G.B. Schaller 2011. Diet of Mongolian gazelles and Tibetan antelopes from steppe habitats using premaxillary shape, tooth mesowear and microwear analyses. *Mammalian Biology* 76(3):358–364. doi.org/10.1016/j.mambio.2011.01.005

Rohlf, F.J. 2003. *tpsSmall 1.20. Ecology & Evolution.* State University at Stony Brook, New York. life.bio. sunysb.edu/morph/index.html (accessed 1 January 2023).

Rohlf, F.J. 2004. *tpsDig 1.40-Thin Plate Spline Digitizer 1.40.* State University at Stony Brook, New York. life.bio.sunysb.edu/morph/index.html (accessed 1 January 2023).

Schutz, H., P.D. Polly, J.D. Krieger and R.P. Guralnick 2009. Differential sexual dimorphism: Size and shape in the cranium and pelvis of grey foxes (*Urocyon*). *Biological Journal of the Linnean Society* 96(2):339–353. doi.org/10.1111/j.1095-8312.2008.01132.x

Seetah, T.K., A. Cardini and P.T. Miracle 2012. Can *morphospace* shed light on cave bear spatial-temporal variation? Population dynamics of *Ursus spelaeus* from Romualdova Pécina and Vindija, (Croatia). *Journal of Archaeological Science* 39:500–510. doi.org/10.1016/j.jas.2011.10.005

Skelton, R. 1985. Aspartic Acid Racemization Dating of Southeast Asian Sites. Unpublished report. University of Montana, Missoula.

Smith, A.T. and Y. Xie (eds) 2008. *A Guide to the Mammals of China*. Princeton University Press, Princeton NJ.

Smith, H.E., G.J. Price, M. Duval, K. Westaway, J. Zaim, Y. Rizal, Aswan, M.R. Puspaningrum, A. Trihascaryo, M. Stewart and J. Louys 2021. Taxonomy, taphonomy and chronology of the Pleistocene faunal assemblage at Ngalau Gupin cave, Sumatra. *Quaternary International* 603:40–63. doi.org/10.1016/j.quaint.2021.05.005

Sykes, N., R.F. Carden and K. Harris 2011. Changes in the size and shape of fallow deer—evidence for the movement and management of a species. *International Journal of Osteoarchaeology* 23:55–68. doi.org/10.1002/oa.1239

Tacutu, R., D. Thornton, E. Johnson, A. Budovsky, D. Barardo, T. Craig, E. Diana, G. Lehmann, D. Toren, J. Wang, V.E. Fraifeld and J.P. de Magalhaes 2018. Human ageing genomic resources: New and updated databases. *Nucleic Acids Research* 46(1):1083–1090. doi.org/10.1093/nar/gkx1042

Timmins, R., K. Kawanishi, B. Giman, A. Lynam, B. Chan, R. Steinmetz, H. Sagar Baral and N. Samba Kumar 2015. *Rusa unicolor* [article]. *The IUCN Red List of Threatened Species* 2015:e.T41790A85628124. doi.org/10.2305/IUCN.UK.2015-2.RLTS.T41790A22156247.en

van den Bergh, G.D., J. de Vos and P.Y. Sondaar 2001. The Late Quaternary palaeogeography of mammal evolution in the Indonesian Archipelago. *Palaeogeography, Palaeoclimatology, Palaeoecology* 171(3–4):385–408. doi.org/10.1016/S0031-0182(01)00255-3

van Mourik, S. and V. Schurig 1985. Hybridization between sambar (*Cervus (Rusa) unicolor*) and rusa (*Cervus (Rusa) timorensis*) deer. *Zoologischer Anzeiger* 214:177–184.

Viscosi, V. and A. Cardini 2011. Leaf morphology, taxonomy and geometric morphometrics: A simplified protocol for beginners. *PLoS One* 6:1–20. doi.org/10.1371/journal.pone.0025630

von Koenigswald, G.H.R. 1933. Beitrag zur Kenntnis der fossilen Wirbeltiere Javas I. Teil. *Wetenschappelijke Mededelingen Dienst Mijnbouwkunde Nederlandsch-Indië* 23:1–127.

von Koenigswald, G.H.R. 1934. Zur Stratigraphie des Javanischen Pleistocän. *De ingenieur Nederlandsch-Indië* 1(4):185–201.

von Koenigswald, G.H.R. 1935. Die fossilen Saugetierfaunen Javas. *Proceedings of the Koninklijke Nederlandse Akademie van Wetenschappen* 38:88–98.

Voris, H.K. 2000. Maps of Pleistocene sea levels in Southeast Asia: Shorelines, river systems and time durations. *Journal of Biogeography* 27:1153–1167. doi.org/10.1046/j.1365-2699.2000.00489.x

Walker, J.A. 2000. The ability of geometric morphometric methods to estimate a known covariance matrix. *Systematic Biology* 49(4):686–696.

Westaway, K.E., J. Louys, R. Due Awe, M.J. Morwood, G.J. Price, J.X. Zhao, M. Aubert, R. Joannes-Boyau, T. Smith, M.M. Skinner, T. Compton, R.M. Bailey, G.D. van den Bergh, J. de Vos, A.W.G. Pike, C. Stringer, E.W. Saptomo, Y. Rizal, J. Zaim, W.D. Santoso, A. Trihascaryo, L. Kinsley and B. Sulistyanto 2017. An early modern human presence in Sumatra 73,000–63,000 years ago. *Nature* 548:322–325. doi.org/10.1038/nature23452

Westaway, K.E., M.J. Morwood, R.G. Roberts, A.D. Rokus, J.X. Zhao, P. Storm, F. Aziz, G. van den Bergh, P. Hadi, Jatmiko and J. de Vos 2007. Age and biostratigraphic significance of the Punung Rainforest Fauna, East Java, Indonesia, and implications for *Pongo* and *Homo*. *Journal of Human Evolution* 53:709–717. doi.org/10.1016/j.jhevol.2007.06.002

Whitten, T.J., Dmanik, J., Sengli, Anwar, Janzanul, Hisyam and Nazaruddin 2000. *The Ecology of Sumatra*. Periplus, Singapore.

Wirkner, M. and C. Hertler 2019. Feeding ecology of Late Pleistocene *Muntiacus muntjak* in the Padang Highlands (Sumatra). *Comptes Rendus Palevol* 18(5):541–554. doi.org/10.1016/j.crpv.2019.03.004

Zelditch, M.L., D.L. Swiderski, H.D. Sheets and W.L. Fink 2004. *Geometric Morphometrics for Biologists: A Primer*. Elsevier, Berlin.

7

Environments, terrestrial ecosystems and mammalian species: An overview of Southeast Asia in the Late Pleistocene

Anne-Marie Bacon and Pierre-Olivier Antoine

Abstract

During the highly dynamic, climate-driven Pleistocene period, mammalian communities from the Indomalayan region faced major environmental changes. In the late Middle to the Late Pleistocene, the Sunda Shelf surface was particularly affected under the influence of multiple parameters—tectonic, eustatic and climatic—leading to alternating phases of exposure and flooding. The fossil faunas from the Padang Highlands in Sumatra discovered by Eugène Dubois illustrate episodes of species dispersal during the periods of exposure of land areas. Here, we analyse the assemblages of Sibrambang and Lida Ajer in the light of a selection of mammalian faunas located in continental and insular regions during two possible periods of dispersion, c. 130 ka at the Marine Isotope Stage (MIS) 6–5 transition and c. 71 ka at the beginning of MIS 4. We investigated (1) the taxonomic composition of herbivore communities in terms of archaic versus modern taxa; (2) the functions of ecosystems, based on the type of digestive physiology of herbivores (ruminant versus non-ruminant) per body mass category; and (3) the relative abundance of some Artiodactyla, Perissodactyla and Primates. Our results show that, at the time of the earliest range expansion of modern species into Sundaland c. 130 ka, diverse functional herbivore communities containing local archaic taxa coexisted in Southeast Asia. Overall, Sundaland seems to have always been less rich in large-bodied herbivore diversity compared to the Indochinese subregion, most probably reflecting the lower heterogeneity of Sundaic ecosystems, even during the period of large connections between land masses. By comparing Duoi U'Oi, Vietnam (*Homo* sp.; 70–60 ka) and Lida Ajer, Sumatra (*Homo sapiens*; 73–63 ka), two sites located at different latitudes, the results underscore the different availability to humans of herbivore prey species depending on their relative abundance in highly forested habitats.

Keywords: Megafauna, herbivore, Indochinese peninsula, Sundaland, mammalian communities, hominins

Abstrak

Selama periode Pleistosen yang sangat dinamis akibat pengaruh iklim, komunitas mamalia dari wilayah Indo-Melayu menghadapi perubahan lingkungan yang sangat kontras. Pada akhir Pleistosen Tengah hingga Akhir, permukaan Paparan Sunda sangat dipengaruhi oleh beberapa parameter— tektonik, eustatik, dan iklim—, yang menyebabkan perselingan fase daratan dan genang laut. Fauna dari Dataran Tinggi Padang di Sumatra yang ditemukan oleh Eugène Dubois menggambarkan episode-episode penyebaran spesies melalui periode-periode wilayah daratan yang terbuka ini. Di sini, kami menganalisis kumpulan fosil dari Sibrambang dan Lida Ajer berdasarkan seleksi fauna mamalia yang terletak di wilayah kontinental dan kepulauan, selama dua kemungkinan periode penyebaran, c. 130 ka pada transisi Tahap Isotop Laut/*Marine Isotope Stage* (MIS) 6–5 dan c. 71 ka pada awal MIS 4. Penelitian kami meliputi (1) komposisi taksonomi komunitas herbivora; (2) fungsi ekosistem berdasarkan jenis fisiologi pencernaan (ruminansia terhadap non-ruminansia) menurut kategori massa tubuh; dan (3) kelimpahan relatif beberapa taksa Artiodactyla, Perissodactyla dan Primata. Hasil kami menunjukkan bahwa pada saat penyebaran paling awal spesies modern di Sunda c. 130 ka, beragam komunitas herbivora fungsional dengan taksa primitif lokal hidup berdampingan di Asia Tenggara. Secara keseluruhan, Sundaland tampaknya selalu kurang kaya akan keanekaragaman herbivora bertubuh besar dibandingkan dengan subkawasan Indocina, kemungkinan besar mencerminkan heterogenitas ekosistem Sunda yang lebih rendah, bahkan selama periode hubungan besar antara daratan. Dengan membandingkan Duoi U'Oi, Vietnam (*Homo* sp.; 70–60 ka) dan Lida Ajer, Sumatera (*Homo sapiens*; 73–63 ka), dua lokasi yang terletak di garis lintang berbeda, hasilnya sangat jelas menunjukkan adanya perbedaan keterdapatan spesies mangsa herbivora bagi manusia, berdasarkan kelimpahan relatif mereka di habitat hutan lebat.

Kata kunci: Megafauna, herbivora, Indochina, Sundaland, komunitas mamalia, hominin

Introduction

The deposits at Lida Ajer, Sibrambang and Djambu caves are, so far, the most prolific fossiliferous deposits recovered in the karstic caves of the Padang Highlands in Sumatra. Assemblages were collected by Eugène Dubois between 1887 and 1890 as part of his visionary project to find human ancestors in Southeast Asia (Chapter 2, this volume; Wood 2020). Both the selective preservation of these remains, which consist mainly of isolated teeth of large mammals embedded in cemented breccia, and the rarity of associated hominin remains (no human bones or teeth are mentioned in the locality of Sibrambang, but Lida Ajer yielded, at that time, two human teeth), prompted Dubois to relocate to the island of Java, which had different depositional contexts and environments (Dubois 1894).

From the 1940s onwards, Dirk Albert Hooijer described and inventoried the species in the abovementioned Sumatran assemblages (e.g. Hooijer 1946a, 1946b, 1947, 1948, 1960, 1962), a work continued by John de Vos (de Vos 1983; Long et al. 1996). The faunas of these caves are comparable with each other and fully modern in terms of species composition, with most of the mammals still living in Sunda (Figure 7.1). Sunda was a floristic and faunistic geographic unit whose northern limit separated it from the Indochinese subregion and was initially placed in the Malay Peninsula, close to the Isthmus of Kra, by Alfred Russel Wallace (1860). Further east, the so-called Wallace's Line separates Sunda from Wallacea, and extends northward between the Indonesian archipelago and the Philippines, excluding Palawan, as drawn by Thomas Henry Huxley (1868). The patterns of the distribution of species throughout the Indochinese peninsula and Sunda are profoundly affected by a north–south temperature gradient, and the boundary between the regions varies according to the type of plants or animals studied, within a transitional zone between the Kangar-Pattani Line at c. 6°N and the Isthmus of Kra at c. 14°N (Woodruff 2010). How this boundary fluctuated during the Pleistocene glacial cycles is unknown, but several works have demonstrated that during the Late Pleistocene it was probably south of the Isthmus of Kra (Suraprasit et al. 2019; Tougard and Montuire 2006; Woodruff and Turner 2009). Today, Southeast Asia has one of the highest percentages of plant and vertebrate endemic species, especially in the Sundaic and Indo-Burmese subregions (as defined by Myers et al. 2000), which have been identified as biodiversity hotspots. The biodiversity of large mammals in the Indochinese and Sundaic subregions over the last 500,000 years is still poorly known.

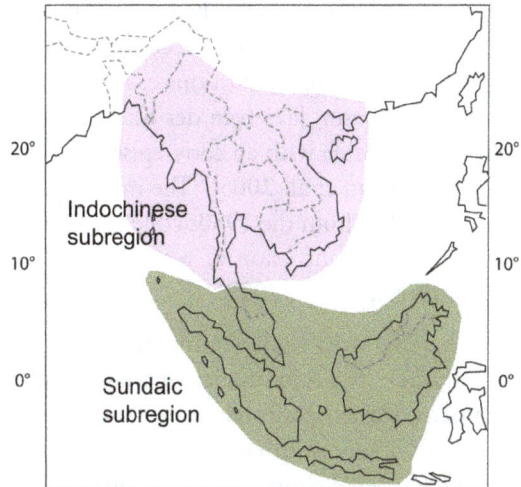

Figure 7.1: Southeast Asian map showing the limits of the biogeographic Indochinese and Sundaic subregions.

Source: Map by authors.

The age range of the historical faunas from the Padang Highlands was first estimated to be recent or Late Holocene. Based on biochronology, it was placed at c. 80–60 ka (de Vos 1983), or c. 81–70 ka according to relative dating using amino-acid racemisation (AAR) on bones (Skelton 1985). More recently, however, new dating, using coupled uranium-series (U-series) and electron spin resonance (ESR) techniques on mammalian teeth, and luminescence and U-series techniques on sediments and speleothems in various caves in Sunda, including Lida Ajer, has led to a precise chronological framework for the assemblages and thus to a precise timing for the dispersal of modern species onto the exposed continent. The new, robust age range of the fauna of Lida Ajer, c. 73–63 ka (Westaway et al. 2017), which was reconfirmed recently on the basis of the dating of the fossiliferous Unit 5 within this cave at 71–68 ka (Louys et al. 2022), postdates by about 50 ka the oldest expansion of modern taxa in Sunda. The timing of this event has been specified following the discovery of an in situ fauna at the Gunung Dawung site, also named Punung III, on Java (Storm et al. 2005; Storm and de Vos 2006), which was dated to c. 128–118 ka using luminescence and U-series methods on breccia deposits and flowstones (Westaway et al. 2007). The site, located near the village of Punung, produced a modern fauna comparable to those collected by Ralph von Koenigswald in the early 1930s (von Koenigswald 1939) in the Punung I and Punung II karstic localities (Badoux 1959).

Recently, the discovery of a faunal assemblage in a newly discovered cave of the Padang Highlands, Ngalau Gupin, with an estimated age range of 160–115 ka based on U-series and ESR dates of mammalian teeth from the breccia deposits coded NG-A (Smith et al. 2021), confirmed the antiquity of this event, which potentially extended into Marine Isotope Stage (MIS) 6 (191–130 ka; Lisiecki and Raymo 2005). Shortly before this discovery, the time range of the resulting turnover that led to the replacement of archaic taxa in Sunda was also reassessed based on a new geochronological and palaeontological study of the Ngandong site in Java (Rizal et al. 2020). Rizal et al. introduced a new chronological framework, based on U-series and ESR dating on teeth, for the vertebrate bed (facies C) in which *Homo erectus* was discovered during the 1930s. Dated to c. 117–108 ka, this bone bed still mostly contained archaic taxa endemic to the region (Rizal et al. 2020). These data suggest that this turnover took place in Java c. 120 ka, close to the oldest limits previously suggested,

c. 135–70 ka (van den Bergh et al. 2001) or c. 120–90 ka (Storm et al. 2005). This timing is consistent with palaeoclimatic records for the western region of Java, which indicate shifts towards very warm and humid conditions c. 126 ka, based on sedimentological and palynological data from the Bandung basin, Java (van der Kaars and Dam 1995). One question remains, however: did this event also coincide with an early episodic spread of *Homo sapiens* into Southeast Asia as previously proposed (Storm et al. 2005)? The modern-human nature of the single remaining tooth (an upper third premolar) from the 1930s collections from Punung has been challenged (Polanski et al. 2016), and the possible intrusion of recent human remains into older stratigraphic levels has also been suggested (Kaifu et al. 2022).

There is still a need to determine precise ages for the Djambu and Sibrambang faunas (Chapter 5, this volume). The fully modern nature of Sibrambang—the collection contains more than 3,000 specimens, without any archaic elements—suggests that this site probably postdates Ngalau Gupin (c. 160–115 ka; Smith et al. 2021), but, if we accept the AAR age of c. 81–70 ka proposed for Sibrambang by Skelton (1985), it could pre-date Lida Ajer (c. 73–63 ka; Westaway et al. 2017). New investigations at Ngalau Sampit, a historical Dubois site, confirmed the presence of MIS 5 faunas on Sumatra >105 ka based on U-series/ESR dating of teeth at 105 ± 9 ka and post-infrared infrared-stimulated luminescence dating of breccia at 93 ± 6 ka (Duval et al. 2021).

In a recent analysis, we showed that, during the Late Pleistocene, extensive rainforests coincided with cold stages in northern latitudes of the Indochinese peninsula (Bacon et al. 2021). Indeed, our results, based on carbon (δ^{13}C) and oxygen (δ^{18}O) records from a large spectrum of mammals from northern Laos and Vietnam, underscored that two phases of C_3-dominated vegetation occurred, during MIS 6 and MIS 4 (191–130 ka and 71–57 ka respectively; Lisiecki and Raymo 2005). In contrast, MIS 5, an interglacial stage (130–71 ka; Lisiecki and Raymo 2005), was marked by the presence of more open environments (C_3–C_4 intermediate forests and woodlands and C_4 savanna-type habitats), in conjunction with the contraction of closed-canopy forests. The two C_3 phases indicated by our results, based on the relative similarity in the δ^{13}C and δ^{18}O values of the faunas of Coc Muoi (148–117 ka; Bacon et al. 2018a) and Duoi U'Oi (70–60 ka; Bacon et al. 2008, 2015, 2018b), have been associated with two large drops in monsoon intensity: in oxygen isotope substage 6.2 and at the onset of stage 4 respectively, based on the curves of δ^{18}O records from the speleothems in the Sanbao, Dongee and Hulu Chinese caves (Wang Y. et al. 2008). The oldest of these climatic and vegetational shifts with extensive forests on the mainland might coincide with the end of the penultimate glacial phase at c. 130 ka, when the sea-level was low and modern faunas dispersed into Sunda, as possibly illustrated by Ngalau Gupin in the Padang Highlands (160–105 ka; Duval et al. 2021; Smith et al. 2021). However, whether this synchronicity occurred remains speculative.

The climate shift at the beginning of MIS 4 (71–57 ka), short and abrupt with a notable change in the amount of precipitation and a temperature drop of c. 5–6°C (Wang Y. et al. 2008), was severe enough to lead to a turnover of plant taxa, with dense rainforests being replaced by forests dominated by conifers (Zheng and Lei 1999). New herbivore populations that might have dispersed into the new forested biome include those of Duoi U'Oi (70–60 ka), which were better adapted to this new environment (Bacon et al. 2021). At the latitude of Duoi U'Oi in northern Vietnam, the forest expansion would have occurred in opposite phase with the savanna expansion through the central north–south corridor in Sundaland (Bird et al. 2005). In contrast, for the same time period in southwestern Sumatra, the palynological record from deep-sea cores dated to c. 71 ka does not indicate major changes in vegetation, showing a predominance of Dipterocarpaceae rainforests and a climate, which remained humid as in the preceding interglacial MIS 5 (van der Kaars et al. 2010). This underscores the sharp climatic contrast between Duoi U'Oi (70–60 ka; Bacon et al. 2015) and Lida Ajer (73–63 ka; Westaway et al. 2017).

Thus, Indochinese and Sundaic areas share a common biogeographical history (see also Heaney 1986; Woodruff 2010). In relation to the period analysed herein—from the late Middle Pleistocene to the Late Pleistocene—simulation of the landscape evolution using various parameters, including tectonics, eustatic sea-level variations, and rainfall, has shown how the Sunda Shelf surface was affected by them, with long phases of exposure (>80% exposed) that alternated with short partially flooded (>50% exposed) and fully marine periods (Salles et al. 2021: figure 1). The faunas from Ngalau Gupin, Sibrambang and Lida Ajer in Sumatra, along with those from Punung in Java, might reflect at least two episodes of species dispersal via connected land areas; a 40 m drop in sea-level was sufficient to connect the Thai-Malay Peninsula, Sumatra, northwestern Java and Borneo (van den Bergh et al. 2001; van der Geer et al. 2021).

Given this background, the present chapter presents an overview of Dubois' Sumatran Pleistocene faunal assemblages—from Sibrambang and Lida Ajer—in the light of a selection of 23 mammalian faunas that inhabited continental regions (Southern China, Laos, Vietnam, Thailand and Malaysia) and insular regions (Sumatra, Java, and Borneo) at the MIS 6–5 transition and at the beginning of MIS 4. The sites examined here are limited to those with new chronologies (using various geochronological techniques on fossil remains and/or sediments) and/or that have been subjected to new investigations (carbon and oxygen isotopic analyses of mammalian teeth). Therefore, the present chapter does not deal with old collections that have already been comprehensively explored (e.g. Louys 2012; Louys and Meijaard 2010; Louys et al. 2007; Tougard and Montuire 2006; van den Bergh et al. 2001).

In undertaking this overview of past Southeast Asian mammalian faunas, we attempted to explore how terrestrial environments, ecosystems and species changed during the period c. 500–40 ka; our exploration focuses on primary consumers. We analysed the structure of communities of herbivores at various points in space and time by investigating: (1) the taxonomic composition of assemblages (archaic versus modern taxa from Artiodactyla, Perissodactyla and Proboscidea); (2) the functioning of ecosystems, based on the type of digestive physiology of herbivores (ruminant versus non-ruminant) per body mass category; and (3) the relative abundance of taxa among Artiodactyla, Perissodactyla and Primates, using the minimum number of individuals (MNI) as the best ecological indicator. For the purposes of this review, we also used carbon and oxygen isotope data from fossil faunas as complementary sources of information on palaeodiets and palaeoenvironments.

Faunal assemblages, although rare and poorly preserved, are nevertheless critical for understanding *H. sapiens*' adaptation across Southeast Asia. Therefore, this analysis also provides valuable insights into the environmental conditions during the dispersal and settlement of *H. sapiens* around 70 ka by comparing the data from Duoi U'Oi and Lida Ajer. Sediment infill chronology for Duoi U'Oi indirectly dates two hominin teeth (*Homo* sp.) to 70–60 ka (Bacon et al. 2008, 2015, 2018b), and that for Lida Ajer constrains two modern human teeth (*H. sapiens*) to 73–63 ka (Westaway et al. 2017). Our overview gave us the opportunity to compare the resource availability of herbivore species at Duoi U'Oi and Lida Ajer and, therefore, to investigate aspects of human foraging behaviour in different latitudinal conditions and different forested habitats (Bacon et al. 2021; Louys et al. 2022; Roberts et al. 2016). We also attempted to assess potential hunting pressure by predators, using mortality profiles of Rhinocerotidae, Tapiridae, Cervidae and Suidae, including novel results on Lida Ajer (for *Tapirus indicus* and *Sus* spp.).

Materials

Selected faunas

Our review surveyed published faunas from 23 Southeast Asian continental and insular sites; the details of their location and chronology are shown in Appendix 7.1 and Figures 7.2 and 7.3. The species or genus compositions of the assemblages of large mammals are listed in Appendices 7.2 and 7.3. The record of $\delta^{18}O$ values from benthic foraminifera presented in Figure 7.3, as indicators of temperatures of oceans, shows how climates fluctuated for the last ~200,000 years, at a global scale (Lisiecki and Raymo 2005; Railsback et al. 2015).

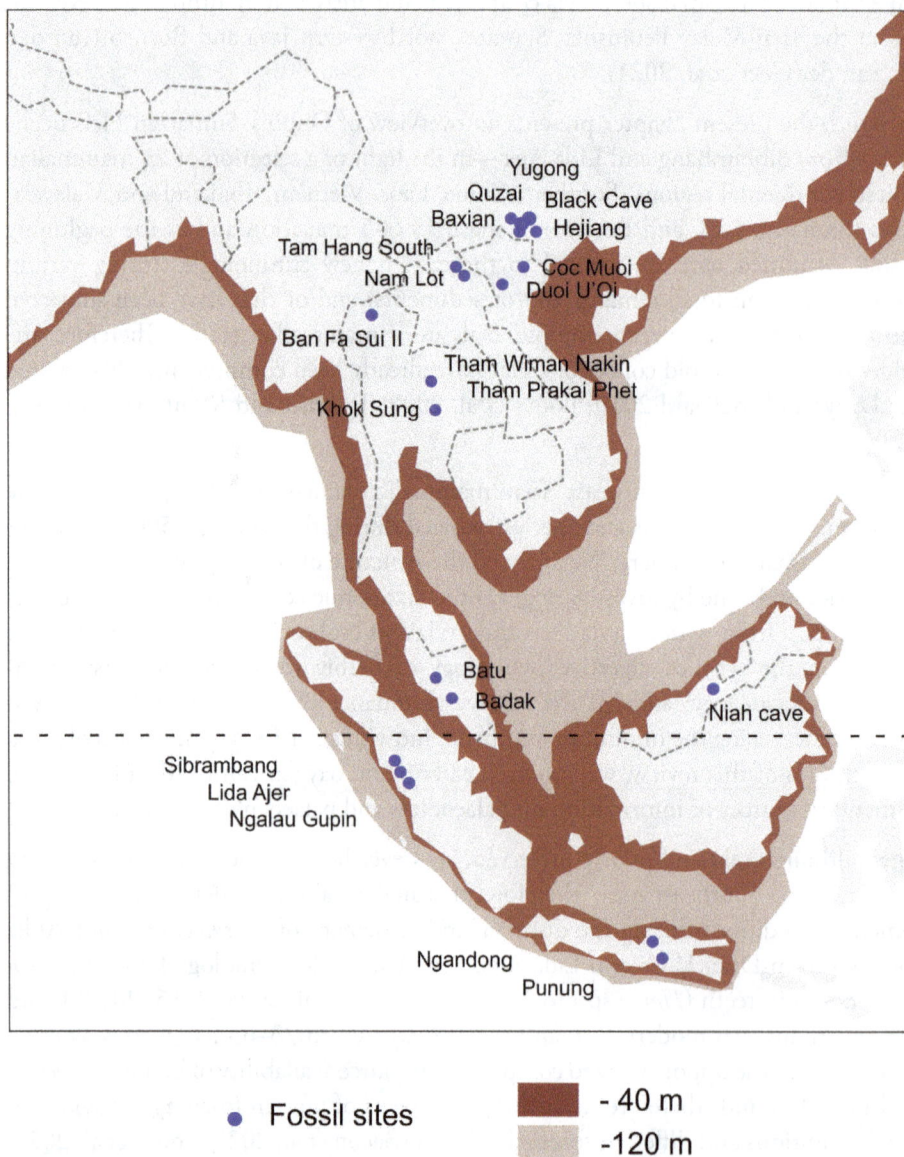

Figure 7.2: Locations of the Southeast Asian sites included in the study.

Note: We have represented the extent of land area during sea-level changes of −40 m and −120 m relative to the current level (Sathiamurthy and Voris 2006).

Source: Map by authors.

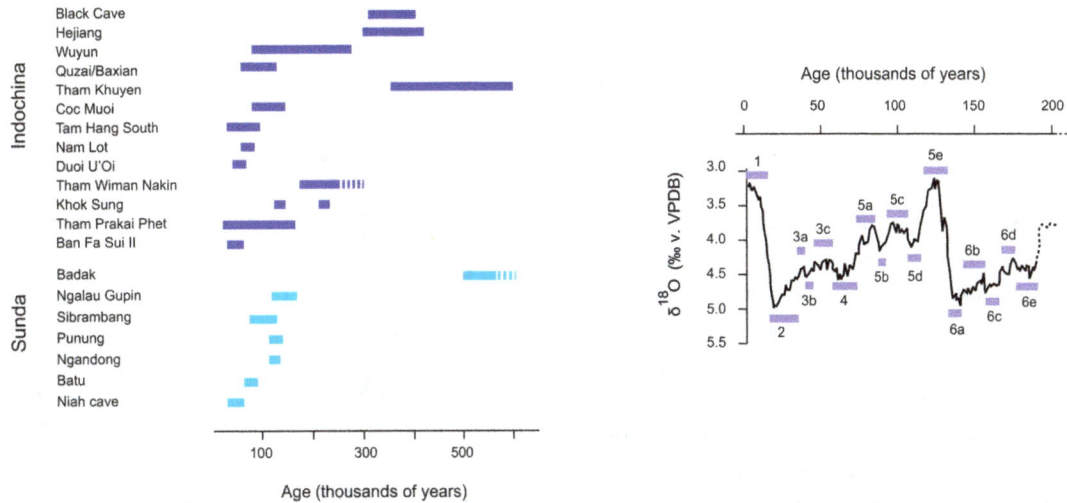

Figure 7.3: (A) Chronology of Southeast Asian sites included in the study and (B) chart of benthic foraminifera δ¹⁸O data during the Marine Isotope Substages for the last 200,000 years.

Note: In the chart (B), the horizontal bars labelled 1, 2, 3a and so on represent the Marine Isotope Substages. On the y-axis, oxygen isotopic values are presented in delta 'δ' notation expressed as deviation ‰ compared to the International Standard Vienna Pee Dee Belemnite (VPDB).

Source: Chronology by authors; chart modified from Railsback et al. (2015: figure 3).

Depositional contexts and composition of assemblages

With the exception of Ngandong, Java, where fossil bones are found in a terrace context formed over the Middle Pleistocene by successive alluvial deposits of the Solo River (Rizal et al. 2020), and Khok Sung, Thailand, where the bone bed is associated with the Mun River terrace deposits (Duval et al. 2019; Suraprasit et al. 2018), the faunas studied here come from breccias in a karstic context. Due to differences in depositional processes, the two sites located in river valleys yielded some complete skeletal elements, whereas the cave sites located in karsts produced isolated teeth and very occasionally bones. The latter have been associated with taphonomic and geological processes of transport and deposition inside the karsts (the taphonomic processes being the actions of biotic and abiotic agents that modified the skeletal remains). In most cases, the cave-context remains have been transported throughout the karstic network under high-energy hydrological conditions (rainfalls or river flooding) that led to the loss of the smallest elements.

This complex action of biotic and abiotic agents generated preservation biases, and assemblages from cave sites consisted of isolated teeth—the majority gnawed by porcupines—from a wide array of mammals ranging from c. 5 kg to c. 5,000 kg belonging to Artiodactyla, Perissodactyla, Proboscidea, Carnivora, Primates and Rodentia. First, the capacity of porcupines to collect a wide range of remains of predated or scavenged animals, either partial remains (mandibles of large ungulates like water buffaloes and maxillae of smaller ones like muntjacs) or complete jaws (of wild pigs) (Brain 1981) appears to be the cause of the differing quantitative representation of teeth within Artiodactyla, Perissodactyla and Proboscidea (Bacon et al. 2015). Second, the taxonomic groups also appear to be differently represented. In a previous investigation (Bacon et al. 2015), we mentioned that the species diversity of small mammals (up to c. 5 kg) is frequently underestimated, especially for carnivores and primates versus ungulates. In such assemblages, this underreported diversity coincides with the different representation of elements between groups, giving the false impression of a low abundance of small species and, conversely, a high abundance of larger species (Louys 2012). This is particularly the case for small carnivores. Current subtropical and tropical habitats harbour the greatest richness of small carnivore species, with up to 29 inventoried species, at mid-latitudes (Corbet and Hill 1992) (Table 7.1), a level of diversity rarely found in fossil assemblages. Another bias in species diversity exists, which is of a taxonomic nature and tied to the difficulty of identifying the different species of small primates (macaques, gibbons, and langurs) and carnivores. Finally, the Dubois historical collections, particularly that of Sibrambang, may have been affected by a recovery bias due to the discarding of tooth fragments (Bacon et al. 2015).

Data analysed

This review uses a combination of mostly published data and newly analysed data. The original data concern the taxonomic revision of Perissodactyla of Lida Ajer, Sibrambang and Punung, along with the estimate of dental eruption sequences and wear stages of *Tapirus indicus intermedius* and *Sus* sp. (*S. scrofa* and *S. barbatus*) from the collection of Lida Ajer. They were collected in 2016 by the authors at Naturalis Biodiversity Center, Leiden, the Netherlands. The tapir specimens in this collection include 24 permanent and 12 deciduous dental specimens, whereas the pig specimens include 78 permanent molars.

Table 7.1: Species richness of current mammalian faunas from China, Myanmar, Vietnam, Thailand, Malaysia, Sumatra, Borneo and Java in the six orders of large mammals, following a north–south gradient.

	Southern China 25–30°N	Central Myanmar 20–25°N	Northern Vietnam 20–25°N	Northern Thailand 15–20°N	Southern Malaysia 0–5°N	Northern Sumatra 0–5°N	Northern Borneo 0–5°N	Central Borneo 0–5°S	Central Java 5–10°S
Artiodactyla	6	10	8	8	8	7	7	3	5
Perissodactyla	–	2	1	2	2	2	1	–	1
Proboscidea	–	1	–	1	1	1	–	–	–
Carnivora	14	23	26	29	27	24	18	9	14
Primates	3	4	8	6	7	9	9	7	4
Rodentia	1	2	2	2	1	1	1	1	1

Note: Richness is defined as number of species. Among Primates, lorises and tarsiers not recovered in fossil assemblages have been excluded, as have other small mammals, such as moles, shrews, flying lemurs and bats. Among Rodentia, we included only the large rodents (*Hystrix* and *Atherurus*).

Source: Data from Corbet and Hill (1992).

Methods

Our analysis focused on the taxonomic composition of herbivores (Artiodactyla, Perissodactyla and Proboscidea) by examining the proportion of archaic versus modern taxa at the species or genus level within each fauna, based on data listed in Appendices 7.2 and 7.3. Taxa defined at upper ranks (subfamily, family or order) have been excluded, with the exception of the Rhinocerotidae. 'Archaic' here means an extinct, fossil taxon, in contrast to 'modern', which means a current taxon, for both genera or species.

We plotted the type of digestive physiology, ruminant versus non-ruminant (hindgut fermenting herbivore) by body mass category, using the categories A (18–80 kg), B (80–350 kg), C (350–1,000 kg) and D (>1,000 kg) (Faith et al. 2019), as in a prior analysis of Southeast Asian ecosystems (Bacon et al. 2021) (Appendices 7.2 and 7.3). These indicators allowed us to describe the functional diversity of terrestrial ecosystems by time period: MIS 6 (130–123 ka) and earlier stages up to c. 500 ka, MIS 5 (123–71 ka) and MIS 4 (71–29) (Lisiecki and Raymo 2005). We also considered the carrying capacity of ecosystems to be the maximum load, that is, the largest amount of a given group of organisms that can sustainably feed using the resources locally available (Del Monte-Luna et al. 2004). We analysed the mammalian communities by period: MIS 6 (130–123 ka) and earlier stages up to c. 500 ka, MIS 5 (123–71 ka) and MIS 4 (71–29 ka) (Lisiecki and Raymo 2005).

Most of the reviewed assemblages are composed of isolated teeth; one tooth is considered here as one specimen. Therefore, to estimate the relative abundance of some Artiodactyla, Perissodactyla and Primates along a north–south latitudinal gradient, we used a MNI based on the frequency of the most common permanent and deciduous teeth, whether left or right, upper or lower, by taxon (species or genus) (Mayr 1942).

To investigate the potential signature of predators, including hominins, on prey species from Duoi U'Oi and Lida Ajer, we used a combination of published and new analysed data. The previously published data are the three-cohort profiles (showing the proportions of the juvenile, subadult and adult/mature remains) of *Rusa unicolor*, *Sus scrofa* and Rhinocerotidae for Duoi U'Oi (Bacon et al. 2015), and those of Rhinocerotidae for Lida Ajer (Bacon et al. 2018a). In these publications, we used crown height measurements as wear stages to estimate the age of *R. unicolor* individuals of Duoi U'Oi, divided into 10 age classes (10% lifespan intervals), following Klein et al. (1981). We then grouped the individuals into three cohorts: infants (< c. 1.6 years), young adults (c. 1.6–3.2 years), and mature and old adults (c. 3.2–16 years).

In the mortality profile of *S. scrofa* from Duoi U'Oi, the ages of individuals were distributed into 13 age classes [A-N], based on occlusal wear stages of lower molars (m1/m2/m3) following the criteria defined by Grant (1982). The three cohorts represented piglets (up to c. 14 months), young adults (up to c. 26 months) and mature and old adults (>6 years).

For Rhinocerotidae from Lida Ajer and Duoi U'Oi, we used wear stages of all teeth, permanent and deciduous, lower and upper, to characterise age classes following a procedure adapted from Hillman-Smith et al. (1986). The three cohorts—calves (<3 years), subadults (3–6 years) and adults (>6 years)—coincide with the age classes—0–V, VI–VIII and IX–XVI respectively—defined by these authors.

In the present analysis, we merged the juvenile and subadult cohorts of recent populations of *Rhinoceros unicornis* and *Rusa unicolor*, and of fossil samples of rhinocerotids and *R. unicolor*, in order to compare the results for two versus three cohorts for all the concerned taxa consistently, as data were merged a priori for juveniles and subadults of *Sus scrofa* from Nagarhole and Pench

National Parks that we here use for comparison (Biswas and Sankar 2002; Karanth and Sunquist 1995). Given the scope of our comparisons (i.e. multiple usage of a simple test), we did not use Bonferroni corrections for the relevant χ^2 tests, following the recommendations of Sharpe (2015).

Concerning the original age profiles of *Tapirus indicus intermedius* from Lida Ajer presented here, the age of individuals was estimated using the dental eruption sequence and wear stages defined for a natural lowlands population of *Tapirus terrestris* by Maffei (2003), and the individuals were then divided into three cohorts: calves (<1 year), subadults (1–2 years), and adults (>2 years). For the pigs, *Sus* sp. (*S. scrofa* and *S. barbatus*), recovered at the site, the protocol used to build the novel age profile was the same as described by Bacon et al. (2015).

Results

Proportion of archaic versus modern ungulates and proboscideans

Figure 7.4 illustrates the proportion of archaic taxa versus modern ungulate and proboscidean taxa based on the data compiled in Appendices 7.2 and 7.3. For MIS 6 and earlier stages (before c. 120 ka), the fossil records from the continental sites showed various mixed compositions: 41.6% (*n* = 11) of the taxa were archaic at Tham Khuyen (*Sus lydekkeri, Megatapirus augustus, Rhinoceros sinensis, Stegodon orientalis, Palaeoloxodon namadicus*), 50% (*n* = 8) at Hejiang and 54.5% (*n* = 11) at Black Cave (*Dicoryphochoerus ultimus, Megalovis guangxiensis, S. bijiashanensis, M. augustus, R. sinensis, S. orientalis*). In contrast, the taxa from sites further south on the mainland, such as Tham Wiman Naking (*n* = 15) and Khok Sung (*n* = 13), were 100% modern or little archaic (7.6%). In the insular Java, the Ngandong ungulate and proboscidean fauna was composed of 73% (*n* = 11) archaic species (*Axis lydekkeri, Bibos palaeosondaicus, Bubalus palaeokerabau, Sus macrognathus, S. brachygnathus, Hexaprotodon sivajavanicus, Elephas hysudrindicus,* and *Stegodon trigonocephalus*) with a high level of endemism superimposed.

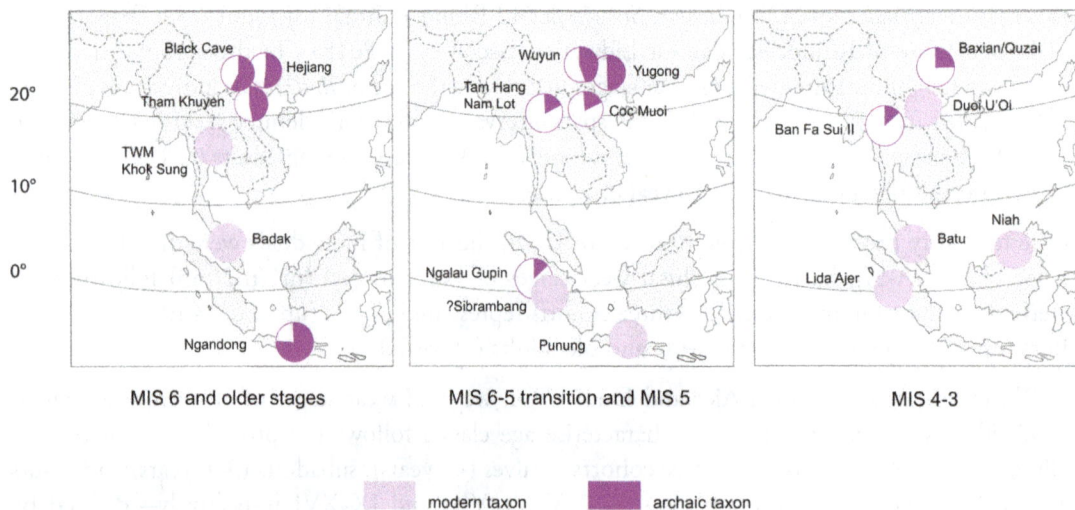

Figure 7.4: Proportion of archaic taxa (extinct genera or species) versus modern taxa among ungulates and proboscideans in fossil faunas.

Note: We considered three time periods: MIS 6 (130–123 ka) and earlier stages up to c. 500 ka, MIS 5 (123–71 ka) and MIS 4 (71–29 ka). MIS = Marine Isotope Stage.

Source: Maps by authors, using data compiled in Appendices 7.2 and 7.3.

We will now consider MIS 5 and the transition from MIS 6 to MIS 5. The mainland ungulate faunas from this period were represented in various local assemblages. In China, Yugon's ungulate taxa (*n* = 8) were 62.5% archaic (*M. augustus, S. orientalis, S. peii, S. xiaozhu, Leptobos* sp.) and Wuyun's (*n* = 9) were 44.4% archaic (*M. augustus, S. orientalis, Tapirus sinensis*); whereas the assemblages from sites in the more southern latitudes of Laos and Vietnam harboured fewer archaic elements, with 16.6% (*n* = 12) at Coc Muoi (*M. augustus, Stegodon* sp.), 14.2% (*n* = 14) at Tam Hang South (*M. augustus* and *Stegodon* sp.) and 9% (*n* = 11) at Nam Lot (*S. orientalis*). The centre of the Malay Peninsula did not contain any sites representing this transition period. On Sumatra, Ngalau Gupin's ungulate fauna showed a similarly low percentage of archaic taxa (8%, *n* = 12, representing a single archaic taxon, the hippopotamus *Hexaprotodon* sp.), whereas Sibrambang's appeared 100% modern.

From MIS 4 onwards, the mainland herbivores were almost entirely modern, but there were some areas where *Stegodon* may have persisted locally, such as those of Ban Fa Sui II (12.5%; *n* = 8) and, further north, Baxian, where *S. orientalis* and the giant tapir *M. augustus* are recorded (25%, *n* = 8). It should be added, however, that the Baxian site not dated accurately could be older than MIS 4. Given the available data, the ungulate fauna on the Greater Sunda Islands, Sumatra (Lida Ajer) and Borneo (Niah) appear to have been 100% modern during this period.

Diversity and carrying capacity of ecosystems: Ruminants versus non-ruminants

Figure 7.5 shows the distribution of ruminant versus non-ruminant taxa in fossil faunas by body size category, based on data compiled in Appendices 7.2 and 7.3. Despite limitations imposed by a small dataset, differences in sample size, and taxonomic constraints on the differentiation of taxa within Muntiacinae, medium-sized Cervidae and large Bovidae at the species level, three main trends emerge regarding the period studied: (1) The functional diversity of the ecosystems on the mainland was greater overall than of that on the Sunda Shelf; (2) there seems to have been a difference in the carrying capacities of ecosystems between, on the one hand, the Indochinese peninsula and, on the other hand, southern China and Sunda; and (3) there seems to have been a loss of biodiversity in large-bodied mammals from c. 70 ka onward throughout Southeast Asia. Each of these trends will now be considered in the light of our results.

First, the ecosystems on the mainland during the period MIS 6–3 were highly functionally diverse; they were dominated either by large-bodied non-ruminant herbivore taxa (*Rhinoceros, Dicerorhinus, Elephas, Megatapirus,* and *Tapirus* of body size categories C and D), as found in Black Cave, Tham Khuyen, Coc Muoi, Tam Hang South, Duoi U'Oi, Quzai and Baxian, or by medium-sized ruminant taxa (*Muntiacus, Cervus, Axis, Rucervus, Capricornis,* and *Naemorhedus* of body size categories A and B), as found in Tham Wiman Nakin, Khok Sung and, to a lesser extent, Ban Fa Sui II. In contrast, in Sunda, the functional diversity of the ecosystems was relatively low, as shown by the proportions of ruminant versus non-ruminant taxa.

Second, the carrying capacity of ecosystems on the Indochinese peninsula was shown to be different from that of the ecosystems in southern China and Sunda. This seems to have been the case throughout the period studied. It is particularly notable for MIS 6 and earlier stages, as indicated by the numbers of ungulate and proboscidean species recorded at Khok Sung (*n* = 13) and Tham Wiman Nakin (*n* = 15) compared to the numbers recorded at Black Cave (*n* = 11) in southern China and at Badak (*n* = 6) and Ngandong (*n* = 11) south of the Isthmus of Kra.

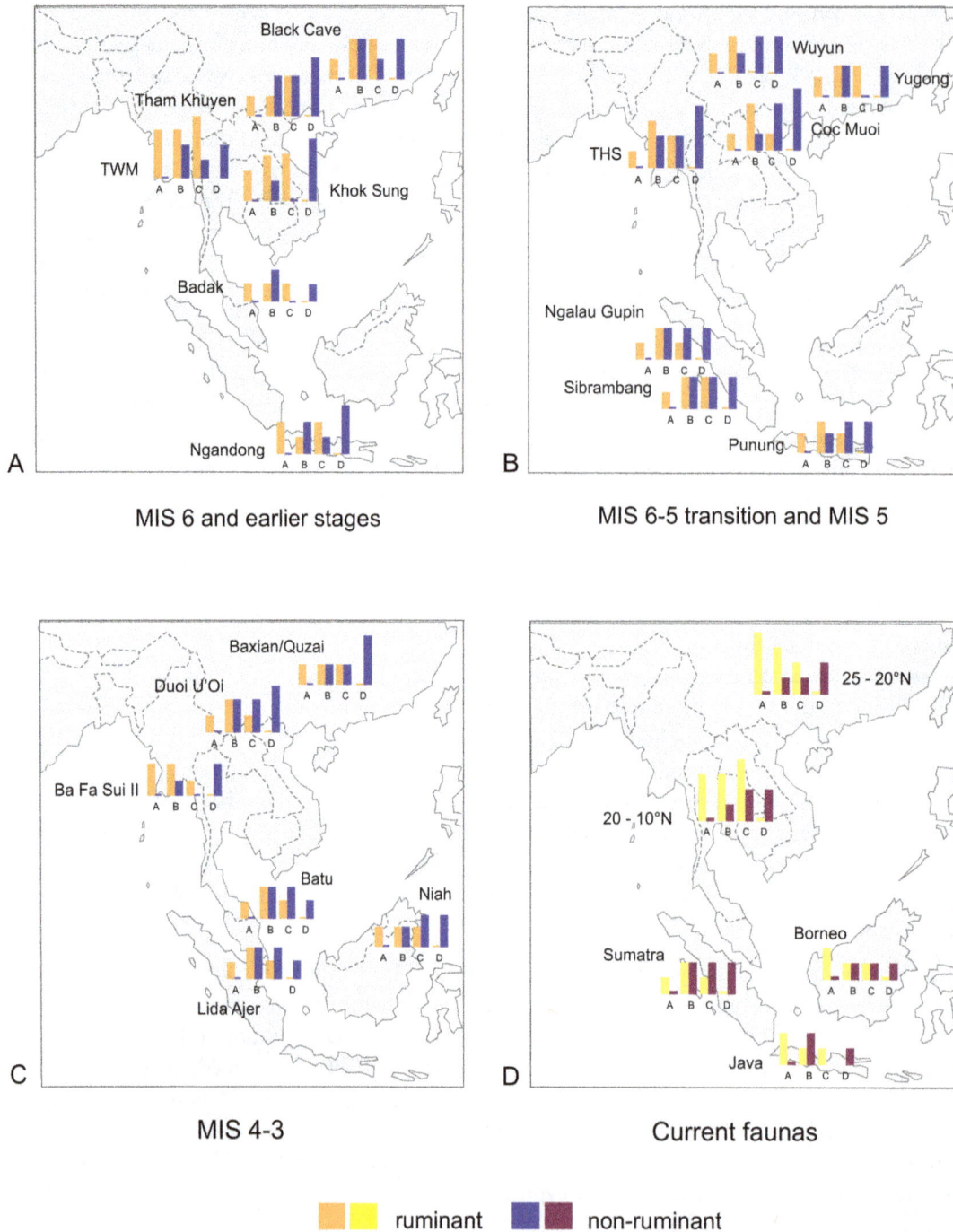

A   MIS 6 and earlier stages

B   MIS 6-5 transition and MIS 5

C   MIS 4-3

D   Current faunas

ruminant   non-ruminant

Figure 7.5: Distribution of ruminant and non-ruminant taxa from Southeast Asian sites in fossil and recent faunas, by body size category.

Note: We considered three time period: MIS 6 (130–123 ka) and earlier stages up to c. 500 ka, MIS 5 (123–71 ka) and MIS 4 (71–29 ka). MIS = Marine Isotope Stage. A: 18–80 kg. B: 80–350 kg. C: 350–1,000 kg. D: >1,000 kg.

Source: Maps by authors, using data compiled in Appendices 7.2 and 7.3.

This difference remained significant during the MIS 6–5 transition, as indicated by the numbers of ungulate taxa recorded at Coc Muoi ($n = 12$) and Tam Hang South ($n = 14$) compared to the numbers recorded at Wuyun ($n = 9$) and Yugong ($n = 8$) in southern China and Punung ($n = 9$) in Java.

The contrast appears to have been less marked in MIS 4–3. There is not a substantial difference between the numbers of ungulate taxa recorded at Quzai/Baxian ($n = 8$) and Duoi U'Oi ($n = 11$) and those recorded at Lida Ajer ($n = 10$), Batu ($n = 10$), Niah Cave ($n = 6$, without Tragulidae) and Sibrambang ($n = 11$); Ngalau Gupin ($n = 12$, without Tragulidae) showed an ungulate diversity close to that of Sibrambang.

Third, when considering the faunas dominated by non-ruminant taxa and comparing MIS 5 and earlier stages with MIS 4–3 (see Figure 7.5 for the stages of the sites and Appendices 7.2 and 7.3 for the species details), we noted a decrease in the species diversity of large-bodied herbivores, in particular, an absence of *Megatapirus* and *Stegodon* specimens at Duoi U'Oi (MIS 4) that did not occur at Tam Hang South, Tham Khuyen or Coc Muoi. We observed a comparable difference between small to medium-sized ruminants (*Axis porcinus*, *Rucervus eldii*, and *Capricornis sumatraensis*) at Tham Wiman Nakin (MIS 6) and Ban Fa Sui II (MIS 4–3), with none recorded at the latter site. Ban Fa Sui II also had a lower diversity of large ruminants, but this result is biased because the species diversity of large Bovidae (*Bos* sp. of body size category C) could not be determined at Ban Fa Sui II, whereas four species were identified at Tham Wiman Nakin.

Species abundance

As shown in Figure 7.6, the proportions of individuals (MNIs) were used to investigate the abundance distribution of species in fossil faunas from all the studied periods combined, within various taxonomic groups, namely Artiodactyla, Perissodactyla and Primates. The results in Table 7.2 clearly indicate differences following a north–south gradient.

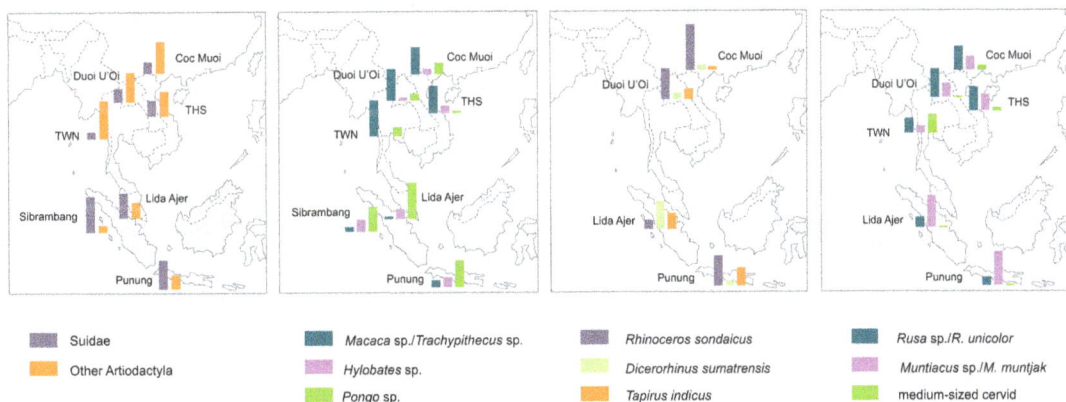

Legend:
- Suidae
- Other Artiodactyla
- *Macaca* sp./*Trachypithecus* sp.
- *Hylobates* sp.
- *Pongo* sp.
- *Rhinoceros sondaicus*
- *Dicerorhinus sumatrensis*
- *Tapirus indicus*
- *Rusa* sp./*R. unicolor*
- *Muntiacus* sp./*M. muntjak*
- medium-sized cervid

Figure 7.6: Proportions of individuals (using minimum numbers of individuals or MNIs) showing the relative abundance of taxa within taxonomic groups recorded in fossil Southeast Asian faunas from Marine Isotope Stages 6 to 3.

Note: Data on southern Chinese faunas are not available.

Source: Maps by authors, using data compiled in Table 7.2.

The habitats at the latitudes of Sunda harboured a relative abundance of pigs (*Sus* sp., up to 85% at Sibrambang), muntjacs (*Muntiacus* sp., 73.5% at Lida Ajer), tapirs (*Tapirus indicus*, 33.3% at Punung), two-horned rhinoceroses (*Dicerorhinus sumatrensis*, 55.5% at Lida Ajer), orangutans (*Pongo* sp., 78% at Lida Ajer), and gibbons (*Hylobates* sp., 30% at Sibrambang). In contrast, the prevailing environments at the latitudes of Coc Muoi, Duoi U'Oi and Tam Hang South, on the Indochinese peninsula, were the preferred habitats of sambar (*Rusa unicolor*, 65.8% at Duoi U'Oi), one-horned rhinoceroses (*R. sondaicus*, 86.3% at Coc Muoi and 66.6% at Duoi U'Oi; versus *D. sumatrensis* with 9% at Coc Muoi and 13.3% at Duoi U'Oi), and monkeys (*Macaca* sp. and *Trachypithecus* sp., 62.5% at Coc Muoi and 75% at Duoi U'Oi).

Two sites stand out within this north–south pattern: Tham Wiman Nakin, whose habitats were favourable to medium-sized cervids (44.4% versus 38.8% of large cervids), and Punung, whose results indicate a greater abundance of *R. sondaicus* (60%) than that of *D. sumatrensis* (6.6%), unlike at Lida Ajer (16.6% versus 55.5%).

Another aspect of the studied ecosystems concerns the body mass distribution of mammals. The warm, humid climates were more suitable for the smaller species within some taxonomic groups: *D. sumatrensis* (900–1,000 kg) versus *R. sondaicus* (1,500–2,000 kg) within the rhinocerotids, and *Muntiacus* sp. (20–28 kg) versus *Rusa unicolor* (180–260 kg) within the cervids (see also Francis 2008).

Table 7.2: Relative abundance of mammalian taxa, showing minimum number of individuals (MNI) and percentages within Primates, Perissodactyla and Artiodactyla at sites in Sumatra, Java, Laos, Vietnam and Thailand.

	Lida Ajer	Sibrambang	Punung	Coc Muoi	Duoi U'Oi	Tam Hang South	Nam Lot	Tham Wiman Nakin
	73–63 ka	~120–80 ka or 73–63 ka	128–118 ka	148–117 ka	70–60 ka	94–60 ka	86–72 ka	>169 ka
Primates								
Macaca sp./ *Trachypithecus* sp.	2 (2.4%)	17 (13.0%)	4 (16.6%)	5 (62.5%)	18 (75.0%)	10 (71.4%)	5 (83.3%)	7 (77.7%)
Hylobates sp.	16 (19.5%)	39 (30.0%)	6 (25.0%)	1 (12.5%)	2 (8.3%)	3 (21.4%)	—	—
Pongo sp.	64 (78.0%)	74 (56.9%)	14 (58.3%)	2 (25.0%)	4 (16.6%)	1 (7.1%)	1 (16.6%)	2 (22.2%)
Perissodactyla								
Rhinoceros sondaicus	3 (16.6%)	21 (84.0%)[1]	9 (60.0%)	38 (86.3%)	10 (66.6%)	5 (71.4%)	1	—[2]
Dicerorhinus sumatrensis	10 (55.5%)	—	1 (6.6%)	4 (9.0%)	2 (13.3%)	—	—	—[2]
Tapirus indicus	5 (27.7%)	4 (16.0%)	5 (33.3%)	2 (4.5%)	3 (20.0%)	2 (28.5%)	2	1
Artiodactyla								
Suidae	59 (59.5%)	244 (85.0%)	25 (60.9%)	18 (25.3%)	18 (29.0%)	15 (35.7%)	11 (37.9%)	6 (13.0%)
Other Artiodactyla	40 (40.4%)	43 (14.9%)	16 (39.0%)	53 (74.6%)	44 (70.9%)	27 (64.2%)	18 (62.0%)	40 (86.9%)
Rusa sp./ *R. unicolor*	9 (26.4%)	14 (41.1%)	2 (22.2%)	17 (53.1%)	27 (65.8%)	13 (56.5%)	4 (57.1%)	7 (38.8%)
Muntiacus sp./ *M. muntjak*	25 (73.5%)	20 (58.8%)	7 (77.7%)	11 (34.3%)	14 (34.1%)	9 (39.1%)	3 (42.8%)	3 (16.6%)

	Lida Ajer	Sibrambang	Punung	Coc Muoi	Duoi U'Oi	Tam Hang South	Nam Lot	Tham Wiman Nakin
Medium-sized cervid taxa	—	—	—	4 (12.5%)	—	1 (4.3%)	—	8 (44.4%)

Note: The taxonomic determination of Perissodactyla from Lida Ajer, Sibrambang and Punung was revised by POA based on material at Naturalis Biodiversity Center, Leiden, the Netherlands. Within Perissodactyla, *R. unicornis* (Tam Hang South, Nam Lot, Coc Muoi, Duoi U'Oi, Tham Wiman Nakin) and *Megatapirus augustus* (Coc Muoi and Tam Hang South) were also recorded.

[1] Rhinocerotids from Sibrambang were assigned to *R. sondaicus* or *D. sumatrensis*.

[2] In relation to Tham Wiman Nakin, Suraprasit et al. (2021) did not find the *R. sondaicus* previously identified by Tougard (1998).

Sources: Fossil occurrence data: Tham Wiman Nakin: Suraprasit et al. (2021), Tougard (1998). With the exception of the data for Lida Ajer (authors; present study), the MNI data have been published in our earlier works (Bacon et al. 2015, 2018a).

Mortality profiles of ungulate taxa: Duoi U'Oi versus Lida Ajer

Figure 7.7 illustrates the three-cohort (juvenile, subadult, and adult) mortality profiles of various ungulate taxa recorded at Duoi U'Oi and Lida Ajer. The distribution of individuals among the cohorts was compared to the J-shaped patterns (adult > juvenile > subadult) observed in natural populations (see Table 7.3). For some recent populations used as references, juveniles and subadults are merged, which led us to also consider two-cohort profiles: juvenile plus subadult, and adult.

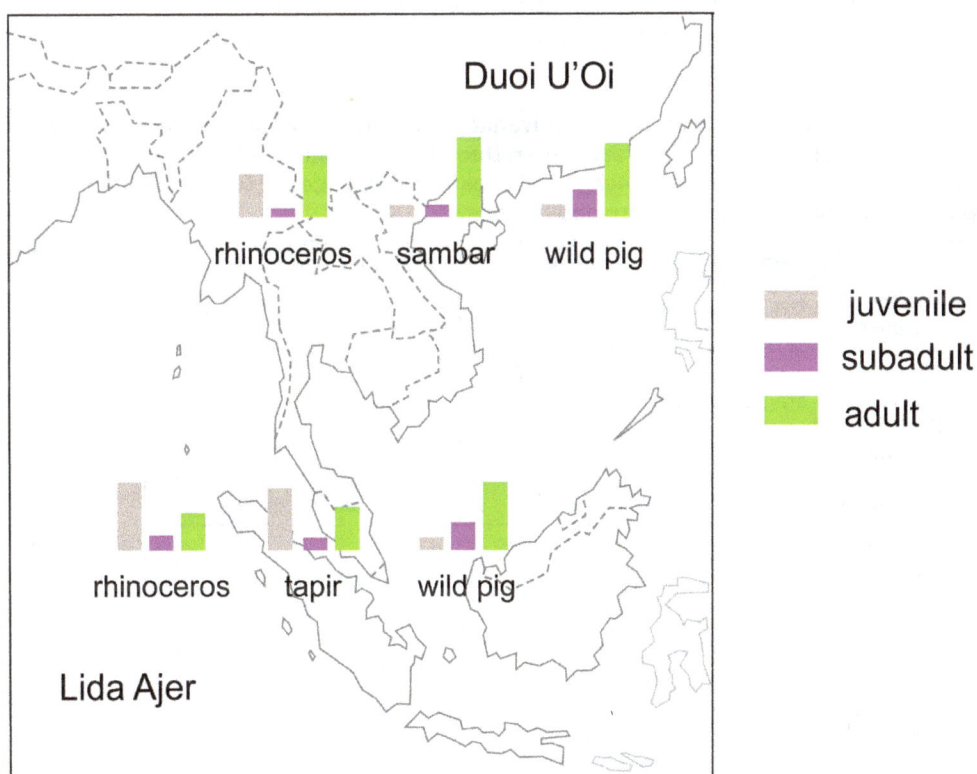

Figure 7.7: Three-cohort (juvenile, subadult, and adult) mortality profiles of taxa: rhinoceros (*Rhinoceros, Dicerorhinus*), tapir (*Tapirus*), sambar (*Rusa unicolor*), and wild pig (*Sus*) from Duoi U'Oi (Vietnam) and Lida Ajer (Sumatra).

Source: Image by authors, using data compiled in Table 7.3.

The three-cohort profiles of sambar (*R. unicolor*) at Duoi U'Oi and tapir (*T. indicus intermedius*) and rhinoceros (*D. sumatrensis*) at Lida Ajer indicate selective pressures on some age classes. At Duoi U'Oi, adult sambar individuals are overrepresented, at 75% compared to 59–72% in two natural populations from Indian reserves (Biswas and Sankar 2002; Karanth and Sunquist 1995) and include only prime-adult individuals (3–9 years, c. 180–260 kg; Francis 2008). This hints at a human signature (Bacon et al. 2015) rather than the tiger (*Panthera tigris*) signature, which always contains old individuals in addition to prime-adult individuals (Karanth and Sunquist 1995).

Among the tapirs from Lida Ajer, there is a bias towards calves less than one year old: 53% compared to 25% in a natural population of *Tapirus terrestris* from Amazonian forests (Maffei 2003). (To our knowledge, no data are available for Malayan tapirs, *Tapirus indicus*.) The body weight of juveniles ranged between c. 10 and c. 160 kg (Donny et al. 2019), which suggests a selective pressure by either pack-hunting dholes (*Cuon alpinus*), small felids (*Felis temmincki*) or humans, all three having the capacity to hunt at least small tapirs, such as newborns and young calves of tapirs given their body weight (Gearty 2012; Hayward et al. 2014).

We will now compare the age profiles of rhinocerotids (all species combined) between sites. The distribution pattern at Duoi U'Oi coincides with that of a natural population, *R. unicornis* (Laurie et al. 1983), with no apparent bias (three-cohort or two-cohort), whereas the pattern at Lida Ajer shows an overrepresentation of juveniles (57% v. 27%). Only pack-hunting dholes or humans could have hunted Lida Ajer's newborn rhinoceroses, which would have weighed up to 300 kg (Groves and Leslie Jr 2011).

In relation to suids, no selective pressure or taphonomic bias can be clearly assessed from either the three-cohort or the two-cohort profiles found at Duoi U'Oi (*S. scrofa*) and Lida Ajer (*S. scrofa* and *S. barbatus*).

Table 7.3: Data and results of the three-cohort (juvenile, subadult, and adult) mortality profiles of rhinocerotids, tapirids, large cervids and suids from Duoi U'Oi (Vietnam) and Lida Ajer (Sumatra); method, tooth type and number of specimens used to estimate the ages of fossil individuals; and demographic data of the reference modern populations.

Locality	Taxa	Method	Teeth	No.	Juvenile	Subadult	Adult	χ^2	Sources
Chitwan, Nepal	*Rhinoceros unicornis*	—	—	—	27% 48%[1]	21%	52%	—	Laurie et al. 1983
Duoi U'Oi, Vietnam	*Rhinoceros sondaicus, Rhinoceros unicornis, Dicerorhinus sumatrensis*	wear stages	all teeth	51	37.2% 47.9%[1]	10.6%	52.1% 0 (>0.90)	5.04 (>0.05)	Bacon et al. 2015
Lida Ajer, Sumatra	*Rhinoceros sondaicus, Dicerorhinus sumatrensis*	wear stages	all teeth	77	57.4% 72%[1]	14.5%	28% 23.08 (<0.001)	19.34 (<0.001)	Bacon et al. 2018a
Amazonia, Bolivia	*Tapirus terrestris*	—	—	—	25% 44.5%[1]	19.5%	55.5%	—	Maffei 2003
Lida Ajer, Sumatra	*Tapirus indicus intermedius*	eruption sequence, wear stages	all teeth	36	52.7% 63.9%[1]	11.1%	36.1% 14.47 (<0.001)	16.29 (<0.001)	Authors

Locality	Taxa	Method	Teeth	No.	Juvenile	Subadult	Adult	χ²	Sources
Nagarhole National Park, India	*Rusa unicolor*	—	—	—	19% 40.7%[1]	21.7%	59.3%	—	Karanth and Sunquist 1995
Pench National Park, India	*Rusa unicolor*	—	—	—	21% 27.8%[1]	6.8%	72.2%	—	Biswas and Sankar 2002
Duoi U'Oi, Vietnam	*Rusa unicolor*	wear stages	d4/m3	25	12% 24%[1]	12%	76%	N: 6.43 (<0.05) P: 4.55 (>0.10) N: 10.88 (<0.01) P: 0.54 (>0.50)	Bacon et al. 2015
Nagarhole National Park, India	*Sus scrofa*	—	—	—	39.4%[1]	60.6%		—	Karanth and Sunquist 1995
Pench National Park, India	*Sus scrofa*	—	—	—	28.4%[1]	71.6%		—	Biswas and Sankar 2002
Duoi U'Oi, Vietnam	*Sus scrofa*	wear stages	m1/ m2/ m3	21	38%[1] (14 + 24%)	62%		N: 0.04 (>0.70) P: 0.73 (>0.30)	Bacon et al. 2015
Lida Ajer, Sumatra	*S. scrofa, S. barbatus*	wear stages	m1/ m2/ m3	78	38.5%[1] (12.8 + 25.6%)	61.5%		N: 0.44 (>0.80) P: 2.29 (>0.10)	Authors

Note: Shaded rows represent natural populations.

[1] Juveniles plus subadults.

χ2 values include the confidence interval. Two χ2 values were available for *Rusa* and *Sus*: N = Nagarhole National Park; P = Pench National Park.

Juveniles and subadult percentages were merged at Nagarhole and Pench for *Sus scrofa*, which led us to consider similarly merged percentages for Duoi U'Oi and Lida Ajer juveniles and subadults assigned to *Sus* spp. for the sake of χ2 comparison. We similarly merged the juvenile and subadult cohorts of recent populations of *R. unicornis* and *R. unicolor*, and of fossil samples of rhinocerotids and *R. unicolor*, in order to compare consistently the results for two-cohort and three-cohort profiles.

Sources: As shown in the table.

Discussion

Diverse functional herbivore communities

Our overview of Southeast Asian mammalian faunas shows that over the period c. 500–40 ka, communities were organised into a biogeographic pattern similar to that of today's, following a north–south temperature gradient, regarding the structure of ecosystems and their carrying capacities (Corlett 2010; Woodruff 2010). In the period before MIS 6 (c. 500–130 ka) and during the MIS 6–5 transitional period, megafaunas on the mainland were largely archaic (c. 40–60% archaic taxa versus c. 10–50% modern taxa), and there were various local associations between herbivores. The Ngandong fauna from Java is composed of c. 70% archaic endemic taxa, indicating the long-term isolation of this mammalian community due to insular conditions until c. 120 ka (Rizal et al. 2020).

At the time of the earliest range expansion of modern faunas into Sunda c. 130ka diverse functional herbivore communities coexisted in the Southeast Asian mainland (Louys and Roberts 2020). Extensive savanna, open woodlands and dense forests covered the central plains of the continent, as shown by the data of Tham Wiman Nakin and Khok Sung; these extended to the southernmost boundary of the Indochinese subregion, including the Yai Ruak cave site located between the Isthmus of Kra and the Kangar-Pattani line (Suraprasit et al. 2019). These habitats were home to browsers such as rhinoceros and tapir and to a great number of small, medium-sized and large mixed-feeding and grazing cervids and bovids. Within the ruminant taxa, the great diversity of bovids (e.g. Bovinae and Caprinae) is particularly notable (Bocherens et al. 2017; Pushkina et al. 2010; Suraprasit et al. 2021).

The taxonomic diversity in ungulates, including, for example, 15 taxa at Tham Wiman Nakin, reflects a high environmental heterogeneity, with notably the presence of open woodlands and savanah in the central plains of the Indochinese Peninsula that allowed greater niche partitioning between taxa (Graham et al. 1996). This contrasts with the much less diverse southern Chinese mammalian communities (Black Cave, Wuyun, Hejiang and Yugong) containing 8 to 10 ungulate taxa and reflecting conversely predominant forested environments. Some other faunas have suggested the same pattern: Ganxian Cave, with 11 taxa (Liang 2020; 360–160 ka); Zhiren Cave, with 9 taxa (Jin et al. 2009; Ge et al. 2020; 116–106 ka or 190–130 ka); Fuyan Cave, with 10 taxa (Li et al. 2013; 180–120 ka); and Mocun Cave with 12 taxa (Fan et al. 2022; 101–66 ka).

The newly recovered faunal assemblage at Ngalau Gupin in the Padang Highlands tells us more about the composition of mammalian communities in the early phase of expansion of mammals in Sunda in Sumatra at c. 130 ka (Duval et al. 2021). This expansion brought about the emergence of a new modern guild combining taxa from the mainland source area able to adapt to new, humid tropic conditions, associated with one local archaic hippopotamus *Hexaprotodon* sp. (>70 ka; direct U-series age estimated from one specimen; Smith et al. 2021). The example of the Ngalau Gupin fauna shows how climate-driven biogeographical events contributed to new associations between herbivore taxa in new communities balanced differently to the preceding ones (Barnosky 2001; Stewart 2009).

Meanwhile, in more northern latitudes, *Stegodon orientalis* and *Megatapirus augustus* belonged to herbivore communities composed of a greater diversity of large-bodied non-ruminants (rhinocerotids, proboscideans, and tapirids) living predominantly in forested landscapes (Antoine 2012; Bacon et al. 2015, 2018a; Ma et al. 2017; Rink et al. 2008; Sun et al. 2019). *Stegodon orientalis* and *M. augustus* on the mainland and *Hexaprotodon* sp. in Sunda were the last relicts of Early to Middle Pleistocene archaic megafaunas, either being browsers ($\delta^{13}C < -14‰$) adapted to C_3-canopy forests (Bacon et al. 2018b, 2021; Bocherens et al. 2017; Li et al. 2017; Ma et al. 2017, 2019; Stacklyn et al. 2017; Wang W. et al. 2007), or C_3–C_4 mixed feeders ($\delta^{13}C > -8‰$) and C_4 grazers ($\delta^{13}C > -2‰$) living in a predominantly open environment with large areas of swamps and/or lakes (Janssen et al. 2016; Puspaningrum et al. 2020).

The turnover of the mammalian composition in Java shows how drastic the shift was, with all the archaic endemic ungulate species found at Ngandong (Rizal et al. 2020) replaced by the modern species found at Punung (Storm and de Vos 2006). However, our data seem to indicate that this turnover did not result in a noticeable change in the diversity of ungulates within body size categories, suggesting that either the carrying capacity or the structure (or both) of the inferred ecosystems did not change so significantly. Archaic species adapted to open landscapes were replaced by their modern congenerics from the mainland; these had broad ecological ranges and included large-bodied ruminants. For example, *Bubalus palaeokerabau* was replaced by *B. arnee* (Janssen et al. 2016). The relative abundance of specialised browsers such as tapirs (*T. indicus*) and of mixed feeders such as wild pigs (*Sus* sp.) or muntjacs (*M. muntjac*), as shown by our analysis, along with the relative abundance of orangutans (*Pongo pygmaeus*), gibbons (*Hylobates syndactylus*) and bears (*Helarctos malayanus*) (de Vos 1983), leaves no doubt about the presence of rainforests and associated warm, humid conditions (van der Kaars and Dam 1995). However, some evidence hints at the presence of grassy clearings within the rainforest habitat around Punung, probably associated with higher seasonality. This evidence takes two forms: the carbon isotope signal of large bovids that relied exclusively on a C_4 diet (Janssen et al. 2016), and, as shown in the present analysis, the predominance of *R. sondaicus* at Punung, which is known to have different ecological constraints from those of *D. sumatrensis*. Regarding the old collection from Punung studied here, however, the alternative hypothesis that it contains a mixture of elements from different stratigraphic levels remains viable (Kaifu et al. 2022).

In the biogeographical history of Southeast Asia, it is difficult to assess the effects of the other postulated turnover in the middle of the Late Pleistocene, which is much less detectable in the fossil records, as it involves modern lineages of herbivores discriminated at the infraspecific level, as shown by the Duoi U'Oi evidence from 70–60 ka (Bacon et al. 2021). This turnover of populations on the mainland was associated with a rapid climatic shift at the beginning of MIS 4 (Wang et al. 2008) that had profound effects on temperatures, seasonality and vegetation, with an increase in temperate plants, which was particularly noticeable in conifers and ferns (Zheng and Lei 1999). This, in turn, affected the faunal communities, leading to the occurrence of populations better adapted to this new C_3-dominated environment and the local loss of archaic taxa.

This climatic change had seemingly less impact in southern latitudes. At this time, the lowlands rainforests of Sumatra, consisting of dipterocarps, remained very humid, with precipitation over 2,000 mm per year (van der Kaars et al. 2010) that had comparatively less effect on faunal communities. In our results, the faunal communities from Southeast Asia may seem to appear more depleted of ungulates during MIS 4–3 compared with those from the previous MIS 6–5 period, but our results are not convincing due to the small size of the datasets. More evidence is needed to reliably assess the effects of this climatic episode on Southeast Asian mammalian herbivore communities.

Besides the evidently greater herbivore biomass on the mainland—either ruminants or non-ruminants depending on the carrying capacity of grassy versus forested habitats and the extent of areas and resource availability (Woodruff and Turner 2009)—overall, our results suggest a lower carrying capacity of ecosystems in the Sundaic region than in the Indomalayan region and a relative continuity there, even during the period of broad connections between land masses that led to diverse, balanced faunas, that is, faunas with large predators and a broad array of prey (as found at Niah Cave in Borneo and Sibrambang in Sumatra). This contrast between the mainland and the islands appears more marked today due to the global decline in megafauna since c. 50 ka, which has been particularly great in insular environments (Corlett 2010; Koch and Barnosky 2006).

Availability of prey species to humans

Our results indicate that the Indomalayan region experienced differing past ecological conditions depending on latitude, that affected the structure of mammalian communities. These conditions played a significant role in the abundance distribution of ungulate species and, therefore, in the availability of prey species to predators, including modern humans.

The comparison between Duoi U'Oi and Lida Ajer provides some clues to this question around 70 ka. At Duoi U'Oi, in a highly forested habitat including a significant proportion of closed-canopy forests (Bacon et al. 2021), hunting pressure on the sambar deer (*R. unicolor*) was high, most probably due to its relative abundance in the environment. This abundance could explain why humans (*Homo* sp.) targeted this prey preferentially, as we suggested previously (Bacon et al. 2015). At Lida Ajer, in an environment dominated by dipterocarp rainforests (Louys et al. 2022), hunting pressure might likewise have been higher on the most abundant species, tapir (*T. indicus*) and Sumatran rhinoceros (*D. sumatrensis*), but if so, it is not possible to say if one was preferentially targeted by humans.

In relation to suids, results appear fairly similar at both sites, with no evidence of selective pressure on *S. scrofa* at Duoi U'Oi or on *S. scrofa* or *S. barbatus* at Lida Ajer. It has been demonstrated that, at Niah Cave in the forests of Borneo, during the earliest phase of occupation (from c. 50 ka), the bearded pig (*S. barbatus*) was the primary prey of humans, with no particular selection of age classes (Barker et al. 2017; Piper and Rabett 2009). The question remains as to whether humans also hunted pigs in the forests around Duoi U'Oi (Bacon et al. 2021). It is also unknown whether pigs were hunted by humans from Lida Ajer, who might have frequently encountered abundant pigs in areas of relatively open-canopy vegetation (Louys et al. 2022). Currently, due to the absence of convincing archaeological evidence (e.g. evidence of lithic or organic industry, bones with butchery marks, etc.), firm knowledge of human foraging behaviour in Southeast Asia remains elusive.

Conclusion

This study investigated the composition and structure of the mammalian communities of Southeast Asia at the time of dispersal events in Sunda. Despite the limited dataset, the comparative analysis of Indochinese and Sundaic ungulate guilds provides an overview of the diversity of the ecosystems, which was strongly modulated by environmental conditions. The difference between the species-rich ungulate communities in the centre of the mainland and the less diverse ones from southern China and Sunda might reflect the degree of heterogeneity of the biomes. Comparatively, Sundaland seems to have been relatively impoverished in large-bodied species throughout the Late Pleistocene, apparently with a continuity in the carrying capacity of ecosystems. The results also illustrate the stark contrast between past and present ecosystems. In the changing climates of the Late Pleistocene, modern humans faced a wide range of rainforest conditions, and probably adapted their foraging to focus on different prey species according to their abundance.

Acknowledgements

We thank the curators of the Naturalis Biodiversity Center, Leiden, the Netherlands, for their assistance, and the editors, Julien Louys, Paul Albers and Alexandra van der Geer, for giving us the opportunity to contribute to this volume.

References

Antoine, P.-O. 2012. Pleistocene and Holocene rhinocerotids (Mammalia, Perissodactyla) from the Indochinese Peninsula. *Comptes Rendus Palevol* 11:159–168. doi.org/10.1016/j.crpv.2011.03.002

Bacon, A.-M., P.-O. Antoine, Nguyen Thi Mai Huong, K. Westaway, Nguyen Anh Tuan, P. Duringer, J.-X. Zhao, J.-L. Ponche, Sam Canh Dung, Truong Huu Nghia, Tran Thi Minh, Pham Tranh Son, M. Boyon, Nguyen Thi Kim Thuy, A. Blin and F. Demeter 2018a. A rhinocerotid-dominated megafauna at the MIS 6-5 transition: The late Middle Pleistocene Coc Muoi assemblage, Lang Son province, Vietnam. *Quaternary Science Reviews* 186:123–141. doi.org/10.1016/j.quascirev.2018.02.017

Bacon, A.-M., N. Bourgon, E. Dufour, C. Zanolli, P. Duringer, J.-L. Ponche, P.-O. Antoine, L. Shackelford, Nguyen Thi Mai Huong, T. Sayavonkhamdy, E. Patole-Edoumba and F. Demeter 2018b. Nam Lot (MIS 5) and Duoi U'Oi (MIS 4) Southeast Asian sites revisited: Zooarchaeological and isotopic evidences. *Palaeogeography, Palaeoclimatology, Palaeoecology* 512:132–144. doi.org/10.1016/j.palaeo.2018.03.034

Bacon, A.-M., N. Bourgon, F. Welker, E. Cappellini, D. Fiorillo, O. Tombret, Nguyen Thi Mai Huong, Nguyen Anh Tuan, T. Sayavonkhamdy, V. Souksavatdy, P. Sichanthongtip, P.-O. Antoine, P. Duringer, J.-L. Ponche, K. Westaway, R. Joannes-Boyau, Q. Boesch, E. Suzzoni, S. Frangeul, E. Patole-Edoumba, A. Zachwieja, L. Shackelford, F. Demeter, J.-J. Hublin and E. Dufour 2021. A multi-proxy approach to exploring *Homo sapiens*' arrival, environments and adaptations in Southeast Asia. *Scientific Reports* 11:21080. doi.org/10.1038/s41598-021-99931-4

Bacon, A.-M., F. Demeter, P. Duringer, C. Helm, M. Bano, Vu The Long, Nguyen Thi Kim Thuy, P.-O. Antoine, Bui Thi Mai, Nguyen Thi Mai Huong, Y. Dodo, F. Chabaux and S. Rihs 2008. The Late Pleistocene Duoi U'Oi cave in northern Vietnam: Palaeontology, sedimentology, taphonomy, palaeoenvironments. *Quaternary Science Reviews* 27:1627–1654. doi.org/10.1016/j.quascirev.2008.04.017

Bacon, A.-M., K. Westaway, P.-O. Antoine, P. Duringer, A. Blin, F. Demeter, J.-L. Ponche, J.-X. Zhao, L. Barnes, T. Sayavongkhamdy, Nguyen Thi Kim Thuy, E. Patole-Edoumba, Vu The Long and L. Shackelford 2015. Late Pleistocene mammalian assemblages of Southeast Asia: New dating, mortality profiles and evolution of the predator–prey relationships in an environmental context. *Palaeogeography, Palaeoclimatology, Palaeoecology* 422:101–127. doi.org/10.1016/j.palaeo.2015.01.011

Badoux, D.M. 1959. *Fossil Mammals From Two Deposits at Punung (Java)*. Kemink en Zoon, Utrecht.

Barker, G., H. Barton, M. Bird, P. Daly, I. Datan, A. Dykes, L. Farr, D. Gilbertson, B. Harrison, C. Hunt, T. Higham, L. Kealhofer, J. Krigbaum, H. Lewis, S. McLaren, V. Paz, A. Pike, P. Piper, B. Pyatt, R. Rabett, T. Reynolds, J. Rose, G. Rushworth, M. Stephens, C. Stringer, J. Thompson and C. Turney 2007. The 'human revolution' in lowland tropical Southeast Asia: The antiquity and behavior of anatomically modern humans at Niah cave (Sarawak, Borneo). *Journal of Human Evolution* 52:243–261. doi.org/10.1016/j.jhevol.2006.08.011

Barker, G., C. Hunt, H. Barton, C. Gosden, S. Jones, L. Lloyd-Smith, L. Farr, B. Nyiri and S. O'Dennell 2017. The 'cultured rainforests' of Borneo. *Quaternary International* 448:44–61. doi.org/10.1016/j.quaint.2016.08.018

Barnosky, A.D. 2001. Distinguishing the effects of the Red Queen and Court Jester on Miocene mammal evolution in the northern Rocky Mountains. *Journal of Vertebrate Paleontology* 21(1):172–185. doi.org/10.1671/0272-4634(2001)021[0172:DTEOTR]2.0.CO;2

Bird, M.I., D. Taylor and C. Hunt 2005. Palaeoenvironments of insular Southeast Asia during the Last Glacial Period: A savanna corridor in Sundaland? *Quaternary Science Reviews* 24:2228–2242. doi.org/10.1016/j.quascirev.2005.04.004

Biswas, S. and S. Sankar 2002. Prey abundance and food habit of tigers (*Panthera tigris tigris*) in Pench National Park, Madhya Pradesh, India. *Journal of Zoology* 256:411–420. doi.org/10.1017/S095283690 2000456

Bocherens, H., F. Schrenk, Y. Chaimanee, O. Kullmer, D. Mörike, D. Pushkina and J.-J. Jaeger 2017. Flexibility of diet and habitat in Pleistocene South Asian mammals: Implications for the fate of the giant fossil ape *Gigantopithecus*. *Quaternary International* 434:148–155. doi.org/10.1016/j.quaint.2015.11.059

Brain, C.K. 1981. *The Hunters and the Hunted? An Introduction to African Cave Taphonomy*. The University of Chicago Press, Chicago and London.

Ciochon, R.L., V.T. Long, R. Larick, L. Gonzalez, R. Grün, J. de Vos, C. Yonge, L. Taylor, H. Yoshida and M. Reagan 1996. Dated co-occurrence of *Homo erectus* and *Gigantopithecus* from Tham Khuyen Cave, Vietnam. *Proceedings of the National Academy of Sciences of the USA* 93:3016–3020. doi.org/10.1073/pnas.93.7.3016

Corbet, G.B. and J.E. Hill 1992. *The Mammals of the Indomalayan Region*. Natural History Museum Publications. Oxford University Press, Oxford.

Corlett, R.T. 2010. Megafaunal extinctions and their consequences in the tropical Indo-Pacific. In S.G. Haberle, J. Stevenson and M. Prebble (eds), *Altered Ecologies: Fire, Climate and Human Influence on Terrestrial Landscapes*, pp. 117–131. Terra Australis 32. ANU Press, Canberra. doi.org/10.22459/TA32. 11.2010.08

Cuong, N.L. 1985. Fossile Menschenfunde aus Nordvietnam. In J. Herrmann and H. Ullrich (eds), *Menschwerdung—Biotischer und Gesellschaftlicher Entwicklungsprozess*, pp. 96–102. Akademieverlag, Berlin.

de Vos, J. 1983. The *Pongo* faunas from Java and Sumatra and their significance for biostratigraphical and paleoecological interpretations. *Proceedings of the Koninklijke Nederlandse Akademie van Wetenschappen, Series B* 86:417–425.

Del Monte-Luna, P., B.W. Brook, M.J. Zetina-Rejón and V.H. Cruz-Escalona 2004. The carrying capacity of ecosystems. *Global Ecology and Biogeography* 13:485–495. doi.org/10.1111/j.1466-822X.2004.00131.x

Dong, W., Y. Wang, C. Jin, D. Qin, Q. Xu and L. Zhang 2014. Artiodactyla associated with *Homo sapiens* from Gongjishan, Chongzuo, Guangxi, South China. *Acta Anthropologica Sinica* 33:355–368.

Donny, Y., Z.Z. Zainal, R.R. Jeffrine Japning, M.Z. Che Ku, Z.Z. Cwar Mohd, J. Enos, T. Rahmat and A.A.H. Kadir 2019. Growth rate and pelage colour changes of a captive bred Malayan tapir (*Tapirus indicus*). *Malaysian Journal of Veterinary Research* 10:25–31.

Dubois, M.E.F.T. 1894. *Pithecanthropus erectus, Eine Menschenaehnliche Uebergangsform aus Java*. Landesdruckerei, Batavia.

Duval, M., F. Fang, K. Suraprasit, J.-J. Jaeger, M. Benammi, Y. Chaimanee, J. Iglesias Cibanal and R. Grün 2019. Direct ESR dating of the Pleistocene vertebrate assemblage from Khok Sung locality, Nakhon Ratchasima Province, Northeast Thailand. *Palaeontologia Electronica* 22.3.69:1–25. doi.org/10.26879/941

Duval, M., K. Westaway, Y. Zaim, Y. Rizal, Aswan, M.R. Puspaningrum, A. Trihascaryo, P.C.H. Albers, H.E. Smith, G.M. Drawhorn, G.J. Price and J. Louys 2021. New chronological constraints for the Late Pleistocene fossil assemblage and associated breccia from Ngalau Sampit, Sumatra. *Open Quaternary* 7:1–24. doi.org/10.5334/oq.96

Esposito, M., J.-L. Reyss, Y. Chaimanee and J.-J. Jaeger 2002. U-series dating of fossil teeth and carbonates from Snake cave, Thailand. *Journal of Archaeological Science* 29:341–349. doi.org/10.1006/jasc.2002.0718

Esposito, M., Y. Chaimanee, J.-J. Jaeger and J.-L. Reyss 1998. Datation des concrétions carbonatées de la 'Grotte du serpent' (Thaïlande) par la méthode Th/U. *Comptes Rendus de l'Académie des Sciences, Series IIA, Earth and Planetary Science* 326(9):603–608. doi.org/10.1016/S1251-8050(98)80250-4

Faith, J.T., J. Rowan and A. Du 2019. Early hominins evolved within non-analog ecosystems. *Proceedings of the National Academy of Sciences of the USA* 116:21478–21483. doi.org/10.1073/pnas.1909284116

Fan, Y., Q. Shao, W. Liao, A.-M. Bacon and W. Wang 2022. Late Pleistocene large-bodied mammalian fauna from Mocun cave in south China: Palaeontological, chronological and biogeographical implications. *Quaternary Science Reviews.* doi.org/10.1016/j.quascirev.2022.107741

Filoux, A., A. Wattanapituksakul, C. Lespes and C. Thongcharoenchaikit 2015. A Pleistocene mammal assemblage containing *Ailuropoda* and *Pongo* from Tham Prakai Phet cave, Chaiyaphum Province, Thailand. *Geobios* 48:341–349. doi.org/10.1016/j.geobios.2015.07.003

Francis, C.M. 2008. *A Field Guide to the Mammals of Southeast Asia.* New Holland Publishers, London.

Ge, J.Y., C. Deng, Y. Wang, Q. Shao, X. Zhou, S. Xing, H. Pang and C. Jin 2020. Climate-influenced cave deposition and human occupation during the Pleistocene in Zhiren Cave, southwest China. *Quaternary International* 559, 14–23. doi.org/10.1016/j.quaint.2020.01.018

Gearty, W. 2012. *Tapirus indicus.* Animal Diversity Web. animaldiversity.org/accounts/Tapirus_indicus (accessed 19 January 2022).

Graham, R.W., E.L. Lundelius Jr, M.A. Graham, E.K. Schroeder, R.S. Toomey III, E. Anderson, A.D. Barnosky, J.A. Burns, C.S. Churcher, D.K. Grayson, R.D. Guthrie, C.R. Harington, G.T. Jefferson, L.D. Martin, H.G. McDonald, R.E. Morlan, H.A. Semken Jr, S.D. Webb, L. Werdelin and M.C. Wilson 1996. Spatial response of mammals to Late Quaternary environmental fluctuations. *Science* 272(5268):1601–1606. doi.org/10.1126/science.272.5268.1601

Grant, A. 1982. The use of tooth wear as a guide to the age of domestic ungulates. In B. Wilson, C. Grigson and S. Payne (eds), *Ageing and Sexing Animal Bones From Archaeological Sites*, pp. 91–108. BAR British Series 109. BAR Publishing, Oxford, England. doi.org/10.30861/9780860541929

Groves, C. and D. Leslie Jr 2011. *Rhinoceros sondaicus* (Perissodactyla: Rhinocerotidae). *Mammalian Species* 43(887):190–208. doi.org/10.1644/887.1

Hayward, M.W., S. Lyngdoh and B. Habib 2014. Diet and prey preferences of dholes (*Cuon alpinus*): Dietary competition within Asia's apex predator guild. *Journal of Zoology* 294(4):255–266. doi.org/10.1111/jzo.12171

Heaney, L.R. 1986. Biogeography of mammals in SE Asia: Estimates of rates of colonization, extinction and speciation. *Biological Journal of the Linnean Society* 28(1–2):127–165. doi.org/10.1111/j.1095-8312.1986.tb01752.x

Hillman-Smith, A.K.K., N. Owen-Smith, J.L. Anderson, A.J. Hall-Martin and J.P. Selaladi 1986. Age estimation of the white rhinoceros (*Ceratotherium simum*). *Journal of Zoology* 210:355–379. doi.org/10.1111/j.1469-7998.1986.tb03639.x

Hooijer, D.A. 1946a. Prehistoric and fossil rhinoceroses from the Malay Archipelago and India. *Zoologische Mededelingen* 26:1–138.

Hooijer, D.A. 1946b. Some remarks on recent, prehistoric and fossil porcupines from the Malay Archipelago. *Zoologische Mededelingen* 26:251–267.

Hooijer, D.A. 1947. On fossil and prehistoric remains of *Tapirus* from Java, Sumatra and China. *Zoologische Mededelingen* 27:253–299.

Hooijer, D.A. 1948. Prehistoric teeth of man and of the orang-utan from central Sumatra, with notes on the fossil orang-utan from Java and southern China. *Zoologische Mededelingen* 29:175–301.

Hooijer, D.A. 1960. Quaternary gibbons from the Malay Archipelago. *Zoologische Verhandelingen* 46:1–41.

Hooijer, D.A. 1962. Quaternary langurs and macaques from the Malay Archipelago. *Zoologische Verhandelingen* 55:1–64.

Huxley, T.H. 1868. On the classification and distribution of the Alectoromorphae and Heteromorphae. *Proceedings of the Zoological Society of London* 1868:294–319.

Ibrahim, Y.K., L.T. Tshen, K.E. Westaway, Earl of Cranbrook, L. Humphrey, R.F. Muhammad, J-X. Zhao and L.C. Peng 2013. First discovery of Pleistocene orangutan (*Pongo* sp.) fossils in Peninsular Malaysia: Biogeographic and palaeoenvironmental implications. *Journal of Human Evolution* 65:770–797. doi.org/10.1016/j.jhevol.2013.09.005

Janssen, R., J.C.A. Joordens, D.F. Koutamanis, M.R. Puspaningrum, J. de Vos, J.H.J.L. van der Lubbe, J.J.G. Reijmer, O. Hampe and H.B. Vonhof 2016. Tooth enamel stable isotopes of Holocene and Pleistocene fossil fauna reveal glacial and interglacial paleoenvironments of hominins in Indonesia. *Quaternary Science Reviews* 144:145–154. doi.org/10.1016/j.quascirev.2016.02.028

Jin, C., W. Pan, Y. Zhang, Y. Cai, Q. Xu, Z. Tang, W. Wang, Y. Wang, J. Liu, D. Qin, R.L. Edwards and H. Cheng 2009. The *Homo sapiens* cave hominin site of Mulan mountain, Jiangzhou district, Chongzuo, Guangxi with emphasis on its age. *Chinese Science Bulletin* 54:3848. doi.org/10.1007/s11434-009-0641-1

Kaifu, Y., I. Kurniawan, D. Yurnaldi, R. Setiawan, E. Setiyabudi, H. Insani, M. Takai, Y. Nishioka, A. Takahashi, F. Aziz and M. Yoneda 2022. Modern human teeth unearthed from below the ~128,000-year-old level at Punung, Java: A case highlighting the problem of recent intrusion in cave sediments. *Journal of Human Evolution* 163:103122. doi.org/10.1016/j.jhevol.2021.103122

Karanth, K.U. and M.E. Sunquist 1995. Prey selection by tiger, leopard and dhole in tropical forests. *Journal of Animal Ecology* 64:439–450. doi.org/10.2307/5647

Klein, R.G., C. Wolf, L.G. Freeman and K. Allwarden 1981. The use of dental crown heights for constructing age profiles of red deer and similar species in archaeological samples. *Journal of Archaeological Science* 8(1):1–31. doi.org/10.1016/0305-4403(81)90010-8

Koch, P.L. and A.D. Barnosky 2006. Late Quaternary extinctions: State of the debate. *Annual Review of Ecology Evolution and Systematics* 37:215–250. doi.org/10.1146/annurev.ecolsys.34.011802.132415

Laurie, W.A., E.M. Lang and C.P. Groves 1983. *Rhinoceros unicornis*. *Mammalian Species* 211:1–6. doi.org/10.2307/3504002

Li, D., C. Hu, W. Wang, J. Chen, F. Tian, S. Huang and C.J. Bae 2017. The stable isotope record in cervid tooth enamel from Tantang Cave, Guangxi: Implications for the Quaternary East Asian monsoon. *Quaternary International* 434:156–162. doi.org/10.1016/j.quaint.2015.11.049

Li, Y.-Y., S.-W. Pei, H.-W. Tong, X.-X. Yang, Y.-J. Cai, W. Liu and X.-J. Wu 2013. A preliminary report on the 2011 excavation at Houbeishan Fuyan Cave, Daoxian, Hunan Province. *Acta Anthropologica Sinica* 32:133–143.

Liang, H. 2020. Middle Pleistocene Orangutan Fossil from Ganxian Cave, Tiandong County, Guangxi, South China and its Significance for Evolution. Unpublished masters thesis. Guilin University of Technology, Guilin, China.

Lisiecki, L.E. and M.E. Raymo 2005. A Pliocene-Pleistocene stack of 57 globally distributed benthic δ^{18}O records. *Paleoceanography* 20:PA1003. doi.org/10.1029/2004PA001071

Long, V.T., J. de Vos and R.L. Ciochon 1996. The fossil mammal fauna of the Lang Trang caves, Vietnam, compared with Southeast Asian fossil and recent mammal faunas: The geographical implications. *Indo-Pacific Prehistory Association Bulletin* 14:101–109.

Louys, J. 2007. Limited effect of the Quaternary's largest super-eruption (Toba) on land mammals from Southeast Asia. *Quaternary Science Reviews* 26:3108–3117. doi.org/10.1016/j.quascirev.2007.09.008

Louys, J. 2012. Mammal community structure of Sundanese fossil assemblages from the Late Pleistocene, and a discussion on the ecological effects of the Toba eruption. *Quaternary International* 258:80–87. doi.org/10.1016/j.quaint.2011.07.027

Louys, J., D. Curnoe and H. Tong 2007. Characteristics of the Pleistocene megafauna extinctions in Southeast Asia. *Palaeogeography, Palaeoclimatology, Palaeoecology* 243:152–173. doi.org/10.1016/j.palaeo.2006.07.011

Louys, J., M. Duval, G.J. Price, K. Westaway, Y. Zaim, Y, Rizal, Aswan, M. Puspaningrum, A. Trihascaryo, S. Breitenbach, O. Kwiecien, Y. Cai, P. Higgins, P.C.H. Albers, J. de Vos and P. Roberts 2022. Speleological and environmental history of Lida Ajer cave, western Sumatra. *Philosophical Transactions of the Royal Society B*. 377:20200494. doi.org/10.1098/rstb.2020.0494

Louys, J. and E. Meijaard 2010. Palaeoecology of Southeast Asian megafauna-bearing sites from the Pleistocene and a review of environmental changes in the region. *Journal of Biogeography* 37:1432–1449. doi.org/10.1111/j.1365-2699.2010.02297.x

Louys, J. and P. Roberts 2020. Environmental drivers of megafauna and hominin extinction in Southeast Asia. *Nature* 586:402–406. doi.org/10.1038/s41586-020-2810-y

Ma, J., Y. Wang, C. Jin, Y. Hu and H. Bocherens 2019. Ecological flexibility and differential survival of Pleistocene *Stegodon orientalis* and *Elephas maximus* in mainland Southeast Asia revealed by stable isotope (C, O) analysis. *Quaternary Science Reviews* 212:33–44. doi.org/10.1016/j.quascirev.2019.03.021

Ma, J., Y. Wang, C. Jin, Y. Yan, Y. Qu and Y. Hu 2017. Isotopic evidence of foraging ecology of Asian elephant (*Elephas maximus*) in South China during the Late Pleistocene. *Quaternary International* 443:160–167. doi.org/10.1016/j.quaint.2016.09.043

Maffei, L. 2003. The age structure of tapirs (*Tapirus terrestris*) in the Chaco. *Newsletter of the IUCN/SSC Tapir Specialist Group* 12(2):18–19.

Mayr, E. 1942. *Systematics and the Origin of Species*. Columbia University Press, New York.

Myers, N., R.A. Mittermeier, C.G. Mittermeier, G.A.B. da Fonseca and J. Kent 2000. Biodiversity hotspots for conservation priorities. *Nature* 403:853–858. doi.org/10.1038/35002501

Piper, P.J. and R.J. Rabett 2009. Hunting in a tropical rainforest: Evidence from the Terminal Pleistocene at Lobang Hangus, Niah Caves, Sarawak. *International Journal of Osteoarchaeology* 19:551–565. doi.org/10.1002/oa.1046

Polanski, J.M., H.E. Marsh and S.D. Maddux 2016. Dental size reduction in Indonesian *Homo erectus*: Implications for the PU-198 premolar and the appearance of *Homo sapiens* on Java. *Journal of Human Evolution* 90:49–54. doi.org/10.1016/j.jhevol.2015.09.008

Pushkina, D., H. Bocherens, Y. Chaimanee and J.-J. Jaeger 2010. Stable carbon isotope reconstructions of diet and paleoenvironment from the late Middle Pleistocene Snake Cave in northeastern Thailand. *Naturwissenschaften* 97:299–309. doi.org/10.1007/s00114-009-0642-6

Puspaningrum, M.R., G.D. van den Bergh, A.R. Chivas, E. Setiabudi and I. Kurniawan 2020. Isotopic reconstruction of Proboscidean habitats and diets on Java since the Early Pleistocene: Implications for adaptations and extinction. *Quaternary Science Reviews* 228:106007. doi.org/10.1016/j.quascirev.2019. 106007

Railsback, L.B., P.L. Gibbard, M.J. Head, N.R.G. Voarintsoa and S. Toucanne 2015. An optimized scheme of lettered marine isotope substages for the last 1.0 million years, and the climatostratigraphic nature of isotope stages and substages. *Quaternary Science Reviews* 111:94–106. doi.org/10.1016/j.quascirev.2015. 01.012

Rink, W.J., W. Wang, D. Bekken and H.L. Jones 2008. Geochronology of *Ailuropoda-Stegodon* fauna and *Gigantopithecus* in Guangxi Province. *Quaternary Research* 69(3):377–387. doi.org/10.1016/j.yqres.2008. 02.008

Rizal, Y., K.E. Westaway, Z. Yahdi, G.D. van den Bergh, E. Arthur Bettis III, M.J. Morwood, O.F. Huffman, R. Grün, R. Joannes-Boyau, R.M. Bailey, Sidarto, M.C. Westaway, I. Kurniawan, M.W. Moore, M. Storey, F. Aziz, Suminto, J.-X. Zhao, Aswan, M.E. Sipola, R. Larick, J.-P. Zonneveld, R. Scott, S. Putt and R.L. Ciochon 2020. Last appearance of *Homo erectus* at Ngandong, Java, 117,000–108,000 years ago. *Nature* 577:381–385. doi.org/10.1038/s41586-019-1863-2

Roberts, P., N. Boivin, J. Lee-Thorp, M. Petraglia and J. Stock 2016. Tropical forests and the genus *Homo*. *Evolutionary Anthropology* 25(6):306–317. doi.org/10.1002/evan.21508

Salles, T., C. Mallard, L. Husson, S. Zahirovic, A.C. Sarr and P. Sepulchre 2021. Quaternary landscape dynamics boosted species dispersal across Southeast Asia. *Communications Earth & Environment* 2:1–12. doi.org/10.1038/s43247-021-00311-7

Sathiamurthy, E. and Voris, H.K. 2006. Maps of Holocene sea level transgression and submerged lakes on the Sunda Shelf. *The Natural History Journal of Chulalongkorn University* 2:1–44.

Shao, K., Y. Wang, P. Voinchet, M. Zhu, M. Lin, W.J. Rink, C. Jin and J.-J. Bahain 2017. U-series and ESR/U-series dating of the *Stegodon-Ailuropoda* fauna at Black Cave, Guangxi, southern China with implications for the timing of the extinction of *Gigantopithecus blacki*. *Quaternary International* 434:65–74. doi.org/10.1016/j.quaint.2015.12.016

Sharpe, D. 2015. Chi-Square test is statistically significant: Now what? *Practical Assessment, Research, and Evaluation* 20:8. doi.org/10.7275/tbfa-x148

Skelton, R. 1985. Aspartic Acid Racemization Dating of Southeast Asian Sites. Unpublished report.

Smith, H.E., G.J. Price, M. Duval, K. Westaway, J. Zaim, Y. Rizal, Aswan, M.R. Puspaningrum, A. Trihascaryo, M. Stewart and J. Louys 2021. Taxonomy, taphonomy and chronology of the Pleistocene faunal assemblage at Ngalau Gupin cave, Sumatra. *Quaternary International* 603:40–63. doi.org/10.1016/ j.quaint.2021.05.005

Stacklyn, S., Y. Wang, C.-Z. Jin, Y. Wang, F. Sun, C. Zhang, S. Jiang and T. Deng 2017. Carbon and oxygen isotopic evidence for diets, environments and niche differentiation of early Pleistocene pandas and associated mammals in South China. *Palaeogeography, Palaeoclimatology, Palaeoecology* 468:351–361. doi.org/10.1016/j.palaeo.2016.12.015

Stewart, J.R. 2009. The evolutionary consequence of the individualistic response to climate change. *Journal of Evolutionary Biology* 22:2363–2375. doi.org/10.1111/j.1420-9101.2009.01859.x

Storm, P., F. Aziz, J. de Vos, D. Kosasih, S. Baskoro, Ngaliman and L.W. van den Hoek Ostende 2005. Late Pleistocene *Homo sapiens* in a tropical rainforest fauna in East Java. *Journal of Human Evolution* 49:536–545. doi.org/10.1016/j.jhevol.2005.06.003

Storm, P. and J. de Vos 2006. Rediscovery of the Late Pleistocene Punung hominin sites and the discovery of a new site Gunung Dawung in East Java. *Senckenbergiana Lethaea* 86(2):121–131. doi.org/10.1007/BF03043494

Sun, F., Y. Wang, Y. Wang, C.-Z. Jin, T. Deng and B. Wolff 2019. Paleoecology of Pleistocene mammals and paleoclimatic change in South China: Evidence from stable carbon and oxygen isotopes. *Palaeogeography, Palaeoclimatology, Palaeoecology* 524:1–12. doi.org/10.1016/j.palaeo.2019.03.021

Suraprasit, K., H. Bocherens, Y. Chaimanee, S. Panha and J.-J. Jaeger 2018. Late Middle Pleistocene ecology and climate in northeastern Thailand inferred from the stable isotope analysis of Khok Sung herbivore tooth enamel and the land mammal cenogram. *Quaternary Science Reviews* 193:24–42. doi.org/10.1016/j.quascirev.2018.06.004

Suraprasit, K., S. Jongautchariyakul, C. Yamee, C. Pothichaiya and H. Bocherens 2019. New fossil and isotope evidence for the Pleistocene zoogeographic transition and hypothesized savanna corridor in peninsular Thailand. *Quaternary Science Reviews* 221:105861. doi.org/10.1016/j.quascirev.2019.105861

Suraprasit, K., R. Shoocongdej, K. Chintakanon and H. Bocherens 2021. Late Pleistocene human paleoecology in the highland savanna ecosystem of mainland Southeast Asia. *Scientific Reports* 11:16756. doi.org/10.1038/s41598-021-96260-4

Tougard, C. 1998. Les faunes de grands mammifères du Pléistocène moyen terminal de Thaïlande dans leur cadre phylogénétique, paléoécologique et biochronologique. Unpublished doctoral thesis. Université de Montpellier II, Montpellier, France.

Tougard, C. and S. Montuire 2006. Pleistocene paleoenvironmental reconstructions and mammalian evolution in South-East Asia: Focus on fossil faunas from Thailand. *Quaternary Science Reviews* 25:126–141. doi.org/10.1016/j.quascirev.2005.04.010

van den Bergh, G.D., J. de Vos and P.Y. Sondaar 2001. The Late Quaternary palaeogeography of mammal evolution in the Indonesian Archipelago. *Palaeogeography, Palaeoclimatology, Palaeoecology* 171(3–4):385–408. doi.org/10.1016/S0031-0182(01)00255-3

van der Geer, A., G. Lyras and J. de Vos 2021. *Evolution of Island Mammals.* Wiley-Blackwell, London.

van der Kaars, W.A., F. Bassinot, P. De Deckker and F. Guichard 2010. Changes in monsoon and ocean circulation and the vegetation cover of southwest Sumatra through the last 83,000 years: The records from marine core BAR94-42. *Palaeogeography, Palaeoclimatology, Palaeoecology* 296:52–78. doi.org/10.1016/j.palaeo.2010.06.015

van der Kaars, W.A. and M.A.C. Dam 1995. A 135,000-year record of vegetational and climatic change from the Bandung area, West-Java, Indonesia. *Palaeogeography, Palaeoclimatology, Palaeoecology* 117:55–72. doi.org/10.1016/0031-0182(94)00121-N

von Koenigswald, G.H.R. 1939. Das Pleistocän Javas. *Quartär* 2:28–53.

Wallace, A.R. 1860. On the zoological geography of the Malay Archipelago. *Journal of the Proceedings of the Linnean Society* 4(16):172–184. doi.org/10.1111/j.1096-3642.1860.tb00090.x

Wang, Y., H. Cheng, R.L. Edwards, X. Kong, X. Shao, S. Chen, J. Wu, X. Jiang, X. Wang and Z. An 2008. Millennial- and orbital-scale changes in the East Asian monsoon over the past 224,000 years. *Nature* 451:1090–1093. doi.org/10.1038/nature06692

Wang, W., R. Potts, Y. Baoyin, W. Huang, H. Cheng, R.L. Edwards and P. Ditchfield 2007. Sequence of mammalian fossils, including hominoid teeth, from the Bubing Basin caves, South China. *Journal of Human Evolution* 52:370–379. doi.org/10.1016/j.jhevol.2006.10.003

Westaway, K.E., J. Louys, R. Due Awe, M.J. Morwood, G.J. Price, J.X. Zhao, M. Aubert, R. Joannes-Boyau, T. Smith, M.M. Skinner, T. Compton, R.M. Bailey, G.D. van den Bergh, J. de Vos, A.W.G. Pike, C. Stringer, E.W. Saptomo, Y. Rizal, J. Zaim, W.D. Santoso, A. Trihascaryo, L. Kinsley and B. Sulistyanto 2017. An early modern human presence in Sumatra 73,000–63,000 years ago. *Nature* 548:322–325. doi.org/10.1038/nature23452

Westaway, K.E., M.J. Morwood, R.G. Roberts, A.D. Rokus, J.X. Zhao, P. Storm, F. Aziz, G. van den Bergh, P. Hadi, Jatmiko and J. de Vos 2007. Age and biostratigraphic significance of the Punung Rainforest Fauna, East Java, Indonesia, and implications for *Pongo* and *Homo*. *Journal of Human Evolution* 53:709–717. doi.org/10.1016/j.jhevol.2007.06.002

Wood, B. 2020. Birth of *Homo erectus*. *Evolutionary Anthropology* 29:293–298. doi.org/10.1002/evan.21873

Woodruff, D.S. 2010. Biogeography and conservation in Southeast Asia: How 2.7 million years of repeated environmental fluctuations affect today's patterns and the future of the remaining refugial-phase biodiversity. *Biodiversity and Conservation* 19:919–941. doi.org/10.1007/s10531-010-9783-3

Woodruff, D.S. and L.M. Turner 2009. The Indochinese-Sundaic zoogeographic transition: A description and analysis of terrestrial mammal species distributions. *Journal of Biogeography* 36:803–821. doi.org/10.1111/j.1365-2699.2008.02071.x

Zeitoun, V., W. Chinnawut, L. Arnaud, C. Bochaton, K. Burdette, J. Thompson, J.-B. Mallye, S. Frere, R. Debruyne, P.-O. Antoine, J.R. William and A. Prasit 2019. Dating, stratigraphy and taphonomy of the Pleistocene site of Ban Fa Suai II (northern Thailand): Contributions to the study of paleobiodiversity in Southeast Asia. *Annales de Paléontologie* 2:275–285. doi.org/10.1016/j.annpal.2019.03.005

Zhang, Y., J. Changzhu, Y. Cai, R. Kono, W. Wang, Y. Wang, M. Zhu and Y. Yan 2014. New 400–320 ka *Gigantopithecus blacki* remains from Hejiang Cave, Chongzuo City, Guangxi, South China. *Quaternary International* 354:35–45. doi.org/10.1016/j.quaint.2013.12.008

Zheng, Z. and Z.-Q. Lei 1999. A 400,000 year record of vegetational and climatic changes from a volcanic basin, Leizhou Peninsula, southern China. *Palaeogeography, Palaeoclimatology, Palaeoecology* 145:339–362. doi.org/10.1016/s0031-0182(98)00107-2

Appendix 7.1: The Southeast Asian sites included in the present analysis, listed from north to south.

Site	Country	Age	Sources
Yugong Cave	Guangxi Zuang Autonomous Region, China	late Middle Pleistocene	Dong et al. 2014; Sun et al. 2019
Black Cave	Guangxi Zuang Autonomous Region, China	404–382 ka	Shao et al. 2017
Hejiang Cave	Guangxi Zuang Autonomous Region, China	400–320 ka	Zhang et al. 2014
Wuyun Cave	Guangxi Zuang Autonomous Region, China	279–76 ka	Rink et al. 2008
Quzai Cave	Guangxi Zuang Autonomous Region, China	early Late Pleistocene	Ma et al. 2019
Baxian Cave	Guangxi Zuang Autonomous Region, China	early Late Pleistocene	Ma et al. 2017; Sun et al. 2019
Tham Kuyen	Lang Son Province, Vietnam	475 ± 125 ka	Ciochon et al. 1996; Cuong 1985
Coc Muoi Cave	Lang Son Province, Vietnam	148–117 ka	Bacon et al. 2018a, 2021
Duoi U'Oi Cave	Hoà Bình Province, Vietnam	70–60 ka	Bacon et al. 2008, 2015, 2018b, 2021
Tam Hang South	Huaphan Province, Laos	94–60 ka	Bacon et al. 2015, 2021
Nam Lot Cave	Huaphan Province, Laos	86–72 ka	Bacon et al. 2015, 2021
Tham Wiman Nakin	Chaiyaphum Province, Thailand	>169 ± 15 ka	Esposito et al. 1998, 2002; Suraprasit et al. 2021; Tougard 1998
Tham Prakai Phet	Chaiyaphum Province, Thailand	169–19 ka	Esposito et al. 1998, 2002; Filoux et al. 2015; Tougard 1998
Khok Sung	Nakhon Ratchasima Province, Thailand	217 ka or 130 ka	Duval et al. 2019; Suraprasit et al. 2018
Ban Fa Sui II (Levels 2e–2f)	Chiang Mai Province, Thailand	55–46 ka	Zeitoun et al. 2019
Batu (group of three caves)	Selangor, Peninsular Malaysia	66–33 ka	Ibrahim et al. 2013
Badak Cave	Selangor, Peninsular Malaysia	>500 ka	Ibrahim et al. 2013
Ngalau Gupin	Sumatra	160–115 ka	Smith et al. 2021
Lida Ajer	Sumatra	73–63 ka	Long et al. 1996; Louys 2012; Westaway et al. 2017
Sibrambang	Sumatra	128–118 ka or 73–63 ka	Westaway et al. 2007, 2017
Ngandong	Java	117–108 ka	Rizal et al. 2020
Gunung Dawung (Punung III)	Java	128–118 ka	Storm et al. 2005; Storm and de Vos 2006; Westaway et al. 2007
Niah Cave	Sarawak, Malaysia, Borneo	From c. 50 ka to Holocene 46–34 ka 'Deep skull' layer	Barker et al. 2007, 2017

Source: Authors.

Appendix 7.2: List of taxa (Artiodactyla, Perissodactyla and Proboscidea), dietary strategy (ruminant versus non-ruminant), body size category, and occurrence in the Indochinese subregion at the reviewed sites and in current faunas.

Taxon	Common name	Dietary strategy	Body size category	Yugong	Black Cave	Hejiang Cave	Wuyun Cave	Quzai/Baxian	Tham Khuyen	Coc Muoi	Duoi U'Oi	Tam Hang South	Nam Lot	Tham Wiman Nakin	Tham Prakai Phet	Khok Sung	Ban Fa Sui II	Current faunas 25°–20° N	Current faunas 20°–10° N
Cervus sp.	Deer	R[1]	B[2]		x		x		x										
Cervus nippon	Sika	R	B														cf.	x[3]	
Rusa unicolor	Sambar deer	R	B	x		cf.		x	cf.	x	x	x	x	x	x	x	x	x	x
Axis porcinus	Hog deer	R	A											x	x				x
Axis axis	Chital	R	A														x		
Rucervus eldii	Eld's deer	R	B									(?)		x		(?)		x	x
Muntiacus sp.	Muntjac	R	A	x	x	x	x	x		x				x	x				
Muntiacus muntjak	Red muntjac	R	A						x		x	x	x			x	x	x	x
Muntiacus feae	Fea's muntjac	R	A																x
Muntiacus rooseveltorum	Roosevelt's muntjac	R	A															x	
Megalovis guangxiensis*	Extinct bovid	R	C		x	x													
Leptobos sp.*	Extinct bovid	R	C	x															
Bos sp./Bibos sp.	Large bovid	R	C	x	x	x		x			x		x			x			
Bos javanicus	Banteng	R	C											x	x			x	x
Bos sauveli	Kouprey	R	C					x			x			x	x	x			x
Bos gaurus (B. frontalis)	Gaur	R	C						x					x		x		x	x
Bubalus bubalis (B. arnee)	Water buffalo	R	C						x			x	x	x		x			x
Capricornis sumatraensis	Southern serow	R	B				x					x	x	x	x	x		x	x
Capricornis sp.	Serow	R	B		(?)					x									
Naemorhedus goral	Goral	R	A											x					
Naemorhedus caudatus	Chinese goral	R	A															x	
Naemorhedus sp.	Goral	R	A		(?)											x	(?)		
Dicoryphochoerus ultimus*	Extinct suid	NR	B		x														
Sus xiaozhu*	Extinct suid	NR	B	x		x													
Sus peii*	Extinct suid	NR	B	x															

Taxon	Common name	Dietary strategy	Body size category	Yugong	Black Cave	Hejiang Cave	Wuyun Cave	Quzai/Baxian	Tham Khuyen	Coc Muoi	Duoi U'Oi	Tam Hang South	Nam Lot	Tham Wiman Nakin	Tham Prakai Phet	Khok Sung	Ban Fa Sui II	Current faunas 25°–20° N	Current faunas 20°–10° N
*Sus lydekkeri**	Extinct suid	NR	B						cf.										
*Sus bijiashanensis**	Extinct suid	NR	B		x														
Sus scrofa	Wild pig	NR	B			x	x	x	x	x	x	x	x	x	x	x		x	x
Sus barbatus	Bearded pig	NR	B								x	x		x	x	x			
Rhinoceros sondaicus	One-horned rhinoceros	NR	D	x				x		x	x	x	x		x	x	x	x	x
Rhinoceros unicornis	Indian rhinoceros	NR	D							x	x	x	x	x		x			
*Rhinoceros sinensis**	Extinct rhinocerotid	NR	D		x	x	x		x										
Dicerorhinus sumatrensis	Two-horned rhinoceros	NR	C								x	x						x	x
*Megatapirus augustus**	Giant tapir	NR	C	x			x	x	x	x			x						
Tapirus indicus	Malayan tapir	NR	C							x	x	x			x				x
*Tapirus sinensis**	Extinct tapirid	NR	C			x	x												
Tapirus sp.	Tapir	NR	C					x					x						
Elephas maximus	Asian elephant	NR	D				x	x		x								x	x
*Palaeoloxodon namadicus**	Extinct elephantid	NR	D							x									
Elephas sp.	Elephant	NR	D								x	x	x	x		x			
*Stegodon orientalis**	Extinct stegodontid	NR	D		x		x	x	x				x	x		x			
*Stegodon sp.**	Extinct stegodontid	NR	D	x					x								x		

* Extinct taxa.

[1] Digestive physiology: R = ruminant, NR = non-ruminant.

[2] Body size categories: A 18–80 kg, B 80–350 kg, C 350–1,000 kg, D >1,000 kg (Faith et al. 2019). Body mass of modern species from Francis (2008).

[3] The current faunas are those from the studied latitudinal zone during the pre-industrial period (c. mid-nineteenth century) (Corbet and Hill 1992).

Sources: Fossil occurrence data from the following sources. Yugong: Dong et al. (2014), Sun et al. (2019). Black Cave: Shao et al. (2017). Hejiang Cave: Zhang et al. (2014). Wuyun: Rink et al. (2008). Quzai: Ma et al. (2019). Baxian: Ma et al. (2017), Sun et al. (2019). Tham Khuyen: Cuong (1985). Coc Muoi: Bacon et al. (2018a). Duoi U'Oi: Bacon et al. (2008). Tam Hang South: Bacon et al. (2015). Nam Lot: Bacon et al. (2015). Tham Wiman Nakin: Suraprasit et al. (2021), Tougard (1998). Tham Prakai Phet: Filoux et al. (2015), Tougard (1998). Khok Sung: Suraprasit et al. (2018). Ban Fa Sui II: Zeitoun et al. (2019).

Appendix 7.3: List of taxa (Artiodactyla, Perissodactyla and Proboscidea), dietary strategy (ruminant versus non-ruminant), body size category, and occurrence in the Sundaic subregion at the reviewed sites and in current faunas.

Taxon	Common name	Dietary strategy	Body size category	Badak	Batu	Ngalau Gupin	Sibrambang	Lida Ajer	Niah Cave	Ngandong	Punung	Current faunas 10°N – 5°S	Current faunas 5°–10°S
Tragulus sp.	Mousedeer	R[1]	-			x			x[6]				
Tragulus napu	Greater mousedeer	R	-						x				
Rusa unicolor	Sambar deer	R	B[2]	x	x	(?)			x			x (S, B)[3]	
Rusa sp.	Deer	R	B				x	x		x	x		
Cervus timorensis	Javan rusa	R	B										x (J)
Axis lydekkeri*	Extinct cervid	R	A							x			
Axis kuhlii	Bawean deer	R	A										x (J)
Muntiacus sp.	Muntjac	R	A			x							
Muntiacus muntjak	Red muntjac	R	A	x	x	x	x	x	x	x	x	x (S, B)	x (J)
Muntiacus atherodes	Bornean yellow muntjac	R	A									x (B)	
Bibos palaeosondaicus*	Extinct bovid	R	C							x			
Bos/Bubalus sp.	Large bovid	R	C	x	x	(?)					(?)		
Bos javanicus	Banteng	R	C				x	x	x			x (B)	x
Bos gaurus	Gaur	R	C									x	
Bubalus bubalis (B. arnee)	Water buffalo	R	C				x	x			x[5]		
Bubalus palaeokerabau*	Extinct bovid	R	C							x			
Capricornis sumatraensis	Southern serow	R	B	x	x	x	x	x			x	x (S)	
Sus macrognathus*	Extinct suid	NR	B							x			
Sus brachygnathus*	Extinct suid	NR	B							x			
Sus sp.	Suid	NR	B	x	x	x					x		
Sus scrofa	Wild pig	NR	B	x	x	x	x	x			x[5]	x (S)	x
Sus verrucosus	Javan warty pig	NR	B										x (J)
Sus barbatus	Bearded pig	NR	B		x	x	x	x	x			x (S, B)	
Hexaprotodon sp.*	Extinct hippopotamid	NR	C			x							

Taxon	Common name	Dietary strategy	Body size category	Badak	Batu	Ngalau Gupin	Sibrambang	Lida Ajer	Niah Cave	Ngandong	Punung	Current faunas 10° N – 5° S	Current faunas 5°–10° S
*Hexaprotodon sivajavanicus**	Extinct hippopotamid	NR	C								x		
Rhinoceros sondaicus	One-horned rhinoceros	NR	D	(?)		(?)	x⁴			x	x⁴	x (S, B)	x (J)
Rhinoceros unicornis	Indian rhinoceros	NR	D	(?)		(?)							
Dicerorhinus sumatrensis	Two-horned rhinoceros	NR	C	(?)	x	(?)	(?)⁴	x⁴	x		x⁴	x (S, B)	
Tapirus indicus	Malayan tapir	NR	C		x	x	x⁴	x⁴	x		x⁴	x (S)	
Elephas maximus	Asian elephant	NR	D				x	x			cf.	x (S)	
Elephas sp.	Elephant	NR	D			x							
*Elephas hysudrindicus**	Extinct elephantid	NR	D								x		
*Stegodon trigonocephalus**	Extinct stegodontid	NR	D								x		

* Extinct taxa.

¹ Digestive physiology: R = ruminant, NR = non-ruminant.

² Body size categories: A 18–80 kg, B 80–350 kg, C 350–1,000 kg, D >1,000 kg (Faith et al. 2019). Body mass of modern species from Francis (2008).

³ The current faunas are those from the studied latitudinal zone during the pre-industrial period (c. mid-nineteenth century) (Corbet and Hill 1992). B = Borneo; S = Sumatra; J = Java.

⁴ Perissodactyls revised by POA who identified *Tapirus indicus intermedius* at Sibrambang and Lida Ajer.

⁵ Taxon cited in Louys (2012), missing in Storm et al. (2005).

⁶ Taxon cited in Barker et al. (2017), missing in Louys (2007). Tragulidae are below the body size categories selected in the manuscript.

Sources: Fossil occurrence data from the following sources. Batu and Badak: Ibrahim et al. (2013). Ngalau Gupin: Smith et al. (2021). Lida Ajer and Sibrambang: Long et al. (1996), Louys (2012). Niah Cave: Barker et al. (2017). Ngandong: Rizal et al. (2020). Punung, represented by Punung III and Gunung Dawung: Storm et al. (2005), Storm and de Vos (2006).

Appendix 7.4: Taxa (Rodentia, Carnivora and Primates) found at sites in the Indochinese subregion.

Taxon	Common name	Yugong Middle Pleistocene	Black Cave 404-382 ka	Heijang Cave 400-320 ka	Wuyun Cave 279-76 ka	Quzai Late Pleistocene	Baxian Late Pleistocene	Coc Muoi 148-117ka	Duoi U'Oi 70-60 ka	Tam Hang South 94-60 ka	Nam Lot 86-72 ka	Tham Wiman Nakin >169 ka	Tham Prakai Phet 169-19 ka	Khok Sung 217 ka or 130 ka	Ban Fa Sui II 55-46 ka (Levels 2e-2f)	Current faunas 25°-20° N	Current faunas 20°-10° N
Hystrix sp.	Porcupines							X									X
Hystrix brachyura	Malayan porcupine									X					cf.	X	X
Hystrix subcristata	Malayan porcupine		X		X												
Hystrix indica	Indian porcupine												cf.				
Atherurus sp.	Small porcupines		X					X									X
Atherurus macrourus	Brush-tailed porcupine				cf.											X	
Martes flavigula	Yellow-throated marten									cf.	X	X					
Martes sp.	Martens							X									
Melogale personata	Ferret-badger									X							X
Melogale sp.	Badgers			X													
Paradoxurus sp.	Palm civets				X			X									
Paradoxurus hermaphroditus	Common palm civet									X		X				X	X
Meles leucurus	Asian badger											cf.					
Meles meles	European badger								X	X	X					X	
Meles sp.	Badgers			X													
Paguma larvata	Masked palm civet		X						X			X				X	X
Viverra zibetha	Large Indian civet								X	X	X					X	X
Viverra megaspila	Large-spotted civet								cf.							X	X

Taxon	Common name	Current faunas 20°–10° N	Current faunas 25°–20° N	Ban Fa Sui II 55–46 ka (Levels 2e–2f)	Khok Sung 217 ka or 130 ka	Tham Prakai Phet 169–19 ka	Tham Wiman Nakin >169 ka	Nam Lot 86–72 ka	Tam Hang South 94–60 ka	Duoi U'Oi 70–60 ka	Coc Muoi 148–117 ka	Baxian Late Pleistocene	Quzai Late Pleistocene	Wuyun Cave 279–76 ka	Hejiang Cave 400–320 ka	Black Cave 404–382 ka	Yugong Middle Pleistocene
Small meline	Meline										X						
Viverricula malaccensis	Small Indian civet															X	
Arctonyx collaris	Hog badger	X	X				X		X	X		X	X	X		X	
Canidae indet.	Canid																
Cuon alpinus	Dhole	X	X	cf.				X	X	X	X			cf.		X	
Cuon sp.	Dogs				X								X				
Panthera tigris	Tiger	X	X				cf.		X	X	X	X		X	X		
Panthera pardus	Leopard	X	X							X				X	X		
Panthera sp.	Leopards					cf.											
Small felid	Felid										X		X				
Felis sp.	Cats												X				
Felis temmincki	Asian golden cat	X	X					cf.	cf.								
Felis teilhardi	Extinct felid													X			
Prionailurus bengalensis	Leopard cat	X	X						cf.								
Neofelis nebulosa	Clouded leopard	X	X							X							
Crocuta Crocuta/C. ultima	Spotted hyena					X	X	X									
Hyaena sp.	Hyenas														X		
Helarctos malayanus	Sun bear	X	X						X	X	X	X					
Ursus thibetanus	Asian black bear	X	X	cf.		X	X	X	X	X	X	X	X	X		X	
Ursus sp.	Bears			X											X		
Ailuropoda baconi	Extinct panda						X					X	X		X		X

Taxon	Common name	Yugong Middle Pleistocene	Black Cave 404–382 ka	Hejiang Cave 400–320 ka	Wuyun Cave 279–76 ka	Quzai Late Pleistocene	Baxian Late Pleistocene	Coc Muoi 148–117ka	Duoi U'Oi 70–60 ka	Tam Hang South 94–60 ka	Nam Lot 86–72 ka	Tham Wiman Nakin >169 ka	Tham Prakai Phet 169–19 ka	Khok Sung 217 ka or 130 ka	Ban Fa Sui II 55–46 ka (Levels 2e–2f)	Current faunas 25°–20° N	Current faunas 20°–10° N
Ailuropoda melanoleuca	Giant panda		X		X			X			X		X		cf.	X	
Macaca sp.	Macaques		X	X	X	X	X	X	X	X		X	X	X	X	X	
Macaca nemestrina	Pig-tailed macaque													X	cf.	X	X
Macaca mulatta	Rhesus macaque														cf.	X	X
Trachypithecus/Presbytis sp.	Langurs			X	X			X	X	X		X					
Rhinopithecus sp.	Langurs		X			X	X										
Nomascus sp.	Gibbons			X		X	X										
Hylobates sp.	Gibbons		X					X	X	X							
Pongo sp.	Orangutans		X		X	X	X	X	X	X		X	X				
Pongo pygmaeus	Bornean orangutan														cf.		
Gigantopithecus blacki	Extinct ape		X	X													
Homo sp.	Humans								X			X					

The current faunas are those from the studied latitudinal zone in the pre-industrial period (c. mid-nineteenth century).

Source: Fossil occurrence data from the following sources. Yugong: Dong et al. (2014), Sun et al. (2019). Black Cave: Shao et al. (2017). Hejiang Cave: Zhang et al. (2014). Wuyun: Rink et al. (2008). Quzai: Ma et al. (2019). Baxian: Ma et al. (2017), Sun et al. (2019). Tham Khuyen: Cuong (1985). Coc Muoi: Bacon et al. (2018). Duoi U'Oi: Bacon et al. (2008). Tam Hang South: Bacon et al. (2015). Nam Lot: Bacon et al. (2015). Tham Wiman Nakin: Suraprasit et al. (2021), Tougard (1998). Tham Prakai Phet: Filoux et al. (2015), Tougard (1998). Khok Sung: Suraprasit et al. (2018). Ban Fa Sui II: Zeitoun et al. (2019). Current faunas: Corbet and Hill (1992:161–227, 409–413).

Appendix 7.5: Taxa (Rodentia, Carnivora and Primates) found at sites in the Sundaic subregion.

Taxon	Common name	Badak >500 ka	Batu 066–33 ka	Ngalau Gupin 160–115 ka	Sibrambang 128–118 ka or 73–63 ka	Lida Ajer 73–63 ka	Niah cave ~45 ka	Ngandong 117–108 ka	Punung 128–118 ka	Current faunas 10°N–10°S	Distri-bution[3]
Hystrix sp.	Porcupines			X			X[2]				
Hystrix brachyura	Malayan porcupine	X	X		X	X	X		X	X	S/B/TM
Hystrix indica	Indian porcupine										
Atherurus sp.	Small porcupines										
Atherurus macrourus	Brush-tailed porcupine	X	X							X	TM
Arctogalidia trivirgata	Small-toothed palm civet						X			X	S/B/TM/J
Hemigalus derbyanus	Banded civet						cf.			X	S/B/TM
Herpestes sp.	Mongooses						X				
Martes flavigula	Yellow-throated marten						X			X	S/B/TM/J
Melogale everetti	Bornean ferret-badger						X			X	B
Melogale orientalis	Javan ferret-badger								cf.[1]		J
Paradoxurus hermaphroditus	Common palm civet					X	X			X	S/B/TM/J
Paguma larvata	Masked palm civet						X			X	S/B/TM
Paguma sp.	Civets				X						
Viverra tangalunga	Malayan civet		X				X			X	S/B/TM
Small meline	Meline										
Arctonyx collaris	Hog badger					X				X	TM
Arctonyx sp.	Badgers				X						
Aonyx cinerea	Oriental small-clawed otter						X			X	S/B/J
Lutra sumatrana	Hairy-nosed otter						X			X	S/B/TM
Arcticitis binturong	Binturong						X			X	S/B/TM/J
Cuon alpinus	Dhole					X				X	S/TM/J
Cuon sp.	Dogs				X						
Panthera tigris	Tiger		X	X	X		X	X	X		S/TM
Panthera pardus	Leopard				X					X	TM/J
Felis temmincki	Asian golden cat				X	X				X	S/TM

Taxon	Common name	Badak >500 ka	Batu 066–33 ka	Ngalau Gupin 160–115 ka	Sibrambang 128–118 ka or 73–63 ka	Lida Ajer 73–63 ka	Niah cave ~45 ka	Ngandong 117–108 ka	Punung 128–118 ka	Current faunas 10°N–10°S	Distri-bution[3]
Prionailurus bengalensis	Leopard cat						X		X	X	S/B/TM/J
Neofelis nebulosa	Clouded leopard				X				X	X	S/B/TM
Neofelis diardi	Sunda clouded leopard						X				
Helarctos malayanus	Sun bear	X	X	X	X	X	X		X	X	S/B/TM
Ursus thibetanus	Asian black bear	X	X								
Manis javanica	Sunda pangolin						X				
Manis palaeojavanica	Extinct pangolin						X				
Macaca sp.	Macaques			X				X	X		
Macaca nemestrina	Pig-tailed macaque	X					X		X	X	S/B/TM
Macaca fascicularis	Long-tailed macaque			X			X		X	X	S/B/TM/J
Trachypithecus/Presbytis sp.	Langurs						X		X		
Trachypithecus auratus	Javan langur								X		J
Nasalis sp.	Long-nosed monkeys			X							B
Hylobates syndactylus	Siamang								X	X	S
Hylobates leuciscus	Gibbon				'				X		
Hylobates muelleri	Müller's gibbon						cf.			X	B
Pongo pygmaeus	Bornean orangutan						X		X	X	S
Pongo abelii	Sumatran orangutan		cf.							X	B
Pongo sp.	Orangutans	X									
Homo erectus	Extinct *Homo erectus*							X			
Homo sapiens	Modern humans					X	X		X		X

[1] Taxon cited in Kaifu et al. (2022) in complement to Louys (2012) and Storm et al. (2005).

[2] Taxon cited in Barker et al. (2017) in complement to Louys (2007).

[3] B = Borneo; S = Sumatra; J = Java; TM = Thai-Malay Peninsula.

The current faunas are those from the studied latitudinal zone in the pre-industrial period (c. mid-nineteenth century).

Source: Fossil occurrence data from the following sources. Batu and Badak: Ibrahim et al. (2013). Ngalau Gupin: Smith et al. (2021). Lida Ajer and Sibrambang: Long et al. (1996), Louys (2012). Niah Cave: Barker et al. (2017). Ngandong: Rizal et al. (2020). Punung III, Gunung Dawung, Java: Storm et al. (2005), Storm and de Vos (2006). Current faunas: Corbet and Hill (1992:161–227, 409–413).

8

Investigating super osteons in fossil Asian elephant (*Elephas maximus*) bone from Bangka Island, southeastern Sumatra

Pauline Basilia, Justyna J. Miszkiewicz, Jahdi Zaim, Yan Rizal, Aswan, Mika R. Puspangingrum, Agus Tri Hascaryo, Gilbert J. Price and Julien Louys

Abstract

Previous histological analysis of Asian forest elephant (*Elephas maximus*) cortical bone samples revealed the occurrence of an atypical secondary osteon variant, which was termed as a 'super osteon'. The area of these unusually large osteons is at least 100,000 μm^2, but their other features are similar to those of typical secondary osteons. The function of these super osteons in elephant biology is unknown. Following on from the extant elephant research, this study documents super osteons in the cortical bone of a fossil Asian elephant from Bangka Island, southeastern Sumatra, Indonesia. The area of intact secondary osteons occurring in cortical bone was compared between humerus, rib and vertebral samples. Less than 10% of the studied cortex surfaces were occupied by super osteons. We identified for the first time super osteons characterised by an unusually large size, which we refer to as 'extreme' super osteons. The weight-bearing humerus and largely non-weight-bearing rib had similar super osteon occurrence percentages, while the vertebra had a higher percentage of super osteons. Hence, the presence and number of super osteons appear to be unrelated to bone biomechanics. It is possible that super osteons are influenced by bone homeostasis requirements. The presence of super osteons in extinct and extant elephants invites future research to investigate the link between elephants' cortical bone histology and their biology. This study demonstrates the value of applying osteohistology to Indonesian fossil bones for furthering our understanding of mammalian palaeobiology in the region.

Keywords: bone histology, histomorphometry, palaeohistology, Proboscidea

Abstrak

Analisis histologis terdahulu dari sampel tulang kortikal gajah hutan Asia (*Elephas maximus*) mengungkapkan terjadinya varian osteon sekunder atipikal, yang dikenal sebagai 'super osteon'. Area pada osteon yang besarnya tidak biasa ini setidaknya berukuran 100,000 m², namun selain itu ciri-ciri lainnya serupa dengan osteon sekunder lain yang khas. Fungsi dari super osteon ini dalam biologi gajah masih belum diketahui. Merujuk penelitian gajah yang masih hidup saat ini, studi ini mendokumentasikan super osteon yang terdapat di tulang kortikal fosil gajah Asia dari Pulau Bangka, tenggara Sumatra, Indonesia. Area osteon sekunder utuh yang terdapat di tulang kortikal dibandingkan antara tulang lengan/humerus, tulang rusuk, dan tulang belakang/vertebrae. Kurang dari 10 persen dari permukaan korteks yang dipelajari ditempati oleh super osteon. Kami mengidentifikasi super osteon unik dengan ukuran luar biasa besar, yang kami sebut sebagai super osteon 'ekstrim'. Humerus yang menahan beban dan sebagian besar tulang rusuk yang tidak menahan beban memiliki persentase keberadaan super osteon yang serupa, sedangkan tulang belakang memiliki persentase keberadaan super osteon yang lebih tinggi. Dengan demikian, keberadaan dan jumlah super osteon tampaknya tidak berhubungan dengan biomekanik tulang. Ada kemungkinan bahwa super osteon dipengaruhi oleh kebutuhan homeostasis tulang. Kehadiran osteon super pada jenis gajah yang punah dan masih ada saat ini tengah mengundang penelitian masa depan untuk menyelidiki hubungan antara histologi tulang kortikal dan biologi mereka. Studi ini menunjukkan nilai penerapan osteohistologi pada fosil tulang di Indonesia guna menambah pemahaman kita mengenai paleobiologi mamalia di wilayah tersebut.

Kata kunci: histologi tulang, histomorfometri, palaeohistologi, Proboscidea

Introduction

Cortical bones of some mammals typically contain secondary osteons (hereafter, 'osteons'), which are cylindrical structures that form as a result of bone cellular resorption and formation activity known as remodelling (Burr 2002; Martin 2003). Remodelling serves to maintain adult bone density, structural integrity (Martin 2003) and mineral homeostasis (Burr 2002). Variations in osteonal micromorphology are caused by the plasticity of basic multicellular units (BMUs)—teams of osteoblasts and osteoclasts—that execute remodelling (Parfitt 1994). Histologically, the most common type of osteons, Type I, present with uninterrupted concentric lamellae formed around a central Haversian canal (Lee et al. 2013) (see Figure 8.1), and are on average 200–300 μm in diameter (Hennig et al. 2015). However, osteon micromorphology, regardless of size, exhibits variants (Skedros et al. 2006). Other osteon types, such as Type II through to IV, are considered 'atypical' (Skedros et al. 2007:286). The complexity of osteon morphology is hypothesised to be an effect of variation in bone mechanical function (Frost 1983) and repair of microdamage (Parfitt 2002). While BMUs are known to respond to both of these factors, the relationship between remodelling and osteon variants has yet to be fully understood (Cooke et al. 2021; Raguin and Drapeau 2020). Recent histological analysis of osteon variants in human cortical bone suggests that there are no correlations between remodelling and variant occurrence (Cooke et al. 2021). There has been no strong evidence for a correlation between atypical osteons and biomechanical factors either (Skedros et al. 2007).

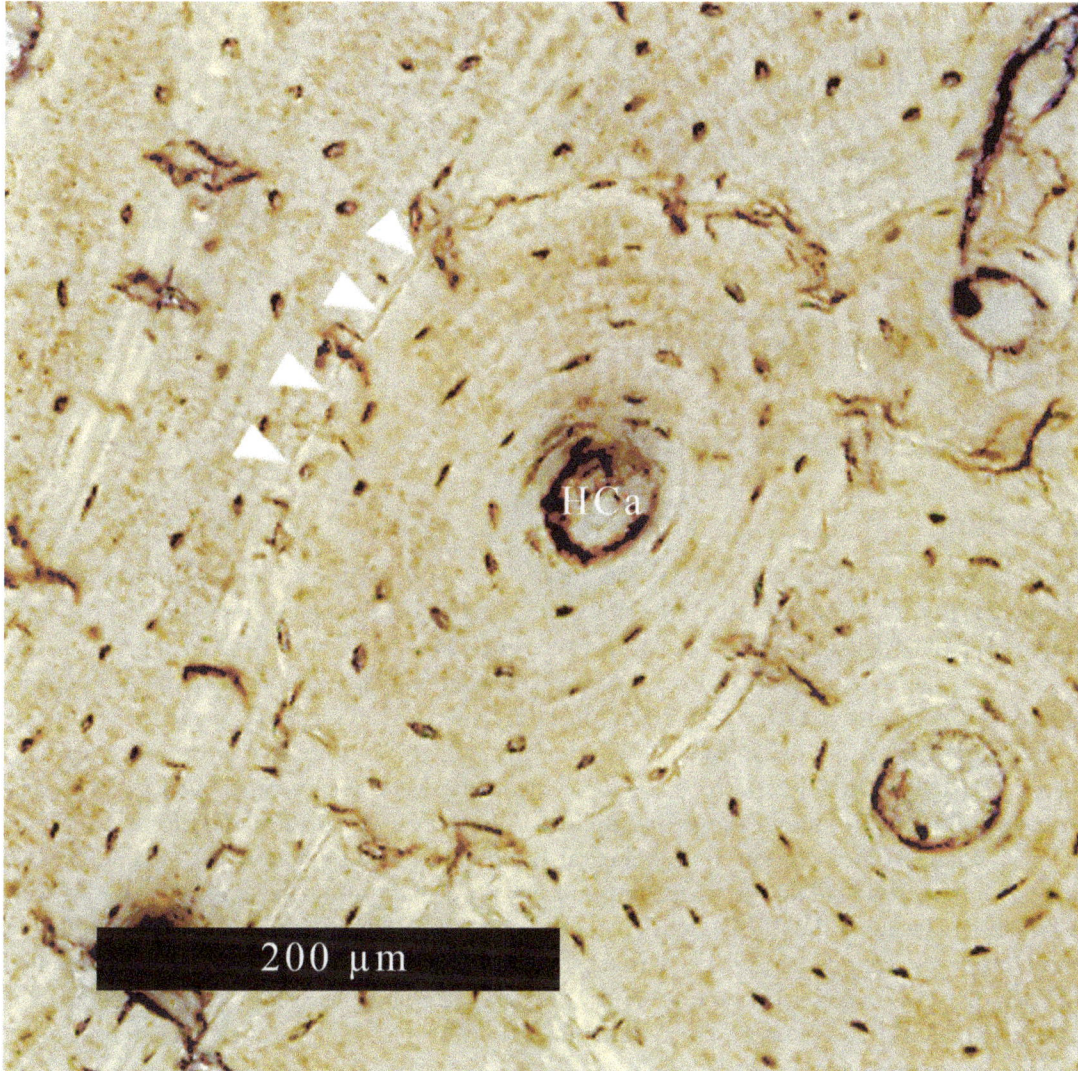

Figure 8.1: Typical osteon with Haversian canal and cement line.

Note: HCa = Haversian canal. White arrows indicate cement line.

Source: Photograph by Pauline Basilia.

In extant Asian elephants (*Elephas maximus*), histological analysis has identified atypical osteons, in particular, secondary osteons with double cement lines (Nganvongpanit et al. 2017). These atypical osteon types are characterised by a hypercalcified ring within the cement line of the osteon (Skedros et al. 2007). Another atypical osteon type that has been identified in Asian elephant post-cranial osteohistology is a 'super osteon' (Nganvongpanit et al. 2017:556) individually measuring more than 100,000 μm^2. Nganvongpanit et al. (2017) reported that 20% of osteons in their rib samples were super osteons. These are not to be confused with the 'super-osteons' discussed in human bone histology studies, where the term is used to refer to normal osteons clustering and converging into larger pores (Bell et al. 2001; Cooper et al. 2006). Goodyear et al. (2009:899) also used the term 'super-osteon' colloquially to refer to mouse bone histology reflecting unremodelled cortical bone, and Mori et al. (1999:105) and Mori et al. (2003:50) used the term 'giant osteon' colloquially when describing radius laminar bone histology in a giant Holstein cow with dermal dysplasia. Otherwise, to our knowledge, super osteons in mammal bone histology have not been discussed.

Bone samples from a fossil Asian forest elephant from Bangka Island, southeastern Sumatra, Indonesia, are currently being investigated histologically by our research group (Basilia et al. 2023). During these analyses, we preliminarily identified the occurrence of atypical osteons in the humerus, rib and vertebral samples. Building on this observation, we developed a research question asking whether super osteon presence differs between bone types. This could possibly occur as a result of varying mechanical capacities throughout the elephant skeleton—that is, the weight-bearing humerus compared with the largely non-weight-bearing rib and vertebrae (Stewart et al. 2021).

Investigating the occurrence of these atypical, unusually large osteons in the bones of large mammals allows us to further hypothesise its possible function. Their analysis could also lead to a better understanding of fossil elephant palaeobiology.

Materials and methods

Sampling

Fossil samples were collected from Late Pleistocene alluvial deposits on Bangka Island, Indonesia (Louys et al. 2023) and are currently stored in the Institut Teknologi Bandung (ITB), Java, Indonesia. The fossils, probably belonging to a single individual, were highly fragmented but appeared to have suitable preservation for histological sampling. Species identification was possible through examination of the accompanying dental fragments. The fragment of the mid-diaphysis of the humerus, the mid-diaphysis of the rib, and the spinous processes of two vertebra fragments were selected for histological sampling. These fragments were documented, photographed and osteologically examined prior to invasive sampling. Thin sections were made of the selected fragments following standard methods used for histological purposes (e.g. Walker et al. 2019). Briefly, the steps were as follows: embedding the bone samples in epoxy resin, cutting the embedded blocks with a low-speed saw, mounting the cut blocks on glass slides, and grinding and polishing the mounted sections down to approximately 100 μm thick. The ground and polished slides were then dehydrated in ethanol, cleared using xylene and covered with a glass slip glued on using DPX. For the present case study, five slides were selected: one humerus slide, two rib slides from the same bone, and two vertebra slides from different bones.

Imaging and analytical steps

Imaging was conducted using an AmScope 2000X trinocular compound microscope fitted with an AmScope 1.3 MP microscope digital camera. Rather than taking selective images of specific regions of interest, we took sequence of images from the periosteal border to the opposite periosteal border (PP band), as well as images from the periosteal border to the endosteal border (PE band) (Figure 8.2a). The selection of PP and PE bands was determined by the completeness of the fossil sample: PP bands were taken from fossil samples with preserved periosteal border. This imaging approach allowed us to compensate for the small number of slides. These series of images were montaged manually in Adobe Photoshop CC 23.1, where additional corrections (hue and saturation, brightness and contrast, dehaze, and sharpness) were applied to enhance osteon cement lines, improving their visibility. This increased the accuracy of the measurements we took from the images. Additional imaging of super osteons occurring in the humerus was completed using an Olympus BX53 microscope equipped with an Olympus DP72 camera.

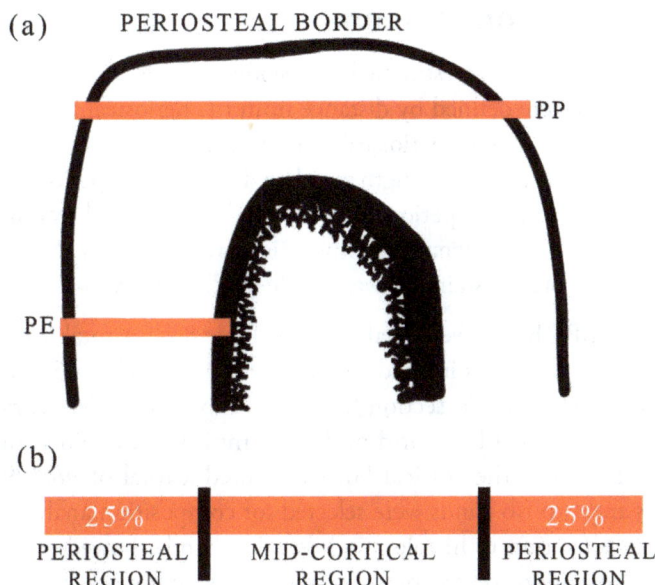

Figure 8.2: Schematic diagram of bone sampling bands. (a) The two types of bands (PP and PE) examined in the study. (b) The arbitrary division used for PE band cortical bone.

Note: P: periosteal border. E: endosteal border.

Source: Drawing by Pauline Basilia.

First, we identified the various bone tissues present in the cortical bone of each skeletal element. The histology descriptions were based on Francillon-Vieillot et al. (1990). The area of each identified bone tissue section was measured in ImageJ (Schneider et al. 2011) to determine cortical bone composition expressed in percentages. Secondly, we applied histomorphometry to quantify osteons and their features. We determined whether the area (On.Ar) of intact osteons—defined as unremodelled osteons with at least 90% of their cement lines unobscured by remodelling (Felder et al. 2017)—varies between bones. We also determined the frequency of super osteon occurrence by comparing the number of super osteons with the total number of intact osteons (N.On) and recorded the sections where they occurred in the examined cortical bone. The On.Ar and intact osteon number variables were based on histology of Haversian bone, and interstitial or circumferential lamellae.

Since super osteons in elephants have previously been defined using area measurements (Nganvongpanit et al. 2017), we followed the same technique to identify atypical osteons. The On.Ar variable accounted for the total area occupied by the Haversian canal and the surrounding lamellae deposited circumferentially by the BMU (Skedros et al. 2011). Tracing of cement lines was done using a WACOM graphics tablet with a handheld stylus.

The measured osteons were grouped into three size classes: small, regular and large. The parameters of each osteon group size were based on the size of the intact osteon compared to the skeletal element. Small osteons were defined as smaller than 25% and large osteons as larger than 75%, with the remaining osteons labelled as regular. Per Nganvongpanit et al. (2017), osteon areas measuring at least 100,000 μm^2 were defined as super osteons.

Intra-observer error was minimised by taking the average of multiple histomorphometric measurements. Using PAST (Hammer et al. 2001), the Shapiro-Wilk test for normality was used to check data distribution. We took the average of each measurement and compared the resulting values intraskeletally. As the data were not normally distributed, they were compared using a Kruskal-Wallis test for unequal medians ($p < 0.05$) with a Mann-Whitney U pairwise post-hoc test.

Identification and description of super osteons

The position of super osteons in the cortical bone was estimated by dividing the PE band into distinct sections (Figure 8.2b). These divisions were defined by distance from the periosteal border. The total length of the PE band, from the outer edge of periosteal bone to the outer edge of the endosteal bone, was measured using the ImageJ line tool. The length was then divided into a periosteal section comprising the first 25% of the distance from the periosteal border and an endosteal section comprising the last 25%. The middle section was designated as the mid-cortical section. Some taphonomic alteration, which appeared as dark orange staining, was visible in all samples.

From the five slides, four PP bands and eight PE bands were analysed (see Table 8.1). A total thin-section area (combining all slides) of 100,627 mm^2 was imaged (see Figure 8.3). Vertebra #5 and the proximal rib had both PE and PP bands, the rib mid-section had only PE bands and Vertebra #7 and humerus had only PP bands. A total cortical bone area of 36,758 mm^2 was examined in the PE bands and 61,552 mm^2 in the PP bands. The cortical bone measured a total of 98,309 mm^2 from all bands. The humerus bands and two rib bands were selected for composition analysis. These bands showed the least taphonomic alteration to histology, while other bands showed more extreme histology alterations. However, observations on osteon morphometry were not affected by taphonomic alterations because cement lines were clearly defined despite uneven bone preservation. Additional images were taken of fragmentary (partially remodelled) super osteons that we termed 'extremely' large (apparent On.Ar ≥500,000 μm^2). These were found only within the mid-cortical section of the humerus.

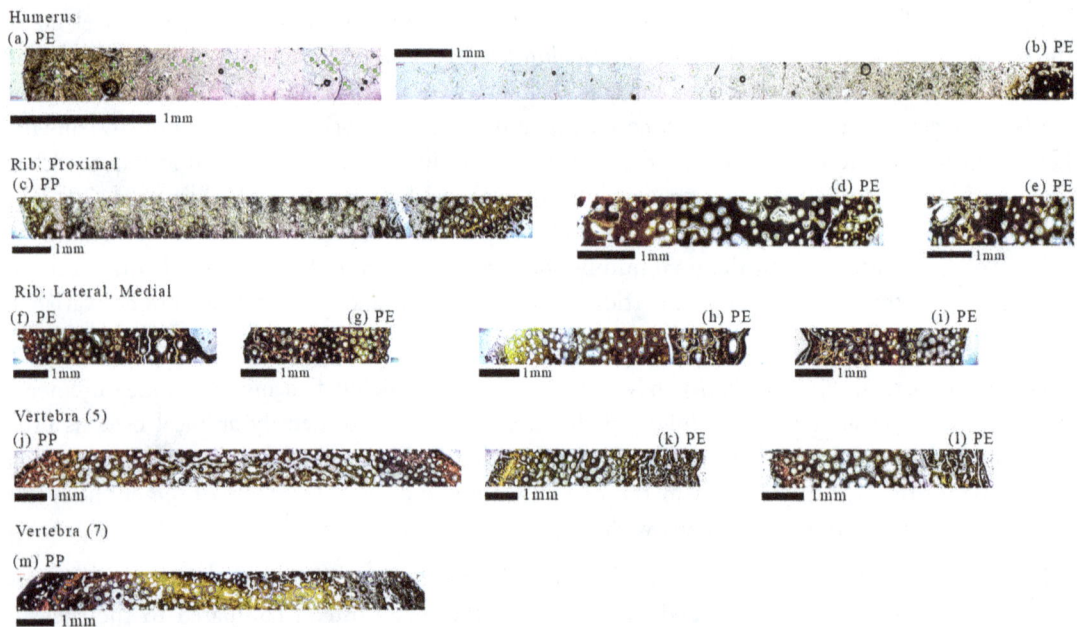

Figure 8.3: The elephant bone PP and PE band montaged micrograph images that were examined for intact osteons.

Note: Taphonomic effects are seen as deep-orange to yellow discolouration. The labels (a) to (m) are used in Table 8.1.

Source: Photographs by Pauline Basilia.

Table 8.1: Cortical area and composition of the elephant humerus and rib sample bands that had minimal taphonomic alterations.

Skeletal element[1]	Sample band	Cortical area μm²	Composition (%)	
			Interstitial	Haversian
Humerus (a, b)	PE, PE	24,489	22%	62%
Rib (c)	PP	12,589	7%	73%
Rib (d)	PE	4,541	n/a	n/a
Rib (e)	PE	3,381	n/a	n/a
Rib (f)	PE	4,740	n/a	n/a
Rib (g)	PE	4,030	n/a	n/a
Rib (h)	PE	5,046	n/a	n/a
Rib (i)	PE	3,803	0%	100%
Vertebra #5 (j)	PP	13,975	n/a	n/a
Vertebra #5 (k)	PE	6,788	n/a	n/a
Vertebra #5 (l)	PE	4,430	n/a	n/a
Vertebra #7 (m)	PP	10,499	n/a	n/a

[1] (a) to (m) refer to the micrographs in Figure 8.3 and the bands in the schematic illustration of the samples in Figure 8.4.

[2] Only humerus sample bands a and b and rib sample bands c and i were selected for compositional analysis.

Source: Authors' data.

Results

The cortical bone of the adult elephant samples examined in this study consisted of secondary bone tissue histologically described as primarily dense avascular Haversian systems (Nganvongpanit et al. 2017; Thitaram et al. 2018) (Figure 8.4). Only the humerus retained circumferential secondary lamellae. Further, the humerus had the highest cortical bone area of all the samples at 24,489 mm², while one of the vertebrae showed the smallest cortical area at 4,430 mm². Bone tissue differentiation was visible only in the humerus bands, one proximal rib band and one rib mid-section band. The humerus had the highest percentage of interstitial lamellae (22%), while the ribs recorded only 7% at most. Consequently, of the rib and humerus sample bands selected for the compositional analysis, the rib sample bands had more widespread Haversian bone (73% and 100%).

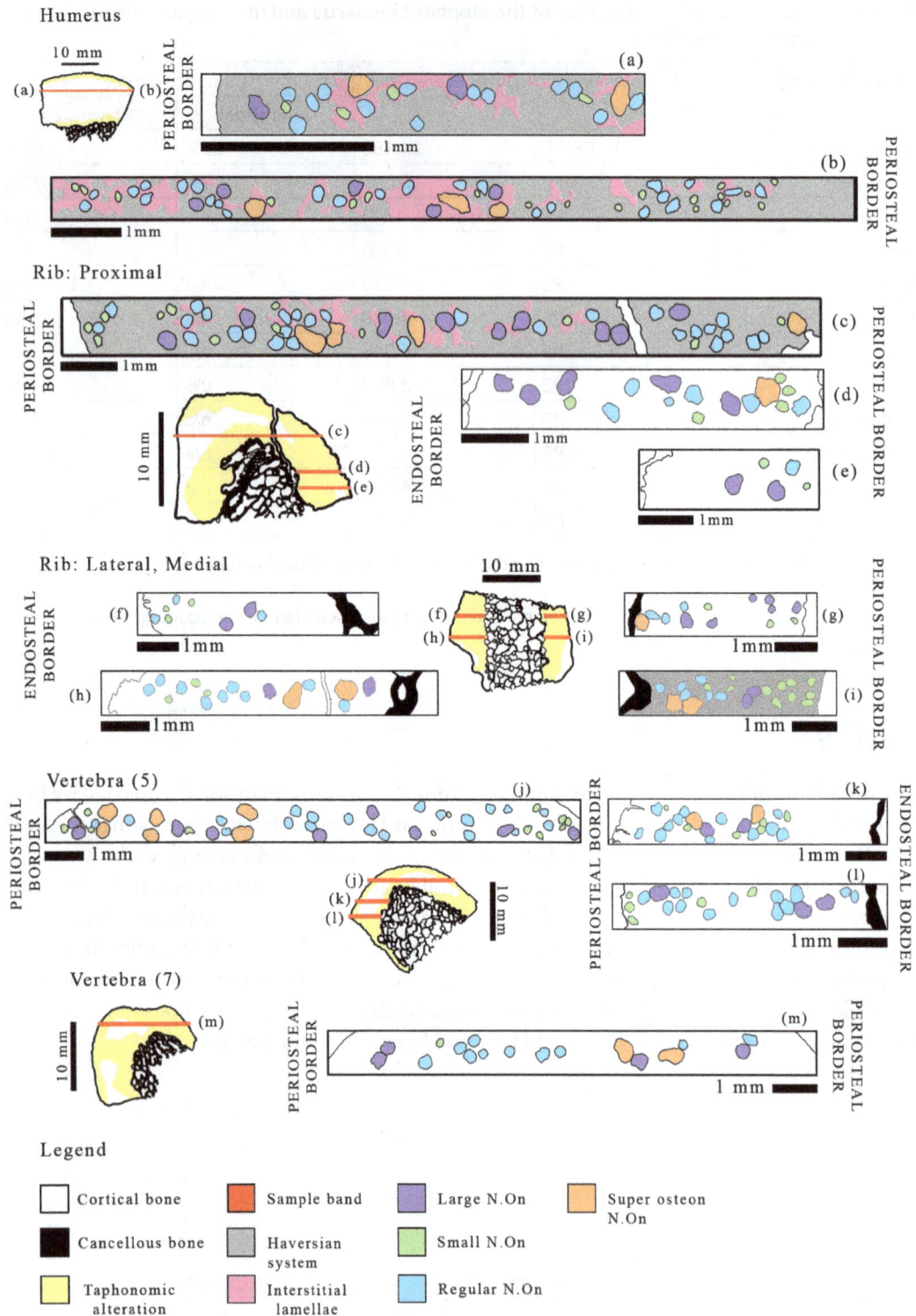

Figure 8.4: Line drawing of bone samples showing visible taphonomic alteration and schematic of sample bands showing cortical bone composition (Haversian system, interstitial lamellae), and osteons.

Note: N.On = number of intact osteons. Vertebra numbers are sample names and are not anatomical.

Source: Drawing Pauline Basilia.

Osteon area trends

From all the bands, 314 intact osteons were identified and measured. (The intact osteon data are shown in Table 8.2.) The ribs had the highest N.On: 134. The largest osteon recorded from all the samples measured 172,776.4 μm² and was found in one of the vertebra samples. The smallest osteon area was 9,928 μm² and was located in the rib. In the humerus, small osteons measured < 27,000 μm², and large osteons measured > 64,000 μm². In the rib, small osteons measured < 25,000 μm², and large osteons measured > 58,000 μm². In the vertebrae, small osteons measured < 32,000 μm², and large osteons measured > 76,000 μm². Most of the intact osteons were regular-sized, and super osteons comprised the lowest N.On at 8%.

Table 8.2: Total number of intact osteons from all sample bands, listed by size category.

Osteon size	Humerus	Rib	Vertebrae
Small	22	32	25
Regular	39	68	54
Large	7	25	18
Super	5	9	10
Total	73	134	107

Note: For the humerus, small osteons measured < 27,000 μm², and large osteons measured > 64,000 μm². For the rib, small osteons measured < 25,000 μm², and large osteons measured > 58,000 μm². For the vertebrae, small osteons measured < 32,000 μm², and large osteons measured > 76,000 μm². Super osteons for all bones measured > 100,000 μm².

Source: Authors' data.

The On.Ar data (see Table 8.3) were not normally distributed. When compared to the other bones, the vertebrae had the highest mean On.Ar, 57,934 μm² ($p < 0.05$). The Mann-Whitney U pairwise post-hoc test showed that only the difference between the rib and vertebra values was significant.

Table 8.3: Statistical analysis of On.Ar (area of intact osteons) values.

Statistical analysis		Humerus	Rib	Vertebra
Summary statistics	N	73	134	107
	Min.	9866.1	9928.0	9860.3
	Max.	211455.1	171134.7	172776.4
	Mean	49831.8	47468.3	57933.9
Normality test	Shapiro-Wilk W	0.8079	0.8637	0.9072
	p (normal)	2.39×10^{-08}	9×10^{-10}	1.585×10^{-6}
Kruskal-Wallis	H (χ^2)			7.352
	p			0.02532
Mann-Whitney pairwise post-hoc	—	v. rib	v. vertebra	v. humerus
	U	4759	5746	3280
	p value	0.7495	0.00816	0.06863

Source: Authors' data.

Super osteons and 'extreme' super osteons

Super osteons were observed in all bone samples, but at varying percentages. The super osteons in the humerus and the rib formed only 7% of their samples' total intact osteon number; this percentage was 9% in the vertebra samples. The vertebrae also had the highest occurrence of super osteons ($n = 6$) in a single band. Most bands had two super osteons, and one band showed no super osteons (see Figure 8.4). Further, super osteons occurred in three sections of each PE band of the rib and vertebra (bands d and g–k in Figure 8.4). A total of eight super osteons were observed in PE bands. Most super osteons were seen in the mid-cortical section. However, the rib lateral and medial PE bands showed higher super osteon occurrence in the endosteal region (bands g–I in Figure 8.4). Only one super osteon was recorded in the periosteal section of the rib PE band (d in Figure 8.4).

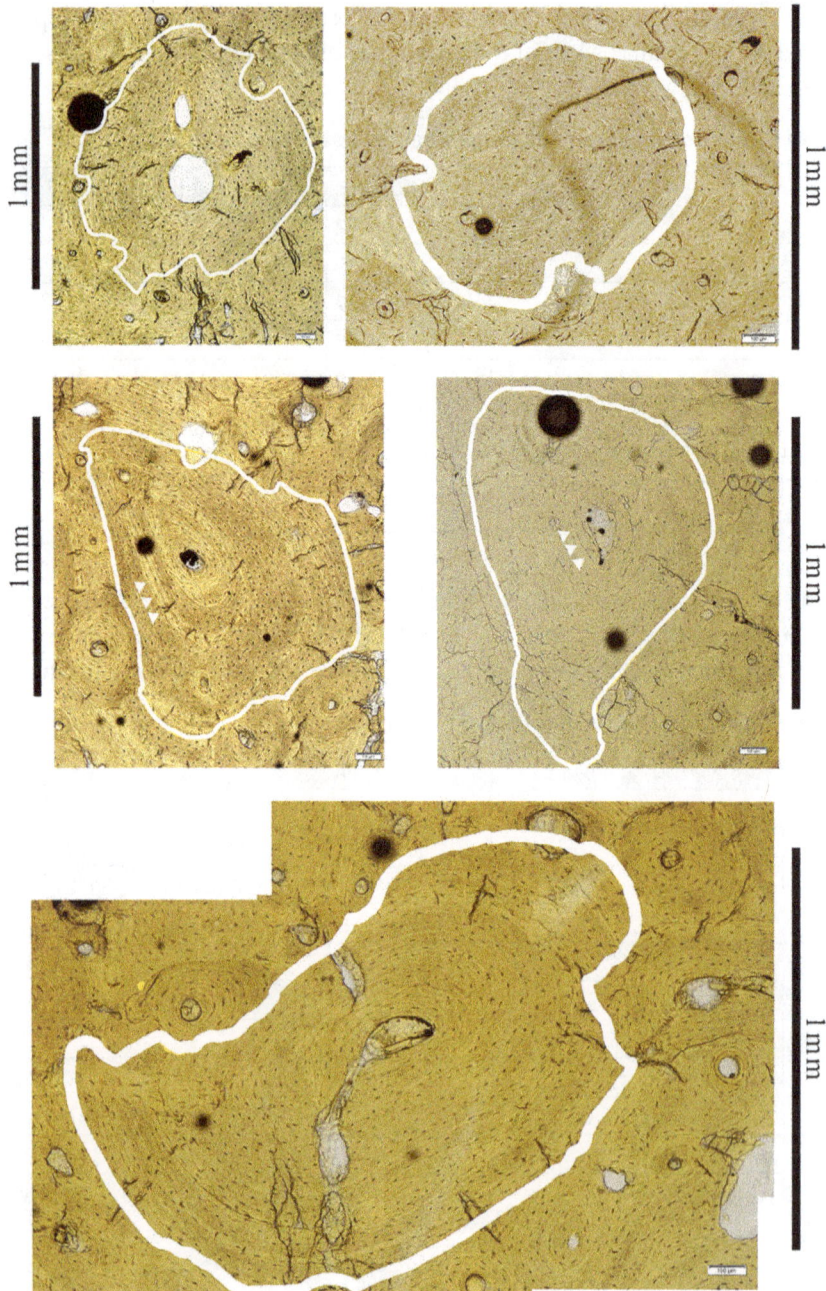

Figure 8.5: Targeted sampling of fragmented 'extremely' large super osteons from the intercortical bone of the humerus.

Note: White arrows indicate double cement lines.

Source: Photograph by Pauline Basilia.

The cortical bone of the humerus showed 'extremely' large super osteons that far exceeded known super osteon sizes (see Figure 8.5). Five of these osteons were imaged. The smallest measured 590,000 μm^2, while the biggest measured 1,200,000 μm^2. All these osteons were fragmentary (partially remodelled) and surrounded by smaller osteons. Most lacked the typical circular shape, and two appeared to be drifting osteons, or Type IV osteons, which show tails that curl through the bone. At least two of the 'extreme' super osteons showed double cement lines, another trait atypical of elephant Haversian tissue. However, apart from their 'extreme' size, the appearance of these super osteons was similar to their smaller counterparts.

Discussion

The histology slides we produced from fossil bone fragments representing an Asian elephant from Bangka Island showed bone histology and super osteons similar to those reported for extant Asian elephants by Nganvongpanit et al. (2017). Among the bands from the Bangka specimen with less-obtrusive taphonomic alterations, the highest concentration of Haversian bone consisting of both typical and atypical osteons was noted for the rib slide. Ribs are hypothesised to experience relatively fast remodelling compared to other bones due to a less variable mechanical environment than that of, for example, limb bones (Fahy et al. 2017). As such, cortical bone remodelling of the rib might have effectively erased interstitial and circumferential lamellae in the Bangka specimen, as also occurs in older individuals as remodelling progresses with age (Frost 1987; Miszkiewicz and van der Geer 2022; Waskow and Mateus 2017). A widespread presence of Haversian bone in the selected rib sample bands compared with the humerus sample bands conforms with this observation, implying that the remodelling processes in the Bangka rib may have occurred earlier compared to those in the vertebrae and the humerus. Further, it has been reported that in the case of older individuals, an accumulation of bone tissue in the periosteal border of limb bones may be a response to bending resistance (Robling et al. 2006), or more intense physical activity (Zedda et al. 2019). If all bones in the Bangka elephant were remodelled at the same rate and age, the humerus and the rib should show identical Haversian bone remodelling. However, the retention of interstitial and circumferential lamellae in the humerus confirms some degree of disparity in intraskeletal remodelling. Because remodelling disparity between these elements exists, differences in intraskeletal super osteon distribution could be explained by the animal's internal skeletal physiology and functional processes acting differently across different elements.

The vertebrae also experienced a different type of strain from that experienced by the humerus, wherein stiffness is typically exhibited (Smit 2002). The Bangka elephant vertebra samples showed significantly higher concentrations of super osteons than the humerus and rib samples, and the super osteons in the vertebrae were also larger, whereas the osteons of the rib and humerus were not much different in either size or number.

The high percentage of super osteons in the interior of the cortical bone suggests that super osteons occur there preferentially. However, we have a limited sample size, so more samples from larger numbers of individuals would need to be collected and examined. Further, it is possible that super osteons might have developed in bone tissues near the periosteal border but were remodelled by newer and smaller osteons.

Super osteons in mammalian bone

If elephant super osteons developed in a similar way to those that have been reported for humans, in whom they were detrimental to bone integrity (Bell et al. 2001), the weight-bearing bones of the Bangka specimen would be expected to develop fewer super osteons compared to largely non-weight-bearing bones. The results of this study do not agree with this assumption because the percentages of super osteons were similar in the rib and humerus and highest for the vertebrae. Further, the elephant's super osteons' appearance was comparable to that of typical osteons, with concentric lamellae around the Haversian canal (Francillon-Vieillot et al. 1990) and variation only in size.

Further, the super osteons identified in the elephant's humerus reached unprecedented sizes. These 'extreme' super osteons occurred only as fragmentary osteons, with remodelled smaller osteons obscuring the cement lines occurring in the intercortical region. However, despite the unusually large osteon size, there was no indication of super osteons having merged to create these osteons. To the best of our knowledge, there is no documented evidence for similarly sized osteons in other mammals, suggesting that they may be unique to elephants. For these osteons, we propose the term 'extreme' super osteons and define them as atypical osteons reaching >500,000 μm^2 in area as found in *Elephas maximus* cortical bone. We note that although these osteon variants can be considered 'extreme' on the basis of the osteon sizes that are known for a range of other mammals (Felder et al. 2017), they might reflect normal variation in cortical bone histology among elephants.

Are super osteons unique to elephants?

Elephants are the largest terrestrial mammals, with body mass reaching 3,200 kg for Indian *Elephas maximus* (Sukumar 2003). Elephant forelimbs directly carry most of the weight, while the remainder of the weight is indirectly distributed over the hindlimbs (Panagiotopoulou et al. 2012). The great weight carried by elephant limb bones is expected to promote high bone density and integrity. Results of prior histological analysis of modern elephant bones supported the assumption that to preserve bone integrity, super osteons did not develop in the limb bones (Nganvongpanit et al. 2017). In contrast, our study documented super osteons in both weight-bearing and non-weight-bearing bones. Further, we also documented size variation among super osteons and the presence of 'extreme' (unusually large) super osteons.

Since biomechanical signals might have not been responsible for the formation of super osteons in the Bangka specimens (at present, this is suggested by bone form and function, rather than by experimental evidence), there are several other possible reasons why these atypical osteons have developed. Simple physiological needs, or scaling relationships between histology and body and bone size, may account for these super osteons. One major difference between elephant and other mammalian bones is that there is little or no medullary cavity in the long bones: it occupies at most 1% of total bone volume in the straight-tusked elephant *Palaeoloxodon antiquus*, for example (Boschian et al. 2019). Instead, the bone cavity is filled with cancellous bone (Nganvongpanit et al. 2017). Elephant bones show a relatively high level of iron in bones with minimal medullary cavity. This may indicate that bones play a role in iron storage (Nganvongpanit et al. 2017). Iron, which is usually stored in the bone marrow, is essential for haematopoiesis and bone metabolism (Fontenay et al. 2006). Since super osteons, like iron, occur in bones with minimal medullary cavity, it is possible that there is a link between super osteon occurrence and iron storage. Whether super and 'extreme' osteons help maintain iron stores is unclear and warrants further study. Further, we cannot exclude the simple effect of body size on the underlying histology; this might mean large elephants tend to produce relatively large osteons. Felder et al. (2017) demonstrated allometric relationships between mammal body size and osteon size and proposed that larger mammals require more osteonal bone to maintain osteocyte viability. Bone robustness has also been shown to relate to the size of histological units in bone in other large mammals, including humans (Goldman et al. 2014; Miszkiewicz and Mahoney 2019). Hence, the occurrence of super osteons in elephants could arise from a combination of factors, ranging from simple anatomical variation to biology.

The present study was limited by its small sample size, the fossil nature of the bone, which meant the sex, age and other life history variables of the elephant were unknown, the two-dimensional analysis of osteon size, the lack of comparative data on super osteons in other mammals, and the extremely limited super osteon data from other elephants. Future research should aim to validate our findings using documented specimens under experimental conditions. Nevertheless, this preliminary study has identified and described unique atypical osteon variants, namely super and 'extreme' osteons, and therefore contributes to our understanding of fossil elephant osteohistology.

Conclusion

We investigated the occurrence of unusually large, atypical osteons found in fossil *Elephas maximus* cortical bone from Bangka Island, Indonesia. This osteon variant was documented in rib, humerus and vertebra samples. We also documented, for the first time, particularly large super osteons, which we have termed 'extreme' super osteons in the context of elephant bone histology. We speculated about the various possible factors underlying the formation of these atypical osteons in elephants, including bone form and function, iron storage and bone physiology, as well as macro- and micro-anatomical variation and allometric scaling relationships. We demonstrated the value of applying histology to Indonesian proboscidean fossil bones for furthering our understanding of both palaeobiology and fundamental bone biology principles such as remodelling.

Acknowledgements

Permission for the research was granted by the Indonesian government via a RISTEK Foreign Research Permit (Louys 2483/FRP/E5/Dit.KI/V/2018). Staff at the Coral Reef Algae Laboratory, Griffith University, facilitated access to microscopes. PB's work is funded by a Griffith University International Postgraduate Research Scholarship. Research and fieldwork were supported by an Australian Research Council Future Fellowship awarded to JL (FT160100450). Laboratory facilities at The Australian National University (ANU) were funded by an Australian Research Council grant awarded to JJM (DE190100068) and the ANU College of Arts and Social Sciences.

References

Basilia, P., J.J. Miszkiewicz, K. Nganvongpanit, J. Zaim, Y. Rizal, Aswan, M.R. Puspaningrum, A. Trihascaryo, G.J. Price, A.A.E. van der Geer and J. Louys 2023. Bone histology in a fossil elephant (*Elephas maximus*) from Pulau Bangka, Indonesia. *Historical Biology* 35: 1356–1367.

Bell, K.L., N. Loveridge, J. Reeve, C.D. Thomas, S.A. Feik and J.G. Clement 2001. Super-osteons (remodeling clusters) in the cortex of the femoral shaft: Influence of age and gender. *The Anatomical Record* 264:378–386. doi.org/10.1002/ar.10014

Boschian, G., D. Caramella, D. Saccà and R. Barkai 2019. Are there marrow cavities in Pleistocene elephant limb bones, and was marrow available to early humans? New CT scan results from the site of Castel di Guido (Italy). *Quaternary Science Reviews* 215:86–97. doi.org/10.1016/j.quascirev.2019.05.010

Burr, D.B. 2002. Targeted and nontargeted remodeling. *Bone* 30:2–4. doi.org/10.1016/s8756-3282(01) 00619-6

Cooke, K.M., P. Mahoney and J.J. Miszkiewicz 2021. Secondary osteon variants and remodeling in human bone. *The Anatomical Record* 305(6):1299–1315. doi.org/10.1002/ar.24646

Cooper, D.M., C.D.L. Thomas, J.G. Clement and B. Hallgrímsson 2006. Three-dimensional microcomputed tomography imaging of basic multicellular unit-related resorption spaces in human cortical bone. *The Anatomical Record* 288:806–816. doi.org/10.1002/ar.a.20344

Fahy, G.E., C. Deter, R. Pitfield, J.J. Miszkiewicz and P. Mahoney 2017. Bone deep: Variation in stable isotope ratios and histomorphometric measurements of bone remodelling within adult humans. *Journal of Archaeological Science* 87:10–16. doi.org/10.1016/j.jas.2017.09.009

Felder, A.A., C. Phillips, H. Cornish, M. Cooke, J.R. Hutchinson and M. Doube 2017. Secondary osteons scale allometrically in mammalian humerus and femur. *Royal Society Open Science* 4:170431. doi.org/10.1098/rsos.170431

Fontenay, M., S. Cathelin, M. Amiot, E. Gyan and E. Solary 2006. Mitochondria in hematopoiesis and hematological diseases. *Oncogene* 25:4757–4767. doi.org/10.1038/sj.onc.1209606

Francillon-Vieillot, H., V. de Buffrénil, J. Castanet, J. Géraudie, F. Meunier, J. Sire, L. Zylberberg and A. de Ricqlès 1990. Microstructure and mineralization of vertebrate skeletal tissues. In J.G. Carter (ed.), *Skeletal Biomineralization: Patterns, Processes and Evolutionary Trends 1*, pp. 471–530. Van Nostrand Reinhold, New York. doi.org/10.1029/SC005p0175

Frost, H.M. 1983. A determinant of bone architecture: The minimum effective strain. *Clinical Orthopaedics and Related Research* 175:286–292. doi.org/10.1097/00003086-198305000-00047

Frost, H.M. 1987. Secondary osteon population densities: An algorithm for estimating the missing osteons. *American Journal of Physical Anthropology* 30(S8):239–254. doi.org/10.1002/ajpa.1330300512

Goldman, H.M., N.A. Hampson, J.J. Guth, D. Lin and K.J. Jepsen 2014. Intracortical remodeling parameters are associated with measures of bone robustness. *The Anatomical Record* 297:1817–1828. doi.org/10.1002/ar.22962

Goodyear, S.R., I.R. Gibson, J.M. Skakle, R.P. Wells and R.M. Aspden 2009. A comparison of cortical and trabecular bone from C57 Black 6 mice using Raman spectroscopy. *Bone* 44:899–907. doi.org/10.1016/j.bone.2009.01.008

Hammer, Ø., D.A. Harper and P.D. Ryan 2001. PAST: Paleontological statistics software package for education and data analysis. *Palaeontologia Electronica* 4:1–9.

Hennig, C., C.D.L. Thomas, J.G. Clement and D.M. Cooper 2015. Does 3D orientation account for variation in osteon morphology assessed by 2D histology? *Journal of Anatomy* 227:497–505. doi.org/10.1111/joa.12357

Lee, A.H., A.K. Huttenlocker, K. Padian and H.N. Woodward 2013. Analysis of growth rates. In Padian, K. and E.-T. Lamm (eds), *Bone Histology of Fossil Tetrapods*, pp. 217–252. University of California Press, Berkeley, USA.

Louys, J., Y. Zaim, Y. Rizal, G.J. Price, A. Aswan, M.R. Puspaningrum, H. Smith and A.T. Hascaryo 2021. Palaeontological surveys in Central Sumatra and Bangka. *Berita Sedimentologi* 47(3):50–56. doi.org/10.51835/bsed.2021.47.3.358

Martin, R.B. 2003. Fatigue damage, remodeling, and the minimization of skeletal weight. *Journal of Theoretical Biology.* 220:271–276. doi.org/10.1006/jtbi.2003.3148

Miszkiewicz, J.J. and P. Mahoney 2019. Histomorphometry and cortical robusticity of the adult human femur. *Journal of Bone and Mineral Metabolism* 37:90–104. doi.org/10.1007/s00774-017-0899-3

Miszkiewicz, J.J. and A.A.E. van der Geer 2022. Inferring longevity from advanced rib remodelling in insular dwarf deer. *Biological Journal of the Linnean Society* 136(1):41–58. doi.org/10.1093/biolinnean/blac018

Mori, R., T. Kodaka and Y. Naito 1999. Delayed osteon formation in long-bone diaphysis of an 11-year-old giant cow with dermal dysplasia. *Journal of Veterinary Medical Science* 61:101–106. doi.org/10.1292/jvms.61.101

Mori, R., T. Kodaka, T. Sano, N. Yamagishi, M. Asari and Y. Naito 2003. Comparative histology of the laminar bone between young calves and foals. *Cells Tissues Organs* 175:43–50. doi.org/10.1159/000073436

Nganvongpanit, K., P. Siengdee, K. Buddhachat, J.L. Brown, S. Klinhom, T. Pitakarnnop, T. Angkawanish and C. Thitaram 2017. Anatomy, histology and elemental profile of long bones and ribs of the Asian elephant (*Elephas maximus*). *Anatomical Science International* 92:554–568. doi.org/10.1007/s12565-016-0361-y

Panagiotopoulou, O., T.C. Pataky, Z. Hill and J.R. Hutchinson 2012. Statistical parametric mapping of the regional distribution and ontogenetic scaling of foot pressures during walking in Asian elephants (*Elephas maximus*). *Journal of Experimental Biology* 215(9):1584–1593. doi.org/10.1242/jeb.065862

Parfitt, A.M. 1994. Osteonal and hemi-osteonal remodeling: The spatial and temporal framework for signal traffic in adult human bone. *Journal of Cellular Biochemistry* 55(3):273–286. doi.org/10.1002/jcb.240550303

Parfitt, A.M. 2002. Parathyroid hormone and periosteal bone expansion. *Journal of Bone and Mineral Research* 17(10):1741–1743. doi.org/10.1359/jbmr.2002.17.10.1741

Raguin, E. and M.S.M. Drapeau 2020. Relation between cross-sectional bone geometry and double zonal osteon frequency and morphology. *American Journal of Physical Anthropology* 171(4):598–612. doi.org/10.1002/ajpa.23954

Robling, A.G., A.B. Castillo and C.H. Turner 2006. Biomechanical and molecular regulation of bone remodelling. *Annual Review of Biomedical Engineering* 8:455–498. doi.org/10.1146/annurev.bioeng.8.061505.095721

Schneider, P., M. Meier, R. Wepf and R. Müller 2011. Serial FIB/SEM imaging for quantitative 3D assessment of the osteocyte lacuno-canalicular network. *Bone* 49(2):304–311. doi.org/10.1016/j.bone.2011.04.005

Skedros, J.G., G.C. Clark, S.M. Sorenson, K.W. Taylor and S. Qiu 2011. Analysis of the effect of osteon diameter on the potential relationship of osteocyte lacuna density and osteon wall thickness. *The Anatomical Record* 294(9):1472–1485. doi.org/10.1002/ar.21452

Skedros, J.G., M.R. Dayton, C.L. Sybrowsky, R.D. Bloebaum and K.N. Bachus 2006. The influence of collagen fiber orientation and other histocompositional characteristics on the mechanical properties of equine cortical bone. *Journal of Experimental Biology* 209(15):3025–3042. doi.org/10.1242/jeb.02304

Skedros, J.G., S.M. Sorenson and N.H. Jenson 2007. Are distributions of secondary osteon variants useful for interpreting load history in mammalian bones? *Cells Tissues Organs* 185(4):285–307. doi.org/10.1159/000102176

Smit, T.H. 2002. The use of a quadruped as an in vivo model for the study of the spine—biomechanical considerations. *European Spine Journal* 11:137–144. doi.org/10.1007/s005860100346

Stewart, T.J., J. Louys and J.J. Miszkiewicz 2021. Intra-skeletal vascular density in a bipedal hopping macropod with implications for analyses of rib histology. *Anatomical Science International* 96:386–399. doi.org/10.1007/s12565-020-00601-8

Sukumar, R. 2003. *The Living Elephants: Evolutionary Ecology, Behaviour, and Conservation*. Oxford University Press, New York.

Thitaram, C., P. Matchimakul, W. Pongkan, W. Tangphokhanon, R. Maktrirat, J. Khonmee, A. Sathanawongs, P. Kongtueng and K. Nganvongpanit 2018. Histology of 24 organs from Asian elephant calves (*Elephas maximus*). *PeerJ* 6:e4947. doi.org/10.7717/peerj.4947

Walker, M.M., E.M. Street, R. Pitfield, J.J. Miszkiewicz, S.L. Brennan-Olsen and P. Mahoney 2019. Ancient human bone microstructure case studies from medieval England. In J.J. Miszkiewicz, S.L. Brennan-Olsen and J.A. Riancho (eds), *Bone Health: A Reflection of the Social Mosaic*, pp. 35–52. Springer, Singapore. doi.org/10.1007/978-981-13-7256-8_3

Waskow, K. and O. Mateus 2017. Dorsal rib histology of dinosaurs and a crocodylomorph from western Portugal: Skeletochronological implications on age determination and life history traits. *Comptes Rendus Palevol* 16(4):425–439. doi.org/10.1016/j.crpv.2017.01.003

Zedda, M., D. Brits, S. Giua and V. Farina 2019. Distinguishing domestic pig femora and tibiae from wild boar through microscopic analyses. *Zoomorphology* 138:159–170. doi.org/10.1007/s00435-018-0426-7

9

How did *Homo erectus* reach Java? Least-cost pathway models and a consideration of possible Sumatran routes

Julien Louys and Shimona Kealy

Abstract

The earliest *Homo erectus* remains in Southeast Asia are in opposite reaches of this geographical region. *H. erectus* material from Gongwangling, China, and Mojokerto, Java, represent some of the earliest body fossils recovered for this species, but very few *H. erectus* records exist from between these regions. We examine possible routes that *H. erectus* could have taken on their journey southward, using a least-cost pathway analysis. Our models suggest that the easiest pathway ran through the centre of Sundaland, an area now almost entirely submerged. During periods of higher sea-levels, however, the pathway moved west and could coincide with emergent areas on or just off the east coast of Sumatra. Geological conditions on the east coast of Sumatra, while of the right age to contain early hominin remains, are not conducive to the preservation of fossil material or the retention of suitable quarries for stone artefact production. The Riau archipelago also lies on probable migration routes; however, geological outcrops of the right age will probably be difficult to find there.

Keywords: Indomalayan, Indonesia, island Southeast Asia, hominin dispersal, palaeogeographic reconstruction, remote survey, sea-level rise, Sunda Shelf

Abstrak

Peninggalan Homo erectus paling awal di Asia Tenggara secara geografis berada di jangkauan yang berlawanan arah pada wilayah ini. Sisa-sisa Homo erectus dari Gongwangling, Cina, dan Mojokerto, Jawa, mewakili beberapa fosil tubuh paling awal yang ditemukan untuk spesies ini, tetapi sangat sedikit catatan yang ditemukan di antaranya. Kami meneliti kemungkinan rute yang dapat ditempuh Homo erectus dalam perjalanannya ke selatan menggunakan analisis jalur paling optimal dengan upaya paling rendah. Model kami menunjukkan bahwa jalur paling optimum terletak di tengah-tengah Sundaland, daerah yang sekarang hampir seluruhnya terendam di bawah permukaan laut. Namun, selama periode permukaan laut yang lebih tinggi, jalur tersebut bergeser ke barat dan mungkin berhimpitan dengan daerah yang terpapar atau di lepas pantai timur Sumatra. Kondisi geologi di pantai timur Sumatra, meskipun secara umur sesuai dengan okupansi hominin awal, tidak kondusif untuk pengawetan material fosil atau retensi sumber alat-alat batu yang melimpah. Kepulauan Riau juga terletak pada rute migrasi yang memungkinkan; namun, singkapan geologi dengan umur yang sesuai kemungkinan sulit ditemukan di sini.

Kata kunci: Indomalaya, Indonesia, Kepulauan Asia Tenggara, penyebaran hominin, rekonstruksi paleogeografi, survei jarak jauh, kenaikan muka air laut, Paparan Sunda

Introduction

Situated between China and Java is a region that has, surprisingly, been mostly free of direct physical traces of the first Asian hominin *Homo erectus*. The earliest dated evidence of the presence of hominins in Asia is currently that obtained from the sites of Majuangou in the Nihewan Basin of northern China and Shangchen in the southern Loess Plateau of north-central China. Magnetostratigraphic dating at Majuangou identified geomagnetic events bracketing artefact layers between 1.77 Ma and 1.24 Ma and provides an interpolated age of c. 1.66 Ma for the lowest artefact level (Ao et al. 2013; Zhu R.X. et al. 2004). Shangchen has been dated to approximately 2.1 Ma based on magnetostratigraphic and loess profile correlations (Zhu Z.Y. et al. 2018). However, these sites preserve only Mode 1 chopper–chopping tools, not body fossils, and without the latter, the identity of the tool-makers remains somewhat speculative.

The earliest dated hominin fossils from Asia, assigned to *Homo erectus,* are derived from the paleosol sequences of the Luochuan Sequence in Gongwangling, only about 4 km south of Shangchen, near the base of the Qinling Mountains, north-central China. Although originally correlated with either an upper sandy loess dated to 0.78 Ma or a lower sandy loess dated to 1.2–1.09 Ma, (An and Ho 1989; Liu et al. 1985), these dated fossil beds were recently re-examined and correlated with paleosol sequences dated to 1.65–1.54 Ma (Zhu Z.Y. et al. 2015). The presence of the fossils in these paleosol deposits, in addition to the identity of most mammalian fossils found in association with the Gongwangling hominin, suggests that subtropical to tropical environments were predominant in the region at this time. Such environmental conditions are more reminiscent of the Indomalayan biogeographic realm than of the drier and cooler conditions of the Palaearctic realm where Gongwangling is now located (Chow and Li 1965; Hu and Qi 1978; Louys et al. 2009). Further early Pleistocene hominin material attributable to *H. erectus* has been recovered from the Chinese sites Yuanmou, in Yunnan Province, and Yunxian, in Hubei Province, both in the Indomalayan realm, and dated to approximately 1.7 Ma and 1.15 Ma (or 0.8 Ma) respectively (Guo et al. 2013; Zhu R.X. et al. 2003, 2008). Most recently, fossil material preserving features typical of *H. erectus* has been recovered from Hualongdong in Anhui Province, eastern China (Wu Xiu-Jie et al. 2019), dated to 331–271 ka.

H. erectus material has been recovered from the Palaearctic realm as well, most famously from the extensive Zhoukoudian deposits, which may be as old as 0.8 Ma or as young as 230 ka depending on the dating technique favoured (Shen et al. 2009; Wu Xinzhi 2004). However, fossil hominins in southern China share more similarities with the Southeast Asian samples than with those in northern China (Lee and Hudock 2021), suggesting a divergence of evolutionary trajectories between the two biogeographical realms inhabited by *H. erectus* (Kaifu et al. 2005). It would seem, then, that the Indomalayan *H. erectus* fossils probably come from a single evolutionary group who migrated from north to south into Indonesia along the 'Sino-Malayan' route, which is the most parsimonious and probable based on evidence from the biogeography of other Pleistocene mammals (e.g. Kahlke 1972; Long et al. 1996; Tougard 2001).

South of southern China and north of Java, Indonesia, fossils of *H. erectus* are scarce. Isolated dental remains recovered from Tham Khuyen Cave and Tham Hai in northern Vietnam, dated to approximately 475 ka, have been identified as *H. erectus* (Ciochon et al. 1996; Olson and Ciochon 1990), although some of these attributions have been questioned based on the degree of wear on the teeth (Demeter et al. 2004).

The earliest dated *H. erectus* fossil from Java may be the Mojokerto skull, with dates ranging from 1.8 Ma to 1.43 Ma depending on which dating methods and materials are accepted (Morley et al. 2020; Morwood et al. 2003; Swisher et al. 1994). The Sangiran hominin fossil ages, which are more tightly constrained and more accepted, are approximately 1.5–1.3 Ma based on fission-track and uranium-series dating (Matsu'ura et al. 2020). Younger fossils have been recovered from other sites in Java, including Trinil and Sambungmacan, and the youngest ever fossil remains of *H. erectus* were probably found at Ngandong, dated to 117–108 ka (Rizal et al. 2019).

The vast area between southern China and northern Vietnam, which were at the northern extent of the *H. erectus* range in the early Pleistocene, and central and eastern Java, which were at the southern end, can reasonably be expected to preserve evidence of the passage and migration of this hominin. The lack of fossils from this region is probably at least partly due to both limited fieldwork and the subsidence of the Sunda Shelf since the Middle Pleistocene. Even though palaeontological fieldwork has increased dramatically in Southeast Asia in the last 20 years (e.g. review in Smith et al. 2020), the focus of this work has been largely on limestone caves. This makes sense as cave sites often preserve fossil material and are a natural feature of the landscape that are relatively easy to locate, particularly in dense forest (Louys et al. 2017). Nevertheless, the preservation of fossils in these sites is heavily biased towards the late Middle and Late Pleistocene. While deposits of these ages could theoretically host *H. erectus* fossil material, other than a few teeth only identifiable as *Homo* sp.— such as those found at Tham Wiman Nakin, Thailand (Tougard et al. 1998) and Ma U'Oi, Vietnam (Demeter et al. 2004)—no other hominin material has been recovered. The notable but rare open-air Pleistocene fossil mammal deposits from Southeast Asia, such as Khok Sung, Thailand (Duval et al. 2019; Suraprasit et al. 2018), have likewise failed to yield hominin fossils. Stone tools recovered from Southeast Asia, such as the Acheulean-like bifaces from southern Sumatra (Chapter 10, this volume), have yet to be dated or definitively associated with any particular hominin species.

The subsidence of the Sunda Shelf had profound effects on the biogeography and environments of Southeast Asia. The subsidence of the shelf is estimated as beginning at c. 400 ka based on geomorphological observations, numerical simulations of coral reef growth, and shallow seismic stratigraphy (Sarr et al. 2019). The continuous exposure of the shelf prior to 400 ka probably provided a natural savanna corridor for migration, as well as habitats for numerous large-bodied mammals including *H. erectus* (Husson et al. 2020; Louys and Roberts 2020), and these savannah environments may have been a population source for hominin population sinks in northern Asia (Dennell 2020; Louys and Turner 2012).

The eventual loss of the Sundaland corridor and the relatively open forest and savanna ecosystems it promoted probably disrupted gene flow between populations; it is associated with the extinction of several megafauna, including *H. erectus* (Husson et al. 2020; Louys and Roberts 2020). In addition, it is probable that the inundation of the Sunda Shelf submerged many potential archaeological and palaeontological sites, contributing to the dearth of fossil hominin records between southern China and Java. Here, we explore the question of which paths *H. erectus* may have taken through this corridor, paying particular attention to routes possibly taken following the inundation of the Sunda

Shelf. Following previous research examining modern human movements through Southeast Asia (Kealy et al. 2018), we take a least-cost pathway approach to that question in an effort to determine if any pathways may still be at least partially above water today.

Methods

Sea-levels and palaeogeographic reconstructions

We reconstructed the palaeogeography of Southeast Asia for seven time-and-sea-level slices (see Table 9.1) with the aim of covering a random but representative sample of times and sea-levels encompassing the last 400 ka. The first two slices were selected based on sea-levels present during the hypothetical scenario that Sundaland subsidence occurred prior to 400 ka, namely (1) the initial arrival of hominins in the region at 2.1 Ma (a date chosen as indicative of the earliest arrival of *H. erectus* on mainland Asia) and (2) 1.6–1.5 Ma, the earliest secure record of *H. erectus* in Java. The other five reconstructions aimed to account for variations in sea-level that would have significantly influenced land extent during the periods when hominins moved through the region and that cover most scenarios of sea-level and degree of Sundaland subsidence. Plate tectonic models and palaeogeographic reconstructions of the region suggest that, with the exceptions of continuing uplift and volcanism local to the Wallacean islands, Southeast Asia had largely reached the present geographic layout before 2.1 Ma (Hall 2001; Nugraha and Hall 2018). The aim of our sampling strategy was not to capture every time period and its associated sea-levels, but rather to randomly sample across the period after the subsidence of the Sunda Shelf and across fluctuating sea-levels to observe whether any patterns emerged.

Here we used the Miller et al. (2011) sea-level model, which is based on data from the LR04 $\delta^{18}O$ stack and provides a continuous model of global sea-level fluctuations for the last 180 Ma. Due to the broad geographic scope (India–New Guinea, China–Indonesia) and temporal range (2.1–0 Ma) of our study, we found the Miller et al. (2011) model to be the most applicable. The only exception to this was for the minimum (i.e. lowest) sea-level from the last 2.1 Ma, the Last Glacial Maximum (LGM). For our LGM sea-level reconstruction we used the most extreme depth of −135 m (135 m below present sea-levels), from the model by Lambeck et al. (2014), which is based on more detailed and regionally relevant data from the nearby Huon Peninsula, New Guinea. Thus, our LGM reconstruction represents an absolute maximum land extent scenario.

Our five additional time-and-sea-level slices were therefore developed based on these sea-level models. The additional five are: (3) 25–22 ka, the LGM and maximum sea-level lowstand, (4) 123 ka, the maximum sea-level highstand, (5) 2.1–0 Ma mean sea-level; (6) 2.1–0 Ma upper quartile (75th percentile) sea-level; and (7) 2.1–0 Ma lower quartile (25th percentile) sea-level. All seven slices are shown in Table 9.1.

Seven palaeogeographic reconstructions were then developed based on the slices' sea-levels (shown in Table 9.1). We used the General Bathymetric Chart of the Oceans (GEBCO_19) dataset (Smith and Sandwell 1997) to extract contours corresponding to each of our seven different sea-levels. These contours were then used to define the relevant palaeoland extent, and the corresponding sea-level difference was added to the GEBCO_19 dataset to model the palaeotopography.

Table 9.1: Sea-level slices used for palaeogeographic reconstructions.

Model number	Name	Time period	Sea-level m bpl[1]	Ages[2] ka
1	*Asia*	2.1 Ma	−14	415–414, 400–397, 323, 240–237, 118, 8
2	*Java*	1.6–1.5 Ma	−46*	394–388, 217, 287, 219, 195–193, 129, 113, 104–98, 93, 85–80, 75, 12
3	*LGM*, lowstand	25–22 ka	−135	27–21
4	Highstand	123 ka	+9	405, 123
5	*Mean*	2.1–0 Ma	−54	386–382, 306–300, 289–288, 244, 229, 112–107, 91–86, 79–76, 74, 13
6	*75%*	2.1–0 Ma	−33	418, 396, 335, 311, 235, 218–197, 128, 115, 96
7	*25%*	2.1–0 Ma	−75	374–364, 294, 275–246, 222, 183–173, 64–45

Note: LGM = Last Glacial Maximum.

[1] Depth in metres relative to present sea-levels.

[2] Approximate ages, over the last c. 400 ka, that correspond with the reconstructions.

* Averaged measurement.

Source: Authors' analysis.

We then used our palaeotopography to model river and lake systems for each of these scenarios. Each reconstructed digital elevation model (DEM) was hydrologically conditioned using the 'sink' and 'fill' tools in ArcGIS v10.7 (ESRI 2018) to smooth out depressions and small errors in the dataset. This enabled us to clearly establish flow direction and accumulation across our DEM's using the Hydrology toolset in ArcGIS v10.7. A drainage threshold of 1,000 cells was applied to the flow accumulation model to delineate major palaeostreams and rivers. A surface area threshold of >100 km² was also applied to the modelled palaeolakes. Both these thresholds were employed to minimise overestimations of reconstructed waterways and focus on those most likely to represent major, permanent water bodies in the palaeolandscape.

Least-cost pathway models

The construction of our least-cost pathway models for the seven different palaeogeographic reconstructions largely followed the methodology of Kealy et al. (2018). 'Slope cost' and 'river distance cost' were both calculated per Kealy et al. (2018: table 1). We also added an additional cost variable not considered by Kealy et al., that of lakes. While the Kealy et al. models focused on the island region of Wallacea, where lakes are generally both rare and small, in our region of interest, lakes comprise a more substantial proportion of the landscape. Therefore, we included lakes with a surface area >100 km² in our modelling.

As *Homo erectus* is not generally considered to have possessed the capabilities required for purposeful crossing of major water bodies, and presumably avoided such activity where possible, we assigned our lakes a cost value of 15. This value corresponds to Field and Lahr's (2005) 'sand seas' value that means crossings are unlikely, but remotely possible for short distances. However, while lake surface was assigned a high cost, we consider lake edges to represent particularly attractive zones, similarly to river systems but to a greater extent (see also Shipton et al. 2018). We therefore assigned a cost value of zero to a 0.5 km buffer extending outwards from our lake edges. These additional lake cost values were combined with the existing river cost values to create a 'waterways cost' surface. The equations used are shown in Table 9.2.

Table 9.2: Equations used in the development of the cost surfaces for the seven palaeogeographic reconstructions modelled.

Output	Code	Formula
Distance from rivers (km)	DR	Euclidean distance calculated in ArcGIS 10.5.1
River distance cost	RC	$RC = (TfExp(DR,0.1,maxDR)) + (\frac{DR}{10})$ *TfExp* base factor calculated in ArcGIS based on upper and lower values
Lake surface cost	LC	$LC = 15$
Lake distance cost	LDC	$LDC = 0.5$ km buffer from lake edge = 0
Waterways cost surface	WC	$WC = RC + LC + LDC$
Slope (degrees)	S	Slope function in ArcGIS 10.5.1 calculated in degrees
Slope cost	SC	$SC = \frac{\tan \tan S}{\tan \tan 1°}$
Total cost surface	TCS	$TCS = SC + WC$

Source: Authors' analysis; table modified from Kealy et al. (2018: table 1).

In contrast to the modelling by Kealy et al. (2018), which was focused on *Homo sapiens* crossing the seas of Wallacea, here we returned to the Field and Lahr (2005) model and classified the ocean as impermeable. This classification had the additional effect of halting the least-cost paths at the coast, making direct access to the islands of Sumatra or Java impossible (according to our model) when the Sunda Shelf was submerged. In these scenarios, we also followed the example of Field and Lahr (2005) to simply pause our pathway model at the coast and restart it at the closest point on the opposite landmass, chosen based on a direct line across the channel.

Numerous studies suggest archaic hominins were incapable of purposeful voyaging (O'Connor et al. 2017; Shipton et al. 2021), unlike *H. sapiens* (Bird et al. 2019; Kealy et al. 2018). Archaic hominins were, however, clearly capable of accidental sea crossings, as evidenced by the early records of Flores, Sulawesi and the Philippines (Brumm et al. 2010; Ingicco et al. 2018; van den Bergh et al. 2016). Recent efforts by D'Cunha et al. (2021) attempted to model such drift dispersal routes, but their study focused on the major crossing of the Makassar Strait (i.e. Wallace's Line) and interactions with the Indonesian Throughflow. For our study, the longest sea crossing required is c. 26 km (across the Sunda Strait between Sumatra and Java) during the period of highest sea-level, significantly shorter than the narrowest point of the Makassar Strait. Our methodology reflects this scenario: sea crossings are not considered by our pathway model, but minor accidental dispersal across short distances is accounted for by the abovementioned 'stop-start' approach of Field and Lahr (2005), thus allowing path continuation across regions which would otherwise be unreachable within the model's parameters.

To capture migration pathways hypothesised from large-mammal biogeography, namely the Siva-Malayan and Sino-Malayan routes (de Vos et al. 1999; Tougard 2001; von Koenigswald 1935, 1939), least-cost pathway models were run from India and China towards Java (specifically, the sites of Narmada in India, Gongwangling in China and Sangiran in Java). Not only did we then model our least-cost path from these two sources to the Java destination—as in the cases of both Kealy et al. (2018) and Field and Lahr (2005)—but we also ran our pathway model in reverse to detect any differences between the favourabilities of potential pathways for travel back from Java. Unlike the southward paths, the reverse models were not forced to return to particular destinations (i.e. Narmada or Gongwangling) as we felt it more realistic to let the model choose its own path with a termination option anywhere along the outer rim of our modelled region. This also provided useful ways to compare fixed-destination and non-fixed-destination models. The analysis used the Cost Distance, Cost Back-Link and Cost Path tools in the ArcGIS 10.7 (ESRI 2018) Spatial Analyst Toolbox.

Results

Palaeogeographic reconstructions

The ages covered by the sea-levels examined, which ranged over the last 400 ka, follow a Poisson distribution for point events (p = 0.087) with no density trend detected (Laplace test, U = −1.3447, p = 0.179). This means our sea-level sampling covers an even spread of the palaeogeographic scenarios of the last 400 ka, including maximum and minimum extent of sea-level changes. Because we also examined the mean and quartiles for sea-levels over the last 2.1 Ma, we feel confident that the variable palaeogeography experienced by *H. erectus* in Southeast Asia has been captured by our sampling approach.

The seven palaeogeographic reconstructions (Figures 9.1–9.7) included three scenarios in which portions of the Sunda Shelf are submerged to the extent that Java is not connected by land to mainland Southeast Asia: *Asia* (Figure 9.1); *Highstand* (Figure 9.4), and *75%* (Figure 9.6). In these scenarios, the Sunda Strait would have to be crossed to reach Java from mainland Southeast Asia. However, unlike *Asia* and *Highstand*, the *75%* reconstruction does model land connectivity between mainland Southeast Asia and Sumatra, so it does not include the additional necessity of crossing the Malacca and Singapore Straits. In our four other scenarios, sufficient expanses of the Sunda Shelf are exposed to allow travel by land at all times between Java and mainland Asia.

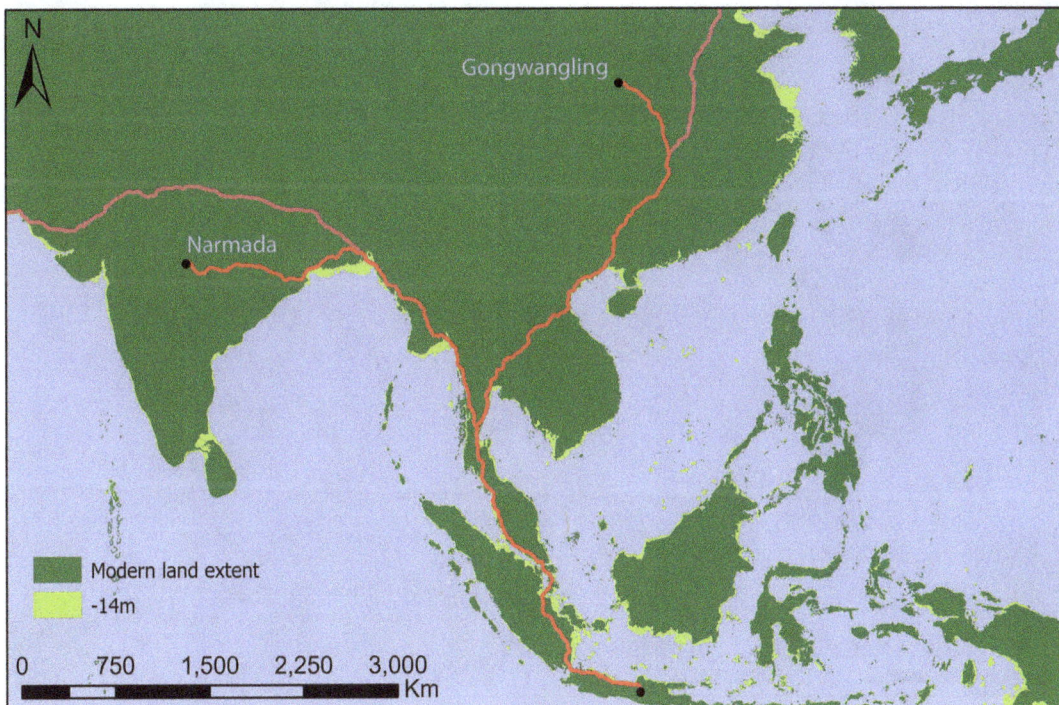

Figure 9.1: Least-cost pathways from India (left) and China (right) to Sangiran, Java (red), and return pathways (pink) for the *Asia* scenario with sea-level −14 m relative to present.

Source: doi.org/10.6084/m9.figshare.25255141. Map by authors.

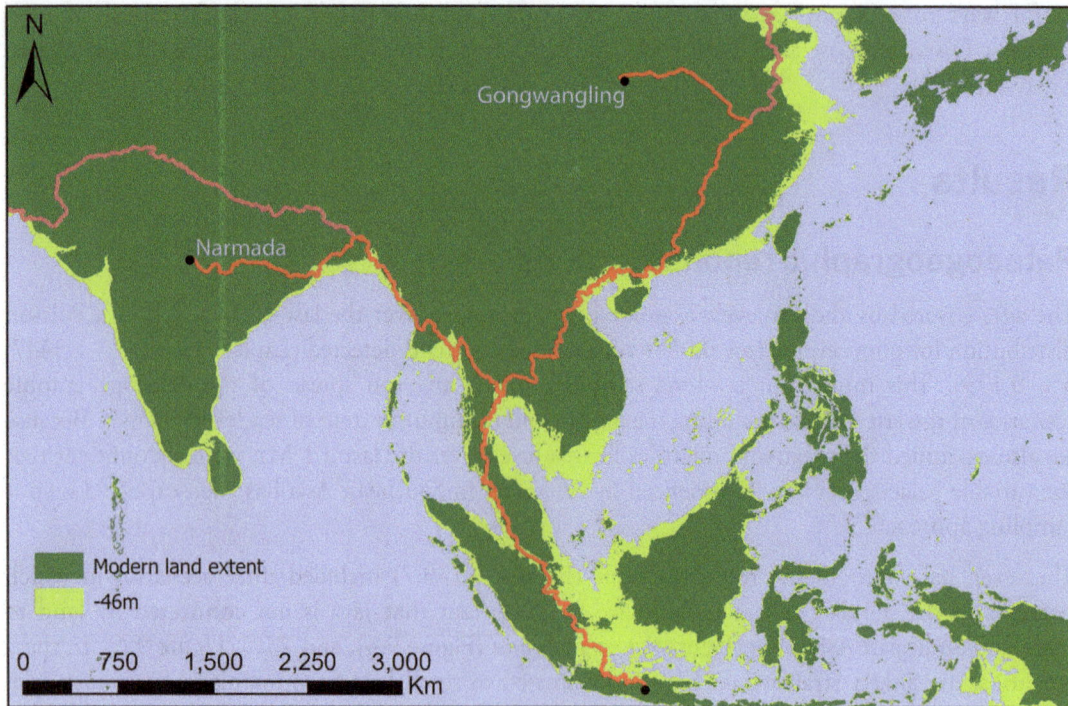

Figure 9.2: Least-cost pathways from India (left) and China (right) to Sangiran, Java (red), and return pathways (pink) for the _Java_ scenario with sea-level −46 m relative to present.
Source: doi.org/10.6084/m9.figshare.25255141. Map by authors.

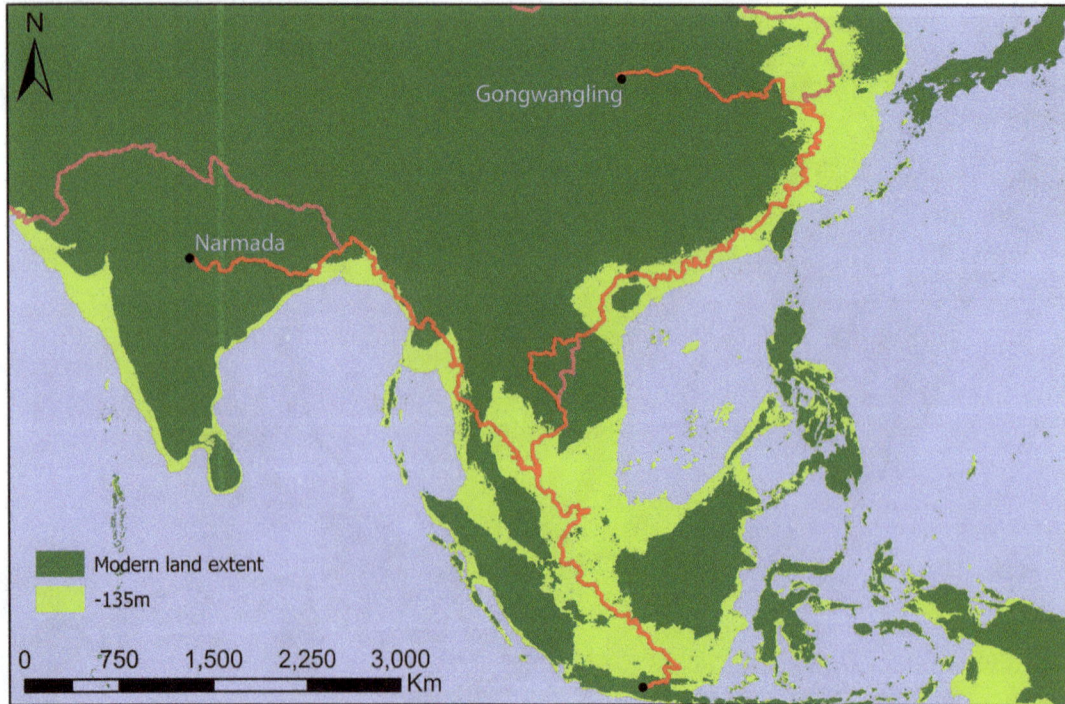

Figure 9.3: Least-cost pathways from India (left) and China (right) to Sangiran, Java (red), and return pathways (pink) for the _LGM_ scenario with sea-level −135 m relative to present.
Source: doi.org/10.6084/m9.figshare.25255141. Map by authors.

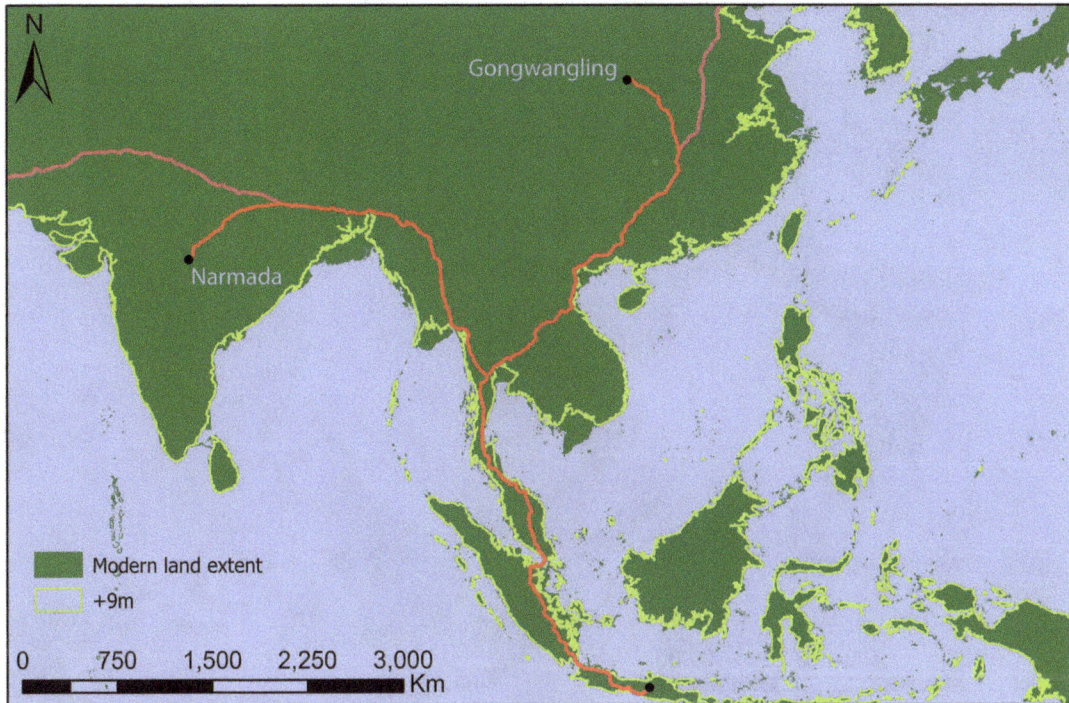

Figure 9.4: Least-cost pathways from India (left) and China (right) to Sangiran, Java (red), and return pathways (pink) for the *Highstand* scenario with sea-level +9 m relative to present.

Source: doi.org/10.6084/m9.figshare.25255141. Map by authors.

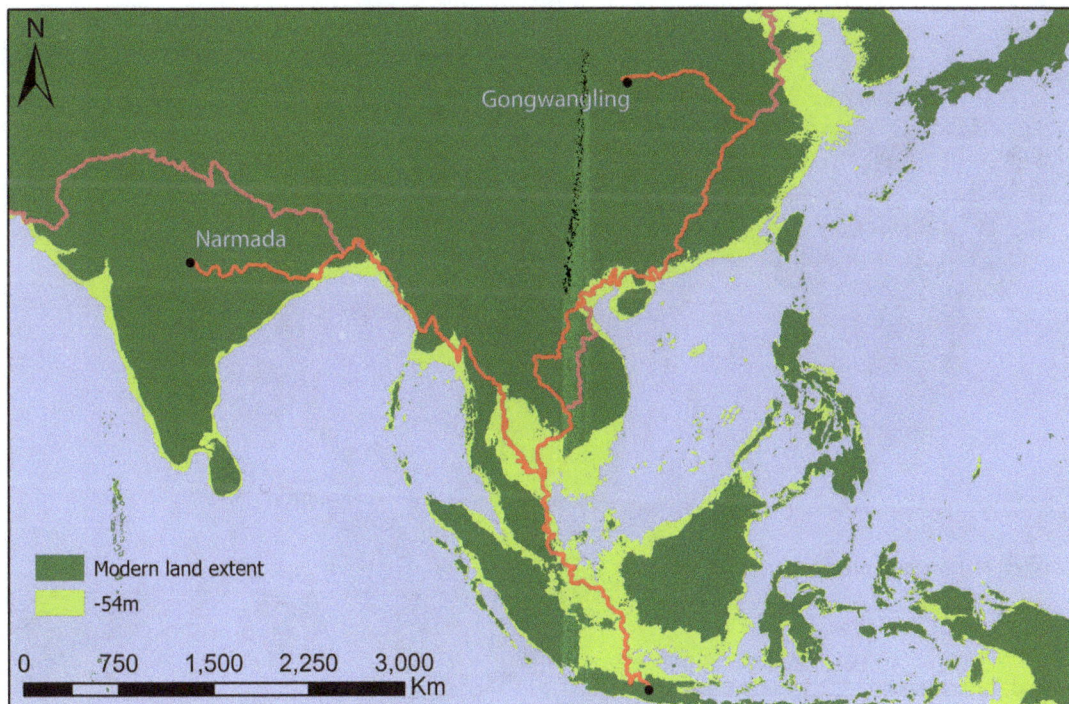

Figure 9.5: Least- cost pathways from India (left) and China (right) to Sangiran, Java (red), and return pathways (pink) for the *Mean* scenario with sea-level –54 m relative to present.

Source: doi.org/10.6084/m9.figshare.25255141. Map by authors.

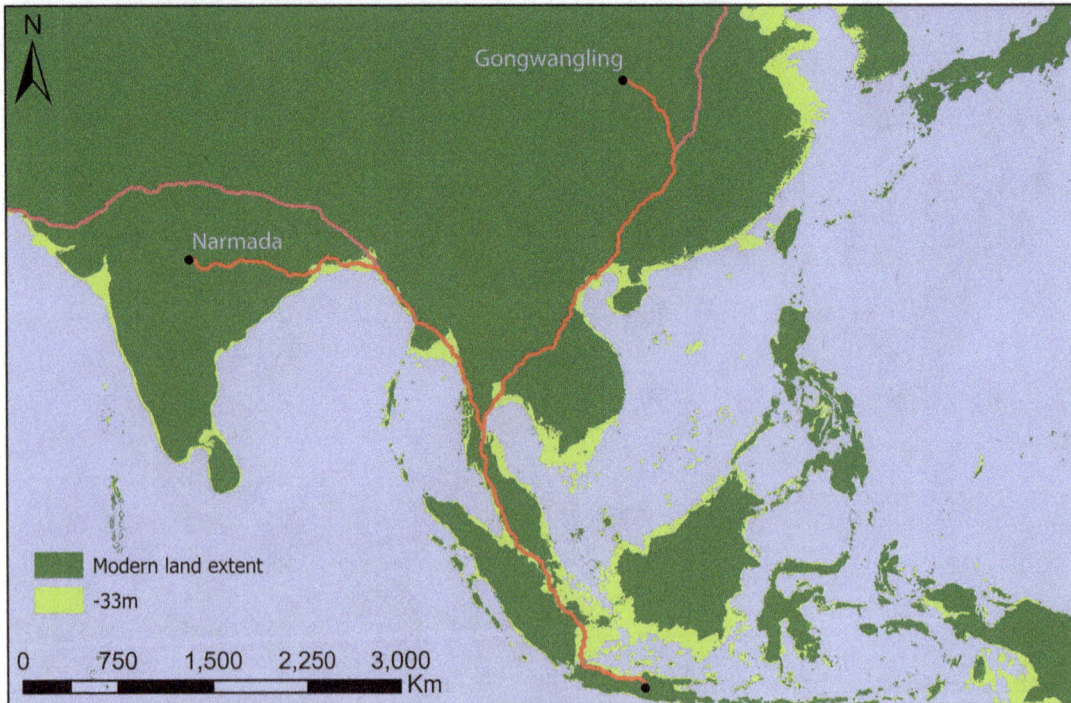

Figure 9.6: Least-cost pathways from India (left) and China (right) to Sangiran, Java (red), and return pathways (pink) for the 75% scenario with sea-level –33 m relative to present.
Source: doi.org/10.6084/m9.figshare.25255141. Map by authors.

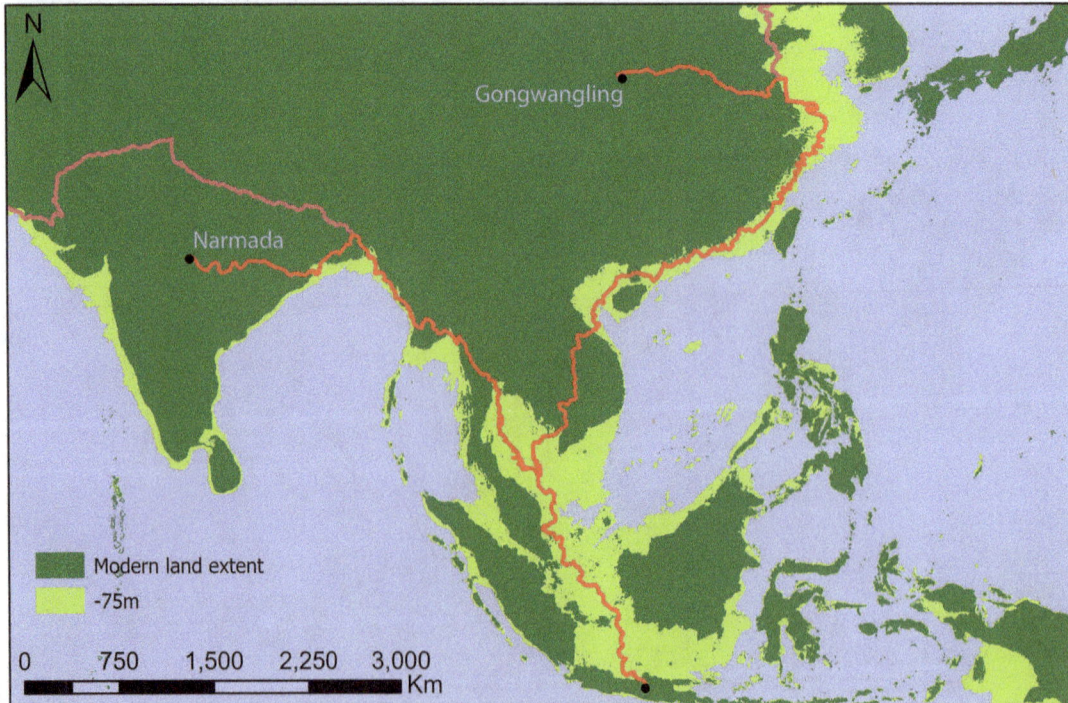

Figure 9.7: Least-cost pathways from India (left) and China (right) to Sangiran, Java (red), and return pathways (pink) for the 25% scenario with sea-level –75 m relative to present.
Source: doi.org/10.6084/m9.figshare.25255141. Map by authors.

The validity of the models is supported by comparisons with known *Homo erectus* traits. In particular, the degree to which our modelled pathways follow river corridors to move inland while avoiding regions of high elevation and slope corresponds with observations from studies of various Acheulean assemblages in western Asia (e.g. Shipton et al. 2018). Unlike the more coastal and maritime-focused pathways of Kealy et al.'s (2018) models of *H. sapiens* Wallacea crossings, our models appear to mirror the more terrestrial, inland focus that has been observed for *H. erectus* (Louys and Roberts 2020; O'Connor et al. 2017; Shipton et al. 2021). This comparison is not being made to provide circular support for previous *H. erectus* lifestyle hypotheses, but to demonstrate that our choice and weighting of cost variables successfully reflect what current research suggests were the probable parameters of *H. erectus* movement. Thus, our models represent potential paths taken by *H. erectus* based on our current understanding of the palaeolandscape and *H. erectus* capabilities and preferences.

Three general observations arise from our least-cost pathway scenarios. First, within our region of interest (mainland Southeast Asia), the routes to and from Java are almost always the same as one another—in other words, it makes little difference in our models if the path followed was from north to south or from south to north. Significant divergence only occurred in India and northern China, both of which lie outside the Southeast Asian biogeographic realm. In only two scenarios, the *LGM* and *Mean* sea-level models (Figures 9.3 and 9.5), did the path back from Java to China diverge temporarily from the China-to-Java path; this occurred in the eastern part of the Indochinese region.

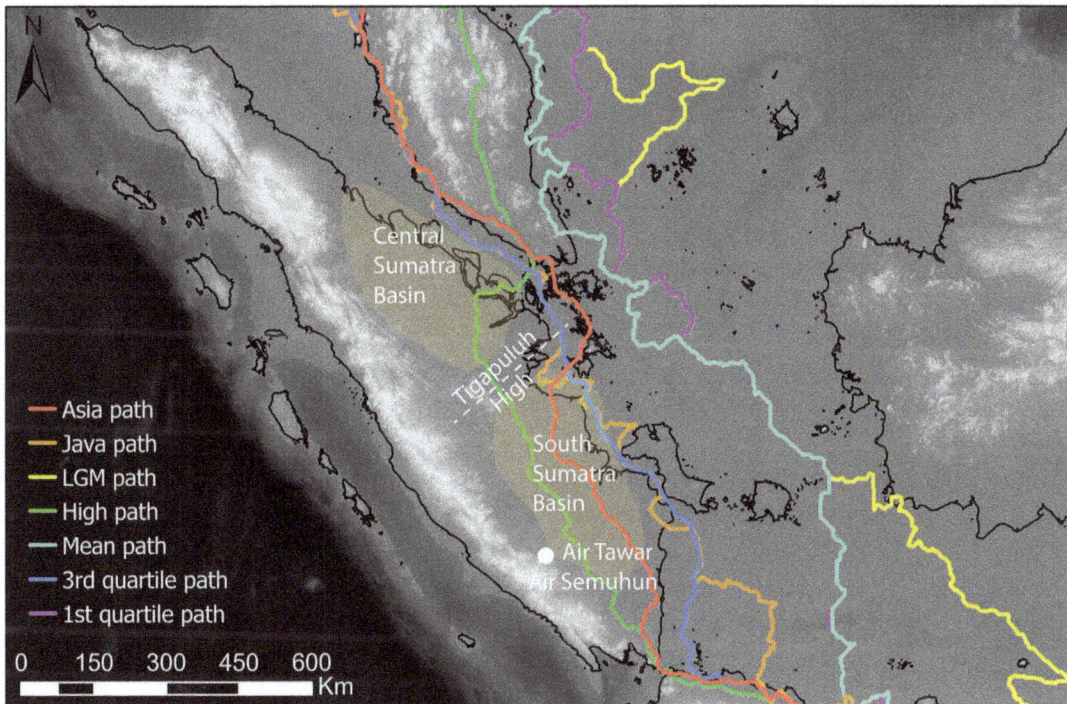

Figure 9.8: Least-cost pathways along the east coast of Sumatra under different sea-level conditions.

Note: The major basins of central and southern Sumatra are shown relative to the Air Tawar and Air Semuhun stone artefact sources.

Source: Map by authors. Basin locations after Barber and Crow (2005).

Second, paths from either India or China eventually converge in Southeast Asia, although the point of convergence differs between sea-level scenarios. In most instances, the higher the sea-level, the further north and west this point of convergence occurs. At its most northern occurrence, in the *Highstand* model (Figure 9.4), it is near the Kanchanaburi Province of Thailand. Its most southern, in the *LGM* model (Figure 9.3), occurs in the now-submerged Johore basin.

Finally, the major difference between the sea-level scenarios occurs in the Siam and East Sunda Basins. In the *LGM* scenario, the least-cost pathway runs through central Sundaland, in a region that is now almost entirely submerged. As the sea-level approaches modern levels, however, the pathway shifts noticeably west, towards and along the east coast of Sumatra (see Figure 9.8). Although the individual pathways through eastern Sumatra differ considerably between the scenarios, this trend suggests that eastern Sumatra may have been occupied or traversed (based on the variables included in our analysis).

Discussion

The most probable route taken by early hominins and associated megafauna southward into Java is indicated by the model with maximum connectivity between landmasses and would thus have been in the middle of the now-submerged Sunda Shelf. Such a route would also have gone through more open environments, particularly during the early to Middle Pleistocene (Louys and Roberts 2020). Unfortunately, identification and recovery of any material from this region will be difficult, although, as demonstrated by underwater recovery efforts elsewhere in the world (e.g. Bailey et al. 2007; Benjamin et al. 2020), perhaps not impossible. Nevertheless, any such sites, if they exist, are unlikely to be found in the near future. Therefore, it is useful to examine areas that are currently emergent and which have some support in the literature for their having been used as a migration corridor.

Recently, Salles et al. (2021) reported on landscape evolution and connectivity models of the Late Pleistocene of Southeast Asia. While the focus of Salles et al.'s (2021) study was on the drivers of increase in Southeast Asian biodiversity, their results have two important implications related to our modelling. First, their modelling showed high-connectivity migration corridors along the east coast of Sumatra coinciding with our westward least-cost pathways (Salles et al. 2021: figure 5). High connectivity exists regardless of whether rainforests were considered corridors or barriers to migration. The east coast of Sumatra appears to become a migration highway for many species over the Late Pleistocene, and, by extrapolation, even during periods of maximum continental shelf connectivity, such as the LGM, and the Pleistocene before 400 ka. This is supported by the recovery of Acheulean-type artefacts in the Air Tawar and Air Semuhun rivers (Chapter 10, this volume), which lie in the regions of high connectivity suggested by Salles et al. (2021), and just west of the pathways predicted by our least-cost modelling.

This area, encompassing the piedmont plains and peneplains of southern and eastern Sumatra, would therefore appear to be ideal for the recovery of early hominin material in Sumatra. Here, however, is where the second implication of the Salles et al. (2021) study for our question is relevant, notably the high net cumulative erosion of the east coast of Sumatra they record (Salles et al. 2021: figure 1). Structurally, southern and eastern Sumatra are characterised by two major basin systems: the South Sumatra Basin and the Central Sumatra Basin, which are separated by the Tigapuluh Hills, an upfaulted pre-Neogene block (Barber and Crow 2005; Figure 9.8). The uppermost formations in these basins, the Plio-Pleistocene-to-recent Kasai Formation in the South Sumatra Block and the similarly aged Minas Formation in the Central Sumatra Basin, unconformably overlie older marine sediments. It is these formations that are likely to preserve material of the right age for early hominins.

Extensive faulting in the Central Sumatra Basin largely controls drainage patterns in this region, which follow a northwest–southeast direction (Verstappen 1973). In the South Sumatra Basin, numerous anticlines control drainage, which is directed more east–west than in the Central Sumatra Basin. Denudation following major orogenic events, such as the uplift and volcanism of the Barisan Mountains, has produced intense base-levelling of high topographic features. Verstappen (1973) reports the loss of 1,000 m, but perhaps up to 5,000 m, of sediment from uplifted blocks and anticlines. Weathering of host rock is largely chemical rather than physical due to the region's high rainfall and dense rainforest vegetation, so that scree fans and coarse alluvial fans are rare, particularly in the area furthest east of the Barisan Mountains (Verstappen 1973). Most fluvial sediment load in the eastern lowlands is therefore composed of silts and clays, and there is extensive erosion, alteration of sediment, and rapid formation of soils, fuelling the growth of the eastern and southern alluvial plains (Verstappen 1973), with outcrops being rare (Katili 1974).

The least-cost pathways through eastern Sumatra (see Figure 9.8) remain relatively close to the east coast—in most instances less than 150 km away. Although some previous authors (e.g. Coleman et al. 1970; Keller and Richards 1967) suggested that a large sediment supply came to the east coast from inland river sources, a convincing study by Cecil et al. (1993) instead suggests that the east coast is an area of net erosion, with the little sedimentation that remains being primarily estuarine and marine rather than alluvial. They suggest that most of the sediment currently exposed in the east is the result of a marine transgression possibly occurring as recently as 5,000 years ago. How far this extends inland is locality-dependent; however, Cecil et al. (1993) suggest that the Kampar estuary is tidally influenced for up to 180 km, and flood tide–dominated more than 100 km inland. This is consistent with other studies that constructed this zone as a humid, tropical deltaic system (Boyd and Peacock 1986; Louys et al. 2021). Any early Pleistocene outcrops within the area identified by our modelling were exposed to repeated marine transgressions and regressions, with concomitant erosional events and marine sedimentation, over the last 400 ka. Thus, while the area of eastern Sumatra is very likely, from a modelling perspective, to preserve remains of early hominins in conditions that are today emergent, geological conditions are not highly favourable for such deposits. Both sedimentological constraints on preservation and the lack of suitable outcrops for stone tool production (e.g. Dennell 2008), as much as a lack of active exploration, probably explain why no Pleistocene early hominin fossil material has been recovered from this region.

These factors may also help to explain the absence of hyena fossils from Sumatra. Two species of hyena were widespread in Southeast Asia throughout the Pleistocene (Louys 2014). These hyenas probably fed in open environments on medium and large herbivores, especially rhinocerotids and bovids (Bacon et al. 2015, 2018), but potentially also including Southeast Asian hominins. Nevertheless, no hyena fossils have been recovered from any of the cave sites in Sumatra. As predators tend to follow prey closely, hyenas, like *Homo erectus*, may have been restricted to regions currently submerged. However, as noted in Chapter 5, more open areas may have existed in the Padang Highlands during the Middle Pleistocene, and the possibility remains that *Homo erectus* and hyena fossils may yet be recovered from the western side of Sumatra.

One final possible emergent area that our models identified as likely to have been traversed by *Homo erectus* and its potential predators and prey—one with less cumulative erosion than the east coast of Sumatra (Salles et al. 2021: figure 1)—is the Riau archipelago. Four of our seven models suggest pathways close to these islands, with two (*High* and *Asia*) suggesting pathways that traverse the modern, emergent islands of Karimun Besar and Bulan. Prospecting difficulties do arise in the Riau archipelago due to the age of the rocks there (they are mostly Mesozoic). Other factors, such as the ready availability of geological resources for tool manufacture (e.g. Dennell 2008) or the distribution of regional topographic and edaphic constraints (e.g. Devès et al. 2014; Kübler et al. 2016), may be equally important in determining the success for the recovery of early hominins and associated faunas from these islands.

Conclusion

Our least-cost pathway modelling suggests that the most probable route southward through Sundaland would have been through the middle of the now-sunken continental shelf. This route would have benefited hominins such as *Homo erectus* by being much more open than today's tropical rainforests (Louys and Roberts 2020). Nevertheless, any material preserved by these early hominins is currently submerged and inaccessible. The presently unsubmerged (and hence accessible) areas that are potentially on a major migration route southward into Java are mostly situated on the east coast of Sumatra. As sea-levels approach the highs seen today, our least-cost modelling moves the most probable such route westward within Sumatra, towards the Barisan Mountains. These routes coincide with biodiversity connectivity corridors identified through other researchers' landscape evolution modelling (Salles et al. 2021). Unfortunately, these areas are also net erosive regions, highly susceptible to chemical erosion and pedogenesis, hosting relatively few outcrops, and largely overlaid with marine sedimentation, particularly along the east coast. In such conditions, long-term preservation of early Pleistocene material is unlikely, so such material will continue to be difficult to find. Based on our modelling results and previously established erosion patterns, the islands of the Riau archipelago may be an alternative option for future research efforts.

Acknowledgements

Funding for this research was generously provided by the Australian Research Council (FT160100450) and the National Geographic Society (NGS-59859R-19). We thank Paul Albers, Alexandra van der Geer and two anonymous reviewers for helpful comments on this manuscript.

References

An, Z.S. and C.K. Ho 1989. New magnetostratigraphic dates of Lantian *Homo erectus*. *Quaternary Research* 32(2):213–221. doi.org/10.1016/0033-5894(89)90077-X

Ao, H., M.J. Dekkers, Q. Wei, X. Qiang and G. Xiao 2013. New evidence for early presence of hominids in North China. *Scientific Reports* 3:2403. doi.org/10.1038/srep02403

Bacon, A.M., K. Westaway, P.O. Antoine, P. Duringer, A. Blin, F. Demeter, J.L. Ponche, J.X. Zhao, L.M. Barnes, T. Sayavonkhamdy, N.T.K. Thuy, V.T. Long, E. Patole-Edoumba and L. Shackelford 2015. Late Pleistocene mammalian assemblages of Southeast Asia: New dating, mortality profiles and evolution of the predator–prey relationships in an environmental context. *Palaeogeography, Palaeoclimatology, Palaeoecology* 422:101–127. doi.org/10.1016/j.palaeo.2015.01.011

Bacon, A.M., P. Duringer, K. Westaway, R. Joannes-Boyau, J.X. Zhao, N. Bourgon, E. Dufour, S. Pheng, S. Tep, J.L. Ponche, L. Barnes, A. Blin, E. Patole-Edoumba and F. Demeter 2018. Testing the savannah corridor hypothesis during MIS2: The Boh Dambang hyena site in southern Cambodia. *Quaternary International* 464(Part B):417–439. doi.org/10.1016/j.quaint.2017.10.047

Bailey, G.N., N.C. Flemming, G.C. King, K. Lambeck, G. Momber, L.J. Moran, A. Al-Sharekh and C. Vita-Finzi 2007. Coastlines, submerged landscapes, and human evolution: The Red Sea Basin and the Farasan Islands. *The Journal of Island and Coastal Archaeology* 2(2):127–160. doi.org/10.1080/155648907016 23449

Barber, A.J. and M.J. Crow 2005. Structure and structural history. In A.J. Barber, M.J. Crow, J.S. Milsom (eds), *Sumatra: Geology, Resources and Tectonic Evolution*, pp. 175–233. Geological Society Memoir No. 31. Geological Society, London. doi.org/10.1144/GSL.MEM.2005.031.01.13

Benjamin, J., M. O'Leary, J. McDonald, C. Wiseman, J. McCarthy, E. Beckett, P. Morrison, F. Stankiewicz, J. Leach, J. Hacker, P. Baggaley, K. Jerbić, M. Fowler, J. Fairweather, P. Jeffries, S. Ulm and G. Bailey 2020. Aboriginal artefacts on the continental shelf reveal ancient drowned cultural landscapes in northwest Australia. *PLoS ONE* 15:e0233912. doi.org/10.1371/journal.pone.0233912

Bird, M.I., S.A. Condie, S. O'Connor, D. O'Grady, C. Reepmeyer, S. Ulm, M. Zega, F. Saltré and C.J. Bradshaw 2019. Early human settlement of Sahul was not an accident. *Scientific Reports* 9:8220. doi.org/10.1038/s41598-019-42946-9

Boyd, J.D. and S.G. Peacock 1986. Sedimentological analysis of a Miocene deltaic systems: Air Benakat and Muaraenim Formations, Central Merangin Block, South Sumatra. *Proceedings of the Indonesian Petroleum Association 15th Annual Convention 1986*, pp. 245–258. Indonesian Petroleum Association, Jakarta. ipa. or.id/en/publications/sedimentological-analysis-of-a-miocene-deltaic-systems-air-benakat-and-muara-enim-formations-central-merangin-block-south-sumatra

Brumm, A., G.M. Jensen, G.D., van den Bergh, M.J. Morwood, I. Kurniawan, F. Aziz and M. Storey 2010. Hominins on Flores, Indonesia, by one million years ago. *Nature* 464(7289):748–752. doi.org/10.1038/nature08844

Cecil, C.B., F.T. Dulong and J.C. Cobb 1993. Allogenic and autogenic controls on sedimentation in the Central Sumatra basin as an analogue for Pennsylvanian coal-bearing strata in the Appalachian basin. In J.C. Cobb and C.B. Cecil (eds), *Modern and Ancient Coal-Forming Environments*, pp. 3–22. GSA Special Papers 286. Geological Society of America, Boulder, CO. doi.org/10.1130/SPE286-p3

Chow, M.C. and C.K. Li 1965. Mammalian fossils in association with the mandible of Lantian Man at Chenchiaou, in Lantian, Shensi. *Vertebrata PalAsiatica* 9:377–393.

Ciochon, R., V.T. Long, R. Larick, L. González, R. Grün, J. de Vos, C. Yonge, L. Taylor, H. Yoshida and M. Reagan 1996. Dated co-occurrence of *Homo erectus* and *Gigantopithecus* from Tham Khuyen cave, Vietnam. *Proceedings of the National Academy of Sciences of the USA* 93(7):3016–3020. doi.org/10.1073/pnas.93.7.3016

Coleman, J.M., S.M. Gagliano and W.G. Smith 1970. Sedimentation in a Malaysian high tide tropical delta. In J.P. Morgan (ed.), *Deltaic Sedimentation, Modern and Ancient*, pp. 185–197. Society of Economic Paleontologists and Mineralogists Special Publication 15. Society for Sedimentary Geology, Tulsa, OK. doi.org/10.2110/pec.70.11.0185

D'Cunha, M.G.T., A. Montenegro and J.S. Field 2021. Modeling water crossings leading to the arrival of early *Homo* in Sulawesi, Indonesia, via paleoclimate drift experiments. *Journal of Archaeological Science: Reports* 40(Part A):103194. doi.org/10.1016/j.jasrep.2021.103194

Demeter, F., A. Bacon, N. Thuy, V. Long, H. Matsumura, H. Nga, M. Schuster, N. Huong and Y. Coppens 2004. An archaic *Homo* molar from northern Vietnam. *Current Anthropology* 45(4):535–541.

Dennell, R.W. 2008. The taphonomic record of Upper Siwalik (Pinjor stage) landscapes in the Pabbi Hills, northern Pakistan, with consideration regarding the preservation of hominin remains. *Quaternary International* 192(1):62–77. doi.org/10.1016/j.quaint.2007.06.024

Dennell, R.W. 2020. *From Arabia to the Pacific: How Our Species Colonised Asia*. Routledge, London. doi.org/ 10.4324/9781003038788

Devès, M., D. Sturdy, N. Godet, G.C.P. King and G.N. Bailey 2014. Hominin reactions to herbivore distribution in the Lower Palaeolithic of the Southern Levant. *Quaternary Science Reviews* 96:140–160. doi.org/10.1016/j.quascirev.2014.04.017

de Vos, J., F. Aziz, P.Y. Sondaar and G.D. van den Bergh 1999. *Homo erectus* in S.E. Asia. Time, space and migration routes; a global model III. Migration routes and evolution. In J. Gibert, F. Sanchez, L. Gibert and F. Ribot (eds), *The Hominids and Their Environment During the Lower and Middle Pleistocene of Eurasia*, pp. 369–381. Proceedings of the International Conference of Human Paleontology, Orce 1995. Museo de Prehistoria y Paleontología, Orce, Granada, Spain.

Duval, M., F. Fang, K. Suraprasit, J.J. Jaeger, M. Benammi, C. Yaowalak, J. Iglesias Cibanal and R. Grün 2019. Direct ESR dating of the Pleistocene vertebrate assemblage from Khok Sung locality, Nakhon Ratchasima Province, Northeast Thailand. *Palaeontologia Electronica* 22.3:69. doi.org/10.26879/941

Environmental Systems Research Institute (ESRI) 2018. *ArcGIS 10.7 for Desktop*. ESRI, Redlands, California.

Field, J.S. and M.M. Lahr 2005. Assessment of the southern dispersal: GIS-based analyses of potential routes at oxygen isotopic stage 4. *Journal of World Prehistory* 19:1–45. doi.org/10.1007/S10963-005-9000-6

Guo, Y., C.C. Huang, J. Pang, X. Zha, Y. Zhou, Y. Zhang and L. Zhou 2013. Sedimentological study of the stratigraphy at the site of *Homo erectus yunxianensis* in the upper Hanjiang River valley, China. *Quaternary International* 300:75–82. doi.org/10.1016/j.quaint.2012.12.036

Hall, R. 2001. Cenozoic reconstructions of SE Asia and the SW Pacific: Changing patterns of land and sea. In I. Metcalfe, J.M. Smith, M. Morwood and I. Davidson (eds), *Faunal and Floral Migration and Evolution in SE Asia-Australasia*, pp. 35–56. A.A. Balkema Publishers, Lisse.

Hu, C. and T. Qi 1978. Gongwangling Pleistocene mammalian fauna of Lantian, Shaanxi. *Palaeontologia Sinica* 155:1–6.

Husson, L., F.C. Boucher, A.C. Sarr, P. Sepulchre and S.Y. Cahyarini 2020. Evidence of Sundaland's subsidence requires revisiting its biogeography. *Journal of Biogeography* 47(4):843–853. doi.org/10.1111/jbi.13762

Ingicco, T., G.D. van den Bergh, C. Jago-On, J.J. Bahain, M.G. Chacón, N. Amano, H. Forestier, C. King, K. Manalo, S. Nomade, A. Pereira, M.C. Reyes, A.-M. Sémah, Q. Shao, P. Voinchet, C. Falguères, P.C.H. Albers, M. Lising, G. Lyras, D. Yurnaldi, P. Rochette, A. Bautista and J. de Vos 2018. Earliest known hominin activity in the Philippines by 709 thousand years ago. *Nature* 557(7704):233–237. doi.org/ 10.1038/s41586-018-0072-8

Kahlke, H.D. 1972. A review of the Pleistocene history of the orangutan (*Pongo* Lacepede, 1799). *Asian Perspectives* 15:5–14.

Kaifu, Y., H. Baba, F. Aziz, E. Indriati, F. Schrenk and T. Jacob 2005. Taxonomic affinities and evolutionary history of the early Pleistocene hominids of Java: Dentognathic evidence. *American Journal of Physical Anthropology* 128(4):709–726. doi.org/10.1002/ajpa.10425

Katili, J.A. 1974. Sumatra. In *Geological Society, London, Special Publications*, Volume 4, pp. 317–331. Geological Society, London. doi.org/10.1144/GSL.SP.2005.004.01.18

Kealy, S., L. Louys and S. O'Connor 2018. Least-cost pathway models indicate northern human dispersal from Sunda to Sahul. *Journal of Human Evolution* 125:59–70. doi.org/10.1016/j.jhevol.2018.10.003

Keller, G.H. and A.F. Richards 1967. Sediments of the Malacca Strait, Southeast Asia. *Journal of Sedimentary Petrology* 37:102–127. doi.org/10.1306/74D7166D-2B21-11D7-8648000102C1865D

Kübler, S., S. Rucina, S. Reynolds, P. Owenga, G. Bailey and G.C.P. King 2016. Edaphic and topographic constraints on exploitation of the Central Kenya Rift by large mammals and early hominins. *Open Quaternary* 2:1–18. doi.org/10.5334/oq.21

Lambeck, K., H. Rouby, A. Purcell, Y. Sun and M. Sambridge 2014. Sea level and global ice volumes from the Last Glacial Maximum to the Holocene. *Proceedings of the National Academy of Sciences of the USA* 111(43):15296–15303. doi.org/10.1073/pnas.1411762111

Lee, S.H. and A. Hudock 2021. Human evolution in Asia: Taking stock and looking forward. *Annual Review of Anthropology* 50:145–166. doi.org/10.1146/annurev-anthro-101819-110230

Liu, T., Z. An, B. Yuan and J. Han 1985. The loess–paleosol sequence in China and climatic history. *Episodes* 8:21–28. doi.org/10.18814/epiiugs/1985/v8i1/003

Long, V.T., J. de Vos and R. Ciochon 1996. The fossil mammal fauna of the Lang Trang caves, Viet-nam, compared with Southeast Asian fossil and recent mammal faunas: The geographical implications. *Bulletin of the Indo-Pacific Prehistory Association* 14:101–109.

Louys, J. 2014. The large terrestrial carnivore guild in Quaternary Southeast Asia. *Quaternary Science Reviews* 96:86–97. doi.org/10.1016/j.quascirev.2013.06.014

Louys, J., S. Kealy, S. O'Connor, G.J. Price, S. Hawkins, K. Aplin, Y. Rizal, Y. Zaim, Mahirta, D.A. Tanudirjo, W.D. Santoso, A.R. Hidayah, A. Trihascaryo, R. Wood, J. Bevitt and T. Clark 2017. Differential preservation of vertebrates in Southeast Asian caves. *International Journal of Speleology* 46:379–408. doi.org/10.5038/1827-806X.46.3.2131

Louys, J. and P. Roberts 2020. Environmental drivers of megafauna and hominin extinction in Southeast Asia. *Nature* 586:402–406. doi.org/10.1038/s41586-020-2810-y

Louys, J., K.J. Travouillon, M. Bassarova and H. Tong 2009. The use of natural protected areas in palaeoecological analyses: Assumptions, limitations and application. *Journal of Archaeological Science* 36(10):2274–2288. doi.org/10.1016/j.jas.2009.06.012

Louys, J. and A. Turner 2012. Environment, preferred habitats and potential refugia for Pleistocene *Homo* in Southeast Asia. *Comptes Rendus Palevol* 11:203–211. doi.org/10.1016/j.crpv.2011.03.003

Louys, J., Y. Zaim, Y. Rizal, G.J. Price, Aswan, M.R. Puspanigrum, H. Smith and A. Trihascaryo 2021. Palaeontological surveys in Central Sumatra and Bangka. *Berita Sedimentologi* 47: 50–56.

Matsu'ura, S., M. Kondo, T. Danhara, S. Sakata, H. Iwano, T. Hirata, I. Kurniawan, E. Setiyabudi, Y. Takeshita, M. Hyodo, I. Kitaba, M. Sudo, Y. Danhara and F. Aziz 2020. Age control of the first appearance datum for Javanese *Homo erectus* in the Sangiran area. *Science* 367(6474):210–214. doi.org/10.1126/science.aau8556

Miller, K.G., G.S. Mountain, J.D. Wright and J.V. Browning 2011. A 180-million-year record of sea level and ice volume variations from continental margin and deep-sea isotopic records. *Oceanography* 24(2):40–53. doi.org/10.5670/oceanog.2011.26

Morley, R.J., H.P. Morley, Y. Zaim and O.F. Huffman 2020. Palaeoenvironmental setting of Mojokerto *Homo erectus*, the palynological expressions of Pleistocene marine deltas, open grasslands and volcanic mountains in East Java. *Journal of Biogeography* 47(3):566–583. doi.org/10.1111/jbi.13770

Morwood, M.J., P. O'Sullivan, E.E. Susanto and F. Aziz 2003. Revised age for Mojokerto 1, an early *Homo erectus* cranium from East Java, Indonesia. *Australian Archaeology* 57(1):1–4. doi.org/10.1080/03122417.2003.11681757

Nugraha, A.M.S. and R. Hall 2018. Late Cenozoic palaeogeography of Sulawesi, Indonesia. *Palaeogeography, Palaeoclimatology, Palaeoecology* 490:191–209. doi.org/10.1016/j.palaeo.2017.10.033

O'Connor, S., J. Louys, S. Kealy and S.C. Samper Carro 2017. Hominin dispersal and settlement east of Huxley's Line: The role of sea level changes, island size, and subsistence behavior. *Current Anthropology* 58(S17):S567–S582. doi.org/10.1086/694252

Olsen, J.W. and R.L. Ciochon 1990. A review of evidence for postulated Middle Pleistocene occupations in Viet Nam. *Journal of Human Evolution* 19(8):761–788. doi.org/10.1016/0047-2484(90)90020-C

Rizal Y, K.E. Westaway, Y. Zaim, G.D. van den Bergh, E.A. Bettis III, M.J. Morwood, O.F. Huffman, R. Grün, R. Joannes-Boyau, R.M. Bailey, Sidarto, M.C. Westaway, I. Kurniawan, M.W. Moore, M. Storey, F. Aziz, Suminto, J.-X. Zhao, Aswan, M.E. Sipola, R. Larick, J.-P. Zonneveld, R. Scott, S. Putt and R.L. Ciochon 2019. Last appearance of *Homo erectus* at Ngandong, Java, 117,000–108,000 years ago. *Nature* 577:381–385. doi.org/10.1038/s41586-019-1863-2

Salles, T., C. Mallard, L. Husson, S. Zahirovic, A.C. Sarr and P. Sepulchre 2021. Quaternary landscape dynamics boosted species dispersal across Southeast Asia. *Communications Earth & Environment* 2:240. doi.org/10.1038/s43247-021-00311-7

Sarr, A.C., L. Husson, P. Sepulchre, A.M. Pastier, K. Pedoja, M. Elliot, C. Arias-Ruiz, T. Solihuddin, S. Aribowo and Susilohadi 2019. Subsiding Sundaland. *Geology* 47(2):119–122. doi.org/10.1130/G45629.1

Shen, G., X. Gao, B. Gao and D.E. Granger 2009. Age of Zhoukoudian *Homo erectus* determined with ^{26}Al/^{10}Be burial dating. *Nature* 458:198–200. doi.org/10.1038/nature07741

Shipton, C., J. Blinkhorn, P.S. Breeze, P. Cuthbertson, N. Drake, H.S. Groucutt, R.P. Jennings, A. Parton, E.M. Scerri, A. Alsharekh and M.D. Petraglia 2018. Acheulean technology and landscape use at Dawadmi, central Arabia. *PLoS ONE* 13(7):e0200497. doi.org/10.1371/journal.pone.0200497

Shipton, C., S. O'Connor and S. Kealy 2021. The biogeographic threshold of Wallacea in human evolution. *Quaternary International* 574:1–12. doi.org/10.1016/j.quaint.2020.07.028

Smith, H.E., M.W. Morley and J. Louys 2020. Taphonomic analyses of cave breccia in southeast Asia: A review and future directions. *Open Quaternary* 6(1).

Smith, W.H.F. and D.T. Sandwell 1997. Global sea floor topography from satellite altimetry and ship depth soundings. *Science* 277(5334):1956–1962. doi.org/10.1126/science.277.5334.1956

Suraprasit, K., H. Bocherens, Y. Chaimanee, S. Panha and J.J. Jaeger 2018. Late Middle Pleistocene ecology and climate in northeastern Thailand inferred from the stable isotope analysis of Khok Sung herbivore tooth enamel and the land mammal cenogram. *Quaternary Science Reviews* 193:24–42. doi.org/10.1016/j.quascirev.2018.06.004

Swisher, C.C. III, G.H. Curtis, T. Jacob, A.G. Getty, A. Suprijo and Widiasmoro 1994. Age of the earliest known hominids in Java, Indonesia. *Science* 263(5150):1118–1121. doi.org/10.1126/science.8108729

Tougard, C. 2001. Biogeography and migration routes of large mammal faunas in South–East Asia during the Late Middle Pleistocene: Focus on the fossil and extant faunas from Thailand. *Palaeogeography, Palaeoclimatology, Palaeoecology* 168(3–4):337–358. doi.org/10.1016/S0031-0182(00)00243-1

Tougard, C., J.J. Jaeger, Y. Chaimanee, V. Suteethorn and S. Triamwichanon 1998. Discovery of a *Homo* sp. tooth associated with a mammalian cave fauna of Late Middle Pleistocene age, northern Thailand. *Journal of Human Evolution* 35(1):47–54. doi.org/10.1006/jhev.1998.0221

van den Bergh, G.D., B. Li, A. Brumm, R. Grün, D. Yurnaldi, M.W. Moore, I. Kurniawan, R. Setiawan, F. Aziz, R.G. Roberts and M. Storey 2016. Earliest hominin occupation of Sulawesi, Indonesia. *Nature* 529:208–211. doi.org/10.1038/nature16448

Verstappen H.T. 1973. *A Geomorphological Reconnaissance of Sumatra and Adjacent Islands (Indonesia)*, Volume 1. Wolters-Noordhoff, Groningen.

von Koenigswald G.H.R. 1935. Die fossilen Säugetierfaunen Javas. *Proceedings of the Koninklijke Nederlandse Akademie van Wetenschappen* 38:188–198.

von Koenigswald G.H.R. 1939. The relationship between the fossil mammalian faunae of Java and China, with special reference to early man. *Peking Natural History Bulletin* 13:293–298.

Wu Xinzhi 2004. On the origin of modern humans in China. *Quaternary International* 117:131–140. doi.org/10.1016/S1040-6182(03)00123-X

Wu Xiu-Jie, S.W. Pei, Y.J. Cai, H.W. Tong, Q. Li, Z. Dong, J.C. Sheng, Z.T. Jin, D.D. Ma, S. Xing, X.L. Li, X. Cheng, H. Cheng, I. de la Torre, R. L. Edwards, X.C. Gong, Z.S. An and E. Trinkaus 2019. Archaic human remains from Hualongdong, China, and Middle Pleistocene human continuity and variation. *Proceedings of the National Academy of Sciences of the USA* 116(20):9820–9824. doi.org/10.1073/pnas.1902396116

Zhu, R.X., Z. An, R. Potts and K.A. Hoffman 2003. Magnetostratigraphic dating of early humans in China. Earth-Science Reviews 61(3–4):341–359. doi.org/10.1016/S0012-8252(02)00132-0

Zhu, R.X., R. Potts, F. Xie, K.A. Hoffman, C.L. Deng, C.D. Shi, Y.X. Pan, H.Q. Wang, R.P. Shi, Y.C. Wang, G.H. Shi and N.Q. Wu 2004. New evidence on the earliest human presence at high northern latitudes in northeast Asia. *Nature* 431:559–562. doi.org/10.1038/nature02829

Zhu, R.X., R. Potts, Y.X. Pan, H.T. Yao, L.Q. Lü, X. Zhao, X. Gao, L.W. Chen, F. Gao and C.L. Deng 2008. Early evidence of the genus *Homo* in East Asia. *Journal of Human Evolution* 55(6):1075–1085. doi.org/10.1016/j.jhevol.2008.08.005

Zhu, Z.Y., R. Dennell, W.W. Huang, Y. Wu, Z.G. Rao, S.F. Qiu, J.B. Xie. W. Liu, S.Q. Fu, J.W. Han and H.Y. Zhou 2015. New dating of the *Homo erectus* cranium from Lantian (Gongwangling), China. *Journal of Human Evolution* 78:144–157. doi.org/10.1016/j.jhevol.2014.10.001

Zhu, Z.Y., R. Dennell, W. Huang, Y. Wu, S. Qiu, S. Yang, Z. Rao, Y. Hou, J. Xie, J. Han and T. Ouyang 2018. Hominin occupation of the Chinese Loess Plateau since about 2.1 million years ago. *Nature* 559:608–612. doi.org/10.1038/s41586-018-0299-4

10

Stone tools in Palaeolithic Sumatra, Indonesia: From *Homo erectus* to the Hoabinhian

Hubert Forestier

Abstract

Sumatra is regarded as a land bridge between mainland Southeast Asia and the Indonesian archipelago. This island played an important and strategic role in human migrations during the Pleistocene and the settlement of Indonesia. Since early prehistoric times, humans would have crossed the ancient Sundaland subcontinent, and would thus have inevitably passed through Sumatra before reaching Java. From the ancient Palaeolithic to the Neolithic, traces in the form of stone tools were left in Sumatra, initially by the first migrants, *Homo erectus*, then by Hoabinhian foragers and later the first farmers. Here, I present a comprehensive overview of stone tools as cultural markers preserved through time. First, this contribution briefly reviews the history of prehistoric research in Sumatra from the colonial period to the present. Second, I present new discoveries resulting from recent fieldwork, attempting to provide new insights into the prehistoric cultural steps on this vast and often-forgotten island.

Keywords: ancient prehistory, hunter-gatherer, *Homo sapiens*, stone artefacts

Abstrak

Sumatra selama ini dianggap sebagai jembatan darat antara Daratan Asia Tenggara dan kepulauan Indonesia. Pulau ini telah memainkan peran penting dan strategis dalam migrasi dan okupansi manusia di Indonesia selama Pleistosen. Sejak zaman prasejarah awal, manusia pasti telah melintasi sub-benua Sundaland kuno dan mau tidak mau melewati Sumatra sebelum mencapai Jawa. Migran pertama, Homo erectus, peramu Hoabinhian dan petani pertama mulai dari periode Palaeolitik purba hingga Neolitik, semuanya meninggalkan jejak peralatan batu mereka di Sumatra. Di sini, saya menyajikan gambaran lengkap tentang alat-alat batu sebagai penanda budaya sepanjang perjalanan waktu. Pertama, kontribusi ini mengulas secara singkat sejarah penelitian prasejarah di Sumatra dari masa kolonial hingga saat ini. Kedua, saya menyajikan penemuan-penemuan baru yang dihasilkan dari kerja lapangan baru-baru ini, mencoba memberikan wawasan baru tentang capaian langkah budaya prasejarah pada pulau yang luas dan terlupakan ini.

Kata kunci: Prasejarah purba, pemburu-peramu, Homo sapiens, artefak batu

The history of prehistoric research in Sumatra

Sumatra, at 473,000 km², can be considered the main gateway to the world's largest archipelago, the Indonesian archipelago. It is the westernmost of the 17,508 islands in the archipelago and the closest large island to the Indochinese peninsula. Situated on either side of the Equator, it stretches for almost 1,600 km in a northwest–southeast direction and has a pronounced tropical climate (see Figure 10.1).

Figure 10.1: Relief map of Sumatra showing the location of all areas and sites mentioned in the text and general physiographical information.

Source: Map by author.

For many years, Sumatra was not a region of focus in prehistoric and palaeoanthropological research. Rather, researchers were attracted by the fossil wealth of its neighbouring island, Java. Sumatra is also a difficult, often mountainous and forested environment, which makes fieldwork challenging and limits standardised surveys. For these reasons, Sumatra did not gain the same palaeontological glory as Java (Widianto 2009), despite Eugène Dubois' stay in its western area until around 1890.

Although archaeological research in Sumatra is more than a century old, the island's prehistory is poorly documented, and few archaeological discoveries have been made. The research can be divided into four consecutive periods or events of scientific interest:

1. At the end of the nineteenth century, the well-known palaeoanthropologist, Eugène Dubois, travelled to Sumatra in search of the 'missing link'; after his stay on Sumatra, he moved to Java, where he discovered *Pithecanthropus* (Shipman 2001).

2. During the first half of the twentieth century, van Heekeren presented the first discoveries about the Sumatran Hoabinhian culture at the First Congress of Prehistorians of the Far East (Congrès des Préhistoriens d'Extrême Orient) on 30 January 1932 in Hanoi, Vietnam.

3. During the second half of the twentieth century, research focused on Sumatra as the first place of settlement of *Homo erectus*, who arrived in Indonesia from mainland Southeast Asia and left traces in the form of stone tools (Simanjuntak 2009; Soejono 1961; van Heekeren 1972).

4. The last decades of the twentieth century heralded modern research and fieldwork, including my own team's work in Palaeolithic prehistory and recent and historical archaeology (Tjoa-Bonatz 2019).

Evidence of *Homo erectus* in South Sumatra

Surveys undertaken in South Sumatra by a French–Indonesian team between 2000 and 2004 discovered unique and ancient lithic tools in the beds of two small rivers called Air Tawar and Air Semuhun, tributaries of the Ogan River in South Sumatra near Padang Bindu village in the karstic area of Baturaja (see Figures 10.1 and 10.2). These hundreds of pieces present an astonishing diversity in terms of size but also in the raw materials selected for knapping. These tools can be described as 'ancient' based on their size, weight and overall morphology, because they resemble what is usually associated with *Homo erectus*, that is, an abundance of massive bifacial pieces shaped from large rocks (mainly cobbles and boulders). The raw material varies in quality and type: it includes local chert, silicified wood, breccia, silicified limestone, quartz and andesite.

Massive, highly patinated Sumatran pieces are characteristic of the so-called 'Acheulean' complex, composed of hand axes, cleavers, cores and choppers. These types of tools are associated with the Lower Palaeolithic in Europe, Africa, and Asia; and in eastern Java, specifically with the Pacitanian artefacts collected in the Baksoka River. Although these stone artefacts were discovered in the absence of a stratigraphic or geochronological context, the Padang Bindu surface finds introduce compelling evidence for the presence of archaic stone tools in South Sumatra.

The Padang Bindu assemblage also includes some exceptional pieces, such as huge hand axes (>20 cm long), trihedral picks, thick horse-hoof-shaped cores, choppers and chopping tools, and cleavers (Figure 10.3). The large cutting tools (LCTs) have been produced from giant prismatic cores weighing about 25 kg with a single large striking platform (Figure 10.4). The LCTs include thick cortical-backed flakes, retouched into simple scrapers, convergent scrapers, notches, and denticulate or even bifacial retouches.

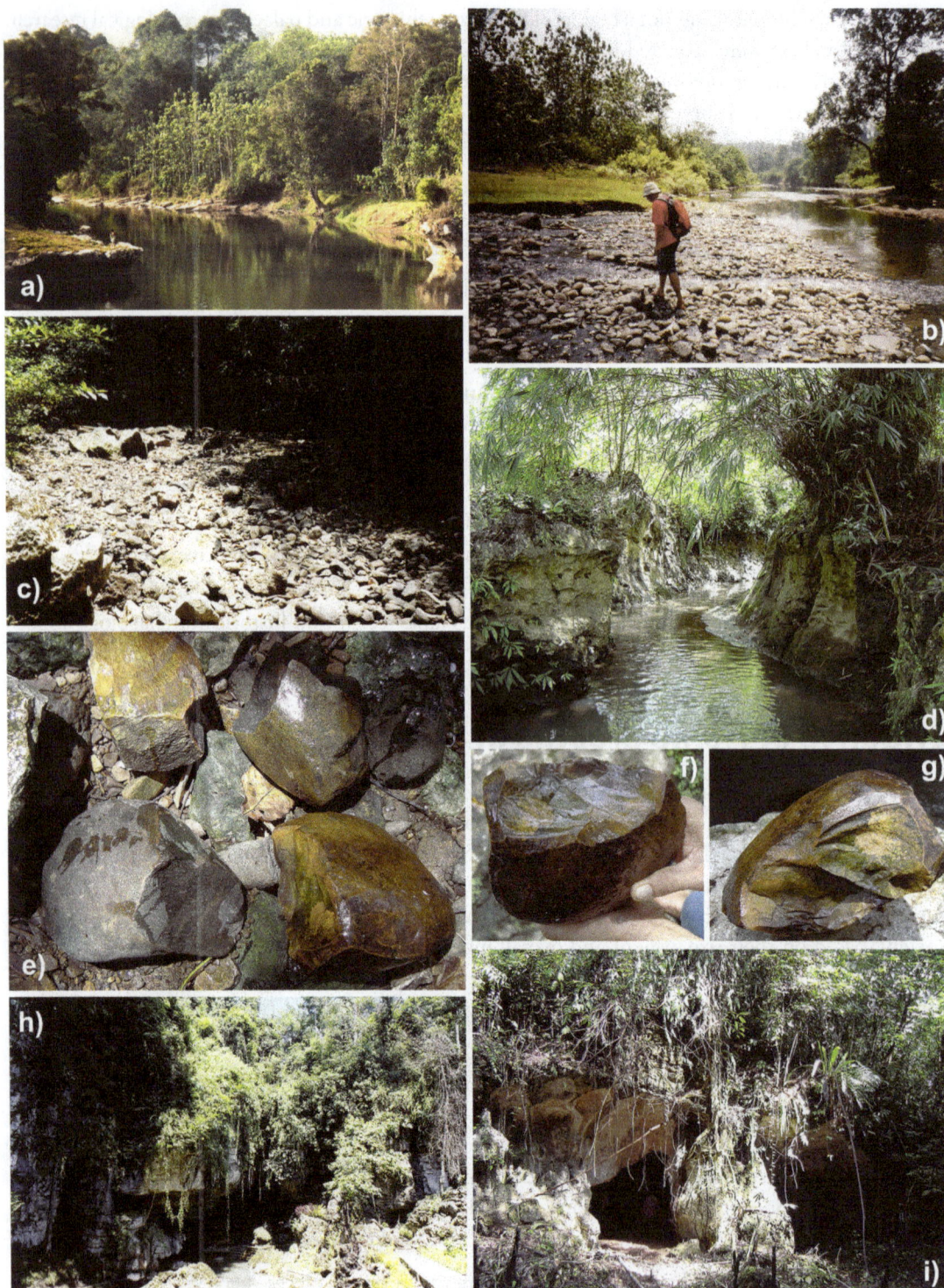

Figure 10.2: Views of the environments associated with the Palaeolithic open-air sites in South Sumatra.

a, b: Ogan river.

c: Air Tawar river.

d: Air Semuhun river.

Source: Photographs by author.

e–g: Massive Palaeolithic implements found in situ.

h: Karst of Padang Bindu.

i: Gua Pandan cave.

Figure 10.3: Examples of ancient Palaeolithic implements found in the Air Tawar and Air Semuhun rivers.

a–c: Massive handaxes.

d: Trihedral pick.

e, f: Choppers.

g: Pebble with an isolated convex removal.

h, i: Cleavers.

Source: Photograph by author.

Figure 10.4: Examples of ancient Palaeolithic implements found in the Air Tawar and Air Semuhun rivers.

a–f: Large cutting tools.

g, h: Giant cores.

Source: Photograph by author.

The hand axe morphologies from Sumatra and Java (Sémah et al. 2014; Simanjuntak et al. 2010) and Sulawesi (Keates and Bartstra 2001) can be categorised as thick, cortical, massive and heavy, compared to those of African or South Asian artefacts, which display varied and changing forms over the Quaternary (Brumm and Moore 2012; Simanjuntak and Forestier 2008, 2009). The diversity of Acheulean tools makes it difficult to define this industry, and Sumatran tools add to its diversity.

The presence of this Lower Palaeolithic facies in South Sumatra is almost certainly linked to *Homo erectus* passing through Sumatra on their way to Java. The 'Sumatran Acheulean' further challenges the already somewhat dubious concept of the 'Movius line' (Brumm and Moore 2012). This theoretical line across northeastern South Asia aims to separate the biface and cleaver industries occurring between Africa and South Asia from the strictly pebble-and-cobble industries in the rest of eastern Asia. The Sumatran ancient stone tool assemblage thus invalidates the Movius model because it contains numerous hand axes and cleavers and has a surprising diversity of tool-kits compared to the Pacitanian corpus in Java (Sémah et al. 1992; Simanjuntak et al. 2010). The only artefact that is so far absent in Sumatra is the bola; this could be a definite 'signature' of Javanese *Homo erectus*.

Homo sapiens in Sumatra and the Hoabinhian

Recent reinvestigation of the Sumatran caves by Westaway et al. (2017) evidenced the presence of *Homo sapiens* on Sumatra about 70,000 years ago. The earliest Sumatran presence of modern humans is certainly that found in the northern provinces of Sumatra, namely the Hoabinhian stone artefacts discovered in the 1920s (Congrès des Préhistoriens d'Extrême Orient 1932).

Hoabinhians were hunter-gatherer groups who came from mainland Southeast Asia via the Malay Peninsula (Majid 2003) and settled in Sumatra (Brandt 1976). They probably occupied coastal areas, as evidenced by the vast shell middens on the northeast coast of Sumatra between Medan and North Aceh (see Figure 10.1), middens which have subsequently disappeared. Several factors influenced their settlement patterns: the environment (its physical relief, coastline, tides, etc.), access to resources (beaches, mangroves and forests) and the availability of raw materials to make unifacial stone tools. Van Stein Callenfels was one of the first researchers to excavate a shell midden, at Saentis near Medan, where he noted a high concentration of animal bones, single-sided pebbles, mortars, millstones and, above all, thousands of shell remains dominated by *Meretrix meretrix* (van Heekeren 1972). This shell midden (Sukajadi) was associated with numerous unifacial and chopper-type pebbles (see Figure 10.5) and was dated to 7,340 ± 360 BP (uncalibrated; Bronson and Glover 1984). This dating was later confirmed by Edwards McKinnon's excavation of the Sukajadi Pasar site, which was dated to c. 7,500 BP (McKinnon 1991).

During the 1970s, an archaeological survey was conducted from the north to the south, covering 9,000 km in a period of two months, to investigate the archaeological potential of Sumatra (Bronson and Wisseman 1974). Apart from reporting information about the Hoabinhian, this survey included an excavation in Tianko Panjang Cave, in Jambi near Lake Kerinci, that revealed an industry of small obsidian flakes dated to c. 10,000 BP (Bellwood 1997; Bronson and Asmar 1975; Simanjuntak 2006).

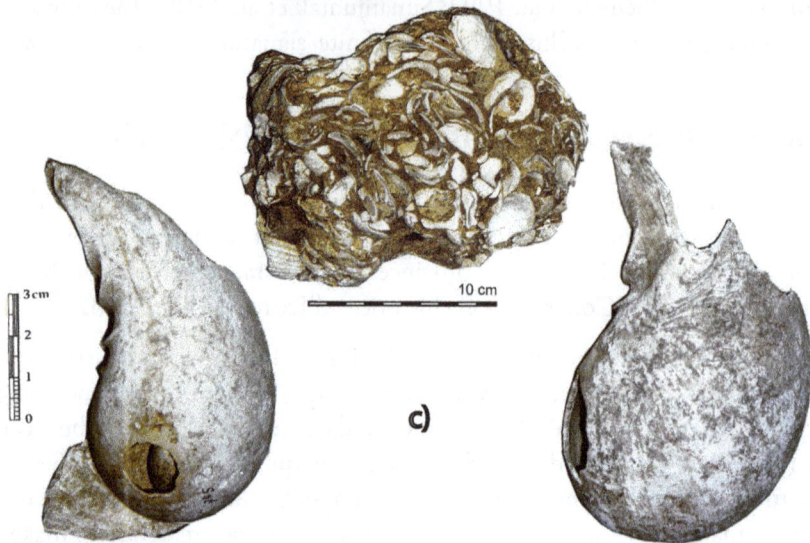

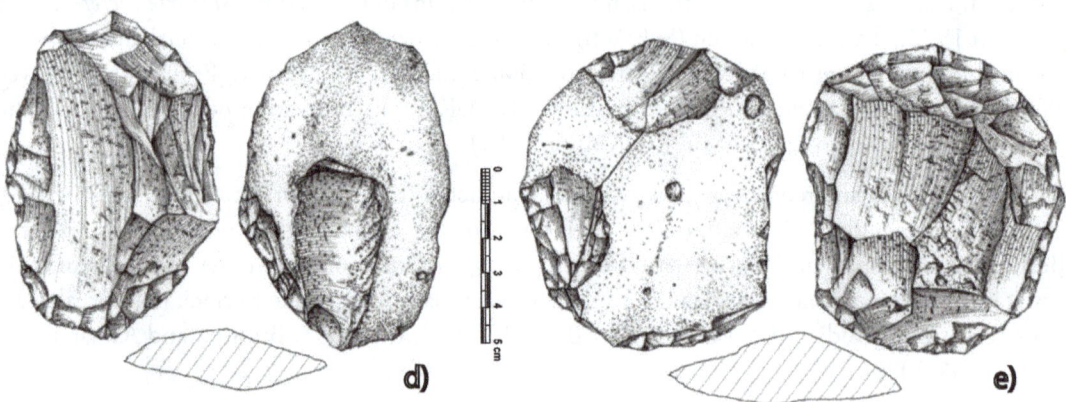

Figure 10.5: The Hoabinhian site of Sukajadi, near Medan, North Sumatra.

a, b: Hoabinhian shell midden, now empty of shell and used as a fish pool.

c: Indurated fragment of shell midden deposit.

d, e: Unifacial pebble tools.

Source: Photographs by author.

Figure 10.6: Tögi Ndrawa Cave site, Nias Island, North Sumatra.

a: Eastern view of Nias landscape.

b: Tögi Ndrawa Cave entrance.

c: Western section of the excavation, showing an important shell and bone deposit.

Source: Photographs by author.

d: Single chopper.

e: Unifacial pebble.

f: Single convex chopper.

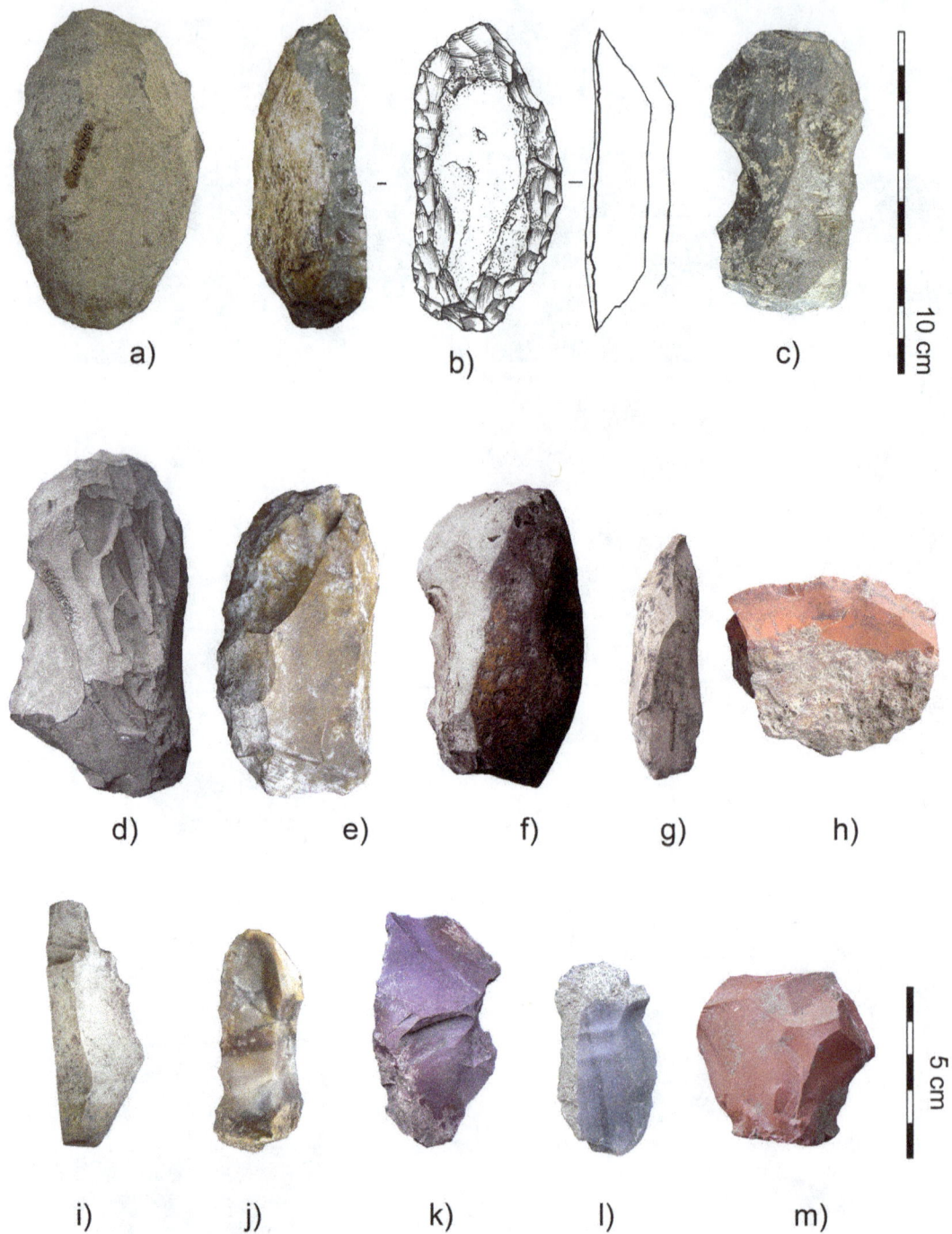

Figure 10.7: Examples of Hoabinhian implements, Gua Pandan, South Sumatra.

a–d: Unifacial pebble.

e, f: Lateral side choppers.

g: Blade-like flake.

h: Red jasper flake with proximal convex denticulation.

i–l: Blade products.

m: Jasper flake.

Source: Photograph by author.

Further west, on the small island of Nias, the Tögi Ndrawa Cave contains a 3 m–deep archaeological deposit with thousands of burnt consumed shells, burnt bones and pebble tools within several interstratified ash levels dated to between 12,000 and 900 BP (uncalibrated; Forestier et al. 2005). The assemblage consists of Hoabinhian tools (choppers, chopping tools, and unifaces) made from limestone, andesite or basalt pebbles (see Figure 10.6). These tools' raw materials, of rather poor quality, were collected from the surrounding rivers and beach and then brought back to the cave. This excavation confirms that the Hoabinhian occupations in Sumatra date from around the Pleistocene-Holocene transition, as proposed by Edwards McKinnon (1991).

Finally, Gua Pandan Cave (Figure 10.7), in the Padang Bindu karst, is the southernmost Hoabinhian site and therefore represents the furthest Hoabinhian extension into Southeast Asia. Its archaeological layer is dated to between 9,000 and 6,500 BP (uncalibrated), and contains not only heavy unifacial tools made from limestone pebbles with many unifaces but also lateral choppers, micro-flakes and blade tools made from chert and red jasper, which gives this layer a mixed identity (Forestier et al. 2006). This Hoabinhian site shows a high diversity of tool and raw material types, demonstrating adaptation to the different environments that occur between Sumatra's coast and its interior.

Conclusion, and perspective on prehistoric research in Sumatra

The prehistory of Sumatra reveals a long and rich cultural chronology that begins in the ancient Palaeolithic and extends up to the Metal Age and historical times. The history of settlement and the anthropogenic landscape have been fundamental issues in the research of this large island. Modern humans settled in cave sites in the Sumatran lowlands and foothills as early as the Lower Palaeolithic, then again during the Hoabinhian period, and the Neolithic. In contrast, the highlands were not settled until the Neolithic and Metal Age periods, probably because they were relatively poor in lithic raw materials but rich in fertile volcanic soils suitable for agricultural communities. Prehistoric research is just beginning again in Sumatra, which remains an underexplored island where important Palaeolithic discoveries are to be expected.

References

Bellwood, P. 1997. *Prehistory of the Indo-Malaysian Archipelago*. 2nd edition. University of Hawaii Press, Honolulu. doi.org/10.26530/OAPEN_459472

Brandt, R.W. 1976. The Hoabinhian of Sumatra: Some remarks. *Modern Quaternary Research in Southeast Asia* 2:49–52.

Bronson, B. and T. Asmar 1975. Prehistoric investigations at Tianko Panjang cave, Sumatra. *Asian Perspectives* 18:128–145.

Bronson, B. and I.C. Glover 1984. Archaeological radiocarbon dates from Indonesia. *Indonesia Circle* 12(34): 37–44. doi.org/10.1080/03062848408729585

Bronson, B. and N. Wisseman 1974. An archaeological survey in Sumatra, 1973. *Sumatra Research Bulletin* 4(1):87–94.

Brumm, A.A. and M.W.M. Moore 2012. Biface distributions and the Movius Line: A Southeast Asian perspective. *Australian Archaeology* 74:34–46. doi.org/10.1080/03122417.2012.11681933

Congrès des Préhistoriens d'Extrême Orient 1932. *Praehistorica Asiae Orientalis 1: Premier Congrès des Préhistoriens d'Extrême Orient Hanoi (1932)*. Imprimerie de l'Extrême-Orient, Hanoi.

Edwards McKinnon, E. 1991. The Hoabinhian in the Wampu/Lau Biang valley of northeastern Sumatra: An update. *Bulletin of the Indo-Pacific Prehistory Association* 10:132–142.

Forestier, H., D. Driwantoro, D. Guillaud and Budiman 2006. New data about Prehistoric chronology of South Sumatra. In H.T. Simanjuntak, M. Hisyam, B. Prasetyo and T.S. Nastiti (eds), *Archaeology, Indonesian perspective: R.P. Soejono's Festschrift*, pp. 177–192. Lipi, Jakarta.

Forestier, H., T. Simanjuntak, D. Guillaud, D. Driwantoro, K. Wiradnyana, D. Siregar, R. Due Awe and Budiman 2005. Le site de Tögi Ndrawa, île de Nias, Sumatra Nord: Les premières traces d'une occupation hoabinhienne en grotte en Indonésie. *Comptes Rendus Palevol* 4(8):727–733. doi.org/10.1016/j.crpv.2005.08.004

Keates, S.G. and G.J. Bartstra 2001. Observations on Cabengian and Pacitanian artefacts from island Southeast Asia. *Quartär* 51/52:9–32. doi.org/10.7485/QU51_01

Majid, Z. 2003. *Archaeology in Malaysia*. University Sains Malaysia Press, Penang.

Sémah, F., A.M. Sémah, T. Djubiantono and H.T. Simanjuntak 1992. Did they also make stone tools? *Journal of Human Evolution* 23(5):439–446. doi.org/10.1016/0047-2484(92)90092-n

Sémah, F., T. Simanjuntak, B. Dizon, C. Gaillard and A.M. Sémah 2014. Insular Southeast Asia in the Lower Paleolithic. In C. Smith (ed.), *Encyclopedia of Global Archaeology*, pp. 3904–3918. Springer, New York. doi.org/10.1007/978-1-4419-0465-2_1907

Shipman, P. 2001. *The Man who Found the Missing Link: Eugène Dubois and His Lifelong Quest to Prove Darwin Right*. Simon and Schuster, New York.

Simanjuntak, T. 2006. Indonesia–Southeast Asia: Climates, settlements, and cultures in Late Pleistocene. *Comptes Rendus Palevol* 5(1–2):371–379. doi.org/10.1016/j.crpv.2005.10.005

Simanjuntak, T. 2009. *Archaeological Discoveries in Indonesia, 1950–1980*. Pusat Penelitian dan Pengembangan Arkeologi Nasional, Jakarta.

Simanjuntak, T. and H. Forestier 2008. Handaxe in Indonesia. A question on the Movius Line. *Human Evolution* 23(1):97–107.

Simanjuntak, T. and H. Forestier 2009. Once upon a time in South Sumatra: The Acheulean stone tools of the Ogan River? In M. Saidin and K. Razak (eds), *Proceedings of the International Seminar on Sharing our Archaeological Heritage*, pp. 233–241. Warisan Johor, Penang, Malaysia.

Simanjuntak, T., F. Sémah and C. Gaillard 2010. The Palaeolithic in Indonesia: Nature and chronology. *Quaternary International* 223–224:418–421. doi.org/10.1016/j.quaint.2009.07.022

Soejono, R.P. 1961. Preliminary notes on new finds of Lower-Palaeolithic implements from Indonesia. *Asian Perspectives* 5(2):217–32.

Tjoa-Bonatz, M.L. 2019. *A View from the Highlands: Archaeology and Settlement History of West Sumatra, Indonesia*. ISEAS Publishing, Singapore. doi.org/10.1355/9789814843027 van Heekeren, H.R. 1972. *The Stone Age of Indonesia*. 2nd revised edition. Nijhoff, The Hague. doi.org/ 10.1163/9789004286917

Westaway, K.E., J. Louys, R. Due Awe, M.J. Morwood, G.J. Price, J.X. Zhao, M. Aubert, R. Joannes-Boyau, T. Smith, M.M. Skinner, T. Compton, R.M. Bailey, G.D. van den Bergh, J. de Vos, A.W.G. Pike, C. Stringer, E.W. Saptomo, Y. Rizal, J. Zaim, W.D. Santoso, A. Trihascaryo, L. Kinsley and B. Sulistyanto 2017. An early modern human presence in Sumatra 73,000–63,000 years ago. *Nature* 548:322–325. doi.org/10.1038/nature23452

Widianto, H. 2009. The dawn of humanity in Sumatra: Arrival and dispersal from the human remains perspective. In D. Bonatz, J.N. Miksic, J.D. Neidel and M.L. Tjoa-Bonatz (eds), *From Distant Tales: Archaeology and Ethnohistory in the Highlands of Sumatra*, pp. 28–42. Cambridge Scholars Publishing, Newcastle upon Tyne.

11

The rise of the Metal Age in Sumatra: Evidence from Harimau Cave in South Sumatra

Harry Octavianus Sofian and Truman Simanjuntak

Abstract

Sumatra is one of the largest islands in the Indonesian archipelago. Its location at the western edge of Indonesia makes it close to and, when sea-levels are low, frequently connected to the mainland of Southeast Asia. It is thus not surprising that human migrations and cultural diffusions from mainland Asia to Indonesia often passed through Sumatra first and then spread further into the archipelago. Such diffusions influenced the emergence of metal culture in Indonesia (in addition to other cultures such as pottery and agriculture). The archaeological finds at several sites in Sumatra reveal bronze artefacts in the Dong Son style of Vietnam. One of these sites is Harimau Cave in the southern part of Sumatra. Excavations in this cave recovered bronze and iron artefacts from the protohistoric occupation layer. The bronze artefacts are socketed axes and bracelets that date from between the fourth century BC and the first century AD. These are the oldest metal artefacts thus far found in Sumatra and Indonesia in general. Hence, the bronze artefacts from Harimau Cave may be an indication of the rise of the Metal Age on Sumatra, which coincides with the emergence of the international Maritime Silk Road.

Keywords: bronze artefacts, Harimau Cave, protohistory, South Sumatra

Abstrak

Sumatera adalah salah satu pulau terbesar di kepulauan Indonesia. Letaknya yang berada di ujung barat Indonesia membuatnya dekat dan sering berhubungan dengan daratan Asia Tenggara. Tidak mengherankan jika migrasi manusia atau difusi budaya dari daratan Asia ke Indonesia seringkali terlebih dahulu melewati wilayah ini dan kemudian menyebar lebih luas di Nusantara. Salah satu pengaruh tersebut adalah munculnya budaya logam di Indonesia. Temuan arkeologis di situs Sumatera mengungkapkan artefak logam perunggu bergaya Dong Son berasal dari Vietnam. Salah satu situs tersebut adalah Gua Harimau di bagian selatan Sumatera. Ekskavasi di gua ini menemukan artefak-artefak perunggu dan besi dari lapisan protosejarah. Artefak yang terbuat dari perunggu terdiri dari kapak corong yang berasal dari antara abad ke-4 SM dan abad ke-1 Masehi. Hal ini merepresentasikan artefak logam tertua yang ditemukan di Sumatera dan bahkan Indonesia. Atas dasar ini, artefak perunggu dari gua Harimau dapat menjadi indikasi kebangkitan zaman logam di pulau ini, yang bertepatan dengan munculnya Jalur Sutra Maritim internasional.

Kata kunci: artefak perunggu, Gua Harimau, protosejarah, Sumatra Selatan

Introduction

Sumatra is a large island at the western edge of the Indonesian archipelago (see Figure 11.1). Extending in a northwest–southeast direction, this island consists of three areas, with the middle area consisting of the Bukit Barisan mountains. With an altitude of 900–1,200 m above sea-level, these mountains form a kind of high ridge that occupies almost the entire length of the island. This mountainous region separates the west-coast part of the island from the eastern plains. The location of Sumatra, which is close to the mainland of Southeast Asia and separated from the Malay Peninsula only by the Malacca Strait, resulted in frequent connections with mainland Asia during glacial periods of the Pleistocene; during these, the island formed the western part of the exposed Sunda Shelf.

Physiographically, the island of Sumatra has an elongated shape with a northwest–southeast orientation and latitudes from 6° N to 6° S and longitudes from 95° E to 107° E. It has an area of about 435,000 km² with a length of 1,650 km measured from Banda Aceh in the north to Tanjungkarang in the south and maximum widths of about 100–200 km in the north and about 350 km in the south (Darman and Sidi 2000). Like the other islands in Indonesia in general, the formation of Sumatra is controlled by tectonics, including the subduction process between the Tethys Sea and the Sunda Shelf. In the Tethys Sea, the Indian Plate is moving northward towards the Sunda Shelf, resulting in subduction and the origination of a series of volcanoes. This geological process has produced rocks of Mesozoic, Cenozoic and Quaternary age and a series of active Quaternary volcanoes.

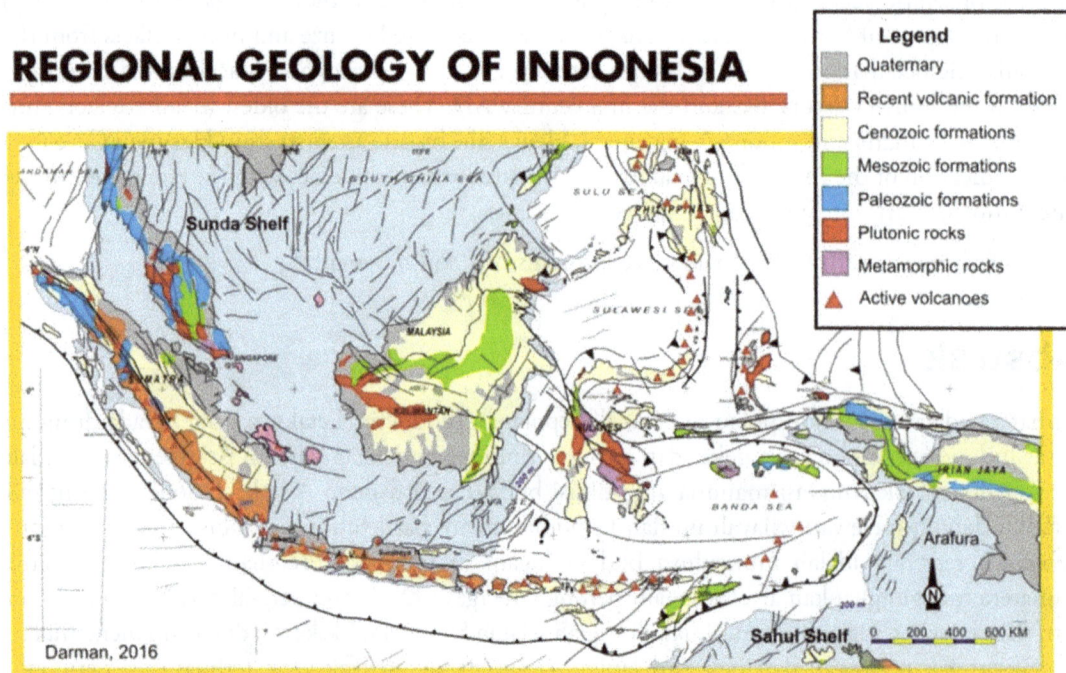

Figure 11.1: Map of Indonesian regional geology.

Source: Herman Darman (commons.wikimedia.org/wiki/File:Geology_indonesia_map.jpg), CC-BY 3.0 (creativecommons.org/licenses/by/3.0).

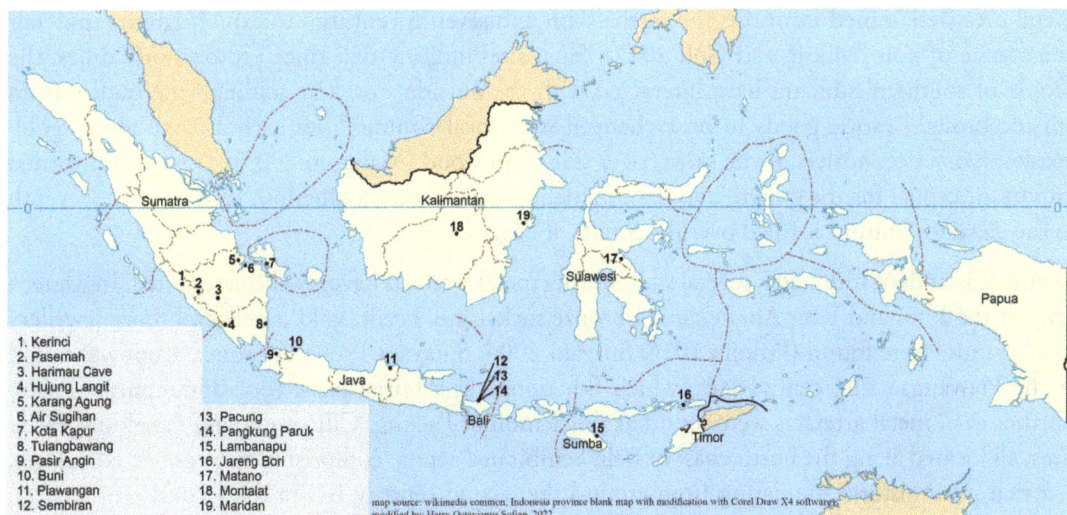

Figure 11.2: Location map of metal sites in Indonesia mentioned in the text.

Source: Wikimedia Commons (commons.wikimedia.org/wiki/File:Indonesia_provinces_blank_map.svg), CC-BY-SA 3.0 (creativecommons.org/licenses/by-sa/3.0), modified by Harry Octavianus Sofian.

Studies on archaeometallurgy in Sumatra, and Indonesia in general, are very limited, with most of the island unexplored (see Figure 11.2). This presents a challenge for the development of this field. When did metal culture develop in this region, where did it originate, what was the process of developing metallurgical technology, and how did the potential for metal ores from ancient mining sites support its development and distribution? These are fundamental questions that have not been answered satisfactorily. The current limitations in this field can be seen from an overview of research to date and its most important findings. This will now be presented.

We will first consider Sumatra, which is the focus of this chapter. Attention to its early metal culture began early, even though it was merely exploratory. Some of these early studies were conducted in the highlands of Jambi, Bengkulu, South Sumatra and Lampung, and reported discoveries in the form of metal artefacts associated with megalithic or jar burial sites (Indriastuti 2010; Parmentier 1918; Sukendar 2003; van Heekeren 1958). Later, other researchers reported the discovery of bronze drums, which are still sacred to the local peoples, in the Jambi highlands (Purwanti 2016; Sunliensyar 2017), and the image of a dagger similar to those of the Dong Son style, engraved in a stone inscription from AD 997 at Hujung Langit in West Lampung Regency, Lampung Province (Rusyanti 2013). There is also a depiction of metal tools with Dong Son drums, bracelets, earrings and accessories on the Pasemah megalithic statue in South Sumatra (Indriastuti 2000; Sukendar 2003). Also worth mentioning is a report about the exploitation of gold around the Batanghari River, Jambi, during Srivijaya periods (Do 2013; Edwards McKinnon 1985). In addition, the metal research discussed in the present chapter was conducted by Harry Sofian (2020 and ongoing) as part of his doctoral research at Nanterre University, Paris. That research focused on the exploitation and exchange of non-ferrous metals in Sumatra from the end of prehistoric times to the first millennium.

Other research has been conducted in the swampy regions of southern Sumatra and the regions along the east coast of southern Sumatra. In this area, there are protohistoric sites, such as Air Sugihan, Karang Agung and Cengal. Dating from between the second century AD and the emergence of the Srivijaya kingdom in the mid-seventh century, these sites are rich in artefacts made of gold, bronze and tin. They include coins, coin moulds, beads and intaglio (Budisantosa 2007; Koestoro et al. 1994; Pelaksana 2010; Soeroso et al. 1994). Close to Sumatra, on Bangka Island, tin remains and a star-shaped tin ingot were found at the Kota Kapur site (Budisantosa 2007; Pelaksana 2010).

Metal ores were mined from this site in the sixth and seventh centuries to exploit laterite minerals as a source of iron (Miksic and Goh 2017). Such sites indicate that since protohistoric times, the people of southern Sumatra have interacted with the outside world by trading. The traders from outside brought exotic goods to be exchanged with local commodities such as pine resins, gold, textiles, ivory, deer antlers, turtle skins, tiger skins and wood (Manguin 2009). This trade provided important capital for the growth and development of Srivijaya as a kingdom, and from the seventh to the eleventh century it ruled over the Straits of Malacca.

On other islands of Indonesia, several sites bearing metal artefacts have also been reported. In western Java, at the Buni and Pasir Angin sites, a bronze socket axe, beads, gold jewellery, bronze jewellery and ceramics were found (Prijono 2016; Suryani 2004; Sutayasa 1969). A bronze drum was found at the Plawangan site, central Java, which functioned as a burial place (Boedhisampurno 1990). Further east, metal artefacts were found at the Sembiran-Pacung, Gilimanuk and Pangkung Paruk sites, all located along the north coast of Bali. Sembiran-Pacung, comprising two connected villages, is a rich protohistoric site dating from around the second century BC to the second century AD. Excavations conducted at this site unearthed bronze artefacts such as bracelets, socketed axes, and other metal artefacts. It is interesting to note that the presence of local bronze casting at this site indicates the possibility of the introduction of metallurgical technology to the local people. From the microstructural analysis of bronze artefacts, it has been recognised that the bronze source material was not from Bali but from mainland Southeast Asia (Calo et al. 2015; Pryce et al. 2018). Another metal artefact found at this site is a golden bead. The presence of these metal artefacts, together with Indian rouletted pottery and other imported goods, show that Sembiran-Pacung was a port connecting Bali with India and mainland Southeast Asia from the late first millennium BC.

Another interesting find is from the Lambanapu site in eastern Sumba, which has been occupied since the Neolithic. In the Palaeometallic occupation layer of this site, a large metal bowl was found, which functioned as a container for the bones of a secondary burial (Sofian 2020). Also, in Kalimantan, in the Montalat River region along the Upper Barito River, metal smelting sites were recently found in at least 19 locations. Based on the results of radiocarbon analyses, these smelting activities were dated to the fourteenth to nineteenth centuries AD (Hartatik et al. 2021). As well as at Kalimantan, iron smelting sites were found in Matano, central Sulawesi, dating to the eighth century AD (Adhityatama et al. 2021). This latter region is famous for iron ore containing nickel, which is a source material for making kris daggers. Via trade contacts with the Majapahit kingdom in eastern Java, Matano people exported iron from Sulawesi to Java (Do 2013). Lastly, at the Jareng Bori site in Pantar Island, eastern Indonesia, an iron fragment was recently discovered (Hawkins et al. 2020).

The research described above shows the great potential of Indonesia for the study of metal culture, which is one of the global milestones of civilisation. The finding of metal artefacts at several sites indicates the emergence of metal culture in the protohistoric period, a development that has continued into historical times. It is immediately apparent that the development of metal culture in this area began through exchange, with the importation of metal objects, and then developed further through the transfer of metallurgical technology to the local people.

Exactly when this metallurgic culture emerged in Indonesia is a question that has often been raised. Fortunately, the recovery of metal objects in Harimau Cave, which will now be described, provides important new data to answer this question. Ongoing studies using radiometric dating are providing a preliminary picture of the emergence of the oldest metal culture in Indonesia.

Harimau Cave and its metal artefacts

Harimau Cave (Figure 11.3) is one of dozens of prehistoric caves in the Padang Bindu karst environment in South Sumatra. A series of excavations conducted in this cave from 2009 to 2015 by a team from Indonesia's National Research Center for Archaeology led by the senior author (TS), showed that the cave has been inhabited by humans since at least 22 ka. These excavations reached a depth of more than 5 m. From the excavation, cultural layers were identified, with the Palaeolithic represented in the bottom layer, the pre-Neolithic and Neolithic in the middle layers and the Palaeometallic in the top layer. Lithic artefacts, generally in the form of flake tools, and faunal remains dominated the findings in the Palaeolithic and Pre-Neolithic layers. In the Neolithic and Palaeometallic layers, in addition to stone tools and faunal remains, pottery, bone tools, burnt remains and freshwater molluscs were found. Among the lithic artefacts, as well as flakes, there are hammers and anvils made of andesite, chert, chalcedony and jasper. The Palaeometallic layer is indicated by the presence of metal artefacts (Simanjuntak et al. 2013).

Figure 11.3: The appearance of Harimau Cave when it was discovered in 2008.
Source: Tim Penelitian Padang Bindu (2009), reproduced by permission of Truman Simanjuntak.

The most prominent findings at Harimau Cave were human burials, which, including all found up to the final year of excavation in 2015, represent 81 individuals in anatomical association. The oldest burial came from the Pre-Neolithic layer dated back to 5,712–5,591 cal. BP (4,910 ± 30 BP [Beta 450669]; Matsumura et al. 2018). This individual was buried in a flexed position; the physical character shows an Australomelanesoid affinity. Human burials continued into the Neolithic and Palaeometallic cultural layers, with the youngest burial dated to 1,864–1,719 cal. BP (1,852 ± 20 BP [BTN12002]; Matsumura et al. 2018). In these layers, most of the skeletons bear Mongoloid characters. These findings show that Harimau Cave was probably inhabited by an Australomelanesian group before being used by a Mongoloid population between c. 4,000 BP to early years AD (Matsumura et al. 2018). Rock art was another important discovery in Harimau Cave. This was the first finding of rock art in the karstic region of Sumatra. The images have been painted on the walls and ceiling of the cave and represent figurative and non-figurative forms. Some of the images bear motifs of nets, concentric circles, parallel curves, combs, parallel lines and points (Simanjuntak 2016).

Another important finding was metal objects above the Neolithic layer. The existence of these objects is a marker that shows a cultural change among the inhabitants of the cave from the Neolithic to the Palaeometallic, a culture which, in the periodisation of prehistoric Indonesia, is included in the protohistoric era (Simanjuntak 2020). A total of 12 metal artefacts were found in the top layer of the stratigraphic unit (see Figures 11.4 and 11.5): eight of them were made of bronze and four of iron. These objects are fragmentary and highly corroded. Our study focused on the bronze artefacts, which are socketed axes (three pieces), bracelets (three pieces) and two unidentified pieces. Bronze is a metal alloy of the elements copper (Cu), tin (Sn), lead (Pb), and arsenic (As). When copper is combined with other metals, the melting range of the resulting alloy is narrower than that of copper. Producing metal objects is not an easy task, because multiple complicated production steps are needed, as well as knowledge about metals, furnaces and fire control (Haryono 2001; Scott 1991).

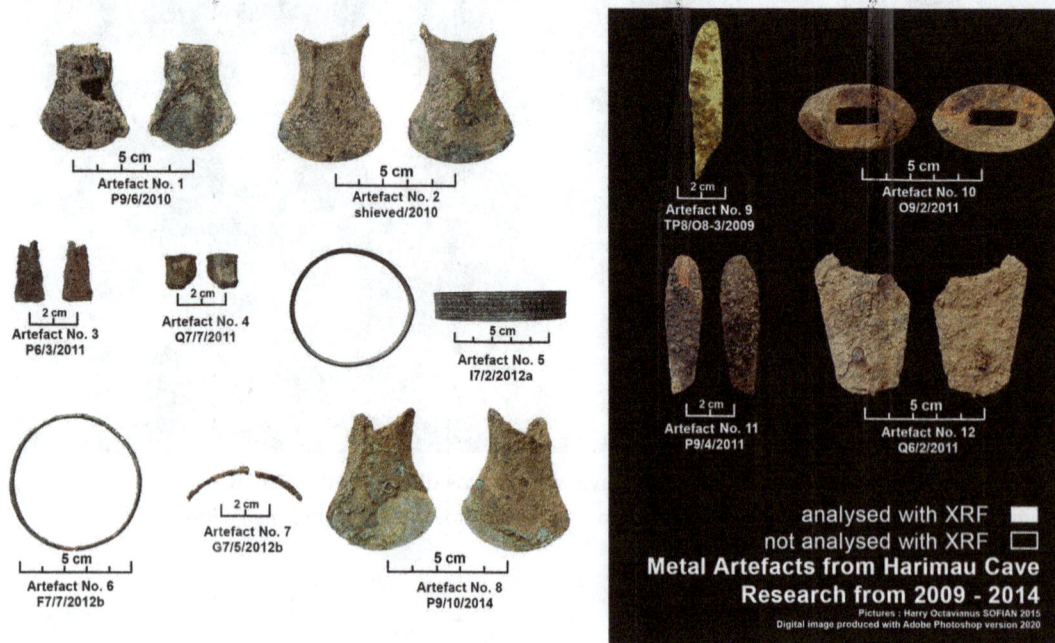

Figure 11.4: Metal artefacts from Harimau Cave.

Note: Artefact Nos 1–8, on the left, have been examined with X-ray fluorescence.

Source: Photographs by Harry Octavianus Sofian. Artefacts: Azis et al. (2011), Oktaviana et al. (2012), Oktaviana et al. (2014), Tim Penelitian Padang Bindu (2009) and Simanjuntak et al. (2013).

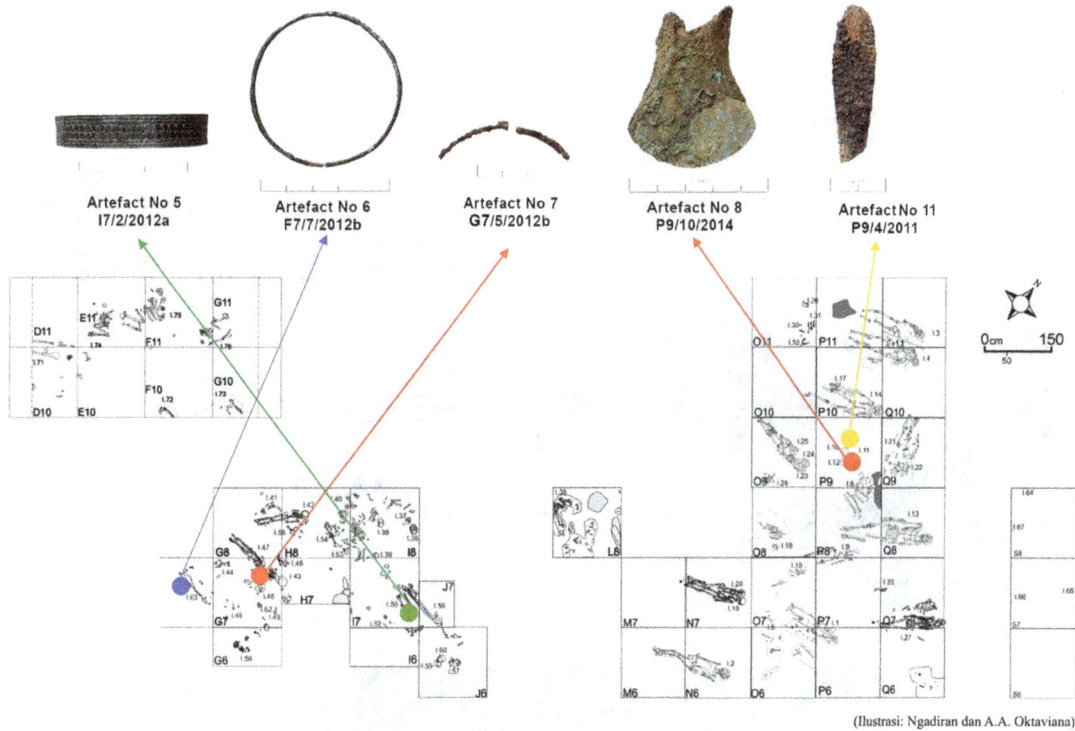

Figure 11.5: Burials associated with metal artefacts at Harimau Cave.

Source: Sofian (2015), reproduced with permission from the author.

The socketed axes were found in association with human burials (Individuals I.10, I.11 and I.12). The context of the discovery implies that the socketed axes are a rare object and were probably used not as ordinary tools but as ceremonial tools and burial gifts. The average size of the socketed axes is 5 cm. There are two types. In type 'Soejono I', at the baseline, the axe handle is straight, whereas in type 'Soejono II', the base is wide and the tip is split like the tail of a swallow; the latter type functioned as a burial gift (Prijono 2016; Soejono 1975). From their morpho-stylistic appearance, the socketed bronze axes from Harimau Cave are of a different type than the socketed bronze axes from Gilimanuk (Indonesia), Ban Chiang (Thailand) and Prohear (Cambodia), which have a longer handle with a narrower base. The Soejono II type from Harimau Cave is of the same type as the socketed bronze axes from Samon valley (Myanmar).

There are three bracelets: one with motifs (Figure 11.6) and two without. The bracelet with motifs has a fishbone motif (Simanjuntak et al. 2013) and a hook motif (Buckley 2012). Like the socketed axes, the bronze bracelets are associated with human burials. The one with motifs is associated with the burial of Individual I.50, while the two without motifs are associated with the burials of Individuals I.43 and I.63. From a morpho-stylistic point of view, the fishbone and hook motifs are common in Southeast Asia and found on Dong Son bronze drums, where they are usually located on the handle and body of the drum. In our cave, the same ornate motifs were also found, along with other motifs, on the bodies of pottery and in the rock paintings on the cave ceiling (see Figure 11.6). The similarity of motifs indicates that an imitation of the bronze bracelet motif decoration was applied to pottery decorations and rock paintings. If this is justified, then the bronze bracelet that comes from outside would have been in Harimau Cave first, and then the decorations were imitated when making the pottery and paintings.

Artefact No 5
I7/2/2012a

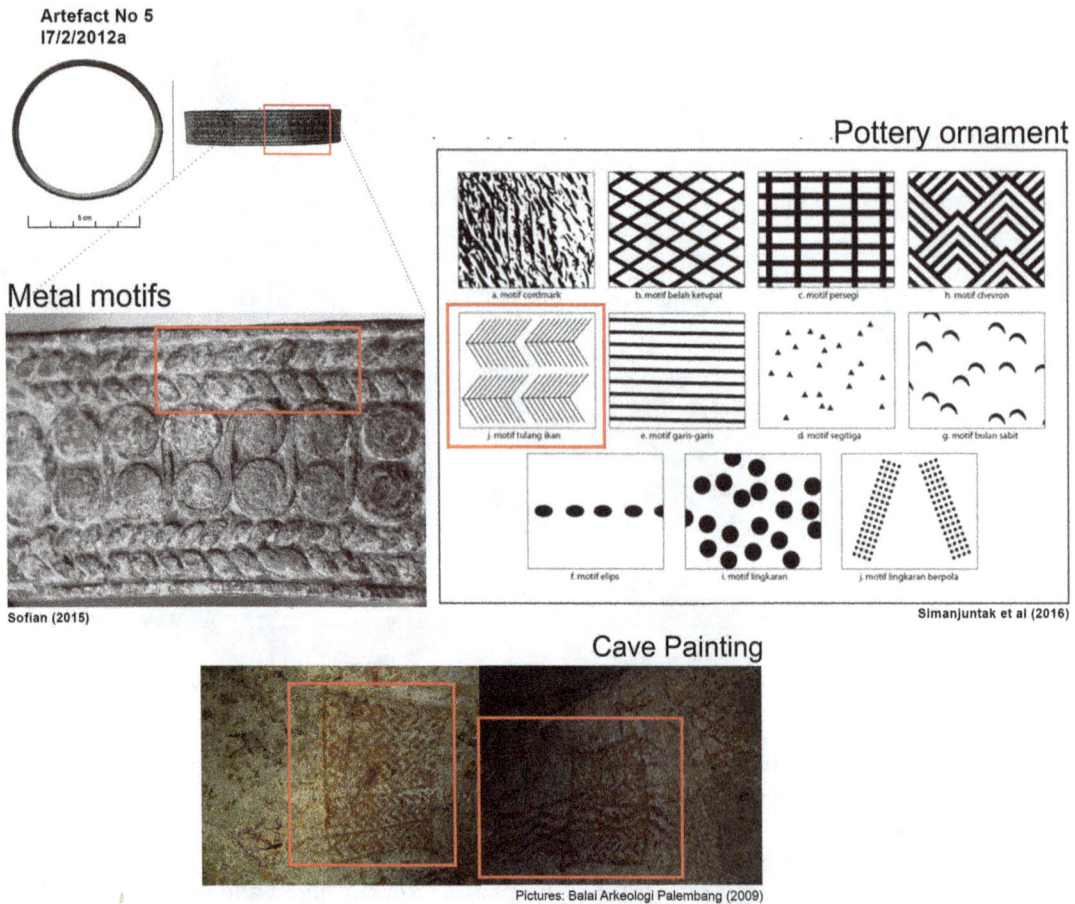

Metal motifs

Pottery ornament

Sofian (2015)

Simanjuntak et al (2016)

Cave Painting

Pictures: Balai Arkeologi Palembang (2009)

Figure 11.6: Similar motifs found at Harimau Cave on a bronze bracelet, on pottery and in cave paintings.

Source: Sofian (2015:32) and Simanjuntak et al. (2016:150, figure 5.13), reproduced with permission from the authors.

To determine the age of the bronze artefacts, we dated human bones that were in direct contact with each artefact. At least 12 bone samples were taken from each relevant burial (those of Individuals I.2, I.3, I.4, I.8, I.13, I.27, I.40, I.44, I.43, I.54, I.56 and I.58) and sent to the laboratory of *Pusat Aplikasi Teknologi Isotop dan Radiasi, Badan Tenaga Atom Nasional,* Indonesia. Surprisingly, our results show that dates spanned the period between the eighth century BC to the first century AD. Given the regional context of the emergence of metal, it seems that the oldest of these dates is too old: 2,760–2,518 cal. BP (2,575 ± 30 BP [BTN12006]; Matsumura et al. 2018). For the time being, we have assumed that the oldest that is reliable is from the fourth century BC; this is the second-oldest, 2,352–2,206 cal. BP (2,290 ± 20 BP [BTN12022]; Matsumura et al. 2018), from burial I.43, where a bronze bracelet without motifs was in contact with the left hand of the individual. The youngest date, 1,879–1,737 cal. BP (1,880 ± 20 BP [BTN12003]; Matsumura et al. 2018), from burial I.8, seems in line with the generally accepted view of the early development of metal culture in Indonesia.

The methodology we use to study metal artefacts from Harimau Cave—metallography—includes the microscopical examination of examine ancient metal artefacts to obtain information about their composition, microstructural components, production techniques and corrosion. Further, to determine the chemical composition of the objects, we use X-ray fluorescence (XRF), a non-destructive analytical technique. We also use morpho-stylistic typology to understand the form and the style of the object (Sofian 2015).

From the results of the metallographic analysis, the metal artefacts from Harimau Cave can be divided into two overall groups: those produced by metal casting and those produced by metalworking. Casting is the operation of pouring metal into a mould and allowing it to cool down and solidify; moulds can be made from stone, ceramics, clay or similar materials. Working is hammering the metal at low temperatures to make it harder and stronger. During the metalworking process, twin boundaries are annealed due to the release of work-hardened stresses in the metal; a twin boundary is a type of planar surface defect in the orientation of the microstructure of metals, whereby one side mirrors the orientation of the other (Dungworth et al. 2015). The metalworking technique was common in the Bronze and Iron Ages.

The majority of the Harimau Cave metal artefacts had been produced by casting. The results for one artefact (a socketed bronze axe, Artefact No. 2) indicated that the two techniques of metal production (casting and working) had been combined, while all the other artefacts' results indicated that only casting had been used.

The chemical composition of the artefacts, as shown by the XRF analysis, is summarised in Table 11.1. (Detailed spectra are provided in the appendix.) From our analysis, copper (Cu) appears to be the main metal and was alloyed with other metals, primarily tin (Sn) and lead (Pb). The single sample containing a significant amount of Pb is the bracelet with motifs, showing that the Pb was deliberately added along with Sn to make the alloy more liquid so it would be easier to apply the motifs during the solidification process.

Table 11.1: Chemical composition of metal artefacts from Harimau Cave.

Artefact no. and description	Code	Copper (Cu)	Tin (Sn)	Lead (Pb)
1. Socketed bronze axe	P9/6/2010	X	X	
2. Socketed bronze axe	shieved/2010	X	X	
3. Bronze fragment	P6/3/3011	X	X	
4. Bronze fragment	Q7/7/2011	X	X	
5. Bracelets with motifs	I7/2/2012a	X	X	X
6. Bracelets without motifs	F7.7/2012b	X	X	
7. Fragment bracelets without motifs	G7/5/2012b	X	X	
8. Socketed bronze axe	P9/10/2014	X	X	

Note: Artefact numbers refer to Figure 11.4.
Source: Authors' data.

Discussion

Mainland Southeast Asia is an interesting area for metallurgical studies. The development of metal culture in this area is thought to be based on exchange contacts with China that resulted in the transfer of bronze technology, encouraging the development of metallurgy in Southeast Asia (Higham et al. 2011). This is why this area is considered one of the centres of the ancient development of metal technology. Bronze discoveries at the Ban Chiang site in northeastern Thailand date from the middle of the second millennium BC, while iron discoveries from that site date from c. 500 BC (Shaw and Jameson 1999). Similarly, according to O'Reilly (2000), Bronze Iron Age technology developed in

Thailand over the period c. 1700–500 BC and Iron Age technology c. 500 BC. These dates are still under debate (Higham 2014; White and Hamilton 2014) because they are considered too old with respect to similar findings in the region.

Another centre of metal development was the area around the Red River Valley, Tang Hoa Province, in northern Vietnam. The culture that has been found here is known as the Dong Son culture based on the location where it was first discovered. The Red River Valley area developed an industry that produced bronze objects between c. 500 BC and c. AD 100 (Kipfer 2007). Excavations conducted by E. Payot in 1924 at this site yielded bronze vessels, spearheads, axes and bracelets; these artefacts have similarities with metal objects from the Han Dynasty period in China (Higham 1996; Pryce et al. 2011). This Dong Son culture spread to various large areas in Southeast Asia, including Indonesia. Kettledrums, vessels, axes, jewellery and other bronze objects found on various islands in the archipelago are thought to be Dong Son cultural objects traded through exchange with local commodities such as handicrafts, camphor, spices and sandalwood, as mentioned above.

In this context, the presence of bronze artefacts in Harimau Cave is thought to be the result of an exchange between the cave's inhabitants and traders who came from outside. It is interesting that the oldest dated bronze objects date back to around the fourth century BC, indicating that the inhabitants of Harimau Cave, and the Sumatran interior in general, were involved in exchanges with the outside world not long after the development of the Dong Son culture in Vietnam. These exchanges would have been possible due to two factors. First, the lifestyle of the people in the interior of Sumatra at this time was sufficiently complex to allow interaction with the outside world. Second, the geographical position of Sumatra, directly opposite mainland Southeast Asia, would have made it the first island in Indonesia to be reached during travel to Indonesia.

Another factor contributing to the early introduction of metals into Sumatra's interior is the presence of rivers that originate in the Bukit Barisan mountains and empty into the sea at the east coast (see Figure 11.7). These rivers were used by outside traders to enter the interior by boat. The Musi River and its tributary, the Ogan River, are thought to be the means of transportation that connected Harimau Cave and other caves around the Padang Bindu karst mountains to the coast. These are broad, calm rivers that can support shipping well into their upstream areas, even as far as the Pasemah megalithic complex, as shown by the images of Dong Son objects carved on megalithic remains there.

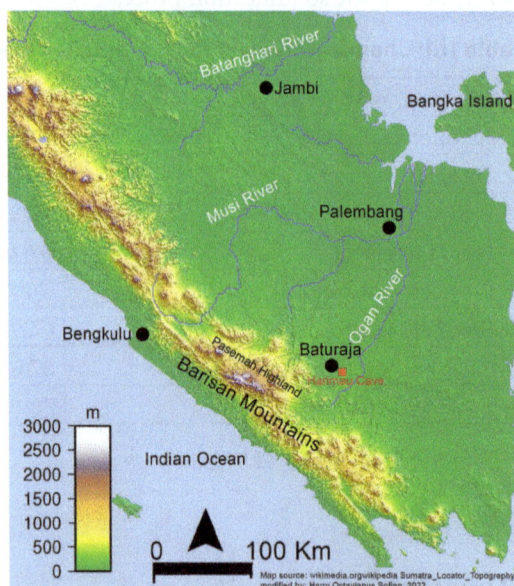

Figure 11.7: Map showing the Musi River, running from the hinterland to the coast, and its tributaries.

Source: Sadalmelik (id.m.wikipedia.org/wiki/Berkas: Sumatra_Locator_Topography.png), CC-BY-SA 3.0 (creativecommons.org/licenses/by-sa/3.0), via Wikimedia Commons, modified by Harry Octavianus Sofian.

As they were a new product made from newly introduced materials, bronze objects are expected to have had a special meaning in rural communities. It is evident that not all inhabitants of the interior regions possessed them, but that they were limited to certain circles. Therefore, these objects most probably did not function as tools for daily use but had a special meaning in community life. The bronze objects would at least have represented a kind of status symbol or served as ceremonial tools. Their discovery in the context of graves also shows their function as burial gifts.

The oldest and youngest dates inferred for the bronze objects show that the inhabitants of Harimau Cave were interacting with the outside world for about five centuries (from around the fourth century BC to the first century AD). This means that the habitation of Harimau Cave and its metal culture coincided with the establishment of the so-called spice trade route, when the spice wealth of the archipelago became the object of attention and global trade. Outside traders came to the archipelago bringing exotic goods to be exchanged for local commodities such as cloves, nutmeg, sandalwood, agarwood, camphor and incense. The 'spice route' trade increased during historical times and contributed to the background of the colonialism that began in the archipelago in the sixteenth century AD.

The presence of bronze and other metal objects in Harimau Cave marked the beginning of a new period in the history of Sumatran civilisation. In the periodisation of the prehistory of Indonesia, this period is referred to as the protohistoric era. In addition to the presence of a metal culture, this era is characterised by the presence of a megalithic culture—a large-stone culture that was established as a means of glorifying ancestral spirits in order to bring prosperity, fertility and other benefits to the living. The presence and growth of these two new cultures increasingly contributed to the complexity of life in the archipelago, until they eventually became social capital that supported the growth of Srivijaya into a large maritime empire, which controlled the waters of the Malacca Strait and the surrounding area in the seventh to eleventh centuries AD.

Conclusion

The discovery of metal objects at Harimau Cave provides a new view of the early development of metal culture in Sumatra and Indonesia in general. Probably dating from the fourth century BC, these objects are by far the oldest metal artefacts found in Indonesia, and are only slightly younger than the early development of the Dong Son culture in Southeast Asia in the fifth century BC. The geographical position of Sumatra, which is close to mainland Southeast Asia, may explain the presence of an early metal culture on this island. An interesting note regarding the presence of this early metal culture is that it was not limited to coastal areas but was also present in the interior of Sumatra. Discoveries in Harimau Cave, the Pasemah megalithic complex and other inland sites demonstrate this. In the development of this culture, the existence of rivers connecting the interior with the coast was an important factor because it allowed metal objects and other cultural items and technologies to be quickly introduced into the interior. Because traders could navigate the rivers from the coast to well upstream, the inland areas received outside influences very soon after their carriers arrived at the coast.

The discoveries at Harimau Cave represent the beginning of the growth and development of metal culture in Sumatra and Indonesia in general. The presence of these objects shows the emergence of a metal culture in this region, initially when outside influences introduced metal objects to the residents, both at the coast and in the interior. Subsequently, this culture spread to other islands in the archipelago, and the inhabitants of the archipelago began to produce their own objects through the transfer of technology. Indonesia's rich metal ore deposits made this possible. Further research is needed to help us better understand the development of metal culture in Indonesia, the background of its relationship with mainland Southeast Asia, and the environmental and other factors that supported its sustained development in Indonesia.

Acknowledgements

Harry Octavianus Sofian expresses gratitude and the highest appreciation to Professor François Sémah for the opportunity to undertake masters studies in Quaternary and Prehistory at the National Museum d'Histoire Naturelle Paris. HS also thanks Dr Thomas Oliver Pryce, Center d'Etude Atomique (CEA) UMR 7065 IRAMAT, who supervised HOS for a masters studies in archaeometallurgy, and the French Embassy in Jakarta for providing scholarships to study archaeometallurgy in France with *Bourse du Gouvernement Français*.

References

Adhityatama, S., R R Triwurjani, D. Yurnaldi, R. Janssen, M.D.K. Dhony, Suryatman, A. Abbas, A. Lukman and D. Bulbeck 2021. Pulau Ampat site: A submerged 8th century iron production village in Matano Lake, South Sulawesi, Indonesia. *Archaeological Research in Asia* 29:100335. doi.org/10.1016/j.ara.2021.100335

Azis, F., A. Budiman, A. Octaviana, S.E. Prasetyo, V.P. Sari, Vita and Dariusman 2011. *Penelitian Hunian Prasejarah Di Gua Harimau, OKU, Sumatera Selatan*. Unpublished report. Pusat Penelitian Arkeologi Nasional, Jakarta.

Boedhisampurno, S. 1990. *Temuan Sisa Manusia Dari Situs Kubur Paleometalik Plawangan, Rembang, Jawa Tengah*. Analisis Hasil Penelitian Arkeologi I. Pusat Penelitian Arkeologi Nasional, Jakarta.

Buckley, C.D. 2012. Investigating cultural evolution using phylogenetic analysis: The origins and descent of the Southeast Asian tradition of Warp Ikat weaving. *PLoS ONE* 7(12):e52064. doi.org/10.1371/journal.pone.0052064

Budisantosa and T. Marhaeni 2007. *Penelitian Situs Kota Kapur, Kabupaten Bangka Provinsi Sumatera Selatan*. Unpublished report. Balai Arkeologi Palembang, Palembang.

Calo, A., B. Prasetyo, P. Bellwood, J.W. Lankton, B. Gratuze, T.O. Pryce, A. Reinecke, V. Leusch, H. Schenk, R. Wood, R.A. Bawono, I.D.K. Gede, N.L.K.C. Yuliati, J. Fenner, C. Reepmeyer, C. Castillo and A.K. Carter 2015. Sembiran and Pacung on the north coast of Bali: A strategic crossroads for early Trans-Asiatic exchange. *Antiquity* 89:378–96. doi.org/10.15184/aqy.2014.45

Darman, H. and F. Hasan Sidi 2000. *An Outline of the Geology of Indonesia*. The Indonesian Association of Geologists (Ikatan Ahli Geologi Indonesia), Jakarta.

Do, M. 2013. Iron-Nickel Alloy Smelting Production in Luwu, South Sulawesi during the Pre-Islamic Period. Unpublished masters thesis. University College London, London.

Dungworth, D., J. Bayley, S. Paynter, P. Crew, V. Fell, B. Gilmour, G. McDonnell, C. Mortimer, P. Northover, D. Starley and T. Young 2015. *Archaeometallurgy*. Revised edition. Centre for Archaeology Guidelines. Historic England, London.

Edwards McKinnon, E. 1985. Early politics in southern Sumatra: Some preliminary observations based on archaeological evidence. *Indonesia* 40:1–36. doi.org/10.2307/3350873

Hartatik, H.O. Sofian, Sunarningsih, N.N. Susanto and R.B. Sulistiyo 2021. The sustainability of the iron industry based on local wisdom in the Barito watershed. *IOP Conference Series: Materials Science and Engineering* 980:012046. doi.org/10.1088/1757-899X/980/1/012046

Haryono, T. 2001. *Logam Dan Peradaban Manusia.* Philosophy Press, Yogyakarta.

Hawkins, S., F.S. Arumdhati, M. Litster, T.S. Lim, G. Basile, M. Leclerc, C. Reepmeyer, T.R. Maloney, C. Boulanger, J. Louys, Mahirta, G. Clark, G. Keling, R.C. Willan, P. Yuwono and S. O'Connor 2020. Metal-Age maritime culture at Jareng Bori rockshelter, Pantar Island, eastern Indonesia. *Records of the Australian Museum* 72(5):237–262. doi.org/10.3853/j.2201-4349.72.2020.1726

Higham, C.F.W. 1996. A review of archaeology in mainland Southeast Asia. *Journal of Archaeological Research* 4(1):3–49. doi.org/10.1007/BF02228837

Higham, C. 2014. *Early Mainland Southeast Asia: From First Humans to Angkor.* River Books, Bangkok.

Higham, C., T. Higham, R. Ciarla, K. Douka, A. Kijngam and F. Rispoli 2011. The origins of the Bronze Age of Southeast Asia. *Journal of World Prehistory* 24(4):227–74. doi.org/10.1007/s10963-011-9054-6

Indriastuti, K. 2000. Perekonomian masa prasejarah di dataran tinggi pasemah. *Jurnal Arkeologi Siddhayatra* 5:1–12. Balai Arkeologi Palembang, Palembang, Indonesia.

Indriastuti, K. 2010. *Laporan Penelitian Fajar Bulan.* Unpublished report. Balai Arkeologi Palembang, Palembang, Indonesia.

Kipfer, B.A. 2007. *Dictionary of Artifacts.* Blackwell Publishing, Malden, MA. doi.org/10.1002/978047069 0901

Koestoro, L.P., Soeroso and P.-Y. Manguin 1994. An ancient site reascertained: The 1994 campaigns at Kota Kapur (Nangka South Sumatra). In P.-Y. Manguin (ed.), *Proceedings of the 5th International Conference of The European Association of Southeast Asian Archaeologists 24–28 October 1994*, pp. 61–81. Centre for Southeast Asian Studies, University of Hull, England.

Manguin, P.-Y. 2009. Southeast Sumatra in Protohistoric and Srivijaya times: Upstream-downstream relations and the settlement of the Peneplain. In D. Bonatz, J.N. Miksic, J.D. Neidel and M.L. Tjoa-Bonatz (eds), *From Distant Tales: Archaeology and Ethnohistory in the Highlands of Sumatra*, pp. 43–74. Cambridge Scholars Publishing, Newcastle upon Tyne.

Matsumura, H., K.-I. Shinoda, T. Simanjuntak, A.A. Oktaviana, S. Noerwidi, H.O. Sofian, D. Prastiningtyas, L.C. Nguyen, T. Kakuda, H. Kanzawa-Kiriyama, N. Adachi, H.-C. Hung, X. Fan, X. Wu, A. Willis and M.F. Oxenham 2018. Cranio-morphometric and aDNA corroboration of the Austronesian dispersal model in Ancient Island Southeast Asia: Support from Gua Harimau, Indonesia. *PLoS ONE* 13(6):e0198689. doi.org/10.1371/journal.pone.0198689

Miksic, J.N. and G.Y. Goh 2017. *Ancient Southeast Asia.* Routledge, New York. doi.org/10.4324/97813156 41119

O'Reilly, D.J.W. 2000. From the Bronze Age to the Iron Age in Thailand: Applying the heterarchical approach. *Asian Perspectives* 39(1–2):1–19.

Oktaviana, A.A., M.R. Fauzi, D. Prastiningtyas, M. Ansyori, S. Noerwidi, T. Marhaeni and Ngadiran 2014. Peradaban di Lingkungan Karst Kabupaten OKU, Sumatera Selatan. Unpublished report. Pusat Arkeologi Nasional, Jakarta.

Oktaviana, A.A., F.S. Intan, R. Handini, Vita, S.E. Prasetyo, M. Anshori, W. Saptomo and T. Simanjuntak 2012. Penelitian Hunian prasejarah di Gua Harimau, Padang Bindu OKU, Sumatera Selatan. Unpublished report. Pusat Penelitian dan Pengembangan Arkeologi Nasional, Jakarta.

Parmentier, H. 1918. Anciens tambours de bronze. *Bulletin de l'École française d'Extrême-Orient* 18:1–30. doi.org/10.3406/befeo.1918.5884

Pelaksana, T. 2010. *Studi Mintakat Dan Kelayakan Kawasan Situs Kota Kapur*. Unpublished report. Dinas Kebudayaan dan Pariwisata Provinsi Kepulauan Bangka-Belitung, Pangkal Pinang, Bangka, Indonesia.

Prijono, S. 2016. Artefak Perunggu Prasejarah Situs Pasir Angin Bogor: Hubungannya Dengan Aspek Sumber Bahan. *Berkala Arkeologi* 36(1):71–82. doi.org/10.30883/jba.v36i1.225

Pryce, T.O., A. Calo, B. Prasetyo, P. Bellwood and S. O'Connor 2018. Copper-base metallurgy in metal-age Bali: Evidence from Gilimanuk, Manikliyu, Pacung, Pangkung Paruk and Sembiran. *Archaeometry* 60(6):1271–1289. doi.org/10.1111/arcm.12384

Pryce, T.O., M. Pollard, M. Martinón-Torres, V.C. Pigott and E. Pernicka 2011. Southeast Asia's first isotopically defined prehistoric copper production system : When did extractive metallurgy begin in the Khao Wong Prachan Valley of central Thailand ? *Archaeometry* 53(1):146–163. doi.org/10.1111/J.1475-4754.2010.00527.X

Purwanti, R. 2016. Nekara Perunggu Di Kerinci. In *Kerincimu Kerinciku: Dataran Tinggi Jambi Dalam Perspektif Arkeologi*, pp. 87–106. Penerbit Ombak, Palembang, Indonesia.

Rusyanti, R. 2013. Tembikar-tembikar di situs Hujung Langit Lampung Barat. The potteries of Hujung Langit sites, West Lampung. *Purbawidya: Jurnal Penelitian Dan Pengembangan Arkeologi* 2(2):206–217. doi.org/10.24164/pw.v2i2.49

Scott, D.A. 1991. *Metallography and Microstructure of Ancient and Historic Metals*. The Getty Conservation Institute/Archaetype Books, Singapore.

Shaw, I. and R. Jameson 1999. *A Dictionary of Archaeology*. Penguin, London. doi.org/10.1002/97804707 53446

Simanjuntak, T. 2020. *Manusia-Manusia Dan Peradaban Indonesia*. UGM Press, Yogyakarta.

Simanjuntak, T., A.A. Oktaviana and D. Prastiningtyas 2013. Peradaban Di Lingkungan Karst, Kabupaten OKU, OKU Timur, dan OKU Selatan. Unpublished report. Pusat Penelitian dan Pengembangan Arkeologi Nasional, Jakarta.

Simanjuntak, T. (ed.). 2016. *Harimau Cave and the Long Journey of OKU Civilization*. Gadjah Mada University Press, Yogyakarta.

Soejono, R.P. 1975. Sejarah Nasional Indonesia I. In R.P. Soejono (ed.), *Jaman Prasejarah di Indonesia*, pp. 1–310. Balai Pustaka, Jakarta.

Soeroso, L., P. Koestoro and P.-Y. Manguin 1994. *Pemetaan geomorfologi situs Kota Kapur, Bangka*. Unpublished report. Balai Arkeologi Palembang, Palembang, Indonesia.

Sofian, H.O. 2015. Metal Artifacts Analysis From Gua Harimau, South Sumatera, Indonesia. Unpublished masters thesis. Muséum national d'histoire naturelle, Paris.

Sofian, H.O. 2020. Ketika Logam Memasuki Lambanapu. In T. Simanjuntak (ed.), *Lambanapu Perjalanan Perkampungan Tua Leluhur Austronesia*, pp. 101–112. Yayasan Pustaka Obor Indonesia, Jakarta.

Sukendar, H. 2003. *Megalitik Bumi Pasemah Peranan Serta Fungsinya*. Deputi Bidang Pelestarian dan Pengembangan Budaya, Jakarta.

Sunliensyar, H.H. 2017. Prospek Penelitian Artefak Perunggu Temuan Kerinci Melalui Analisis Metalurgi. *Jurnal Arkeologi Siddhayatra* 22(2):89.

Suryani, D. 2004. *Artefak Perunggu Situs Pasir Angin; Analisis Komposisi Unsur.* Unpublished BA (Hons) Thesis. Universitas Indonesia, Jakarta.

Sutayasa, I.M. 1969. Ragam hias prasejarah dari kompleks Buni. *Manusia Indonesia* 3(1–6):127–135.

Tim Penelitian Padang Bindu 2009. *Penelitian Hunian Prasejarah Di Padang Bindu—Baturaja Sumatera Selatan*. Unpublished report. Pusat Penelitian Arkeologi Nasional, Jakarta.

van Heekeren, H.R. 1958. *The Bronze-Iron Age of Indonesia*. Verhandelingen van het Koninklijk Instituut van Taal-, Land- en Volkenkunde 22. Martinus Nijhoff, The Hague. doi.org/10.26530/OAPEN_613360

White, J.C. and E.G. Hamilton 2014. The transmission of early bronze technology to Thailand: New perspectives. In B. Roberts and C. Thornton (eds), *Archaeometallurgy in Global Perspective*, pp. 805–852. Springer, New York. doi.org/10.1007/978-1-4614-9017-3_28

Appendix

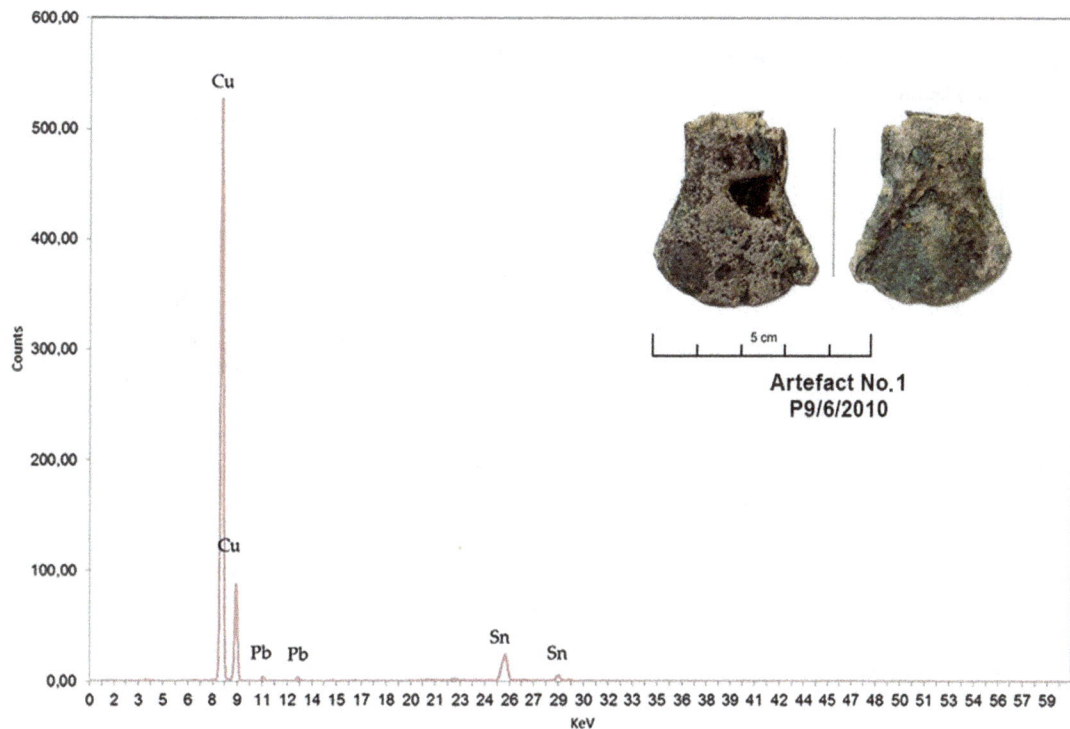

Figure 11.A1: p-XRF spectra result from artefact no. 1.
Source: Harry Octavianus Sofian.

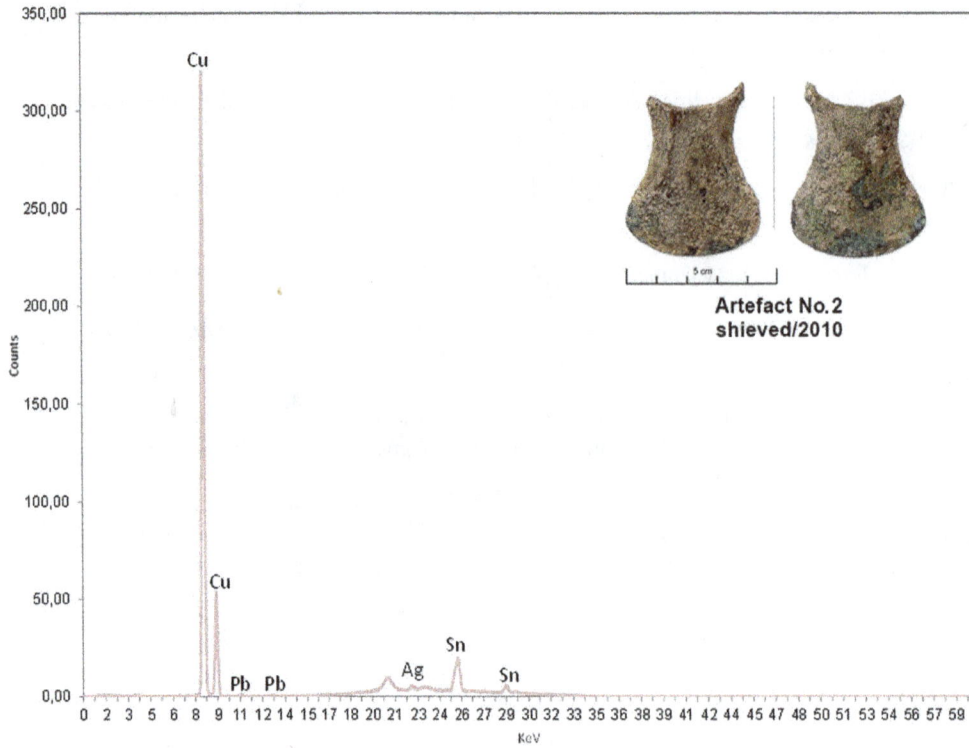

Figure 11.A2: p-XRF spectra result from artefact no. 2.

Source: Harry Octavianus Sofian.

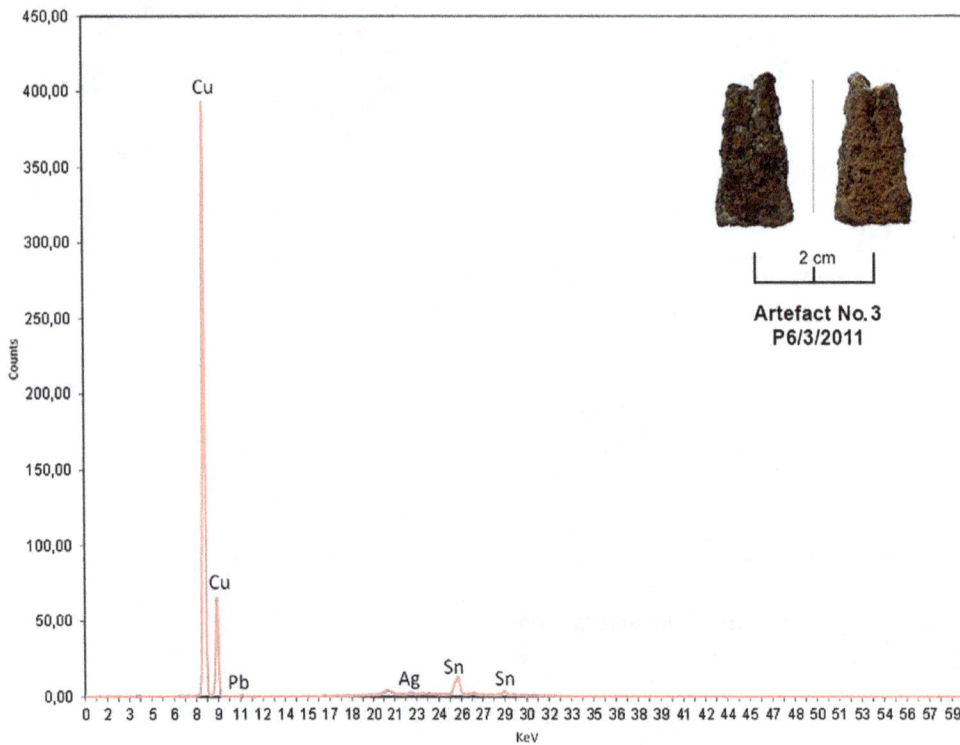

Figure 11.A3: p-XRF spectra result from artefact no. 3.

Source: Harry Octavianus Sofian.

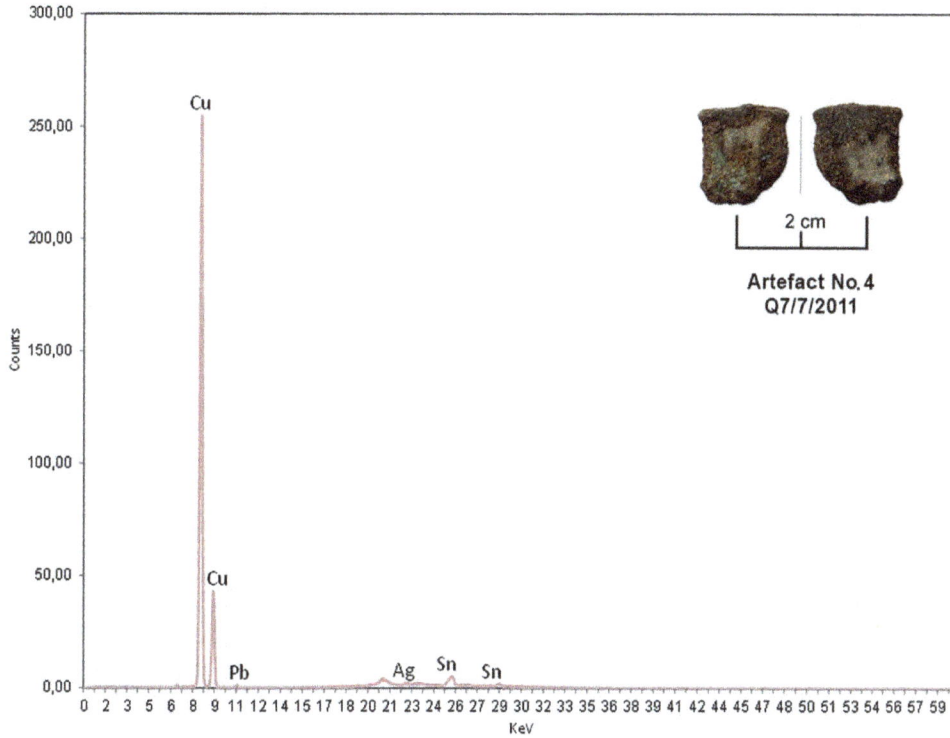

Figure 11.A4: p-XRF spectra result from artefact no. 4.
Source: Harry Octavianus Sofian.

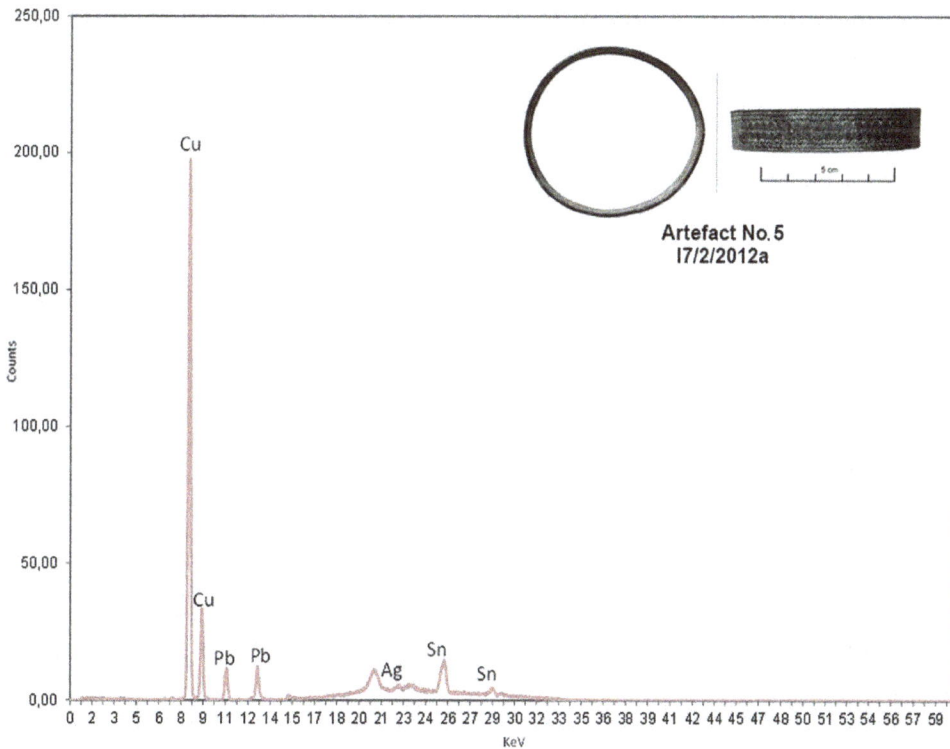

Figure 11.A5: p-XRF spectra result from artefact no. 5.
Source: Harry Octavianus Sofian.

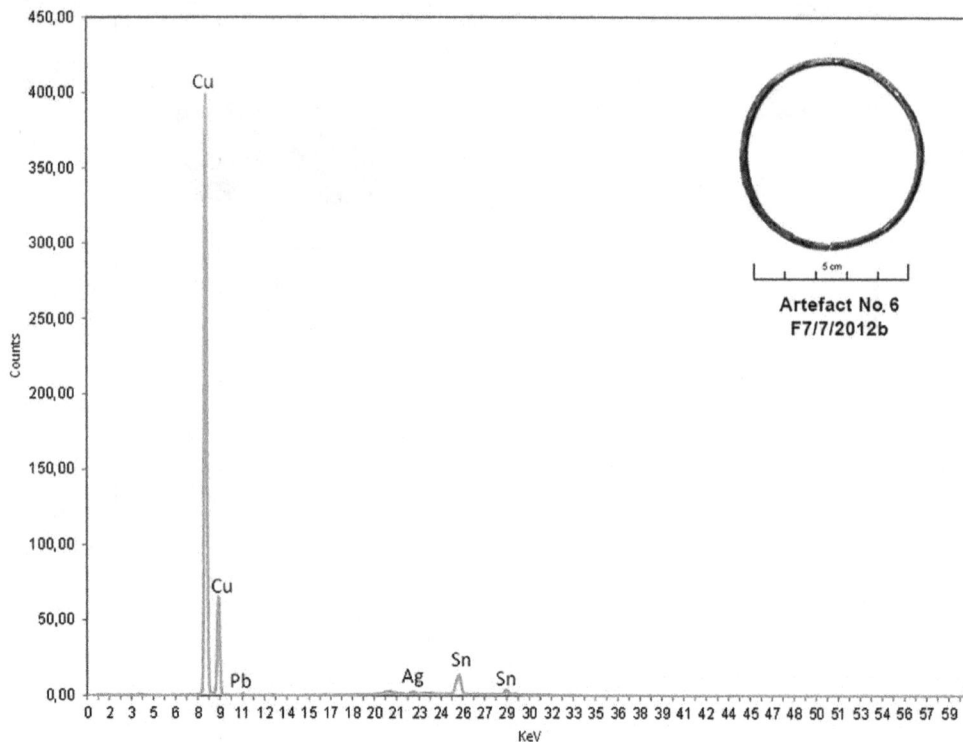

Figure 11.A6: p-XRF spectra result from artefact no. 6.
Source: Harry Octavianus Sofian.

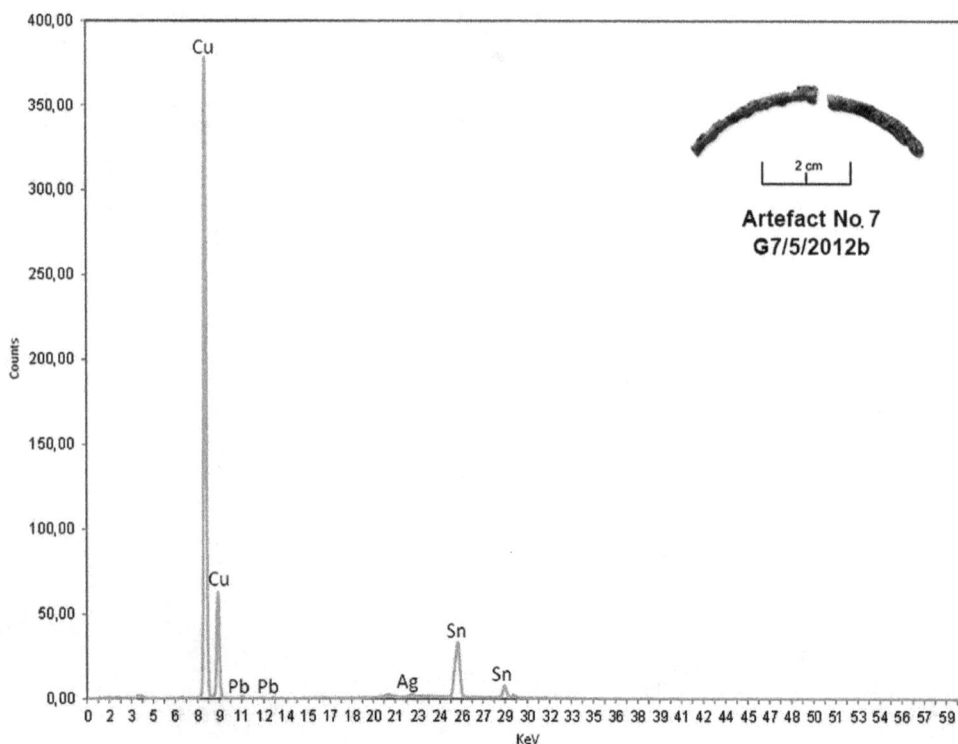

Figure 11.A7: p-XRF spectra result from artefact no. 7.
Source: Harry Octavianus Sofian.

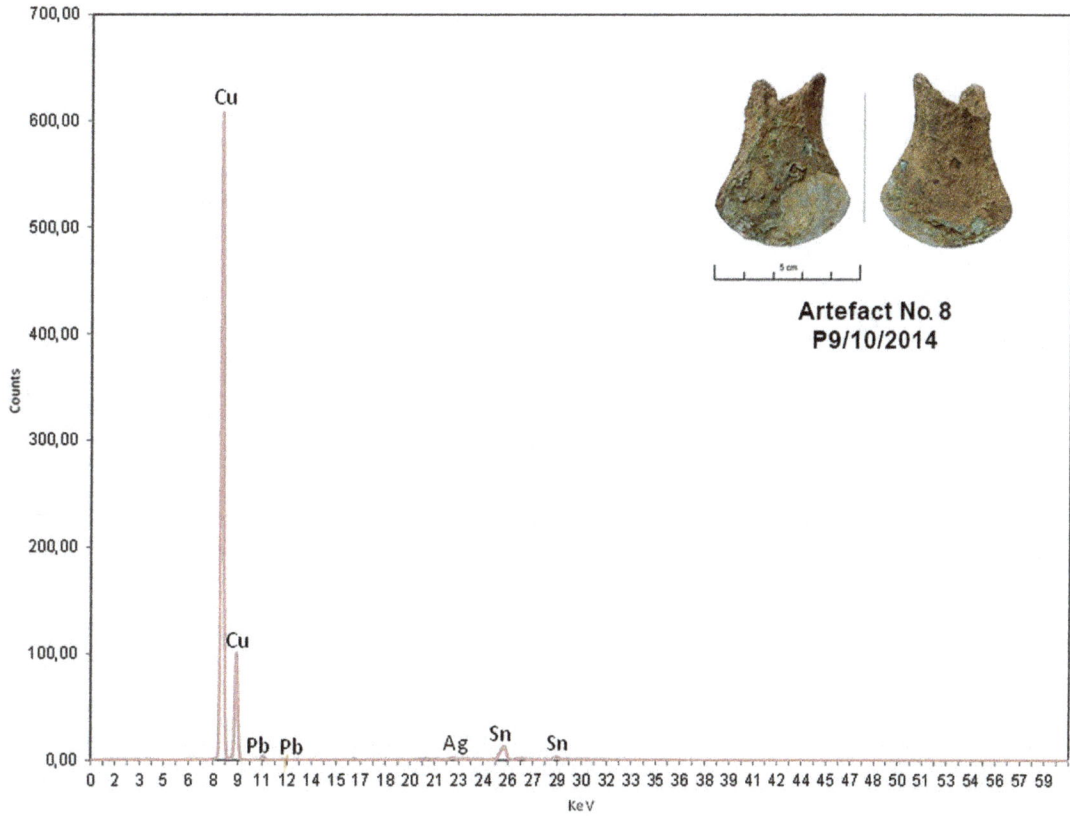

Figure 11.A8: p-XRF spectra result from artefact no. 8.
Source: Harry Octavianus Sofian.

12

Across the highlands: Ethnicity, archaeology and monuments in the lands of the Rejang, Minangkabau and Batak

Dominik Bonatz

Abstract

Since its beginnings, prehistoric archaeology in the highlands of Sumatra has been mainly concerned with stone monuments, generally labelled as megaliths. They have survived in large quantities in various highland regions, exhibit a variety of formal and iconic characteristics, and date to a number of periods, from the early first millennium AD to the present. Given this spatial and diachronic extent, the variety of megalithic forms of expression and their differing social contexts present an important field of inquiry. In this chapter, I show how these megaliths represent cultural developments that are intertwined with other developments in the lowlands and coastal areas of Sumatra. Furthermore, I argue for the need to consider the megalithic remains from the perspective of the local communities in which they are nowadays embedded. Major ethnic groups in the highlands of Sumatra, such as the Rejang, Minangkabau and Batak, attach different values to their megalithic heritage. In archaeology, it is very helpful to make use of these values when prehistoric monuments are reviewed from a historical perspective.

Keywords: Sumatra, megaliths, stone monuments, archaeology, ethnicity

Abstrak

Sejak awal, arkeologi prasejarah di dataran tinggi Sumatra umunya berkaitan dengan monumen batu, umumnya disebut sebagai megalit, yang masih dapat dijumpai dalam jumlah banyak di berbagai daerah di dataran tinggi dan menunjukkan karakteristik formal dan ikonik yang berbeda pula. Monumen-monumen ini berasal dari periode yang berbeda, dari awal milenium pertama Masehi hingga saat ini. Mengingat luasnya jangkauan spasial dan diakronisnya, keragaman bentuk ekspresi megalitik dan konteks sosial yang berbeda memunculkan bidang penyelidikan yang krusial. Dalam bab ini akan diperlihatkan keberadaan monmen dalam konteks perkembangan budaya, dan dalam kaitannya dengan perkembangan lain di dataran rendah dan daerah pesisir Sumatra. Selanjutnya akan dikemukakan perlunya melihat peninggalan megalitik dari perspektif yang tertanam dalam masyarakat lokal saat ini. Kelompok etnis besar di dataran tinggi Sumatra seperti Rejang, Minangkabau dan Batak memberikan nilai yang berbeda pada warisan megalitik mereka. Untuk arkeologi, hal tersebut sangat membantu untuk memanfaatkan nilai-nilai tersebut ketika monumen prasejarah ditinjau dari sebuah perspektif sejarah.

Kata kunci: Sumatera, megalit, monumen batu, arkeologi, kesukuan

Preliminary remark

This chapter includes documentations and observations from field research that a team from the Freie Universität Berlin, under my direction, pursued in cooperation with Indonesian research institutions from 2005 to present in Sumatra. During this research, much information was gathered with the help of local informants. This information cannot be substantiated with references to scientific literature. DB, therefore, assumes full responsibility for its reliability. He thanks all the people in Indonesia for their warm hospitality, guidance and willingness to share all the knowledge we asked for.

Introduction: Archaeology and ethnicity in the highlands of Sumatra

Favourable living conditions in the fertile valleys and plateaus of Sumatra's mountains probably led to earlier human settlement there than in the regions near the coast. Archaeologists and historians who study Sumatra therefore assume that important processes of settlement began in the highlands (Reid 1997; Miksic 2009). Then, at the beginning of the first century AD, the highlands' contact with the trading sites in the lowlands and subsequent integration into the network of international maritime trade relations led to dynamic exchange relations that fostered the establishment of the earliest political systems, Srivijaya and Melayu, in Sumatra's southeastern lowlands (Bonatz 2021:39–41; Manguin 2009; Miksic 2009; Miksic 1996:45). This process lasted several centuries and marked a clear shift from the dominance of the ports in the upper Thai-Malay Peninsula and the Mekong Delta to the dominance of those in Sumatra. On the island of Bangka and in the Palembang area in southeastern Sumatra, there are Sanskrit inscriptions from a range of dates starting in the seventh century AD, attesting to a political system that reached as far as Kedah on the Thai-Malay Peninsula and controlled the trade in the Malacca Straits (Miksic and Goh 2017:291–298). It is suggested that the success of Srivijaya was based on a system that involved direct access to its trading partners (Miksic and Goh 2017), who included people living in the mountains, where the most valuable natural resources for trade were found. However, for a long time, these developments did not entail any loss of integrity for the communities in the various highland regions. In the relative isolation of their natural living spaces, they created and preserved distinctive cultural characteristics and developed their own languages and ethnicities. Three ethnic groups were particularly prominent in the Bukit Barisan highlands in this historical process: the Rejang in the south, the Minangkabau in the middle and the Batak in the north (see Figure 12.1).

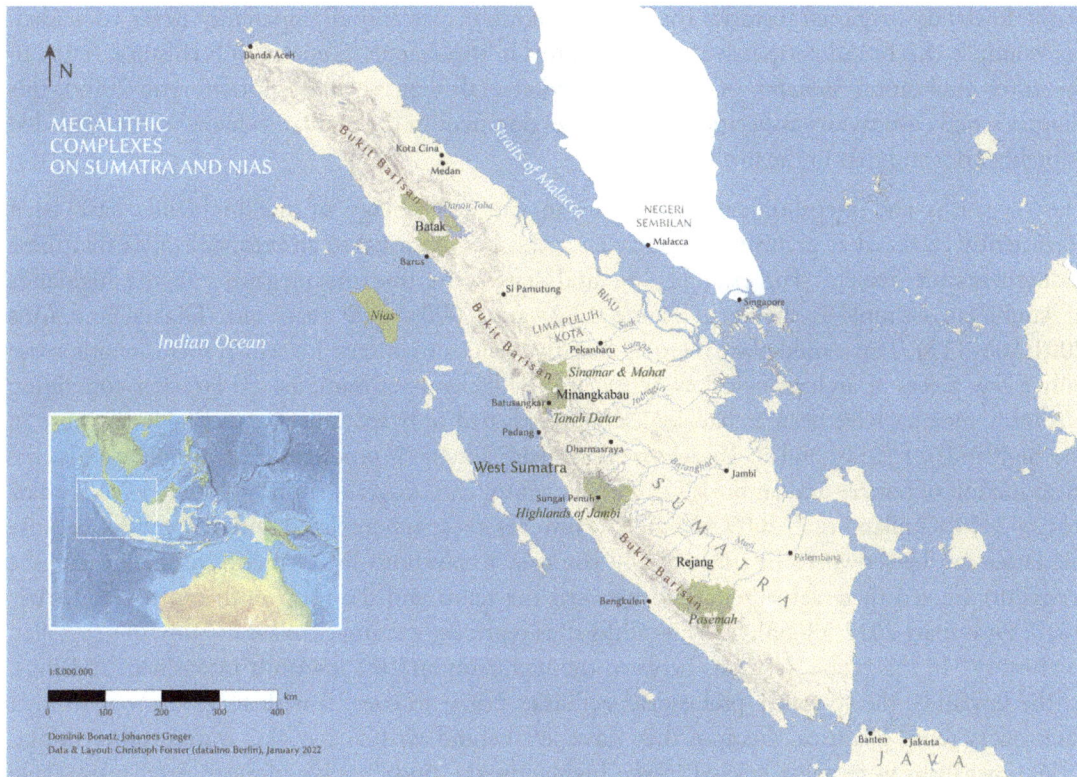

Figure 12.1: Map showing the core regions of the three ethnic groups discussed in this text.

Note: The areas with megalithic complexes on Sumatra and Nias are shown in green.

Source: Dominik Bonatz and Johannes Greger, with data and layout by Christoph Forster.

First, we need to explain why a contribution to a book covering the archaeology of the highlands of Sumatra is also concerned with questions about ethnicity in this region. This is essential, because the problem of connecting ethnic groups and material legacies is well known in science. In the case of Sumatra, the groups are contemporary ethnic groups, of which two, namely the Batak and Minangkabau, still stand out as dominant within the overall multiethnic composition of Sumatra, while the third group, the Rejang, still exist as a minority in the primarily Malay south of the island. These groups', and their regional subgroups', strong consciousness of their own culture and common descent, however, raises two scientifically relevant questions. First, what is their stance towards the archaeological monuments in their home regions? Second, might these monuments provide information about these groups' past, including their period of origin? In the following three main sections of this contribution, the purpose of the discussion is not to ethnicise the material legacies and monuments, but rather to include their present ethnic context in this volume's considerations.

Another important preliminary remark concerns the idea of prehistoric archaeology and prehistoric periods in the highlands of Sumatra. This idea initially resulted from an essentially European conception of the periodisation of phases of societal development and is, to this day, a scientific inheritance from the Dutch colonial era in Indonesia (Bloembergen and Eickhoff 2015). In this context, Indonesian archaeology uses the term 'Classical Era' to refer to a period that began during the seventh century and lasted until the end of the fifteenth century, when writing systems were adopted and Hindu and Buddhist influences became predominant in certain areas of Sumatra, Java and Bali (Miksic 2004a). For Sumatra, this results in a preconceived distinction between a prehistoric past, to which most of the highlands remains were assigned, and the early historic period or 'Classical Era' in the lowlands—regional histories that, in the common perception, apparently never coincided. For example, this biased perspective was maintained in the chapter 'Sumatra in Prehistoric times' in the 2009 publication *Sumatra—Crossroads of Cultures* (Brinkgreve and Sulistianingsih 2009); this chapter strictly avoids any association between development in the highlands (consistently regarded as prehistoric) and that in the lowlands.

The megaliths and megalith cultures salient to the archaeology of the highlands have been consistently classified as prehistoric monuments; this has often led to an erroneous idea that these monuments are ancient. For example, we find statements that the megaliths in the highlands of Jambi (an example is shown in Figure 12.2) are 4,000–4,500 years old (Djakfar and Idris 2001:108–113). That would place them in an early Neolithic context, for which there are otherwise only a few pieces of archaeological evidence in the highlands of Sumatra. So far, sites containing Neolithic remains have been archaeologically investigated only sporadically; this includes those in the highlands of Jambi and in Pasemah. Along with intensive production of obsidian tools, the introduction of pottery and jar burials can be shown to have occurred (Bonatz 2009:54–59; Bonatz 2012:42–54; Guillaud et al. 2009:425–426). However, these are unrelated to the megaliths, because the latter can be shown to be substantially younger. Excavations in Kerinci have shown that the megaliths erected there actually date to between the tenth and the fourteenth century AD (Aziz 2010:29; Bonatz 2012:58–63). The megaliths thus represent a younger phase of Sumatra's so-called 'prehistory'. In this phase, relations between the highlands and the lowlands intensified, and thus, in the lowlands, the so-called 'prehistoric' activities began to overlap with societal processes that researchers term 'historical' because they have left behind written records, among other things. While megaliths were being erected in the highlands, the Buddhist kingdom of Srivijaya-Melayu expanded its international network of maritime trade, which was based at the harbours along the rivers Batang Musi and Batang Hari. The coexistence of differing forms of society in the highlands and in the lowlands involved a number of important points of contact, which are discussed below. Nonetheless, for much of the history of Sumatran archaeological research, the preliterate highlands stood in the shadow of the Buddhist kingdoms and the subsequent Islamic sultanates. Until the end of the twentieth century, research interests definitely shifted to the early lowlands polities, which were 'depicted as outposts of civilization at the edge of jungles inhabited by barbarians' (Miksic 2009:10).

In principle, there is no turning point in the history of Sumatra that allows us to distinguish between prehistoric and historic time for the entire region. To illustrate this, let us take the example of the island of Nias, off Sumatra's west coast, whose unusual megalith culture reached its zenith in the eighteenth and nineteenth centuries (e.g. Bonatz 2021:86–112; Steimer-Herbet 2018:86–97; Ziegler and Viaro 1999). Strictly speaking, up to this time, this was a prehistoric culture, and only a very few external sources had reported on it. Much of that which characterises this culture's social, political, and art and craft practice can be taken as analogous to prehistoric societies that existed markedly earlier. The ethnographic character of Nias, however, puts it tellingly outside the scope of archaeological research, which is why van Heekeren's standard work *The Bronze-Iron Age of Indonesia*, for example, summarily dismisses the megalith culture on this island by saying that one should leave it to the ethnologists (van Heekeren 1958:79). From today's perspective, this position seems too near-sighted because it precludes a knowledgeable examination of culturally significant developments that cannot be shoehorned into the rigid model of archaeological periodisation.

Figure 12.2: Megalith in Dusun Tuo, Highlands of Jambi, Sumatra.
Note: The local guide in this picture is Pak Andri from the village close to Dusun Tuo.
Source: Photograph by Dominik Bonatz.

Therefore, what I propose instead is a *longue durée* approach, in the sense used by Braudel. He takes account of the importance of slow-changing geographic factors that influence human economies and communication. In the first volume of his masterwork, *The Mediterranean and the Mediterranean World in the Age of Philip II*, Braudel recognises the tension between mountain dwellers and plain dwellers as a basic feature of Mediterranean history over thousands of years, although both sides exhibit different cultural and economic models (Braudel 1972). This puts emphasis on long-term historical structures instead of making deliberate choices among chronological realities (Braudel 2009:173–176). In a similar sense, the archaeology of the Sumatran highlands indeed presents the possibility of focusing on historical developments that may extend into the present. Overlaps between parallel historical processes and forms of society repeatedly appear. This long history of coexistence underlies the especially dynamic nature of societal development on Sumatra; it has formed the complex overall cultural shape of the island and fostered its cultural characteristics, which have been preserved in many places, especially among the ethnic groups of the highlands.

Archaeological sites and monuments in the lands of the Rejang

The Pasemah Plateau in the south of Sumatra played a special role in the beginnings of archaeological research on the island. As early as 1850, in a short report, Ullman mentioned the impressive stone monuments in this region (Ullmann 1850). In 1870, Tombrink discussed them more thoroughly, connecting them with immigrant Hindus (Tombrink 1870). In 1922, Westenenk published an inventory of the monuments in Pasemah, which he, too, termed 'Indian' (Westenenk 1922). Then, in 1931, the relative renown of the Pasemah complex led van der Hoop to conduct a first systematic investigation in this region, which must be regarded as pioneering work in the field of Sumatran archaeology (van der Hoop 1932). Van der Hoop established the term 'megalith culture', which Schnitger adopted in his overview of the prehistoric monuments in the highlands of Sumatra and on the island of Nias (Schnitger 1939a:126–154). Since then, the prehistoric cultures in the highlands have been considered, above all, megalith cultures; this, however, long obscured the view of other forms of societal development in this region outside the megalithic perspective.

Van der Hoop recognised that the iconography of the megaliths in Pasemah, especially the depiction of the kettledrum (see Figure 12.3), displayed close parallels to the so-called Dong Son culture of northern Vietnam; therefore, he and subsequent scientists assumed there had been a temporal closeness between the creation of these megaliths and the Dong Son culture and assigned the complex in Pasemah in general to the 'Early Metal Age' in Indonesia (Guillaud et al. 2009:416–420). As a result, in the aforementioned work *The Bronze-Iron Age of Indonesia*, van Heekeren also labelled Pasemah an outstanding example of an 'Early Metal Age' megalith culture (van Heekeren 1958:63–77).

Figure 12.3: Carved rock near Desa Air Puar, Pasemah.
Source: Photograph by Dominik Bonatz.

What makes Pasemah so special? It is primarily the impressive number of stone monuments and megalithic constructions found at 25 sites in the region. It is not clear whether the settlements of the builders of the megaliths were located at these sites, because not a single standard excavation in this region has been conducted since van der Hoop's days. Good current overviews are provided by Rangkuti et al. (2017), Steimer-Herbet (2018:21–29) and Bonatz (2021:17–41), but these are based on the monuments visible on site and can hardly be used to interpret other archaeological data and finds. Only the stone cist graves that van der Hoop excavated in Tegurwangi and Tanjung Aro in 1931 produced material-culture remains; these included stone and glass beads, small gold, bronze and iron objects, and vessels or shards of vessels made of simple earthenware (van der Hoop 1932:47–52, figures 171–172). Apart from the depictions on the megaliths, these are the only glimpses of the material culture of the inhabitants of Pasemah who erected the megaliths.

Indonesian archaeologists such as Rangkuti et al. (2017:22–24) have slightly modified the classifications of van der Hoop and van Heekeren to subdivide the megaliths in Pasemah into nine groups: (1) completely three-dimensionally elaborated statues (*arca batu*); (2) stones left in their natural state but decorated with a relief (*batu bergores*); (3) stones erected to stand upright (*menhir*); (4) stones lying horizontally (*batu datar*); (5) groups of four stones left in their natural state (*tetralith*); (6) stone basins (*lesung batu*); (7) stone mortars (*lumpang*); (8) below-ground stone cist graves (*bilik batu*); and (9) above-ground dolmens (*dolmen*). As a rule, monuments from different groups appear together. Thus, near the graves and dolmens there are usually also statues, menhirs and groups of stones. The spatial context of the burials underscores the interpretation that the human depictions are images of ancestors. To this interpretation, the narrative character of the images can be added; this is described below.

If we consider the geographic locations of the sites containing these collections of stones (and occasionally single stones), then two patterns of distribution can be recognised that hypothetically correspond with the old pattern of settlement. One area with megaliths extends from the eastern foothills of Gunung Dempo, a volcano with altitude 3,159 m above sea-level, through the valley between that volcano and the low Barisan mountain chain in the north. Here, the fertile volcanic soils and easily accessed watercourses offer optimal conditions for agriculture and are hence an ideal area for human settlement. The other area with megaliths, in contrast, is found on the slopes and narrow ridges of the northern edge of the plateau. Here, the main river in Pasemah—the Lematang—and its tributaries have cut deep, impenetrable canyons in the terrain. Only a single easily traversable path runs beside these slopes down to Lahat, where the landscape opens up to the lowlands. It is easy to see why several sites with megaliths are found in this area. They seem to guard the sole approach to the plateau, marking the territory of a tribal community whose very individual cultural imprint reveals itself directly through the impression these striking stone monuments made on the visitor.

The complex iconography of the statues and other stones decorated with reliefs lends the megalith culture in Pasemah its emphatically pictorial character. About 100 depictions of people, of people together with animals and of animals alone are known.[1] Most are depictions of men, but many women and a surprisingly large number of children are part of the pictorial repertoire. The interactions between adults and children and the relationships between people and animals form the special, almost narrative character of the megaliths in Pasemah.

---

1   A good overview of this is provided in the *Megalitik Pasemah* (Rangkuti et al. 2017), edited and richly illustrated by Nurhadin Rangkuti. Unfortunately, this, like most of the other relevant archaeological publications, is not available outside Indonesia.

Figure 12.4: Statue in Pulau Panggung, Pasemah.
Source: Photograph by Johannes Greger.

An example of this is the statue in Pulau Panggung (Figure 12.4), which stands near a collapsed megalith. In this statue, a man is sitting on an elephant's back and pressing it to the ground. The man's hands grasp the right-hand side of the animal's forehead and its left cheek. At the same time, the man is holding two small persons, probably children, clamped under the crooks of his arms. With their heads turned towards the rear, each clings with one hand to the man's waist and with the other to the elephant's forehead. This impressively concentrated and dynamic sculptural composition conveys an expression of control and power, even as it shows the considerable effort the man is having to make to tame both the animal and the people at the same time.

In other sculptures, a protective or helping gesture towards children is foregrounded, and animals such as elephants are not merely tamed but also become pets at the side of a man or a woman (Bonatz 2021: figures 7–10).

The protective function is also suggested in the more static statues that show a single man or woman (e.g. Bonatz 2021: figures 11–12, 21). They stand like guardian figures in the landscape and guard sites where the graves of important deceased members of the community lie. Because building a stone cist grave or dolmen requires much effort, it can be assumed that this form of burial was an honour only for selected personages, which, in turn, suggests a high degree of hierarchisation in the society of Pasemah. Expressions of status, power and prestige appear in almost all the depictions of men, in particular: these men are equipped as warriors, with helmet, sword, and heavy metal rings or armour plates protecting their arms and legs. A depicted object that in this context points to an especially high degree of prestige and probably also wealth is the aforementioned kettledrum, whose original must have been made of bronze. As on the well-known *batu gajah* ('elephant stone'; Bonatz 2021: figures 13a–c), which originally stood in Kota Raya Lembak, this kettledrum is shown being carried on the backs of warriors, or they hold it with both hands in front of their bodies, as can be seen in the statues in Belumai and Tegurwangi (Bonatz 2021: figures 11–12). On a large oval stone in Air Puar (see Figure 12.3), whose front side is entirely decorated with a shallow relief, two men hold the kettledrum as well as leashes on which they lead dogs. Two frontally depicted water buffalo heads fill the remainder of the pictorial space. In this scene, which is difficult to interpret, the kettledrum is clearly the focus of the action. Because it is depicted in this manner in Pasemah's megalith art, it must have been an object of overarching and symbolic significance. The value of the kettledrum is further stressed by the fact that such rare items were imported in trade with the lowlands. As an archaeological object, the kettledrum depicted in the megalithic art points to transregional exchange that connected Pasemah with the network of early international trade relations.

The similarity of these depictions to the type of kettledrum produced by the Dong Son culture in northern Vietnam, a type defined as Heger I, led to the probably erroneous assumption that the depictions on the megaliths in Pasemah and the real kettledrums found in other parts of Sumatra dated from the same time, namely the period of the Dong Son culture between 500 BC and AD 200 (van der Hoop 1932:166). However, Peter Bellwood pointed out as early as 1985 that the networks generated by the Dong Son people existed long after the demise of that culture, and that artefacts such as the kettledrums therefore circulated for many more centuries in the Southeast Asian archipelago (Bellwood 1985:272; see also Miksic and Goh 2017:109–111 on the spread of the kettledrums). It is thus possible that the kettledrums did not enter the Pasemah region until much later than AD 200.

For this reason, a preferable approach to dating the megalith culture in Pasemah is to situate it closer in time to the development of the first politically united trade empire in the eastern lowlands. Since it has to be assumed that the conveyance of kettledrums and other valuable import goods to the highlands depended on reliable trading stations in the lowlands and on the coast, then evidence of their existence before the sixth century AD is clearly lacking. However, after this, the kingdom of Srivijaya arose along the shore of the Batang Musi estuary in Sumatra's southeast. In what is called a mandala system, it united a large number of small tribal principalities in the lowlands and at the same time rose to become the most important maritime trading power in the Indo-Pacific region (Miksic and Goh 2017:289–306). Srivijaya's merchant fleets crossed the Indian Ocean to India and

Arabia and reached the ports of the Tang and Song dynasties in China via the Java Sea. Srivijaya acquired its special strategic importance by controlling the vital maritime trade route through the Strait of Malacca. Srivijaya's capital, Palembang, on the Batang Musi, flourished into the eleventh century as a political and economic centre of this great power, which was not decisively weakened until it was invaded by an army of the southern Indian Chola dynasty in 1071.

The local resources important for trade during the time of Srivijaya are all found exclusively in Sumatra's highlands: gold, tropical woods, camphor and benzoin, ivory, rhinoceros horn and the horns of the hornbill are merely a selection of the highlands products that promised huge wealth through trade (Wolters 1967). Because of its geographical proximity, it is highly probable that the Pasemah region was one of the primary destinations of Srivijaya's economic activities (Manguin 2009). Therefore, intensive lowlands–highlands relations probably started to develop in the sixth or seventh century AD, providing powerful mutual impetus to both regions' societal development. For Pasemah's people, the possibility of acquiring new possessions such as jewellery, metal weapons, metal tools, textiles and salt led to new forms of reputation, power and prestige, and also influenced the emergence of new political structures—because, in turn, it now became important to control and to exploit more intensively the resources one had in order to make them available for exchanging for goods from the lowlands. Given this context of dynamic development, it is easy to explain why territorial claims, group alliances and elites gained importance. The megaliths and megalith graves are another logical consequence of this development, because they serve related functions: marking territories, preserving group identities and giving visibility to elites. This is probably the essential reason for the emergence of the megalith tradition, not only in Pasemah but also in other regions of the Indonesian archipelago. It is this tension between highlands and lowlands that is typical of the *longue durée* in the history of Sumatra.

The further chronology of Pasemah's development cannot be determined in detail. However, we can assume that the megalith tradition dwindled as Palembang lost its political and economic predominance after the eleventh century. In the fourteenth century, the Majapahit empire, based in Java, took power over southern Sumatra and was never displaced. Popular legends from that time equate the arrival of a new ruling elite in the highlands with the displacement of an autochthonous population who are regarded as having been Rejang. The Rejang were forced to leave the Pasemah Plateau and settle in areas further north and west of it. In essence, these tales revolve around two legendary founding figures, Atung Bungsu and Serunting Sakti, better known by his nickname Lidah Pahit ('Bitter Tongue'). The new settlement of the highlands is attributed to them, and many of the communities living there today invoke them as their mythical progenitors (Barendregt 2002; Collins 1998; Westenenk 1922). Their holy graves, still visited by pilgrims, are both in Pasemah, Atung Bungsu's in Benua Keling Lama and Lidah Pahit's near the village of Pelang Kenidai (Guillaud et al. 2009:426–430).

The mythology around Lidah Pahit includes him being able to turn people to stone with a word, which is the origin of the epithet Bitter Tongue. Pasemah's indigenous people, some of whom suffered this fate after Bitter Tongue's arrival, are called Rejang in the oral tradition. This suggests a direct connection between the Rejang and the megaliths in this region, because according to the legend, of course, the statues in Pasemah are none other than the rivals whom Bitter Tongue turned to stone. Similarly, it is related that Atung Bungsu made himself the tribal chief of the Rejang and that those who did not follow him emigrated to neighbouring regions. Indeed, today, remnant groups of the ethnic Rejang live outside Pasemah, for example in the administrative district named after them, Rejang Lebong, which is in the northwestern province of Bengkulen. This migratory narrative, which is connected with the megaliths and natural stones in Pasemah, is analysed in detail by Barendregt (2002).

This narrative cannot be historically or, as yet, archaeologically evidenced, of course. Nonetheless, it contextualises the Pasemah archaeological monuments in a historical process that must have been strongly shaped by migrations. Thus, the connection between the megaliths and the early history of the Rejang creates a form of identity that differentiates the Indigenous people of southern Sumatra, who consider themselves descendants of the early Rejang, from the Malay people who are now the majority. The megaliths thereby retrospectively receive their own ethnic identity as markers of a long-gone era.

Archaeological sites and monuments in the lands of the Minangkabau

The fertile high plains and valleys at the foot of Gunung Merapi in western Sumatra are the homeland of the Minangkabau, whose matrilineal and matrilocal structures, still preserved today, make them one of the best-known ethnic minorities in Indonesia. In their main areas of settlement in Tanah Datar, Agam and Lima Puluh Kota (see Figure 12.1), the Minangkabau long isolated themselves from strangers, although their region's reputation for wealth aroused fantasies and desires among people far beyond Sumatra (Barnard 2013:20–25). In early Indian sources, Sumatra is referred to as the island of gold (*suvarnadvīpa*), and from the sixteenth century onward, various European travellers believed there was a legendary land of gold in the core area of the Minangkabau (Drakard 1999:25–29). Reports from Portuguese and Dutch envoys followed, describing the extraordinary splendour at the courts of local rulers and the extravagant plenitude of gold with which they surrounded themselves (Tjoa-Bonatz 2019:74–79).

As early as the fourteenth century, Javanese and Chinese sources perceived the Minangkabau as a political unit. At this time, in their central area in Tanah Datar, a kingdom existed that constitutes the earliest example of foreign rule in the highlands of Sumatra. Its founder was Adityavarman, a Buddhist king from Melayu, who apparently felt that his own political destiny was too insecure in the lowlands and therefore shifted his seat of government to Tanah Datar in the highlands in 1347 (Tjoa-Bonatz 2019b:30–41). One of the main sites of his kingdom was at Bukit Gombak. It was archaeologically investigated in 2011 and 2012 in the context of a German–Indonesian research project (Bonatz 2019b). Elsewhere in the region, 15 of Adityavarman's Sanskrit inscriptions chiselled in stone are known. In them, Adityavarman styles himself the divine ruler of the Gold Land and announces that several major construction plans will be implemented during his reign, which ended with his death in 1375 (Kulke 2009; Tjoa-Bonatz 2019a:30–72). After that, there is no further evidence of a kingdom in the highlands characterised by Buddhism. But evidence of continued settlement into the seventeenth century can be found, near Bukit Gombak and elsewhere. During this time, the rajas of the Minangkabau made new political alliances and began their conversion to Islam. Not far from Bukit Gombak, which was abandoned after the seventeenth century, one of the most important royal families of the Minangkabau settled in Pagaruyung and erected a palace there. Rebuilt several times, it is now one of the region's best-known monuments.

Figure 12.5: Islamic tombs in Saruaso, Tanah Datar.
Source: Photograph by author.

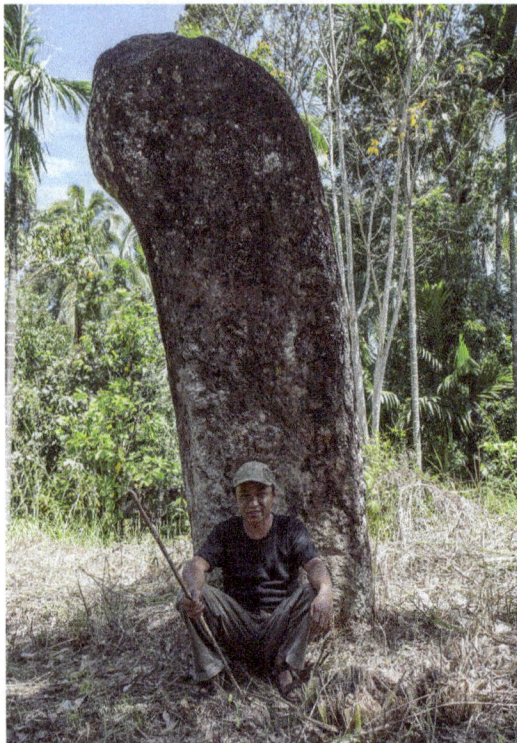

Figure 12.6: Megalith in Tabagak, Mahat.
Source: Photograph by author.

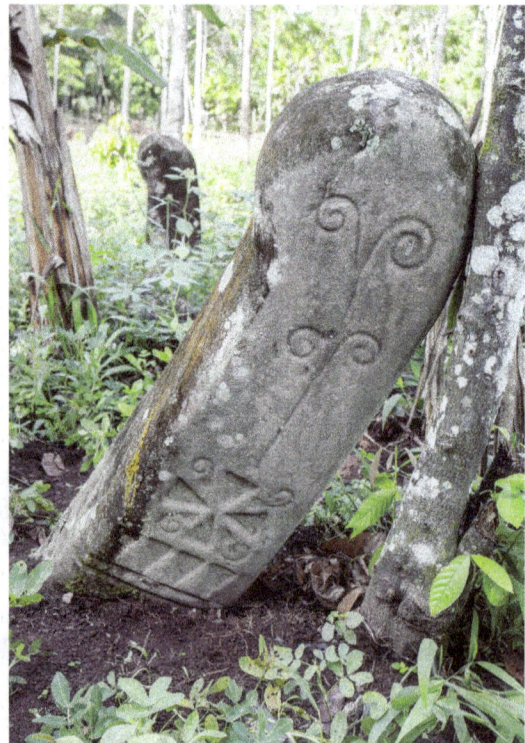

Figure 12.7: Megalith in Tanjung Bunga, Mahat.
Source: Photograph by Anselm Kissel.

The memory of Adityavarman's epoch is still strong among the Minangkabau and plays a special role in traditional common law (*adat*). Adityavarman's Sanskrit inscriptions, known as *prasasti*, are not his epoch's only material legacies. The owners of objects from his reign, such as the dagger called Si Mandang Giri that is in the possession of the royal family of Pagaruyung (Tjoa-Bonatz 2019a: figure 2.2), have looked after them as *pusaka* (heirlooms) for generations. Another form of material remembrance appears at the burial sites of the royal families and nobles of the Minangkabau. Carefully hewn stones with their tops bent or curled forwards are erected over the graves (see Figure 12.5). This shape is clearly an adaptation of the commonly seen shape of the megaliths in the region of the Minangkabau (see Figures 12.6 and 12.7), which were erected over pre-Islamic burial grounds, as discussed below. Unlike the megaliths, which are all oriented towards one of the prominent volcanoes in the highlands, the Islamic headstones are all oriented towards Mecca. Terminologically, we distinguish between *batu tagak* ('upright stone') for 'megalith' and *batu nisan* for 'Islamic gravestone'. Despite these differences, the two share a tradition (see also Miksic 2004b) that goes far back into the past and originated before the time of the historically traceable Minangkabau.

Origin and continuity of the megalith tradition

In the northeast of the Minangkabau lands, near Payakumbuh, the seat of one of their most prestigious royal houses, is the Sinamar River valley and—accessible from there only via a high mountain pass— the remote Mahat Valley. In this region, today called the Lima Puluh Kota administrative district, several sites have larger collections of megaliths, most of them in Mahat, in a concentration that is uniquely dense for the Indonesian archipelago.

In our own documentation works in Mahat Valley in 2014, my team counted a total of 788 megaliths distributed across 18 sites (Bonatz 2019a:416–422; Bonatz 2021:55–64). In the past, however, there must have been far more, because many stones have been destroyed, hauled away or reused as construction material.

In 1985, Indonesian excavations in Bawah Parit—with 368 stones, the largest megalithic site in the valley—turned up remnants of human skeletons at a depth of almost 2 m, beneath the megaliths (Aziz and Siregar 1997). This suggests that places with megaliths can be interpreted as cemeteries. Excavations in Guguk Nunang and Sati, megalith sites in the neighbouring valley of the Sinamar also unearthed human bones, confirming this assumption (Triwurjani 2013:7–28).

Radiocarbon dating of one of the individuals buried in Bawah Parit yields a date of c. 180–120 BC, while two markedly different age determinations were found for the individuals buried at the Sinamar sites: in one case, between AD 220 and 580; in the other, c. AD 1000 (Triwurjani 2013:44). These datings provide what is so far the sole valid reference for determining the age of the megaliths in the Mahat and Sinamar valleys. The dates are far apart, but not so far apart that a theoretical continuation of the megalith culture in this region can be excluded for the period between the second century BC and the tenth to eleventh century AD.

All the megaliths in the Mahat and Sinamar valleys have the same basic form (Figures 12.6 and 12.7): pillar-like andesite monuments, with heights ranging from 0.5 m to almost 4 m, whose upper ends are bent, so that their appearance may be compared to the handle of a kris dagger. Most of the stones are carved, which emphasises their natural pillar-like form. In a small portion (about 15%) of them, geometrical and vegetative motifs are engraved in the stone. The vegetative motifs are clearly borrowed from the natural world, but the triangles at the base of the stones may also indicate a natural phenomenon, namely volcanoes. A close metaphysical relationship to nature is expressed in particular by the fact that the bent ends of all these stones are oriented towards Gunung Sago, the most prominent volcano in this region. This orientation is all the more remarkable because Gunung Sago cannot even be seen from the valley, where the view of it is blocked by high mountains. Nonetheless, the volcano appears to have been strongly anchored in the minds of the region's inhabitants as a source of fertility and a symbol of power. It can also be assumed that the megaliths were perceived as a medium for communicating with this force of nature. But they also incorporate a human symbolism that can be deduced from the unusual design of one megalith in Ikua Labuah (Bonatz 2021: figure 49). A schematic face and a triangular head covering have been sculpted into the bent end of this stone (Bonatz 2021: figure 49). Used to interpret all the other stones, this means that their bent ends, too, can be construed as abstract representations of human heads. This suggests that they are symbols of people gazing towards the volcano as well as being symbols over graves, so they may symbolise the people for whom they were erected at the time of burial.

The phenomenon of the megaliths of Mahat should surely also be considered in terms of a competitive behaviour among the communities settling in the valley. The places with megaliths are on the hills and small plateaus high above the valley of the Mahat River. In 18 sites in the area, which is only 50 km² in area, one finds an astonishingly high concentration of probable burial grounds with megaliths. The number and size of the stones on such a field can be understood as analogous to the power and prestige of the community or clan behind it. But the problem arising from such considerations is that sites with megaliths have to be assigned to settlements. Archaeological inspections in the surroundings of megaliths have found evidence of nearby settlement sites in only two cases. In particular, in one of them, Aur Guri, large numbers of ceramic shards are found on the surface. Schnitger (1939a:126–128) had already investigated this important site as early as 1935. It was later mentioned in an article by Miksic (1986), who travelled through the Mahat Valley in 1982 but was unable to locate Aur Guri. DB identified it in 2014 and examined the ceramic evidence (Bonatz 2021:62–64, figures 52–53). Most of them are from simple pottery for everyday use, but some are remnants of Chinese porcelain from the Yan Dynasty (1279–1368) or Ming Dynasty (1368–1644). This finding contradicts the aforementioned dating of the megaliths, which was markedly earlier. This may mean we must assume a much longer duration of megalith production, or it may mean the megaliths were already present when the archaeologically tangible settlements were founded. If the latter case applies, the stones would be visible testimony to an unknown prehistory, a testimony that residents faced every day when they left and entered the village.

The people in the village community living in the Mahat Valley and Sinamar do not connect themselves with the megaliths. They do not perceive them as monuments erected by their early ancestors. Their only explanation for the megaliths' existence, a trivial one, is that the people who erected them left the valley a long time ago. Thus, the tradition of the megaliths was not continued in Mahat or Sinamar. Rather, it moved to the plateau of Tanah Datar at the foot of Gunung Merapi. There, it initially mixed with the cultural practice newly introduced under Adityavarman in the fourteenth century. During his reign, stone monuments already had a special meaning and included not only the stones with Sanskrit inscriptions that he erected but also stones with exclusively pictorial decorations (Tjoa-Bonatz 2019a:42–72). For example, in Kaburajo, the site of the royal cinerary urns, there is a large stone whose pictorial surface displays the disc of the sun and a stylised tree motif (Bonatz 2021: figure 56). The branches with spirals on this tree recall the motifs on the megaliths in Mahat. We can therefore assume that, when erecting his stones, Adityavarman took inspiration from the megalith tradition existing in the highlands. Next to Bukit Gombak, the centre of his dominion, a wide burial ground was unearthed during excavations on Bukit Kincir (Greger 2019). The stones erected there as grave markers are almost too small to be called megaliths, but in their function and uniform orientation towards the volcano, they correspond to the established pattern of the megalithic traditions in the highlands of the Minangkabau. There is hardly any other region in which these traditions stand so clearly at the threshold between prehistorical and historical research. Sometime in between, the Minangkabau, too, entered the historical stage, beyond all legends. Their appearance in the region's long history can be concretely grasped only together with the aforementioned written records dating from the fourteenth century onwards. If the history of the Minangkabau goes further back, to the period of the megaliths, remains a matter of future research.

Archaeological sites and monuments in the lands of the Batak

The Batak people are divided into six groups, each with its own language and alphabetic script: Angkola Batak, Mandailing Batak, Toba Batak, Pakpak Batak, Simalungun Batak and Karo Batak. These groups live around the Lake Toba in North Sumatra. Due to the proselytisation in the second half of the nineteenth century, today, the majority of the Batak profess Christianity, but there are also significant Muslim minorities, especially among the Mandailing Batak and Pakpak Batak. At the centre of the cultural heritage, which the Batak continue to cultivate intensively, and of the Batak mythology is the region around Lake Toba with its island, Samosir, which is also the centre of what is called Batak art. Today, this art enriches ethnological collections around the world and creates the impression of a culture with unusual social and pagan customs. Archaeologically, little is known about the Batak. There have never been excavations in their lands. The Batak thus appear to outsiders as a people who feature in myths and legends but do not have their own history (Reid 2009).

In two Batak regions, that of the Toba Batak and the Pakpak Batak, stone monuments are part of the material cultural heritage.

The reason why there are no important stone monuments in other regions is simply that these areas have stone-poor geology. The lack of stones as resources for building and for creating monuments is an important problem for archaeology on Sumatra in general. Without this resource, the most visible and lasting characteristic of 'prehistoric' communities is lacking on Sumatra. A natural environment in which most constructed and handcrafted objects are made of organic and hence perishable materials makes it especially difficult to find the traces of early human activities. The visibility of so-called megalith cultures should therefore not lead us to lose sight of regions without megaliths. As the chapters in this volume show, there are many approaches to conducting interdisciplinary scientific research on the earliest developments of settlement on Sumatra. Here, the work of Indonesian archaeologists should be underscored; it repeatedly unearths interesting contexts of findings but is unfortunately perceived only to a limited extent at the international level (cf. Bonatz 2009:54–60).

Sarcophagi and stone urns of the Toba Batak

In the 1930s, Schnitger conducted the first systematic inventory of Batak monuments. He speaks of Batak people having a 'megalith culture' and a 'megalith cult' (Schnitger 1939a:105–110, 1939b, 1941–1942). His classification essentially refers to the large stone sarcophagi and stone urns that were in the area of the Toba Batak at the time of his research, some of which are still there today. Both stone sarcophagi and stone urns are precursors of the grave monuments called *tugu*, which are extremely important today in the Christian Batak's cult of the dead and ancestors. Everywhere on Samosir and around Lake Toba, large cement graves, clad in colourful tiles and decorated with sculptures, stand out conspicuously from the landscape. These *tugu* are the pride of a whole family group; they can cost a fortune and thereby drive individual families to the verge of financial ruin.

To be precise, the *tugu* are ossuaries. That means they store the bones of several deceased persons; these bones have been taken from their original burial place and transferred to this final burial site. Not every individual is honoured in this way, a long time after death, only those considered especially distinguished and who have much prestige in a family group.

The effortful ritual of reburial in a *tugu* has a deeper eschatological meaning. It helps the soul (*begu*) of the deceased ascend to a higher rank. This is why the bones of the ancestors who stand very high in the hierarchy of the dead are collected in the *tugu*. They are symbols of the ruling elite of a family group or of a whole clan (*marga*) and thus also function as political monuments to a high degree (Sibeth 1990:76–80).

As noted, the *tugu* are based on older forms of stone urns and stone sarcophagi, because the bones of significant ancestors were transferred into those, too, with the sarcophagi being reserved for the rajas and their closest family members. Most of the traditional stone urns (e.g. Bonatz 2021: figure 61) have now vanished from the villages. Many of the stone sarcophagi remain, however. They still contain the bones of the deceased rajas and their spouses, and they still sometimes receive new secondary burials to bring special members of the royal family into the circle of higher ancestors. They continue to be important memorials for the collective memory of a societal descent group.

The sarcophagi are monolithic structures, each made of a large boulder up to 3.5 m long (see Figure 12.8). They consist of two parts, the sarcophagus basin and the lid. Procuring a suitably large block of stone to produce a sarcophagus, transporting it over long distances and elaborating it into an artistically sculpted grave (*parholian*) is one of the most impressive achievements of the Batak culture; in this sense, they can indeed be termed megalithic monuments.

Figure 12.8: Stone sarcophagus of the *marga* (clan) Sidaputar in Tomok, Samosir, Sumatra.
Source: Photograph by author.

These are complex iconographic structures that unite various figurative components (as shown in Figure 12.8). The front end of the lid flaunts the mighty head of a chimeric mythical creature that the Batak call a *singa*. The word *singa*, like some other loan words in the Batak languages, derives from the Sanskrit *siṃha*, which means 'lion'. But the head on the sarcophagus has little in common with that of a lion. The face is that of a human, while the high comb and small horns on the head and the usually crest-like coiffure are reminiscent of a reptile. Additionally, on some sarcophagi, a tail-like component protrudes at the rear end of the lid; moreover, on a single, unfortunately now lost example, feet were mounted on the lower corners of the basin (Barbier 1999: figure 114). This makes it clear that the entire sarcophagus was understood as the body of a chimera with a human face. For this reason, it is assumed that the creature called *singa* today rather can be equated with the snake Naga Padoha, who is originally anchored in the mythology of the Batak (Barbier 1988:89). Naga Padoha bears the middle world, where humans live, on his back. When this mighty snake stirs, the earth quakes. The souls of the distinguished deceased find their final residence with Naga Padoha after being allowed to rest for two years in the seventh heaven. So it makes sense that the sarcophagus, which is the final resting place of the bones of the dead, has the shape of Naga Padoha.

Early Indian influences, such as those found in the mythology and language of the Batak, may have partly determined the iconography of the sarcophagi. However, almost all these monuments feature two human sculptures, and these originated in Indigenous ideas, because they are not found in other cultures. At the front of the basin, the figure of a man or—rarely—a woman crouches beneath the head of the *singa*. It is assumed that these figures are representations of the royal ancestor for whom the sarcophagus was built.

In addition to the figure on the front, there is a usually female figure sitting on the back end of the sarcophagus' lid (see Figure 12.8). She grips her bent legs tightly with her arms, pressing them against her body. On her head she bears a bowl that the Batak say was used to receive purifying lemon water. In some cases, there is a second bowl in front of this figure.

There are different views of the significance of this figure. Older statements claim that it embodies an old woman who functions as a medium to take on the soul of the deceased to make the sarcophagus lighter as it is being transported to where it will be set up (Schnitger 1939a: 106–107). However, it is also often viewed as the wife of the deceased raja or, for the rare male depictions, as the raja himself. Important in any case is these figures' function, underscored by the bowls, of receiving offerings, because making offerings to one's ancestors (*ompu*) is considered one's foremost duty. As powerful ghosts (*begu*), they can not only protect their surviving relatives but also punish them with illness or other misfortunes if the offerings are not brought. Cases are even known in which a sarcophagus was moved from the village because the villagers thought that the ghost of the dead ancestor had turned on them.

The sarcophagi are not only symbolically charged containers for the bones of the deceased but also a means of communicating with the ancestors. Today, as noted above, the Christian *tugu* also fulfil similar functions, because there, too, all kinds of offerings are made in the form of donations of food and drink, but also of small presents of money and cigarettes. Also, in rare cases, the descendants of the rajas erect their own sarcophagi, which are made of cement and colourfully painted. However, these easily fabricated monuments do not have the significance of the old megalith-like sarcophagi.

As a rule, a sarcophagus is associated with the name of an important raja or with the name of a clan (*marga*). Individual such names reach back as far as the sixteenth century, but most of the sarcophagi still extant today are dated to the eighteenth or nineteenth century (Barbier 1999:92–98). Thus, the sarcophagi do not take us very far back in the history of the Toba Batak. Strictly speaking, they are not prehistoric monuments, either, since the names of some of their donors are known and still remembered in oral histories. Further, it is questionable whether the stone sarcophagi and urns, in themselves, are enough to justify our speaking of a megalith culture. Be that as it may, as monuments from the pre-Christian history of the Toba Batak, they offer glimpses of cultural practices and religious ideas that have survived into the present with their meanings unchanged.

The rider statues in the lands of the Pakpak Batak

The region of the Toba Batak is a heavily visited tourist area. Far less well known are the lands of the Pakpak Batak, which extend from the extremely rugged hilly country west of Lake Toba down to the coastal region between Sibolga and Barus (see Figure 12.1). The Pakpak Batak have their own language, script and culture, but they have been little-researched by outsiders to date. Viner and Kaplan (1981) is the only source that provides information on the social changes in this region during the recent past. The cultural heritage of the Pakpak only has been the interest of very few Western authors. Not until the late nineteenth century did research begin, as reports from Dutch colonial administrators and Christian missionaries weakly illuminated their history. In 1878, one of the first European travellers in this region, Baron H. von Rosenberg, published a drawing of an equestrian sculpture from the area around Dairi (von Rosenberg 1878: figure on p. 61; reproduced in Barbier 1999: figure 151). The works of missionary Warneck—especially Warneck (1909)—offer the most comprehensive glimpse of the religious and cultural life of the various Batak groups at the beginning of the twentieth century, but are entirely silent about the stone monuments of the Pakpak Batak.

Figure 12.9: Stone statue of a horse and rider in Santar Jehe, Pakpak Dairi.
Source: Photograph by author.

Figure 12.10: Stone rider statue, female statue and cremation urns in Lebuh Kitepapan, Pakpak Dairi.

Source: Photograph courtesy of Johannes Greger.

The leitmotif of Pakpak art is the slightly smaller than life-sized statues of riders (see Figures 12.9 and 12.10); these are depictions of rajas on especially prestigious mounts, namely horses. In the past, one or more examples of these monuments must have stood in almost every village. However, as the Swiss art collector Barbier documented in the 1980s, a large proportion of them have been lost to art theft (Barbier 1988, 1999). The research of our team in 2019 showed that many of the monuments Barbier was able to record have also now disappeared (Bonatz 2021:75–82, figure 69). Although people in the villages use every means to protect the sculptures from theft, such as cementing them in the ground or placing them in huts shielded with bars, they are nevertheless often stolen and sold on the antiquities market.

Originally, these equestrian likenesses were often accompanied by small statues of women (as in Figure 12.10). Today, they are regarded as representing the wives of the rajas of earlier times. In general, these figures are depicted sitting on the ground with tightly pulled-in legs. Until recently in Lebuk Artitum in the Pakpak Dairi territory, there was an intact group in which the statue of a rider was accompanied by two statues of women. However, on 4 July 2015, the rider figure was stolen. Subsequently, the residents of the nearby village built a protective hut over the remaining sculptures and set up a memorial plaque beside it to commemorate the stolen equestrian statue (Bonatz 2021: figures 79–80).

Collectors' and museums' interest in stolen art from the region of the Pakpak Batak can be explained by the uniqueness of both the motifs and the style of the rider figures. The riders are male and sit naked on their horses with their thighs horizontal and their lower legs vertical (Figures 12.8 and 12.9; Bonatz 2021: figures 70–71, 73–75, 77). There are also variants with two or even three riders on a single horse, but art theft has led to the disappearance of almost all of those from the region. In the 1930s, Schnitger documented a particularly impressive group in Salak with four sculptures, each of which showed two riders sitting on one horse (Schnitger 1939b:24, plates 6.6 and 6.8).

The mounts have short, stocky legs and, as a rule, bodies stretched long but lowered in the middle, so that it sometimes looks as if the rider is sitting on a hobbyhorse. The anus and testicles are rendered on the horses' rears, indicating that importance was placed on the fact that these are stallions. The horses' tails are bent upward and combine elegantly with the backs of the riders. But most impressive is the design of the heads. One recognises the horses primarily because their long muzzles are depicted with wide nostrils. In some of them, the mouth is open, revealing the powerful row of teeth typical of horses. The tongue hangs out of the mouth or grows directly out of the muzzle, like a long trunk. It either trails down to the ground or reaches the horse's throat. The end of the tongue is often rolled up, which gives the depictions a playful demeanour but sometimes leads to confusion with the trunk of an elephant.

In addition, the bridle typical of horses is presented: the reins, which are attached to the mouth with rein guides and a snaffle, and in some cases bolt-like handles at the ends of the reins. So there is no doubt that these represent trained mounts. However, the fact that these are horses and not elephants, which are otherwise so popular in the iconography of rule in Southeast Asia and, for example, prominent in the megalithic art of Pasemah (see above), deserves special consideration. Evidence of the existence of horses among the Pakpak Batak is found only when one examines the distant past of this region.

To date, there has not been a single archaeological excavation in the region of the Pakpak Batak. The few sites where the sculptures have not been moved or removed nonetheless convey at least a vague impression of their original context. They are located high above the settlement sites in the river valleys and offer commanding views of the surrounding area (Figures 12.9 and 12.10). One finds on the surface the shards from simple clay vessels that indicate past settlement activities. Today, most of these old village squares are deserted, but the people in the surrounding areas remember their names and consider themselves partly descended from the families that once lived there. Some individual equestrian statues are connected with the names of famous rajas whose family trees extend up to 15 generations back. Assuming an average of 25 to 30 years per generation, this is 375 to 450 years. This hard-to-verify information is all that is known so far about the age of the sculptures.

When working in their fields in the neighbourhoods of the statues, the farmers often find small stone urns with lids. The farmers collect these urns and put them with the statues of riders and women (see Figures 12.9 and 12.10). The urns have been found to contain the ashes of cremated bodies. This finding is significant, because almost nowhere else on Sumatra are the dead burned. Cremation of the dead is known to have occurred elsewhere only among the royal family of Adiyavarman in Tanah Datar (see above), and this was apparently intended to distinguish them from the way the Indigenous people's bodies were buried. The only region in the whole Indonesian archipelago where cremation has been practised for centuries is the Hindu island of Bali. We can thus suspect that the former practice of cremation in the region of the Pakpak Batak arose from Indian influences. In fact, a direct influence is plausible, because, from the ninth to the twelfth century, an important port that was the seat of a trade guild of India's Tamil Chola empire was located in Barus on Sumatra's west coast (Guy 2011; Perret and Surachman 2011). A Tamil inscription found in Lobu Tua near Barus has been dated to 1088 (Subbarayalu 1998). French–Indonesian excavations in Lobu Tua were able to confirm the wealth of this trade colony (Guillot 1998; Guillot 2003; Perret and Surachman 2009). Along with large amounts of southern Indian ceramics, glazed ceramics from Persia and porcelain and glass beads from China were found. However, the Tamil traders, who conducted their activities under the patronage of the powerful Chola dynasty, were primarily interested in gold and the fragrant resins camphor and benzoin. All these precious wares could be found in Barus's hinterland, the hill country of the Pakpak Batak. It is thus probable that, starting in the ninth century, trade with the Tamils brought cultural influences into the region, apparently including the custom of cremation and perhaps even the motif of the horse rider, which was very common in southern India, especially among statues made of terracotta (Alexandra van der Geer pers. comm. 2022).

Among the desirable commodities that the Tamils brought from India to the trading ports on the Malay Peninsula and in Indonesia were horses (Edwards McKinnon 2011:138). Until now, it has been assumed that horses reached northern Sumatra, via Aceh, only during Islamisation in the fifteenth century (Clarence-Smith 2004). However, in the case of Barus, it is quite possible that the Tamils exchanged horses for camphor, benzoin and gold much earlier. That is the only way to explain why the statues in the Pakpak Batak region depict riders on horses. It is easy to imagine the powerful impression these exotic animals must have made on the local people. The heads of the villages that were involved in trade with the Tamils adopted the horse as a very prestigious mount, and the reproduction of the bridle on the statues shows that they were indeed instructed in the art of riding.

Finally, an iconographic detail points to Indian influences on the ensembles of statues. The bun hairstyle visible on some of the men and women (see Figures 12.9 and 12.10) recalls the hairstyle of Buddha in Indian art—the hairstyle called *ushnisha* (*uṣṇīṣa*)—but is also often a feature displaying the social status of a member of the religious aristocracy in the early Hindu and Buddhist cultural realms.

The inspirations for creating the unusual rider figures can thus be connected in various ways with the presence of Tamil traders on the west coast of Sumatra from the ninth to the twelfth century. It cannot be proven whether the oldest equestrian statues of the Pakpak Batak were actually produced at that time. However, it is very probable that a tradition began back then that developed over the centuries and lastingly influenced the art of the Pakpak Batak, starting earlier than can be evidenced for the traditions of the Toba Batak.

As well as influencing material culture, the region of the Pakpak Batak must have played an important role in the transfer of language and script, because it is well known that many elements of Sanskrit entered the various Batak languages (pers. comm. Kozok cited in Sibeth 1990:100–114). For example, an inscription in the language of the Toba Batak in Lae Langae, documented in 2019, shows that this language was present in the Dairi area of the Pakpak Batak and that, for whatever reasons, it was even eternalised on a stone monument (Bonatz 2021: figure 81). There are thus enough indications to demonstrate that there was direct cultural exchange among the various Batak groups. Nonetheless, each of them developed its own cultural characteristics. The Pakpak Batak, of whom 60% are Christian and 40% are Muslim, observe to this day the New Year festival Nyepi, which is otherwise known only on Bali, where it is firmly anchored in religion: it is the day of driving away the evil spirits, and is followed by a day of absolute quiet and purification. This, too, is a tradition that arose from Indian influences—in this case, an unbroken tradition. Nevertheless, among the Pakpak Batak, the rider figures and other statues erected long ago also have great societal significance. They are respected as efficacious depictions of the ancestors. On every visit, one lights cigarettes for them and lays fruit, rice and beverages at their feet. The Pakpak Batak maintain a living understanding that the centuries-old stone monuments are part of their history as a people.

Concluding discussion

The megalithic monuments in the highlands of Sumatra occupy different positions in the collective memories of the different ethnic groups who live there today. In the highlands of Jambi, only briefly mentioned in the introduction, the megaliths (see Figure 12.2) are probably most clearly attributable to a mythical past that has nothing to do with the descent or history of the current inhabitants of this region. Kerinci and the adjoining regions of Serampas and Sungai Tenang have a very complex and patchwork-like ethnic composition. Each village community here has its own legend about its origins, and in these stories the migration narratives point in different directions. In part, they concern the arrival of groups of Minangkabau people from the north, but immigrants from the lowlands of Palembang-Srivijaya are also named as important founding figures (Bakels 2009:370; Watson 2009:260–262). In all these narratives, which can be traced back no further than the fifteenth century, the megaliths play no role (see also Znoj 2009:360–362). That is why myths explain the megaliths' existence as the work of the ghosts of the original inhabitants of the region, generally termed *mambang*, or to primordial Indian godheads (Bonatz et al. 2006:509; Bakels 2009:368–369). It is said that, in a quarrel, these latter godheads threw big stones down from the volcanoes, leaving the megaliths, locally termed *batu patah* ('smashed stone'), strewn across the landscape. Local people approach the *mambang* with respect and with fear of their still effective magic, but they have nothing to do with one's own ancestors, who, according to a common saying, entered the highlands 'like grasshoppers, not like bees' (Bakels 2009:369). This metaphor expresses the idea that the ancestors settled the country one after the other, rather than as a huge swarm.

This distancing by mythologising the megaliths in Kerinci and its neighbouring regions follows a different pattern from that of the legends that formed about the stone monuments in Pasemah. There, the megalithic remains are part of a historical discourse that equates the arrival of the people's own ancestors with the displacement of the Indigenous ethnic group, the Rejang. The stone monuments also have an established place in the tradition of the Minangkabau. The inhabitants of the remote Mahat Valley, where the earliest traces of a megalithic tradition can be found, call themselves newcomers who have nothing in common with the people who once erected the stones; but the tradition of the megaliths is carried forward in the material culture and cultural practices of the Minangkabau. The history of the Minangkabau and the process of the formation of their identity as an ethnicity may have been decisively shaped by Adityavarman's interregnum in the fourteenth century. Behind the etymology of the name Minangkabau stands the well-known legend of the victorious (*minang*) fight of a calf against an overpowering water buffalo (*kabau*) from Java. In collective memory, this legend is equated with the overcoming of the 'Javanese' foreign rule under Adityavarman (Kulke 2009:247) and thereby marks the date of this event as an effective founding date of the historical Minangkabau. But the continuum of cultural traditions goes back much further and permits us to deduce a long, unbroken process of settlement behind the ethnically self-contained identity of today's Minangkabau.

The Batak have the closest ancestral relationship with the stone monuments. In the case of the stone sarcophagi in the lands of the Toba Batak, this is easily understood due to the relatively recent age of these monuments and their still vital function as containers of bones. With the statues, especially the rider figures in the region of the Pakpak Batak, however, the archaeological traces and evidence from secondary sources lead far back into the past, possibly as far as the tenth century. Independently of their actual age or the attempt to determine their age by counting generations, the stone sculptures are considered to be connected with the local people's own ancestors, whether these are anonymous or part of a historical tradition. The close relationship here is very similar to that between the inhabitants of Nias and their stone monuments, which are considered to have been erected by their own group. The political context of the stones as monuments honouring specific personalities seems comparable between these regions. However, the zenith of megalith art on Nias, as shown above, was in the eighteenth and nineteenth centuries, whereas the traditions surrounding the equestrian figures among the Pakpak Batak probably go back much further.

Of course, excavations in the areas of the Batak, as well as in other places with megaliths on Sumatra, are urgently needed to be able to make more precise statements about the chronology of the megalithic traditions. What is greatly lacking are contexts that make it possible to locate the stones more precisely in their erstwhile societal surroundings and connect them with other material and immaterial legacies of vanished cultures. But the cultural legacy carved in stone and the few contexts researched so far nevertheless permit us to make a historical sketch of the past two millennia. Despite all its gaps, this sketch reveals many facets of the extremely dynamic developments in the history of the highlands and points repeatedly to overlaps with processes in other parts of the island. Finally, the modern ethnic context of these stone monuments should be considered, because it emphasises information about the self-understanding of the ethnic groups that live on Sumatra today and can supplement the archaeological and the few written sources that tell of the early history of these ethnic groups. Even if the combination of archaeology and ethnography is a problematic field of science that is beset with many misunderstandings (see Jones 1997 for an extensive discussion of this), the special situation in the highlands of Sumatra invites us to view the two as a closely tied interdisciplinary pair, especially from the perspective of the *longue durée*.

References

Aziz, F.A. 2010. Potensi situs arkeologi kawasan Kerinci. Jambi: Ikon Budaya Austronesia. *Amerta Jurnal Penelitian dan Pengembangan Arkeologi* 28:17–44.

Aziz, F.A. and D.A. Siregar 1997. Pertanggalan kronometrik sisa rangka manusia dari situs Bawah Parit, Mahat, Sumatera Barat. *Jurnal Arkeologi Siddhayatra*½ 2:12–22.

Bakels, J. 2009. Kerinci's living past: Stones, tales and tigers. In D. Bonatz, J.N. Miksic, J.D. Neidel and M. Tjoa-Bonatz (eds), *From Distant Tales: Archaeology and Ethnohistory in the Highlands of Sumatra*, pp. 367–382. Cambridge Scholars Publishing, Newcastle upon Tyne.

Barbier, J.P. 1988. A stone rider of the Batak of Sumatra. In J.P. Barbier and D. Newton (eds), *Islands and Ancestors*, pp. 50–65. The Metropolitan Museum of Art, New York.

Barbier, J.P. 1999. Batak Monuments. In J.P. Barbier (ed.), *Messages in Stone: Statues and Sculptures from Tribal Indonesia in the Collections of the Barbier-Mueller Museum*, pp. 35–78. Skira, Milan; Musée Barbier-Mueller, Geneva.

Barendregt, B. 2002. Representing the Ancient Other. *Indonesia and the Malay World* 30(88):277–308. doi.org/10.1080/1363981022000064366

Barnard, T.P. 2013. Thomas Dias' journey to Central Sumatra. In Harta Karun (ed.), *Hidden treasures on Indonesian and Asian-European History from the VOC Archives in Jakarta*, document 1. Arsip Nasional Republik, Jakarta.

Bellwood, P. 1985. *Prehistory of the Indo-Malaysian Archipelago*. Academic Press, Sydney.

Bloembergen, M. and M. Eickhoff 2015. The colonial archaeological hero reconsidered: Postcolonial perspectives on the 'discovery' of pre-historic Indonesia. In G. Eberhardt and F. Link (eds), *Historiographical Approaches to Past Archaeological Research*, pp. 133–164. Edition Topoi, Berlin.

Bonatz, D. 2009. The Neolithic in the Highlands of Sumatra: Problems of definition. In D. Bonatz, J.N. Miksic, J.D. Neidel and M. Tjoa-Bonatz (eds), *From Distant Tales: Archaeology and Ethnohistory in the Highlands of Sumatra*, pp. 43–74. Cambridge Scholars Publishing, Newcastle upon Tyne.

Bonatz, D. 2012. A Highland perspective on the archaeology and settlement history of Sumatra. *Archipel* 84:35–81. doi.org/10.3406/arch.2012.4361

Bonatz, D. 2019a. Megalithic landscapes in the Highland of Sumatra. In J. Müller, M. Hinz and M. Wunderlich (eds), *Megaliths—Societies—Landscapes. Early Monumentality and Social Differentiation in Neolithic Europe*, Volume 1, pp. 407–428. Proceedings of the international conference 'Megaliths—Societies—Landscapes', Kiel, Germany, 16–20 June 2015. Rudolf Habelet, Bonn.

Bonatz, D. 2019b. Adityvarman's Royal Centre? The settlement site on Bukit Gombak. In M.L. Tjoa-Bonatz (ed.), *A View from the Highlands. Archaeology and Settlement History of West Sumatra, Indonesia*, pp. 96–120. ISEAS Publishing, Singapore.

Bonatz, D. 2021. *Megalithen im Indonesischen Archipel*. Philipp von Zabern, Mainz.

Bonatz, D., J.D. Neidel and M.L. Tjoa-Bonatz 2006. The megalithic complex of highland Jambi. An archaeological perspective. *Bijdragen tot de Taal-, Land- en Volkenkunde / Journal of the Humanities and Social Sciences of Southeast Asia* 162(4):490–522. doi.org/10.1163/22134379-90003664

Braudel, F. 1972. *The Mediterranean and the Mediterranean World in the Age of Philip II*, Volume 1 (S. Reynolds, trans.). Harper & Row, New York.

Braudel, F. 2009. History and the Social Sciences. The *Longue Durée* (I. Wallerstein, trans.). *Review* 32(2): 171–203.

Brinkgreve, F. and R. Sulistianingsih 2009. *Sumatra: Crossroads of Cultures*. KITLV Press, Leiden.

Clarence-Smith, W.G. 2004. Elephants, horses, and the coming of Islam in northern Sumatra. *Indonesia and the Malay World* 32:271–284. doi.org/10.1080/1363981042000320161

Collins, W.A. 1998. *The Guritan of Radin Suane. A Study of the Besemah Oral Epic from South Sumatra*. Bibliotheca Indonesia 28. KITLV Press, Leiden.

Djakfar, H.I. and I. Idris 2001. *Menguak tabir prasejarah di alam kerinci*. Dinas Pariwisata dan Kebudayaan Kabupaten Kerinci, Pangkalan Kerinci, Indonesia.

Drakard, J.A. 1999. *Kingdom of Words: Language and Power in Sumatra*. Oxford University Press, Oxford.

Edwards McKinnon E. 2011. Continuity and change in South Indian involvement in northern Sumatra: The inferences of archaeological evidence from Kota Cina and Lamreh. In P.-Y. Manguin, A. Mani and G. Wade (eds), *Early Interactions between South and Southeast Asia: Reflections on Cross-Cultural Exchange*, pp. 137–160. ISEAS Publishing, Singapore. doi.org/10.1355/9789814311175-009

Greger, J.D. 2019. The burial site on Bukit Kincir. In M.L. Tjoa-Bonatz (ed.), *A View from the Highlands. Archaeology and Settlement History of West Sumatra, Indonesia*, pp. 120–127. ISEAS Publishing, Singapore.

Guillaud, D., H. Forestier and T. Simanjuntak 2009. Mounds, tombs, and tales: Archaeology and oral tradition in the South Sumatra Highlands. In D. Bonatz, J.N. Miksic, J.D. Neidel and M. Tjoa-Bonatz (eds), *From Distant Tales: Archaeology and Ethnohistory in the Highlands of Sumatra*, pp. 416–433. Cambridge Scholars Publishing, Newcastle upon Tyne.

Guillot, C. (ed.) 1998. *Histoire de Barus. Le site de Lobu Tua, I: Études et documents*. Cahiers d'Archipel 30. Archipel, Paris.

Guillot, C. (ed.) 2003. *Histoire de Barus. Le site de Lobu Tua, II: Études archéologiques et documents.* Cahiers d'Archipel 30. Archipel, Paris.

Guy, J. 2011. Tamil merchants and the Hindu-Buddhist diaspora in early Southeast Asia. In P.-Y. Manguin, A. Mani and G. Wade (eds), *Early Interactions between South and Southeast Asia: Reflections on Cross-Cultural Exchange*, pp. 243–262. ISEAS Publishing, Singapore. doi.org/10.1355/9789814311175-014

Jones, S. 1997. *The Archaeology of Ethnicity: Constructing Identities in the Past and Present.* Routledge, New York.

Kulke, H. 2009. Adityawarman's highland kingdom 2009. In D. Bonatz, J.N. Miksic, J.D. Neidel and M. Tjoa-Bonatz (eds), *From Distant Tales: Archaeology and Ethnohistory in the Highlands of Sumatra*, pp. 229–252. Cambridge Scholars Publishing, Newcastle upon Tyne.

Manguin, P.-Y. 2009. Southeast Sumatra in Protohistoric and Srivijaya times: Upstream-downstream relations and the settlement of the peneplain. In D. Bonatz, J.N. Miksic, J.D. Neidel and M. Tjoa-Bonatz (eds), *From Distant Tales: Archaeology and Ethnohistory in the Highlands of Sumatra*, pp. 434–451. Cambridge Scholars Publishing, Newcastle upon Tyne.

Miksic, J.N. 1986. A valley of megaliths in West Sumatra. Mahat (Schnitger's Aoer Doeri) revisited. *Journal of the Malaysian Branch of the Royal Asiatic Society* 59:27–32.

Miksic, J.N. 1996. *Indonesian Heritage, Volume 1: Ancient History.* Editions Didier Millet; Archipelago Press, Singapore.

Miksic, J.N. 2004a. The classical cultures of Indonesia. In I. Glover and P. Bellwood (eds), *Southeast Asia. From Prehistory to History*, pp. 234–256. Routledge, London.

Miksic, J.N. 2004b. From megaliths to tombstones: The transition from prehistory to the early Islamic period in highland West Sumatra. *Journal of the Malaysian Branch of the Royal Asiatic Society* 32:191–210. doi.org/10.1080/1363981042000320134

Miksic, J.N. 2009. Highland-lowland connections in Jambi, South Sumatra, and West Sumatra, 11th to 14th centuries. In D. Bonatz, J.N. Miksic, J.D. Neidel and M. Tjoa-Bonatz (eds), *From Distant Tales: Archaeology and Ethnohistory in the Highlands of Sumatra*, pp. 75–103. Cambridge Scholars Publishing, Newcastle upon Tyne.

Miksic, J.N. and G.Y. Goh 2017. *Ancient Southeast Asia.* Routledge, London. doi.org/10.4324/9781315641119

Perret, D. and H. Surachman 2011. South Asia and the Tapanuli area (north-west Sumatra): Ninth-fourteenth centuries CE. In P.-Y. Manguin, A. Mani and G. Wade (eds), *Early Interactions between South and Southeast Asia: Reflections on Cross-Cultural Exchange*, pp. 161–176. ISEAS Publishing, Singapore. doi.org/10.1355/9789814311175-010

Perret, D. and H. Surachman (eds) 2009. *Histoire de Barus-Sumatra, III: Regards sur une place marchande de l'océan Indien (XIIe-milieu du XVIIe s.).* Cahiers d'Archipel 38. Archipel, Paris.

Rangkuti, N. Nasruddin, Triwuryani, A. Gultom, R. Fahlen and R. Setyorini 2017. *Megalitik Pasemah: Warisan Budaya Penanda Zaman.* Balai Pelestarian Cagar Budaya, Jambi, Indonesia.

Reid, A. 1997. 'Inside out': The colonial displacement of Sumatra's population. In P. Boomgaard, F. Colombijn and D. Henley (eds), *Paper Landscapes. Explorations in the Environmental History of Indonesia*, pp. 61–87. KITLV Press, Leiden.

Reid, A. 2009. Is there a Batak history? In D. Bonatz, J.N. Miksic, J.D. Neidel and M. Tjoa-Bonatz (eds), *From Distant Tales: Archaeology and Ethnohistory in the Highlands of Sumatra*, pp. 104–119. Cambridge Scholars Publishing, Newcastle upon Tyne.

Schnitger, F.M. 1939a. *Forgotten Kingdoms in Sumatra*. Reprint 1989. Oxford University Press, Singapore.

Schnitger, F.M. 1939b. Monuments mégalithiques de Sumatra-septentrional. *Revue des Arts Asiatiques* 13(1):23–27.

Schnitger, F.M. 1941–1942. Megalithen vom Batakland und Nias. *Jahrbuch für prähistorische und ethnographische Kunst* 16:220–252.

Sibeth, A. 1990. *Mit den Ahnen leben: Batak Menschen in Indonesien*. Edition Hansjörg Mayer, Stuttgart.

Steimer-Herbet, T. 2018. *Indonesian Megaliths. A Forgotten Cultural Heritage*. Archaeopress, Oxford.

Subbarayalu, Y. 1998. The Tamil merchant-guild inscription at Barus: A rediscovery. In Guillot, C. (ed.), *Histoire de Barus. Le site de Lobu Tua, I: Études et documents*, pp. 25–33. Cahiers d'Archipel 30. Archipel, Paris.

Tjoa-Bonatz, M.L. (ed.) 2019a. *A View from the Highlands. Archaeology and Settlement History of West Sumatra, Indonesia*. ISEAS Publishing, Singapore. doi.org/10.1355/9789814843027

Tjoa-Bonatz, M.L. 2019b. The Minangkabau and Adityavarman. In M.L. Tjoa-Bonatz (ed.), *A View from the Highlands. Archaeology and Settlement History of West Sumatra, Indonesia*, pp. 30–42. ISEAS Publishing, Singapore.

Tombrink, E.P. 1870. Hindoe-Monumenten in de Bovenlanden van Palembang, als bron van geschiedkundig onderzoek. *Tijdschrift van het Bataviaasch Genootschap van Kunsten en Wetenschappen* 19:1–45.

Triwurjani, R. 2013. *Tradisi Megalitik di Lima Puluh Koto*. Penerbit Wedatama Widya Sastra, Jakarta.

Ullmann, L. 1850. Hindoe-beelden in de Binnenlanden van Palembang. *Indisch Archief. Tijdschrift voor de Indien* 1:493–494.

van der Hoop, A.N.J.Th. à Th. 1932. *Megalithic Remains in South-Sumatra* (W. Shirlaw, trans.). W.J. Thieme, Zutphen, the Netherlands.

van Heekeren, H.R. 1958. *The Bronze-Iron Age of Indonesia*. Verhandelingen van het Koninklijk Instituut van Taal-, Land- en Volkenkunde 22. Martinus Nijhoff, The Hague. doi.org/10.26530/OAPEN_613360

Viner, A.C. and E.L. Kaplan 1981. The Changing Pakpak Batak. *Journal of the Malaysian Branch of the Royal Asian Society* 45(1):93–105.

von Rosenberg, H. 1878. *Der Malayische Archipel. Land und Leute. Land und Leute in Schilderungen, gesammelt während eines 30jährigen Aufenthaltes in den Kolonien*. Gustav Weigel, Leipzig.

Warneck, J. 1909. *Die Religion der Batak. Ein paradigma für die Animistischen Religionen des Indischen Archipels*. Vandenhoeck & Ruprecht, Göttingen.

Watson, C.W. 2009. Tambo Kerinci. In D. Bonatz, J.N. Miksic, J.D. Neidel and M. Tjoa-Bonatz (eds), *From Distant Tales: Archaeology and Ethnohistory in the Highlands of Sumatra*, pp. 253–271. Cambridge Scholars Publishing, Newcastle upon Tyne.

Westenenk, L.C. 1922. De Hindoe oudheden in de Pasemah Hoogvlakte (Residentie Palembang). *Oudheidkundig Verslag* 1:31–37.

Wolters, O.W. 1967. *Early Indonesian Commerce: A Study of the Origins of Sri Vijaya*. Cornell University Press, Ithaca, NY.

Ziegler, A. and A. Viaro 1999. Stones of power: Statues and megalithism in Nias. In J.P. Barbier (ed.), *Messages in Stone: Statues and Sculptures from Tribal Indonesia in the Collections of the Barbier-Mueller Museum*, pp. 35–78. Skira, Milan; Musée Barbier-Mueller, Geneva.

Znoj, H. 2009. Social structure and mobility in historical perspective: Sungai Tenang in Highland Jambi. In D. Bonatz, J.N. Miksic, J.D. Neidel and M. Tjoa-Bonatz (eds), *From Distant Tales: Archaeology and Ethnohistory in the Highlands of Sumatra*, pp. 347–366. Cambridge Scholars Publishing, Newcastle upon Tyne.

13

The material culture and heritage value of Lida Ajer Cave in West Sumatra

Gilbert J. Price, Gerrell M. Drawhorn, Sue O'Connor, Yahdi Zaim, Yan Rizal, Aswan, Mika R. Puspaningrum, Agus Tri Hascaryo and Julien Louys

Abstract

Lida Ajer Cave, in West Sumatra, Indonesia, is the location of remarkable fossils that document the evolution of humans. The cave is known for its palaeontological significance, but its historical record has received considerably less attention. It was first documented in written records by the Dutch palaeoanthropologist Eugène Dubois in the late 1880s. Not finding what he had hoped for, Dubois abandoned his work there and shifted his attention to Java, where he later famously reported the discovery of 'Java Man' (known today as *Homo erectus*). Specimens from Lida Ajer became the focus of renewed investigations in 1948, when the fossilised remains of modern humans were recognised in Dubois' collection. Later dating of these fossils demonstrated that people occupied the region around 70,000 years ago, making them the world's oldest record of *Homo sapiens* in rainforest environments. Relics of Dubois' time in the cave are still evident there, including excavation pits and refuse. More recent oral histories and physical objects (e.g. grenade shards) relate to the cave's connections with the military activities of World War II and the birth of modern Indonesia. Abandoned infrastructure for bird's nest harvesting in the cave provides a tangible reminder of rapidly diminishing native species that have been exploited for commercial gain on a global scale. This insignificant-looking hole in the ground has, remarkably, provided major insights into human evolution, human use of speleological resources, and cultural appropriation in historic times.

Keywords: cultural heritage, scientific and historic significance, Padang Highlands, bird's nest soup

Abstrak

Gua Lida Ajer berada di Provinsi Sumatra Barat, Indonesia, merupakan lokasi ditemukannya fosil-fosil luar biasa yang menyimpan bukti evolusi manusia. Gua ini dikenal karena signifikansi sejarah temuan fosil paleontologis Zaman Kuarter, tetapi catatan sejarah penemuannya kurang mendapat perhatian. Temuan paleontologi ini, pertama kali didokumentasikan dalam catatan tertulis oleh ahli paleoantropologi Belanda bernama Eugène Dubois pada akhir tahun 1880-an. Tidak menemukan apa yang dia harapkan di awal, Dubois kemudian menghentikan penelitiannya di Gua Lida Ajer dan kemudian beralih ke Pulau Jawa, di mana ia melaporkan temuannya yang paling terkenal yaitu 'Manusia Jawa' (sekarang dikenal sebagai *Homo erectus*). Spesimen dari Lida Ajer menjadi fokus penyelidikan kembali sejak tahun 1948 ketika sisa-sisa fosil manusia modern ditemukan pada koleksi Dubois. Hasil analisis pertanggalan fosil-fosil ini menunjukkan bahwa hominid telah berada di wilayah tersebut sekitar 70 ribu tahun yang lalu, sebagai *Homo sapiens* tertua secara global di lingkungan hutan hujan. Benda-benda peninggalan Dubois ketika melakukan penelitian di dalam ruang gua masih dapat dilihat berupa kotak galian ekskavasi dan lubang sampah. Selain itu benda-benda masa kolonial ditemukan pula misalnya pecahan granat, yang berhubungan dengan agresi militer Perang Dunia II serta masa kemerdekaan Indonesia. Kondisi Gua Lida Ajer saat ini sangat terbengkalai, hanya dimanfaatkan untuk pengambilan sarang burung Walet yang sebagai bahan makanan sup sarang burung, padahal bukti paleontologis di dalam gua ini merupakan bukti nyata tentang spesies endimik yang cepat mengalami kepunahan akibat eksploitasi untuk komersialisasi global. Kotak ekskavasi Dubois tampaknya tidak signifikan, namun telah memainkan peran yang luar biasa dalam memberikan wawasan mengenai evolusi manusia, eksploitasi antropogenik sumber daya speleologis, dan pengaruh budaya pada masa sejarah.

Kata kunci: warisan budaya, keilmuan, signifikansi sejarah, tinggian daratan Padang, sup sarang burung

Introduction

Lida Ajer is a small cave in the uplifted limestone of the Padang Highlands of West Sumatra, Indonesia. It is remarkable for its contribution to palaeoanthropology and palaeontology, but its historic significance has received considerably less attention. It was first explored and documented in the writings of Eugène Dubois in the late 1880s. Dubois soon abandoned his Sumatran work to continue his search in Java, which culminated in the discovery of 'Java Man', now *Homo erectus* (Dubois 1894). In the 1940s, Dutch palaeontologist Dirk Hooijer identified teeth of *Homo sapiens* among Dubois' Lida Ajer fossil collection (Hooijer 1948). Our recent palaeontological work in Lida Ajer in 2015 and 2018 focused on placing these fossil human teeth into a temporal framework; this is critical for understanding the timing of the arrival and spread of humans in the region. Dating the depositional context of these human fossils indicated that they are around 70,000 years old, making them the world's oldest record of *H. sapiens* in rainforest environments and among the earliest evidence for the migration of our species into Asia (Louys et al. 2022; Westaway et al. 2017). This finding is particularly significant, given that anatomically modern human populations had left Africa by 85 ka (Groucutt et al. 2018) and, before that time, are not known to have occupied rainforest habitats. The earliness of the Lida Ajer date thus testifies to the adaptability of the species.

Lida Ajer clearly has outstanding global scientific heritage value due to the probable age of its human fossils, a discovery that provides major insights into human evolution. It also has outstanding global historical and heritage value as a result of its special association with the lives and work of Dubois and Hooijer and their contributions to the development of the disciplines of palaeoanthropology and palaeontology.

During our visits to Lida Ajer, we observed artefacts relating to Dubois' time working the fossil deposits in the cave, including his excavation pits and refuse. Discussions with local townspeople also revealed an intriguing local history of the cave, with several individuals recounting the cave's use by Japanese and Allied forces during the military activities of World War II as well as its role in the birth of the Indonesian resistance movement that arose from the war. A grenade found in one of the chambers supports these local accounts. This finding has considerable historical significance, exemplifying the story of the Indonesian islands' role in the Asian arena of the war and Indonesia's subsequent independence. Most recently, the cave has been used by local people as a source of swiftlet nests to be sold and made into bird's nest soup. The cave contains the remains of the physical structures they used to ascend the high cave walls to collect the nests. These finds demonstrate continuous cave use through to today and constitute a tangible reminder of the unsustainable exploitation of wild resources for commercial gain that is occurring on a global scale. The aim of this chapter is to discuss all these different findings in the context of the broader heritage value of the cave.

Lida Ajer: A significant place in the story of human evolution

Biographical details of Dubois' life can be found in Theunissen (1985) and Albers and de Vos (2010). More detailed examinations of Dubois' time in Sumatra are provided in Chapters 2 and 3. Upon arriving in western Sumatra, Dubois channelled his energies into fossil hunting. One of the first caves he visited was called Ngalau Lida Ajer ('water tongue cave'). This cave is in the uplifted limestones of the Padang Highlands, southwest of Payakumbuh City (see Figures 13.1 and 13.2). During the second half of 1888, Dubois regularly visited the cave, and with the support of the Dutch military and the assistance of local workers, hundreds of fossil remains were excavated (Albers and de Vos 2010).

Figure 13.1: Map of the Sumatra region showing Lida Ajer and other major locations mentioned in this chapter.

Source: Map by Gilbert Price.

The diversity of this fossil assemblage is quite remarkable and includes orangutans, pigs, rhinoceroses, tigers, deer, elephants and porcupines (de Vos 1983; Louys et al. 2021b). However, as far as Dubois was concerned, fossils of the 'missing link' (i.e. a species ancestral to *Homo sapiens*) were not apparent in the deposit. He thought that because (in his understanding) the fossils belonged to relatively modern animals, the deposits were probably too young to contain the ancestral human that he was convinced once inhabited Southeast Asia (Hooijer 1948).

In 1948, another Dutchman, Dirk Albert Hooijer, re-examined the fossils from Lida Ajer and other Sumatran caves that had been worked Dubois. In investigating these assemblages, Hooijer not only formulated new understandings about the evolution and diversity of orangutans, but also described two teeth of *Homo sapiens* (Hooijer 1948).

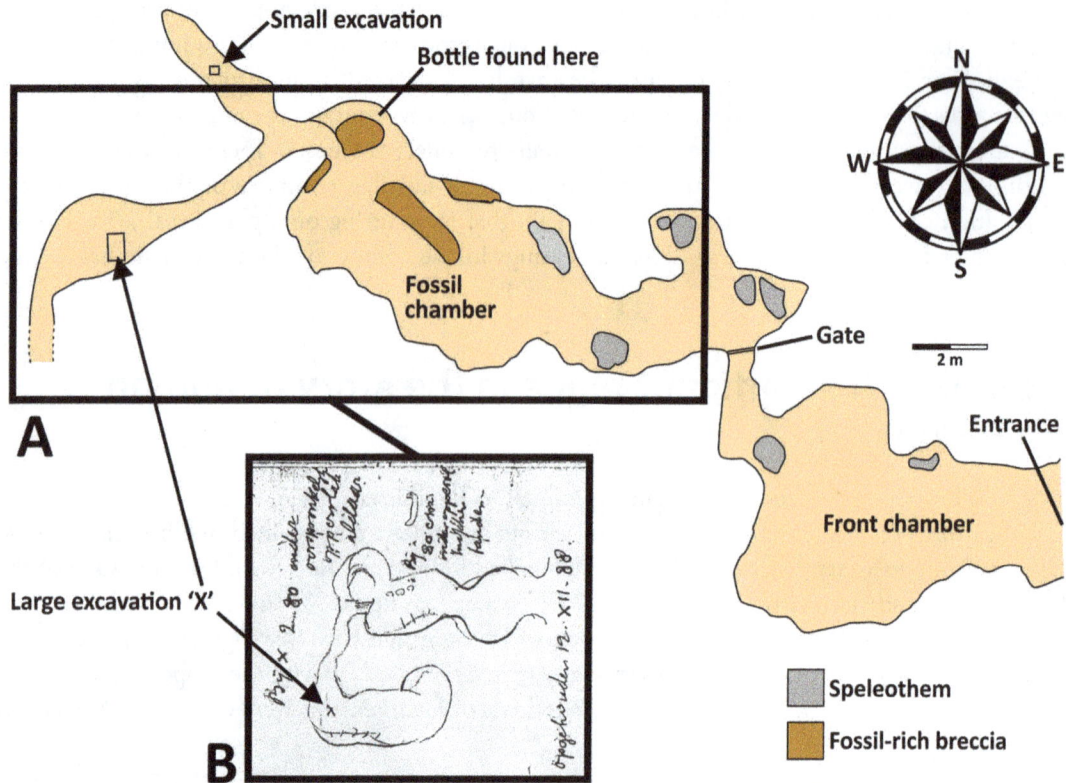

Figure 13.2: Plan views of Lida Ajer Cave.

A: Modern cartographic map. B: Rough sketch from Dubois' field notes.

Source: Map and drawings by Gilbert Price and Julien Louys with inset by Eugène Dubois (Dubois n.d.).

X Marks the spot: Early modern humans in the rainforest

Lida Ajer itself is situated high above a valley in the Payakumbuh region. It has a horizontal entrance approximately 4.8 m wide by 2.1 m high that opens into a large cavern (see Figure 13.2). The entrance chamber then narrows to a tight spot (where a gate has been installed) before widening again into the main fossil chamber, which is oriented east–west. It was in this chamber that datable geological and palaeontological samples were sought (Louys et al. 2021b, 2022; Smith et al. 2021; Westaway et al. 2017).

To the modern visitor, the cave offers a quiet, dry shelter protected from the heavy rains that fall throughout the year. Despite this, an analysis of the fossil assemblage indicates that ancient humans did not necessarily use the cave as a site of habitation. Rather, the bones and teeth of humans and other fauna were brought into the cave as a result of the scavenging activities of porcupines, as noted early on by Dubois (Chapter 2, this volume). These rodents commonly scavenge skeletal elements from carrion scattered across their local environment and bring them to the caves, where they are gnawed. Thus, these remains periodically accumulate in the caves and over time make their way into the fossil record. Unlike bone, the outer layers of (most) teeth are composed of tough, durable enamel, a biological compound that porcupines are unwilling to gnaw on. This probably explains the preponderance of fossil teeth (such as the one in Figure 13.3) among the skeletal elements.

Figure 13.3: Fossil orangutan tooth collected from the fossil chamber of Lida Ajer Cave.

Source: Photograph by Gilbert Price.

During our recent surveys of the cave (Louys et al. 2021a), guided by a copy of Dubois' original field notes (see Chapter 2, this volume for details of these), we identified two specific areas in the cave that were subjected to his 1888 excavations. The first area occurs towards the end of a small chamber below and directly northwest of the main fossil chamber. To the west of the small chamber, a passage heads southwest and leads to a larger excavation pit halfway along another small chamber. The pit, marked with an 'X' in Dubois' field notes, is 1.3 × 0.9 m across, and around 1.1 m deep (Figure 13.2b). We took geological samples from this pit for dating and geomorphological investigation (Smith et al. 2021).

Time in a bottle: Lida Ajer and Dubois' search for the 'missing link'

During the 2018 survey, a fragment of a glass bottle (see Figure 13.4) was collected as a surface specimen in a cramped but wide subchamber at the northwestern edge of the main fossil chamber (see Figure 13.2). The entrance to the subchamber is only 30–40 cm high, and the height decreases to only a few centimetres about 3 m in from the entrance. Thus, the passage is very difficult to access, and in historical times, was clearly not a thoroughfare.

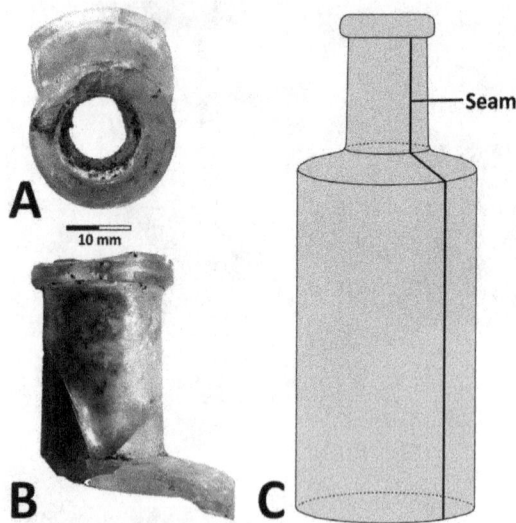

Figure 13.4: Bottle fragment from Lida Ajer Cave.

A: Top view. B: Side view. C: Reconstruction.

Source: Photograph and drawing by Gilbert Price.

The bottle fragment includes the bore, finish, neck and part of the shoulder (Figure 13.4). The bore is circular, with an inner diameter of 12 mm and an outer diameter of 22 mm. The finish is 4 mm deep and has no distinct lip or collar. Its edges are vertical relative to the depth of the bottle. It connects to the neck at an angle of c. 90°. The neck is 18.5 mm in outer diameter and 24 mm deep. It connects to the shoulder at an angle of c. 100°. Assuming that the bottle was symmetrical, it is evident that its body was cylindrical. In these aspects, the bottle resembles those used for storing medicine or tonics (see Figure 13.4c).

Although the bottle fragment lacks maker markings, aspects of its manufacture allow it to be dated to the late nineteenth century. A faint straight seam extends up the bottle through the neck but does not extend into the finish. Bottle moulds showing such features were commonly used between AD 1880 and 1890 (Polak 2016).

Significantly, this finding corresponds well with the time when Dubois conducted his palaeontological investigations of the cave. Although we are not able to definitely link the bottle to a Dutch manufacturer, we would be surprised if the bottle was not, at least, associated with Dubois or his workforce. Future archaeological investigations in this part of the cave would probably yield additional artefacts potentially associated with Dubois' endeavours.

Bombs among bones: Lida Ajer and the World War II Asian arena

The Japanese invasion of Sumatra during World War II marked a significant turning point in the quest for the independence of the Dutch East Indies. The island had been under the control of the Netherlands since 1819. Many Sundanese welcomed the Japanese invasion of early 1942 and considered the Japanese as potential liberators. Of course, that sentiment soon changed when the hardships of the war became apparent (Nieuwenhof 1984).

Sensing that a threat from the Japanese was imminent, the Allies assembled the American-British-Dutch-Australian Command in late 1941. Troops were rallied, with Australia sending more than 3,000 servicemen to Sumatra. Neighbouring Singapore fell in February 1942, and Sumatra fell during the following month. Although huge numbers of Allies were either captured or killed in Singapore, some escaped and travelled west through Sumatra (Wigmore 1957). Many eventually made their way to Padang, where they were evacuated from the coastal port of Emmahaven, today known as Teluk Bayur (Walker 1956). Significantly, the Padang Highlands are west-southwest of Singapore, thus it is probable that many of the escapees from Singapore passed through the highlands.

Anecdotal information from local villagers indicates that Sundanese present at the time used the caves in the highlands to avoid the Japanese. No physical evidence for this exists, as far as we are aware. However, during our 2018 survey of Lida Ajer, the half-shell of a grenade was discovered in the main fossil chamber of the cave (see Figure 13.5).

This fragment is approximately 9 cm in length and 6 cm in diameter and is of the classic 'pineapple' shape, narrowing at both the top and bottom. Deep grooves extend vertically and horizontally over the shell, providing a raised and elongated 'waffle' or rectangular-patterned grip. The hole for the filling plug is intact (see Figure 13.5b), although the plug itself is missing. On the basis of its morphology and context, the grenade is clearly a 36M grenade, a British-made model otherwise known as a 'Mills bomb' (Gordon 2011). The 36M differs from similar US-made pineapple-shaped grenades (e.g. the Mk 2 grenade) in that the rectangles in the grip are oriented with their long sides vertical rather than horizontal (some US-made models have a pattern of almost-square shapes). The preservation state of the grenade (i.e. as a half-shell) suggests that it was wet at the time of detonation and did not shatter in the intended manner.

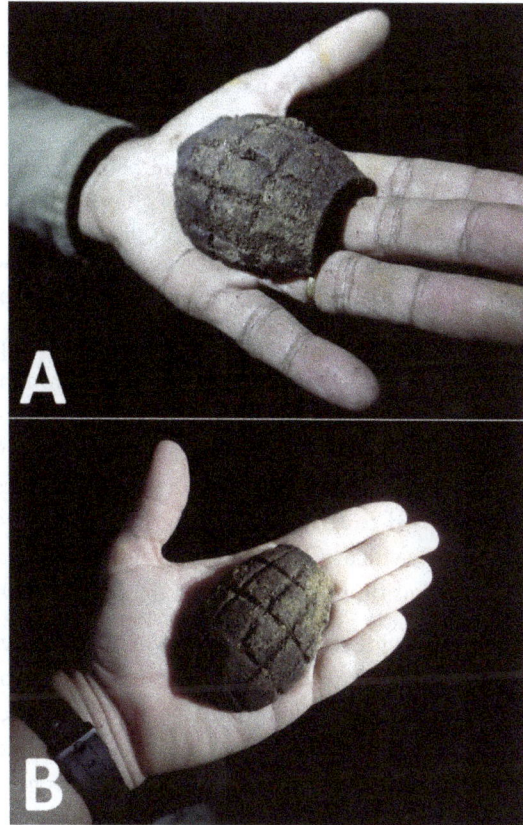

Figure 13.5: Half-shell of 36M grenade found inside Lida Ajer Cave.

A: Oblique view. B: Side view.

Source: Photograph by Gilbert Price.

The 36M model was a defensive fragmentation grenade developed in 1918 by the Mills Munitions Factory in Britain (Prenderghast 2018) and was British military standard issue from 1930 to 1972 (Gordon 2011). Its design was based on earlier Mills grenade models, such as the No. 5 and No. 23. During World War II, 36M grenades were also supplied to non-British Allies, including the Australian and Indian forces, which also had prominent roles in the Southeast Asian region during the conflict. The fact that the earlier Mills grenade models were not manufactured after 1918, together with the preponderance of the 36M model in Sumatra during World War II, excludes the Lida Ajer specimen from being an earlier model.

How the 36M grenade casing came to be in Lida Ajer Cave remains unknown, but it was probably brought to the region during or soon after World War II. It is possible that British, Australian or Indian escapees from Singapore, or from Sumatra itself, brought the grenade to the cave while travelling west to Padang.

An alternative hypothesis was mentioned to GMD on his first visit to Lida Ajer in 1996. He was told by local people in the nearby village of Sialang Indah that the cave was used as a hideout for Indonesian revolutionaries who were fighting the returning Dutch colonial army. On 15 January 1949, a meeting of West Sumatran militia leaders was to be held in the nearby town of Sitajuh Batur to develop a strategy for fighting the rising Dutch forces. Having received intelligence that the meeting was to take place, Dutch commandos attacked before dawn, killing 49 participants (Kahin 1974:109). A recollection of the event (which is called Peristiwa Sitajuh Batur, 'Incident at Sitajuh Batur') from a survivor named Syamsulbahar confirms that caves near Lida Ajer were used at least temporarily as places of refuge after the attack:

> Selasi memeriksa mayat, kami berjumpa dengan Sdr. Dahlan Ibrahim sedang basuh-kayub menutar-mutar mengeringkan pistol kosongya. Rupaaya ia semput didalam ngalau (Gua) dalam bendang yang memang dalam ditepi tebing itu. [After examining the corpses, we met with Capt. Dahlan Ibrahim, who was still soaking wet, drying his empty pistol. He had managed to hide in a cave in a cliff face after crossing the paddy.] (Damhoeri 1949:20)

Local Indonesian fighters, such as the Tentara Republik Indonesia Resimen Istim ewa Komandemen Sumatera (established in 1948), may have brought the grenade to the cave after capturing munitions during British occupation (e.g. Hamka 1966). In particular, a raid on the 26th British Indian Division's military arsenal at Rimbo Kalueng, north of Padang, provided a cache of Allied vehicles, weapons and munitions, including hand grenades (Handayani 2021). Also, after the Dutch military were allowed to return to Padang in August 1946, there was an increase in desertions of Punjabi troops; McMillan (2006:157–158) estimates that as many as 137 deserters from the 26th British Indian Division may have joined the rebels with their weapons.

Anecdotal evidence from local townspeople provided to GMD suggests that the Dutch later threw hand grenades into Lida Ajer Cave. Fragments of a detonated hand grenade, mistaken as ceramics until handled, were found in the mouth of the cave by GMD in 1998. The grenade may have exploded accidentally as a result of the unstable nature of the explosive. It is important to note here that the Dutch manufactured their own grenades and did not use the pineapple-shaped design (and nor did the Japanese); thus, the recently found Lida Ajer specimen cannot have had a Dutch origin (unless it came from the 'Free' Dutch Forces, who might have received British munitions after the Australian and Indian interim forces were recalled).

Spit in the soup: Local ways of life and diminishing wild resources

Lida Ajer has continued to be of use to local people until recent times. Although the cave's fossils are of no interest to them, the cave is still regularly visited for the harvesting of swiftlet nests. Swiftlets (various species of *Aerodramus*) use the cave as a roosting site, constructing intricate nests on the walls and ceiling (see Figure 13.6). The nest is made from the bird's hardened saliva and comprises up to c. 60% protein, with the remainder being a mixture of carbohydrates, water, and inorganic ash (Thorburn 2015). The nests are whitish in colour and resemble the flesh of a coconut, being dense and damp (Shaw 1992).

The nests are used for making soup. Despite being affectionately regarded as the 'caviar of the East' (Marcone 2005), the nests lack flavour and require the addition of broths and sugars to make them delectable (Thorburn 2015). Bird's nest soup is a sought-after delicacy among Chinese gourmands, especially for its supposed health benefits, which include cellular proliferation, fast recovery from illness, and resistance to the effects of ageing (e.g. Kong et al. 1987; Ng et al. 1986). The nests are a valuable commodity, fetching up to US$3,000 for 1 kg of well-formed, clean nests (Thorburn 2015).

Figure 13.6: Long striations on cave walls and ceilings indicative of harvested swiftlet nests in Lida Ajer Cave (former PhD student Holly Smith for scale).

Note: The striations are the result of a special knife used to scrape the surface of the cave wall without leaving human oils (from hands) on the surface.

Source: Photograph by Gilbert Price.

The swiftlet nests are clearly highly valued by the local people, as evidenced by a metal gate that has been installed inside the cave between the first and second chambers (Figure 13.2). The purpose of the gate is to prevent insidious over-harvesting of the nests. The gate was locked when we visited in 2015 but was found open during our 2018 survey. Evidently, despite preventive measures, the cave had been over-exploited during that time: no active swiftlets were observed in the cave in 2018. Extensive, but temporarily abandoned, infrastructure for harvesting the swiftlet nests still existed in the cave. This included timber for erecting scaffolds to aid in the monitoring and collection of the nests. It is probable that swiftlets will reoccupy the cave, given time.

Discussion

In addition to being a site of critical importance for understanding the origin of our species, Lida Ajer preserves material culture from three distinct but equally important periods of Sumatra's history that underline the cave's heritage significance. The first, represented by the remains of Dubois' excavations and a glass bottle, provide physical evidence of Dubois' nineteenth-century exploration of the cave during his search for the 'missing link'. Hominins were described from Dubois' Lida Ajer fossils by Hooijer and are, to date, the oldest examples of *Homo sapiens* from Indonesia (Louys et al. 2022; Westaway et al. 2017), establishing the cave as a heritage site of both scientific and historical importance.

Dubois' focus on caves in looking for the 'missing link' is unsurprising. He was aware that caves commonly produced well-preserved fossils, often in abundance, and thus represented an obvious place to begin his investigations. This belief was probably bolstered by Dubois' own personal experience exploring caves in his youth. This focus might also have been partly due to the then-common belief that wild, primitive people inhabited caves, a belief enshrined biologically by Linnaeus, who erected the species *Homo troglodytes* in 1758; this species was said to be a resident of the Malay world (Skott 2014). Dubois, or, often more accurately, Dubois' workers, extracted hundreds of fossils from Lida Ajer. Dubois clearly made a considerable effort to conduct systematic excavations: the pit observed in Lida Ajer is roughly square in outline, with sheer sides, quite unlike any examples of guano-mining or goldmining pits we have previously observed in Sumatran caves. Likewise, Dubois took extensive field notes during the Lida Ajer excavations. The tangible record of Dubois' exploration in Lida Ajer, together with Hooijer's later descriptions, can be considered one record of the philosophical progression of nineteenth-century thinking about the evolution of our species. (During his later efforts in the region, fewer details were recorded. It is clear from his writings that Dubois became progressively disenchanted by his lack of fortune during the Sumatran period of his investigations. Of course, this changed remarkably once he reached Java.)

The second phase of occupation of Lida Ajer Cave, represented by the grenade, exemplifies a period of transition in Sumatra. The island was occupied by the Dutch until 1942, then the Japanese until 1945. Indonesian independence was declared immediately after the capitulation of the Japanese in August 1945. The Dutch then tried to re-establish rule, leading to bitter fighting with Indonesian revolutionaries, including near Lida Ajer (e.g. Kahin 1974), before ceasing their attempts as a result of public pressure in 1949. As to what the grenades were doing in Lida Ajer, we can only speculate. However, oral tradition described by various local people in Payakumbuh City records that during World War II, caves were commonly used by local townspeople seeking shelter, by Japanese soldiers expanding tunnels to make bunkers, and as secure places for munition dumps. It would not be surprising if the cave was also visited during the war by Australian, Indian or British military escapees fleeing the atrocities that were happening in neighbouring Singapore (as well as Sumatra itself) or by Indonesian revolutionaries immediately after the war. This record complements other records of cave use in the Asia-Pacific Theater of World War II (Dixon et al. 2012). Although cave use by the military was probably ubiquitous during this conflict, it has rarely been recorded in the archaeological literature.

Third, the exploitation of swiftlet nests during the late twentieth and early twenty-first centuries signifies the economic importance of cave resources for local townspeople. The broken wooden remains of infrastructure in Lida Ajer, as well as the abandonment of the locked gate between chambers, indicate that the harvest of the nests has ended. We did not observe swiftlets during our visits, suggesting they are functionally extinct within the cave system, although we did see some active nests in other caves of the Padang Highlands during our broader 2018 surveys. Physical evidence of the management of dwindling wildlife resources in a context of increased population growth and the allure of commercial markets—or of its opposite, the over-exploitation of a species to its extinction—will probably continue to dominate the cultural record of the West Sumatran caves of the present century.

Finally, we note the recent report of rock art in the entrance chamber of the cave, adjacent to the main entry point (Arifin and Permana 2022). The age of this art, which contains human figures and other motifs as well as graffiti with Latin characters, is likely to be somewhat recent: less than 150 years old or perhaps substantially younger. This style of rock art has not been found any further into the cave than the entrance chamber and does not appear to have any relationship with the artefacts related to Dubois, World War II or swiftlet nest harvesting. Indeed, Arifin and Permana (2022) proposed a connection between this art and traditional *tasawwuf* rituals (*tasawwuf* is a form of Islamic mysticism, namely Sufism), an unexpected finding considering that continuing Indonesian societies tend not to have been founded on traditional Islamic or Christian beliefs. The style of Lida Ajer's rock art seems different from that of other sites across Indonesia and may be worthy of further investigation (Arifin and Permana 2022).

Conclusions

This seemingly insignificant hole in the ground has outstanding intrinsic heritage value due to its special association with the life and work of Dubois and Hooijer and the role it played in their contribution to the development of the disciplines of palaeoanthropology and palaeontology. Lida Ajer also has outstanding scientific heritage value due to its fossils, which provide major insights into human evolution; significantly, they provide the oldest geological evidence that humans lived in and exploited rainforest environments around 70,000 years ago. As such, Lida Ajer meets UNESCO's Criteria V and VI for nomination for World Heritage status as an 'outstanding example of a traditional human settlement, land-use […] or human interaction with the environment' and one that is 'directly or tangibly associated with events or living traditions, with ideas, or with beliefs, with artistic and literary works of outstanding universal significance' (UNESCO 2021:30).

The cave's use during World War II and the oral histories and archaeology surrounding it exemplify the place of the Indonesian islands in the Asian arena and the birth of Indonesian independence, making it a site of national significance. The material cultural artefacts associated with the extraction of swiftlet nests are physical testament to the ongoing conflict about conserving species that are consumed by humans. This conflict is one that is central to the twentieth- and twenty-first-century discourses of the global conservation movement (e.g. Sodhi and Kenneth 2000).

It is hoped that the diverse heritage value of Lida Ajer will be recognised in a management plan that will see the historic objects and activity areas within the cave system documented and preserved into the future. If Lida Ajer is properly managed in a way that involves local community members, its heritage value has the potential to alleviate some of the pressure on its wild resources by providing another income stream via cultural tourism.

Acknowledgements

We thank Holly Smith and townsfolk from the area surrounding Lida Ajer for their support in the field. Rod Bellars and David Gordon kindly provided assistance with the interpretation of the Mills bomb. Our work was funded by an Australian Future Fellowship (FT160100450) to JL, with additional support from The University of Queensland and the Institut Teknologi Bandung.

References

Albers, P.C.H. and J. de Vos 2010. *Through Eugène Dubois' Eyes: Stills of a Turbulent Life*. Brill, Leiden. doi.org/10.1163/ej.9789004183001.i-186

Arifin, K. and C.E. Permana 2022. Recent rock art sites from West Sumatra. *Asian Perspectives* 61(2):285–316. doi.org/10.1353/asi.2022.0017

Damhoeri, A. 1949. *Peristiwa Sitadjuah Batur 15-1-1949: Pewarta Hayat Syamsul Bahar*. Wikimedia Commons. commons.wikimedia.org/w/index.php?title=File:ADH_0009_A._Damhoeri_-_Peristiwa_Situjuh_Batur_15-1-1949.pdf (accessed 1 February 2022).

de Vos, J. 1983. The *Pongo* faunas from Java and Sumatra and their significance for biostratigraphical and paleo-ecological interpretations. *Proceedings of the Koninklijke Nederlandse Akademie van Wetenschappen, Series B* 86:417–425.

Dixon, B., L. Gilda and L. Bulgrin 2012. The archaeology of World War II Japanese stragglers on the island of Guan and the Bushido Code. *Asian Perspectives* 51:110–127. doi.org/10.1353/asi.2012.0000

Dubois, M.E.F.T. n.d. Unpublished field notes. The Dubois Archive, Naturalis Biodiversity Center, Leiden.

Dubois, M.E.F.T. 1894. *Pithecanthropus erectus. Eine Menschenähnliche Übergangsform aus Java*. G.E. Stechert, New York.

Gordon, D. 2011. *Weapons of the WWII Tommy*. Pictorial Histories Publishing Co., Missoula, MT.

Groucutt, H.S., R. Grün, I.A. Zalmout, N.A. Drake, S.J. Armitage, I. Candy, R Clark-Wilson, J. Louys, P.S. Breeze, M. Duval, L.T. Buck, T.L. Kivell, E. Pomeroy, N.B. Stephens, J.T. Stock, M. Stewart, G.J. Price, L. Kinsley, W.W. Sung, A. Alsharekh, A. Al-Omari, M. Zahir, A.M. Memesh, A.J. Abdulshakoor, A.M. Al-Masari, A.A. Bahameem, K.M.S. Al Murayyi, B. Zahrani, R.L.M. Scerri and M.D. Petraglia 2018. *Homo sapiens* in Arabia by 85,000 years ago. *Nature Ecology & Evolution* 2(5):800–809. doi.org/10.1038/s41559-018-0518-2

Hamka 1966. *Kenang-Kenangan Hidup 2nd Edition*. Pustaka Antara, Kuala Lumpur.

Handayani, R. 2021. Hesbollah Kuranji at the Front Padang Area (1945–1948). *Islam Transformatif: Journal of Islamic Studies* 5(1):85–98.

Hooijer, D.A. 1948. Prehistoric teeth of man and of the orang-utan from central Sumatra, with notes on the fossil orang-utan from Java and southern China. *Zoologische Mededelingen* 29:175–301.

Kahin, A.R. 1974. Some preliminary observations on West Sumatra during the revolution. *Indonesia* 18:77–117. doi.org/10.2307/3350695

Kong, Y.C., W.M. Keung, T.T. Yip, K.M. Ko, S.W. Tsao and M.H. Ng 1987. Evidence that epidermal growth factor is present in swiftlet's (*Collocalia*) nest. *Comparative Biochemistry and Physiology Part B: Comparative Biochemistry* 87(2):221–226. doi.org/10.1016/0305-0491(87)90133-7

Louys, J., M. Duval, G.J. Price, K. Westaway, Y. Zaim, Y. Rizal, Aswan, M. Puspaningrum, A. Trihascaryo, S. Breitenbach, O. Kwiecien, Y. Cai, P. Higgins, P.C.H. Albers, J. de Vos and P. Roberts 2022. Speleological and environmental history of Lida Ajer cave, western Sumatra. *Philosophical Transactions of the Royal Society B* 377:20200494. doi.org/10.1098/rstb.2020.0494

Louys, J., Y. Zaim, Y. Rizal, G.J. Price, Aswan, M.R. Puspaningrum, H. Smith and A.T. Hascaryo 2021a. Palaeontological surveys in Central Sumatra and Bangka. *Berita Sedimentologi* 47(3):50–56. doi.org/10.51835/bsed.2021.47.3.358

Louys, J., Y. Zaim, Y. Rizal, M. Puspaningrum, A. Trihascaryo, G.J. Price, A. Petherick, E. Scholtz and L.R.G. DeSantis 2021b. Sumatran orangutan diets in the Late Pleistocene as inferred from dental microwear texture analysis. *Quaternary International* 603:74–81. doi.org/10.1016/j.quaint.2020.08.040

Marcone, M.F. 2005. Characterization of the edible bird's nest the 'Caviar of the East'. *Food Research International* 38(10):1125–1134. doi.org/10.1016/j.foodres.2005.02.008

McMillan, R. 2006. *British Occupation of Indonesia: 1945-1946: Britain, the Netherlands and the Indonesian Revolution*. Routledge, London. doi.org/10.4324/9780203001943

Ng, M.H., K.H. Chan and Y.C. Kong 1986. Potentiation of mitogenic response by extracts of the swiftlet's (*Collocalia*) nest. *Biochemistry International* 13(3):521–531.

Nieuwenhof, F. 1984. Japanese film propaganda in World War II: Indonesia and Australia. *Historical Journal of Film, Radio and Television* 4(2):161–177. doi.org/10.1080/01439688400260161

Polak, M. 2016. *Antique Trader Bottles. 8th Edition*. Krause Publications, Iola, WI.

Prenderghast, G. 2018. *Repeating and Multi-Fire Weapons: A History from the Zhuge Crossbow Through the AK-47*. McFarland, Jefferson, NC.

Shaw, T.R. 1992. *History of Cave Science. The Exploration and Study of Limestone Caves, to 1900*. 2nd edition. Sydney Speleological Society, Sydney.

Skott, C. 2014. Linnaeus and the troglodyte: Early European encounters with the Malay world and the natural history of man. *Indonesia and the Malay World* 42(123):141–169. doi.org/10.1080/13639811.2014.915084

Smith, H.E., J.J. Bevitt, Y. Zaim, Y. Rizal, Aswan, M.R. Puspaningrum, A. Trihascaryo, G.J. Price, G.E. Webb and J. Louys 2021. High-resolution high-throughput thermal neutron tomographic imaging of fossiliferous cave breccias from Sumatra. *Scientific Reports* 11(1):1–16. doi.org/10.1038/s41598-021-99290-0

Sodhi, N.S. and B.H. Kenneth 2000. Conservation meets consumption. *Trends in Ecology and Evolution* 15(10):431. doi.org/10.1016/S0169-5347(00)01979-0

Theunissen, L.T.G. 1985. *Eugène Dubois en de Aapmens van Java*. Rodopi, Amsterdam.

Thorburn, C.C. 2015. The edible nest swiftlet industry in Southeast Asia: Capitalism meets commensalism. *Human Ecology* 43(1):179–184. doi.org/10.1007/s10745-014-9713-1

UNESCO 2021. *Operational Guidelines for the Implementation of the World Heritage Convention.* UNESCO World Heritage Centre, Paris.

Walker, A.S. 1956. *Australia in the War of 1939–1945, Volume II: Middle East and Far East.* Australian War Memorial, Canberra.

Westaway, K.E., J. Louys, R. Due Awe, M.J. Morwood, G.J. Price, J.X. Zhao, M. Aubert, R. Joannes-Boyau, T. Smith, M.M. Skinner, T. Compton, R.M. Bailey, G.D. van den Bergh, J. de Vos, A.W.G. Pike, C. Stringer, E.W. Saptomo, Y. Rizal, J. Zaim, W.D. Santoso, A. Trihascaryo, L. Kinsley and B. Sulistyanto 2017. An early modern human presence in Sumatra 73,000–63,000 years ago. *Nature* 548:322–325. doi.org/10.1038/nature23452

Wigmore, L. 1957. *Australia in the War of 1939–1945, Volume IV: The Japanese Thrust.* Australian War Memorial, Canberra, Australia.

14

Concluding remarks: Continuing the work in Sumatran connections

Julien Louys, Paul C.H. Albers and Alexandra A.E. van der Geer

Abstract

The island of Sumatra is at a critical crossroads of biodiversity and cultural diversity in Southeast Asia. Despite its central geographical position, the island has received relatively limited archaeological and palaeontological attention in comparison with its immediate neighbours to the north (the Thai-Malay Peninsula) and the south (Java), particularly regarding the Pleistocene. This volume has drawn together the history and current status of Sumatran archaeological and palaeontological research and, it is hoped, provides a firm baseline from which understanding of the island can progress. As hinted throughout the contributions presented in this volume, we are barely scratching the surface in our understanding of the biotic and cultural history of Sumatra, and it is telling that the first large-scale explorations and collections from the island, those conducted by Dubois in the late 1880s, still form the basis of much of the current research presented in these pages. The common theme emerging from all the chapters is one of connection—within Sumatra, but more importantly with the rest of Southeast Asia—biologically, culturally and through time and space. We echo the call of researchers from the 1970s—Edwards McKinnon, Bronson and others—for wider and more numerous field expeditions and greater research attention to this island.

Keywords: Southeast Asia, Sundaland, history of science, archaeology, palaeontology

Abstrak

Pulau Sumatra berada pada persimpangan kawasan Paparan Sunda yang penting artinya terhadap keanekaragaman hayati dan keragaman budaya di Asia Tenggara. Terlepas dari posisi geografisnya yang berada di tengah dan memiliki peran penting, pulau ini secara signifikan menjadi perhatian bidang arkeologi dan paleontologi walaupun belum terlalu intensif penelitiannya, jika dibandingkan dengan tetangga terdekat di utara (semenanjung Thai-Malaya) dan selatan (Jawa), khususnya untuk Pleistosen. Volume ini telah mengumpulkan sejarah dan status terkini berdasarkan hasil penelitian serta diharapkan memberikan dasar yang kuat pada pemahaman lebih lanjut tentang arti penting keberadaan Pulau Sumatra. Kontribusi yang ditunjukkan di seluruh data yang disajikan dalam volume ini, memberikan pemahaman kita tentang sejarah biotik dan budaya Sumatra. Data tersebut menginformasikan bahwa eksplorasi serta koleksi penemuan dalam skala besar pertama dari pulau ini dilakukan oleh Dubois pada akhir tahun 1880-an. Informasi hasil penelitiannya, juga masih menjadi dasar dari sebagian besar penelitian terkini yang disajikan pada bab-bab dalam volume ini. Secara umum, tema yang tertuang pada semua bab merupakan suatu koneksitas penelitian di wilayah Pulau Sumatra, tetapi yang lebih penting adalah hubungannya dengan seluruh Asia Tenggara mengenai bidang biologi maupun budaya, dalam relung ruang dan waktu. Kami menggemakan seruan kepada para peneliti dari tahun 1970-an, Edwards McKinnon, Bronson, dan lainnya, untuk melakukan ekspedisi lapangan yang lebih luas dan lebih intensif serta perhatian penelitian yang lebih besar ke pulau ini.

Kata kunci: Asia Tenggara, Paparan Sunda, sejarah ilmu pengetahuan, arkeologi, paleontologi

Introduction

The contributions to this volume have been wide-ranging in scope, befitting the range needed to cover an island as diverse in its natural and cultural history as Sumatra. While treating this one island as an independent subject is understandable both conceptually and geographically, the reality is that there can be no one definition of Sumatra in prehistory, in much the same way that Reid (1988) argues there is no single identity of Sumatra in history. Instead, the natural and cultural history of the island can be thought of in terms of connections; that is, internal connections and commonalities between the very different regions on the island—the highlands and lowlands, the upland catchment and the lowland floodplain rivers, the mainland and the offshore islands to the east and those of the west. Then there are the connections beyond the island of Sumatra—to Java, to the now-sunken Sunda shelf, to Indomalaya and beyond. It is difficult to capture all these strands in a single book, but nevertheless, they can be discerned and traced through time in the contributions of this volume. These contributions can be broadly grouped into three temporal perspectives—historical, palaeontological and archaeological—that explore the cultural and biodiversity connections and highlight the unique appeal of studying this island's past.

Historical perspectives

Two of the chapters concerning this theme deal entirely with caves and the history of cave use and exploration in Sumatra (Chapters 2 and 4, this volume), and the other two (Chapters 3 and 5, this volume) also consider them to some extent. This is no coincidence—most of the major Pleistocene finds in Sumatra, both palaeontological and archaeological, have been made in caves. Such finds include older materials from Lida Ajer, Sibrambang and Jambu and more recent material from caves such as Gua Harimau and Tianko Panjang. This situation is understandable: caves are a feature of the landscape known to both fauna and humans and can provide resources or shelter for both. Because caves are a prominent geological feature, the location of the caves and the resources preserved therein can also be predicted with a reasonable level of success, and the caves are often known and named by local people. The familiarity and ubiquitousness of caves are aptly demonstrated by Drawhorn, who has provided a comprehensive overview of the documented historical significance of speleology in Sumatra. That this extended beyond historical or written records is clearly evidenced by the preservation of *Homo sapiens* material, from early sites such as Lida Ajer to the more recent burials found in Gua Harimau.

Despite this ubiquitousness, finding and working in caves presents considerable difficulties, particularly in the tropical rainforest conditions covering much of the island. That these were experienced by Dubois is clearly documented in his notebooks and reports (Chapter 2, this volume). These difficulties ranged from lack of cooperation from the local people, diseases, and cave and passage collapses to the logistical challenges of working in remote and undeveloped terrains. Dubois did not simply stumble on fossils in the Sumatran caves; rather, his finds resulted from a well-coordinated plan based on published sources and the best available geological information. That Dubois benefited from the colonial situation in Sumatra is undoubtable (Chapter 3, this volume), and this may well have been part of the reason Dubois chose Sumatra as the starting point for his searches. Although Wood (2020:294) suggested that Dubois' biographer Theunissen (and by implication Wood himself) is 'none the wiser' about when or why Dubois decided to travel to Sumatra, there are several indications in Dubois' notes and letters of the strategy Dubois employed for finding the 'missing link', and the reasons why he thought the Sumatran caves would give him the best chance of success. That Dubois endured for two years working in the difficult and sometimes unpleasant caves in the Padang Highlands, even after he had been urged to consider Java, where conditions were better, perhaps indicates a stubbornness and an innate conviction that he was correct in choosing this area.

Dubois was enormously scientifically successful in Sumatra (though not in his stated goal). But he was convinced that the Sumatran deposits were too young for his purposes, and he became significantly less enthused about them over the course of his time in Sumatra. His negative attitude to the material may have been compounded by the knowledge that his initial conviction regarding the choice of the Padang Highlands had been wrong. However, it was undoubtedly the huge success Dubois subsequently found on Java that eclipsed the Sumatran fossils and their significance, as is well noted by Drawhorn (Chapter 4). Research on Java continued to be enormously successful into the 1930s and beyond, and in the 1940s, when Hooijer began to describe the Sumatran fossils, interest in Sumatra did not dramatically increase. In fact, the decades from the 1940s to the 1970s were a quiescent time for research into the prehistory of Sumatra. Prior to this time, in the 1920s and 1930s, there had been considerable activity and interest, fuelled by the discoveries in the northern Sumatran midden deposits (Chapter 1, this volume), but after that, for several decades, no significant finds or excavations were conducted on the island. A brief flurry of activity in the 1970s was spurred by the University of Hull Centre for South-East Asian Studies and one of its publications, the *Sumatra Research Bulletin*, a short-lived periodical covering aspects of Sumatran ethnography, history and archaeological research.

During the 1980s, field research programs were initiated by Indonesian teams, and since the 1990s, joint Indonesian–international teams have had considerable success in expanding our knowledge of the island's history and prehistory, working in both caves and open-air sites. Given this context, the fact that Dubois' collections still constitute one of the most important resources for understanding the deep-time history of the island demonstrates the huge contribution Dubois' expedition provided to science and his considerable achievements in Sumatra.

Palaeontological perspectives

Three of the four chapters on palaeontology in Sumatra deal explicitly with the Dubois fossils collected from the Padang Highlands. All three of these contributions demonstrate that, far from representing modern faunas of little interest to specialists in Indonesian palaeontology, the deposits are of considerable antiquity and are valuable for understanding the ecological, environmental and biogeographic history of the broader region.

The reconstructed environment of the Padang cave faunas, as presented in the chapters in this volume as well as previous studies (e.g. de Vos 1983; Janssen et al. 2016; Louys et al. 2021, 2022), indicates that rainforest habitats have dominated western Sumatra since at least Marine Isotope Stage 4 (57–71 ka). However, what is also clear from these studies is that there were probably important, although subtle (at the level of resolution available through vertebrate fossil proxies), differences between the Late Pleistocene rainforests and those of today. Janssen et al. (2016), Louys et al. (2021, 2022, Chapter 5, this volume) and Chapter 6 (this volume) examine different palaeodietary proxies that not only reveal the ready availability of rainforest habitats in Padang but also hint at the presence of slightly or significantly more open environments or greater seasonality during some parts of the Pleistocene. This is clearest in the stable isotope studies of Janssen et al. (2016) and Chapter 5 (this volume) but could also be reflected in the dental wear patterns in the Padang deer (Gruwier et al. this volume; Wirkner and Hertler 2019). Of course, these are only hints, and need to be confirmed with more extensive analyses, preferably of well-dated and well-provenanced specimens. As Chapter 5 (this volume) demonstrates, understanding the chronological and depositional context of Jambu, Sibrambang and the other still-unlocated Padang caves investigated by Dubois, is complicated at best.

Nevertheless, the new dates reported in this volume contribute important new data on fossils excavated by Dubois. They unambiguously demonstrate that these fossils are of considerable antiquity: Late Pleistocene—and perhaps Middle Pleistocene—specimens are represented in the deposits. Chapters 6 and 7 (this volume) also show how new biogeographic insights can be derived from these historical collections. Gruwier et al. show that there were complex faunal exchanges, possibly involving hybridisation, between Sumatra and Java throughout the Late Pleistocene. It is unlikely that such patterns were restricted to deer. Indeed, as Chapter 5 (this volume) discusses, the taxonomy (and by implication, biogeography) of the Late Pleistocene orangutans is not straightforward, and the relationship between Sumatran and Javan fossil orangutans has yet to be fully explored.

At a broader scale, both geographic and temporal, Chapter 7 (this volume) compares the Sumatran and Sundanese mammal communities with those of Indochina, examining their similarities and differences. The former appear to have had far fewer large herbivorous taxa than the latter. This, the authors argue, would have meant prey availability for carnivores differed between the regions. One meat-eating taxon of particular interest is the Homininae, the subfamily including *Homo erectus* and *H. sapiens*. This study again underscores the differences between rainforests across the region—no two rainforests are exactly alike, and the way they differ might have profound implications for understanding the distribution, evolution and extinction of faunas in their regions.

Finally, Chapter 8 (this volume) presents novel data from another part of Sumatra: Bangka Island. Although administratively separate from Sumatra today, geographically, Bangka was connected to eastern Sumatra for most of the last two million years. Hence, the recovery of fossils from fluvial (as opposed to cave) deposits there provides indications that further such deposits might be found in the peneplains of eastern Sumatra. More importantly, Basilia et al.'s study indicates just how little is known about the biology of even the extant species found in Sumatra today. Their chapter reports a novel microanatomical feature of elephants that has implications for understanding the growth of these large mammals. The palaeontological work done thus far in Sumatra has barely scratched the surface, and there remain more unanswered or even unasked questions than there are specialists working in the field.

Archaeological perspectives

The chapters in this part of the volume are united by what they reveal about temporal and spatial connections to and within Sumatra. The chapter by Louys and Kealy does this explicitly by modelling and discussing the potential routes to and through Sumatra of hominins (and other large-bodied mammals) travelling between mainland Southeast Asia and Java. The focus here is on the geographical aspects of the terrain that might help or hinder movements, especially its topography and hydrology. Chapter 9 (this volume) suggests that some routes through Sumatra might still be above water, although their discussion of the geology of those routes suggests that the preservation of fossil and archaeological material of the required antiquity is unlikely. Likewise, Chapter 10 (this volume) stresses the similarities of the stone tool technologies present in Sumatra to those used in Java and the rest of Southeast Asia. The similarities in typologies, particularly in the Palaeolithic-like tools recovered from several Sumatran fluviatile deposits, suggest direct connections and suggest the presence of early hominins, namely *Homo erectus*, on Sumatra at some point in the Pleistocene.

Continuing the theme of spatial connections, Chapters 11 and 12 discuss the metal and megalith periods[1] in Sumatra respectively, providing convincing narratives of not only the transfer of cultural and technological material into Sumatra from South and Southeast Asia but also the interconnections within Sumatra itself. In this context, the river systems of Sumatra have played a major role in the relationships between the highlands and the lowlands; hence, these chapters also bring to mind the routes into the island suggested for earlier humans or other species Chapter 9 (this volume). Far from being an isolated or backwater region, in these chapters, Sumatra emerges as an important regional nexus, facilitating the flow and subsequent diffusion of fauna, people, technologies and cultures into the wider Indonesian archipelago. Although it is not discussed in any detail in the chapters presented here, the possibility, indeed likelihood, of fauna, people, technologies and cultures originating in Sumatra and flowing out to the larger Asian diaspora must also be acknowledged and is readily evoked by the term sumatralith (Chapter 1, this volume).

The contributions in this section also stress the temporal connections that exist among the subjects discussed. Chapter 12 (this volume) is most emphatic in blurring the lines between the prehistoric, historical and modern periods, arguing convincingly that these arbitrary boundaries and definitions are more of a hindrance than a help in understanding the island and its people. This idea is also echoed in the consideration of Lida Ajer Cave in Chapter 13 (this volume), which examines the scientific and cultural heritage value of a 'seemingly insignificant hole in the ground'. They bring this volume full circle, examining the physical records of the excavations in the cave—especially those of Dubois—and of the search for the 'missing link' and an understanding of Sumatra's deep past. The cave was subsequently used for other purposes; physical evidence also links it to World War II and Indonesian independence and shows that in very recent times it has been used for bird's nest

---

1   Note, however, that, as Bonatz (Chapter 12) makes clear, the creation of megaliths may have started as early as the second century BC and continued until at least the nineteenth century AD. This temporal span overlaps with, for example, the metal and historical periods, which seemingly refutes the idea that there was a distinct 'megalith period' in Sumatra.

harvesting. The latest use of the cave is probably by the large proportion of this volume's authors who continue to explore and further sample the deposits in an effort to understand the past (Louys et al. 2022).

The future of research in Sumatra

A great deal of work remains to be done to further our understanding of the biological, anthropological and cultural history of Sumatra. As the contributions in this volume have demonstrated, the island is a rich depository of information. Research there has the potential to provide insights into events and conditions that occurred within and around this central node of Asia during periods from the early Pleistocene through to today. It is hoped that this volume will stimulate continued interest and work in Sumatran research and generate efforts to connect Sumatra's records with those of other significant regions as well as efforts to further our understanding of the dynamics that have existed, and continue to exist, within Sumatra itself.

References

de Vos, J. 1983. The *Pongo* faunas from Java and Sumatra and their significance for biostratigraphical and paleo-ecological interpretations. *Proceedings of the Koninklke Nederlandse Akademie van Wetenschappen, Series B* 86:417–425.

Drawhorn, G.M. this volume. Dubois and beyond: The historical background of cave exploration in Sumatra. In J. Louys, P.C.H. Albers and A.A.E. van der Geer (eds), *Quaternary Palaeontology and Archaeology of Sumatra*, pp. 77–97. Terra Australis. ANU Press, Canberra. doi.org/10.22459/TA56. 2024.04

Janssen, R., J.C. Joordens, D.S. Koutamanis, M.R. Puspaningrum, J. de Vos, J.H. van der Lubbe, J.J. Reijmer, O. Hampe and H.B. Vonhof 2016. Tooth enamel stable isotopes of Holocene and Pleistocene fossil fauna reveal glacial and interglacial paleoenvironments of hominins in Indonesia. *Quaternary Science Reviews* 144:145–154. doi.org/10.1016/j.quascirev.2016.02.028

Louys, J., M. Duval, G.J. Price, K. Westaway, Y. Zaim, Y, Rizal, Aswan, M. Puspaningrum, A. Trihascaryo, S. Breitenbach, O. Kwiecien, Y. Cai, P. Higgins, P.C.H. Albers, J. de Vos and P. Roberts 2022. Speleological and environmental history of Lida Ajer cave, western Sumatra. *Philosophical Transactions of the Royal Society B* 377:20200494. doi.org/10.1098/rstb.2020.0494

Louys, J., Y. Zaim, Y. Rizal, M. Puspaningrum, A. Trihascaryo, G.J. Price, A. Petherick, E. Scholtz and L.R.G. DeSantis 2021. Sumatran orangutan diets in the Late Pleistocene as inferred from dental microwear texture analysis. *Quaternary International* 603:74–81. doi.org/10.1016/j.quaint.2020.08.040

Reid, A. 1988. The identity of 'Sumatra' in history. In R. Carle (ed.), *Cultures and Societies of North Sumatra*, pp. 25–42. Dietrich Reimer Verlag, Berlin.

Wirkner, M. and C. Hertler 2019. Feeding ecology of Late Pleistocene *Muntiacus muntjak* in the Padang Highlands (Sumatra). *Comptes Rendus Palevol* 18(5):541–554. doi.org/10.1016/j.crpv.2019.03.004

Wood, B. 2020. Birth of *Homo erectus*. *Evolutionary Anthropology: Issues, News, and Reviews.* 29(6):293–298. doi.org/10.1002/evan.21873

Contributors

Paul C.H. Albers
Naturalis Biodiversity Center, Darwinweg 2, 2333 CR Leiden, the Netherlands. palbers@xs4all.nl. ORCID: 0000-0001-5896-1021

Pierre-Olivier Antoine
Institut des Sciences de l'Evolution, Université Montpellier, CNRS, IRD, 34095 Montpellier, France. pierre-olivier.antoine@umontpellier.fr

Aswan
Paleontology and Quaternary Geology Research Group, Department of Geological Engineering, Faculty of Earth Sciences and Technology, Institut Teknologi Bandung (ITB), Jl. Ganesha 10 Bandung, Jawa Barat, Indonesia. aswan_gl@gl.itb.ac.id

Anne-Marie Bacon
Université Paris Cité, CNRS, BABEL, 75012 Paris, France. anne-marie.bacon@u-paris.fr

Pauline Basilia
Australian Research Centre for Human Evolution, Griffith University, Brisbane, Australia. Archaeological Studies Program, University of the Philippines, Diliman, Philippines. pauline.basilia@griffithuni.edu.au. ORCID: 0000-0003-3219-4789

Dominik Bonatz
Institut für Vorderasiatische Archäologie, Freie Universität Berlin, Fabeckstrasse 23–25, 14195 Berlin, Germany. dominik.bonatz@fu-berlin.de

John de Vos
Naturalis Biodiversity Center, Darwinweg 2, 2333 CR Leiden, the Netherlands. john.devos@naturalis.nl

Gerrell M. Drawhorn
Department of Anthropology, California State University, California, United States of America. piltdown@csus.edu

Hubert Forestier
Muséum National d'Histoire Naturelle, UMR 7194 HNHP, Musée de l'Homme, 17, Place du Trocadéro, 75116 Paris, France. hubforestier@gmail.com. ORCID: 0000-0002-9720-8515

Ben Gruwier
HALMA—UMR 8164 (CNRS), Université de Lille, Campus Pont-de-Bois, Rue du Barreau, 59653 Villeneuve d'Ascq, France. Maritime Cultures Research Institute, Department of Art Sciences and Archaeology, Vrije Universiteit Brussel, Pleinlaan 2, 1050 Brussels, Belgium. Research Unit: Analytical, Environmental and Geochemistry, Department of Chemistry, Vrije Universiteit Brussel, Pleinlaan 2, 1050 Brussels, Belgium. ben.gruwier@hotmail.com. ORCID: 0000-0002-3512-6629

Christine Hertler
The Role of Culture in Early Expansions of Humans, Senckenberg Research Institute, Senckenberganlage 25, 60325 Frankfurt, Germany. ROCEEH Research Center, Heidelberg Academy of Sciences and Humanities, Karlstrasse 4, 69117 Heidelberg, Germany. christine.hertler@senckenberg.de. ORCID: 0000-0002-8252-9674

Pennilyn Higgins
EPOCH Isotopes, 6606 E Townline Rd, Williamson NY 14589, United States of America. pennilyn.higgins@gmail.com. ORCID: 0000-0001-6048-8106

Shimona Kealy
Archaeology and Natural History, College of Asia and the Pacific, The Australian National University, Canberra ACT 2600, Australia. ARC Centre of Excellence for Australian Biodiversity and Heritage, The Australian National University, Canberra ACT 2600, Australia. shimona.kealy@anu.edu.au

Kris Kovarovic
Department of Anthropology, Durham University, South Road, Durham, DH1 3LE, United Kingdom. kris.kovarovic@durham.ac.uk. ORCID: 0000-0002-6056-4591

Julien Louys
Australian Research Centre for Human Evolution, Griffith University, 170 Kessels Road, Nathan QLD 4111, Australia. Archaeology and Natural History, College of Asia and the Pacific, The Australian National University, Canberra ACT 2600, Australia. j.louys@griffith.edu.au. ORCID: 0000-0001-7539-0689

Justyna J. Miszkiewicz
Naturalis Biodiversity Center, Darwinweg 2, 2333 CR Leiden, the Netherlands. School of Social Science, The University of Queensland, St Lucia QLD 4072, Australia. j.miszkiewicz@uq.edu.au. ORCID: 0000-0002-9769-2706

Sue O'Connor
Archaeology and Natural History, College of Asia and the Pacific, The Australian National University, Canberra ACT 2600, Australia. ARC Centre of Excellence for Australian Biodiversity and Heritage, The Australian National University, Canberra ACT 2600, Australia. sue.oconnor@anu.edu.au. ORCID: 0000-0001-9381-078X

Gilbert J. Price
School of Earth and Environmental Sciences, The University of Queensland, St Lucia QLD 4072. Australia. g.price1@uq.edu.au. ORCID: 0000-0001-8406-4594

Mika Rizki Puspaningrum
Paleontology and Quaternary Geology Research Group, Department of Geological Engineering, Faculty of Earth Sciences and Technology, Institut Teknologi Bandung (ITB), Jl. Ganesha 10 Bandung, Jawa Barat, Indonesia. mika.puspaningrum@itb.ac.id

Yan Rizal
Paleontology and Quaternary Geology Research Group, Department of Geological Engineering, Faculty of Earth Sciences and Technology, Institut Teknologi Bandung (ITB), Jl. Ganesha 10 Bandung, Jawa Barat, Indonesia. yan@gl.itb.ac.id

Truman Simanjuntak
Center for Prehistory and Austronesian Studies, Jl. Ahmad Dahlan IV No. 20, Kelurahan Kukusan, Depok—Jawa Barat 16425, Indonesia. simanjuntaktruman@gmail.com

Harry Octavianus Sofian
Research Center for Archaeometry, National Research and Innovation Agency (BRIN), Jl. Condet Pejaten No. 4, Jakarta Selatan 12510, Indonesia. Center for Prehistory and Austronesian Studies, Jl. Ahmad Dahlan IV No. 20, Kelurahan Kukusan, Depok—Jawa Barat 16425, Indonesia. harry.octa@gmail.com. ORCID: 0000-0002-5427-4803

Agus Tri Hascaryo
Paleontology and Quaternary Geology Research Group, Department of Geological Engineering, Faculty of Earth Sciences and Technology, Institut Teknologi Bandung (ITB), Jl. Ganesha 10 Bandung, Jawa Barat, Indonesia. agusgeoar@yahoo.com

Alexandra A.E. van der Geer
Naturalis Biodiversity Center, Darwinweg 2, 2333 CR Leiden, the Netherlands. alexandra.vandergeer@naturalis.nl. ORCID: 0000-0002-9588-4739

Mathias Wirkner
Department of Messel Research and Mammalogy, Senckenberg Research Institute, Senckenberganlage 25, 60325 Frankfurt, Germany. Department for Geosciences, University Frankfurt, Altenhöferallee 1, 60325 Frankfurt, Germany. mathias.wirkner@senckenberg.de. ORCID: 0000-0002-9526-5401

Jahdi Zaim
Paleontology and Quaternary Geology Research Group, Department of Geological Engineering, Faculty of Earth Sciences and Technology, Institut Teknologi Bandung (ITB), Jl. Ganesha 10 Bandung, Jawa Barat, Indonesia. zaim@itb.ac.id

Terra Australis reports the results of archaeological and related research within the south and east of Asia, though mainly Australia, New Guinea and island Melanesia — lands that remained terra australis incognita to generations of prehistorians. Its subject is the settlement of the diverse environments in this isolated quarter of the globe by peoples who have maintained their discrete and traditional ways of life into the recent recorded or remembered past and at times into the observable present.

List of volumes in Terra Australis